THE CANADIAN YEARBOOK OF INTERNATIONAL LAW

1994

ANNUAIRE CANADIEN DE DROIT INTERNATIONAL

The Canadian Yearbook of International Law

VOLUME XXXII 1994 TOME XXXII

Annuaire canadien de Droit international

Published under the auspices of
THE CANADIAN BRANCH, INTERNATIONAL LAW ASSOCIATION
AND
THE CANADIAN COUNCIL ON INTERNATIONAL LAW

Publié sous les auspices de
LA SECTION CANADIENNE DE L'ASSOCIATION DE DROIT INTERNATIONAL
ET
LE CONSEIL CANADIEN DE DROIT INTERNATIONAL

UBC Press
VANCOUVER, B.C.

Printed in Canada on acid-free paper ∞

ISBN 0-7748-0527-7
ISSN 0069-0058

Canadian Cataloguing in Publication Data

The National Library of Canada has catalogued this
publication as follows:

*The Canadian yearbook of international law — Annuaire
canadien de droit international*

Annual.
Text in English and French.
"Published under the auspices of the Canadian
Branch, International Law Association and the
Canadian Council on International Law."
ISSN 0069-0058

1. International Law — Periodicals. I.
International Law Association. Canadian Branch.
II. Title: Annuaire canadien de droit international.
JX21.C3   341'.05   C75-34558-6E

Donnés de catalogage avant publication (Canada)

Annuaire canadien de droit international — Canadian
yearbook of international law

Annuaire.
Textes en anglais et en français.
"Publié sous les auspices de la Branche canadienne
de l'Association de droit international et le Conseil
canadien de droit international."
ISSN 0069-0058

1. Droit international — Périodiques. I.
Association de droit international. Section canadienne.
II. Conseil canadien de droit international.
III. Titre: The Canadian yearbook of international law.
JX21.C3   341'.05   C75-34558-6F

UBC Press
University of British Columbia
6344 Memorial Road
Vancouver, BC V6T 1Z2
(604) 822-3259
Fax: 1-800-668-0821
E-mail: orders@ubcpress.ubc.ca

Contents / Sommaire

BOOK REVIEWS / RECENSIONS DE LIVRES

THE CANADIAN YEARBOOK OF INTERNATIONAL LAW

1994

ANNUAIRE CANADIEN DE DROIT INTERNATIONAL

Le Canada et l'unification internationale du droit privé

L E PRÉSENT ARTICLE TRAITE des efforts d'harmonisation et d'unification au plan international de cette partie du droit interne
des États qu'est le droit privé et de la pratique canadienne à cet
égard. On entend par droit privé aux fins de cet article non seulement les règles substantielles de droit privé en vigueur dans chaque
État mais aussi les règles de procédure, appelées droit international
privé,[1] qui s'appliquent lorsqu'il y a des relations juridiques internationales ou un élément étranger et visent à régler les conflits entre

---

* Ministère de la Justice, Ottawa. Les opinions exprimées dans cet article sont
celles de l'auteur et ne sauraient en aucune manière être attribuées au ministère
de la Justice.

---

[1] L'expression droit international privé peut prêter à confusion vu que les règles de
droit international privé ne font partie du droit international que lorsqu'elles sont
contenues dans des conventions, l'existence de droit coutumier en la matière
étant controversée. Donc, à par ces règles supranationales conventionnelles, les
règles de droit international privé sont tout simplement des règles de droit interne.
Voir P. Guggenheim, *Traité de droit international public*, t. 1 (Genève: Librairie de
l'Université, Georg & Cie S.A., 1953), à la p. 28, note 2 et J.-G. Castel, *Introduction
to Conflict of Laws*, 2d ed. (Toronto and Vancouver: Butterworths, 1986), à la p. 4.
Voir aussi la décision de la Cour Permanente de Justice Internationale dans
l'affaire des emprunts franco-serbes et franco-brésiliens citant les sources du droit
international privé: "Tout contrat qui n'est pas un contrat entre des États en tant
que sujets du droit international a son fondement dans une loi nationale. La
question de savoir quelle est cette loi fait l'objet de la partie du droit
qu'aujourd'hui on désigne le plus souvent sous le nom de droit international privé
ou de théorie du conflit des lois. Les règles en peuvent être communes à plusieurs
États et même être établies par des conventions internationales ou des coutumes,
et dans ce dernier cas avoir le caractère d'un vrai droit international, régissant les
rapports entre des États. Mais, à part cela, il y a lieu de considérer que lesdites
règles font partie du droit interne." Rapporté dans H. Batiffol, "Contributions de
la juridiction internationale au droit international privé" dans *Mélanges offerts à
Charles Rousseau* (Paris: Pédone, 1974) 17 à la p. 19.

ordres juridiques différents, soit les conflits de lois et de juridictions qui peuvent survenir dans de telles situations.

Comme les règles de droit privé et de droit international privé varient d'un État à un autre, les États en sont venus à apprécier l'importance d'avoir des règles admises universellement dans un monde où les personnes et les biens peuvent traverser de plus en plus facilement les frontières. L'uniformité de ces règles de droit offre un cadre juridique plus familier pour les transactions internationales et contribue ainsi à développer le commerce international. Les États ont tout intérêt à faire en sorte que leurs résidents puissent connaître à l'avance le régime juridique qui les régira dans des situations internationales. C'est aussi dans leur intérêt que les lois soient respectées et que, par exemple, le simple fait de franchir une frontière n'exempte pas le débiteur de l'exécution de ses obligations. Mais un État ne peut, à lui seul, édicter les conséquences juridiques de toutes les situations comportant un élément étranger. Seule une norme supranationale peut avoir cet effet et fournir un plus grand degré de certitude au contexte juridique sous-jacent aux relations internationales entre individus. Par conséquent, les États ont cherché à coordonner et harmoniser le développement du droit privé en négociant des traités bilatéraux ou multilatéraux.[2] Ils ont aussi par de tels traités voulu régler des problèmes très concrets en instaurant des mécanismes d'entraide judiciaire ou administrative.

Cet article porte sur la participation du Canada à l'élaboration de règles de droit international privé ou de droit privé qui sont supranationales du fait de leur incorporation dans un traité bilatéral ou multilatéral négocié souvent, dans ce dernier cas, au sein d'une organisation internationale gouvernementale. Il se limitera à l'unification internationale du droit privé applicable aux activités des individus en général et ne traitera pas de la participation canadienne au développement international du droit international privé dans des domaines d'activités spécialisées, comme le transport aérien ou maritime. La première partie de l'article identifiera les principales organisations internationales qui travaillent à l'unification internationale du droit privé. La deuxième partie se penchera sur le contexte canadien et les règles constitutionnelles appli-

---

[2] Pour J. G. Castel, "Canada and The Hague Conference" (1967) 45 R.du B.can.1 note 1: "the field of commercial law is one in which uniformity is most desirable and can easily be obtained as there are almost no irreconcilable differences of policy among the rules in force in the various countries of the world."

cables. La troisième partie examinera la pratique internationale eu égard à la participation des États fédéraux à des conventions portant en partie sur des matières relevant de la compétence législative de leurs unités territoriales constituantes. La quatrième partie traitera de la participation du Canada aux activités internationales d'unification du droit privé et de la mise en oeuvre de traités ou de lois types internationales portant sur ce domaine. Un bilan sera finalement tracé des réalisations canadiennes.

I LES ORGANISATIONS INTERNATIONALES

Les principales organisations internationales oeuvrant dans le domaine du doit international privé ou de l'harmonisation du droit privé auxquelles le Canada participe sont la Conférence interaméricaine de droit international privé (CIDIP) de l'Organisation des États américains (OEA), la Conférence de La Haye de droit international privé, l'Institut international pour l'unification du droit privé (Unidroit) et la Commission des Nations Unies pour le droit commercial international (CNUDCI).[3]

A CONFÉRENCE INTERAMÉRICAINE DE DROIT INTERNATIONAL PRIVÉ (CIDIP)

Il y a plus d'un siècle que l'Amérique latine, "continent" de droit civil, s'intéresse au droit international privé.[4] La Charte de l'OEA

---

[3] Au plan régional, le Conseil de l'Europe a établi en 1963 un comité européen de coopération juridique (CDCJ) qui coordonne l'harmonisation des législations des États membres. Le Canada participe comme observateur aux travaux du Conseil de l'Europe dans différents domaines mais il n'a accédé à aucune convention portant sur l'harmonisation du droit privé ou du droit international privé. Parmi les conventions de droit privé élaborées au sein du Conseil de l'Europe, mentionnons la Convention sur la reconnaissance des décisions en matière de garde d'enfants, la Convention sur la preuve de la loi étrangère et la Convention sur la signification et la notification de documents administratifs.

[4] L'Amérique latine a développé une approche régionale au droit international privé et ce, depuis le Congrès de Panama de 1826. Une première conférence de codification du droit international privé eut lieu à Lima en 1877. À l'ordre du jour y figuraient la capacité, la propriété, les contrats, le mariage, la succession et la compétence des tribunaux. Un Congrès sud-américain de droit international privé se réunit en 1888-89 à Montevideo où furent adoptés des traités portant sur diverses questions dont le droit civil international, le droit commercial international, la propriété littéraire et artistique, la procédure, qui constituent selon Calvo, "un véritable Code de Droit international privé." Voir M. C. Calvo, *Le droit international théorique et pratique*, t.VI, 5e éd. (Paris: Rousseau, 1896), à la

établit un comité juridique interaméricain appelé à promouvoir le développement et la codification du droit international et étudier la possibilité d'unifier les lois des différents pays américains en autant que cela semble approprié.[5] Le Comité entreprend des études et recommande la convocation de conférences juridiques spécialisées. Il est composé de onze juristes, élus par l'Assemblée générale de l'OEA à partir de candidats proposés par les États membres. L'Assemblée générale de l'OEA a décidé de confier à des conférences spécialisées la tâche de codifier le droit international privé. La première conférence, CIDIP I, eut lieu en 1975 et la plus récente, CIDIP V, en 1994.[6] Le Canada a participé aux quatre premières conférences à titre d'observateur et à la cinquième en tant que membre de l'OEA.

Les travaux des conférences spécialisées interaméricaines ont été influencés par ceux de la Conférence de La Haye de droit international privé et bien des conventions développées au sein des conférences spécialisées portent sur les mêmes sujets que les conventions de La Haye. Mais l'approche suivie est souvent plus globale. Par exemple, la Convention sur les lettres rogatoires s'applique aussi en matière d'arbitrage et la Convention sur le trafic international des mineurs couvre à la fois le domaine civil et criminel. D'autres conventions contiennent à la fois des dispositions relatives à la loi applicable et au droit substantiel. Le Canada ne s'est pas beaucoup

---

p. 93. La Conférence de La Havane de 1928 a établi une codification du droit international privé (Code Bustamente) qui a recueilli l'adhésion de tous les participants à la Conférence sauf les États-Unis. Voir Guggenheim, *supra* note 1, à la p. 165, note 2.

5 Articles 104-10 de la Charte de l'Organisation des États américains, Treaty Series No. 1-D OEA/Ser.A/2 (English) Rev.2, General Secretariat, Organization of American States, Washington, DC, 1989.

6 CIDIP I, qui eut lieu à Panama en 1975, a adopté deux résolutions et six traités portant sur les lettres de change, les chèques, l'arbitrage commercial international, les lettres rogatoires, l'obtention des preuves à l'étranger et le régime juridique des procurations utilisées à l'étranger. CIDIP II, qui se réunit à Montevideo en 1979, a adopté entre autres des conventions sur la reconnaissance et l'exécution des jugements et la preuve de la loi étrangère. CIDIP III qui eut lieu à La Paz en 1984, a adopté, entre autres, une convention portant sur l'adoption internationale. L'ordre du jour de CIDIP IV qui eut lieu à Montevideo en 1989, comprenait l'enlèvement des mineurs et leur retour, le transport terrestre, les arrangements contractuels internationaux et les obligations alimentaires. Deux conventions ont été adoptées par CIDIP V qui eut lieu à Mexico du 14 au 18 mars 1994, la Convention interaméricaine sur le trafic international des mineurs et la Convention interaméricaine sur la loi applicable aux contrats commerciaux.

impliqué dans les activités de droit international privé de l'OEA. Il s'est plus impliqué dans les activités de la Conférence de La Haye de droit international privé, d'Unidroit et de la Commission des Nations Unies pour le droit commercial international.

B CONFÉRENCE DE LA HAYE DE DROIT INTERNATIONAL PRIVÉ

La Conférence de La Haye existe depuis 1893.[7] Lors de sa septième session en 1951,[8] elle se dota d'un statut et devint véritablement une organisation internationale. Tel que mentionné dans le Statut de 1951, la Conférence de La Haye a pour but de travailler à l'unification progressive des règles de droit international privé. Sont membres de la Conférence les États qui ont participé à des sessions de la Conférence. Peuvent devenir membres de la Conférence les autres États dont la participation présente un intérêt de nature juridique pour les travaux de la Conférence. L'admission de nouveaux membres est décidée par une majorité des États participants. La Conférence est composée d'un secrétariat appelé Bureau permanent et se réunit en sessions tous les quatre ans sauf excep-

---

7 Il y a eu quelques tentatives européennes au siècle dernier de convoquer des conférences diplomatiques pour réaliser une certaine uniformité dans les règles de droit international privé, mais c'est la Conférence de La Haye de droit international privé qui a réussi à le faire. La première conférence fut convoquée à La Haye par le gouvernement des Pays-Bas en 1893 et 13 États européens y participèrent (Allemagne, Autriche-Hongrie, Belgique, Danemark, Espagne, France, Italie, Luxembourg, Pays-Bas, Portugal, Roumanie, Russie, Suisse). Les sujets à l'ordre du jour comprenaient le mariage, la forme des actes, la procédure (signification d'actes judiciaires et extra-judiciaires, les commissions rogatoires), les successions, testaments et donations. D'autres sessions eurent lieu en 1894, 1900 et 1904 (le Japon fut le premier État non-européen à y participer) et six traités ont résulté des quatre premières sessions de la Conférence. Les sessions suivantes eurent lieu en 1925 et 1928. Aucune convention n'y fut adoptée mais un Protocole acceptant la juridiction de la Cour Permanente de Justice internationale pour l'interprétation des conventions de La Haye fut signé le 27 mars 1931. Le Royaume-Uni participa pour la première fois à une session de la Conférence de La Haye en 1925. Plusieurs périodiques de droit international ont consacré des articles, sinon une publication entière, au centenaire de la Conférence de La Haye. Voir, entre autres, K. Lipstein, "One Hundred Years of Hague Conference on Private International Law" (1993) 42 *International and Comparative Law Quarterly* 553; (1993) XL *Netherlands International Law Review*, Issue 1; (1993) *Revue suisse de droit international et de droit européen*, 2/93, numéro spécial. Voir aussi A. E. Von Overbeck, "La contribution de la Conférence de La Haye au développement du droit international privé," dans *RCADI*, tome 233, (1992-II), à la p.9.

8 Seize États, dont quinze d'Europe de l'Ouest et le Japon, y ont participé à titre d'invités.

tion. Au cours de la période intersessionnelle des "Commissions spéciales" formées de représentants des États membres élaborent des projets de conventions qui seront adoptées à la session suivante. Des Commissions spéciales sont aussi convoquées pour discuter du programme de travail futur de la Conférence et examiner le fonctionnement de conventions adoptées par la Conférence.

Dans les années 1950-60 la Conférence de La Haye devint plus universelle avec l'admission d'États non européens comme les États-Unis et le Japon.[9] C'est en 1968 que le Canada devint membre de la Conférence de La Haye et il assista à la onzième session, qui eut lieu la même année. En 1995 l'on compte quarante-et-un États membres de la Conférence provenant de diverses régions du monde.

La Conférence a adopté trente-deux conventions depuis 1951 dont vingt-quatre sont entrées en vigueur.[10] Elles portent sur la loi applicable, la procédure civile internationale, y compris la reconnaissance et l'exécution des jugements, et l'entraide judiciaire et administrative.[11] Parmi les conventions les plus récentes, l'on note la Convention relative à la loi applicable au trust et à sa reconnaissance adoptée en 1984, la Convention relative à la loi applicable aux successions à cause de mort adoptée en 1988 et la Convention sur la protection des enfants et la coopération en matière d'adoption internationale adoptée en 1993. Le programme de travail de la Conférence de La Haye pour la période 1993-96 comprend l'élaboration d'une convention sur la protection des mineurs et l'examen de la possibilité de développer une convention multilatérale sur la reconnaissance et l'exécution des jugements en matière civile ou commerciale.

Les États non membres de la Conférence de La Haye peuvent adhérer aux conventions adoptées par la Conférence et les conven-

---

9 Les États-Unis assistèrent pour la première fois à la huitième session de 1956 à titre d'observateurs et, encore à titre d'observateurs, à la neuvième session en 1960. Ils assistèrent à titre de membre à la dixième session de la Conférence en 1964.

10 La *Revue critique de droit international privé* publie chaque année l'état des signatures, ratifications et adhésions.

11 Ce sont les conventions sur la procédure civile et celles d'entraide administrative qui ont eu le plus de succès. Ainsi la Convention de 1965 relative à la signification et la notification à l'étranger des actes judiciaires et extrajudiciaires en matière civile ou commerciale est en vigueur dans trente-deux États, la Convention de 1961 supprimant l'exigence de la légalisation des actes publics étrangers dans quarante-cinq États et la Convention de 1980 sur les aspects civils de l'enlèvement international d'enfants dans trente-cinq États.

tions auxquelles ils adhèrent s'appliquent entre eux et les États parties qui acceptent ces adhésions. Plusieurs États non membres ont adhéré à des conventions de La Haye.[12]

C   INSTITUT INTERNATIONAL POUR L'UNIFICATION DU DROIT PRIVÉ

C'est aussi en 1968 que le Canada devint membre de l'Institut international pour l'unification du droit privé (Unidroit). Unidroit a été créé en 1926 à l'initiative du gouvernement italien, avec l'appui de la Société des Nations. Il a joué entre les deux guerres un rôle important dans les mouvements d'unification du droit privé en Europe. Lorsque l'Italie s'est retirée de la Société des Nations Unidroit est devenu indépendant et a repris ses travaux en 1940 dans le cadre d'un accord multilatéral. Tout comme la Conférence de La Haye, Unidroit était au début composé d'États en majorité civilistes bien que le Royaume-Uni ait participé à ses travaux entre les deux guerres et soit redevenu membre en 1948. Les États-Unis sont devenus membres en 1964. En 1992, il y avait cinquante-trois États membres d'Unidroit provenant des diverses régions du monde.

L'objectif d'Unidroit est d'examiner la manière d'harmoniser et de coordonner le droit privé et de préparer pour adoption par les États des règles uniformes de droit privé. À cette fin, il prépare des projets de lois ou de conventions visant à établir un droit interne uniforme, entreprend des études en droit comparé et organise des conférences. L'Institut a travaillé traditionnellement dans le domaine de l'unification des règles de droit substantiel.

Le programme de travail d'Unidroit est développé lors des réunions annuelles du Conseil de direction.[13] Les États membres sont ensuite consultés sur les suggestions retenues par le Conseil de

---

12 Par exemple, vingt-et-un États non membres de la Conférence de La Haye ont adhéré à la Convention supprimant l'exigence de la légalisation, treize à la Convention de 1961 sur les conflits de loi en matière de forme des dispositions testamentaires et douze à la Convention sur l'enlèvement d'enfants.

13 Les vingt-cinq membres du Conseil de direction sont des experts présentés par les États membres et élus par l'Assemblée générale d'Unidroit pour un mandat de cinq ans. Ils ne représentent pas leur gouvernement. Deux Canadiens ont été élus au Conseil de direction, Me T. B. Smith qui en a fait partie de 1984 à 1989, et Madame le Juge Anne-Marie Trahan qui en fait partie depuis 1989. Deux sujets inscrits au programme de travail d'Unidroit, le contrat de franchisage international et la question des sûretés sur le matériel pouvant être déplacé l'ont été suite à la proposition de Me T. B. Smith.

direction. S'ils expriment leur intérêt pour un sujet particulier, le Secrétariat, responsable de la réalisation du programme de travail, convoque un groupe d'experts non gouvernementaux qui développe un projet de convention qui sera ensuite revu par des experts gouvernementaux. Une conférence diplomatique est ensuite convoquée par un pays membre d'Unidroit pour adopter la convention.

Depuis sa création, Unidroit a préparé plus de soixante-dix études et projets de conventions ou autres documents portant principalement sur la vente, le crédit, le transport, la loi applicable à la responsabilité civile, etc. et a préparé sept conventions qui furent adoptées lors de conférences diplomatiques.[14] Les travaux d'Unidroit ont aussi mené à l'adoption de conventions internationales au sein d'autres organisations internationales.[15] Unidroit publie la *Revue de droit uniforme* et a développé les *Principes d'Unidroit relatifs aux contrats du commerce international, 1994*. Une conférence diplomatique aura lieu en juin 1995 à Rome pour adopter un projet de convention élaboré par un groupe d'experts gouvernementaux sur les biens culturels volés ou illicitement exportés.

D   COMMISSION DES NATIONS UNIES POUR LE DROIT
     COMMERCIAL INTERNATIONAL

Quant à la Commission des Nations Unies pour le droit commercial international (CNUDCI) elle a été créée par résolution de l'Assemblée générale des Nations Unies en 1966. C'est l'organe principal des Nations Unies dans le domaine du droit commercial international et elle a pour mandat d'encourager l'harmonisation et l'unification progressives du droit commercial international, entre autres, en préparant de nouvelles conventions internationales et lois types ainsi qu'en encourageant la codification et une acceptation plus générale des termes, règles, usages et pratiques du commerce international, en recherchant les moyens d'assurer l'inter-

14 Ce sont, entre autres, la Convention sur la représentation en matière de vente internationale de marchandises, la Convention internationale de 1973 sur la loi uniforme sur la forme d'un testament international, la Convention d'Unidroit sur le crédit-bail international et la Convention d'Unidroit sur l'affacturage international, les deux dernières conventions ayant été adoptées lors d'une conférence diplomatique qui a eu lieu à Ottawa en 1988.

15 Ce fut le cas de la Convention de 1954 de l'Unesco pour la protection des biens culturels en temps de conflit armé, de la Convention de La Haye de 1958 concernant la reconnaissance et l'exécution des décisions en matière d'obligations alimentaires envers les enfants et de la Convention des Nations Unies sur les contrats de vente internationale de marchandises.

prétation et l'application uniformes des conventions internationales
et des lois uniformes dans le domaine du droit commercial et en
rassemblant et en diffusant des informations sur les législations nationales et sur l'évolution juridique moderne, y compris celle de la
jurisprudence, dans le domaine du droit commercial international.[16]
   La CNUDCI est composée de 36 États membres représentant les
diverses régions du monde, élus par l'Assemblée générale des
Nations Unies pour un mandat de six ans. Tout État membre des
Nations Unies peut aussi assister aux réunions de la CNUDCI et de
ses groupes de travail comme observateur. Le Canada a participé
comme observateur aux travaux de la CNUDCI depuis 1973 et a été
élu membre en 1988.[17]
   La Commission décide de son programme de travail après examen des propositions faites par les gouvernements et en consultation avec d'autres organisations internationales. Les travaux préparatoires des questions inscrites au programme de travail de la
Commission sont confiés à des groupes de travail gouvernementaux
dont la composition varie selon le sujet à traiter. Il y a maintenant
trois groupes de travail, le Groupe de travail sur les échanges de
données informatisées, le Groupe de travail des pratiques en
matière de contrats internationaux et le Groupe de travail sur le
nouvel ordre économique international. Les groupes de travail font
rapport à la Commission lors de sa session annuelle. Les projets de
lois types et de conventions et les guides juridiques ou autres
documents qu'ils développent sont soumis pour adoption à la Commission. Ils sont ensuite adoptés par l'Assemblée générale des
Nations Unies qui convoque en général, dans le cas des conventions, une conférence diplomatique lors de laquelle la convention
sera finalement adoptée et ouverte à la signature et ratification des
États membres des Nations Unies.
   C'est au sein de la CNUDCI que la Convention des Nations Unies
sur les contrats de vente internationale de marchandises et la Loi
type sur l'arbitrage commercial ont été développées.[18] La CNUDCI

[16] CNUDCI, La Commission des Nations Unies pour le droit commercial international, Nations Unies, New York (1987) (no de vente F.86.V.8) p.57.

[17] À partir de mai 1995, l'Australie remplacera le Canada pour une période de six
ans. Le Canada participera alors comme observateur aux travaux de la
CNUDCI.

[18] La CNUDCI a en outre adopté la Convention de 1974 sur la prescription en
matière de vente internationale de marchandises, la Convention de 1978 sur le
transport de marchandises par mer, la Convention de 1988 sur les lettres de

publie des résumés des décisions rendues sur les conventions et lois types qu'elle adopte. Trente-et-un des soixante-dix-huit résumés publiés à date sont des résumés de décisions rendues par des tribunaux canadiens portant sur la Loi type de la CNUDCI sur l'arbitrage commercial international.[19]

Parmi les sujets à l'ordre du jour de la session de 1995 figurent le projet de convention concernant les garanties et les lettres de crédit stand-by développé par le Groupe de travail des pratiques en matière de contrats internationaux et les règles en matière d'échanges de données informatisées développées par le Groupe de travail sur les échanges de données informatisées.

Le Canada a une grande expérience de l'unification du droit privé[20] et du développement du droit international privé[21] vu l'exis-

change internationales et les billets à ordre internationaux et la Convention de 1991 sur la responsabilité des exploitants de terminaux de transport dans le commerce international, la Loi type sur les virements internationaux, deux lois types sur la passation des marchés et divers guides juridiques dont ceux sur l'établissement de contrats internationaux de construction d'installations industrielles et sur les opérations internationales d'échanges compensés.

[19] Voir Nations Unies, Assemblée Générale, Commission des Nations Unies pour le droit commercial international, A/CN.9/SER.C/ABSTRACTS/1 à 5.

[20] La Conférence des commissaires sur l'uniformisation des lois, devenue la Conférence sur l'uniformisation des lois, fut créée en 1918 suite à la recommandation de l'Association du Barreau canadien et a pour mandat de promouvoir l'uniformité des lois des provinces. Organisation non gouvernementale formée de professeurs, de membres de commissions de réforme du droit, de praticiens et de fonctionnaires des ministères de la Justice, la Conférence adopte des lois uniformes qui sont ensuite soumises aux provinces pour adoption. Chaque province est libre de les adopter, avec ou sans amendements. Le gouvernement fédéral participe depuis 1935 à ces réunions et il en est résulté une certaine uniformité entre lois provinciales et fédérales dans les domaines où des lois semblables sont adoptées par les deux juridictions. Voir le rapport écrit en 1970 par J. W. Ryan en collaboration avec G. Lehoux, pour publication dans l'Annuaire d'Unidroit, *Proceedings of the Fifty-third Annual Meeting of the Conference of Commissioners on Unification of Legislation in Canada* (1971), à la p. 414. Les auteurs notent qu'à l'époque la Conférence avait adopté cinquante-deux lois types portant sur le droit de la famille, les testaments et les trusts, le droit commercial, la procédure et des questions diverses. L'article 94 de la *Loi constitutionnelle de 1867* aborde la question de l'uniformité des lois pour les provinces de common law en permettant au Parlement du Canada de pourvoir à l'uniformité de lois relatives à la propriété et aux droits civils et de la procédure des tribunaux si la législature de la province adopte cette loi. Mais cet article n'a pas été utilisé.

[21] Le Code civil du Bas-Canada de 1866 contenait quelques règles de droit international privé (en particulier les articles 6, 7, 7.1, 8, et 8.1). Le nouveau

tence de règles de droit et de systèmes juridiques différents au sein
de la fédération canadienne, mais ce n'est qu'en 1968 que le
Canada est devenu membre de la Conférence de La Haye et d'Unidroit et il n'est pas devenu partie à des conventions multilatérales
dans le domaine du droit international privé avant les années 70.[22]

Code Civil du Québec, entré en vigueur le 1er janvier 1994, en contient
presque cent. Voir Livre dixième, Droit international privé, art. 3076-3168, qui
s'inspire largement des conventions de La Haye et de la codification suisse tel
qu'énoncé à la Loi fédérale sur le droit international privé, du 18 décembre
1987. Voir P. Glenn, "Droit International privé: La réforme du Code civil,
textes réunis par le Barreau du Québec et la Chambre des Notaires du Québec,
1993," tome III, à la p. 779, note 4. Les règles de droit international privé des
provinces de common law sont d'origine britannique. Nos tribunaux ont
développé le droit international privé applicable dans les provinces de common
law et au Québec. Voir E. Groffier, *Précis de droit international privé québecois*, 4e
éd. (Cowansville: Yvon Blais, 1990), à la p. 14. Jusqu'à très récemment, les
conflits entre les lois de diverses provinces, y compris, dans certains cas, celles
du Québec, ainsi que la reconnaissance et l'exécution par les tribunaux d'une
province de jugements rendus par les tribunaux d'une autre province étaient
réglés en s'inspirant des règles britanniques de droit international privé applicables dans les relations juridiques internationales sans tenir compte des
exigences constitutionnelles. En 1990, la Cour Suprême du Canada a jugé que
les tribunaux avaient fait une erreur en transposant les règles élaborées pour la
reconnaissance et l'exécution de jugements étrangers dans l'Angleterre du
dix-neuvième siècle à la reconnaissance et l'exécution par les tribunaux d'une
province de jugements rendus par les tribunaux d'une province "soeur." De
l'avis de la Cour, les règles britanniques vont à l'encontre de l'intention de
créer en vertu de la constitution canadienne un marché commun et un système
judiciaire unifié. Par conséquent, les tribunaux d'une province doivent
accorder pleine confiance et crédit aux jugements rendus par un tribunal
d'une autre province à condition qu'il ait exercé sa compétence à bon droit ou
de façon appropriée. Un tribunal ne peut exercer sa compétence que s'il a un
lien réel et substantiel avec l'action. *Morguard Investments Ltd.* c. *De Savoye*
[1990] 3 R.C.S. 1077. Le caractère constitutionnel de cette exigence a depuis
été confirmé dans *Hunt* c. *T & N plc*, [1993] 4 R.C.S. 289. Voir aussi *Tolofson* c.
Jensen et *Lucas* c. *Gagnon*, rendus le 15 décembre 1994, sur le choix de la loi
applicable dans le cas d'un accident automobile impliquant des résidents de
différentes provinces. Un grand nombre d'articles ont été publiés depuis l'arrêt
Morguard. Voir, entre autres, ceux publiés dans (1993) 22 Can. Bus. L. J. Voir
aussi P. W. Hogg, *Constitutional Law of Canada*, vol. 1, 3d ed.(Supplemented),
(Toronto: Carswell, 1992) aux pp. 13-13 à 13-24, sur le lien entre le droit
international privé et la constitution.

22 Entre 1928 et 1939, le Canada a conclu des traités avec dix-neuf États portant
sur la procédure en matière civile et commerciale. Ces traités se basaient sur
des traités conclus par le Royaume-Uni en matière de signification de documents judiciaires et autres et obtention des preuves. Ces traités sont encore en
vigueur et sont utilisés avec la coopération des provinces. Lors de son adhésion

Cette participation tardive du Canada aux activités internationales de développement du droit international privé s'explique en partie par la situation géographique du Canada qui a sans doute contribué à minimiser les cas d'application de lois avec un élément étranger, et au fait que la tradition de la common law a fourni des règles flexibles pour régler les questions qui se posaient. Le contexte constitutionnel canadien explique aussi l'inactivité du Canada dans ce domaine.

II LE CONTEXTE CONSTITUTIONNEL CANADIEN

La participation du Canada aux activités d'organisations internationales dans le domaine de l'unification du droit privé soulève la question de la compétence dans le domaine des affaires extérieures, plus précisément l'appartenance à des organisations internationales, la négociation, signature et ratification de traités et leur mise en oeuvre. C'est dans la constitution canadienne, dont le préambule énonce qu'elle repose sur les mêmes principes que celle du Royaume-Uni, que l'on retrouve les règles applicables à la conduite des relations internationales. La compétence du Canada dans ce domaine a suivi l'évolution du statut du Canada, qui est passé de colonie en 1867 à État souverain entre 1919 et 1931.

Il n'y a rien dans la Loi constitutionnelle de 1867 sur la participation du Canada à des organisations internationales ni sur la conclusion de traités par le Canada ou leur mise en oeuvre parce que cette situation n'avait pas été envisagée. Le Canada était à l'époque une colonie britannique et la conduite des affaires internationales au sein de l'Empire britannique relevait de la Couronne impériale et n'avait pas été déléguée aux gouverneurs coloniaux.[23] Les colonies n'avaient pas la souveraineté extérieure et leurs pouvoirs exécutifs ne s'étendaient pas à l'extérieur de leur territoire. Elles ne pou-

---

à la Convention de La Haye relative à la signification et la notification à l'étranger des actes judiciaires et extrajudiciaires en matière civile ou commerciale, le Canada, après consultation avec les provinces, a déclaré qu'il continuerait à être lié par ces traités, tel que le permet l'article 25 de la Convention. Ces traités sont mentionnés à l'Annexe A de la publication du ministère des Affaires extérieures relative à l'entraide judiciaire internationale et certaines autres matières, 1987, p.75. Voir aussi Castel, "International Civil Procedure," dans *Canadian Perspectives on International Law and Organization, infra* note 38, à la p. 855, note 1.

[23] Voir F. Chevrette et H. Marx, *Droit constitutionnel* (Montréal: Presses de l'Université de Montréal, 1982), aux pages 1181-82.

vaient pas, par exemple, signer de traités.[24] La seule disposition de la Loi constitutionnelle de 1867 qui touche à un aspect des affaires internationales, l'article 132, reflète la situation de l'époque et se réfère aux traités conclus par l'Empire britannique, c'est-à-dire par le gouvernement britannique, qui s'appliquent au Canada. Son principal effet semble avoir été de donner au parlement et au gouvernement fédéral le pouvoir de mettre en oeuvre les traités de l'empire, et ce, même s'ils portent sur des matières relevant de la compétence législative provinciale.[25]

En droit constitutionnel britannique, l'appartenance à une organisation internationale et la conclusion de traités relèvent de la prérogative royale et il n'y a pas d'obligation juridique d'y associer le Parlement.[26] Mais la compétence de l'Exécutif de conclure des traités n'équivaut pas à une compétence indirecte de légiférer. En d'autres termes, l'Exécutif ratifie le traité, le Parlement adopte les lois. Un traité conclu par l'Exécutif, bien que créant des obligations en vertu du droit international, ne fait pas partie automatiquement du droit interne et ne crée pas de droits privés. Dans les rares cas où son exécution relève de la prérogative, il pourra être mis en oeuvre

24 Voir D. P. O'Connell, *International Law*, vol. 1, 2d ed. (London: Stevens & Sons, 1970), aux pp. 346-47; P. W. Hogg, *supra* note 21, et pp. 11-12; *Renvoi relatif au plateau continental de Terre-Neuve* [1984] 1 R.C.S.86, aux pp. 99-101.

25 L'article 132 de la *Loi constitutionnelle de 1867* a donné au Parlement et au gouvernement du Canada le pouvoir de "remplir envers les pays étrangers, comme portion de l'Empire Britannique, les obligations du Canada ou d'aucune de ses provinces, naissant de traités conclus entre l'empire et ces pays étrangers." En 1867, les traités portaient surtout sur la paix, les alliances, la navigation et le commerce mais ils pouvaient, à l'occasion, toucher au domaine du droit privé. Par exemple, le Traité de commerce avec le Japon accordait aux Japonais le traitement de la nation la plus favorisée dans l'exercice de leur profession. Une loi provinciale visant à empêcher l'emploi de Chinois et de Japonais fut jugée invalide parce qu'elle allait à l'encontre de la loi fédérale de mise en oeuvre du Traité. Voir *A.-G. of British Columbia* v. *A.-G. of Canada* [1923] A.C. 384. L'article 132 a aussi écarté l'application de la doctrine de l'incompétence législative territoriale des colonies dans la mesure où les obligations imposées par ces traités pouvaient avoir un aspect extraterritorial. Le Traité sur les eaux limitrophes de 1909 et la Convention de 1916 sur la protection des oiseaux migrateurs, conclus entre la Grande-Bretagne et les États, sont des traités de l'Empire au sens de l'article 132.

26 Le Parlement approuve à l'occasion le traité par résolution ou par une loi mais cette approbation ne doit pas être confondue avec la ratification du traité, qui relève de l'Exécutif, et ne suffit pas, en tant que telle, pour donner force de loi au traité. Voir l'*arrêt sur les conventions du travail, A.-G. for Canada* v. *A.-G. for Ontario*, [1937] A.C. 326 aux pp. 347-48.

directement par le pouvoir exécutif sans qu'une loi interne ne soit requise pour l'incorporer au droit canadien. Dans la plupart des cas cependant, on ne peut donner effet au traité que si le droit interne en permet l'application. Si le droit interne est différent du traité, il est nécessaire de le modifier car le traité ne fait pas, à lui seul, partie du droit interne. Dans ce cas, seul le Parlement peut donner force de loi au traité ou en transposer autrement les obligations en droit interne.[27] Le droit britannique est différent sur ce point du droit en vigueur dans des pays comme les États-Unis et la France où la constitution associe le pouvoir législatif à la ratification des traités et dispose que le traité, une fois ratifié par l'exécutif, fait partie du droit interne.

La situation constitutionnelle du Canada a évolué progressivement. Ainsi, dès 1871, des représentants du gouvernement canadien ont participé aux négociations du Traité de Washington, un traité de l'Empire s'appliquant au Canada.[28] Les traités de commerce conclus par l'Empire ne furent plus étendus au Canada sans son consentement après 1880[29] et des représentants canadiens ont co-signé des traités commerciaux affectant le Canada. Des clauses coloniales ont été insérées dans les traités conclus par le Royaume-Uni permettant au Royaume-Uni d'étendre les traités aux colonies ou à certaines d'entre elles. Le Canada a participé avec les autres Dominions à la conférence de paix de 1919, a co-signé le Traité de Versailles et est devenu membre de la Société des Nations et de l'Organisation internationale du Travail. La Convention de 1923 avec les États-Unis sur la protection du flétan a été le premier traité

---

[27] "The government may negotiate, conclude, construe, observe, breach, repudiate or terminate a treaty. Parliament may alter the laws of the United Kingdom. The courts must enforce those laws; judges have no power to grant specific performance of a treaty or to award damages against a sovereign state for breach of a treaty or to invent laws or misconstrue legislation in order to enforce a treaty. . . . Except to the extent that a treaty becomes incorporated into the laws of the United Kingdom by statute, the courts of the United Kingdom have no power to enforce treaty rights and obligations at the behest of a sovereign government or at the behest of a private individual." *J. H. Rayner (Mincing Lane) Ltd.* v. *Dept. of Trade and Industry* [1990] 2 A.C. 418 à la page 476. Voir aussi McNair, *The Law of Treaties* (Oxford: Clarendon Press, 1961) aux pp. 81-97; *The Parlement Belge* [1880] 5 PD 197; *Walker* v. *Baird* [1892] AC 491; *A.-G. for Canada* v. *A.-G. for Ontario, supra* note 26, aux pp. 347-48.

[28] Voir A. E. Gotlieb, *Canadian Treaty-Making* (Toronto: Butterworths, 1968), à la p. 7.

[29] McNair, *supra* note 27, à la p. 112, note 1.

conclu par le Canada de son propre chef.[30] La Conférence impériale de 1926 adopta la déclaration Balfour acceptant le principe de l'égalité de statut du Royaume-Uni et des Dominions et reconnut aux Dominions le pouvoir de négocier, signer et ratifier des traités.[31] Enfin le Statut de Westminster de 1931 consacrait la dernière étape de l'indépendance des dominions en reconnaissant qu'aucune loi du Royaume-Uni ne s'étendrait à un dominion sauf si elle stipulait expressément que le dominion a demandé la loi et consenti à son adoption et en déclarant le pouvoir des parlements des dominions d'adopter des lois avec effet extraterritorial.[32] C'est dans les lettres patentes de 1947 constituant la fonction de gouverneur général que l'on trouve l'octroi formel au gouverneur général du pouvoir de conclure des traités. En vertu de l'article 2, le gouverneur général est autorisé à exercer tous les pouvoirs appartenant légalement au souverain en ce qui concerne le Canada.[33]

---

[30] Treaties and Agreements Affecting Canada 1814-1924, (1927), p. 505. La Cour Suprême du Canada a noté que le Gouvernement du Canada avait obtenu la reconnaissance internationale de son pouvoir indépendant de contracter des obligations extérieures lors de la négociation du Traité sur le flétan et que les conférences impériales subséquentes l'avaient confirmé. Voir *Renvoi sur la résolution pour amender la Constitution du Canada*, [1981] 1 R.C.S. 753, pp. 802-3.

[31] La Conférence adopta le rapport du comité sur les relations inter-impériales déclarant les dominions et la Grande-Bretagne communautés autonomes au sein de l'Empire britannique, égales du point de vue statut et n'étant pas subordonnées les unes aux autres dans leurs affaires internes ou extérieures. Voir McNair, *supra* note 27, à la p. 113 et Hogg, *supra* note 21, aux pp. 3-5.

[32] Articles 4 et 3. Les provinces ne possèdent pas ce pouvoir d'adopter des lois extraterritoriales. La Cour Suprême du Canada a jugé que "la souveraineté canadienne a été acquise dans la période entre la signature séparée par le Canada du Traité de Versailles en 1919 et le Statut de Westminster en 1931." Voir *Renvoi: Offshore Mineral Rights of British Columbia* [1967] R.C.S. 792 à la p. 816.

[33] Même sans cette délégation expresse, l'accession du Canada à l'indépendance entraînerait nécessairement la compétence de conclure des traités. Voir Hogg, *supra*, note 21, c.11.2. Certains auteurs ont allégué que les provinces auraient le pouvoir de conclure des traités dans les domaines de compétence provinciale. Voir entre autres J.-Y. Morin, (1967) 45 R. du B. Can. 160. La théorie d'un éventuel pouvoir provincial de conclure des traités a été rejetée par le gouvernement fédéral et en pratique ce dernier exerce un pouvoir exclusif en la matière. Dans "The Labour Conventions Case Revisited," (1974) A.C.D.I. 137 à la p. 138, M. le Juge La Forest rappelle que déjà dans l'*arrêt sur les conventions internationales du travail* la majorité des juges de la Cour Suprême était d'avis que le statut international du Canada lui permettait de conclure des traités et que d'ailleurs la question est réglée depuis le *Renvoi sur les droits miniers*

La question qui s'est posée dès les années 1920 était de savoir si le pouvoir de mettre en oeuvre les traités, corollaire de la compétence de conclure des traités (*treaty-making power*), relevait aussi du fédéral.

Un premier jugement répond en partie à cette question, le *Renvoi sur la réglementation et le contrôle de la radiocommunication.*[34] Afin que le Canada se conforme à la Convention internationale sur la radiotélégraphie de 1927 il fallait réglementer les fréquences radio au Canada. Le comité judiciaire du Conseil Privé a jugé que ce pouvoir ne pouvait être fondé sur l'article 132 puisque la convention en question n'était pas un traité de l'Empire ayant été conclue par le Canada de son propre chef. Le pouvoir de réglementer les radiocommunications reposait plutôt sur le pouvoir de légiférer relativement aux ouvrages interprovinciaux (article 92 (10) a)) et pour la paix, l'ordre et le bon gouvernement du Canada. Le Comité judiciaire a vu dans ce dernier pouvoir un pouvoir de mise en oeuvre des traités conclus par le Canada comme il n'y avait pas dans les articles 91 et 92 de pouvoir explicite à ce sujet. Mais ce raisonnement fut rejeté dans l'arrêt sur les *conventions du travail.*[35]

Dans cet arrêt, le comité judiciaire du Conseil Privé était appelé à se prononcer sur la validité de lois fédérales de mise en oeuvre de conventions de l'Organisation internationale du Travail portant sur la durée des heures de travail, le repos hebdomadaire, et le salaire minimum. Le jugement est bien connu, l'article 132 n'autorise pas la mise en oeuvre de traités conclus par le Canada en vertu de son nouveau statut de personne internationale et, comme il n'y a pas dans notre constitution de compétence législative portant sur les traités en tant que tels, les règles normales de partage des compétences législatives s'appliquent. Par conséquent même si l'Exécutif fédéral peut conclure un traité portant sur des matières relevant de la compétence législative des provinces, le Parlement fédéral ne peut légiférer pour le mettre en oeuvre si la matière couverte par le traité ne tombe pas sous un chef de compétence fédérale. Le Comité judiciaire du Conseil Privé a conclu:

---

sous-marins [1967] R.C.S. 792. Voir aussi *Renvoi: résolution pour modifier la Constitution* [1981] 1 R.C.S. 753 à la p. 823 et *Renvoi relatif au plateau continental de Terre-Neuve* [1984] 1 R.C.S. 86. Voir aussi Hogg, *supra*, note 21, c.11-17 à 19. Voir aussi *A.-G. Ont.* v. *Scott* [1956] S.C.R. 137 et *Bazylio c. Collins* (1985) 11 D.L.R. (4th) 679.

[34] 1932 A.C. 304.

[35] Voir *supra* note 26.

It must not be thought that the result of this decision is that Canada is incompetent to legislate in performance of treaty obligations. In totality of legislative powers, Dominion and Provincial together, she is fully equipped. But the legislative powers remain distributed, and if in the exercise of her new functions derived from her new international status Canada incurs obligations they must, so far as legislation be concerned, when they deal with Provincial classes of subjects, be dealt with by the totality of powers, in other words by co-operation between the Dominion and the Provinces.[36]

L'arrêt des *conventions du travail* a suscité bien des commentaires. Certains l'ont critiqué et ont estimé que le tribunal avait privé le Canada des moyens dont il avait besoin pour affirmer sa personnalité internationale et le paralysait ni plus ni moins dans le domaine des affaires étrangères. D'autres ont salué la clairvoyance du tribunal qui avait su préserver l'équilibre délicat entre le fédéral et les provinces au sein de la fédération canadienne. Quoi qu'il en soit, l'arrêt représente toujours l'état du droit canadien en matière de traités.[37] Il est indéniable qu'il a eu un impact sur la participation du Canada à des traités portant sur l'unification du droit privé vu que le droit privé relève en grande partie de la compétence législative des provinces et que chaque province a ses règles de droit

---

[36] *Ibid.*, à la p. 354.

[37] Des commentateurs ont vu dans certains *obiter dicta* dans les arrêts *John A. Macdonald and Railquip Enterprises Ltd.* c. *Vapour Canada Ltd.* [1977] 2 R.C.S. 134, aux pages 169, 171 et *Schneider* v. *The Queen* [1982] 2 R.C.S. 112, aux pages 134-35, une indication que certains juges seraient prêts à le reconsidérer. M. le Juge La Forest, quant à lui, estimait dans un article publié en 1974 que ce n'est pas en renversant l'*arrêt sur les conventions du travail* que les tribunaux reconnaîtront plus de pouvoirs au Parlement pour mettre en oeuvre des mesures internationales. Il voyait plutôt que les tribunaux pourraient développer certains domaines ayant des répercussions internationales évidentes et ce, non seulement en vertu du pouvoir de légiférer pour la paix, l'ordre et le bon gouvernement du Canada, mais aussi en vertu de chefs de compétence comme la naturalisation et les aubains, l'immigration, le mariage et le divorce ainsi que la réglementation du commerce. Quant au traité, il pourrait servir dans certains cas à établir qu'une question a atteint des dimensions nationales. Voir *supra* note 33, à la p.151. Hogg, lorsqu'il traite de révisions possibles de *l'arrêt des conventions internationales du travail*, suggère une distinction entre les traités qui visent l'harmonisation du droit interne, qui continueraient d'être soumis à l'arrêt de 1937, et ceux en vertu desquels les parties s'obligent à des obligations réciproques dont le caractère international ne fait pas de doute et qui seraient mis en oeuvre par législation fédérale. Voir *supra* note 21, aux pp.11-16.

international privé qui font partie de la *common law*, du droit statutaire ou du Code civil.[38]

Mais le Canada n'est pas le seul État fédéral et la pratique internationale montre comment les États fédéraux ont tenté de limiter leurs
obligations conventionnelles lorsque le traité qu'ils négociaient portait sur des matières relevant de la compétence de leurs unités
constituantes afin de faciliter leur participation à ces traités ou comment ils ont permis la participation d'une de leurs unités constituantes à un traité qui n'intéressait pas les autres unités constituantes.

III   LES RÉSERVES, LES CLAUSES FÉDÉRALES ET LES ACCORDS-
CADRES DANS LA PRATIQUE INTERNATIONALE

Il arrive qu'un État fédéral fasse, lorsqu'il ratifie un traité, une
réserve visant à exclure les matières relevant de la compétence
législative de ses unités constituantes.[39] Dans d'autres cas, des
clauses dites "clauses fédérales"[40] ont été insérées dans les traités

38 Voir, entre autres, J. E. C. Brierley, "International Trade Arbitration: The
Canadian Viewpoint" dans R. St. J. MacDonald, G. L. Morris & D. M. Johnston,
eds., *Canadian Perspectives on International Law and Organization* (Toronto: University of Toronto Press, 1974), 826 à la p.835 qui attribuait (en 1974)
l'absence de participation du Canada aux traités multilatéraux dans le domaine
de l'arbitrage au problème de la mise en oeuvre des traités portant sur des
matières de compétence provinciale. Voir, au même effet, P. J. Davidson,
"Uniformity in International Trade Law: The Constitutional Obstacle" (1987)
11 Dalhousie L.J. 677 aux pp. 678-80. Voir aussi *supra* note 21. Le gouvernement des Pays-Bas avait demandé au gouvernement du Canada en 1955 s'il était
intéressé à devenir membre de la Conférence de La Haye de droit international
privé. Le gouvernement canadien répondit qu'il avait consulté l'Association du
Barreau canadien (dont l'un des objectifs est de promouvoir l'unification du
droit privé au Canada) et qu'elle n'avait pas exprimé d'intérêt particulier pour
les travaux de la Conférence et qu'il ne pouvait envoyer de délégation, même à
titre d'observateur, à la prochaine session, car il outrepasserait sa compétence
constitutionnelle vu que la matière traitée ne relevait pas de la compétence
législative fédérale. Rapporté dans Castel, *supra* note 2, à la p. 31.

39 La Convention sur les droits politiques de la femme ne comportant pas de
clause fédérale, le gouvernement canadien a fait une réserve au moment de la
ratification de la Convention par le Canada "au sujet des droits qui relèvent de
la compétence législative des provinces." Voir A.-M. Jacomy-Millette, *L'introduction et l'application des traités internationaux au Canada* (Paris: Librairie générale
de droit et de jurisprudence, 1971), à la p. 64.

40 La pratique internationale connaît un autre type de clauses, les clauses
d'application territoriale, qu'il ne faut pas confondre avec les clauses fédérales.
Ces clauses d'application territoriale permettent à un État de déclarer que la
convention à laquelle il devient partie s'étendra à l'ensemble des territoires

afin de tenir compte de la situation constitutionnelle des États fédéraux lorsque le traité porte sur des matières relevant de la compétence législative des unités constituantes de l'État fédéral. La pratique des clauses fédérales n'est pas nouvelle et l'on en trouve des exemples dans des traités bilatéraux conclus par les États-Unis au siècle dernier.[41]

Une des premières clauses dites fédérales dans une convention multilatérale se retrouve dans la Constitution de l'Organisation internationale du travail rédigée en 1919. Elle résulte d'un compromis entre le Royaume-Uni et les États-Unis. Le Royaume-Uni désirait voir dans la Constitution de l'Organisation internationale du travail une obligation pour les États membres de ratifier toutes les conventions adoptées par l'OIT à moins que le parlement de l'État membre n'exprime son refus.[42] La délégation américaine s'est objectée vigoureusement à cette proposition, estimant que vu qu'aux États-Unis le droit du travail relevait de la compétence des États, le gouvernement fédéral ne pourrait souscrire à des obligations qu'il ne pourrait respecter.[43] Le compromis retenu apparaît à l'article 405 du Traité de Versailles. Il dispose que dans le cas d'un

---

qu'il représente sur le plan international ou à l'un ou plusieurs d'entre eux. Ce type de clauses remonte au siècle dernier et les traités conclus par la Grande-Bretagne en contiennent plusieurs exemples ainsi que les conventions de La Haye. Il s'agit en vérité d'une clause coloniale et la référence aux territoires vise des territoires autres que le territoire métropolitain de l'État, des territoires d'outre-mer en quelque sorte. La principale différence entre les clauses d'application territoriale et les clauses fédérales est que la clause fédérale est une clause de *compétence* visant à limiter les obligations de l'État fédéral en ce qui concerne les articles du traité portant sur des matières relevant de la compétence législative de ses unités constituantes, tandis que la clause d'application territoriale est une clause *territoriale* qui n'a aucune application dans le cas d'un État fédéral composé de provinces, d'états ou de cantons et qui n'a pas de possessions à l'extérieur de son territoire. Voir I. Bernier, *International Legal Aspects of Federalism* (1973), aux pp. 172-73.

41 *Ibid.*, aux pp. 173-74.

42 Le Premier Ministre du Canada d'alors, Sir Robert Borden, aurait soulevé la question de l'application d'une telle proposition à des États fédéraux mais il estimait que cela pourrait être réglé. Voir R. B. Looper, "'Federal State' Clauses in Multilateral Instruments," (1955-56) 32 B.Y.B.I.L. 162 à la p. 165.

43 L'arrêt *Missouri v. Holland*, qui a reconnu le pouvoir de conclure des traités dans les domaines de compétence étatique ne fut rendu que l'année suivante. Voir Looper, *ibid.*, à la p. 169. Comme l'a noté M. Hudson, "Membership of the United States in the International Labour Organization," (1934) 28 American Journal of International Law à la p. 673, il y avait nettement confusion entre le pouvoir de conclure un traité et le pouvoir de le mettre en oeuvre.

État fédéral dont le pouvoir de conclure des conventions en matière de travail est limité, le gouvernement de cet État pourra traiter le projet de convention comme une recommandation.[44] Quant aux recommandations de l'OIT, elles doivent être portées par ce gouvernement à l'attention des parlements concernés pour qu'ils puissent décider s'ils sont prêts à leur donner effet.

La Constitution de l'OIT fut amendée en 1946[45] afin d'améliorer le processus d'approbation des conventions et la clause fédérale alors introduite et toujours en vigueur impose à l'État fédéral les mêmes obligations qu'aux États unitaires en ce qui concerne les conventions et recommandations que le gouvernement fédéral juge appropriées pour une action fédérale. Quant aux conventions et recommandations que le gouvernement fédéral juge appropriées pour une action provinciale, le gouvernement fédéral est tenu de les référer aux autorités compétentes afin qu'elles adoptent la législation requise.[46] Cette clause ouvre la porte à une interprétation peut-être encore plus large que la précédente en ce qu'elle permet à un État fédéral qui a la compétence de mettre en oeuvre une convention par législation fédérale de la référer à ses autorités provinciales ou cantonales pour la simple raison qu'il ne lui semble pas approprié de recourir au pouvoir de mise en oeuvre fédéral.

Des clauses fédérales ont été insérées dans d'autres traités des Nations Unies comme, par exemple, la Convention relative au statut des réfugiés du 28 juillet 1951,[47] la Convention des Nations Unies de 1956 sur le recouvrement des aliments à l'étranger[48] et la

---

[44] Même si, en théorie, cette clause n'aurait pas dû s'appliquer aux États-Unis et aux autres États fédéraux comme le Canada où le pouvoir de *conclure* des traités n'est pas limité, certains États fédéraux ont interprété cette clause comme si elle leur permettait de considérer les conventions de l'OIT comme des recommandations tandis que les États unitaires étaient soumis à des obligations nettement plus onéreuses. Le Canada a adopté un décret en 1920 affirmant que les obligations imposées par le Traité de Versailles seraient respectées si les projets de conventions et les recommandations étaient soumis aux autorités compétentes fédérales ou provinciales. Voir Looper, *supra* note 42, à la p. 176.

[45] Entre-temps, la Cour Suprême du Canada avait confirmé dans *In the Matter of Legislative Jurisdiction over Hours of Labour* (1925) R.C.S. 505 que les obligations conventionnelles du Canada pouvaient être satisfaites en référant les conventions et recommandations de l'OIT aux autorités fédérales ou provinciales et le Comité Judiciare du Conseil privé avait rendu son arrêt sur les *conventions du travail*. Voir *supra* note 26.

[46] Voir Looper, *supra* note 42, à la p. 182.

[47] Article 41 R.T.N.U. 1954 aux pp.180-82.

[48] Article 11 268 R.T.N.U. à la p. 32.

Convention des Nations Unies de 1958 pour la reconnaissance et l'exécution des sentences arbitrales étrangères.[49] Ces clauses s'inspirent de la clause de l'OIT en ce qu'elles établissent une distinction entre les articles du traité qui relèvent de la compétence législative du pouvoir fédéral et ceux qui relèvent de la compétence législative des états ou provinces constituants. Dans le premier cas, les obligations de l'État fédéral partie à la convention sont les mêmes que celles des États unitaires parties à la convention; dans le deuxième cas, l'État fédéral est tenu de porter le plus tôt possible et avec une recommandation favorable le traité à l'attention de ses états ou provinces.[50]

Ces clauses fédérales ont été critiquées parce qu'elles créent un manque de réciprocité entre les obligations des États fédéraux et celles des États unitaires dans l'application d'un traité.[51] En outre, elles introduisent beaucoup d'incertitude car les parties au traité ne connaissent pas les détails de la constitution de l'État fédéral et on ne peut présumer qu'elles sauront dans quel cas le traité peut ou non être appliqué par l'État fédéral. Il est arrivé que des propositions d'insérer une clause fédérale de ce type dans un traité aient été refusées.[52]

Les clauses fédérales que connaissait la pratique internationale de l'époque n'étaient pas satisfaisantes pour des conventions en matière de droit privé. En effet, en plus du manque de réciprocité et de l'incertitude qu'elles créent quant à l'étendue des obligations de l'État fédéral elles ne favorisent pas l'uniformité recherchée par les conventions qui unifient le droit. C'est pourquoi le Canada estimait que les clauses fédérales du type "OIT" ne facilitaient pas

[49] L.R.C. (1985) ch. 16 (2e suppl.).

[50] La clause fédérale qui figure à l'article XXIV de l'Accord général sur les tarifs douaniers et le commerce (GATT) (RTNU 1950, p. 273) est différente. Cette clause impose aux parties contractantes l'obligation de prendre toutes mesures raisonnables en leur pouvoir pour que les autorités gouvernementales ou administratives, régionales et locales, de leur territoire observent les dispositions de l'Accord. L'interprétation que lui ont donnée certains panels permet de se demander si elle accorde quoi que ce soit de plus à l'État fédéral qu'un délai, avant d'être jugé coupable de manquement à ses obligations, afin de lui permettre de convaincre les autorités régionales et locales de son territoire de prendre les mesures d'application appropriées.

[51] Voir Looper, *supra* note 42, aux pp. 200-3.

[52] Ce fut le cas pour les Pactes des Nations Unies sur les droits civils et politiques et sur les droits sociaux et économiques qui contiennent un article (article 50 dans le cas du premier pacte, 28 dans le cas du deuxième pacte) stipulant qu'ils s'appliquent à toutes les parties d'un État fédéral.

la participation des États fédéraux dans les conventions de droit international privé. Il fallait une clause qui permettrait au Canada de devenir partie à une convention même si certaines provinces n'y voyaient pas d'intérêt et qui établirait avec clarté et certitude dans quelle mesure le Canada sera lié par la convention dans son entier.

À part la clause ou la réserve fédérale une autre technique à laquelle le Canada a recouru est celle de l'accord-cadre conclu avec un État étranger permettant à des provinces de conclure des ententes avec cet État.[53]

IV   LA PARTICIPATION DU CANADA À L'UNIFICATION INTERNATIONALE DU DROIT PRIVÉ

Entre 1960 et 1970, plusieurs voix se firent entendre en faveur d'une participation canadienne aux efforts internationaux d'uniformisation du droit privé. Dans un article qu'il écrivait en 1965, le professeur Castel recommandait que le Canada devienne membre de la Conférence de La Haye et d'Unidroit estimant que c'était tout à fait réalisable en autant que les provinces soient consultées et que les traités élaborés par ces organisations contiennent des clauses fédérales.[54] L'attitude des gouvernements, de la Conférence des commissaires pour l'uniformisation de la législation ainsi que de l'Association du Barreau canadien a évolué et les problèmes constitutionnels n'apparaissaient plus insurmontables.[55] En 1966, le ministère fédéral de la Justice informait la Conférence des commissaires sur l'uniformisation des lois des étapes envisagées pour la participation du Canada à la Conférence de La Haye et à l'Institut international pour l'unification du droit privé.[56] En 1967, le premier ministre du Canada a écrit à ses collègues provinciaux pour les informer de l'intention du Canada de devenir membre de la Conférence de La Haye de droit privé et d'Unidroit et de recourir à la

---

[53] Voir J.-Y. Morin, *supra* note 33, aux pp. 170-71 qui cite l'échange de lettres entre le Canada et la France du 27 février 1965 par lequel le Canada donnait son consentement à l'Entente France-Québec du même jour sur les échanges et la coopération dans le domaine de l'éducation ainsi que l'Accord culturel entre le Canada et la France du 17 novembre 1965 et de l'échange de lettres l'accompagnant qui permettait aux provinces de conclure des ententes avec la France. Voir aussi Castel, *supra* note 2, aux pp. 29-30.

[54] Voir *supra* note 2.

[55] *Ibid.*, à la p. 32.

[56] Voir *Proceedings of the Forty-Ninth Annual Meeting of the Conference of Commissioners on Uniformity of Legislation in Canada* (1967), à la p. 19.

Conférence des commissaires sur l'uniformisation des lois pour faciliter la participation des provinces aux conférences organisées par ces deux organisations. Après consultation avec les provinces le Canada a adhéré en 1968 à la Conférence de La Haye et à Unidroit. Pour satisfaire aux exigences du Statut de la Conférence, le Ministère de la Justice a été nommé "organe national."

Trois questions importantes devaient être adressées: comment aider et conseiller le ministère de la Justice qui était responsable de la participation canadienne au sein des organisations internationales de droit privé, comment faciliter la ratification de conventions portant en tout ou en partie sur des matières relevant de la compétence législative des provinces et comment faciliter la mise en oeuvre au Canada de telles conventions?

A   LES MÉCANISMES DE CONSULTATION FÉDÉRALE-PROVINCIALE

La participation des provinces à toutes les étapes a été jugée essentielle dès le départ.[57] Des représentants provinciaux font partie des délégations canadiennes aux conférences et aux réunions des groupes de travail élaborant les conventions internationales portant sur des matières relevant de la compétence provinciale. La pratique suivie par le ministère de la Justice est de faire en sorte que les délégations canadiennes comprennent des représentants des deux systèmes de droit et tiennent compte de la dualité linguistique du Canada. Une consultation étroite, allant de contacts informels aux échanges de correspondance ministérielle, se poursuit aux différentes phases de la négociation de conventions ou lois types portant sur des matières provinciales. Toujours dans le but d'assurer une participation effective aux travaux des organisations internationales de droit international privé, des experts du milieu universitaire ou de la pratique privée ont fait partie des délégations canadiennes.

Le nouveau rôle du Canada dans l'unification internationale du droit privé exigeait un appui soutenu. La formule retenue pour obtenir cet appui était celle d'un comité formé de quatre membres

---

57 La délégation canadienne à la Onzième session comprenait le sous-ministre délégué de la Justice du Canada, un représentant de la Conférence des commissaires sur l'uniformisation des lois et quatre personnes choisies parmi les personnes nommées par les procureurs généraux des provinces. Une de ces personnes avait été nommée par le procureur général du Québec pour assurer la représentation du droit civil, les trois autres représentaient les provinces de common law. Voir *Proceedings of the Fifty-First Annual Meeting of the Conference of Commissioners on Uniformity of Legislation in Canada* (1969), à la p. 75.

représentant la région de l'Atlantique, de l'Ouest, de l'Ontario et du Québec qui conseillerait le ministère de la Justice dans la formulation des politiques relatives à la Conférence de La Haye et Unidroit et dont les membres feraient à l'occasion partie des délégations canadiennes aux sessions de ces organisations internationales et pourraient ensuite travailler à la mise en oeuvre des conventions adaptées. Le Groupe consultatif de droit international privé et de l'unification du droit fut créé en août 1973.[58] Les membres du Groupe sont nommés pour une période de quatre ans par le sous-ministre fédéral de la Justice après consultation de ses collègues provinciaux. Chaque province a eu l'occasion d'être représentée au sein du groupe. Le Groupe, qui se réunit deux fois l'an, discute de façon informelle de questions de droit international privé et d'unification du droit privé. Il passe en revue les travaux des organisations internationales qui oeuvrent dans le domaine de l'unification du droit privé et du droit international privé et discute de l'intérêt que diverses conventions peuvent représenter pour le Canada ainsi que des modalités de la consultation à entreprendre avec les provinces et groupes intéressés. Il aide aussi le ministère de la Justice à établir des priorités dans ce domaine et participe à la promotion des conventions dans les provinces. Le Groupe a joué et continue à jouer un rôle essentiel dans la participation canadienne à l'unification internationale du droit privé. Grâce à lui un véritable réseau de personnes-ressources au niveau provincial et dans la pratique privée a été établi au cours des ans.

Une autre question à régler après l'adhésion du Canada à la Conférence de La Haye et d'Unidroit, au plan international cette fois, était celle de la participation du Canada aux conventions internationales de droit privé portant en partie sur des matières de compétence provinciale. Il s'agissait de faciliter la participation du Canada à ces conventions en lui permettant de devenir partie à ces conventions si une province ou plusieurs provinces le demandaient, sans avoir à obtenir l'appui de toutes les provinces.

---

[58] Le Groupe comprend maintenant cinq membres représentant la région de l'Atlantique, le Québec, l'Ontario, les provinces des Prairies et la Colombie-Britannique ainsi qu'un observateur, le Président de la Section du droit international de l'Association du Barreau canadien. Un avocat du ministère des affaires étrangères assiste aux réunions du Groupe. La région de l'Atlantique est actuellement représentée par l'Île-du-Prince-Édouard tandis que celle des prairies l'est par le Saskatchewan. Les représentants provinciaux au sein du groupe sont des avocats des ministères de la Justice ou du procureur général de ces provinces. Il est arrivé qu'une province soit représentée par un praticien.

B LA CLAUSE FÉDÉRALE-PROVINCIALE TERRITORIALE

Dans son rapport à la Conférence sur l'uniformisation des lois le représentant de la Conférence à la Onzième session de la Conférence de La Haye avait exprimé l'espoir qu'une formule puisse être trouvée qui permette la ratification de conventions de La Haye.[59] La Conférence des commissaires sur l'uniformisation des lois a adopté une résolution recommandant que les délégations canadiennes prenant part à l'élaboration de conventions d'unification du droit fassent insérer dans ces conventions une clause fédérale dont le texte serait finalisé après consultation et qui permettrait la mise en oeuvre intégrale de ces conventions dans toute province qui le désirerait.[60]

[59] Les conventions adoptées lors de la Onzième Session de la Conférence de La Haye portaient sur des matières relevant en grande partie de la compétence législative des provinces. Deux d'entre elles, celle sur la reconnaissance des divorces et des séparations de corps et celle sur la loi applicable en matière d'accidents de la circulation routière, contiennent une clause qui va au-delà de l'habituelle clause coloniale. En vertu de cette clause, l'État contractant qui comprend deux ou plusieurs systèmes de droit pourra déclarer que la convention qu'il ratifie s'étendra à tous ces systèmes de droit ou à l'un ou plusieurs d'entre eux et pourra à tout moment modifier cette déclaration. Cette clause était plus proche de ce que le Canada voulait mais elle n'était pas idéale vu qu'elle pouvait être interprétée comme renvoyant seulement aux systèmes de droit civil et de common law et non pas aux différentes lois en vigueur dans les provinces de common law et dans les territoires. Lors de la session de 1972, la délégation canadienne a cherché à faire clarifier par la Conférence que l'expression "systèmes de droit" pouvait viser non seulement le droit civil et la common law mais aussi que chaque province ou territoire sera considéré comme constituant un système distinct de droit pour cette fin. L'interprétation canadienne a été acceptée par la Conférence. Conférence de La Haye de droit international privé, Actes et Documents de la Douzième session, Tome I Matières diverses, Document de travail no 5: Note de la délégation canadienne, I-91 et Procès-verbal No 4.

[60] Le rapport de 1970 préparé pour la Conférence par les commissaires du Québec passe en revue la pratique canadienne en matière de traités qui, selon eux, démontre que vu l'absence de moyens adéquats de consultation avec les provinces et de ratification des traités, les traités portant sur des matières de compétence provinciale n'ont pas été mis en oeuvre au Canada. Il constate l'insuffisance des clauses fédérales existantes et note qu'une clause fédérale qui permettrait au gouvernement fédéral de rendre la convention applicable dans toute province qui le désirerait pourrait régler le problème de la mise en oeuvre des conventions portant sur des matières relevant de la compétence législative des provinces. L'avantage de cette technique serait que la convention s'appliquerait dans cette province comme dans un pays unitaire tout en préservant la structure fédérale du Canada et protégeant la responsabilité fédérale dans le

C'est en 1972 que les délégations canadienne et américaine à la Douzième Session de la Conférence de La Haye ont proposé la clause fédérale territoriale qui a été incluse depuis lors dans les conventions de droit international privé.[61] La clause fédérale proposée était nouvelle.[62] Ce n'est pas une clause basée sur la répartition des compétences au sein de l'État fédéral comme la clause "OIT." C'est une clause "territoriale." Elle s'applique à un État qui a deux ou plusieurs unités territoriales, c'est-à-dire des unités composantes (provinces, cantons, états) situées sur le territoire de l'État, qui ont leurs propres règles de droit. Elle permet à l'État fédéral lorsqu'il ratifie la convention de l'étendre à une ou plusieurs de ses "unités territoriales." La déclaration peut être modifiée afin d'étendre la convention à d'autres unités territoriales.[63] En pratique, dans le cas du Canada, elle permet au Canada de ratifier une convention qui aurait été mise en oeuvre par une ou plusieurs provinces et de ne pas attendre que toutes les provinces l'ait mise

---

domaine des relations internationales. Voir *Proceedings of the Fifty-Second Annual Meeting of the Conference of Commissioners on Uniformity of Legislation in Canada* (1970), à la p. 42.

[61] H. A. Leal, "Federal State Clauses and the Conventions of The Hague Conference on Private International Law," (1984) 8 Dalhousie L.J. 257-83. La clause fédérale a été proposée du côté canadien, par le chef de la délégation canadienne, le sous-ministre fédéral de la Justice. D'autres délégations, comme le Royaume-Uni et l'Israël, ont appuyé la proposition canado-américaine.

[62] La pratique internationale de l'époque contenait plusieurs exemples de clauses fédérales mais aucune ne ressemblait à celle proposée par les délégations canadienne et américaine. En présentant le document de travail le délégué des États a indiqué qu'il s'agissait là d'une question très importante pour les deux délégations qui le proposaient et que la proposition visait à standardiser les clauses fédérales dans les conventions de La Haye. Voir Conférence de La Haye de droit international privé, Actes et documents de la douzième session, Tome I, Matières diverses, Document de travail No 9 — Joint Proposal of the United States and Canada for a Standard Model of "Federal State" Clauses, I-107; Procès-verbal No 4, I-108-10.

[63] La Convention de La Haye sur l'administration internationale des successions contient une clause fédérale territoriale à l'article 35 qui se lit ainsi: "Tout État contractant qui comprend deux ou plusieurs unités territoriales dans lesquelles des systèmes de droit différents s'appliquent en ce qui concerne l'administration des successions, pourra déclarer que la présente Convention s'étendra à toutes ces unités territoriales ou seulement à l'une ou à plusieurs d'entre elles, et pourra à tout moment modifier cette déclaration en faisant une nouvelle déclaration. Ces déclarations indiqueront expressément l'unité territoriale à laquelle la Convention s'applique. . . . ."

en oeuvre.[64] Elle permet aussi d'étendre par la suite la convention aux autres provinces au fur et à mesure qu'elles ont pris les mesures de mise en oeuvre requises.

La clause fédérale territoriale conduit à un résultat clair et précis. Elle spécifie les unités constituantes dans lesquelles les autres parties au traité pourront s'attendre à une application pleine et entière du traité. Elle indique précisément où le traité s'applique plutôt que dans quelle mesure il s'applique.[65]

En plus de la clause fédérale territoriale, dite aussi clause fédérale de ratification, une clause fédérale d'interprétation a été insérée dans quelques conventions de droit international privé. Avec la présence

[64] Leal, *supra* note 61, à la p. 273 note que la clause fédérale territoriale développée pour les conventions de droit international privé donne plein effet au *treaty-making power* fédéral et au pouvoir provincial de mise en oeuvre des traités portant sur des matières relevant de la compétence provinciale.

[65] Le ministère de la Justice a déployé de nombreux efforts pour faire accepter la clause fédérale territoriale dans diverses instances internationales. En 1973, une clause fédérale territoriale a été insérée dans la Convention de Washington sur la forme internationale des testaments qui avait été développée par Unidroit. En 1974, elle fut insérée dans la Convention des Nations Unies sur la prescription en matière de vente internationale de marchandises et dans les conventions adoptées par la Conférence spécialisée interaméricaine en droit international privé (CIDIP I). Voir *Proceedings of the Fifty-Sixth Annual Meeting of the Uniform Law Conference of Canada* (1974), aux pp. 149-54, App. R. et *Proceedings of the Fifty-Seventh Annual Meeting of the Uniform Law Conference of Canada* (1975), aux pp. 261-64, App. Y. Lors de la quatorzième session de la Conférence de La Haye, l'Australie, qui venait de devenir membre de la Conférence, a proposé une addition à la clause fédérale territoriale. L'addition stipule que la ratification de la convention par un État qui a un système de gouvernement en vertu duquel les pouvoirs exécutif, judiciaire et législatif sont partagés n'emportera aucune conséquence quant au partage interne des pouvoirs dans cet État. Cette addition figure dans les deux conventions adoptées en 1980, la Convention sur les aspects civils de l'enlèvement international d'enfants, article 41, et la Convention tendant à faciliter l'accès international à la justice, article 27. Cette clause avait été demandée par l'Australie pour des raisons de politique constitutiónnelle. Dans son rapport, le rapporteur spécial remarque qu'un grand nombre de délégations estimaient inutile l'introduction de cet article dans les deux conventions, Actes et Documents de la Quatorzième session (1980), tome III, enlèvement d'enfants, Rapport explicatif de Mlle Elisa Pérez-Vera, p. 472. En raison des développements jurisprudentiels dans ce pays (en particulier l'arrêt *Commonwealth v. Tasmania* (Franklin Dam), (1983) 158 C.L.R.1, l'Australie n'a plus besoin de ce genre de clauses et n'a pas demandé à ce qu'elle soit insérée dans d'autres conventions. Voir P. Brazil, "The Experience of Federal States," *Droit uniforme international dans la pratique*, Actes du troisième Congrès de droit privé organisé par l'Institut international de droit privé, Unidroit, Rome, 7-10 septembre 1987, Unidroit (Rome: Oceana Publications, 1988), 66 à la p. 76 et Leal, *supra* note 61.

des clauses fédérales territoriales/ratification il est devenu nécessaire de préciser le sens de termes que l'on retrouve fréquemment dans les conventions de droit privé comme, par exemple, la loi applicable de l'État ou la résidence habituelle dans l'État. Les conventions précisent qu'il s'agit alors de la loi applicable ou de la résidence dans l'unité territoriale. Le principal but de ces clauses est d'aider le juge étranger dans un système de droit unitaire à comprendre les systèmes fédéraux. C'est une clause interprétative et non substantive.[66]

Enfin, la mise en oeuvre des conventions fut facilitée grâce à la préparation de lois uniformes par la Conférence sur l'uniformisation des lois.

C   LA MISE EN OEUVRE DES CONVENTIONS DE DROIT
     INTERNATIONAL PRIVÉ

La pratique canadienne révèle plusieurs façons de mettre en oeuvre les traités.[67] Le traité peut être incorporé dans une courte loi qui donne expressément force de loi au traité ou à certaines de ses dispositions et le traité ou certaines de ses dispositions sont reproduits en annexe dans la loi.[68] Dans d'autres cas, le traité est mis en oeuvre par une loi qui édicte des dispositions équivalentes à celles du traité sans toutefois s'y référer.[69] Il arrive aussi que bien que le traité soit reproduit en annexe la loi ne lui donne pas force de loi et se contente d'édicter des clauses qui ont pour objet de permettre l'application du traité en droit interne en autant qu'il est nécessaire pour respecter les obligations que le traité impose au Canada.[70]

La méthode à laquelle la Conférence des commissaires sur l'uniformisation des lois a recouru dans la plupart des cas est de rédiger

---

66 Pour une explication de la distinction entre clauses fédérales/ratification et clauses fédérales/interprétation, voir Leal, *supra* note 61.

67 Voir C. C. Emmanuelli et S. Slosar, "L'application et l'interprétation des traités internationaux par le juge canadien" (1978) 13 R.J.T. 69, aux pp. 73-74.

68 C'est le cas des conventions visant à éviter la double imposition. Voir par exemple, la Loi de 1980 sur la Convention Canada-Espagne en matière d'impôt sur le revenu L.C. 1980-81-82-83 ch.44. Voir aussi la Loi sur les missions étrangères et les organisations internationales mettant en oeuvre certaines dispositions des conventions sur les relations diplomatiques et consulaires, L.C. 1991, ch.14.

69 Voir l'article 7 du *Code criminel* qui donne effet aux engagements du Canada pris en vertu de conventions internationales dans le domaine du droit aérien et du droit maritime.

70 Voir la Loi de mise en oeuvre de l'Accord de libre-échange Canada-États-Unis, L.C. 1988 ch.65.

une courte loi uniforme donnant force de loi à la convention reproduite en annexe[71] et prescrivant qu'en cas de conflit entre la loi, la convention ou toute autre loi, la présente loi et la convention l'emportent. Les lois fédérales mettant en oeuvre les conventions de droit privé ont en général donné force de loi aux conventions reproduites en annexe. Un des avantages de cette technique de mise en oeuvre est d'encourager les tribunaux à interpréter la convention qui a reçu force de loi en faisant appel aux règles et principes d'interprétation des traités tels que reconnus en droit international.[72] Les lois uniformes n'ont pas toujours été adoptées sans modification par les législatures provinciales.[73]

[71] C'est le cas, par exemple, des lois uniformes sur la Convention sur les aspects civils de l'enlèvement international d'enfants, sur la Convention de La Haye sur la loi applicable aux trusts et à leur reconnaissance, sur la Convention des Nations Unies sur les contrats de vente internationales de marchandises et sur la Convention entre le Royaume-Uni et le Canada sur la reconnaissance et l'exécution des jugements en matière civile et commerciale.

[72] Dans l'arrêt *Thomson* c. *Thomson* [1994] 3 R.C.S.551, la Cour Suprême du Canada a eu recours aux articles 31 et 32 de la Convention de Vienne sur le droit des traités pour interpréter la Convention de La Haye sur les aspects civils de l'enlèvement d'enfants à laquelle la loi manitobaine avait donné force de loi. En ce qui a trait aux travaux préparatoires, le Juge La Forest a indiqué qu'il "serait étrange qu'un traité international auquel la législature a tenté de donner effet ne soit pas interprété dans le sens que les États parties au traité doivent avoir souhaité. Il n'est donc guère surprenant que les parties aient fréquemment recours à ce moyen complémentaire d'interpréter la Convention, et je ferai de même. Je remarque que notre Cour a récemment adopté cette position à l'égard de l'interprétation d'un traité international dans *Canada (Procureur général)* c. *Ward* [1993] 2 R.C.S. 689." La Cour a aussi eu recours à un article publié par le président de la Commission de la Conférence de La Haye qui a élaboré la Convention auquel elle semble donner un statut quasi égal à celui des travaux préparatoires ainsi qu'à la jurisprudence d'États parties à la Convention vu que "la Cour doit déterminer du mieux qu'elle peut l'état du droit en se rapportant aux décisions pertinentes." *Ibid.*, à la p. 30.

[73] Dans l'arrêt *Thomson* c. *Thomson*, la Cour Suprême du Canada note la manière diverse selon laquelle chaque province a légiféré pour mettre en oeuvre la Convention de La Haye sur les aspects civils de l'enlèvement d'enfants. Le Manitoba a adopté la Convention dans une loi générale portant sur les aspects civils des enlèvements d'enfants et ne donnant pas primauté à la Convention en cas de conflit avec une autre loi. La question était de savoir si les deux régimes législatifs s'appliquaient, celui de la Convention et celui de la loi générale. La question était d'importance car si régime général s'appliquait en plus de la Convention, les tribunaux manitobains auraient eu le pouvoir d'ordonner la garde provisoire de l'enfant (et ce alors même que la Convention l'interdit). La Cour a conclu que le régime général ne s'appliquait pas à une demande de retour faite en vertu de la Convention. *Ibid.*

V LE BILAN

Le bilan de ces années est positif. Non seulement le Canada participe avec les autres États au développement de règles qui peuvent lui être applicables par la suite mais, grâce à la clause fédérale territoriale, le Canada a trouvé la formule la plus appropriée qui soit pour permettre aux provinces selon leur propre choix d'intégrer à leur droit les conventions développées au plan international et faire bénéficier leurs résidents des avantages de ces conventions.

Depuis 1968, le Canada est devenu partie à sept conventions et a mis en oeuvre une loi type de la CNUDCI.[74] Tous ces instruments portent sur des matières relevant en tout ou en partie de la compétence provinciale et devaient être mis en oeuvre par les provinces. Deux de ces conventions, la Convention sur la reconnaissance et l'exécution des sentences arbitrales et la Convention sur la signification des documents ne comportaient pas la clause fédérale territoriale.

La Convention de 1958 des Nations Unies sur la reconnaissance et l'exécution des sentences arbitrales porte sur des matières relevant à la fois de la compétence législative du fédéral et des provinces. Elle contient une clause fédérale type OIT qui n'est pas acceptable pour le Canada et il a fallu des lois de mise en oeuvre en place dans toutes les provinces et territoires ainsi qu'au fédéral[75] avant que le Canada n'y devienne partie. Le Canada y a adhéré en 1986. Pendant des années la complexité des efforts nécessaires pour entreprendre les consultations requises avec toutes les provinces sur la mise en oeuvre de la Convention a joué contre une participation canadienne à cette convention.[76] La situation a

74 Ce sont la Convention de New York sur la reconnaissance et l'exécution des sentences arbitrales, la Convention de La Haye sur les aspects civils de l'enlèvement international d'enfants, la Convention de La Haye sur la notification et la signification de documents judiciaires ou quasi-judiciaires, la Convention de La Haye sur la loi applicable aux trusts et à leur reconnaissance, la Convention d'Unidroit sur la forme internationale des testaments, la Convention des Nations Unies sur les contrats de vente internationale de marchandises, la Convention Canada-Royaume-Uni sur la reconnaissance et l'exécution des jugements en matière civile ou commerciale et la Loi type sur l'arbitrage commercial.

75 S.C. 1986, c. 22.

76 Ainsi qu'en témoigne une lettre du Ministre fédéral de la Justice citée dans J.-G. Castel, "Canada and International Arbitration" (1981) 36 Arb. J. 5, aux

changé au début des années 1980 et des consultations fédérales-provinciales intensives ont été engagées en 1984-85 qui ont mené dans un délai relativement court à l'adhésion canadienne. L'expérience de la mise en oeuvre de cette convention démontre qu'il est possible avec beaucoup de travail et une grande motivation de la part des gouvernements provinciaux et fédéral de devenir partie à une convention dans un délai relativement court. Les lois de mise en oeuvre de cette convention ont été introduites en même temps que les lois mettant en oeuvre la loi type de la CNUDCI sur l'arbitrage commercial international de 1985.[77] Cette loi type constitue un code de procédure de l'arbitrage et le Canada fut parmi les premiers États à l'incorporer à son droit interne.

Il a fallu aussi que toutes les provinces et les territoires prennent des mesures de mise en oeuvre de la Convention de 1964 sur la notification et signification de documents judiciaires ou quasi-judiciaires car cette convention, ayant été adoptée par la Conférence de La Haye avant 1972, ne contient pas de clause fédérale. L'absence de clause fédérale dans ce cas a ralenti de beaucoup le processus d'adhésion à cette convention à laquelle le Canada est devenu partie en 1988. La consultation fédérale-provinciale s'est étendue sur une période de plus de quinze ans.[78]

Les cinq autres conventions auxquelles le Canada est devenu partie ont été développées après 1972 et contiennent la clause fédérale territoriale négociée par le Canada.[79] Le Canada a accédé en 1977 à la Convention d'Unidroit sur la forme internationale des testaments adoptée en 1973 et elle a alors été étendue à deux provinces. Il a ratifié en 1983 la Convention de La Haye sur les

---

pp. 9-10 et dans J. L. Friesen, "The Distribution of Treaty-Implementing Powers in Constitutional Federations: Thoughts on the American and Canadian Models" (1994) Columbia Law Rev. 1415, à la p. 1436.

77 S.C. 1986, c. 21.

78 Cette convention fut portée à l'attention des provinces en 1979 et en 1980 l'appui de principe de toutes les provinces était gagné. Plusieurs échanges de correspondance eurent lieu pour déterminer les modalités de son application au Canada.

79 Ce sont la Convention de La Haye sur les aspects civils de l'enlèvement international d'enfants, la Convention de La Haye sur la loi applicable aux trusts et à leur reconnaissance, la Convention d'Unidroit sur la forme internationale des testaments, la Convention des Nations Unies sur les contrats de vente internationale de marchandises, la Convention Canada-Royaume-Uni sur la reconnaissance et l'exécution des jugements en matière civile ou commerciale. Les lois types ne contiennent pas de clause fédérale vu qu'elles peuvent être mises en vigueur en tout ou en partie à la convenance des États.

aspects civils de l'enlèvement international d'enfants adoptée en 1980 qui a alors été étendue à quatre provinces. Il a ratifié en 1986 la Convention Canada-Royaume-Uni sur la reconnaissance et l'exécution des jugements de 1984, a ratifié en 1988 la Convention de La Haye sur la loi applicable aux trusts et à leur reconnaissance adoptée en 1984 qui fut étendue à cinq provinces et a adhéré en 1991 à la Convention de 1980 sur les contrats de vente internationale de marchandises. En devenant partie à ces conventions le Canada a déclaré qu'elles s'étendraient à certaines provinces seulement, celles qui avaient adopté les lois de mise en oeuvre requises. Les déclarations canadiennes ont été modifiées par la suite et les conventions ont été étendues à d'autres provinces au fur et à mesure qu'elles adoptaient les lois de mise en oeuvre requises. La Convention de Vienne sur la vente et la Convention de La Haye sur l'enlèvement d'enfants sont maintenant en vigueur partout au Canada.

Les délais de ratification des conventions contenant la clause fédérale territoriale ont été relativement courts si on les compare au temps mis par des États unitaires pour les ratifier. Par exemple, le Canada était l'un des trois États dont la ratification a contribué à faire entrer en vigueur la Convention sur l'enlèvement d'enfants et a été parmi les premiers États qui ont ratifié la Convention sur les trusts. Quant à la Convention sur la vente, ce n'est qu'à partir de 1987 que la consultation fédérale-provinciale a été engagée et lorsque l'adhésion canadienne est intervenue en 1991 presque toutes les provinces avaient mis en oeuvre la convention. En plus de permettre au Canada de ratifier la Convention sur la vente ainsi que la Convention de La Haye sur l'enlèvement d'enfants avant que toutes les provinces et les deux territoires qui appuyaient ces conventions aient adopté les lois de mise en oeuvre requises, la clause fédérale territoriale a permis aux juridictions qui le désiraient de bénéficier de la participation à l'effort international d'unification du droit en matière de loi applicable aux trusts et de forme du testament international ainsi qu'à la Convention sur la reconnaissance et l'exécution des jugements entre le Royaume-Uni et le Canada, et ce, même si toutes les juridictions canadiennes n'étaient pas prêtes à le faire.[80]

---

[80] La Convention sur la forme internationale des testaments est en vigueur en Alberta, au Manitoba, en Ontario, à l'Île-du-Prince-Édouard, en Saskatchewan et à Terre-Neuve; la Convention sur la loi applicable aux trusts et à leur

Le bilan est positif aussi du point de vue de la coopération qui s'est instaurée entre le ministère de la Justice et les provinces, que ce soit au sein du Groupe consultatif de droit international privé, au sein de la Conférence sur l'uniformisation des lois ou lors de contacts directs à divers niveaux. Il faut aussi rappeler la consultation et l'échange d'informations avec la profession juridique et avec les organismes intéressés par l'unification internationale du droit privé.

Il reste cependant encore beaucoup à faire. Par exemple, il existe des conventions qui ont fait leur preuve, qui semblent apporter une solution utile à des problèmes qui se posent dans les relations internationales et qui ne sont toujours pas en vigueur au Canada. La Convention de La Haye sur l'obtention des preuves en est une.[81] Déjà dans les années 70 la Conférence sur l'uniformisation des lois recommandait que le Canada y adhère. L'Association du Barreau canadien l'a aussi recommandé. Vingt ans plus tard, la consultation avec les provinces quant à l'opportunité pour le Canada d'y adhérer n'est pas concluante.

Ce qui peut sembler être un faible taux de ratifications par le Canada n'est pas toujours dû au système constitutionnel canadien. La clause fédérale territoriale et les mécanismes de consultation et de coopération fédérale-provinciale ont réglé ce problème en grande partie. Mais il faut reconnaître que la codification du droit international privé n'est pas la principale préoccupation des gouvernements et que les projets de loi mettant en oeuvre ces conventions ne trouvent pas toujours une place sur les calendriers législatifs chargés. Si les groupes à qui ces conventions peuvent bénéficier ne manifestent pas leur intérêt il est normal que les conventions ne soient pas ratifiées dans les meilleurs délais. Car ce ne sont pas les gouvernements, fédéral ou provinciaux, qui bénéficieront de ces conventions dans le domaine de l'unification du droit privé. Ce sont plutôt les résidents du Canada qui ont des relations avec l'étranger qui en bénéficieront. La coopération fédérale-provinciale a ses limites, surtout si les groupes susceptibles de bénéficier de ces conventions ne manifestent pas leur intérêt à ce que le Canada y participe. S'il existe un intérêt, comme ce fut le

---

reconnaissance est en vigueur en Alberta, en Colombie-Britannique, au Manitoba, au Nouveau-Brunswick, à l'Île-du-Prince-Édouard, en Saskatchewan et à Terre-Neuve; la Convention Canada-Royaume-Uni est en vigueur dans toutes les provinces et territoires, à l'exception du Québec.

81 La Suisse vient d'y adhérer et a déclaré lors de son adhésion qu'elle considérait la Convention comme moyen exclusif d'obtenir des preuves.

cas, par exemple, pour la Convention sur la reconnaissance et l'exécution des sentences arbitrales commerciales et pour la Convention sur l'enlèvement d'enfants, les mécanismes de consultation fédérale-provinciale sont en place pour permettre d'agir assez rapidement. Il n'est pas toujours facile de susciter un tel intérêt et dans certains cas la communauté juridique elle-même hésite à recourir à ce nouveau droit.[82] Il reste à espérer que cette attitude changera au fur et à mesure que ces conventions auront été interprétées par les tribunaux et que la plus grande certitude juridique qu'elles offrent sera appréciée à cette époque où la globalisation des marchés et les relations économiques internationales multiplient les risques de conflit entre systèmes juridiques.

Enfin, la question de l'uniformisation des lois de mise en oeuvre des conventions dans chaque province et territoire ainsi qu'au plan fédéral devra être surveillée de près afin d'éviter que la même convention ne reçoive des interprétations différentes d'une juridiction à l'autre.

Conclusion

Le Canada a pris sa place dans les efforts d'unification du droit privé auxquels il apporte une contribution appréciée en tant que pays bilingue et bijuridique. Il y a beaucoup de pain sur la planche, beaucoup de conventions à l'horizon susceptibles d'être intéressantes pour les Canadiens. Des mécanismes efficaces de consultation fédérale-provinciale sont en place permettant une pleine participation des provinces dans l'élaboration et la mise en oeuvre de conventions internationales portant sur des matières relevant de la compétence législative exclusive des provinces. Il y a eu beaucoup de chemin de parcouru depuis l'époque où les exigences constitutionnelles étaient invoquées pour justifier l'inactivité du Canada en matière d'unification internationale du droit privé. Grâce à la clause fédérale territoriale et aux mécanismes de coopération fédérale-provinciale en place le Canada peut participer à l'unification internationale du droit privé et y apporter son expérience de pays bijuridique et devenir partie aux conventions portant sur des matières de compétence provinciale qui offrent un intérêt pour une ou plusieurs provinces.

---

[82] Plusieurs praticiens conseillent à leurs clients d'exclure l'application de la Convention sur la vente dans leurs contrats internationaux.

Summary

Canada and the International Unification of Private Law

This article reviews Canada's participation in the international unification of private law and private international law that is carried out by international organizations such as The Hague Conference on Private International Law, Unidroit, the United Nations Commission on International Trade Law, and the Specialized Conferences on Private International Law of the Organization of American States. It describes the new mechanisms that have been established to facilitate this participation, since the conventions developed in these organizations often deal with matters that fall within provincial legislative competence and thus need to be implemented by the provinces. The new "territorial federal State clause" that Canada has had inserted in these conventions and the federal-provincial consultation mechanisms that have been put in place have been instrumental in facilitating Canada's ratification of conventions that unify private law and private international law.

Sommaire

L'unification du droit privé

Cet article examine la participation du Canada à l'unification internationale du droit et du droit international privé telle qu'entreprise par les institutions internationales: la Conférence de la Haye sur Droit International Privé (UNIDROIT), la Commission des Nations Unies sur le Droit Commercial International ainsi que les Conférences Spécialisées sur le Droit Privé International de l'Organisation des État américains. Cet article décrit les nouveaux mécanismes mis en place afin de faciliter la participation du Canada puisque les conventions rédigées par ces organisations font souvent partie de la compétence législative des provinces canadiennes doivent donc par la suite les adopter. La nouvelle "clause territoriale de l'État fédéral" — que le Canada a inclus dans ces conventions — ainsi que les mécanismes de consultation entre l'État fédéral et les provinces permettent aisément au Canada de ratifier ces conventions qui prévoient une unification du droit privé et du droit international privé.

Reservations to Human Rights Treaties: Time for Innovation and Reform

WILLIAM A. SCHABAS*

INTRODUCTION

MOST RECENT INTERNATIONAL human rights treaties will allow any state to "sign on" unilaterally.[1] All too often, however, these actions are not entirely unconditional. A declaration of ratification or accession is frequently accompanied by reservations or "interpretative declarations,"[2] in which the state designates

---

* Professor of Law, Département des sciences juridiques, Université du Québec à Montréal.

---

[1] Convention Against Torture and Other Cruel, Inhuman and Degrading Treatment or Punishment, Dec. 10, 1984, [1987] C.T.S. No. 36, G.A. Res. 39/46, Art. 25; Convention on the Rights of the Child, Nov. 20, 1989, [1992] C.T.S. No. 3, G.A. Res. 44/25, Art. 46. Earlier human rights treaties were somewhat restrictive, requiring as a prerequisite to adhesion that the state be a United Nations member (Convention for the Prevention and Punishment of the Crime of Genocide, Dec. 9, 1948, [1948] C.T.S. No. 27, 78 U.N.T.S. 277, Art. 11), or a member of a specialized United Nations body (International Covenant on Civil and Political Rights, Dec. 16, 1966, [1946] C.T.S. No. 46, 999 U.N.T.S. 171 [hereinafter International Covenant or Covenant], Art. 48 §1; International Convention for the Elimination of All Forms of Racial Discrimination, Dec. 21, 1965, [1969] C.T.S. No. 28, 660 U.N.T.S. 195, Art. 17 §1).

[2] Art. 2 §1d of the Vienna Convention on the Law of Treaties, May 23, 1969, 1155 U.N.T.S. 331 defines a reservation as "a unilateral statement, however phrased or named, made by a State, when signing, ratifying, accepting, approving or acceding to a treaty, whereby it purports to exclude or to modify the legal effect of certain provisions of the treaty in their application to that State." In this respect, content triumphs over form. An "interpretative declaration" will be deemed a reservation if it purports to modify or exclude the legal effect of a treaty, as was stated by the European Court of Human Rights in *Belilos Case*

those parts of the treaty to which it does not wish to be bound. This technique of reservation allows a party to a multilateral treaty to ratify that instrument only partially.[3]

There are both good and bad sides to this practice. By allowing reservations, human rights treaties encourage participation by states that in general agree with the instrument but are unable or unwilling to accept a few of its provisions. This broad participation enhances the protection provided by these treaties, and generates impressive statistics as to the number of parties to a given instru-

---

(1988), Eur. Ct. H.R. Ser. A, No. 132, 10 E.H.R.R. 466, 88 I.L.R. 635. The same rule has been accepted by the Human Rights Committee: "General Comment No. 24 (52)," UN Doc. CCPR/C/21/Rev.1/Add.6, at §3; *T. K. v. France* (No. 220/1987), UN Doc. A/45/40, Vol. II, p. 118 at §8.6. See also: R. St. J. Macdonald, "Reservations Under the European Convention on Human Rights" (1988) 21 Rev. B.D.I. 428; Donald McRae, "The Legal Effect of Interpretative Declarations" (1978) 49 *British Yearbook of International Law* 160; E. Zoller, "L'affaire de la délimitation du plateau continental entre la France et la Grande-Bretagne" (1977) Ann. fran. dr. int. 370; P.-H. Imbert, "La question des réserves dans la décision arbitrale du 30 juin 1977," (1978) Ann. fran. dr. int. 29; J.-P. Quéneudec, "L'affaire de la délimitation du plateau continental entre la France et le Royaume-Uni" (1983) 83 R.G.D. Int. P. 53; Gérald Cohen-Jonathan, "Les réserves à la Convention européenne des droits de l'homme (à propos de l'arrêt Belilos du 29 avril 1988)" (1989) 93 R.G.D. Int. P. 273; J. G. Merrills, "Belilos Case" (1988) 69 *British Yearbook of International Law* 386; Henry J. Bourguignon, "The Belilos Case: New Light on Reservations to Multi-lateral Treaties" (1989) 29 *Va. J. Int'l L.* 347; Susan Marks, "Reservations Unhinged: the Belilos Case before the European Court of Human Rights" (1990) 39 I.C.L.Q. 300.

[3] On reservations generally, see Kaye Holloway, *Les réserves dans les traités multi-latéraux* (Paris: L.G.D.J., 1958); Pierre-Henri Imbert, *Les réserves aux traités multilatéraux* (Paris: Pédone, 1979); Frank Horn, *Reservations and Interpretative Declarations to Multilateral Treaties* (Amsterdam: Elsevier Science Publishers, 1988); G. Fitzmaurice, "Reservations to Multilateral Conventions" (1953) 2 I.C.L.Q. 1; W. Bishop, "Reservations to Treaties" (1961) 103 Rec. des Cours 245; D. Anderson, "Reservations to Multilateral Conventions — A Reexamination" (1964) 13 I.C.L.Q. 450; J. Nisot, "Les réserves aux traités et la Convention de Vienne du 23 mai 1969," [1973] R.G.D. Int'l P. 200; J. M. Ruda, "Reserva-tions to Treaties" (1975) 146 Rec. des Cours 95; D. W. Bowett, "Reservations to Non-Restricted Multilateral Treaties" (1976-77) 48 *British Yearbook of Interna-tional Law* 155; J. K. Gamble Jr., "Reservations to Multilateral Treaties — A Macroscopic View of State Practice" (1980) 74 AJIL 372; G. Teboul, "Remar-ques sur les réserves aux conventions de codification" [1982] R.G.D. Int'l P. 679; Dinah Shelton, "Reservations to Human Rights Treaties" [1983] *Canadian Human Rights Yearbook* 205; Daniel N. Hylton, "Default Breakdown: The Vienna Convention on the Law of Treaties' Inadequate Framework on Reservations" (1994) 27 Vand. J. Transnat'l L. 119; Massimo Coccia, "Reservations to Multi-lateral Treaties on Human Rights" (1985) 15 Calif. W. Int'l L.J. 1.

ment. The chairpersons of United Nations treaty bodies recognized at their 1992 meeting that "there is an important and legitimate role for reservations to treaties."[4] It appears that the Centre for Human Rights of the United Nations Office at Geneva actually encourages states that are considering ratification of or accession to human rights treaties to consider the technique of reservation, and offers advice on the types of reservation that might be admissible.

On the other hand, because reservations are tolerated the treaty regime may be weakened and in some cases totally undermined. Reservations frequently go well beyond mere details, and may even make the ratification virtually meaningless. A state that makes broad reservations hopes to invoke participation in the treaty regime to enhance its international image, while in fact doing little or nothing to improve the legal protection of the human rights of individuals subject to its jurisdiction. As the Human Rights Committee states in its recent General Comment on reservations to the International Covenant on Civil and Political Rights[5] and to the two Optional Protocols,[6] adopted November 2, 1994, "[t]he number of reservations, their content and their scope may undermine the effective implementation of the Covenant and tend to weaken respect for the obligations of States Parties."[7]

4 "Effective implementation of international instruments on human rights, including reporting obligations under international instruments on human rights," UN Doc. A/47/628, at §60.

5 International Covenant, *supra* note 1.

6 Optional Protocol to the International Covenant on Civil and Political Rights, Dec. 16, 1966, [1966] C.T.S. No. 46, 999 U.N.T.S. 171; Second Optional Protocol to the International Covenant on Civil and Political Rights Aimed at Abolition of the Death Penalty, Dec. 29, 1989, G.A. Res. 44/128, 29 I.L.M. 1464.

7 General Comment No. 24 (52), *supra* note 2 at §1. The Human Rights Committee's interest in the question of reservations was probably provoked by the reservations formulated by the United States of America, and specifically those to Arts. 6 and 7 of the Covenant, which concern use of the death penalty. Eleven European states have objected to the United States' reservations to these provisions. The Committee will be required to address the issue shortly, when the United States presents its initial report under Art. 40 of the Covenant. See also William A. Schabas, "Les réserves des Etats-Unis d'Amérique aux articles 6 et 7 du Pacte international relatif aux droits civils et politiques" (1994) 6 Rev. U.D.H. 137; David P. Stewart, "U.S. Ratification of the Covenant on Civil and Political Rights: The Significance of the Reservations, Understandings and Declarations" (1993) 14 HRLJ 77; V. P. Nanda, "The U.S. Reservation to the Ban on the Death Penalty for Juvenile Offenders: An Appraisal under the International Covenant on Civil and Political Rights" (1993) 42 Depaul L. Rev. 1311; E. F. Sherman Jr., "The U.S.

International human rights treaties have been both widely ratified and widely reserved. As of November 1, 1984, of the 127 parties to the International Covenant on Civil and Political Rights, 46 had formulated a total of 150 reservations to one or more of its provisions.[8] One of the most widely ratified conventions is the Convention on the Rights of the Child, with more than 165 ratifications; yet the significance of this is diluted by the fact that some 40 of the parties have also made reservations to various provisions.[9] The Convention on the Elimination of All Forms of Discrimination Against Women[10] is particularly notorious, with 42 of the 134 parties having formulated reservations.[11]

The issue of reservations to international human rights treaties has become a preoccupation of the treaty bodies charged with monitoring compliance and, in some cases, with adjudicating individual and interstate petitions.[12] At the 1992 meeting of heads of

---

Death Penalty Reservation to the International Covenant on Civil and Political Rights — Exposing the Limitations of the Flexible System Governing Treaty Formation" (1994) 29 Texas Int'l L.J. 69; John Quigley, "Criminal Law and Human Rights: Implications of the United States Ratification of the International Covenant on Civil and Political Rights" (1993) 6 Harv. Hum. Rts. J. 59.

8 Reservations, declarations, and objections to the International Covenant, as well as to other human rights treaties in the United Nations system, are published in an annual volume, "Multilateral Treaties deposited with the Secretary-general," UN Doc. ST/LEG/SER.E/11 (1992) [hereinafter "Multilateral Treaties"]. For the Covenant, a complete list is also published in Manfred Nowak, *CCPR Commentary* (Kehl: Engel, 1993).

9 Canada has formulated reservations to Art. 21 (concerning adoption in indigenous families) and to Art. 37(c) (concerning separation detention for adults and children), as well as a declaration with respect to Art. 30 (minority rights and indigenous peoples). See the discussion of the Committee on the Rights of the Child with respect to reservations in its latest annual report: UN Doc. A/49/41, at §§525-534.

10 Dec. 18, 1979, [1982] C.T.S. No. 31, 1249 U.N.T.S. 13. See also Belinda Clark, "The Vienna Convention Reservations Regime and the Convention on Discrimination Against Women" (1991) 85 AJIL 281; Rebecca Cook, "Reservations to the Convention on the Elimination of All Forms of Discrimination Against Women" (1990) 30 Va. J. Int'l L. 643; Frédéric Sudre, *Droit international et européen des droits de l'homme* 97-98 (Paris: Presses universitaires de France, 1989).

11 As of Aug. 1, 1994: UN Doc. A/49/308.

12 Interest in the issue has also been manifested by the International Law Commission, which has added "The law and practice relating to reservations to treaties" to its agenda, and appointed Prof. Alain Pellet as special rapporteur on the topic: UN Doc. A/49/10, at §382. The decision to add the topic to its agenda was endorsed by the General Assembly: UN Doc. A/RES/48/31, Art. 7.

treaty bodies, a general discussion of the situation labelled the practice "alarming," and concluded that "the States Parties concerned should be urged to withdraw the reservations and that other States Parties should not hesitate to object to such reservations as appropriate."[13] The Committee for the Elimination of Discrimination Against Women has issued a general recommendation that urges parties to reconsider their reservations and to consider the adoption of a procedure for determining the validity of reservations.[14] The Vienna Declaration and Program of Action, adopted in 1993 at the close of the World Conference on Human Rights, suggests that states avoid the practice of reservations as much as possible, and limit the scope of those deemed necessary. The Declaration states:

26. The World Conference on Human Rights welcomes the progress made in the codification of human rights instruments, which is a dynamic and evolving process, and urges the universal ratification of human rights treaties. All States are encouraged to accede to these international instruments; all States are encouraged to avoid, as far as possible, the resort to reservations.[15]

. . .

5. The World Conference on Human Rights encourages States to consider limiting the extent of any reservations they lodge to international human rights instruments, formulate any reservations as precisely and narrowly as possible, ensure that none is incompatible with the object and purpose of the relevant treaty and regularly review any reservations with a view to withdrawing them.[16]

The Declaration repeats this admonition with reference to specific treaties, notably the Convention on the Rights of the Child[17] and the Convention for the Elimination of Discrimination Against Women.[18]

The legal rules governing reservations remain extremely unclear in many respects. The substantive criterion for the legality of reser-

13 UN Doc. A/47/628, at §36 at §§60-65.

14 UN Doc. A/47/38, at 11.

15 "Vienna Declaration and Programme of Action," UN Doc. A/CONF.157/24 (Part I), chap. 3, 14 HRLJ 352.

16 *Ibid.*

17 *Supra* note 1. See also the resolution of the General Assembly: UN Doc. A/RES/47/112, art. 7, and Commission on Human Rights resolution 1992/75.

18 *Supra* note 10. See also the resolution of the General Assembly: UN Doc. A/RES/48/104, Art. 4(a).

vations, the famous "object and purpose" test, is a vague one that jurisprudence and legal scholarship have done little to clarify. It raises fascinating issues of more general import, such as the meaning of peremptory or *jus cogens* norms, the content of customary human rights norms, and the significance of derogation.

Although the practice of reservations is regularly criticized, the criticism is often tempered with caution. Treaty bodies have appeared to be particularly uncomfortable with the issue, perhaps out of fear that states will resent any intervention in this area, and possibly respond by denouncing the treaty.[19] The law has advanced in this field in recent years, with the recognition that international tribunals, other international bodies,[20] and even domestic courts[21] may pronounce on the legality of reservations, and in effect declare conventions to have a scope that the ratifying state may never have intended. Nevertheless, these developments are far from being unanimously accepted; furthermore, their impact is of limited significance in states where treaties are not directly implemented, and therefore are not subject to control by domestic courts, or where treaties do not have petition mechanisms. It is to these issues that the present study turns.

[19] Although the spectre of denunciation is regularly invoked in the context of human rights treaties, states rarely resort to this ultimate weapon. The dictatorial regime that took power in Greece in the late 1960s denounced the European Convention for the Protection of Human Rights and Fundamental Freedoms, Nov. 4, 1950, Eur. T.S. 5, 213 U.N.T.S. 221 [hereinafter European Convention of Human Rights or European Convention] ((1968) 12 *Y.B. Eur. Conv. H.R.* 78-83); when democracy was restored in 1974, Greece ratified the Convention again ((1974) 17 *Y.B. Eur. Conv. H.R.* 2-3). There were rumblings in Switzerland about denunciation of the European Convention after the European Court of Human Rights declared that country's reservation to Art. 6 §1 of the Convention to be inadmissible. Note that denunciation of the International Covenant on Civil and Political Rights is not provided for specifically and, according to some scholars, is impossible: Manfred Nowak, *CCPR Commentary, supra* note 8 at §26.

[20] *Belilos Case, supra* note 2, in the case of the European Court of Human Rights. General Comment No. 24 (52), *supra* note 2, for the Human Rights Committee. See also "The Effect of Reservations on the Entry into Force of the American Convention (arts. 74 and 75)" (1982) Int. Am Ct. H.R. Advisory Opinion OC-2/82, Ser. A, No. 2, 67 I.L.R. 559, 22 I.L.M. 37 at §§29-30, for the Inter-American Court of Human Rights.

[21] Jean-François Flauss, "Le contentieux de la validité des réserves à la CEDH devant le tribunal fédéral suisse: Requiem pour la déclaration interprétative relative à l'article 6 §1" (1993) 5 Rev. U.D.H. 297.

THE SCOPE OF RESERVATIONS

ORIGIN OF THE "OBJECT AND PURPOSE" TEST

The starting point in any analysis of reservations to international human rights treaties is the advisory opinion of the International Court of Justice,[22] which was rendered in 1951 with respect to reservations to the Convention on the Prevention and Punishment of the Crime of Genocide. The General Assembly of the United Nations had sought the opinion of the Court in order to determine the date of coming into force of the Convention, which required twenty ratifications. Certain states had formulated reservations to Article 9, which allowed a party to petition the Court if it considered another state to have breached the Convention.[23] It was suggested that such reservations might be inadmissible, and that the consequence of any inadmissibility would be to invalidate the ratification. If this were the case, then the number of ratifications would be insufficient for the Convention to come into force. Although some international conventions provided specific rules to govern the practice of reservations, because the Genocide Convention was silent on the subject the Court was required to examine the customary rules that might be applicable.

In its seven to five decision, the Court decided that classic rules derived from the law of contracts could not easily be applied in the multilateral treaty context.[24] According to the majority judgment, the contracting parties to the Genocide Convention wanted to stimulate widespread ratification, and did not intend that "an objection to a minor reservation" should result in inapplicability.[25] The Court therefore affirmed that reservations were permitted to the Convention,

---

[22] *Reservations to the Convention on the Prevention of Genocide (Advisory Opinion)*, [1951] I.C.J. Rep. 16. See also G.A. Res. 598(6).

[23] An application under Art. 9 was filed in March 1993 by Bosnia against Serbia: *Application of the Convention on the Prevention and Punishment of the Crime of Genocide, (Bosnia and Herzegovina v. Yugoslavia (Serbia and Montenegro))*, *Order of 8 April 1993*, [1993] I.C.J. Rep. 3; *Application of the Convention on the Prevention and Punishment of the Crime of Genocide, (Bosnia and Herzegovina v. Yugoslavia (Serbia and Montenegro))*, *Order of 13 Sept. 1993*, [1993] I.C.J. Rep. 325. See Christine Gray, "Application of the Convention on the Prevention and Punishment of the Crime of Genocide (Bosnia and Herzegovina v. Yugoslavia (Serbia and Montenegro))" (1994) 43 I.C.L.Q. 704.

[24] *Reservations to the Convention on the Prevention of Genocide (Advisory Opinion)*, *supra* note 22 at 21.

[25] *Ibid.*, 24.

despite the absence of any specific provision. Such reservations were, however, not without limits, and would be acceptable only where they were compatible with the "object and purpose" of the Convention. In the case of Article 9, the Court did not consider a reservation to the provision to be incompatible with the "object and purpose."

The principles governing reservations to multilateral treaties were spelled out in greater detail in the Vienna Convention on the Law of Treaties,[26] a codification treaty usually considered to set out the customary rules in this field. The Vienna Convention repeats the principle affirmed by the Court by which reservations compatible with the "object and purpose" of a treaty are admissible. Article 19 of the Vienna Convention provides:

A State may, when signing, ratifying, accepting, approving or acceding to a treaty, formulate a reservation unless:
(a) the reservation is prohibited by the treaty;
(b) the treaty provides that only specified reservations, which do not include the reservation in question, may be made; or
(c) in cases not falling under sub-paragraphs (a) and (b), the reservation is incompatible with the object and purpose of the treaty.

In the context of human rights treaties, an example of paragraph (a) is Protocol No. 6 to the Convention for the Protection of Human Rights and Fundamental Freedoms Concerning the Abolition of the Death Penalty,[27] which prohibits reservations. An example of paragraph (b) is the Second Optional Protocol to the International Covenant on Civil and Political Rights Aimed at Abolition of the Death Penalty,[28] which permits reservations allowing the application of the death penalty in time of war pursuant to a

---

[26] *Supra* note 2, Arts. 19-23.

[27] Apr. 28, 1983, Eur. T.S. no. 114, Art. 4. See also Supplementary Convention on the Abolition of Slavery, the Slave Trade, and Institutions and Practices Similar to Slavery, Sept. 7, 1956, [1963] C.T.S. No. 7, 266 U.N.T.S. 3, Art. 9; UNESCO Convention Against Discrimination in Education, Dec. 14, 1960, 429 U.N.T.S. 93, Art. 9.7.

[28] *Supra* note 6, Art. 2. See General Comment No. 24 (52), *supra* note 2 at §15. Similar provisions appear in: Convention on the Political Rights of Women, Mar. 31, 1953, [1957] C.T.S. No. 3, 193 R.T.N.U. 135, Art. 7; Convention Relating to the Status of Refugees, July 25, 1951, [1969] C.T.S. No. 29, 189 U.N.T.S. 137, Art. 42 §1; Convention on the Nationality of Married Women, Jan. 29, 1957, [1960] C.T.S. No. 2, 309 U.N.T.S. 65, Art. 8; International Convention on the Elimination of All Forms of Racial Discrimination, *supra* note 1, Art. 20; Protocol Relating to the Status of Refugees, Jan. 31, 1967, [1969] C.T.S. No. 6, 606 U.N.T.S. 267, Art. 7; Convention on the Elimination of All Forms of Discrimination Against Women, *supra* note 10, Art. 28.

conviction for a most serious crime of a military nature committed during wartime.[29] Most human rights treaties fall into the category of paragraph (c), because a provision actually spells out the "object and purpose" test,[30] or makes specific reference to the scheme of the Vienna Convention,[31] or simply because the instrument makes no provision whatsoever for reservations.[32]

In its General Comment the Human Rights Committee refers specifically to Article 19 §3 of the Vienna Convention, noting that it provides "relevant guidance," and that "its terms reflect the general international law on this matter as had already been affirmed by the International Court of Justice in the *Genocide Convention* case of 1951."[33] Furthermore, "[e]ven though, unlike some other human rights treaties, the Covenant does not incorporate a specific reference to the object and purpose test, that test governs the matter of interpretation and acceptability of reservations."[34] State practice with respect to the Covenant confirms this conclusion, with numerous objections citing the object and purpose test in attacking reservations.

It is not normal practice in treaty drafting to spell out the "object and purpose" as if one were defining technical terms. Determining

29 Spain is the only party to the Second Optional Protocol to have made such a reservation. For the Human Rights Committee's discussion of reservations to the Second Optional Protocol, see General Comment No. 24 (52), *supra* note 2 at §15.

30 E.g., Convention on the Rights of the Child, *supra* note 1, Art. 51. According to the *travaux préparatoires*, some states suggested that reference to the "object and purpose" test was unnecessary because it appeared in the Vienna Convention on the Law of Treaties. Others argued that some states were not yet parties to the Vienna Convention, and that it was therefore prudent to include such a provision. See UN Doc. E/CN.4/1989/48, at §§678-82.

31 E.g., American Convention on Human Rights, Nov. 22, 1969, 1144 U.N.T.S. 123, O.A.S.T.S. 36, Art. 75.

32 E.g., International Covenant on Civil and Political Rights, *supra* note 1; African Charter of Human and Peoples Rights, June 17, 1981, O.A.U. Doc. CAB/LEG/67/3 rev. 5, 4 E.H.R.R. 417, 21 I.L.M. 58.

33 General Comment No. 24 (52), *supra* note 2 at §6.

34 *Ibid.* The General Assembly had requested the Commission on Human Rights to include a provision authorizing reservations in the draft Covenant: G.A. Res. 546(6). Denmark and the United Kingdom proposed a reservations provision similar to the text of Art. 64 of the European Convention on Human Rights, but this was not retained: UN Doc. E/CN.4/SR.197; UN Doc. E/CN.4/L.345; UN Doc. E/CN.4/677, at §9; UN Doc. E/2573, at §§262-305; UN Doc. A/6546 at §§142-43.

a treaty's object and purpose is therefore a problem of interpretation. Interestingly, the object and purpose test appears elsewhere in
the Vienna Convention, in Article 31, which states that "[a] treaty
shall be interpreted in good faith in accordance with the ordinary
meaning to be given to the terms of the treaty in their context and
in the light of its object and purpose."[35] We are thus confronted by
a tautology, whereby the object and purpose of a treaty are to be
determined in light of its object and purpose! Among other elements useful in interpretation that are indicated by the Vienna
Convention on the Law of Treaties are the preamble,[36] "[a]ny
subsequent practice in the application of the treaty which establishes the agreement of the parties regarding its interpretation,"[37]
the preparatory work of the treaty, and the circumstances of its
conclusion.[38] Because until recently almost no litigation has
addressed the legality of reservations, and because the treaty bodies
have been extremely reticent to pronounce themselves on the
subject, virtually the only guidance comes from objections formulated by other parties who consider the reservation to be inconsistent with the object and purpose.

The object and purpose may be considerably easier to assess in
single-issue human rights conventions, such as the Genocide Convention, the Torture Convention, and the Racial Discrimination
Convention. Scrutiny of reservations to these instruments will
accordingly be quite strict. On the other hand, where human rights
conventions contemplate a wide range of rights and obligations,
not only is it more understandable that a state wishes to reserve to
one or two specific norms, but also it is more difficult to identify the
real "object and purpose" of the instrument. Two examples of

[35] *Supra* note 2; also, Art. 33 §4. The expression "object and purpose" is also
found in Art. 18, whereby a state "is obliged to refrain from acts which would
defeat the object and purpose of a treaty" if it has signed the treaty or agreed to
be bound by it. Art. 41(b)(ii) permits two states to a multilateral treaty to
modify its terms, if the modification "does not relate to a provision, derogation
from which is incompatible with the effective execution of the object and
purpose of the treaty as a whole." Under Art. 58(b)(ii), two parties to a
multilateral treaty may suspend certain of its terms if this "is not incompatible
with the object and purpose of the treaty." Under Art. 60 §3(b), a treaty may be
suspended for a material breach, which is defined as "the violation of a
provision essential to the accomplishment of the object or purpose of the
treaty."

[36] *Supra* note 2, Art. 31 §2.

[37] *Ibid.*, Art. 31 §3(b).

[38] *Ibid.*, Art. 32.

more general conventions would be the International Covenants and the Convention on the Rights of the Child.

RESERVATIONS TO PEREMPTORY NORMS AND
NON-DEROGABLE PROVISIONS

According to the Human Rights Committee, reservations that offend peremptory norms (*jus cogens*) would be incompatible with the object and purpose of a treaty.[39] A peremptory norm, according to Article 53 of the Vienna Convention, is "accepted and recognized by the international community of States as a whole as a norm from which no derogation is permitted."[40] In *Belilos* v. *Switzerland*, Judge De Meyer, in his individual concurring opinion, suggested that any reservations to the substantive provisions of the European Convention, as well as "the provisions permitting them, are incompatible with the *jus cogens* and therefore null and void, unless they relate only to arrangements for implementation, without impairing the actual substance of the rights in question."[41] Such an extreme view, while initially appealing to human rights activists, is of course totally at variance with the longstanding practice of tolerating such reservations to multilateral human rights treaties.

That there can be no reservation to *jus cogens* norms is not a controversial proposition. But there have been very few serious attempts to identify which human rights norms fall into the privileged category of *jus cogens*. The Human Rights Committee, in its General Comment, provides as examples of peremptory norms the prohibition of torture and of arbitrary deprivation of life.[42] The Arbitration Committee of the Conference on Yugoslavia of the European Communities chaired by Judge Robert Badinter, in two of its 1992 opinions, stated that the protection of minorities, as expressed in Article 27 of the International Covenant, constitutes a norm of *jus cogens*.[43] Also, the Inter-American Commission on

---

[39] General Comment No. 24 (52), *supra* note 2 at §8.

[40] Vienna Convention, *supra* note 2, Arts. 53 and 64.

[41] *Belilos Case*, *supra* note 2. See also Pierre-Henri Imbert, "La question des réserves et les conventions en matière de droits de l'homme," in *Actes du cinquième colloque international sur la Convention européenne des droits de l'homme* 99 (Paris: Pedone, 1982).

[42] General Comment No. 24 (52), *supra* note 2 at §10.

[43] Conference on Yugoslavia Arbitration Committee Opinion No. 1, (1992) 31 I.L.M. 1494 at 1496, 92 I.L.R. 162; Conference on Yugoslavia Arbitration

Human Rights has affirmed that the prohibition of execution for crimes committed by an individual under the age of eighteen was in the process of "emerging" as a norm of *jus cogens*.[44] In its objection to a reservation made by the Arab Republic of Yemen to the International Convention on the Elimination of All Forms of Racial Discrimination, Canada declared that "the principle of non-discrimination is generally accepted and recognized in international law and therefore is binding on all states,"[45] although it did not use the term *jus cogens*.

The reference to derogation in Article 53 of the Vienna Convention may be helpful on this point, since it suggests an overlap between peremptory norms and those deemed to be non-derogable. Yet while reservation to a norm of *jus cogens* is clearly illegal, the same cannot so readily be said of non-derogable norms. The International Covenant designates a relatively small number of provisions that are not subject to derogation even in time of war or national emergency, including the right to life (Article 6), protection against torture (Article 7), prohibition of slavery and servitude (Article 8), imprisonment for debt (Article 11), non-retroactivity of penal law (Article 15), the right to a personality (Article 16), and freedom of religion (Article 18). The regional human rights conventions differ somewhat in the choice of non-derogable provisions,[46] although a core of such rights is common to them all —

Commission, Opinion No. 2 (1992) 31 I.L.M. 1497 at 1498, 92 I.L.R. 167. See also Alain Pellet, "Note sur la Commission d'arbitrage de la Conférence européenne pour la paix en Yougoslavie" (1991) 37 Ann. fran. dr. int. 329; Alain Pellet, "L'activité de la Commission d'arbitrage de la Conférence européenne pour la paix en Yougoslavie" (1992) 38 Ann. fran. dr. int. 220.

44 Case 9647 (United States) (1987), Inter-Am. Comm. H.R. Res. No. 3/87, *Annual Report of the Inter-American Commission on Human Rights: 1986-1987*, OEA/Ser.L/V/II.71 Doc. 9 rev.1 (1987) 147, *Inter-American Yearbook on Human Rights, 1987* 328 (Dordrecht/Boston/London: Martinus Nijhoff, 1990), 8 HRLJ 345 at §60. See also Dinah Shelton, "Note" (1987) 8 HRLJ 355; Dinah Shelton, "The Prohibition of Juvenile Executions in International Law" (1987) 58 Rev. I.D.P. 773; David Weissbrodt, "Execution of Juvenile Offenders by the United States Violates International Human Rights Law" (1988) 3 Am. U. J. Int'l L. & Pol'y 339. See also the reply to Professor Weissbrodt's criticism of the Inter-American Commission's report in Case 9647 ("Roach and Pinkerton") by a lawyer for the Commission: Christina M. Cerna, "U.S. Death Penalty Tested Before the Inter-American Commission on Human Rights" (1992) 10 Netherl. Q.H.R. 155.

45 Multilateral Treaties, *supra* note 8 at 106-107.

46 European Convention of Human Rights, *supra* note 19, Art. 15 §2; American Convention on Human Rights, *supra* note 31, Art. 27 §2.

notably, the right to life, the prohibition of torture and slavery, and the principle of non-retroactivity of penal law. Nevertheless, this criterion is of limited usefulness where human rights treaties make no allowance for derogation.

In making objections to reservations, states have on occasion suggested that reservations to non-derogable provisions are *prima facie* incompatible with the object and purpose of the instrument.[47] For example, when the Congo made a reservation to Article 11 (imprisonment for debt) of the International Covenant on Civil and Political Rights, citing its domestic law, which provided for the possibility of detention when an individual was in default on financial obligations,[48] Belgium and the Netherlands objected, not because they considered that the legislation in question was actually contrary to Article 11, but because they did not want to set a precedent by which reservations to non-derogable articles might be tolerated.[49] Some of the objections to the reservations made by the United States to Articles 6 and 7 of the Covenant have adopted the same reasoning. For example, the Netherlands, in its objection to the reservation by the United States to Article 7, declared that "this reservation has the same effect as a general derogation from this Article, while according to Article 4 of the Covenant, no derogations, even in times of public emergency, are permitted."[50] Most of the European states that have objected to the United States reservation to Article 6 cite the fact that derogation is forbidden by Article 4 §2. On the other hand, in some cases reservations to non-derogable provisions have not inspired any objection or other reaction from other parties.[51]

---

47 See also the comments of A. Pereira and C. Zanghi, and the reply by P. H. Imbert, in *Actes du cinquième colloque international sur la Convention européenne des droits de l'homme, supra* note 41 at 160, 173-74, 178-79.

48 Multilateral Treaties, *supra* note 8 at 125.

49 *Ibid.*, 133-34.

50 Similar statements were made by Denmark, Norway, and Finland.

51 There are several examples with respect to the International Covenant on Civil and Political Rights. Norway and Ireland have formulated reservations to Art. 6 (right to life), Italy, Germany, and Argentina have formulated reservations to Art. 15 (non-retroactivity of criminal law), Mexico has formulated a reservation to Art. 18 (religious freedom), and Trinidad and Tobago have reserved Art. 15 §1. In the context of the European Convention on Human Rights, Malta (590 U.N.T.S. 301) has formulated a reservation to Art. 2 (right to life). Also, Barbados (1298 U.N.T.S. 441), Guatemala (1144 U.N.T.S. 210; this reservation

The Inter-American Court of Human Rights has considered whether a reservation to a non-derogable right — the right to life — should be considered incompatible with the treaty's object and purpose in *Restrictions to the Death Penalty*.[52] At the time of ratification of the American Convention on Human Rights, Guatemala had formulated a reservation to Article 4 §4, a provision that excludes the death penalty for political crimes, and which has no counterpart in the International Covenant.[53] Four politically-related death sentences had been handed down in Guatemala, and the issue submitted to the Inter-American Commission of Human Rights.[54] The four individuals involved were eventually executed by firing squad, after being sentenced by "Courts of Special Jurisdiction."[55]

The Inter-American Court found the reservation to be legal but inadequate in scope, and concluded that Guatemala's reservation was ineffective to block application of Article 4 §2 of the Convention.[56] In its advisory opinion, the Inter-American Court of Human Rights confirmed that blanket reservations to the right to life, as a non-derogable provision, were incompatible with the object and purpose of the Convention.[57] However, reservations seeking only to

---

has since been withdrawn: O.A.S. Doc. OEA/Ser.L/V/II.68 Doc.8 rev.1 at 158), and Trinidad and Tobago (O.A.S. Doc. OEA/Ser.L/V/II.81 rev.1 Doc.6 at 335) have made reservations to Art. 4 (right to life) of the American Convention on Human Rights.

52 *Restrictions to the Death Penalty (Arts. 4 §2 and 4 §4 American Convention on Human Rights)* (1983), Int. Am Ct. H.R. Advisory Opinion OC-3/83, Ser. A No. 3, 4 HRLJ 352, 70 I.L.R. 449.

53 The reservation states: "The Government of the Republic of Guatemala ratifies the American Convention on Human Rights, signed in San José, Costa Rica, on the 22nd of November of 1969, making a reservation with regard to Article 4, paragraph 4 of the same, inasmuch as the Constitution of the Republic of Guatemala, in its Article 54, only excludes from the application of the death penalty, political crimes, but not common crimes related to political crimes": 1144 U.N.T.S. 210. Art. 4 §4 provides: "In no case shall capital punishment be inflicted for political offenses or related common crimes."

54 Case 8094 (Guatemala), Annual Report of the Inter-American Commission on Human Rights: 1983-84, OEA/Ser.L/V/II.66 Doc.10 rev.1 at 81-84.

55 *Restrictions to the Death Penalty (Arts. 4§2 and 4§4 American Convention on Human Rights)*, *supra* note 52 at 155-60, 164. See also Monroe Leigh, "American Convention on Human Rights — Advisory Jurisdiction — Effect of a Reservation — Death Penalty," (1984) 78 AJIL 681.

56 *Ibid.*, §74.

57 Vienna Convention, *supra* note 2, Art. 20 §1.

restrict certain aspects of a non-derogable right, such as that made by Guatemala, could not be presumed contrary to the Convention, providing they did not deprive the right to life as a whole of its "basic purpose." The Court stated:

> It would follow therefrom that a reservation which was designed to enable a State to suspend any of the non-derogable fundamental rights must be deemed to be incompatible with the object and purpose of the Convention and, consequently, not permitted by it. The situation would be different if the reservation sought merely to restrict certain aspects of a non-derogable right without depriving the right as a whole of its basic purpose. Since the reservation referred to by the Commission in its submission does not appear to be of a type that is designed to deny the right to life as such, the Court concludes that to that extent it can be considered, in principle, as not being incompatible with the object and purpose of the Convention.[58]

The Human Rights Committee, in its General Comment, takes a somewhat different perspective. It notes that not all rights of profound importance are deemed non-derogable, citing in this respect Article 9 (protection of persons detained or arrested) and Article 17 (minority rights). Some rights have been made non-derogable, notes the Committee, merely because their suspension is irrelevant to the legitimate control of the state of national emergency. An example is imprisonment for debt, prohibited by Article 11 of the Covenant. In other cases, derogation is prohibited because it is impossible (Article 18, freedom of conscience), states the Committee. The Committee concludes: "While there is no automatic correlation between reservations to non-derogable provisions, and reservations which offend against the object and purpose of the Covenant, a State has a heavy onus to justify such a reservation."[59]

RESERVATIONS TO CUSTOMARY NORMS

A second approach to the "object and purpose" test may involve determining whether a norm is part of customary international law. In its General Comment, the Human Rights Committee declares that provisions in the Covenant that are also norms of customary international law may not be the subject of reservations. It provides a list of such customary norms:

[58] *Restrictions to the Death Penalty (Arts. 4 §2 and 4 §4 American Convention on Human Rights), supra* note 52 at §61.

[59] General Comment No. 24 (52), *supra* note 2 at §12.

Accordingly, a State may not reserve the right to engage in slavery, to torture, to subject persons to cruel, inhuman or degrading treatment or punishment, to arbitrarily deprive persons of their lives, to arbitrarily arrest and detain persons, to deny freedom of thought, conscience and religion, to presume a person guilty unless he proves his innocence, to execute pregnant women or children, to permit the advocacy of national, racial or religious hatred, to deny to persons of marriageable age the right to marry, or to deny to minorities the right to enjoy their own culture, profess their own religion or use their own language. And while reservations to particular clauses of Article 14 may be acceptable, a general reservation to a fair trial would not be.[60]

In the past, the Human Rights Committee has overlooked reservations to such customary provisions, which it now says are illegal. For example, in *C.L.D.* v. *France*,[61] it applied the French reservation to Article 27 of the International Covenant on Civil and Political Rights, which ensures the right of minorities to enjoy their own culture, to profess their own religion, or to use their own language. The General Comment implies that the reservation by the United States to Article 6 §5 of the Covenant, with respect to the execution of individuals for crimes committed while under the age of eighteen, is illegal because it violates a customary norm. The General Comment could have been more explicit because, while it prohibits a state from reserving the right "to execute pregnant women or children," Article 6 §5 of the Covenant speaks of "crimes committed by persons below eighteen years of age." The Inter-American Commission on Human Rights has already held that there is a customary norm prohibiting the execution of children, but that the norm only extends to some unspecified age that is lower than eighteen.[62] Is the Committee hinting that it will take the same approach, and follow the lead of the Inter-American Commission in tolerating the execution of individuals for crimes committed while they are aged sixteen and seventeen? It is notable that the Convention on the Rights of the Child defines a "child," which is the term used in the Human Rights Committee's General Comment, as a person under eighteen.[63]

The guidance of the Human Rights Committee with respect to customary human rights norms is helpful, although its explanation in the General Comment is typically laconic. As Rosalyn Higgins has noted, the claim that human rights exist in customary international

---

[60] *Ibid.*, §8.

[61] Case 228/1987, UN Doc. A/43/40 at 257.

[62] Case No. 9647 (United States), *supra* note 44.

[63] Convention on the Rights of the Child, *supra* note 1, Art. 1.

law "will need to be established by reference to the normal criteria of that source, including state practice."[64] That the Committee will look to customary international law in assessing the legality of reservations is an intriguing prospect. It will be compelled to look well beyond the Covenant, its *travaux préparatoires*, and its jurisprudence in this challenging task.

The enumeration of customary norms presented by the Committee in its General Comment does not appear to be complete; for example, the Committee makes no mention whatsoever of the right of self-determination.[65] The status of self-determination as a customary norm is well-documented by legal scholars,[66] and recognized in Article 1 of the Covenant. On the other hand, it would be useful for the Committee to justify its conclusions with respect to other allegedly customary norms, particularly because the case law of the European and Inter-American commissions and courts, not to mention that of the Committee, authorizes limitations and derogations to these rights. Critical of over-optimistic assessments of the scope of customary rules, Theodor Meron has drawn attention to a "tendency to ignore, for the most part, the availability of evidence of state practice (scant as it may have been) and to assume that noble humanitarian principles that deserve recognition as the positive law of the international community have in fact been recognized as such by states. The 'ought' merges with the 'is', the *lex ferenda* with the *lex lata*."[67]

---

64 Rosalyn Higgins, *Problems and Process, International Law and How We Use It* 103 (Oxford: Clarendon Press, 1994).

65 India has formulated a reservation to Art. 1 of the Covenant (as well as to the identical Art. 1 in the International Covenant on Economic, Social and Cultural Rights, Dec. 16 1966, [1976] C.T.S. No. 46, 993 R.T.N.U. 3. The Federal Republic of Germany, France, and the Netherlands have objected to this reservation as being contrary to the object and purpose of the treaties.

66 Jochen A. Frowein, "Self-Determination as a Limit to Obligations Under International Law," in Christian Tomuschat, ed., *Modern Law of Self-Determination* 211 at 218-21 (Dordrecht: Nijhoff, 1993); Hector Gros Espiell, "The Right to Self-Determination, Implementation of United Nations Resolutions," UN Doc. E/CN.4/Sub.2/405/Rev.1, UN Sales No. E.79.XIV.5 (1980) at 11; A. Cassese, "The Self-Determination of Peoples," in L. Henkin (ed.), *The International Bill of Rights* 96 at 111 (New York: Columbia University Press, 1981); A.-C. Kiss, "The Peoples' Right to Self-Determination" (1986) 7 HRLJ 174; Michla Pomerance, *Self-Determination in Law and Practice* 63-72 (The Hague: Martinus Nijhoff, 1982).

67 Theodor Meron, "The Geneva Conventions as Customary Law" (1987) 81 AJIL 348 at 361.

If a norm is customary, reservation by a state to the corresponding conventional norm does nothing to change its substantive international obligations. However, the reservation, were it to be effective with respect to the conventional norm, would in effect neutralize any monitoring function of a treaty body such as the Human Rights Committee, and would furthermore prevent any individual or inter-state petition mechanism.

VAGUE OR GENERAL RESERVATIONS

Problems may also arise due to the vagueness of reservations. For example, the United Kingdom answered the statement of the Republic of Korea at the time of the latter's accession to the Covenant by indicating it was "not however able to take a position on these purported reservations in the absence of a sufficient indication of their intended effect."[68] It is not unknown for states to make specific references to the domestic legislation that they intend to protect.[69] This specificity gives great precision to a reservation and helps other states, treaty bodies, and individual litigants to establish their own positions with respect to the reservation, in full knowledge of its implications.[70] Under the European Convention of Human Rights, there is no requirement that reservations be compatible with the "object and purpose" of the treaty, but they must not be vague, and the domestic legislation being reserved must be clearly identified. Even where such a requirement is not explicit, vagueness will be an issue. It is submitted that a reservation that is

---

[68] Multilateral Treaties, *supra* note 8 at 134.

[69] E.g., see Austria's reservation to Art. 12 of the Covenant. In some cases, such as the European Convention on Human Rights, *supra* note 19, Art. 64, this is a requirement of the treaty. On reservations to the European Convention, see R. St. J. Macdonald, *supra* note 2; William A. Schabas, "Article 64," in L. E. Pettiti, E. Decaux, P.-H. Imbert, *La Convention européenne des droits de l'homme, théorie et pratique* (Paris: Economica, 1995), 923-44; J. Abr. Frowein, "Reservations to the European Convention on Human Rights," in Franz Matscher, Herbert Petzold, *Protecting Human Rights: The European Dimension; Mélanges en l'honneur de Gérard J. Wiarda* 193 (Cologne: Carl Heymanns, 1988); S. Marcus-Helmons, "L'article 64 de la Convention de Rome ou Les réserves à la Convention européenne des droits de l'homme" (1968) 45 Rev. D.I. & D.C. 7.

[70] On the unacceptability of vague or imprecise reservations, see *Temeltasch* v. *Switzerland* (No. 9116/80) (1983), 31 Eur. Comm. H.R. D.R. 120, 5 E.H.R.R. 417, 88 I.L.R. 619; Pierre-Henri Imbert, "Les réserves à la Convention européenne des droits de l'homme devant la Commission de Strasbourg (Affaire Temeltasch)," [1983] R.D.I.P. 580.

too vague deprives all concerned parties of an accurate picture of the rights and obligations of the reserving state.

For example, Pakistan states in its reservation to the Convention on the Rights of the Child that the "[p]rovisions of the Convention shall be interpreted in the light of the principles of Islamic laws and values."[71] This reservation may conceivably affect the application of every provision of the Convention, in contrast with similar "Islamic" reservations by states such as the Syrian Arab Republic,[72] which at least focus on specific provisions of the Convention. The phrase "Islamic laws and values" is so vulnerable to different interpretations that it is simply impossible to establish the obligations assumed by Pakistan under the Convention. Djibouti's reservation is similarly far-reaching, and even more vague than that of Pakistan: "[The Government of Djibouti] shall not consider itself bound by any provisions or articles that are incompatible with its religion and its traditional values."[73] What religion? What traditional values?

Sweden, Norway, Portugal, Finland, and Ireland, in virtually identical terms, have objected to such reservations, stating:

A reservation by which a State party limits its responsibilities under the Convention by invoking general principles of national law may cast doubts on the commitments of the reserving state to the object and purpose of the Convention and, moreover, contribute to undermining the basis of international treaty law.[74]

Italy, in its objection to the reservation of the Syrian Arab Republic, states that a reservation that "is too comprehensive and too general" is necessarily incompatible with the object and purpose of the Convention. In its objection to the Syrian reservation, Finland speaks of its "unlimited and undefined character."[75]

Iran's reservation to the Convention on the Rights of the Child is so far-reaching as to constitute a total absence of ratification: ". . . the Government of the Islamic Republic of Iran reserves the right not to apply any provisions or articles of the Convention that are incompatible with Islamic laws and the internal legislation in

71 Multilateral Treaties, *supra* note 8 at 193.

72 "Supplement to ST/LEG/SER.E/12," furnished by United Nations Headquarters, Aug. 2, 1994.

73 Multilateral Treaties, *supra* note 8 at 190.

74 *Ibid.*, 194-95.

75 "Supplement to ST/LEG/SER.E/12," furnished by United Nations Headquarters, Aug. 2, 1994.

58   *The Canadian Yearbook of International Law 1994*

effect."[76] It is hardly necessary even to consider whether the reservation is compatible with the object and purpose of the Convention. What possible protection can the Convention provide to children in Iran if it is hierarchically inferior to internal legislation?

In its reservation to Article 7 of the International Covenant on Civil and Political Rights, the United States declares: "The United States considers itself bound to the extent that 'cruel, inhuman or degrading treatment or punishment' means the cruel and unusual treatment or punishment prohibited by the Fifth, Eighth or Fourteenth Amendments to the Constitution of the United States."[77] Portugal, in its objections, states that such a reservation, "in which a State limits its responsibilities under the Covenant by invoking general principles of National Law may create doubts on the commitments of the Reserving State to the object and purpose of the Covenant and, moreover, contribute to undermining the basis of international law." When it ratified the Genocide Convention in 1988, the United States declared that "nothing in the Convention requires or authorizes legislation or other action by the United States of America prohibited by the Constitution of the United States as interpreted by the United States."[78] Several states objected, citing the "uncertainty" of such a reservation.[79] Similar reservations that subordinate the international human rights treaty to national law have been formulated with respect to the International Convention on the Elimination of All Forms of Racial Discrimination.[80]

Occasionally, states invoke the provisions of Article 27 of the Vienna Convention on the Law of Treaties in challenging the legality of reservations. This is suggested in the Finnish objections to the reservations of Indonesia, Pakistan, Qatar, the Syrian Arab Republic, and Japan to the Convention on the Rights of the Child.[81]

---

[76] *Ibid.*

[77] *Ibid.*

[78] Multilateral Treaties, *supra* note 8 at 94.

[79] Italy, Mexico, United Kingdom: Multilateral Treaties, *supra* note 8 at 94-97.

[80] Antigua and Barbuda, Bahamas, Barbados, United States of America (at the time of signature), Guyana, Papua-New Guinea: Multilateral Treaties, *supra* note 8 at 100-106.

[81] "Supplement to ST/LEG/SER.E/12," furnished by United Nations Headquarters, Aug. 2, 1994. It was also invoked by Committee rapporteur Marta Santos Pais: UN Doc. CRC/C/SR.41 at §24. See also objections by Denmark, Estonia, Finland, Greece, Ireland, Mexico, Norway, and the Netherlands to the reservations by the United States of America to the Genocide Convention, which cite

The Republic of Korea's reservation to Articles 14 §5 and §7 and 22 of the Covenant provoked an objection from Czechoslovakia, stating that "these reservations are in contradiction to the generally recognized principle of international law according to which a State cannot invoke the provisions of its own internal law as justification for its failure to perform a treaty."[82] According to Article 27, "[a] party may not invoke the provisions of its internal law as justification for its failure to perform a treaty." Article 27 appears in Part III, entitled "Observance, application and interpretation of treaties," and not in the section dealing with reservations. It is submitted that Article 27 should not be invoked in the context of the legality of reservations. Normally, states make reservations precisely because their internal law is in conflict with the treaty. Indeed, the Human Rights Committee specifically urges states "to indicate in precise terms the domestic legislation or practices which [they believe] to be incompatible with the Covenant obligation reserved."[83] Article 27 should apply only when the extent of the state's obligations have been determined — that is, when the issue of reservations has been addressed and resolved.

The Human Rights Committee, in its General Comment, declares that reservations must be "specific and transparent, so that the Committee, those under the jurisdiction of the reserving State, and other States parties may be clear as to what obligations of human rights compliance have or have not been undertaken."[84] Noting that reservations often indicate a state's intention not to change its particular laws, the Committee expresses particular concern about "widely formulated reservations which essentially render ineffective all Covenant rights which would require any change in national law to ensure compliance with Covenant obligations."[85] As the Committee succinctly observes, "[n]o real international rights or obligations have thus been accepted."[86] Accordingly, although this is only implicit in the Committee's General Comment, such reservations are incompatible.

Art. 27 of the Vienna Convention or allude to it: Multilateral Treaties, *supra* note 8 at 94-97.

[82] *Ibid.*, 133.

[83] General Comment No. 24 (52), *supra* note 2 at §19.

[84] *Ibid.*

[85] *Ibid.*, §12. Also §19.

[86] *Ibid.*

The Committee also makes a certain number of recommendations concerning the formulation of reservations, as follows. First, reservations should not be too numerous. Second, states should not suggest in reservations that the meaning of a provision of the Covenant is the same as that given by an organ of another international treaty body.[87] Third, to promote precision, states should describe in precise terms the domestic legislation or practices that they believe to be incompatible with the Covenant. Finally, the Committee urges states to propose a time frame for adjustment of internal legislation to the requirements of the Covenant.[88]

SUPPORTIVE GUARANTEES, REMEDIES, AND PROCEDURAL PROVISIONS

In its General Comment, the Human Rights Committee declares that reservations to "supportive guarantees" are unacceptable. By supportive guarantees, the Committee means the "necessary framework" for implementing fundamental rights and freedoms at both the national and international levels. As an example, the Committee cites Article 2 §2 of the Covenant, which requires states "to adopt such legislative or other measures as may be necessary to give effect to the rights recognized in the present Covenant." A state could not reserve to Article 2 §2, thereby indicating "that it intends to provide no remedies for human rights violations."[89]

The Committee also considers that any reservation seeking to compromise its monitoring role under the Covenant would be incompatible with its object and purpose:

Reservations that purport to evade that essential element in the design of the Covenant, which is also directed to securing the enjoyment of the rights, are also incompatible with its object and purpose. A State may not reserve the right not to present a report and have it considered by the Committee. The Committee's role under the Covenant, whether under article 40 or under the Optional Protocols, necessarily entails interpreting the provisions of the Covenant and the development of a jurisprudence. Accordingly a reservation that rejects the Committee's competence to interpret the requirements of any provisions of the Covenant would also be contrary to the object and purpose of the treaty.[90]

---

87 *Ibid.*, §19.

88 *Ibid.*, §20.

89 *Ibid.*, §12.

90 *Ibid.*, §11.

These comments can be contrasted with the advisory opinion of the International Court of Justice, which deemed reservations to Article 9 of the Genocide Convention to be compatible with the object and purpose of that instrument. Article 9 provided that differences between states concerning their obligations under the Convention be submitted to the International Court of Justice.[91] In the event of reservation to Article 9, there is no available remedy or mechanism of control.[92] Despite the International Court's Advisory Opinion, the United Kingdom and the Netherlands appear to consider reservations to Article 9 to be incompatible with the Genocide Convention, and they have formulated objections on a number of occasions in this respect.[93] Indeed, the Netherlands considers that states that have formulated reservations to Article 9 are not parties to the Convention.[94]

The Committee also notes that the Optional Protocol, which provides for individual petitions, contains no substantive rights as such and is a distinct treaty, although closely related to the Covenant. It is therefore impossible for a state to limit its obligations under the Covenant by means of a reservation to the Optional Protocol. According to the Committee, reservations aimed at excluding certain rights from the purview of the Committee under the individual petition mechanism are illegal:

because the object and purpose of the first Optional Protocol is to allow the rights obligatory for a State under the Covenant to be tested before the Committee, a reservation that seeks to preclude this would be contrary to the object and purpose of the first Optional Protocol.[95]

The Committee adds:

A reservation to a substantive obligation made for the first time under the first Optional Protocol would seem to reflect an intention by the State

91 A similar provision appears in Art. 22 of the International Convention on the Elimination of All Forms of Racial Discrimination, *supra* note 1. There have been several reservations to this provision: Multilateral Treaties, *supra* note 8 at 106-109.

92 Many parties to the Genocide Convention, *supra* note 1, have formulated reservations to Art. 9: Albania, Algeria, Argentina, Bahrein, Bulgaria, China, Spain, United States of America, India, Morocco, Poland, Rumania, Rwanda, Venezuela, Vietnam, Yemen: *ibid.* at 92-94.

93 *Ibid.*, 96-97. See also the position taken by the Agent for Pakistan in *Case concerning Trial of Pakistani Prisoners of War (Pakistan v. India)*, [1973] I.C.J. Pleadings 1 at 118-120.

94 *Ibid.*, 96.

95 General Comment No. 24 (52), *supra* note 2 at §13.

concerned to prevent the Committee from expressing its views relating to a particular article of the Covenant in an individual case.[96]

The Committee also rules out reservations that relate to its procedures, noting that it "must control its own procedures as specified by the Optional Protocol and its rules of procedure." All of this is quite theoretical, since there are no examples of such reservations.[97]

States may attempt to limit the competence of the Committee *ratione temporis*.[98] For the Committee, this is not in reality a reservation. However, it insists that it is competent when events or acts occurring before the date of entry into force of the first Optional Protocol have continued to affect the rights of the victim after that date.[99]

Several European states have formulated reservations to the Optional Protocol that exclude its competence where substantially the same case has already been litigated before the European Court or Commission of Human Rights.[100] These states have followed the lead of the Committee of Ministers of the Council of Europe, which urged European states to make such a reservation out of fear that the Human Rights Committee would become a "court of appeal" from the Strasbourg organs.[101] Reservations of this type are admissible, according to the Committee, "[i]nsofar as the most basic obligation has been to secure independent third party review of the human rights of individuals."[102]

Some states, including Canada,[103] formulated reservations at the time of the declarations by which they accepted the competence of the Human Rights Committee to receive interstate petitions pur-

---

96 *Ibid.*

97 Multilateral Treaties, *supra* note 8 at 154-56.

98 See, e.g., the declarations of Chile, France, Malta, and the USSR: *ibid.*

99 General Comment No. 24 (52), *supra* note 2 at §14.

100 Dominic McGoldrick, *The Human Rights Committee* 184-86 (Oxford: Clarendon Press, 1991). The states are Austria, Denmark, France, Iceland, Ireland, Italy, Luxembourg, Malta, Norway, Poland, Russian Federation, Spain, and Sweden.

101 A. A. Cançado Trindade, "Co-existence and Co-ordination of Mechanisms of International Protection of Human Rights (at global and regional levels)" (1987) 202 Rec. des Cours 1 at 165-76.

102 General Comment No. 24 (52), *supra* note 2 at §14. See also *K. and C. V. v. Germany* (no. 568/1993), unreported views of Apr. 8, 1994 at §4.2; *V. E. M. v. Spain* (no. 467/1991), unreported views of July 16, 1993 at §§4.1 and 5.2.

103 Multilateral Treaties, *supra* note 8 at 134-36. Also Germany, Belgium, Malta, New Zealand.

suant to Article 41. These reservations impose a condition of reciprocity, by which only states that have themselves previously accepted this competence of the Committee may make such petitions. In the eighteen years since the Covenant came into force, this interstate petition mechanism has never been used. The Committee refers only obliquely to these reservations in its General Comment, suggesting that they are acceptable.[104]

WHO DETERMINES WHETHER RESERVATIONS ARE LEGAL?

THE OBJECTIONS REGIME OF THE VIENNA CONVENTION

Where a treaty expressly authorizes reservations, the Vienna Convention states that no subsequent acceptance is required by the other contracting states, unless the treaty so provides.[105] Two special situations are also provided, neither of which is particularly germane to multilateral human rights treaties: treaties negotiated by a relatively small number of states,[106] and treaties constituting international organizations.[107] In all other cases, the Vienna Convention establishes a presumption that a reservation is acceptable, subject to the right of states to challenge the legality of a reservation by formulating objections.[108] The International Convention on the Elimination of All Forms of Racial Discrimination declares that a reservation will be deemed incompatible with the object and purpose of the treaty if at least two thirds of the parties object to the reservation.[109]

According to the Vienna Convention, objections must be expressed within twelve months of the date when the objecting state is informed of the reservation. Although Article 20 of the Vienna Convention does not specifically link the issue of objection with the grounds of illegality enumerated in Article 19, such a relationship is

104 General Comment No. 24 (52), *supra* note 2 at §17.

105 Vienna Convention, *supra* note 2, Art. 20 §1.

106 *Ibid.* Art. 20 §2. In such cases, a reservation must be accepted by all of the parties.

107 *Ibid.* Art. 20 §3. In such cases, a reservation "requires the acceptance of the competent organ of the organization."

108 *Ibid.* Art. 21 §4, 21 §5.

109 *Supra* note 1, Art. 20 §2. Although there have been objections to various reservations, sufficient numbers have never been attained for this provision to become operative.

generally assumed. In other words, a state could not arbitrarily object to a reservation formulated by a ratifying state, but must base its objection on breach of the "object and purpose" test or of some other rule. Thus, the parties become the judge of the acceptability of reservations in much the same way as jurors vote to admit a new member to a jury.

This mechanism, which evolved in the context of multilateral treaties not concerned with human rights, is based on reciprocity. It views the convention as a contract between states. The reservation is a form of offer, which may be accepted in whole or in part by the states that are already parties. But if a state does not consider a reservation by a new party to be admissible, it may refuse the reservation by formulating an objection. The reserved provision in effect becomes excluded from the treaty regime; neither ratifying state nor objecting state is bound by the provision, but only on a bilateral basis.

As has already been mentioned, a large percentage of parties to the International Covenant on Civil and Political Rights have accompanied their instruments of ratification or accession with reservations or interpretative declarations. The largest number of these reservations have been made to specific provisions of Article 14, which enumerates the procedural guarantees that are essential to a fair trial. A substantial number of reservations have also been made to Articles 9, 10, 13, 19, and 20, and a small number to Articles 1, 4, 6, 7, 8, 12, 15, 21, 22, 23, 25, 26, 27, 48, and 50. Few objections have been made to these reservations. A reservation by Trinidad and Tobago,[110] directed at Article 4 §2, was challenged as being incompatible with the object and purpose of the Covenant in objections formulated by Germany and the Netherlands.[111] Australia's very extensive list of reservations,[112] most of which have since been withdrawn, provoked objections from the Netherlands.[113] Korea's reservation,[114] which subjected certain provisions of the Covenant to its own domestic law, was considered illegal in objections filed by Germany, the Netherlands, the United Kingdom, and Czechoslovakia.[115] The other controversial reservations to the Cove-

---

[110] Multilateral Treaties, *supra* note 8 at 130.

[111] *Ibid.*, 133-34.

[112] 1197 U.N.T.S. 414.

[113] Multilateral Treaties, *supra* note 8 at 133-34.

[114] *Ibid.*, 129.

[115] *Ibid.*, 133-34.

nant on this very short list are those of India to Article 1,[116] Congo to Article 11,[117] and Algeria to Article 22.[118] By far the most impressive display of objections was that of eleven European states, in late 1993, to the reservations formulated by the United States to Articles 6 and 7 of the Covenant. Similarly, a certain number of objections have been formulated with respect to other multilateral human rights treaties.

Suitable as this objections mechanism may be when applied to some multilateral treaties, it has slight significance when applied to human rights provisions. As the European Court of Human Rights has noted on at least two occasions, reciprocity is a concept that does not fully apply to human rights treaties.[119] By their nature, human rights stipulations in international conventions create obligations for a state in favour of individuals. It would be simply absurd to conclude that the objections by the various European states to the United States reservations on the death penalty discharge them from their obligations under Articles 6 and 7 as concerns the United States, and this is surely not their intention in making the objection.[120] Indeed, such a result is expressly prohibited by the Vienna Convention on the Law of Treaties, which declares that two parties to a multilateral convention may not modify or suspend certain of its provisions if this action is incompatible with the object and purpose of the instrument.[121]

Support for these views is found in an advisory opinion of the Inter-American Court of Human Rights. Although no objections were expressed to Guatemala's reservation to Article 4 §4 of the American Convention, this did not prevent either the Inter-American Commission on Human Rights or the Inter-American Court from examining the issue.[122] Another advisory opinion of the Inter-American Court, The Effect of Reservations on the Entry into Force

116 Objections by France, Germany, and the Netherlands: *ibid.* at 127.

117 Objections by Belgium and the Netherlands: *supra* note 48.

118 Objections by Germany, the Netherlands, and Portugal: Multilateral Treaties, *supra* note 8 at 124.

119 *Ireland* v. *United Kingdom* (1978), Eur. Ct. H.R. Ser. A No. 25, 2 E.H.R.R. 25, 59 I.L.R. 188 at §239; *Belilos Case, supra* note 2 at §62.

120 Pierre-Henri Imbert, *supra* note 41 at 119; G. Fitzmaurice, *supra* note 3 at 13-16.

121 Vienna Convention, *supra* note 2, Arts. 41(*b*)(ii), 58(*b*)(ii).

122 *Restrictions to the Death Penalty (Arts. 4 §2 and 4 §4 American Convention on Human Rights), supra* note 52.

of the American Convention (Articles 74 and 75), is even clearer on this point. The Court noted that the principles dealing with reservations and objections found in the Vienna Convention:

. . . reflect the needs of traditional multilateral international instruments which have as their object the reciprocal exchange, for the mutual benefit of the States Parties, of bargained for rights and obligations. . . . It permits States to ratify many multilateral treaties and to do so with the reservations they deem necessary; it enables the other contracting States to accept or reject the reservations and to determine whether they wish to enter into treaty relations with the reserving States; and it provides that as soon as at least one other State Party has accepted the reservation, the treaty enters into force with respect to the reserving State. The Court must emphasize, however, that modern human rights treaties in general, and the American Convention in particular, are not multilateral treaties of the traditional type concluded to accomplish the reciprocal exchange of rights for the mutual benefit of the contracting States. Their object and purpose is the protection of the basic rights of individual human beings. . . .[123]

These words echo similar comments in an early report from the European Commission of Human Rights:

. . . the obligations undertaken by the High Contracting Parties in the European Convention are essentially of an objective character being designed rather to protect the fundamental rights of individual human beings from infringements by any of the High Contracting Parties than to create subjective and reciprocal rights for the High Contracting Parties themselves.[124]

When France lodged an interstate application against Turkey alleging a breach of Article 15 of the European Convention on Human Rights, Turkey submitted that France was barred because it had filed a reservation to Article 15, and could not therefore blame Turkey. The European Commission of Human Rights dismissed the argument, noting the "objective character of the Convention."[125]

In the recent European Court of Human Rights case, *Belilos* v. *Switzerland*, the Swiss government objected that the Court was foreclosed from considering the illegality of its reservation because

---

[123] "The Effect of Reservations on the Entry into Force of the American Convention (arts. 74 and 75)," *supra* note 20 at §§29-30.

[124] *Austria* v. *Italy* (No. 788/60) (1961), 4 *Y.B. Eur. Conv. H.R.* 116 at 140; see also *Cyprus* v. *Turkey* (No. 8007/77) (1979), 21 *Y.B. Eur. Conv. H.R.* 226.

[125] *France* v. *Turkey* (Case 9940/82) (1983), 26 *Y.B. Eur. Conv. H.R.* Part II, Eur. Comm. Case-Law 31 at §42.

there had been no objection by other states or by the depository.[126] The Court replied laconically: "the silence of the depository and the Contracting States does not deprive the Convention institutions of the power to make their own assessment."[127]

The Human Rights Committee has also taken this position in its recent General Comment. The Committee states that the objections mechanism of the Vienna Convention is "inappropriate" to human rights treaties:

[H]uman rights treaties . . . and the Covenant specifically, are not a web of inter-State exchanges of mutual obligations. They concern the endowment of individuals with rights. The principle of inter-State reciprocity has no place, save perhaps in the limited context of reservations to declarations on the Committee's competence under article 41. And because the operation of the classic rules on reservations is so inadequate for the Covenant, States have often not seen any legal interest in or need to object to reservations. The absence of protest by States cannot imply that a reservation is either compatible or incompatible with the object and purpose of the Covenant. Objections have been occasional, made by some States but not others, and on grounds not always specified; when an objection is made, it often does not specify a legal consequence, or sometimes even indicates that the objecting party nonetheless does not regard the Covenant as not in effect as between the parties concerned. In short, the pattern is so unclear that it is not safe to assume that a non-objecting State thinks that a particular reservation is acceptable. In the view of the Committee, because of the special characteristics of the Covenant as a human rights treaty, it is open to question what effect objections have between States *inter se*.[128]

But although objections may have only slight legal significance,[129] they are not without important political value.[130] The Human Rights

---

[126] It had hinted at the same argument in *Temeltasch v. Switzerland, supra* note 70. See also G. Cohen-Jonathan, *La Convention européenne des droits de l'homme* 87-88 (Paris: Economica, 1990).

[127] *Belilos Case, supra* note 2 at §47.

[128] General Comment No. 24 (52), *supra* note 2 at §17.

[129] ". . . si effectivement les objections aux réserves faites aux conventions relatives aux droits de l'homme n'ont pas du tout la même portée que dans le cadre d'autres conventions, elles ne sont pas pour autant absolument inutiles. Elles peuvent permettre en particulier de s'opposer à l'interprétation d'une disposition qui pourrait résulter des réserves et, d'une manière générale, de préserver la force d'un principe": Pierre-Henri Imbert, *supra* note 41 at 116.

[130] In this context, mention should also be made of another practice that is eminently political and of no legal significance in a strict sense — namely, the formulation of reservations or declarations that go beyond the obligations found in an instrument. With respect to the Convention on the Rights of the

Committee does not want to discourage the practice, and adds that objections may provide guidance to the Committee in its task of interpreting the compatibility of a given reservation with the object and purpose of the Covenant. The Human Rights Committee is no doubt being generous in attributing the silence of certain states to the insignificant legal value that these states ascribe to these initiatives. In fact, political considerations rather than principle would often appear to explain the failure to register objections. Canada, for example, has objected to reservations by Yemen but not to those by the United States, although it is difficult to identify any objective criteria that would explain the difference in approach.

ADJUDICATION BY THE TREATY BODIES

It should seem obvious that the courts, commissions, and tribunals charged with monitoring human rights treaties and with adjudicating individual petitions also assume the task of ruling on the legality of reservations. How can they fulfil this task without establishing which obligations bind the party concerned?[131] This issue has been widely debated, principally because of the objections mechanism of the Vienna Convention. It has been argued that the parties themselves are the only appropriate adjudicators of the validity of reservations, and that they do so by means of objections. Such arguments have been advanced before the Strasbourg organs,[132] the Human Rights Committee,[133] and the Committee on the Rights of the Child.[134] The Committee for the Elimination of Racial Discrimination has explicitly refused to assume the role of

---

Child, Uruguay affirms that it would have preferred the minimum age for military service to be eighteen and not fifteen, as specified in Art. 38 of the treaty. Argentina, Austria, Colombia, and Spain have made similar declarations. Such "reservations" may be of interest in establishing the *opinio juris* component of customary norms.

131 Nguyen Quoc Dinh, P. Daillier, A. Pellet, *Droit international public* 178 (4th ed., Paris: L.D.G.J., 1992). For a detailed discussion of this point, see G. Cohen-Jonathan, *supra* note 2 at 279-86.

132 Pierre-Henri Imbert, *supra* note 41 at 127-28, 134. Prof. Imbert cites E. Schwelb and R. Higgins in support of his position, but the quotations are not entirely unequivocal.

133 *C. L. D. v. France* (Case 228/1987), UN Doc. A/43/40 at 257. This is also the view of B. Graefrath, quoted in Manfred Nowak, *supra* note 8, Introduction at §24.

134 UN Doc. CRC/C/SR.41 at §25.

judging the legality of reservations, although this is perhaps justifiable because of a specific regime for objections within the treaty itself.[135]

The European Commission of Human Rights[136] and the European Court of Human Rights[137] have recognized their own competence to rule on the legality of reservations since the 1980s. In its judgment in *Belilos* v. *Switzerland*, the Court relied on Articles 19, 45, and 49 of the European Convention to justify its competence with respect to reservations.[138] According to Judge R. St. J. Macdonald, Articles 19 and 45 are the most relevant.[139]

Until recently, the Human Rights Committee had avoided the issue of whether reservations were admissible, although it was quite willing to consider their scope and urge their withdrawal within the context of the periodic reports.[140] The matter arose more directly in an Optional Protocol communication directed against France, which challenged the reservation to Article 27. Committee member Birame Ndiaye, in an individual opinion, stated that the Committee "has no power to object to the reservations of States parties."[141] Five other members of the Committee, Vojin Dimitrijevic, Rosalyn Higgins, Andreas Mavrommatis, Fausto Pocar, and Bertil Wennergren found it unnecessary under the circumstances to address whether a reservation made by France to Article 27 of the Covenant was

---

[135] UN Doc. A/33/18 at §374. See also the opinion of the Legal Office of the United Nations to the same effect: *U.N. Jur. Y.B.*, 1976, Chapter 6.A.23 at 219-21; UN Doc. CERD/C/SR.286. This refusal is explained by the fact that the International Convention for the Elimination of All Forms of Racial Discrimination provides expressly for a mechanism for determining the legality of reservations — something that is not present in the Covenant. Nevertheless, given that the Convention provides for individual petitions, should not an individual who files a communication be entitled to contest the legality of a reservation? See also Pierre-Henri Imbert, *supra* note 41 at 124-26.

[136] *Temeltasch* v. *Switzerland*, *supra* note 70.

[137] *Belilos Case*, *supra* note 2 at §47; R. St. J. Macdonald, *supra* note 2 at 442-43.

[138] *Ibid.*, §50. See also *Weber Case* (1990), Eur. Ct. H.R. Ser. A, No. 177. See also R. St. J. Macdonald, *supra* note 2 at 442.

[139] R. St. J. Macdonald, *supra* note 2 at 442.

[140] E.g., Finland: Report to the Human Rights Committee, UN Doc A/34/40 at §394; Australia: Report to the Human Rights Committee, UN Doc A/38/40 at §138; France: Report of the Human Rights Committee, UN Doc A/38/40 at §315. See Dinah Shelton, *supra* note 44 at 230-31.

[141] *C.L.D.* v. *France*, *supra* note 133 at 257.

actually a reservation or simply an interpretative declaration.[142] These comments, although not devoid of equivocation, suggested that the Committee might be prepared to pronounce itself on the legality of reservations. Subsequently, the Committee decided that it was without competence to examine a communication directed against France in the light of Article 27, because France's declaration amounted to a reservation.[143]

The Committee has now made it clear, in its General Comment, that it is competent to rule on whether reservations are consistent with the object and purpose of the Covenant. It may do this in the form of conclusions during the presentation of periodic reports, or in its views issued pursuant to individual or interstate petitions. At the top of the agenda are the reservations by the United States to Articles 6 and 7 of the Covenant, due to be examined during presentation of that country's initial report. This new aggressivity of the Committee with respect to reservations may encourage the Committee for the Elimination of Discrimination Against Women,[144] the Committee on the Rights of the Child,[145] and the Committee for the Elimination of Racial Discrimination to do likewise. In 1992, the chairpersons of these bodies agreed:

. . . treaty bodies should systematically review reservations made when considering a report and include in the list of questions to be addressed to reporting Governments a question as to whether a given reservation was still necessary and whether a State party would consider withdrawing

---

[142] *Ibid.*, 255.

[143] *T. K.* v. *France, supra* note 2 at §8.6; see also *M. K.* v. *France* (no. 222/1987), UN Doc. A/45/40, Vol. II at 127, and *C. L. D.* v. *France, supra* note 133 at §4.3. In *T. K.* and *M. K.*, note the dissenting views of Rosalyn Higgins, who stressed the Committee's competence to rule on whether the statement was a declaration or a reservation.

[144] During the presentation of periodic reports, members of the Committee for the Elimination of Discrimination Against Women have questioned states about their reservations to the Convention on the Elimination of All Forms of Discrimination Against Women: e.g., UN Doc. A/39/45, Vol. II at §190 (initial report of Egypt); UN Doc. A/44/38 at §74 (initial report of Ireland); UN Doc. A/44/38 at §273 (initial report of Belgium). More recently, the Committee has in effect declared that certain reservations are unacceptable — e.g., the general reservation by the Libyan Arab Jamahiriya concerning the Shariah: UN Doc. A/49/38 at §130.

[145] For an example of that body's hesitant approach, see "Initial Report of Egypt," UN Doc. CRC/C/3/Add.6 at §174; "Preliminary Observations of the Committee on the Rights of the Child: Egypt," UN Doc. CRC/C/15/Add.5. See also UN Doc. CRC/C/1; UN Doc. CRC/C/SR.66 at §40.

a reservation that might be considered by the treaty body concerned as being incompatible with the object and purpose of the treaty.[146]

By 1994, the chairpersons had become considerably less equivocal, recommending "that treaty bodies state clearly that certain reservations to international human rights instruments are contrary to the object and purpose of those instruments and consequently incompatible with treaty law."[147]

The possibility that parties may denounce the various conventions is sometimes invoked in order to persuade treaty bodies to exercise caution when addressing the issue of reservations. The alleged dangers are twofold: first, when reservations are disallowed, the states concerned will simply denounce the instrument, since they have no intention of being bound by the norms subject to their reservation; second, when reservations are allowed, other parties that have earlier ratified without reservation may find the practice unfair, and denounce the instrument so as to permit a subsequent ratification, this time with the appropriate — and legal — reservation. Threats of denunciation have been invoked for many years, but as yet no state has actually taken the step. Nevertheless, assuming the threat is genuine, would it not be better to suffer a few denunciations, in order to enhance the integrity of the norms and ensure that law triumphs over politics?

CONSEQUENCES OF ILLEGALITY

Great confusion surrounds the consequences of illegality of a reservation. Essentially, however, two hypotheses have been presented. The first holds that a reservation deemed illegal invalidates the ratification altogether. This conclusion is suggested in the objections of the Netherlands, the United Kingdom, and China (Taiwan) to certain reservations to the Genocide Convention.[148] The second deems the illegal reservation to be ineffective, with the result that the reserving state is bound by the instrument as a whole, including the reserved provision. A large number of objections to reservations imply this result by stating that the instrument comes into force between the objecting and the reserving states, despite

[146] *Supra* note 4 at §36.

[147] "Effective implementation of international instruments on human rights, including reporting obligations under international instruments on human rights," UN Doc. A/49/537 at §30.

[148] Multilateral Treaties, *supra* note 8 at 94-96.

the illegality of the reservation.[149] But this latter formulation, although widely used, is apparently ambiguous, since it does not clearly declare that the reserved provision comes into force.[150] Were the instrument to come into force between objecting and reserving states with the exception of the reserved provision, then the reserving state would in effect have accomplished its goal, and this can hardly be an appropriate result. As Judge Macdonald has written, "[t]o exclude the application of an obligation by reason of an invalid reservation is in effect to give full force and effect to the reservation."[151]

Where the legal value of objections is discounted, the real issue is not whether a human rights instrument enters into force between reserving and objecting states, or between a reserving state and all other parties. Rather, it is whether the instrument enters into force between the reserving state and "all individuals within its territory and subject to its jurisdiction," to cite the formulation used in the Covenant and employed with slight variation in the other human rights instruments.[152]

International tribunals have examined the issue of the consequences of an illegal reservation to a multilateral treaty on only a few occasions. The issue was first considered by Sir Hersch Lauterpacht, in his dissenting opinions in the *Norwegian Loans* and *Interhandel* cases of the International Court of Justice. Judge Lauterpacht concluded in the latter case that the criterion was one of intent: if a reserving state would not have ratified had it known the reservation was illegal, then it could not be bound by the convention; if, on the other hand, the reservation was only ancillary to its ratification, then the state could be bound by the convention, including the reserved provision. The learned judge therefore sought to determine the intent of the reserving state — in the above cases, the United States of America. A review of practice over several decades left no doubt that the United States considered the issue of the reservation to be a *sine qua non* of its acceptance of the treaty as a whole:

149 This is the position taken by several states that have objected to the United States reservations to the Covenant.

150 Occasionally states will affirm unequivocally that the instrument, including the reserved provision, comes into force: see Denmark's objection to the reservations by Yemen to the International Convention on the Elimination of All Forms of Racial Discrimination.

151 R. St. J. Macdonald, *supra* note 2 at 449.

152 International Covenant on Civil and Political Rights, *supra* note 1, Art. 2 §1.

If that reservation is an essential condition of the Acceptance in the sense that without it the declaring State would have been wholly unwilling to undertake the principal obligation, then it is not open to the Court to disregard that reservation and at the same time to hold the accepting State bound by the Declaration.[153]

The 1988 judgment of the European Court of Human Rights in *Belilos* v. *Switzerland* was the first occasion in which an international court actually found a reservation to be illegal. The Court summarily considered the consequences, applying the test of intention of the reserving state, and concluded: ". . . it is beyond doubt that Switzerland is, and regards itself as, bound by the Convention irrespective of the validity of the declaration."[154] It is important to note that counsel for Switzerland had admitted this fact during the hearing.

But there was no such admission from Turkey when the European Commission on Human Rights ruled illegal its reservation to Article 25 of the European Convention. Turkey's 1987 declaration recognizing the individual petition mechanism before the European Commission included a statement to the effect that it only applied in territory subject to the constitution of Turkey.[155] Manifestly, Turkey sought to exclude the possibility of any individual petitions concerning the territory in northern Cyprus that it has occupied since 1974. The declaration was objected to by Greece, and several other states reserved their rights to object at a later date.[156] Subsequently, three Greek Cypriots filed applications with the Commission alleging various violations of their rights in the Turkish-occupied portions of northern Cyprus. The Commission concluded that the declaration, which was a form of reservation, was illegal, and that consequently an individual petition concerning occupied Cyprus was admissible.[157] The Commission considered

---

153 *Interhandel case (Switzerland v. United States)*, [1959] I.C.J. Rep. 6 at 117; see also Judge Lauterpacht's dissenting opinion in *Norwegian Loans Case (France v. Norway)*, [1957] I.C.J. Rep. 9 at 43-66.

154 *Belilos Case, supra* note 2 at §60.

155 (1987) 30 *Y.B. Eur. Conv. H.R.* 8.

156 It was also criticized by scholars: Claudio Zanghi, "La déclaration de la Turquie relative à l'Article 25 de la Convention européenne des droits de l'homme" (1989) 93 R.G.D. Int'l P. 69; I. Cameron, "Turkey and Article 25 of the European Convention on Human Rights" (1988) 37 I.C.L.Q. 887.

157 *Chrysostomos, Papachrysostomou, Loizidou v. Turkey* (Nos. 15299/89, 15300/89, 15318/89) (1991), 3 Rev. U.D.H. 193.

that Turkey's principal intention was to be bound by Article 25, which must therefore fully apply despite the reservation. In support, it referred to the European Court judgment in *Belilos* and, making an analogy with contract law, the general principle *ut res magis valeat quam pereat*.[158]

"In principle, the will which ought to prevail is the will to accept the treaty," writes Professor D.W. Bowett.[159] He notes, however, that there is a "patent contradiction" in the will of the state to ratify a treaty while attaching to it an illegal condition and that determining the state's intent is "a question of construction."[160] It may be useful here to distinguish the Strasbourg jurisprudence from the approach of Judge Lauterpacht, in that the latter was not dealing with human rights instruments. Where human rights obligations are concerned, and where the protection of the individual and not that of sovereign states is at issue, there are compelling policy reasons why "the thing may rather have effect than be destroyed." The same approach may be less decisive in areas of international litigation where human rights are not involved.

The Human Rights Committee, in its General Comment, unfortunately does not give any attention to the consequences of illegal reservations. Yet it will soon confront the issue when it considers the reservations made by the United States to Articles 6 and 7 of the Covenant. Are they "essential conditions" of ratification, to use the term of Judge Lauterpacht? The preparatory documents indicate that Washington's focus was on executions for crimes committed by individuals aged 16 and 17, and this matter could have been addressed with a far more specific reservation than the very broad declaration that was in fact submitted. The reference in President Bush's explanatory notes to "serious crimes" is puzzling, because capital punishment is imposed in the United States only for murder, which most certainly qualifies as a "serious crime." As for Article 7, the preparatory documents demonstrate that the concern was with the "death row phenomenon" and the spectre of *Soering*.[161] This too could have been accomplished with a far narrower reservation, also likely to pass the threshold of legality, given the

---

158 "That the thing may rather have effect than be destroyed": *ibid.* at §47.

159 D. W. Bowett, *supra* note 3 at 76.

160 *Ibid.*, 77.

161 *Soering Case* (1989), Eur. Ct. H.R. Ser. A, No. 161, 11 E.H.R.R. 439.

Human Rights Committee's conservative approach to the matter.[162] In any case, the "death row phenomenon" may also be raised under Article 10 of the Covenant, and the United States has not reserved application of this provision.

It is useful to recall that the United States participated thoroughly in the drafting of the American Convention on Human Rights, which includes provisions very similar to, and in fact inspired by, Articles 6 and 7 of the Covenant. Its representative, Richard D. Kearney, intervened frequently in Committee 1 of the San José Conference, which was held in November 1969.[163] Although briefly questioning the juvenile death penalty and the exclusion of political crimes, he did not object in substance to the provisions dealing with the death penalty or torture. The United States signed the Convention on June 1, 1977 without reservation. It is consequently bound to refrain from any acts that would defeat the object and purpose of that Convention.[164]

Furthermore, in 1987 the Inter-American Commission of Human Rights found the United States in breach of the American Declaration of Human Rights with respect to imposition of the juvenile death penalty.[165] The United States was bound by the provisions of the Declaration by virtue of the Charter of the Organization of American States.[166] The United States was free to denounce the Charter in response to this ruling, but has not done so. These elements of recent United States practice with respect to similar and related human rights instruments demonstrate that its government considers the sum to be more important than its parts. Therefore, it is submitted that the general intent of the United States has been to assume the norms contained in the Covenant, even if its reservations concerning the death penalty are deemed inadmissible.

---

[162] *Kindler* v. *Canada* (no. 470/1991), UN Doc. CCPR/C/48/D/470/1991, 14 HRLJ 307. See also William A. Schabas, "Soering's Legacy: the Human Rights Committee and the Judicial Committee of the Privy Council Take a Walk Down Death Row" (1994) 43 I.C.L.Q. 913.

[163] OAS/Ser.K/XVI/1.2, Doc.36; OAS/Ser.K/XVI/1.2, Doc.38, Corr.1; OAS/Ser.K/XVI/1.2, doc.40, Corr.1.

[164] Vienna Convention, *supra* note 2, Art. 18.

[165] *Supra* note 44.

[166] Apr. 30, 1948, [1990] C.T.S. No. 23, 119 U.N.T.S. 4; Case 2141 (United States) (1981), Inter-Am. Comm. H.R. Res. No. 23/81, *Annual Report of the Inter-American Commission on Human Rights: 1980-1981*, OEA/Ser.L/V/II.52 doc. 48 (1981), *Ten Years of Activities, 1971-1981*, Washington, D.C.: Organization of American States, 1982 at 186, 1 HRLJ 110.

CAN RESERVATIONS BE "AMENDED"?

The Vienna Convention on the Law of Treaties allows states to formulate reservations only at the time of ratification or accession. Reservations may of course be withdrawn, but states are foreclosed from any subsequent modification. If the Human Rights Committee rules the reservations by the United States to Articles 6 and 7 of the International Covenant to be illegal, the United States cannot reformulate its reservations in a way more likely to pass muster with the Committee. Yet, as we have shown, in acceding to the Covenant the principal intent of the United States was to reserve on juvenile executions and death row conditions. Should the Committee "read down" the United States reservations, leaving intact those portions that it deems admissible, and thereby encourage the United States to remain a party to the Covenant and to resist any temptation to denounce the instrument? Assuming that precise reservations on these two points are not contrary to the object and purpose of the Covenant, this would respect the intent of the United States to impose conditions and at the same time maintain its accession, thereby enhancing the protection of individuals subject to the jurisdiction of the United States.

The impossibility of subsequent modification of reservations, or of the formulation of new reservations, leads to other difficult situations. For example, since 1991 Canada has been considering possible ratification of the American Convention on Human Rights. In contrast with the United Nations and European systems, ratification of the American Convention renders a state automatically susceptible to individual petitions. Canada is concerned about the possibility of successive applications, first to the organs of the Inter-American system, and subsequently to the Human Rights Committee. When European states were faced with the same situation, they formulated reservations to the Optional Protocol that rendered a determination by the Strasbourg organs to be *res judicata* with respect to the Human Rights Committee.[167] But Canada cannot do likewise; because it has already acceded to the Optional Protocol, it is now too late to formulate a reservation.[168]

In the *Belilos* case, counsel for Switzerland suggested to the court that a revised interpretative declaration might be a way to resolve

167 See *supra* note 100.

168 On this issue, see William A. Schabas, "Substantive and Procedural Issues in the Ratification by Canada of the American Convention on Human Rights" (1991) 12 HRLJ 405.

the problem, allowing a state to reformulate its reservation relying on the guidance of the court.[169] Switzerland did in fact produce a revised declaration following the European Court judgment, without apparent objection from the other parties.[170] Its declaration has since been re-amended, again without objection.[171] Liechtenstein has also amended its reservation to Article 6 §1 of the European Convention.[172] The European Convention specifically provides that reservations must be made at the time of signature or ratification,[173] but the principle that reservations cannot be made or amended subsequent to signature, accession, or ratification is more general, as the Vienna Convention on the Law of Treaties makes clear.[174]

Subsequent modification of reservations or declarations is obviously unacceptable in a contract law context. It is now generally agreed, however, that although the principles of the contract model are enshrined in the Vienna Convention, this model is totally inappropriate to human rights treaties. Treaty bodies might therefore formulate a new rule of international law, relying on this still limited practice under the European regional system, that would allow subsequent modification of reservations in order to render them compatible with the object and purpose of the instrument. Judicial recognition of such a possibility can be found in the dissenting opinion of Judge N. Valticos of the European Court of Human Rights, in the 1993 decision *Chorherr* v. *Austria*:

[I]f, several years after it has been made (when the Convention was ratified), a reservation is found to be contrary to the rules laid down in Article 64 and is therefore held to be null and void, can it be replaced by another reservation which is more consistent with that Article? In principle, that should not be possible, because a reservation may be made only at the moment of ratification. That would, however, be unreasonable, because the governments concerned have been informed of the non-validity of their reservation only several years after the ratification. The governments in question should therefore have the opportunity to rectify the situation and to submit a valid reservation within a reasonable time and on the basis of their former reservation.[175]

---

169 *Belilos Case, supra* note 2, "Verbatim Report of the Public Hearings Held on 26 October 1987," Eur. Ct. H.R. Court Misc (87) 237 at 247.

170 (1988) 31 Y.B. Eur. Conv. H.R. 5.

171 Doc. H/INF (89) 2, Information Sheet No. 24 at 7-8.

172 Doc. H/INF (92) 1, Information Sheet No. 29 at 1.

173 *Supra* note 19, Art. 64 §1.

174 *Supra* note 2, Art. 2 §1(*d*).

175 *Chorherr* v. *Austria* (1993), Eur. Ct. H.R. Ser. A, No. 266-B at 42.

Judge Valticos makes another innovative suggestion in the *Chorherr* case. He proposes a form of consultation by which a treaty body (in the case of the European Convention, this would be the European Court of Human Rights) would rule on the legality of reservations at the time of ratification.[176] This is a function that could be performed by the various committees during presentation of a state's initial report, or by the commissions and courts in the European, American, and African systems. As Judge Valticos explains, in comments addressed to the European system but transposable to the other regional and to the universal systems, "[t]his is a question of the observance of the Convention, which the Court was set up to ensure."[177] An alternative that has already been proposed is to seek advisory opinions from the International Court of Justice, via the Economic and Social Council.[178] States could be given a reasonable grace period following such an examination to reformulate any reservations deemed invalid.

The flexibility provided by such new approaches would serve a number of important objectives. It would promote ratification of human rights treaties by assuring new parties a degree of certainty as to the consequences and effects of any reservations. This is a theme present in the debate upon reservations since the time of the International Court's advisory opinion in the *Genocide* case. Furthermore, the other parties would be in a position to debate, and have determined, the precise legal value of any proposed reservations. Reciprocity would be encouraged, in that an existing party to a human rights convention would be in a position to reduce its treaty obligations, if it were determined that certain reservations, previously thought impossible, would pass muster. Presumably, the latter practice would be used in only the rarest of circumstances, but its possibility would establish equality between early ratifiers and those who have waited for the treaty's jurisprudence to develop before expressing a reservation to those aspects with which they disagree. This practice would result in greater certainty, not only for

[176] *Ibid.*

[177] *Ibid.*

[178] *Supra* note 4 at §16. See also decision 1991/115 and resolution 1992/3 of the Sub-Commission on Prevention of Discrimination and Protection of Minorities. The proposal began in the Sub-Commission's Working Group on Contemporary Forms of Slavery: see UN Doc. E/CN.4/Sub.2/1991/41 at §§51-56, Annex C; UN Doc. E/CN.4/Sub.2/1991/SR.33/Add.1 at §43, although the idea appears to have come from Professor Rebecca Cook, *supra* note 10 at 710-11.

states but also for individuals, and in a wider scope for the application of international human rights law.

Conclusion

In its General Comment, the Human Rights Committee makes a number of proposals to regulate the use of reservations. These proposals, although not legally binding rules, may generate a subsequent practice by states that could give rise to new principles of customary law. The Committee urges a reserving state to "indicate in precise terms the domestic legislation or practices which it believes to be incompatible with the Covenant obligation reserved; and to explain the time period it requires to render its own laws and practices compatible with the Covenant."[179] Furthermore, the Committee asks that states periodically review the need for their reservations, taking into account the observations and recommendations made by the Committee.

It has been proposed that treaty bodies make requests for advisory opinions to the International Court of Justice, via the Economic and Social Council, on the issue of reservations.[180] Despite the interest such an approach may have, it should not encourage the treaty bodies to abdicate their responsibilities. The presentation of initial and periodic reports provides an ideal occasion for the treaty to engage in dialogue with a state, to examine the state's internal legislation, and to assess its real intent with respect to reservations.

The General Comment of the Human Rights Committee should be the final nail in the coffin of the Vienna Convention reservations regime as it applies to human rights treaties. Of course, the "object and purpose" rule set out by the International Court of Justice in the *Genocide* case remains in force. As for objections, they continue to have some value by ensuring reciprocity in interstate petition mechanisms, and may also be helpful politically. The emergence of "reservations" by which states affirm that international norms are inadequate and that they themselves set a higher standard (as in the prohibition of child soldiers in the Convention on the Rights of the Child) demonstrates the evolving view that states themselves take of the function of reservations. The solutions proposed up to the present by international treaty law have proved inadequate, and

---

179 General Comment No. 24 (52), *supra* note 2 at §20.

180 *Supra* note 4 at §16.

the international courts, commissions, and treaty bodies have been responsible for innovation. Although the General Comment opens the door to new solutions, it leaves unaddressed such vital issues as the consequences of illegality of reservations or the possibility of amendment. The promise that the Committee will address such issues as the content of customary law and the scope of *jus cogens* norms indicates just how rich an area the litigation on reservations may become in the second half of the United Nations Decade on International Law.

Sommaire

Les réserves aux conventions de protection des droits de la personne: réforme et innovation

La pratique répandue de la formulation de réserves aux conventions internationales des droits de la personne est une préoccupation des organes de contrôle. Les règles coutumières concernant des réserves, qui sont codifiées dans la Convention de Vienne sur le droit des traités, sont inappropriées pour un régime de protection des droits de la personne où la réciprocité des obligations est d'une importance mitigée. Lors de la ratification du Pacte international relatif aux droits civils et politiques, les États-Unis ont formulé une série de réserves. Ceci a provoqué que le Comité des droits de l'homme aborde le sujet dans une observation générale. Le Comité propose des critères d'application du test de l'objet et le but du traité. Il constate que des réserves aux dispositions non-dérogeables sont acceptables. Toutefois, aucune réserve ne peut être formulée à l'égard d'une norme coutumière. De plus, le Comité clarifie la situation quant à la compétence des organes de contrôle de se prononcer sur la légalité des réserves. Mais la conséquence d'une réserve illégale demeure incertaine. L'intention réelle de l'état en question doit être établie afin de déterminer si l'état sera lié par le traité, et ce malgré l'incompatibilité de sa réserve. Une pratique en évolution suggère que les états peuvent reformuler ou amender des réserves après la ratification, même si la Convention de Vienne n'autorise pas une telle démarche.

Summary

Reservations to Human Rights Treaties: Time for Innovation and Reform

The widespread practice of making reservations to international human rights treaties has become an important issue for treaty bodies. The customary rules governing reservations, codified in the Vienna Convention on the Law of Treaties, are largely inappropriate to a human rights regime in which reciprocity of obligations is of limited consequence. Since, upon ratifying the International Covenant on Civil and Political Rights, the United States formulated a series of broad reservations, the Human Rights Committee has addressed the issue in a General Comment. The Committee suggests a number of guidelines for applying the "object and purpose" test, noting that reservations to non-derogable provisions may be permitted. However, it insists that no reservation may be made to a customary norm that has been included within a human rights treaty. Furthermore, the Committee clarifies the confusion among treaty bodies as to their competence to pronounce on the legality of reservations. Nevertheless, the consequences of illegal reservations remain quite uncertain. The genuine intent of a ratifying state must be examined to determine whether it is bound by the treaty as a whole, once its reservation has been declared incompatible. An emerging practice suggests that States may reformulate or amend reservations subsequent to ratification, despite terms to the contrary in the Vienna Convention.

The Iran-Iraq War Revisited: Some Reflections on the Role of International Law

ERIK B. WANG*

> "Canada will remain in the forefront of those countries working to expand the rule of law internationally. . . . Rules-based regimes of arms control and conflict resolution are key priorities for the Government."
>
> Government statement, *Canada in the World*,
> tabled in Parliament, February 7, 1995

ASTRONOMERS LIKE TO STUDY black holes for what they can tell us about the evolution of the universe. The Iran-Iraq war (1980-88) was a black hole in terms of a massive disregard for the rules. There has always been a painful gap between the letter of international law and the practice of states engaged in armed conflict, painful for combatants and victims of hostilities, and painful for proponents of a more central role for law in international relations. This gap was exceptionally wide during the Iran-Iraq war, perhaps wider than in any other conflict since the First and Second World Wars.

Like its savage predecessors, the first Gulf War tended to become a total war. As the conflict escalated, methods of warfare considered unacceptable at the beginning became common practice by the end. Attacks on civilian populations and on neutral aircraft and shipping, abuse of prisoners-of-war, deployment of chemical weapons, and other violations of well-established rules became almost commonplace. Children were sent in to clear minefields. The war spurred an enormous buildup of conventional arms, together with major advances in the development of weapons of

---

* Formerly of the Department of External Affairs, Ottawa. Canadian Ambassador to Iraq, 1986-8. The views expressed are those of the author.

83

mass destruction and means of delivery. No moderation seemed possible as long as each side perceived the enemy as a satanic force threatening not just its interests but its deepest values. The war represented thus not only a clash of armies but also a contest of competing principles of political organization. As one commentator described it, the war "was fought with the weapons of the 1980s, the tactics of World War I, and the passions of the Crusades."[1]

What is more, the conflict raged with an uncommon level of ineffectiveness on the part of the international community in restoring peace or at least mitigating suffering. The efforts of regional organizations and the United Nations to ensure compliance with international law and to bring the conflict to an end were timid, at best, until the final spasms of the struggle threatened wider interests. Some statesmen seemed content to see the war continue indefinitely.[2]

What can this black hole tell us about the prospects for a rules-based international order? Why did civilized restraints fail? From the many violations committed we may look back at three dimensions in particular which were representative of the brutal nature of the war, and of the response of the international community: illegal use of force, use of chemical weapons, and attacks on neutral shipping. What lessons can we draw for community and Canadian efforts to moderate future regional conflicts and uphold the rule of law? We should start with a broad-brush picture of the belligerents themselves and of their attitude to the law.

CHARACTERISTICS OF THE PARTIES

After the fall of the Shah and the return of Ayatollah Khomeini in February 1979, Iran became a militant revolutionary power seeking radical transformation of its domestic society as well as that of its neighbours. Iran actively fomented sectarian strife between Shia and Sunni within Iraq, supported a Kurdish insurgency in northern Iraq, and launched a pattern of terrorist attacks, including an assassination attempt on the Foreign Minister, Tariq Aziz, aimed at destabilizing the secular government of President Saddam Hussein. Iran also committed a growing number of encroachments and violations of Iraq's territorial integrity along the border, culminating in heavy artillery bombardments of civilian centres and closure

[1] M. A. Heller, "Turmoil in the Gulf," *New Republic* (Apr. 23, 1984) 16.

[2] Henry Kissinger commented, "The only regrettable aspect of this situation is that only one of the parties can lose": *Time* (July 28, 1986) 4.

of international navigation in the Shatt-al-Arab waterway shared by Iraq and Iran.[3]

These Iranian pressures reflected a hostility not just to the regime of Saddam Hussein but also to fundamental principles of international law, when they appeared to stand in the way of Islamic teachings. In a number of statements, Khomeini openly called for efforts to "export the revolution" and declared the irrelevance of international borders. Iranian leaders declared that "the road to Jerusalem passes through Baghdad." Under the dictates of religious zealotry, intervention in Iraq's internal affairs was not only permissible but obligatory.

A defining moment in Iran's attitude towards international law came on November 4, 1979, when student militants overran the compound of the United States Embassy in Tehran and took its personnel as hostages. The government subsequently assumed responsibility for the hostage-taking and defied protests from the international community and the Security Council. Four months before the outbreak of war, the International Court of Justice condemned Iran for violating its obligations to the United States under long established rules of international law. Iran did not appear in the court proceedings, but explained its position in a letter to the Court. It rejected the jurisdiction of the Court on the basis of ". . . the essential character of the Islamic Revolution of Iran, a revolution of a whole oppressed nation against its oppressors and their masters, the examination of whose numerous repercussions is essentially and directly a matter within the national sovereignty of Iran."[4]

In comparison, Iraq may be seen, prior to the outbreak of war in 1980, as essentially a *status quo* power. Oil revenues were flowing into the national treasury. Ambitious development projects were transforming every sector of society, and seemed destined to lift

[3] For a summary presentation of the Iraqi case, see the statement of Saadoun Hammadi, Minister for Foreign Affairs of Iraq, before the Security Council on Oct. 15, 1980, UN Doc. S/PV.2250. For the Iranian reply, see the statement of Mohammed Ali Rajai, Prime Minister of Iran, before the Security Council on Oct. 17, 1980, S/PV.2251.

[4] Letter of March 16, 1980, set out in the judgment of the Court dated May 24, 1980, *United States Diplomatic and Consular Staff in Tehran (United States v. Iran),* [1981] ICJ Rep. 1 at 8. Khomeini expressed views on international law in an interview with *Time* magazine: "What kind of law is this? It permits the U.S. Government to exploit and colonize peoples all over the world for decades. But it does not allow the extradition of an individual who has staged great massacres. Can you call it law?" *Time* (Jan. 7, 1980) 27.

Iraq to unimagined heights of progress and prosperity. Because of domestic tensions generated by Iraq's fragmented ethnic, religious, and social make-up, the Iraqi regime was, however, particularly sensitive and vulnerable to subversive activities supported from outside. As evidence of direct Iranian involvement mounted, Saddam Hussein had genuine grounds for believing that Khomeini was intent on overthrowing his regime. He had survived in power through a ruthless policy of domestic repression. His reaction was to strike no less forcefully against an external threat. If the primary goal was defensive, he also saw a historic opportunity to regain control of the Shatt-al-Arab waterway at a time when Iran appeared to be gravely weakened by internal revolutionary convulsions.[5] Iranian disdain for international law collided head on with Iraqi ambitions.

Each leader demanded of his followers unquestioned personal authority to make decisions on behalf of the state. There were cross currents of advice within the inner councils of government, but on each side the decisions of the leader on the overall conduct of hostilities were unchallenged. Each side had large military capabilities, sustained by enormous oil revenues. They saw little need to defer to outsiders on the course they had set for themselves.

A QUESTION OF RESPONSIBILITY

It is almost conventional today to say that Saddam Hussein should have been condemned for aggression against Iran from the outset, in September 1980, and that the failure of the United Nations to take resolute action encouraged him later to think that he could invade Kuwait with impunity.

In his valedictory report to the Security Council on the Iran-Iraq war, in the final weeks before leaving office in 1991, Secretary-General Perez de Cuellar saw the issue in this light. He said that:

---

[5] Gary Sick provides a pointed summary on the situation on the eve of war: ". . .Iran's behaviour in the immediate post-revolutionary period left it with the worst of all possible worlds. Its rhetoric and meddling with the Shi'i opposition in Iraq was highly provocative, while its military weakness made it a tempting target. The combination proved deadly": "Trial by Error: Reflections on the Iran-Iraq War" (1989) 43 Middle East J. 233. For a portrait of the Iranian revolution, see Fouad Ajami, "Iran: The Impossible Revolution," (1988) 67 Foreign Affairs 135. For a powerful portrayal of Saddam Hussein's leadership, see Samir al-Khalil (Kanan Makiya), *Republic of Fear: The Inside Story of Saddam's Iraq* (New York: Pantheon, 1990).

"the attack of 22 September 1980 against Iran. . . . cannot be justified under the Charter of the United Nations, any recognized rules and principles of international law or any principles of international morality and entails the responsibility for the conflict. . . . Even if before the outbreak of the conflict there had been some encroachment by Iran on Iraqi territory, such encroachment did not justify Iraq's aggression against Iran. . . ." He went on to suggest that if there had been implementation of "a system of good-neighbourly relations based on respect of international law, as was envisaged by the Security Council . . . [it] might have spared the region from the further tragedy that followed."[6]

One may question whether this report qualifies as a considered legal opinion or as a wholly understandable expression of personal exasperation over Iraq's conduct through two gulf wars. But if the events of 1980 were ever to be submitted to third party adjudication, there would seem to be good grounds for arguing that Iraq should bear a preponderant, if not exclusive, burden of responsibility for the initial outbreak. In response to Iranian pressures Saddam Hussein expelled from Iraq some 200,000 residents of Iranian origin. He denounced the 1975 Algiers Agreement as null and void, thereby reclaiming Iraqi rights, *inter alia*, to the waters of the Shatt-al-Arab which, under the Agreement, were to be shared along the *thalweg* (the median line of the main navigable channel).[7] On September 22, 1980, he initiated large-scale hostilities by attacking at the level of an estimated four army divisions (45,000 men) and conducting air strikes on a wide front along the central and southern border.[8]

---

6 Secretary-General Perez de Cuellar's Report to Security Council, Dec. 9, 1991, UN Doc S/23273.

7 Iraqi Note to the Embassy of the Islamic Republic of Iran, Baghdad, Sept. 17, 1980, Iraq Ministry of Foreign Affairs, *The Iraqi-Iranian Conflict: Documentary Dossier* 200 (Baghdad: January, 1981) [hereinafter *Dossier*].

8 This is the conservative estimate of Edgar O'Ballance, *The Gulf War* 30 (London: Brassey's, 1988). Dilip Hiro has estimated the Iraqi attack at about seven divisions (70,000 to 100,000 men): *The Longest War: The Iran-Iraq Military Conflict* 40, 41 (London: Graften Books, 1989). The Iranian estimate of the scale of the initial Iraqi invasion was "12 divisions and more than 2,500 tanks, as well as large quantities of weapons and hundreds of war planes": statement of Mohammed Ali Rajai, Prime Minister of Iran, before the Security Council, Oct. 17, 1980, UN Doc S/PV.2251 at 6. President Saddam Hussein stated in a press conference on Nov. 10, 1980: "Iraqi forces have advanced to a depth ranging from 20 to 110 kilometers inside Iranian territory on a front that extends for

There seem to have been doubts initially even on the Iraqi side as to whether the attack in strength on September 22 could be justified as self-defence or as a preemptive strike. In his first appearance before the Security Council on October 15, Iraqi Foreign Minister Saadoun Hammadi said that, in the light of Iranian "hostile acts," his government "was left with no choice but to direct *preventative* strikes against military targets in Iran. There was, to borrow from a well-known case, 'a necessity of self-defence, instant, overwhelming, leaving no choice of means and no moment of deliberations.'" Mr Hammadi provided the case citation: the *Caroline*, 1837.[9] Later Iraqi statements in justification took the position that Iraq acted in self-defence pure and simple, in response to a consistent pattern of threats, terrorist attacks, and incursions that amounted to armed attacks and aggression against Iraq.

Iraq might be vulnerable on either argument. Self-defence as an exception to the prohibition against armed force in Article 2(4) of the Charter has generally been viewed restrictively by the Security Council and the General Assembly when they have pronounced on claims of self-defence.[10] For example, the Council strongly condemned the pre-emptive Israeli attack on Iraqi nuclear installations

550 kilometers": *Dossier* at 309. Detailed accounts of the course of the war include: A. H. Cordesman, *The Iran-Iraq War and Western Security 1984-87: Strategic Implications and Policy Options* (London: Jane's Publishing, 1987); P. Balta, *Iran-Irak: Une Guerre de 5000 Ans* (Paris: Editions Anthropos, 1987); U.S. Senate Committee on Foreign Relations Staff Report, *War in the Persian Gulf: The U.S. Takes Sides* (1987); E. Karsh, *The Iran-Iraq War: A Military Analysis* (London: Adelphi Papers, IISS, 1987).

9 See *Dossier* at 240. Mr. Hammadi also argued that the attack was preventative in a letter to the Heads of Governments of the European Community, Dec. 2, 1980, *Dossier* at 320. The *Caroline* involved a raid by British/Canadian forces against an armed U.S. vessel on the American side of the Niagara River, in anticipation of an attack in support of a rebellion against Upper Canada. Commentators have questioned whether the *Caroline* dictum is consistent with Charter provisions, and in particular whether the inherent right of self-defence under Art. 51 includes a right to take preventative action against an attack that has not yet occurred but seems imminent. For a restrictive view, see I. Brownlie, *International Law and the Use of Force by States* 275-78 (Oxford: Clarendon Press, 1963). Schachter, on the other hand, accepts the *Caroline* as reflecting customary international law and not inconsistent with Art. 51: O. Schachter, *International Law in Theory and Practice* 151 (Dordrecht: Martinus Nijhoff, 1991). President Saddam Hussein stated in his press conference on Nov. 10, 1980 that heavy shelling of Iraqi border towns on Sept. 4, 1980 marked the start of the war. See *Dossier* at 294.

10 See e.g., Schachter, *supra* note 9 at 144-46.

on June 7, 1981, as a "clear violation of the Charter of the United Nations and the norms of international conduct."[11] The International Court of Justice rejected a claim of collective self-defence in the *Nicaragua* case, which had some features similar to the Iran-Iraq conflict. Border incursions from Nicaragua against El Salvador, in the view of the Court, constituted illegal intervention but were not of sufficient magnitude to amount to an "armed attack" justifying measures in collective self-defence by the United States under Article 51 of the Charter.[12]

The *Nicaragua* judgment reiterated that, in order to sustain a claim of self-defence under customary international law, it must be shown that the use of force was *necessary* and *proportionate* to the initial attack.[13] Had either requirement been met?

Clearly, there were other recourses open to Iraq. The Iranian Prime Minister pointed out to the Security Council that the 1975 Algiers Agreement itself provided for the means of settling whatever disputes might arise between the parties.[14] Article 6 of the treaty carefully sets out the mechanisms to which the parties "shall have recourse" in the event of a dispute, beginning with direct bilateral negotiations, then, failing agreement, the good offices of a friendly third state, and finally, binding arbitration by a court of arbitration consisting of three members, one appointed by each side and an umpire appointed by the two. In the event that one of the parties fails to appoint an arbitrator, or that the two arbitrators fail to agree on the choice of the umpire, the party initiating the proceedings may ask the President of the International Court of Justice to appoint the arbitrators or the umpire. Accordingly, if Iraq had chosen this course, arbitration could not have been blocked by opposition or inaction on the part of Iran.

The Iraqi contention was that, by violating fundamental provisions of the treaty, Iran had abrogated the treaty, and "the whole treaty becomes non-existent."[15] Lawyers could debate this issue at length. Considerable weight would have to be given to the explicit

11 Security Council Resolution 487, June 19, 1981.

12 *Military and Paramilitary Activities in and against Nicaragua (Nicaragua v. United States)*, [1986] ICJ Rep. 14.

13 *Ibid.*, para. 194. See also panel discussion: "Implementing Limitations on the Use of Force: The Doctrine of Proportionality and Necessity" (1992) *ASIL Proceedings* 39.

14 Debate in the Security Council, Oct. 17, 1980, *supra* note 3 at 16.

15 *Ibid.*, 37.

undertaking in the treaty that the fundamental provisions "shall be final and permanent," and to the principle of customary international law, expressed in Article 62 of the Vienna Convention on the Law of Treaties, that treaties fixing boundaries may not be terminated unilaterally on the grounds of a fundamental change of circumstances.

Iraq would have even greater difficulty establishing that the attack on September 22 was proportionate to the hostile acts complained of. In its *Documentary Dossier*, Iraq published a detailed list of 418 "Iranian violations of Iraqi territory and air space and Iranian hostile acts against Iraq" that had been protested by diplomatic note from February 1979 to September 22, 1980.[16] Even if one accepts the accuracy of these allegations, which relate mostly to terrorist acts and border incidents, and if one accepts the Iraqi assertion that these incidents amount to a pattern of "armed attack" under Article 51, an invasion by four army divisions to a depth of 110 kilometres, with widespread air strikes, may be judged an excessive response. The Iraqi case for self-defence would be further weakened by claims to have "liberated" territories inhabited by Arabs, to the extent that these can be attributed to the regime. Iraqi representatives in the Security Council insisted that Iraq had no territorial ambitions in Iran.

Iraq would have stronger grounds for arguing that, whatever responsibility might attach to the invasion launched on September 22, 1980, Iran should bear responsibility for the continuation of the war due to its refusal to accept successive United Nations calls for a ceasefire, especially after the withdrawal of Iraqi troops from Iranian territory in 1982. Iraq could underscore its own prompt acceptance of each resolution of the Security Council, starting with Resolution 479 of September 28, 1980, formally accepted by Saddam Hussein on September 29. The Council gave some colour of credence to a distinction between the early and later stages of the war. Resolution 582 of February 24, 1986 deplored "the initial acts which gave rise to the conflict between Iran and Iraq and deplore[d] the continuation of the conflict . . ." Security Council Resolution 598 of July 20, 1987 made a similar distinction, "*deploring* the initiation and continuation of the conflict, . . ." On the one occasion when the General Assembly debated the conflict, it was even more specific in respect of Iran's failure to accept a ceasefire,

16 *Dossier* at 28-49.

"*considering further* that the prolongation of the conflict constitutes a violation of the obligations of Member States under the Charter"[17]

THE REACTION AT THE UNITED NATIONS

The Security Council declined to take a position on the question of responsibility. It is clear from the debates in the Council in the weeks and months following the outbreak of hostilities that the case Iran tried to make in the United Nations in portraying itself as a victim of aggression was seriously undermined by previous breaches in Iranian conduct, including disregard for its obligations under the Algiers Agreement, support for subversion by Iraqi Shias and Kurds, and active and violent intervention in the internal affairs of Iraq. Iran's case was also heavily burdened by its conduct over the United States hostages, for which Iran had been strongly condemned by the same body. Iran did not come to the Security Council with clean hands.

The major powers had no disposition to intervene on any basis of principle, ideology, or interest. The United States had little sympathy for an Iraqi leader who had been at the forefront of confrontation with Israel, had vigorously opposed the Camp David accords, and was supporting terrorist groups. The United States had even less sympathy for an Iranian regime that was threatening to destabilize the region and was holding American diplomats hostage. The Soviet Union regarded Iraq as a profitable client for weapons sales and, deeply enmired in Afghanistan, was content to see Iran engaged on another front.

The first pronouncement of the Council, in Resolution 479 of September 28, 1980 did not condemn Iraq and did not call for withdrawal of forces. It merely called upon Iran and Iraq "to refrain immediately from any further use of force and to settle their dispute by peaceful means and in conformity with principles of justice and international law. . . ." Almost two years later, when the tide of battle had turned in favour of Iran, the Council expressed concern "about the prolongation of the conflict between the two countries, resulting in heavy losses of human lives and considerable material damage, and endangering peace and security." The Council called

---

[17] UNGA Resolution 37/3, Oct. 22, 1982, adopted by 119 votes in favour (Iraq, Canada), 1 against (Iran) and 15 abstentions.

once again for a ceasefire, and added a call for withdrawal of forces
to internationally recognized boundaries.[18]

A perfunctory attempt by the Council to insert a modest United
Nations observer presence was rejected. Olof Palme, former Prime
Minister of Sweden, was appointed United Nations mediator, but
after three years and five visits to Baghdad and Tehran reported
failure. Similar efforts by the Arab League, the Non-Aligned Movement, and the Islamic Conference Organization were to no avail.
Secretary-General Perez de Cuellar took up the cause but the permanent members of the Council seemed content to leave him
suspended in his mediation efforts without any visible means of
support. He succeeded in negotiating a precarious pause in attacks
on civilian populations but the "war of the cities" resumed spas-
modically, subject only to the destructive impulses of the struggle at
the front.[19]

Iran's leaders felt betrayed by the failure of the United Nations to
condemn Iraq's initial attack and complained bitterly that no moral
or legal distinctions had been drawn between the two belligerents.
In Resolution 522 of October 4, 1982 the Council added to Iran's
sense of injustice and bias by calling again for a ceasefire, while at
the same time welcoming "the fact that one of the parties [i.e.,
Iraq] has already expressed its readiness to co-operate in the implementation" of a United Nations-monitored withdrawal of forces. By
this time Iranian forces had managed to drive up to ten miles into
Iraqi territory at certain points. A year later, as a very tepid gesture
towards Iran, the Council included in Resolution 540 of October
31, 1983 a preambular reference "affirming the desirability of an
objective examination of the causes of the war."

After seven years of hostilities, and in the midst of a further
upsurge of bloodshed, the Security Council, under United States
leadership, decided to take more determined action. Acting
explicitly under Articles 39 and 40 of Chapter 7 of the Charter, the
Council declared for the first time that there was a breach of the
peace, thereby invoking its mandatory powers.[20] Resolution 598,
adopted unanimously, called for the implementation of a package

18 Security Council Resolution 514, July 12, 1982. Saddam had previously
announced, on June 20, 1982, his decision to withdraw his troops from Iran.

19 See United Nations Backgrounder, *Chronology of United Nations Negotiations to
End the Iran-Iraq War* (New York: United Nations, 1988).

20 Security Council Resolution 598, July 20, 1987.

of ceasefire provisions. As a further gesture towards Iran, the Council included two provisions that went well beyond a ceasefire. The Council:

6. *Requests* the Secretary-General to explore, in consultation with Iran and Iraq, the question of entrusting an impartial body with inquiring into responsibility for the conflict and to report to the Security Council as soon as possible;

7. *Recognizes* the magnitude of the damage inflicted during the conflict and the need for reconstruction efforts, with appropriate international assistance, once the conflict is ended and, in this regard, requests the Secretary-General to assign a team of experts to study the question of reconstruction and to report to the Security Council . . .

Khomeini continued to be publicly committed to Saddam's downfall. A finding of responsibility was to be the means to this end. The stakes would be enormous. Any finding of responsibility could involve reparations of hundreds of billions of dollars in material damages alone, and the prosecution of leaders for war crimes. The Secretary-General, who continued tirelessly to pursue his mediation efforts, reported to the Council after a visit to Tehran and Baghdad in September 1987 that his ". . . Iranian interlocutors forcefully emphasized that the goal should be the establishment of peace on the basis of justice so as to ensure its durability. They insisted that the international community should acknowledge that the inquiry into the responsibility for the conflict must be given the highest priority in any attempt to progress towards a negotiated settlement."[21] Iran continued to insist on this point as a precondition to a ceasefire. In a letter of May 31, 1988 to the Secretary-General, the Iranian Foreign Minister, Dr. Ali Akbar Velayati, stated: "As we have repeatedly and emphatically stressed in previous consultations with Your Excellency, any political solution would require as its first element the determination of the aggressor."

The question of who started the war and who prolonged it will remain controversial. There was enough ambiguity to fuel a lively debate of commentators, legal experts, and historians. Each side has its champions.[22] Secretary-General Perez de Cuellar was unable

---

21 Secretary-General's Report to the Security Council, Sept. 16, 1987.

22 For pro-Iran views, see R. K. Ramazani, "Who started the Iran-Iraq War? A Commentary" (1992) 33 Virginia J. of Int'l L. 69, and I. F. Dekker, "Criminal Responsibility and the Gulf War of 1980-1988: The Crime of Aggression" in I. F. Dekker and H. H. G. Post (eds.), *The Gulf War of 1980-1988: The Iran-Iraq War in International Legal Perspective* 249-68 (Dordrecht: Martinus Nijhoff,

to find any common ground between the parties as to how the proposed inquiry should be handled. In his final report he said that, in his opinion, "it would not seem to serve any useful purpose to pursue paragraph 6 of Resolution 598 (1987)." The issue of legal responsibility for the first Gulf War had been overtaken by the second Gulf War and its aftermath. It was, in his words, the "peace and security of the whole region that urgently needs to be tended to."[23]

THE USE OF CHEMICAL WEAPONS

The pattern of response at the United Nations to the use of chemical weapons was only slightly more robust than it had been on the question of responsibility for the conflict. The Security Council launched investigations, subject to the consent and co-operation of the parties, and pronounced judgments that, although often muffled and wholly ineffective in halting the use of chemical weapons, continued until the end of the war and beyond.

The first use of chemical weapons by Iraq (mustard gas and possibly nerve agents) was reported to the Security Council in March 1984 by a United Nations technical team that had been dispatched by the Secretary-General to the Iranian side of the front at the invitation of Iran.[24] The use was defensive, against massive human wave attacks that threatened to cut off the Baghdad-Basra highway and in effect split the country in two.[25] Both Iraq and Iran were party to the 1925 Geneva Protocol prohibiting the use in war of chemical and biological weapons.

The first Security Council resolution to address the issue, in February 1986 (almost two years after reported first use by Iraq), merely deplored ". . . the use of chemical weapons contrary to

---

1992). For pro-Iraq views, see N. M. Renfrew, "Who Started the War?" (1987) 66 Foreign Policy 98; M. Khadduri, *The Gulf War: The Origins and Implications of the Iraq-Iran conflict* 18-87 (Oxford: Oxford University Press, 1988); P. Marr, "The Iran-Iraq War: The View from Iraq" in C. C. Joyner (ed.), *The Persian Gulf War: Lessons for Strategy, Law and Diplomacy* (New York: Greenwood Press, 1990); and E. Karsh and I. Rautsi, *Saddam Hussein: A Political Biography* 135-49 (New York: The Free Press, 1991). Kaiyan Homi Kaikobad concludes that both states incurred international responsibility: see "Self-Defence, Enforcement Action and the Gulf Wars, 1980-88 and 1990-91" (1993) *British Yearbook of International Law* 308.

23 *Supra* note 6.

24 UN Mission Report to the Security Council, Mar. 21, 1984, UN Doc. S/16433.

25 Dilip Hiro, *supra* note 8 at 103-105.

obligations under the 1925 Geneva Protocol," without identifying the user.[26] A month later, after a further report of a mission dispatched to Iran to investigate allegations, the President of the Security Council was authorized by members to make a stronger statement. "Profoundly concerned by the unanimous conclusions of the specialists that chemical weapons on many occasions have been used by Iraqi forces against Iranian forces, most recently in the course of the present Iranian offensive into Iraqi territory, the members of the Council strongly condemn this continued use of chemical weapons, in clear violation of the Geneva Protocol of 1925, which prohibits the use in war of chemical weapons."[27] The Security Council Resolution 598 of July 20, 1987 reverted to merely *deploring* the use of chemical weapons (user unspecified). In November 1987 the General Assembly, for its part, condemned "all actions" (unspecified) that violated the Protocol.[28] After receiving a further report from a field mission in April 1988, the Security Council *vigorously* condemned "the continued use of chemical weapons in the conflict between Iran and Iraq" and expected "both sides to refrain from the future use of chemical weapons. . . ."[29] The Council issued a further and final condemnation after the ceasefire had gone into effect, stating that it was "*[d]eeply dismayed* by the missions' conclusions that there had been continued use of chemical weapons in the conflict between Iran and Iraq and that such use against Iranians had become more intense and frequent. . . ." It concluded with a warning that it would consider "appropriate and effective measures in accordance with the Charter of the United Nations, should there be any future use of chemical weapons in violation of international law, wherever and by whomever committed."[30]

---

26 Resolution 582, Feb. 24, 1986. The Security Council had previously authorized the President to make statements on its behalf on mission reports, but without identifying the user.

27 UN Doc. S/PV.2667, Mar. 21, 1986.

28 UNGA Resolution 42/37C, Nov. 30, 1987.

29 SC Resolution 612, May 9, 1988.

30 Resolution 620, Aug. 26, 1988. For an interesting analysis of the effectiveness of chemical weapons in this war, see T. L. McNaugher, "Ballistic Missiles and Chemical Weapons: the Legacy of the Iran-Iraq War" (1990) 15 Int'l Security 5. See also Howard Mann, "Arms Control Verification and the United Nations: The Chemical Weapons Experience of the 1980s" (1988) 26 *Canadian Yearbook of International Law* 185.

Thus international repugnance over the use of chemical weapons (for the first time since the First World War) was not translated into any United Nations sanctions or enforcement action, even at the lowest level of calling for a ban on supplies of chemical weapons precursors. The evidence of use on both sides (predominantly Iraq) was incontrovertible, gathered by seven successive field missions during the period 1984 to 1988. The reticent and even-handed tone of some of the Security Council's condemnations reflected not only the use on both sides but also the attainable level of consensus, given the political preoccupations of members. From the viewpoint of the belligerents, there seemed to be no significant costs that might have outweighed the perceived military utility of chemical weapons. The final warning about effective measures must have had a hollow ring.

FREEDOM OF NAVIGATION

Among the many transgressions committed by the two sides, the only one that can be said to have provoked a firm and demonstrably effective response by the international community was Iranian interference with navigation in the Gulf. The issue was not Iraqi shipping, since there had been no Iraqi sea transport through the Gulf since the outbreak of war. The issue was Iranian attacks on neutral shipping, which galvanized international opinion in a way that none of the other violations had. The response reflected, in part, a concern for the security of oil supplies, although this factor seems to have been exaggerated. Even if Iran had completely closed off the Gulf (which would have been within its capabilities but wholly contrary to its interests), the alternative network of pipelines that had been extended to the Red Sea and to the Mediterranean would have assured a largely uninterrupted flow of oil to world markets.

More important, here was a potent principle at stake. The United States, it was recalled, had entered the First World War in defence of this principle. The United States was prepared to intervene at least indirectly in the Iran-Iraq War in defence of the principle of freedom of navigation in the Gulf. The United States decision to reflag and protect Kuwaiti tankers in the summer of 1987 led to the buildup of the largest American naval flotilla since the Korean War. Naval units of the USSR, Britain, France, Italy, Belgium, and the Netherlands were also gradually drawn in to protect their respective shipping interests.

Legal distinctions mattered. Iraqi attacks on tankers carrying vital Iranian oil exports could be justified under international law. Whatever the flag, these tankers were deemed to be engaged in "unneutral service" and therefore subject to the declared Iraqi blockade on enemy ports. This was a time of severe overcapacity in the world's tanker fleets. Shipowners knew the risks and accepted them, along with the profits from the premium freight rates that the Iranians were obliged to offer. When tankers were damaged or sunk under Iraqi attack, the shipowner collected its insurance, and the flag state had no legal grounds for complaint.

Iranian attacks on third party vessels in the Gulf bound to or from Kuwait and Saudi Arabia could not be justified, since these countries were neutral. Iran protested that these countries were informally supporting Iraq with funds and transshipment facilities, and should not take shelter behind a purely nominal neutrality. The Security Council did not agree, and in Resolution 552 of June 1, 1984, condemned "attacks on commercial ships en route to and from the ports of Kuwait and Saudi Arabia" — that is to say, Iranian attacks. Resolution 598 of July 20, 1987 expressed concern "that further escalation and widening of the conflict may take place" and deplored, *inter alia*, "attacks on neutral shipping." The Council remained silent on Iraqi attacks on shipping bound to and from Iranian ports.[31]

A Soviet proposal to establish a United Nations naval force to guarantee freedom of navigation was rejected, in part due to Iraqi objections that this would be a diversion from the main conflict on land. The United States took the position in the Security Council that it would be premature and unrealistic to consider a United Nations role before acceptance by both parties of a ceasefire in the context of Resolution 598. The end result was a loose coalition of naval powers committed unilaterally but to the same objective, formally neutral and protecting the rights of neutrals, but clashing ·

---

31 Most commentators have supported the legal distinction reflected in state practice in the Gulf. See, e.g., F. V. Russo, Jr., "The Merchant Vessel as Military Objective in the Tanker War," in Dekker & Post, *supra* note 22 at 193: "As economic activity which effectively and substantially contributed to its overall war-fighting/-sustaining effort, Iran's oil export system and the third country oil tankers supporting it were legitimate military objectives." Similarly, see W. J. Fenrick, "The Exclusion Zone Device in the Law of Naval Warfare" (1986) 24 *Canadian Yearbook of International Law* 91 at 121.

intermittently with Iranian forces in the Gulf.[32] Although peripheral to the main conflict raging on land, the skirmishes between the United States and Iran at sea probably played a part in the eventual Iranian decision to accept the ceasefire. In particular, the tragic loss of life aboard the Iranian airliner shot down in error by a United States warship in July 1988 clearly shook Iranian morale.

Two weeks later, Khomeini agreed to accept unconditionally the terms of Resolution 598, saying "this was more deadly for me than taking poison." Iran was disheartened and exhausted by a string of costly military defeats. Its economy was in a shambles under the strains of war, and the survival of the revolution was in jeopardy.

In August 1990, after his invasion of Kuwait, Saddam withdrew Iraqi forces from Iranian territory and accepted the reinstatement of the 1975 boundary treaty and the *thalweg* line.[33] The conflict had in effect burned itself out and the parties had reverted to the *status quo ante*.

It was no coincidence that the one dimension of the conflict that provoked a firm international response involved a perception that United States national interests were engaged, that the latter was willing to commit significant military resources, and that the war invoked an issue or principle capable of rallying the support of others. United States leadership was crucial, as it had been in negotiating the adoption of Resolution 598.

A UNITED NATIONS ARMS EMBARGO?

Each side was crucially dependent on access to foreign arms supplies to sustain the war effort, and international efforts to

[32] The United States invoked the inherent right of self-defence under Art. 51 of the Charter to justify a U.S. naval attack on an Iranian ocean platform in international waters of the Gulf, on the grounds that the platform had assisted in attacks against U.S. and "other non-belligerent shipping": Letter from the U.S. Permanent Representative to the President of the Security Council, UN Doc S/19219, Oct. 19, 1987.

[33] See the letter of Aug. 14, 1990, from Saddam Hussein to Ali Akbar Hashemi Rafsanjani, President of the Islamic Republic of Iran, UN Doc. S/21528, Aug. 15, 1990, and letter of Aug. 17, 1990, from Ali Akbar Velayati, Minister of Foreign Affairs of the Islamic Republic of Iran, to the UN Secretary-General, UN Doc. S/21556, Aug. 17, 1990. From this oblique exchange of letters, and earlier exchanges between the two Presidents referred to therein, it seems clear that both parties committed themselves to the 1975 Algiers Agreement and to the implementation of Resolution 598. The precise terms of their respective letters were not, however, identical, and there is no doubt room for future misunderstanding.

restore peace focused increasingly on measures to halt the flow. The issue revealed deep divisions within the United Nations and weaknesses in national controls. Each side had secure suppliers. The Soviet Union, France, and Egypt were the main suppliers for Iraq, and China and North Korea for Iran. A legion of resourceful and shadowy intermediaries served one or the other side (or both sides) from a variety of arms manufacturers, east and west. Subsequent revelations of the circumvention of national export controls have led to criminal proceedings in the United Kingdom, Germany, Italy, Sweden, Austria, and Switzerland, among others. According to one estimate, during the period 1982-86 alone, Iraq received arms valued at $31.7 billion and Iran $8.4 billion.[34] United Nations reports of inspections onsite after the second Gulf War have revealed that Iraq's nuclear and ballistic missile programs had received a powerful boost during this period.

In 1983 the United States initiated demarches under "Operation Staunch" to persuade other countries to join voluntarily in a campaign to cut off arms technology and supplies to Iran, as the intransigent party. These efforts suffered a severe setback when it was revealed, in 1986, that the White House had authorized arm sales to Iran in an attempt to free United States hostages held in Lebanon by pro-Iranian groups. The campaign to impede the flow of arms to Iran was intensified after the adoption of Resolution 598 in 1987.

From that time, the Council was in effect primed to adopt a "second resolution" under Chapter 7 to enforce an arms embargo, considered by a number of states as a minimum measure required to restore international peace and security and respect for basic norms of international law. This measure was resisted in particular by China, the major arms supplier to Iran, and by the USSR, which was concerned not to antagonize Iran during efforts to extricate itself from Afghanistan. The threat of a further Security Council

---

34 These figures, derived from tables of the U.S. Arms Control and Disarmament Agency, appear in K. Krause, "International Trade in Arms," Background Paper No. 28, Canadian Institute for International Peace and Security (Mar. 1989). According to Krause, the outlook for wider international controls is "bleak": "The Political Economy of the International Arms Transfer System" (1990) 45 Int.'l J. 687 at 721. In a statement before the U.S. Senate Foreign Relations Committee on May 29, 1987, Richard W. Murphy, Assistant Secretary of State for Near Eastern and South Asian Affairs, described "Operation Staunch" in the following terms: ". . . it complicates, delays, and makes more expensive Iranian arms procurement." State Department Bulletin, July 1987, 65.

resolution "with teeth in it" may not have had much credibility in Tehran, given the strong likelihood that at least one and probably two of the permanent members of the Council were prepared to cast a veto.

Given the massive flows of arms, open and covert, that continued throughout the war, one may conclude that unilateral and voluntary efforts to impede that flow, such as "Operation Staunch," were only marginally effective.

The Iran-Iraq war suggests that any search for weaknesses in the international order in responding to regional conflict may properly begin by addressing the problem of international arms transfers. Escorting neutral shipping may be both effective in its immediate objective and consistent with the right of self-defence under the Charter when carried out unilaterally, or in parallel or concert with others, without any authorization by the Security Council. But, if an arms embargo is to be effective and consistent with the Charter, action under Chapter 7 is clearly required on both counts. Such an embargo would have to involve naval patrols and a policy of search and seizure of contraband. Use of force in the case of resistance could be reconciled with the charter's prohibition only by Security Council authorization. The necessary consensus among the permanent five members, including a willingness to forgo important arms exports, may be elusive in many conflict situations. If a consensus cannot be found even on such minor action, which may be considered at the lower level of United Nations enforcement actions, prospects for agreement on more forceful intervention, involving a greater military commitment and greater risks, may be minimal.

THE ROLE OF INTERNATIONAL LAW

Had the rules counted for anything, or was the conflict precipitated, conducted, and ended only by brute force?

Karl Deutsch has said that in the domain of international law, "rules are being enforced by the costs of transgressing them."[35] The war in itself was a national catastrophe for each side. At a basic level, the human suffering and destruction through eight years would weigh heavily in any assessment of the costs of the conduct of the two parties. This may ultimately be the only rough accounting for the mutual provocations, breaches of obligation, and (no doubt) crimes for which the leaders must take responsibility. As Perez de

---

[35] K. Deutsch & S. Hoffmann (eds.), *The Relevance of International Law* 101 (New York: Anchor Books, 1971).

Cuellar suggested, it seems unlikely that there will ever be a formal process of adjudication of their respective claims and transgressions. In that case, the implicit judgment of the international community may well be that each side bears its own devastating costs. Unfortunately, however, it was the people and not the leaders who bore the full weight of those costs.

The major discernible sanction for each breach of the rules was a reciprocal breach by the adversary. Iraqi use of chemical weapons led to Iranian deployment, although the Iranians were much less effective in offensive military operations. Iraq responded to Iranian shelling of civilians in villages and towns with missile attacks on cities, to which Iran responded in kind. Restraint in reciprocal retaliation probably contributed to some moderation of conduct in respect of treatment of prisoners of war. Abuses of POWs by Iran were not fully matched by Iraq, according to reports of the International Committee of the Red Cross, probably because there were far fewer Iranian prisoners in Iraqi hands than vice versa. Iraq seems to have seen advantage in a greater level of compliance with the Geneva Conventions and in granting Red Cross representatives greater access to POW camps in Iraq, in the hope of bringing greater international pressure to bear on behalf of Iraqis in Iranian POW camps.[36]

The language of successive Security Council resolutions through the eight years of the war had been progressively upgraded and the focus sharpened, but the hostilities ended without agreement on any element of enforcement action or coercion. Whether international condemnation and exhortation, absent any coercive measures, had any moderating effect in this conflict is necessarily very difficult to measure. The most one can say is that the rules set standards as a backdrop to the exhortations. The Geneva Conventions provided the essential benchmark of acceptable conduct against which the treatment of civilians and POWs could be judged. Customary laws of neutrality and freedom of navigation helped to provide the domestic political foundation for a modest level of third party intervention to prevent the widening of the conflict. The rules, and the institutions operating under those rules, offered a process for moving towards a ceasefire, even if resisted until the conflict was "ripe" and the combatants exhausted. The persistent efforts of the Secretary-General, basing himself on Resolution 598,

[36] See e.g., "Revue Internationale de la Croix-Rouge," No. 746, 119-21 (mars-avril 1984) and No. 750, 378-81 (novembre-decembre 1984).

carried a weight that eventually induced acceptance, even if it was like drinking poison. It would be difficult to deny that international law had relevance to the humanitarian, conflict containment, and conflict resolution efforts of third parties. The impact on the belligerents themselves is a matter for speculation.

CANADA'S ROLE

Canada was not a member of the Security Council during the period 1980-88.[37] Moreover, in contacts with the two belligerents Canada was somewhat handicapped by the absence of any direct representation in Tehran during the war, after helping United States diplomats to escape from Tehran in January 1980.[38] What was Canada's role in seeking to moderate and end the hostilities?

Canada's basic orientation, in concert with other western countries, was concisely summarized in the agreed statement of the Chair, Prime Minister Mulroney, at the close of the Toronto Summit of the G7 on June 20, 1988:

We have pursued our consultations about the continuing war between Iran and Iraq, which remains a source of profound concern to us. We reaffirm our support for Security Council Resolution 598, which was adopted unanimously. We express our warm appreciation for the efforts of the Secretary-General to work for a settlement on this basis and reiterate our firm determination to ensure implementation of this mandatory resolution by a follow-up resolution. We condemn the use of chemical weapons by either party, deplore proliferation of ballistic missiles in the region, and renew our commitment to uphold the principle of freedom of navigation in the Gulf.

One element of Canadian policy missing from this statement on behalf of the Seven was an embargo on arms shipments to both belligerents, a policy not shared by France. Established Canadian policy was of general application, to ban arms sales to "countries involved in or under imminent threat of hostilities."[39] Canadian concerns about missiles were reflected in an initiative taken in 1987 with the other G7 countries to establish a "Missile Technology Control Regime" to block exports to the Third World of missile

37 Canada was a member of the Security Council during 1977-78 and 1989-90.

38 Canada and Iran agreed in July 1988 to resume normal diplomatic relations with exchange of ambassadors.

39 Department of External Affairs Communique No. 155, "Export Controls Policy," Sept. 10, 1986.

technology and missiles of a range of more than 300 kilometres.[40] Canadian concerns about chemical weapons were reflected in research, presented to the United Nations, to improve methods of onsite investigation of allegations of chemical weapons use.[41] When the ceasefire came into effect in August 1988, Canada's expertise and experience in United Nations peacekeeping resulted in a request to contribute a contingent to the United Nations Iran-Iraq Military Observer Group (UNIIMOG) established by the Security Council to monitor the ceasefire.[42]

This was not an unworthy set of policies, was in the mainstream, and perhaps in some respects was more activist than the policies of some other western countries in its attachment to the principles and processes of the United Nations Charter. These were policies and principles for the long term, of global application, and should not be judged solely in one context. In the Iran-Iraq context they were backed up by a series of vigorous representations, bilateral and multilateral, in capitals and forums in which influence might be exercised on the issues at stake. But making an effort, however principled and well-intentioned, may not be the same as making a difference. It is only realistic to recognize that what made a difference in bringing this war to an end was the grinding action of Iraqi defences on successive waves of Iranian attacks.

THE PULL TOWARDS FAILURE

Against this background, we may see more clearly why civilized restraints failed.

The two regimes, built on different foundations of fanaticism and ruthlessness, were to an unusual degree impervious to the pres-

---

[40] See Marie-France Desjardins, "Ballistic Missile Proliferation," Background Paper No. 34, Canadian Institute for International Peace and Security, Sept. 1990. From Feb. 1988, an advance in Iraqi technology, with North Korean assistance, made it possible to extend the range of Scud-B missiles to strike Tehran from 600 kms. away: *Jane's Defence Weekly*, March 12, 1988. Ironically, these strikes may have contributed significantly to bringing the war to an end by helping to convince Iran that it could not win the war.

[41] See Miriam E. Shapiro, "Investigating Allegations of Chemical or Biological Warfare: The Canadian Contribution" (1986), 80 A.J.I.L. 678.

[42] Security Council Resolution 619, Aug. 9, 1988. Due to Iranian reservations, the Canadian contingent (numbering approximately 370) was deployed only on the Iraqi side of the border. These reservations were attributed to lingering sensitivities over the Canadian role in assisting U.S. diplomats to escape from Iran in Jan. 1980.

sures, internal and external, that normally induce compliance with the community standards embodied in international law. Deeprooted ethnic, sectarian, and historic antagonisms ignited the conflict, and envenomed and prolonged it beyond the reach of reason or self-interest. Oil wealth on each side fed the war machines. The initial response of the major powers, or more precisely the five permanent members of the Security Council, was conditioned by distaste for the two regimes, reinforced by the ambiguous nature of the conflict, in its origins and in its conduct. A certain complacency set in, a sense that this was a local war that would remain local and not touch on their vital interests. Their detachment was made possible by the gradual transformation of Cold War rivalries throughout this period.

The permanent members sponsored increasingly active mediation efforts, but could not agree on any arms control sanctions or coercive measures. Three of them were actively and openly selling arms to one belligerent or both, thereby sending very mixed signals as to how they viewed the conflict. When it appeared that the conflict might widen to affect third parties and sensitive oil supply routes in the Gulf, the United States and others concerned, including the USSR, moved successfully to contain it through unilateral but parallel action. At the United Nations, the permanent five crafted a ceasefire resolution on minimalist terms that were most likely to gain the grudging acceptance of the warring parties, when they were ready.

Thus both the "pull towards compliance," to borrow Professor Franck's apt phrase, and the "push" of international condemnation were weak.[43] If we look upon the rules of the international system as analogous to the rules of a social club, where members conform because they want to preserve the benefits of membership, neither Iran nor Iraq were strongly motivated to stay in the club, and were not likely to be deterred by unconvincing threats of expulsion from "the Board."

Commentators have raised the question whether the Iran-Iraq war brought to light areas of international law that might be in need of revision or further development.[44] Any imperfections in the clarity or applicability of the law would seem to pale in comparison with the glaring inadequacy of the international response to flagrant violations of the law. The standards of acceptable conduct

[43] T. M. Franck, "Legitimacy in the International System" (1988) 82 A.J.I.L. 705, and *The Power of Legitimacy Among Nations* (Oxford: OUP, 1990).

[44] See the comments of Dieter Fleck in Dekker & Post, *supra* note 22 at 194-96.

were not wanting. What was wanting was the agreement and the political will of the members of the Security Council to take appropriate enforcement action to ensure compliance.

The invasion of Kuwait elicited a very different set of responses by the international community. The contrast could not have been greater. Instead of uncertainty over the untidy exchange of provocations of 1980, there was a consensus that a flagrant and unprovoked violation of the Charter prohibition of the use of force had occurred. Instead of ambivalence in 1980, there was strong United States leadership by a President uniquely qualified by his United Nations experience to build a coalition of "member states co-operating with the Government of Kuwait."[45] Instead of a perception of a distant, localized conflict in 1980, there was concern about a direct impact on regional and world interests, especially in relation to oil. Within four days of the invasion, the Security Council, acting under Chapter 7, imposed a ban on imports from Iraq and exports, including arms, to Iraq. Finally, the Security Council authorized the use of force to expel Iraq from Kuwait, and imposed a comprehensive set of post-war sanctions dealing with demarcation of borders, sale of oil, removal of weapons of mass destruction, and humanitarian relief. Moreover, Iraq was held liable under international law by the Security Council for all losses and damages resulting from the invasion of Kuwait, and was subject to far-reaching sanctions designed to ensure payment of claims and compliance with other terms.[46]

A Look Ahead

Can we expect more vigorous action by "the Board" in response to future violations of the rules? The end of the Cold War has made it possible for the permanent five to co-operate in a reborn United Nations on enforcement measures, as in the Kuwait crisis. Can we not write off the first Gulf War as a tragic aberration, a late relic of an old international order now safely behind us in the post-Cold War period? Was this failure not redeemed by forceful United

---

[45] Security Council Resolution 678, Nov. 29, 1990.

[46] Security Council Resolution 687, Apr. 3, 1991, spelling out peace terms in an unprecedented 34 operative paragraphs, has been called "the mother of all U.N. resolutions." As one measure of the strikingly different level of UN involvement, the Security Council adopted a total of 11 resolutions during the eight years of the Iran-Iraq conflict, compared to 13 resolutions adopted during the seven months of the Kuwait crisis. For a thoughtful analysis of the crisis, see Janice Gross Stein, "Deterrence and Compellence in the Gulf, 1990-91" (1992) 17 Int'l Security 147.

Nations action to defeat aggression and uphold the rule of law in the second Gulf War?

Doubts may be in order. The Iran-Iraq war has been called "the first non-East-West conflict."[47] The failure to restore peace in that conflict was not due to east-west rivalries. A high level of east-west co-operation made possible the unanimous adoption of Resolution 598. The lesson to draw from the war is that east-west co-operation, although necessary, may not be sufficient to implement effectively the Charter system for prohibiting the use of force and preserving international peace and security.

The further conditions required will likely be those that were largely absent in the first Gulf War and resoundingly present in the second. These conditions were: major power leadership and commitment on an issue of self-interest and principle attracting sufficiently wide international support to enable the Security Council to act. These conditions are not likely to be in common supply when the conflict is distant, the issues clouded, the costs heavy, and success doubtful. In this sense, Iran-Iraq may provide more of a model of the new world order than Kuwait. Enforcement action, even at the lowest level of involvement, such as escorting neutral shipping, begins to come into view as a policy option only when significant permanent member interests are seen to be engaged. Moreover, domestic public opinion will insist that governments weigh those interests carefully in relation to the costs, including the risk of casualties, in any enforcement action. Such concerns will apply powerful brakes on intervention in any conflict, whether a classic interstate war (such as Iran-Iraq), civil war (such as Somalia), or a combination of the above (such as Bosnia).

Paradoxically, the end of the Cold War has made co-operation in the Council possible, but by removing east-west rivalry it has also made it less likely when a significant commitment is required.

The Security Council mandate is to maintain international peace and security, not to sit in judgment on the conduct of member states. The Council has only rarely made judgments and assumed powers as it did in Kuwait.[48] Canadians and others who seek a rules-based order may have to accept that the Council, in responding to

[47] Giandomenico Picco, "The U.N. and the Use of Force" (1994) 73 Foreign Affairs 14.

[48] This was the fourth time in the history of the UN that the Council had made a determination that there had been a breach of the peace, after Korea (1950), the Falkland Islands (1982), and Iran-Iraq (1987).

certain kinds of regional conflict, will opt for a lower level of community involvement than Chapter 7 enforcement action. The sombre
conclusion is that many conflicts may resist community efforts to
resolve them and may have to burn themselves out. In the Iran-Iraq
War, the conflict ended in a standoff. The two sides were evenly
matched, since Iran's three-fold advantage in population was offset
by Iraq's access to superior weaponry. In other conflicts where the
parties are ill-matched, a burnout will inevitably be at the expense of
the weaker. Although public opinion will find such outcomes distress-
ing, at the same time voices of greater realism and detachment will
be heard. For example, the recent report of the Joint Committee of
Parliament on Canada's Defence Policy states: "Events in the former
Yugoslavia and in Rwanda remind us that the best efforts of the world
community cannot prevent conflict or restore peace where peace is
not wanted; they cannot protect innocent children from becoming
targets in war; they cannot create an atmosphere of justice or democracy if people themselves reject it."[49]

Acceptance of this conclusion need not be the same as resigna-
tion or passivity. Taking into account the destruction and human
suffering involved in these conflicts, most Canadians would probably argue that regional conflicts should be the focus of some significant community efforts, with which Canada can be associated in
some way, directly or indirectly, depending on the extent to which
our talents and capabilities may be brought to bear. As in the Iran-
Iraq war, legal prescriptions and processes should provide the foundation for such involvement, at whatever level of commitment is
thought appropriate. But expectations as to efficacy may have to be
adjusted accordingly.

There may be one special contribution that Canada would be
well placed to make towards a more secure peace between Iran and
Iraq at some future time. When the two countries move towards a
more co-operative relationship, perhaps only under successor regimes, they may see the irrelevance and the folly of their historic
quarrels over the legal position of the boundary line along the
Shatt-al-Arab. Modern management of the waterway in their mutual
interest will depend on joint management mechanisms, irrespective
of whether the line follows the *thalweg* or the shoreline. The Canada-United States joint management of the St. Lawrence Seaway for
navigation and power development is a model of its kind in the

---

[49] *Report of the Special Joint Committee of Parliament on Canada's Defence Policy: Security
in a Changing World* 11 (Ottawa: Queen's Printer, October 1994).

world. At the right time, a Canadian invitation for a joint Iran-Iraq mission of experts to spend, say, two weeks with Seaway authorities observing joint management rules and practices may be a modest but sound investment towards lasting peace in the region.

The really difficult questions posed by the Iran-Iraq war and other regional conflicts are political questions, not legal ones. When does one move beyond exhortation, condemnation, and mediation to try to uphold the rules, or at least some of them, by the use of force? Do all regional conflicts need to be extinguished? In assessing the extent to which our interests might be engaged, can governments be confident that a seemingly self-contained brush fire will burn itself out without leaving a legacy of violence and resentment that may flare up again, at even greater cost to us all?

Sommaire

Un réexamen du conflit Iran-Irak: quelques réflexions sur le rôle du droit international

Le conflit Iran-Irak a été une guerre d'une extrême violence qui n'a respecté aucune des règles du droit international. L'auteur analyse en particulier trois aspects de ce conflit: l'usage illégal de la force, l'usage des armes chimiques ainsi que les attaques contre les navires neutres. À la lumière de toutes ces violations du droit international, la communauté internationale, dont le Canada, n'a pas su réagir avec succès. Quelle leçon peut-on en retenir pour les autres conflits régionaux? L'intervention active de tierces parties à un conflit est donc plutôt l'exception que la règle. Afin de bénéficier d'une telle intervention de la communauté internationale, il faudrait une initiative américaine ou celle d'un autre membre permanent du Conseil de Sécurité des Nations Unies.

Summary

The Iran-Iraq War Revisited: Some Reflections on the Role of International Law

The Iran-Iraq war was a war of exceptional brutality and disregard for the rules of international law. The author reviews three aspects in particular: the illegal use of force, the use of chemical weapons, and attacks on neutral shipping. The response of the international community, and of Canada, to these and other violations of law was largely ineffective, and the conflict finally burned itself out. What lessons can be drawn from that war regarding the prospects of upholding the rule of law in future regional conflicts? Effective intervention by third parties may be the exception rather than the norm in the new post-Cold War order. It will depend on uncommon elements of leadership and on the commitment of the United States and other permanent members of the Security Council acting within a framework of international law to protect their own interests.

Counting Chickens before They Hatch: New Hope or No Hope for Discipline in International Agricultural Trade

NATHALIE J. CHALIFOUR* AND

DONALD BUCKINGHAM†

INTERNATIONAL TRADE HAS BEEN increasingly liberalized in the past few decades. Agricultural commodities have, however, been virtually excluded from this liberalization, largely because developed countries have shielded their domestic agricultural markets to protect producers and to ensure that there is an ample domestic food supply.[1] What little international trade law did apply to trade in agriculture was used by states both as a sword to assail other states' agricultural policies and as a shield to defend their own policies. Incredibly, more than 33 per cent of Canada's GATT disputes have involved agricultural products, while this figure rises

---

* Student-at-Law, Osler, Hoskin, and Harcourt, Toronto.

† Associate Professor, College of Law, University of Saskatchewan.

The authors wish to thank Professor Marjorie Benson, College of Law, University of Saskatchewan, for her comments and critique.

---

1 See J. S. Markle, "Slaying the Sacred Cow: Looking for Consensus in the Reform of World Agricultural Trade" (1992) 68 North Dakota L. Rev. 609 at 609. See also O. Long, *Law and its Limitation in the GATT Multilateral Trade System* (Dordrecht: Martinus Nijhof, 1988); T. Warley, "Western Trade in Agricultural Products" in *International Economic Relations of the Western World 1959-1971*, Vol. 1, Politics and Trade (London: Oxford University Press); J. Jackson, *World Trade and the Law of GATT* (Indianapolis: Bobbs-Merrill, 1969); *GATT, Trade in Agricultural Products — Second and Third Reports of Committee II* (Geneva: GATT, 1962); J. Evans, *The Kennedy Round in American Trade Policy: The Twilight of the GATT?* (Cambridge: Howard University Press, 1971); W. Miner and D. Hathaway (eds.), *World Agricultural Trade: Building a Consensus* (Halifax, Nova Scotia: Institute for Research on Public Policy, 1988); B. Hockman, "Agriculture and the Uruguay Round" (1989) 23 J. World T. 83; S. Tangemann, "Will Agriculture Always Remain a Problem in GATT?" (1987) 22 Intereconomics 163-67.

to almost 50 per cent for the United States and 100 per cent for Australia.[2]

1994 was a banner year for agreements in international trade, especially agricultural trade. Not only did the North American Free Trade Agreement[3] (NAFTA) come into effect on January 1, 1994, but the product of the Uruguay Round of the General Agreement on Tariffs and Trade (GATT 1994)[4] negotiations was finalized. Agricultural trade was a large part of both agreements. The question to be answered now is whether GATT 1994 and NAFTA will end the lawlessness of international agricultural trade.

After a short overview of GATT 1994 and NAFTA, this paper presents a report card on the new trade agreements and their effects on agriculture. The assessments are delivered in terms of the good, the bad, and the unknown.

GATT 1994

On April 15, 1994, 108 nations signed the GATT 1994 agreement.[5] GATT 1994 incorporates and then significantly modifies the original GATT (GATT 1947). GATT 1947 set out five principal obligations for trading states: the granting of most-favoured-nation status, national treatment, tariff reduction commitments (also

---

[2] R. Hudec, *Enforcing International Trade Law: The Evolution of the Modern GATT Legal System* 329 (New Hampshire: Butterworths, 1990).

[3] (1993) 32 I.L.M. 297.

[4] *The Results of the Uruguay Round of Multilateral Trade Negotiations: The Legal Texts* (Geneva: GATT, 1994).

[5] The terminology to be used when referring to the new GATT as contained in the final Act has not yet crystallized. In the meantime we have adopted the following conventions: (1) GATT 1947 refers to the obligations states assumed up to and including the signing of the "Final Act." Thus, GATT 1947 will include the obligations contained in the original GATT itself, its interpretative notes, its amendments, its schedules of tariff bindings and decisions of the contracting parties of GATT. At times, we will also refer to the Subsidiary Codes of GATT 1947 that were concluded at the end of the Tokyo Round in 1979 as part of GATT 1947, even if, technically, they are separate treaties. (2) GATT 1994 refers to the obligations that states have assumed by signing the Marrakesh Protocol (i.e., the Ministerial Decision and Declarations) and those obligations that have become effective with the coming into force of the Agreement Establishing the World Trade Organization. Technically speaking, however, the WTO Agreement contains GATT 1994 which, in its turn, incorporates GATT 1947. (There was an old woman who swallowed a spider who swallowed a fly who swallowed. . . .)

known as tariff bindings), the gradual removal of non-tariff barriers, and the submission of disputes to dispute resolution mechanisms.[6] Almost forty years after entering into the original GATT (GATT 1947), member states embarked on their eighth round of multilateral trade negotiations. When agreement was finally reached in 1994,[7] the world was presented with a labyrinth of agreements, annexes, schedules, decisions, and understandings pertaining to various issues and sectors.[8] Instead of facing the prospect of a piecemeal acceptance of the instruments, member states agreed to accept the package as an integrated whole.

The World Trade Organization (WTO) Agreement is the umbrella document of GATT 1994. It essentially merges all of GATT 1947 and GATT 1994 by making the various agreements and other legal instruments found in its Annexes (including GATT

6 GATT 1947 contains a preamble and four parts, 38 articles in all. The Preamble and Part 1 relate to the tariff concessions granted under GATT, while Part 2 (Arts. 3 to 23) outlines obligations relating to non-tariff obligations. Part 3 (Arts. 23 to 35) deals with procedural and other matters while Part 4 (Arts. 36 to 38) covers principles, objectives, and commitments relating to trade and development. The principal GATT obligations are set out in Parts 1 and 2. GATT 1947 has been formally amended several times, most recently in 1965. GATT 1947 has also been "informally" amended by several understandings and agreements that have resulted from negotiations during rounds of multilateral trade negotiations. Some of the understandings are interpretations of GATT 1947 provisions and are thus binding on all members, whereas other agreements are separate but related free-standing international agreements that bind only those GATT 1947 members that sign and ratify them. The 1982 Ministerial Declaration is an example of the former, while the Subsidies Code of 1979 is an example of the latter.

7 In Sept. 1986, the eighth round of multilateral trade negotiations under GATT 1947 was commenced in Punte Del Este, Uruguay. The "Uruguay Round" was completed eight years later, with the signing of the Final Act in Marrakesh, Morroco on Apr. 15, 1994. One other key date in the conclusion of the Uruguay Round was Dec. 15, 1993, when substantial agreement on the results of the round were achieved. GATT 1994, as part of the institutional package envisioned by the WTO Agreement, came into force on Jan. 1, 1995.

8 GATT 1994 was based considerably on the Dunkel text, MTN.TNC/W/FA (1991), a report tabled by Arthur Dunkel, the Director-General of GATT in 1991. The report, which was tabled on Dec. 20, 1991, contained, *inter alia*, a detailed proposal for an agricultural agreement. Dunkel recognized that agriculture was the last great stumbling block in the Uruguay Round and hoped that his report would spawn consensus. Some of its ideas were brought into GATT 1994, but the success of the Uruguay Round cannot be attributed solely to this report.

1947) all part of the WTO Agreement.[9] Annex 1 consists of thirteen
Multilateral Agreements on Trade in Goods (Annex 1A),[10] a General Agreement on Trade in Services (Annex 1B) and an Agreement
on Trade-Related Aspects of Intellectual Property Rights (Annex
1C). Annex 2 contains the agreement on the procedural and substantive provisions for dispute resolution. The Understanding on
the Rules and Procedures Governing the Settlement of Disputes
("Understanding"), as will be seen in Part III of this paper, has
revolutionized the GATT 1947 dispute settlement procedure by
incorporating existing informal procedures and improving them,
thereby creating a complete code for settling disputes with clear
rules and strict deadlines. Finally, Annex 3 contains the formal
commitment of members to continue the practice commenced
during the Uruguay Round of periodically reviewing all the trade
policies of each member in order to develop openness, accountability, and confidence.[11]

The WTO Agreement contains the necessary institutional provisions to make the organization a free-standing, fully-functioning
international organization so that it might finally assume its position alongside the World Bank and the International Monetary
Fund to form an international system of trade and investment, as
was intended almost fifty years ago.

---

[9] Art. II.2.

[10] Those 13 agreements are: (1) GATT 1994 containing (a) GATT 1947, as
amended with schedules, (b) protocols of states other than their Protocols of
Provisional Application, (c) GATT 1947 waivers still in force at the time of the
WTO Agreement coming into force, (d) decisions of the contracting parties of
GATT 1947, (e) six Understandings interpreting provisions of various obligations under GATT, and (f) the Marrakesh Protocol and members' schedules of
commitments and concessions to GATT 1994; (2) Agreement on Agriculture;
(3) Agreement on the Application of Sanitary and Phytosanitary Measures; (4)
Agreement on Textiles and Clothing; (5) Agreement on Technical Barriers to
Trade; (6) Agreement on Trade-Related Investment Measures; (7) Agreement
on Implementation of Art. VI of GATT 1994; (8) Agreement on Implementation of Art. VII of GATT 1994; (9) Agreement on Preshipment Inspection;
(10) Agreement on Rules of Origin; (11) Agreement on Import Licensing
Procedures; (12) Agreement on Subsidies and Countervailing Measures; and
(13) Agreement on Safeguards.

[11] GATT 1994 also includes Annex 4 — Plurilateral Trade Agreements, i.e.,
Trade in Civil Aircraft, Government Procurement, International Dairy Arrangement, and the Arrangement Regarding Bovine Meat. These agreements are not
binding on all members but only on those who ratify them.

NORTH AMERICAN FREE TRADE AGREEMENT (NAFTA)

While the Uruguay Round was unfolding, international trade in North America was also experiencing significant liberalization. First, in 1988 the Canada-United States Free Trade Agreement (FTA) came into force. The geographically logical extension of free trade between Canada and the United States was into Mexico, thereby creating a North American trading bloc. Four years after signing the FTA, Canada and the United States pursued this logic with the negotiation of NAFTA, an agreement that is very much like its predecessor, the FTA.

The objectives of both the FTA and NAFTA are to eliminate barriers to trade, to promote fair competition, and to establish a framework within which the trading relationship established under the Agreements can be developed. The most significant way in which trade barriers are reduced is by tariff elimination. All tariffs between Canada and the United States must be eliminated by 1998 under the FTA, and NAFTA mandates the elimination of all tariffs among Canada, the United States, and Mexico by 2008.

Both agreements devote separate chapters to the most contentious sectors. Chapter 7 of each agreement deals with agriculture and sanitary and phytosanitary measures. Thus, NAFTA includes separate bilateral agreements between each of its three signatories relating to agriculture. The bilateral agreement between Canada and the United States concluded under the FTA is incorporated by reference into NAFTA while similar rules are created between Mexico and Canada, and Mexico and the United States.

INTERNATIONAL TRADE IN AGRICULTURAL PRODUCTS IN 1995 AND BEYOND: THE GOOD, THE BAD, AND THE UNKNOWN

THE GOOD

Agriculture in the Fold

Agriculture can no longer be significantly protected from the winds of freer trade by protectionist national agricultural policies. The FTA, NAFTA, and now GATT 1994 make clear the obligation on states to facilitate freer trade in agricultural goods. Tariff barriers are falling and trade-distorting non-tariff barriers are being converted into transparent barriers. New non-tariff barriers are, quite simply, outlawed. Gone are the Article XXV GATT waivers that permitted non-GATT-compatible quantitative restrictions. Gone are absolute prohibitions on market access for agricultural products. Gone is the right to the unfettered use of domestic and export subsidies on agricultural products. Gone is the ability to insulate domestic markets through border measures such as variable import levies and supply management systems. Bringing agriculture into the fold is a significant development and a solid step forward for "freer" trade in agricultural products worldwide.

The way in which GATT 1994 and NAFTA push Canada, the United States, and Mexico closer to free trade in agricultural products is through (1) tariff reductions; (2) improved market access; (3) clearer antidumping duty rules; (4) commitments to reduce domestic support of agriculture; and (5) new rules concerning sanitary and phytosanitary measures.

Tariff Reductions

Under schedules to Article II of GATT 1947, states agreed to reduce tariffs for certain products, including agricultural products. Through successive multilateral trade negotiations, tariffs continued to be reduced, although they were never completely eliminated. The Marrakesh Protocol to GATT 1994 includes a separate schedule for agricultural goods.[12] States agree to a general binding on all agricultural tariffs and each country agrees to reduce its agricultural tariffs overall by 36 per cent with a minimum reduction of 15 per cent for every agricultural commodity by the year 2000.

In the North American context, Canada and the United States had already agreed in the FTA to eliminate all bilateral tariffs by 1998. Now, all tariffs within North America among the three

---

[12] Schedule 5 — Uruguay Round Schedule of Commitments — Final Schedule of Agriculture Commitments, Part I — Most-Favoured Nation Tariff, Section 1 Agricultural Products, Section 1 — A Tariffs. E.g., Canada's commitment includes the following: durum wheat, a reduction of tariff from \$4.41/t to \$1.90/t within access commitment and a reduction from 57.7 per cent to 49.0 per cent over access commitment; milk and cream, not concentrated or containing added sugar or other sweetening matter of a fat content, by weight, exceeding 6 per cent, a reduction of tariff from 17.5 per cent to 7.5 per cent within access commitment and a reduction from 283.8 per cent to 241.3 per cent over access commitment; beef, a reduction of tariff from 4.41 cents/kg. to free within access commitment and a reduction from 37.9 per cent to 26.5 per cent over access commitment.

NAFTA states must be eliminated by 2008.[13] The parties, furthermore, are prohibited under NAFTA from increasing existing tariffs or creating new ones with respect to each other.[14] Therefore, by 1998 agricultural trade between Canada and the United States will be tariff free; by 2000, international agricultural trade will enjoy the reduced tariffs agreed to by states in GATT 1994; and by 2008 all agricultural trade in North America will be tariff free.

Improved Market Access

Agricultural products were, under special circumstances, exempt from the general prohibition against the use of quantitative restrictions contained in Article XI of GATT 1947.[15] These exceptions legitimized domestic programs for agricultural products such as Canada's primary commodity supply management schemes. In addition to the GATT 1947 loopholes for agriculture, member states also generally ignored the GATT prohibition on quantitative restrictions that did apply to agricultural products. Article XXV waivers of unlimited duration were often granted to keep important GATT members in the fold. These waivers were used by member states to legitimize non-GATT-compatible quantitative restrictions on agricultural products.[16]

13 NAFTA requires tariffs on all goods traded between Canada, the U.S., and Mexico to be eliminated according to each party's schedule to Annex 302.2 or as set out in Annex 300-B (NAFTA Art. 300). The tariff elimination provision applies to all goods that meet the rules of origin as set out in Chap. 4 of NAFTA, unless provided otherwise in the Agreement.

14 Art. 302(1).

15 Art. XI, which generally prohibits quantitative restrictions, specifically permits (a) export restrictions on agricultural products to prevent critical shortages of foodstuffs; (b) import or export restrictions to maintain standards for the grading and marketing of commodities; and (c) import restrictions to enforce domestic marketing or production restriction programs, or programs that attempt to remove temporary surpluses of a certain commodity.

16 An amendment to s. 22 of the U.S. Agricultural Adjustment Act of 1933 in the 1950s permitted the President to impose whatever import restrictions were necessary when those imports interfered with any program or operation undertaken under the Act. This was in clear contravention of GATT's prohibition on the proliferation of quantitative restrictions, and forced the Contracting Parties of GATT to grant the U.S. a waiver for the latter's agricultural programs (BISD 3/32 (Geneva: GATT, 1955)). This waiver was used over the years to protect American production of several agricultural commodities. For a general discussion of GATT Art. XXV waivers, see Jackson, *supra* note 1 at 541.

GATT 1994 requires increased market access that will break down the primacy of domestic agricultural trade policy over international law. The improved market access works as a two-tiered mechanism. First, states agree to a minimum level of market access for all agricultural products, even those for which no access existed prior to 1995. Then, within this access commitment, states agree to provide a reduced tariff or tariff-free treatment on an agreed quota of agricultural products. Above these levels, all former import restrictions have been converted to bound tariffs, a process known as "tariffication."[17]

Clearer Antidumping Duty Rules

Under Article VI(7) of GATT 1947, under certain circumstances primary commodities were not subject to the imposition of antidumping and countervailing duties.[18] GATT 1994 contains no special rules that apply to trade in agricultural products and provides clearer definitions of "dumping" and "injury."[19] As well, GATT 1994 prohibits any antidumping measure from lasting for more than five years.[20]

Commitments to Reduce Domestic Support of Agriculture

Articles VI(7) and XVI of GATT 1947 authorized domestic export and production subsidy programs for agricultural commodities destined for the international trading system. Article XVI of GATT 1947 prohibited export subsidies for industrial products but permitted them for primary products, except where such subsidies were "applied in a manner which result[ed] in that contracting

---

[17] Agreement on Agriculture, Art. 4 and state schedules.

[18] Antidumping duties are imposed where the export price of a product is lower than its domestic price. A primary product is excepted from this general rule where a system exists for stabilizing its domestic price, even though this may result in the product's export price being lower than its comparable price in the domestic market. The exception operates, however, only where the product is at times available to export markets at higher prices than in the domestic market, and where the system does not operate to "stimulate exports unduly or otherwise seriously prejudice the interests of other contracting parties."

[19] Agreement on Implementation of Article VI of the General Agreement on Tariffs and Trade 1994, Art. 2 "Determination of Dumping" and Art. 3 "Determination of Injury."

[20] *Ibid.*, Art. 11.3.

party having more than an equitable share of world export trade in that product."[21]

In the North American context, the FTA outlawed export subsidies on agricultural goods traded between Canada and the United States.[22] But there is little more of substance in NAFTA or in the FTA to reduce domestic support measures and/or export subsidization to third states. The FTA states that a party should take into account the export interests of the other party in the use of an export subsidy on any agricultural good, recognizing that such subsidies may have prejudicial effects on the export interests of the other party.[23] NAFTA simply states that the parties shall endeavour to work towards domestic support measures that are exempt from any future GATT commitments and "affirms" that it is inappropriate for a party to provide an export subsidy for an agricultural good exported to another party where the latter does not subsidize similar goods into the former state.[24]

GATT 1994 does a superior job of addressing both domestic support and export subsidies. In the Agreement on Subsidies and Countervailing Measures,[25] subsidies that are contingent upon export performance or upon the use of domestic over imported goods are prohibited, regardless of whether they cause injury.[26] It also prohibits subsidies that are specific to an enterprise or industry within the jurisdiction of a member that cause injury, serious prejudice,

---

[21] The Agreement on the Interpretation and Application of Arts. VI, XVI, and XXIII of the GATT (1947) clarified these provisions: BISD 26S/56 (Geneva: GATT, 1979). Although the definition of "more than an equitable share of world export trade" was fuzzy, the GATT found a violation of it in the Australia/France wheat and wheat flour dispute in 1958: *French Export Subsidy on Wheat Flour (Australia v. France)*, BISD 7S/46 (Geneva: GATT, 1958). But when the definition was later "clarified" in the 1979 Subsidies Code, the Subsidies Committee found in the GATT panel decision *EEC Subsidies on Exports of Wheat Flour*, BISD 31S/259 (Geneva: GATT, 1982) that the rise in market share for wheat flour from 24 per cent in 1964 to 62 per cent in 1979 did not violate this definition! GATT 1994 has eliminated this troublesome definition.

[22] FTA Art. 701(2), incorporated by reference into NAFTA by Annex 702.1.

[23] FTA Art. 701.4.

[24] NAFTA Art. 705(1) and (2).

[25] The agreement defines a subsidy as any financial contribution by a government or any public body (such as a direct transfer of funds, a tax credit, or government purchases of goods) where a benefit is thereby conferred upon the recipient: Art. 1.1.

[26] Subsidies Agreement, Art. 3.1.

or the nullification of GATT benefits in a country receiving those subsidized goods.[27]

The application of this agreement, however, is subject to the Agreement on Agriculture, which sets out clear rules regulating the use of both domestic support measures and export subsidies for agricultural products. States agree to reduce domestic support of agriculture, not by forcing the elimination of specific programs, but by agreeing to reduce the total support offered to their national agricultural sectors.[28] This system is called the Aggregate Measure of Support (AMS).[29] Certain support programs are excluded from the AMS calculation. "Blue box" support programs, such as government programs to limit production, and "green box" programs, such as government programs that have no direct effect on agricultural production, are excluded from the calculation.[30] Domestic support measures that must be included in a member's AMS calculation as per its schedule are classified as "amber." Amber measures are generally linked to production and are countervailable to the extent that they threaten or cause injury.[31]

27 *Ibid.*, Arts. 2 and 5. Injury under Art. 5 is defined on the basis of the volume of imports and the effect of the subsidies on domestic producers. If subsidies are causing injury, a member may impose a countervailing duty unless the subsidy is withdrawn: Art. 19. Any countervailing duty must be imposed in a non-discriminatory way and not in excess of the amount of the subsidy being countervailed. The duty may remain in effect only as long as is necessary to combat the subsidy causing injury, to a maximum of five years: Art. 21. Serious prejudice is deemed to exist in the circumstances set out in Art. 6 of the Agreement, including where a subsidy is granted to cover operating losses sustained by an industry or the direct forgiveness of a debt: Art. 6.1.

28 Agreement on Agriculture, Art. 3. The level of reduction is set out in Part 4 of each member's schedule and is called the "Member's Annual and Final Bound Commitment Level." In Canada, the support provided during the base period of 1986-88 was such that it is unlikely that any cuts will have to be made to meet the year 2000 target.

29 To determine whether a member has exceeded its level, the member's "Current Total Aggregate Measure of Support" is subtracted from the member's "Annual and Final Bound Commitment Level" as specified in Part 4 of each member's schedule. The terms for calculation are defined in Art. 1 of the Agreement. See also Art. 6, which sets out the obligation that a member's actual level is not to exceed the allowable level.

30 Annex 2 of the Agreement on Agriculture lists the domestic support measures that do not have to be included in a member's AMS, including, e.g., government service programs, food aid, regional assistance, and general services.

31 Agreement on Agriculture, Art. 13. "Green box" programs are free from threat of countervail action for nine years.

All direct export subsidies and some indirect export subsidies on agricultural products are subject to reduction under the Agreement on Agriculture.[32] Export subsidy expenditures and volumes must be reduced for each agricultural commodity so that every state agrees to spend 36 per cent less on subsidizing agricultural exports and agrees to subsidize 21 per cent less volume of each of the commodities it exports by the year 2000.[33] As well, no new export subsidies may be introduced, and any other measure designed to circumvent these commitments is prohibited.[34]

New Rules Concerning Sanitary and Phytosanitary Measures

Article XX(b) of GATT 1947 provided that any measure may be imposed by a contracting party that is necessary to protect "human, animal or plant life or health." While this exception had at its origin a *bona fide* purpose, it also had the potential to provide yet another exception justifying the erection of trade barriers for agricultural products.[35] The use of this section for trade distorting protective purposes rather than for legitimate health and safety measures prompted the negotiators of both NAFTA and GATT 1994 to develop stricter measures on the use of sanitary and phytosanitary measures.[36]

[32] Art. 9. The indirect subsidies that must be reduced include transport charges mandated by government that are more favourable for export shipments than for domestic shipments and subsidies intended to reduce the costs of marketing exports of agricultural products. For a complete list of the export subsidies subject to reduction commitments, see Art. 9(1) of the Agreement on Agriculture.

[33] Subsidies that are not prohibited are countervailable if they cause injury: Art. 13.

[34] Agreement on Agriculture, Art. 10. Thus, a member must not veil an export subsidy in such a way that it would not technically fit into an Art. 9 category, if without the veil it would be subject to reduction.

[35] Since there were inadequate, objective controls within the GATT system on what constituted legitimate measures, many states saw this provision not only as providing special treatment for agricultural products, but also as a tool for protecting domestic agricultural production. The EC's imposition under this exception of an import prohibition on all beef treated with growth hormones was seen by the U.S. as completely unjustified, given current scientific evidence. See C. Caspair and E. Neville-Rolfe, "The Future of European Agriculture" (1989) The Economist Intelligence Unit, Special Report No. 2007 at 32-33.

[36] See NAFTA, Chap. 7, Section B, "Sanitary and Phytosanitary Measures," Arts. 709-24; GATT 1994, *Agreement on the Application of Sanitary and Phytosanitary*

Through tariff reductions, improved market access, clearer anti-dumping rules, commitments to reducing domestic support of agriculture, and new rules regarding sanitary and phytosanitary measures, NAFTA and GATT 1994 allow Canada to make the most of its significant agricultural resources and to trade them competitively around the globe. The bringing of agriculture into the fold of international trade regulation will allow Canadian farmers to face competition on an equal footing with their American and Mexican counterparts and keep abreast of an increasingly global economy.

A Long-Term Vision for Agricultural Reform

The bringing of agriculture into GATT through these new disciplines is a first step towards a longer term goal for the normalization of agriculture within the GATT system. The rosiest part of that vision is the replacement of non-tariff barriers with tariffs that can be reduced or eliminated during future negotiations. For instance, the tariffication of Canada's supply management systems, the European Union's variable import levies under the Common Agricultural Policy, and the GATT waivers permitting the United States use of its Agricultural Adjustment Act mean that quantified tariffs can now be subject to reduction in future multilateral trade negotiations. Further, with tariffs falling under GATT 1994 and disappearing under the FTA and NAFTA, states have exchanged non-tariff measures for the predictability and transparency of tariffs as GATT 1994's Agreement on Agriculture requires. While the net trade benefits will be negligible in the short term, because of the exceedingly high tariffs being established under tariffication, the long term holds promise for freer, more transparent trade in agriculture.

Effective Dispute Resolution Mechanisms

Parties' commitments to liberalizing trade are hollow unless an effective implementation, monitoring, and enforcement system is in place. This is especially true of agricultural disputes for two

---

Measures. Under both agreements, parties appeal to all states to base sanitary and phytosanitary measures on international scientific standards, guidelines, or recommendations. Higher or more stringent measures may be used by any state as long as (1) these measures are not a disguised restriction on trade, (2) there is a scientific justification for the measures, and (3) a relevant risk assessment is completed. Sanitary and phytosanitary measures must be transparent and must recognize the equivalence of similar measures of different states.

reasons. First, the majority of disputes that have arisen under the FTA and under GATT 1947 have involved the agricultural sector.[37] Second, agriculture was not subject to significant regulation under GATT 1947. Since the new Agreement on Agriculture will likely face many challenges, a reliable dispute resolving mechanism will be necessary to keep the faith of member states and allow the terms of the Agreement to imbed themselves in international trade practice. Thus, the general dispute resolution mechanisms of GATT 1994 and NAFTA will be responsible for maintaining the predictability, certainty, and stability necessary for the resolution of agricultural trade disputes.

The body responsible for the administration of dispute resolution under NAFTA is the Free Trade Commission ("Commission"), a body comprising cabinet level representatives or designees of each party.[38] The Commission's jurisdiction extends to all disputes except those governed by Chapter 19 or other specific dispute settlement provisions.[39] The body in GATT 1994 responsible for dispute settlement functions is the Dispute Settlement Body (DSB). Comprised of representatives of all member states, its duties include establishing panels, adopting panel and Appellate Body reports, reviewing the implementation of recommendations, and authorizing suspensions of concessions and obligations.[40]

Interstate Dispute Settlement under GATT 1994 and NAFTA

The dispute settlement mechanisms under both GATT 1994 and NAFTA involve a two-tiered process. Disputing states first enter into

---

[37] E.g., close to one half of the panel reports issued by FTA panels have involved agricultural goods: *Free Trade Reporter* (Chicago: CCH, 1991) at Chaps. 29-31. See also Hudec, *supra* note 2.

[38] NAFTA, Art. 2001(1). The Commission's functions also include supervising the implementation of NAFTA.

[39] NAFTA, Art. 2004. Chap. 19 of NAFTA is dealt with *infra*. A dispute settlement provision not found in either Chap. 19 or Chap. 20 is Art. 706, which creates the Commission on Agricultural Trade. Although this Commission is not part of a fully-fledged dispute settlement process, it provides a forum for consultation on issues relating to agricultural trade and is not unlike the Committee on Agriculture of GATT 1994: see Agreement on Agriculture, Arts. 17 and 18.

[40] *Understanding on the Rules and Procedures Governing the Settlement of Disputes*, ("Understanding"), Art. 2.1. Note that the Understanding will only apply to disputes that arise on or after Jan. 1, 1995.

consultations; if this fails to resolve their dispute, they may turn to panel arbitration.[41]

Tier one: consultations

NAFTA allows parties to enter into consultations regarding any actual or proposed measure that might affect the operation of the Agreement.[42] This is a very low threshold for requiring consultations. GATT members may request consultations where an agreement under GATT 1994 allows them to do so. The Agreement on Agriculture, for instance, allows states to consult not only about alleged infringements of the Agreement, but also about their participation in the growth of agricultural trade and its relation to the framework created for eliminating subsidization.[43] Time limits on the consultations are imposed to ensure that dispute resolution flows smoothly and efficiently.[44]

Tier two: panel arbitration

If consultations fail to resolve a dispute under either NAFTA or GATT 1994, the parties may request the establishment of an arbitral panel. NAFTA, however, interposes another step prior to the establishment of a panel. If consultations do not resolve a matter

[41] Under both agreements, the parties also have access to alternative techniques of dispute resolution, such as good offices, conciliation, and mediation. Under NAFTA the Commission can request the use of alternative dispute resolution mechanisms, but under GATT these techniques can be undertaken only with the consent of the parties: Understanding, Art. 5.1. Alternative dispute settlement mechanisms may be requested at any stage in the dispute settlement procedure; in fact, they may be concurrent with a panel proceeding: *ibid.*, Art.5.5.

[42] Art. 2006. A third party may join in the consultations if it has a substantial interest in the issue. Although wider consultation may create a more cumbersome process, dispute resolution techniques should not risk alienating a third party that is interested in the dispute, thereby creating rather than alleviating tension in the disputed area.

[43] Agreement on Agriculture, Art. 18.5.

[44] A respondent to a request to consult under the Understanding must respond within 10 days of the request and enter into consultations within 30 days of the request. If the respondent fails to do this, the complainant may proceed to the establishment of an arbitral panel: Understanding, Art. 4.3. When a third party has a substantial interest in the dispute, it may join in the consultations: Understanding, Art. 4.11.

within thirty days of a request,[45] a party may request a meeting of the Commission that must then convene within ten days to assist the parties in resolving the dispute.[46] If the Commission fails to resolve the problem within thirty days, or such other agreed period, the parties may request the establishment of an arbitral panel.

While it seems clear from the language of NAFTA that consultations are a prerequisite to panel arbitration, it is debatable whether this is the case under GATT 1994. The Understanding states unequivocally that arbitration panels may be established upon the request of any member.[47] Article 4 of the Understanding, on the other hand, states that a party may request a panel after the expiry of a certain period if consulations fail. It further states that members affirm their resolve to strengthen and improve the effectiveness of the consultation procedures.[48] It does not, however, legally require them to consult. This issue may logically be resolved by requiring a party that chooses to proceed by way of consultations to wait the allocated time before requesting a panel.

The panel procedures under both NAFTA and GATT 1994 are quite similar.[49] After a panel hears both sides of a dispute and issues

---

45 The time allowed for consultations is 45 days if a third party has become involved or 15 days if a perishable agricultural good is involved.

46 NAFTA Art. 2007(4) and (5). The Commission may obtain expert opinions or have recourse to alternative dispute resolution techniques in attempting to settle an issue.

47 Understanding, Art. 6.1.

48 *Ibid.*, Art. 4.1.

49 Both NAFTA and GATT 1994 panelists are selected from rosters. The roster of NAFTA panelists is selected by the parties on consent, while the GATT roster is established by its Secretariat: NAFTA, Art. 2009(1) and Understanding, Art. 8.4. Qualifications for being on the NAFTA roster include having expertise in international law and being independent. GATT panelists must be selected with a view to ensuring an independent and diverse panel and they must be well-qualified governmental and/or non-governmental individuals with some GATT experience. Under GATT 1994, citizens of members states that are party to a dispute shall thus not be panelists for that dispute unless the disputing parties agree otherwise: Understanding, Arts 8.2 and 8.3. NAFTA panelists are selected by a fairly convoluted method to ensure that the panel does not appear to favour any one party. If there are two disputing parties, a panel shall comprise five members, two selected by each party, and the chair will be selected by consent. If there are more than two disputing parties, a panel shall comprise five members, two selected by the complainant, two by the party complained against, and the chair by consent: NAFTA, Art. 2011. GATT panels are to be composed of three panelists, unless the disputing parties agree to five

its initial report, the participants may comment on the report. Consequently, the panel considers the comments and issues its final report.[50]

One difference between the NAFTA and the GATT 1994 panel arbitration procedures is that a final report under NAFTA is not binding, whereas it is under GATT 1994. The Commission, under NAFTA, may agree on some final settlement other than the panel's recommendations. In practice under the FTA, if a solution other than that suggested by the panel was reached it tended to be very close to the panel's recommendations.[51] Under GATT 1994, once a final report is submitted to the DSB, the Body must adopt that report unless one of the disputing parties formally notifies of its intention to appeal or the DSB decides by consensus not to adopt the report.[52]

Parties are therefore very involved in the dispute settlement process in both NAFTA and GATT 1994, and they are able to communicate quite freely at various stages with the panel decision-makers. This improved communication is a positive step towards

members within 10 days of the panel's establishment. Selection of panelists is to be by consent, but if there is no Agreement within 20 days of the panel's establishment, the panelists are to be appointed by the Director-General in consultation with the DSB chair and the chair of any relevant committee or council.

50 Under NAFTA, parties must submit written comments to the panel within 14 days of the issuance of the initial report. The panel must then issue a final report within 30 days of the initial report and may take into account the comments made by the parties. If separate opinions are given, panelists delivering the opinions may not be identified. This provision preserves the independence of the panelists and seeks to avoid panelist selection based on apparent biases.

GATT allows for even more participation by the parties. Before issuing an interim report, the panel must first submit the factual and argument portions of its draft decision to the disputants, who then have an opportunity to submit written comments. The panel then issues its interim report in which it states its findings and conclusions. Disputing parties may then submit a request that the panel review particular issues in its interim report. The panel will then issue its final report. Like NAFTA, GATT 1994 requires separate opinions expressed in a panel report to be anonymous: Understanding, Art. 14.3. After the final report is submitted to the DSB, the disputing parties may provide written objections to the decision and may participate in the DSB's consideration of the panel's decision: Understanding, Arts. 16.2 and 16.3.

51 For a discussion of the non-binding nature of NAFTA panels, see G. Horlick and A. DeBusk, "Dispute Resolution Under NAFTA — Building on the U.S.-Canada FTA, GATT and ICSID" (1993) 10 J. Int'l Arb. 51 at 69.

52 Understanding, Art. 16.4.

effective dispute resolution, as is the allowance for ongoing submissions during the decision-making process, which help to ensure that panelists do not misinterpret submissions or confuse complex issues. In essence, this system creates a certain, predictable mechanism that is capable of effectively filtering discourse among disputing states.

While the dispute settlement procedure in NAFTA is largely imported from the provisions of the FTA, the GATT 1994 procedure is more a codification of existing practice under GATT 1947 with some significant improvements. Probably the most important of these is that the process under GATT 1994 ensures a constant progression in dispute resolution. Under GATT 1947, the consensus of all members was required at several stages of the process. A politically influential member of GATT could effectively veto decisions with which it disagreed.[53] Now, the dispute settlement process flows automatically and can only be halted by consensus. For example, a panel is established automatically upon request unless every member of the DSB opposes its establishment. Panel reports are also automatically adopted unless they are rejected by consensus.

One reason for requiring consensus under GATT 1947 was to prevent erroneous panel reports from flowing through the system in their faulty state because of the influence of a member state. The creation of the Standing Appellate Body addresses this concern.[54] The Standing Appellate Body was created to hear appeals from panel decisions that were based on alleged errors of law or errors of legal interpretation.[55] The Appellate Body can modify, uphold, or remand a panel's decision.[56]

[53] Although GATT 1947's system of dispute resolution was clearly problematic in this area, it must be recognized that political pressure played a major role in the progression of a dispute. The less influential member states may have feared withholding their consent, so in fact in most cases disputes tended to progress fairly efficiently. See R. Hudec, *supra* note 2 at 165.

[54] Art. 17.1 of the Understanding requires the DSB to create a Standing Appellate Body, composed of seven persons, to sit in panels of three to hear an appeal from a panel decision. Members of the Appellate Body must demonstrate expertise in law, international trade, and the subjects of the GATT 1994 agreements. They are also to be unaffiliated with any government. The requirement for expertise and independence creates a higher standard for the Standing Appellate Body than for the arbitral panels.

[55] Understanding, Art. 17.6.

[56] *Ibid.* Art. 17.13.

Binational Panel Review under NAFTA

Another dispute settlement mechanism that is included in NAFTA but not in GATT 1994 is a procedure for dealing with antidumping and countervailing duty matters.[57] This procedure involves the replacement of national judicial review of antidumping and countervailing duty determinations with binational panel review.[58] Each state retains its domestic antidumping and counter-vailing duty laws and may even amend those laws as long as they are consistent with NAFTA and GATT 1994. This dispute settlement mechanism is designed to ensure that states apply their domestic law in a fair, impartial way and to circumvent any suggestion that national agencies are engaged in protectionism in what are in effect international disputes.

As well as including provisions to ensure the efficiency of Chapter 19 dispute resolution,[59] NAFTA includes a process by which these binational panel decisions can be appealed to an Extraordinary Challenge Committee (ECC). Appeals are limited to those cases in which (1) an allegation is made that a member of the binational panel was guilty of some misconduct, or the panel exceeded its jurisdiction or departed from some fundamental rule of procedure; (2) this behaviour materially affected the panel's decision; and (3)

57 NAFTA, Chap. 19. GATT 1994 defines and regulates the use by states of domestic support measures and export subsidies. Providing for reviews to ensure that a duty determination accords with a member state's *domestic* law would be beyond the purview of GATT.

58 In Canada, the Special Imports Measure Act, R.S.C. 1985, c. S-15, regulates the imposition of antidumping and countervailing duties. This statute grants the Canadian International Trade Tribunal the authority to make final inquiries for determining injury in antidumping and countervailing cases subsequent to a preliminary determination of dumping and subsidization and the imposition of duties by the Deputy Minister of National Revenue for Customs and Excise. The equivalent bodies in the U.S. are the International Trade Commission, which makes findings of injury, and the Department of Commerce, which determines when dumping and subsidization are occurring.

59 E.g., the parties must amend their domestic law to ensure that they do not frustrate the effective implementation of the panel procedure. Consultations may be entered into if a party's domestic law circumvents some aspect of this procedure. Parties must make certain amendments to their domestic law as specified in NAFTA, and they must notify of, and if requested enter into consultations about, changes in their antidumping and countervailing duty laws. Finally, parties must enter into consultations annually to improve the dispute settlement mechanism. See K. Oelstrom, "A Treaty for the Future — the Dispute Settlement Mechanism of the NAFTA" (1994) 25 Law & Pol'y Int'l Bus. 792.

it threatened the integrity of the system.[60] The ECC's jurisdiction, unlike that of the Standing Appellate Body of GATT 1994, allows it only to remand or confirm a panel decision, not to amend it.

Separate Dispute Avoidance for Agricultural Matters

Another innovation under NAFTA stems from the recognition that trade disputes do not arise only between governments, especially in a contentious sector such as agriculture. NAFTA acknowledges this fact by creating a dispute settlement body that is designed to develop prompt and effective mechanisms for the settlement of private commercial disputes regarding agricultural goods.[61] This commitment to resolving non-governmental disagreements may well enhance the public image of NAFTA.

A dispute settlement procedure that applies only to agricultural trade has also been created under GATT 1994. The Committee on Agriculture, established under Article 17 of the Agreement on Agriculture, is responsible for reviewing the implementation of the terms of that Agreement.[62] Members are obliged to notify the Committee if they intend to undertake any new domestic support measures for which they claim exemption, and the Committee is then responsible for reviewing that action. The Committee is also a forum for members to consult annually on their participation in the growth of world trade in agriculture.[63]

Trade laws rely on some measure of implementation and enforcement. The dispute resolution institutions of NAFTA and GATT 1994 have reached a sufficient level of development and sophistication to ensure a confidence and trust among parties to the respective agreements.

THE BAD

Having reviewed the positive achievements in liberalizing trade in agricultural products, we now turn to some of the potential

---

60 NAFTA, Art. 1904(13). The panelists who are to comprise the ECC are to be chosen from a roster established under Annex 1904.13. The majority of panelists chosen should be lawyers in good standing and are often retired judges.

61 *Ibid.*, Art. 707. An Advisory Committee on Private Commercial Disputes regarding Agricultural Goods makes recommendations to the Committee on Agricultural Trade.

62 Agreement on Agriculture, Art. 18.

63 *Ibid.* Art. 18.5.

downfalls of NAFTA and GATT 1994 in relation to agriculture trade.

The Complex Interrelationship of Trade Agreements

How will conflicts among FTA, NAFTA, and GATT 1994 be resolved?

FTA and NAFTA

Article 103 of NAFTA provides:

(1) The Parties affirm their existing rights and obligations with respect to each other under the *General Agreement on Tariffs and Trade* and other agreements to which *such Parties* are party. (emphasis added)
(2) In the event of any inconsistency between this Agreement and such other agreements, this Agreement shall prevail to the extent of the inconsistency, except as otherwise provided in this Agreement.

The issue of precedence between the FTA and NAFTA is not addressed here since Canada and the United States have agreed to suspend the operation of the FTA as long as both countries are parties to NAFTA.[64]

Now this brings about one curious result. Parties to the FTA agreed unequivocally in Article 701(2) not to maintain or introduce any export subsidies on any agricultural good destined for the territory of the other party. Instead of retaining this clause in NAFTA, Mexico, Canada, and the United States have taken a meeker approach and stipulated only that it is inappropriate to provide export subsidies on agricultural goods exported to the territory of another party.

NAFTA and GATT 1994

Establishing precedence between NAFTA and GATT 1994 is not straightforward. As we have seen, Article 103(1) of NAFTA acknowledges that the "Parties affirm their existing rights and obligations with respect to each other" under GATT. However, NAFTA Article 103(2) states that in the event of any inconsistency between NAFTA and other agreements, unless otherwise provided,[65] NAFTA will prevail to the extent of the inconsistency. Under Article 30 of the

---

[64] Canadian Statement on Implementation, Department of External Affairs, Canada Gazette Part I, no. 128(1), Jan. 1, 1994 at 76.

[65] Art. 103(1).

Vienna Convention,[66] GATT 1994, which is the later in time, will prevail over NAFTA, although it could be argued that Article 103 makes NAFTA superior to GATT 1947. Even then, it might be argued that by virtue of GATT 1947 becoming an integral part of GATT 1994, NAFTA cannot prevail even over GATT 1947. Since the NAFTA and GATT negotiators from Canada, the United States, and Mexico were well aware that any GATT agreement would benefit from the interpretive rule found in Article 30 of the Vienna Convention, it is odd that this issue of precedence was not clarified either through provisions in the GATT itself, or in a side agreement between the NAFTA parties.

This issue of precedence and interpretation is not simply a sterile polemic. A battleground on the debate as to which of the agreements will prevail has arisen over the issue of tariffication.[67] Article 302 of NAFTA states that, as between Canada and the United States, "except as otherwise provided by this Agreement, no Party may increase any existing customs duty, or adopt any customs duty, on an originating good." As well, each party agrees progressively to eliminate its custom duties according to its scheduled commitments. Article 309(1) of NAFTA sets out the following:

Except as otherwise provided in this Agreement, no Party may adopt or maintain any prohibition or restriction on the importation of any good of another Party or on the exportation or sale for export of any good destined for the territory of another Party, except in accordance with Article XI of the GATT, including its interpretative notes, and to this end Article XI of the GATT and its interpretative notes, or any equivalent provision of a successor agreement to which all Parties are party, are incorporated into and made a part of this Agreement.

Under GATT 1994, member states have agreed to dismantle and not to revert to measures such as those that were permitted under Article XI of GATT 1947.[68] Thus, Canada has agreed to dismantle its supply management systems in favour of high tariffs. Canada's tariff equivalents are contained in its schedules to GATT 1994, which are bound by virtue of the Marrakesh Protocol to GATT 1994. As of January 1, 1995, Canada has new tariffs for commodities such as milk, eggs, and chickens that were formerly regulated by supply management. Canada's schedule to the Marrakesh Protocol

66 (1969) 1155 U.N.T.S. 331.

67 See "U.S. milk producers push for greater access to NAFTA territories:" 1(16) *NAFTA Watch* (Sept. 15, 1994) at 8.

68 Agreement on Agriculture, Art. 4.

further sets out reductions to the new tariffs that Canada agrees to make by 2000.[69] Thus, the obligations on Canada to introduce no new tariffs and to have eliminated all tariffs on agricultural products traded in North America by 1998 as required by NAFTA are in direct conflict with the commitments of Canada under GATT 1994. Which agreement prevails?

The United States has argued that NAFTA prevails. Canada's position is that GATT commitments arising from the tariffication of supply management domestic support legislation take precedence over the NAFTA prohibition on new tariffs and the complete elimination of tariffs by 1998. Three arguments can be mounted in support of the Canadian position.

First, under the Vienna Convention, later inconsistent agreements on similar issues take precedence to the extent of the inconsistency. Thus, the creation of new tariffs under GATT 1994 supersedes NAFTA's prohibition on new tariffs.

Second, it can be argued that the subsequent practice of the United States and Canada in concluding GATT 1994 has had the effect of modifying the commitment in NAFTA. Article 31(3) of the Vienna Convention states that any meaning in an agreement may be altered by subsequent agreement between the parties regarding the interpretation of the agreement or the application of its provisions, *or* by any subsequent practice in the application of the agreement that establishes the agreement of the parties regarding its interpretation.[70]

Finally, it may be argued that Article 309 of NAFTA itself prevents any conflict between GATT 1994 and NAFTA because it protects and incorporates the "equivalent provision" in GATT 1994 of Article XI of GATT 1947, which is the tariffication process and schedule for tariff reductions. According to this argument, there is no conflict between the two agreements because the preference granted to NAFTA over GATT in Article 103 of NAFTA is subject to any overriding provisions in NAFTA. Article 309 is one such provision that will preserve later GATT Article XI measures, whatever

[69] Such tariffications for Canada have arisen through the loss of supply management schemes. Sectors that might be vulnerable to U.S. imports are eggs, turkey, chicken, and dairy products. Tariffications for the U.S. have arisen through loss of its exemptions from s. 22 of the Agricultural Adjustment Act. Sectors affected and vulnerable to Canadian imports include sugar products and peanut products.

[70] T. O. Elias, *The Modern Law of Treaties* 71-78 (Dobbs Ferry: Oceana, 1974); A. McNair, *Law of Treaties* 424-31 (Oxford: Clarendon Press, 1961).

form they may take, from NAFTA's requirement of tariff elimination by 1998.

The United States position is based on two arguments. First, NAFTA and GATT 1994 are not "like treaties." One sets general trade rules for the world, the other sets specific rules for a free trade area. Thus, no matter what Canada agrees to do under GATT 1994, if it does not remove all tariffs by 1998 it will be in breach of its NAFTA obligations.

The second argument is that Article 309 of NAFTA does not affect Article 302 obligations because there are no equivalent provisions from Article XI of GATT 1947 to incorporate. Therefore, there is no conflict between the agreements.

In our view, the arguments supporting the modification or abrogation of NAFTA obligations by tariffication commitments under GATT 1994 are superior in law and in logic to those arguments that view NAFTA obligations as overriding or co-existing with those of GATT 1994. It is unfortunate that clearer drafting or a side agreement between Canada and the United States did not address this problem.

Discordant Standards of Review

The dispute settlement mechanism in Chapter 19 of NAFTA is a system designed to ensure that the parties apply their domestic laws fairly. Although overall it functions efficiently, there are two problems with it. First, there is little uniformity in the parties' domestic laws, since NAFTA simply allows them to retain their current laws. Only when a party wishes to amend those laws must it notify the other parties, which may then request consultations to ensure that the proposed changes are not inconsistent with NAFTA or with GATT 1994 obligations. The laws in each state are therefore different, and the panels must review different sets of laws.

A second problem is that there is no tri-national standard of review for these domestic decisions. Each of the NAFTA states has its own standard of review for its administrative tribunals. When a binational panel reviews a duty determination, it must apply the standard of review of the country in which the decision was made.[71] The problem with this is twofold. First, the United States' standard sets a lower threshold of review than that in Canada, meaning that a

---

[71] NAFTA, Art. 1904(3).

determination by a United States agency will be less likely to stand.[72] Second, it is evident from experience under the FTA that Chapter 19 disputes are common. The addition of Mexico to the free trade area only adds another standard to the system. The more differences there are, the less fair and predictable any dispute settlement system will be.

The lack of cohesive laws among these states is understandable, since substantial negotiations would be needed to achieve harmonization. The lack of a unified standard, however, is a weakness that can and should have been addressed. It is especially pertinent to address the issue now, while NAFTA consists of only three parties. The addition of more parties would clog the system with even more standards of review and create more potential for unfairness in an otherwise commendable system.

Forum Shopping

Since Canada is a party to the FTA, to NAFTA, and to GATT 1994, its ability to formulate agricultural trade policy is shaped by a number of international obligations. As we have seen, the obligations embodied in each of these agreements overlap. A violation of one agreement will therefore often be a violation of another. It is also conceivable that a dispute arising under Chapter 7 of NAFTA may also arise under GATT 1994. In what jurisdiction should a state lodge its complaint? Does it have a choice? Chapter 20 of NAFTA states that:

Subject to paragraphs 2, 3 and 4, disputes regarding *any matter* arising under both this Agreement and the GATT, any agreement negotiated thereunder, or any successor agreement, may be settled in either forum at the discretion of the complaining Party (emphasis added).[73]

---

72 The standard of review in the U.S. includes allowing review of a decision that is "arbitrary, capricious [or] an abuse of discretion" or "unsupported by substantial evidence on the record" or otherwise "not in accordance with law" (see the Tariff Act of 1930, 19 U.S.C.S. § 1516a(b)(1)(B). The Canadian standard is set out in the Federal Court Act, R.S.C. 1985, c. 7. It allows review of a decision that "fail[s] to observe a principle of natural justice" or in which the decision-makers act beyond or refuse to exercise their jurisdiction, or base their decision on an "erroneous finding of fact in a perverse or capricious manner." Mexico's standard is considered even more rigorous than that of the U.S. See J. Smith & M. Whitney, "Dispute Settlement Mechanism of the NAFTA and Agriculture" (1992) 68 North Dakota L.R. 567 at 601.

73 Art. 2005.

A complainant thus does have a choice. Once a complainant chooses one forum for a dispute, however, it cannot have recourse to any other forum for that same dispute. If two disputing parties agree to use the GATT 1994 dispute settlement procedure, they must notify the third party of this choice. If the third party does not concede to the use of the GATT procedure, the dispute will "normally" be resolved under NAFTA.[74]

NAFTA parties, therefore, do have a choice between NAFTA and GATT 1994 and will no doubt try to proceed under the agreement most favourable to their position. Why might one or the other be more favourable? Under NAFTA, disputants may request that a panel seek advice from experts[75] or reports from scientific review boards.[76] Under GATT 1994, this right is much more limited.[77] From a practical standpoint, it will be more efficient and less costly for NAFTA parties to make use of NAFTA's dispute resolution mechanism, as a result of proximity and the possibility that panelists will have a greater familiarity with the NAFTA states than will GATT 1994 panelists. Of course, if GATT 1994 jurisprudence develops in favour of a NAFTA party's position, that party will surely want to take the route of GATT dispute settlement.

Other factors that may influence whether a party chooses GATT dispute settlement over NAFTA is the binding power of a panel report and the possibility of appeal. As we have mentioned, a NAFTA panel decision is not necessarily binding, whereas a GATT panel decision is binding unless rejected by consensus within the DSB. Furthermore, in the case of the former there is no chance of appeal.

In the final analysis, the real risk in having two fora open for dispute resolution as between the United States, Canada, and Mexico is that there is a serious potential for the development of divergent jurisprudence and practices that can only lead to confusion and discord among these states.

---

[74] Art. 3005(2). It was agreed in a note to NAFTA that this default to the NAFTA process is not in itself disputable: Canadian Statement on Implementation, *supra* note 64 at 211.

[75] Art. 2014.

[76] Art. 2015.

[77] Under GATT 1994, only the panel, not the parties, have the right to initiate the request for outside assistance: Understanding, Art. 13.

Agriculture Still a Special Case

Despite obvious advances in discipline under GATT 1994 and NAFTA, trade in agricultural goods is still accorded special treatment under both agreements. Not only do the agreements deal with agriculture separately, but also, in NAFTA, Chapter 7 includes three separate agreements between the parties that pertain strictly to agricultural trade: the first between Canada and the United States, the second between Canada and Mexico, and the third between the United States and Mexico. As a result, agriculture is the only sector covered by NAFTA on a bilateral rather than trilateral basis. Furthermore, NAFTA includes special safeguards, over and above the general safeguard rules found in Chapter 8, that apply only to agricultural trade.[78]

Little progress has been made in eliminating agricultural export subsidies under NAFTA. As mentioned, NAFTA actually backtracked from the firm FTA commitments that prohibited export subsidies. They are now only "inappropriate."

The special treatment of agriculture also continues to exist under GATT 1994. Because great strides were needed to "normalize" agriculture within GATT, it was to be expected that agriculture would still receive special treatment, especially in the areas of export subsidization, domestic support, and restricted market access. While one would expect that the integration of agriculture into GATT disciplines would be an incremental process, too many special exceptions for agriculture in GATT 1994 might expose that sector to renewed opportunities for the agricultural protectionism of the past. As long as agriculture remains subject to special treatment, some states will feel free to view national policy objectives in agriculture as paramount to their international obligations. The continuing super-subsidization of agricultural exports and disputes over trade in agricultural products[79] even after Marrakesh illustrate that states are not necessarily eager to accept that trade in agricultural products is like trade in any other commodity.

---

[78] NAFTA Art. 703(3). For a discussion of these provisions, see *NAFTA Handbook: A Practical Guide for Doing Business under the NAFTA* 94 (Chicago: CCH, 1994).

[79] See, e.g., the Canada-U.S. wheat dispute: P. Morton, "Wheat war troops have swords," *The [Toronto] Financial Post* (June 25, 1994) 521 and A. Ewins "Canada and U.S. avoid wheat war," *The [Saskatoon] Western Producer* (Aug. 4, 1994) 1.

THE UNKNOWN

In addition to the potentially positive and negative effects of NAFTA and GATT 1994, a number of unknown factors will bear on the success of bringing trade in agricultural products fully under international discipline.

The Inevitability of Politics

At present, trading states can resort only to NAFTA and to GATT 1994 on paper. Do these instruments have the necessary teeth to bring discipline to agriculture? Although burdened with some shortcomings, both are working consensual documents in which states agree to change their ways. The politics of individual member states will remain, but these may be tempered by a realization that domestic agricultural policies simply cost too much to maintain. As well, consumers and environmentalists may force a shift in national agriculture policy away from production and export support for the agricultural sectors. Nevertheless, as discussed in the following sections, the unknown influence of certain international factors must be considered.

The Prominence, Prestige, and Power of the World Trade Organization

It is hoped that a fully developed World Trade Organization (WTO) will operate as a rudder to keep the trade ship on a freer course when buffeted by the winds of politics and national protectionism. Significant obstacles have already been overcome, especially with the United States' ratification of the WTO Agreement and the Organization's coming into existence on January 1, 1995.[80]

The Director-General of the WTO must command the respect of developed nations but be able to understand the wishes and frustrations of developing countries and of the newly industrialized countries, which are now experiencing the most rapid growth in world trade. The previous Director-General, Peter Sutherland, has been instrumental in garnering support for the WTO and for GATT 1994.

[80] By July 1995, 100 countries were members of the WTO. "WTO Membership Reaches 100," *World Trade Organization Press Release,* July 4, 1995.

Politics and Old Habits of Protectionism

The old habits of nationalism in agricultural policy had a marked effect on the final commitments of both Western and other states tabled in the final days of GATT negotiations that wound up the Uruguay Round. Many compromises were struck to keep the major players happy. Some of the compromises included the watering-down of strict, firm, and uniform commitments for agriculture. For instance, agricultural commitments to uniformity in increasing market access, decreasing domestic support, and decreasing export subsidization, as described in the 1991 Dunkel text, were not, in the end, accepted. Japan was able to obtain an arrangement that did not require it to increase market access as much as other states,[81] while the European Union secured less stringent domestic support commitments. These political concessions resulted in prolonged negotiations and were responsible for delaying the implementation of the agricultural commitments to the period 1995-2001 from the original 1993-96. Even then, the commitment to stagger the subsidy reductions by six equal instalments was watered down so that the heaviest cutting of subsidies will occur only in the later years, nearer the year 2001.

Trade disputes involving agriculture continue. The United States-Canada durum wheat dispute resulted not in the furtherance of free trade, but in a managed trade compromise. The next day, the United States concluded a huge sale of subsidized durum wheat to Egypt, a traditional Canadian market. Clearly, the GATT 1994 rules are not enough on their own. The political will to see GATT 1994 succeed is also needed.

The Inevitability of Litigation

The concept and conclusion of GATT 1994's Agreement on Agriculture was a major accomplishment. The legal framework created by the Agreement, however, sets up new disciplines that may be insufficiently defined. The procedure for calculating levels of domestic support involves a very complex formula. Furthermore, along with this complexity, there is no allocation of responsibility for ensuring that calculations are accurate. Although domestic

---

[81] The argument is that the Japanese paid for this concession elsewhere, but the fact remains that the agricultural commitments are not uniform and might lead to grumbling and retaliation down the road, when other concessions are forgotten by states whose access commitment is higher than that of Japan.

support measures and subsidies are categorized and accorded various levels of treatment, again there is no administrative body that is clearly responsible for monitoring these categorizations. The parties are themselves left with the responsibility for policing the Agreement.

Although, practically, this procedure may be a reasonable way of dealing with a touchy issue in an international agreement, it is likely to lead to disputes in the long run. A better alternative would have been to give the Committee on Agricultural Trade the responsibility for administering the complex procedures. The Committee's current responsibilities are to review the implementation of the Agreement and provide a forum for consultation on the growth of world trade. Therefore, why not make the supervision of the calculations and categorizations required under the Agreement part of the Committee's responsibilities, and expand its consultative jurisdiction to include consultations on these issues? Perhaps this expansion of the Committee's role would create an avenue for crystallizing the AMS formula and preventing technical disputes from arising.

Further, even if the Committee is given this monitoring responsibility and the AMS calculation is clear, the problem will remain of deciding what goes into the calculation. No definition can ultimately define and include all trade-distorting subsidies. GATT 1994 is entering new waters and disputes are going to arise over the calculation of the AMS not only because nations may leave some things out, but because nations will continue to bicker over whether a particular support really is a subsidy.

Earlier, we extolled the virtues of the dispute settlement mechanism in GATT 1994. No matter how efficient the system, however, the parties will have to accept the uncertainty that arises when new substantive rules are created. If the GATT dispute settlement process is unable to respond to these challenges of litigation, and instead produces a garbled body of jurisprudence, then GATT 1994 will face serious difficulty. Its success depends largely on the attitude of states that ostensibly, and perhaps tentatively, gave up the primacy of domestic agricultural policy in favour of international rules. They must be convinced that the system for confronting and resolving differences with other states will, over the long run, provide certainty and predictability and therefore produce more gains than the prior system of limited discipline for agricultural products.

GATT 1994 cures the problem of legislative proliferation experienced by the adoption of free-standing codes at the conclusion of the Toyko Round. The comprehensive package of GATT 1994 cannot be fragmented.[82] Nevertheless, the package is so mammoth and labyrinthine that legal confusion and, ultimately, litigation are bound to result over its general interpretation. For example, while it appears that the agreement establishing the World Trade Organization takes precedence over the other multilateral trade agreements within GATT 1994,[83] the Agreement on Agriculture also purports to take precedence over the "provisions of GATT 1994 and of other Multilateral Trade Agreements in Annex 1A to the WTO Agreement."[84] How the other agreements might rank is not explicit. Once again, the effect of this ranking of agreements will remain unknown for some time.

CONCLUSION

Agricultural trade is now entering a period of international liberalization. States are realizing that they cannot have agricultural trade and commerce in a global market on their own terms. The status of agricultural trade is in a precarious state, and there will likely continue to be many disputes regarding its deregulation. The dispute resolution mechanisms and the substantive rules are progressive, but the success of the new agricultural trade regimes will ultimately be determined by the goodwill of states and their ability to see beyond their own short term interests. The success of the dispute settlement procedures in NAFTA and GATT 1994 is crucial to the successful implementation of the new disciplines for trade in agriculture.

Counting chickens before they hatch? In our opinion, there is real hope that GATT 1994 and NAFTA will bring new order to an otherwise unruly system in the international trade in agricultural products. With enough political will and the solid framework of rules and dispute resolution offered by GATT 1994 and NAFTA, the world stands poised to enjoy new benefits from increased and freer trade in agricultural products.

---

[82] States may however choose to adhere or not adhere to the plurilateral agreements in a piecemeal fashion.

[83] WTO Agreement, Art. 16.3. The "Multilateral Trade Agreements" are those included in Annexes 1 to 3 of the WTO Agreement.

[84] Agreement on Agriculture, Art. 21.

Sommaire

Vendre la peau de l'ours avant de l'avoir tué: nouvel espoir ou aucun espoir de discipline dans le commerce mondial des produits agricoles

Le commerce des produits agricoles a été un des secteurs les plus lents à s'ouvrir au libre-échange mondial. Cependant, l'époque des politiques nationales de protection de l'agriculture pourrait bien être révolue du fait de la conclusion de l'Accord de libre-échange nord américain et de l'Accord général sur les tarifs douaniers et le commerce de 1994. Dans cet article, les auteurs analysent brièvement les dispositions de ces nouveaux accords relatives au commerce des produits agricoles, puis ils discutent de leur efficacité. Selon les auteurs, l'inclusion de l'agriculture dans les échanges commerciaux libéralisés et les mécanismes de règlement des différends est, en général, de bon augure pour le commerce international. Toutefois, affirment-ils, la complexité, l'interrelation de ces accords, certains points faibles du régime de règlement des différends et le traitement toujours spécial accordé à l'agriculture par le droit commercial international représentent, par ailleurs, de "mauvais" signes. Finalement, on ne saurait prévoir si les manoeuvres politiques et les inévitables litiges auront pour effet de miner la nouvelle discipline commerciale en matière agricole.

Summary

Counting Chickens before They Hatch: New Hope or No Hope for Discipline in International Agricultural Trade

Agricultural trade has been one of the slowest sectors to open up to international free trade. However, the era of shielded domestic agricultural policies may have come to an end with the conclusion of the North American Free Trade Agreement and the General Agreement on Tariffs and Trade 1994. This paper provides a brief overview of the new agreements as they apply to trade in agriculture, and discusses their adequacy. The authors regard the inclusion of agriculture in the fold of liberalized trade and the mechanisms for resolving disputes generally to be good signs for international trade, but the complexity of the agreements and their interrelation, certain shortcomings of the dispute settlement regime, and the continued treatment of agriculture as a special case in the international trading system to be bad omens. Finally, it is unknown whether the effects of politics and the inevitability of litigation may undermine new trade disciplines for agricultural products.

Notes and Comments /
Notes et commentaires

Moving on from Rio:
Recent Initiatives on Global Forest Issues*

INTRODUCTION

O F ALL THE DEBATES at the United Nations Conference on Environment and Development (UNCED) in 1992, none exemplified the gulf between the North and the South more clearly than the negotiations relating to forests.[1] UNCED was unable, in the face of Group of 77 (G-77) opposition,[2] to conclude a binding agreement on forests, settling instead for the "Non-legally binding, authoritative statement of principles for a global consensus on the management, conservation and sustainable development of all types of forests."[3] Non-binding in form and often vague in content,

---

* Portions of this comment appear as part of a longer work, "Development Assistance Issues Related to a Convention on Forests" in *Global Forests and International Environmental Law* (London: Graham & Trotman, 1995). The research on this paper was undertaken as part of a project on international forest issues, carried out by the Canadian Council on International Law and funded by the Government of Canada through the Green Plan. The invaluable research assistance of Matthew Latella and Megan Shortreed is gratefully acknowledged. The views and opinions expressed are solely those of the author.

---

1 "No other issue divided North and South more intensely or high-lighted the conflict between environment and development more vividly than forests." M. Jahnke, "Rio Conference on Environment and Development" (1992) 22 Env. Pol'y & L 204 at 222.

2 S. P. Johnson, *The Earth Summit: The United Nations Conference on Environment and Development [UNCED]* 103 (London: Graham & Trotman/Martinus Nijhoff, 1993).

3 Adopted June 13, 1992. UN Doc A/CONF.151/6/Rev.1, reprinted in (1992) 31 I.L.M. 882 (hereinafter "Forest Principles").

this document has been attacked as both toothless and misdirected, with a clear implication in some instances that groups of developing and developed states effectively scuppered the prospects for agreement.[4] From a legal perspective, the lack of any enforceable obligations dismayed some commentators, leading one to refer to the Forest Principles as an example of the "regressive development of international law."[5] But is this an appropriate reaction in light of the experience at Rio and subsequent developments? In particular, should the negotiation of a binding legal document be viewed as the *sine qua non* of progress towards sustainable forest development?

The process of forest negotiations, or at least dialogue, did not die with the end of UNCED. A number of initiatives have gone forward, some centred on the preparation of contributions to the United Nations Commission on Sustainable Development (UNCSD)[6] for its 1995 review of the forests issue.[7] One of the most interesting developments involves the joint sponsorship of the Intergovernmental Working Group on Forests (IWGF)[8] by Canada and Malaysia, two countries clearly identified as antagonists in the forest debates at UNCED. From an initial group of fifteen countries, three intergovernmental organizations and four non-governmental organiza-

---

[4] For a discussion of this issue, and the additional negative impact of inter-agency disputes within the UN system, see A. Szekely, "The Legal Protection of the World's Forests After Rio '92," in L. Campiglio, L. Pineschi, D. Siniscalco, T. Treves (eds.), *The Environment After Rio: International Law and Economics* 65 at 67 (London: Graham & Trotman/Martinus Nijhoff, 1994).

[5] *Ibid.*, 68. See also Johnson, *supra* note 2 at 6: "The Statement of Forest Principles which the Conference finally managed to adopt after anguished debate was immediately condemned by non-governmental groups present in Rio as a Chain-Saw Charter."

[6] The UNCSD was created by resolution of the General Assembly to provide for a progress review on the results of UNCED and to encourage co-operation in its implementation: Institutional Arrangements to Follow up the United Nations Conference on Environment and Development, Dec. 22, 1992, GA Res. A/47/191.

[7] See pp. 163-66, *infra*, for a description of these initiatives.

[8] The working group was initially referred to as the Intergovernmental Working Group on Global Forests: see *Report: First Meeting of the Intergovernmental Working Group on Global Forests* (Kuala Lumpur, Apr. 8-21, 1994) (hereinafter "IWGF First Meeting Report"). The word "global" was subsequently dropped; see *Report: Second Meeting of the Intergovernmental Working Group on Forests* (Ottawa/Hull, Oct. 10-14, 1994) (hereinafter "IWGF Second Meeting Report"). "IWGF" is used here to refer to the process, including the first meeting, except where a direct quote from the record refers to "IWGGF."

tions (NGOs) meeting in Kuala Lumpur in April 1994, the process expanded to include thirty-two countries, five intergovernmental agencies and eleven NGOs at the second meeting in Ottawa/Hull in October 1994.[9] The process might be seen in part as a confidence-building exercise, or a search for common ground between former opponents,[10] but the participants made it clear from the beginning that the IWGF should focus on practical issues and was not to become a reprise of the pre-UNCED forest negotiations.

At the outset of the meeting, it was stated that the IWGF was not a negotiating forum, but rather an opportunity for some countries, intergovernmental organizations and NGOs that were actively involved in the global dialogue on forests to discuss important forest issues with a view to promoting an effective review at the 1995 session of the UNCSD.[11]

What are the implications of the emerging post-UNCED process, and in particular the IWGF, for progress towards sustainable management and development of the world's forests? Further, are there lessons to be learned about the nature of global multilateral treaty-making in the environmental context, and the advantages and disadvantages inherent in this approach? This comment considers these general questions, and offers some suggestions as to the factors that might influence future negotiations on forest issues. It should be noted that the focus of this examination is the process of international law-making in the context of global environmental negotiations; the validity of the substantive positions adopted by participants in the course of recent discussions is a broader debate that is not addressed here.

THE NATURE OF THE CHALLENGE

Any consideration of the questions posed above must still, however, proceed from an understanding of the forests issue and

9 See IWGF First Meeting Report, *supra* note 8 at 1, and IWGF Second Meeting Report, *supra* note 8 at 1.

10 The importance of this role is recognized in the *Discussion Paper For the Canada-Malaysia Inter-Governmental Working Group On Global Forests (IWGGF): Institutional Linkages* 4 (Kuala Lumpur, 1994): "The success of current planned endeavours to move the forest agenda ahead is directly dependent on the building of new alliances and the strengthening of existing partnerships amongst governments, non-government organizations and the private sector, in full collaboration with recognized international institutions charged with this role."

11 IWGF First Meeting Report, *supra* note 8 at 1-2.

the challenges that it poses to international law-making. Although a full review of this complex area is beyond the scope of this comment, two factors seem particularly relevant to an assessment of recent initiatives. The first is the extent to which the question of forests is tied up in a broader debate on the conflicting interests of developed and developing states in the environment and development discourse; the second concerns the scope of obligations that could be imposed upon states in a forest agreement, and the implications this has for developing states in particular. While it would be simplistic to ascribe all of UNCED's failings to a confrontation of values and perceptions between the North and the South,[12] it is clear that important disagreements existed, and still persist, about such fundamental elements as the definition of sustainable development and the conflict between intergenerational and intragenerational equity. The opposing positions on forests brought into sharp focus such concepts as the interrelationship between states' permanent sovereignty over natural resources (including the "right to development") and their global environmental responsibilities. It became apparent at UNCED that the areas of ambiguity and potential contradiction between and among these principles have not been resolved to the degree necessary for any serious consensus on an issue as contentious (and as economically critical to many states) as the conservation and development of forests.

The political and economic dimensions of this dispute are relatively clear, if perhaps too readily oversimplified. Developing countries see themselves being asked to bear the burden, through "foregone development," of addressing conditions that result from generations of industrialization in developed states; to sacrifice future development so that the North can maintain current (excessive) patterns of consumption.[13] It is legitimate to respond that unsustainable development is not development at all, and that destructive forestry practices primarily benefit elite groups, but

---

[12] On the divisions within the two broad categories of states, see M. P. A. Kindall, "Talking Past Each Other at the Summit" (1993) 4 Col. J. Int'l Env. L. & Pol'y 69 at 71. These multiple interests are acknowledged, but for convenience the "shorthand" of North/South and developed/developing is applied to the general positions taken on either side.

[13] See Johnson, *supra* note 2 at 7: "Another reason why the 'global bargain' was not struck in Rio, at least in the eyes of the G-77, was the unwillingness of the OECD countries to do anything about their profligate life-styles, or even to admit there was a problem."

such arguments do not serve to eliminate the concern of many developing countries that they are being asked to absorb a disproportionate share of the environmental challenge at the global level.[14] Particular difficulty is caused by two of the critical values ascribed to the conservation of tropical forests — as a carbon reservoir and as a repository of biodiversity. Both of these benefits of forest conservation accrue primarily at the global level, and their use as a justification for enhanced conservation measures contributes to the suspicions reflected in the following statement by the Prime Minister of Malaysia:

> The poor countries have been told to preserve their forests and other genetic resources on the off-chance that at some future date something is discovered which might prove useful to humanity. This is the same as telling these poor countries that they must continue to be poor because their forests and other resources are more precious than themselves. . . .[15]

The merits of the opposing arguments in this continuing debate are, however, effectively irrelevant, given the outcome of UNCED and the imperatives of the post-UNCED period. The vast majority of the world's current destruction of tropical moist forest occurs in developing nations, in which environmental degradation is fostered in part by pressures to achieve high levels of economic growth in order to service massive international debt.[16] Successful negotiation

14 See Kindall, *supra* note 12 at 73-74: "To the ears of the developed countries, the G-77 refrain sounded suspiciously like: 'If you want us to protect our environment, you have to pick up the tab; otherwise we will not lift a finger.' To developing countries, on the other hand, the richer countries . . . appeared to be saying, 'we want you to implement a 500-page action plan to save the environment; paying for it is your responsibility.'"

15 Statement by Dr. Mahathir Mohamad, Prime Minister of Malaysia, quoted in "Extracts from Statements: Plenary and Summit Segment" (1992) 22 Env. Pol'y & L. 226 at 232.

16 Although there has been some improvement in the state of the "debt crisis" in recent years, the gains have not been uniform and many of the poorest countries still face severe difficulties. The UN Commission On Sustainable Development Inter-sessional Ad Hoc Open-Ended Working Group on Finance, in its *Report of the Secretary General — Financial resources and mechanisms for sustainable development: overview of current issues and developments* (Feb. 22, 1994), E/CN.17/ISWG.II/1994/2 (hereinafter, "UNCSD: Financial Resources") stated at para. 37: "Expanded overall resource flows and the improved debt situation have largely bypassed them. For many, debt obligations are still well beyond their ability to meet service payments, resulting in the build-up of arrears. Even for those that have been able to keep up with obligations, many struggle to do so, leaving little foreign exchange earnings for other purposes."

and implementation of any global legal instrument on forests will still depend, therefore, upon the willing participation of developing states. The integration of the South in any forests regime will face substantial challenges, not least of which is the continuing suspicion with which efforts at international control of forestry practices are viewed in many countries. The entire text of the Forest Principles may be seen as an attempt to bridge this gap, to strike a balance between recognition of the environmental values of forests and a corresponding acknowledgment of the role of forests in economic development.[17] This broad compromise is recognized in the wording of the Preamble, which clearly reflects the fundamental conflict of values inherent in the Forest Principles:

(b) The guiding objective of these principles is to contribute to the management, conservation and sustainable development of forests and to provide for their multiple and complementary functions and uses.
(c) Forestry issues and opportunities should be examined in a holistic and balanced manner . . . taking into consideration the multiple functions and uses of forests, including traditional uses, and the likely economic and social stress when these uses are constrained or restricted. . . .
(g) Forests are essential to economic development and the maintenance of all forms of life.[18]

The tension between a state's rights to use forest resources and its obligations to protect them runs throughout the entire document. On the "rights" side of this equation, one of the overriding concerns of developing states in negotiations leading to the Forest Principles was to ensure that the sovereign rights of states over forest resources were affirmed,[19] as was reflected in Principle 1 (a):

---

17 Many, however, would regard it as an imbalance rather than a balance, in that the obligations side of the equation remains unrealized: see e.g., Szekely, *supra* note 4 at 67.

18 This basic dichotomy is echoed throughout the text, both between and within principles. Thus Principle 2(b) combines recognition of the value of forests to the "social, economic, ecological, cultural, and spiritual human needs of present and future generations,"; a clear balancing of concerns for intergenerational and intragenerational equity. Similarly, Principle 4 recognizes the "vital role of all types of forests in maintaining the ecological processes and balance," while others acknowledge more extractive uses such as energy (Principle 6) and other products (Principle 2(b)).

19 This was a reflection of the broader debates on right to development and permanent sovereignty over natural resources that ran through the UNCED discussions. See C. Mensah, "The Environment After Rio: The Role of the Developing Countries," in Campiglio *et al.*, *supra* note 4, 33 at 41-44.

States have, in accordance with the Charter of the United Nations and the principles of international law, the sovereign right to exploit their own resources pursuant to their own environmental policies. . . .

This right is only slightly curtailed by a corresponding obligation in Principle 2 (a) to use forests in a sustainable manner, an obligation that is qualified by reference to "development needs," "level of socio-economic development," and possible "conversion . . . for other uses." The compromises achieved with respect to the overall objectives, and specific recognition of state sovereignty over natural resources, were clearly crucial to reaching agreement, but it is the structure of states' obligations that will determine any future progress towards sustainable development of the world's forests. What characteristics define these obligations, and what will be required to allow states, in particular developing states, to fulfil them?

The obligations proposed in the Forest Principles are of two general types. First, there are international obligations to co-operate, primarily in support of activities at the national level. Second, there are the national obligations, ranging from broad objectives to relatively specific requirements. What is striking about the national-level obligations is their potential breadth; if pursued in good faith they would amount to nothing less than an agenda for social and economic development as applied to the forest sector. While this is not surprising, given the high priority assigned to the integration of forest issues within overall development planning,[20] it nonetheless represents an ambitious set of priorities, as is indicated by even a partial listing of actions potentially required of states in implementing the Principles:

(1) Principle 5(a), dealing with the rights of indigenous peoples and forest dwellers, would require the promotion of conditions whereby such groups could have "an economic stake in forest use, perform economic activities, and achieve and maintain cultural identity and social organization, as well as adequate levels of livelihood and well-being."

(2) Principle 5(b) calls for the active promotion of the "full participation of women in all aspects of the management, conservation and sustainable development of forests." This has been a longstanding but elusive objective in other sectors.

---

[20] See, e.g., Principle 3(c): "All aspects of environmental protection and social and economic development as they relate to forests and forest lands should be integrated and comprehensive."

(3) Principle 6(c), relating to the assessment of environmental costs and the benefits of forest goods and services, implies the presence of significant data collection and analysis capabilities.

(4) The broad support for reforestation and afforestation in Principle 8 would obviously require substantial new programs.

The forest "problem" as envisioned here is based in a complex set of socio-economic causes that are not primarily legal in their genesis, and are not readily susceptible to solution by legal dictate, nor by use of available models of development assistance.[21] The imposition of legal obligations to deal with issues of such complexity, even assuming a political will to act, must be predicated on the presence of two elements. First, states must have the capability to undertake the necessary development programs — a capability extending to the substantial financial, technical, and human resources that would be needed to pursue these activities. Second, states must have the general economic resources and resilience to allow for the substitution of other economic opportunities and the corresponding promotion of restraint in exploiting forest resources. Given that many of the target states for the Forest Principles are developing states, for which neither precondition can be assumed, it is clear that additional measures will be required to ensure that any obligations imposed in law can be achieved in fact. As a result, the efficacy of any agreement on forests could be judged in large part on how well it addresses the problem of developing states' implementation capacity. This element will be central to achieving the underlying objective of sustainable development and management of forests.

CURRENT RESPONSES

Recent developments in international law, primarily in the context of treaty regimes, have indicated a recognition of the complex challenges that are inherent in global environmental obligations, and the need to link these obligations to special consideration for developing states. These considerations can be justified on the basis

[21] Organizing Committee for the Establishment of An Independent World Commission on Forests and Sustainable Development, *Possible Mandate, Key Issues Strategy and Work Plan* (1993) at 8: "When critical issues concerning the sustainable development of forests are considered in connection with the questions of interdependence, sustainability, equity and security, they become complex geo-political problems that do not respond to existing methods of international discussion and cooperation."

of at least three general assumptions, which operate in the alternative depending on the position of the observer and the content of a particular measure:

(1) Developing countries have a valid claim to recompense for development opportunities foregone in, for example, restricting the pace or scope of resource exploitation.

(2) Developed countries bear a higher degree of fault in the creation of current environmental conditions, and therefore should assume more of the burden involved in remedying those conditions.

(3) Regardless of fault or compensation issues, the practical reality is that developing states will require substantial assistance if they are to acquire the capacity (financial and technical) to take the measures asked of them.[22]

A number of elements or themes have characterized these efforts at special consideration. First, legal instruments have recognized the concept of common but differentiated responsibilities: that is, that states may have differing levels of obligation, whether based upon lesser responsibility for the problem or lower capacity to respond.[23] Special consideration measures range from general acknowledgment of the principle[24] to more specific relief from obligations, including

[22] A debate over which of these underlying assumptions justifies which particular approach is not helpful. The common thread is the recognition that "consideration of [developing countries'] . . . particular situation and needs can provide them with added incentive and improve their capacity to participate in, and implement" environmental treaties: *Conclusions of the Siena Forum on International Law of the Environment* (Apr. 1990), reprinted in (1990) 20 Env. Pol'y & L. 232 at para. 7.

[23] Netherlands National Committee for the IUCN, *Report of the Global Consultation on the Development and Enforcement of International Environmental Law, with a special focus on the Preservation of Biodiversity and the International Environmental Law Conference,* adopted Aug. 16, 1991. Reprinted in S. Bilderbeek, ed., *Biodiversity and International Law* 193 (Washington: IOS Press, 1992). This report, at paragraph 3(f), highlights the dual basis of this principle: "[C]osts [of global environmental protection] should be shared equitably among states, taking into account historic responsibilities and present technical and financial capabilities."

[24] See e.g., Article 3(1) of the *United Nations Framework Convention on Climate Change,* concluded May 9, 1992 at New York, in force Mar. 21, 1994, reprinted in (1992) 31 I.L.M. 849 (hereinafter "Climate Change Convention"), which provides a general statement of this principle: "The Parties should protect the climate system for the benefit of present and future generations of humankind, on the basis of equity and in accordance with their common but differentiated

152   *Annuaire canadien de Droit international 1994*

"delayed compliance (grace periods) . . . [and] . . . differentiated standards and objectives."[25] Second, existing instruments have incorporated more technical measures that are aimed at enhancing implementation capacity in the following areas:

(1) *Technology Transfer*: Provisions promoting access to and transfer of environmentally beneficial technology to developing countries (generally on favourable or concessional terms) appear in both the Biodiversity and the Climate Change conventions.[26]

(2) *Scientific Research and Development*: Both the Biodiversity and the Climate Change conventions provide that parties shall co-operate in stimulating or promoting relevant scientific research.[27] This extends to the need for improved education and training, both "formal" and "non-formal" (public awareness).[28]

(3) *Access to Benefits*: The Biodiversity Convention includes a number of measures related to the distribution of the results and

---

responsibilities and respective capabilities. Accordingly, the developed country Parties should take the lead in combating climate change and the adverse effects thereof."

25 *Conclusions of the Siena Forum on International Law and the Environment, supra* note 22 at para. 11(b). An example of a more specific measure is found in Art. 5 of the *Montreal Protocol On Substances That Deplete The Ozone Layer*, concluded Sept. 16, 1987, in force Jan. 1, 1989, reprinted at (1987) 26 I.L.M. 1550; amended by the *London Adjustments and Amendments*, June 29, 1990, reprinted at (1991) 30 I.L.M. 537, and the *Copenhagen Adjustments and Amendments*, Nov. 25, 1992, reprinted at (1993) 32 I.L.M. 874 (hereinafter "Montreal Protocol"). This Article provides for a ten year compliance delay for developing countries with low consumption levels of certain substances.

26 See *United Nations Convention on Biological Diversity*, concluded June 5, 1992, in force Dec. 29, 1993, reprinted in (1992) 31 I.L.M. 818 (hereinafter "Biodiversity Convention"). Art. 16(1) provides *inter alia* as follows: "Each Contracting Party, recognizing that technology includes biotechnology . . . undertakes subject to the provisions of this Article to provide and/or facilitate access for and transfer to other Contracting Parties of technologies that are relevant to the conservation and sustainable use of biological diversity or make use of genetic resources and do not cause significant damage to the environment." See also Climate Change Convention, Art. 5.

27 See e.g., Biodiversity Convention, Art. 17 (facilitating exchange of information, "taking into account the special needs of developing countries"); Art. 18 (promotion of technical and scientific co-operation, with emphasis on "human resources development and institution building"); Art. 12(b) (promotion of research, "especially in developing countries"). See also Art. 5 of the Climate Change Convention.

28 See e.g., Biodiversity Convention Art. 12(a).

benefits of biotechnology research. These measures relate to the rights of "countries of origin" of the genetic resources used to undertake such research, and focus on determining the terms and conditions of use of the genetic resources.[29]

Finally, all of these co-operation measures are to some extent subsidiary to the financial support that must be present to give real substance to the other avenues of co-operation. The provision of financial support to permit developing states to meet new obligations is an obvious requirement, and one that has been addressed in at least two ways: first, treaties may specifically endorse the allocation of additional funds to developing states in furtherance of its objectives; and, second, financial mechanisms can be created to oversee and facilitate the flow of funds related to implementation of an agreement. Examples of these financial arrangements are found in the Montreal Protocol,[30] the Biodiversity Convention,[31] and the Climate Change Convention.[32]

The Forest Principles contain a number of provisions analogous to those discussed here. First, there are statements related to general principles that function mainly to provide justification and context for the more specific provisions found elsewhere in the text. These include, for example, an endorsement of the basic position that the cost of achieving sustainable forest development necessitates such assistance, and that the costs must be "equitably

[29] Art. 15 provides for access to these resources only on "mutually agreed terms" and "subject to prior informed consent of the Contracting Party providing such resources."

[30] Art. 10(1) of the Montreal Protocol provides for the establishment of a "mechanism for the purposes of providing financial and technical cooperation," intended to "meet all agreed incremental costs of [developing country Parties]. . . ." Under Art. 10(2) it is specified that the mechanism "shall include a Multilateral Fund . . . [and may] also include other means of multilateral, regional and bilateral cooperation."

[31] The Biodiversity Convention deals separately with the commitment of financial resources, the financial mechanism, and an interim arrangement for provision of financial support. Art. 20(2) sets out the general obligations of developed country parties to provide assistance in furthering the objectives of the Convention, including the provision of new and additional financial resources, Art. 21 sets out the broad structure of the permanent financial mechanism, and Art. 39 establishes the Global Environment Facility (GEF) as an interim arrangement. (The issue of the GEF is discussed further, *infra* at note 47.)

[32] The Climate Change Convention takes a similar approach to that found in the Biodiversity Convention, including the use of the GEF as an interim arrangement (under Art. 21).

shared" among states.[33] In addition to these broad statements of principle are provisions that could conceivably be translated into firm obligations in a convention. These include measures relating to technology transfer, access to benefits arising from the use of genetic materials, scientific research and development, and financial assistance. Even in this non-binding document, however, the most obvious characteristic of these elements is the extent to which any appearance of definite commitments is avoided. Thus the reference to technology transfer calls for such transfers on "favourable" terms, which may include but presumably are not required to be on a "concessional or preferential" basis, and in any event need only be "promoted, facilitated and financed" where it is "appropriate."[34] It is hard to imagine how this provision might have been more restricted, short of its outright removal from the text. On an even more contentious issue — access to biological resources and the sharing of benefits with countries where those resources are located[35] — the compromise adopted is not particularly reassuring to developing states, since it speaks only of "due regard" to both the sovereign rights of the country where the resources originated, and to the sharing of technology and benefits arising from use of those resources.[36] The provisions relating to scientific research and development, while useful and well-intentioned, do not make firm commitments to specific action.[37]

33 Forest Principles, Principle 1(b): "The agreed full incremental cost of achieving benefits associated with forest conservation and sustainable development requires increased international cooperation and should be equitably shared by the international community." This Principle is obviously subject to restrictive interpretations should states find it convenient, but it does serve to state the underlying premise for the more specific provisions.

34 Forest Principles, Principle 11.

35 This issue was especially difficult in the context of the Biodiversity Convention. See M. Chandler, "The Biodiversity Convention: Selected Issues of Interest to the International Lawyer" (1993) 4 Col. J. Int'l Env. L. & Pol'y 141 at 161-65.

36 Forest Principles, Principle 8(b).

37 Forest Principles, Principle 12, incorporates at least four basic approaches to the problem of research and development. First, particular research efforts of national institutions "should be strengthened through effective modalities, including international cooperation." Second, beyond individual programmes, the Principle stresses the development of institutional capability in related disciplines such as education, the sciences, and social sciences. Third, international information exchange is to be "enhanced and broadened." Finally, the important role of indigenous knowledge is noted and supported.

The crucial issue of financial assistance flows is addressed by Principles 7(b), 8(c), and 10. The most generally worded of these, 8(c), states that "national policies and programs aimed at forest management, conservation and sustainable development . . . should be supported by international financial and technical co-operation."[38] While Principle 8(c) addresses support for forest-related programs, Principle 7(b) deals with the separate issue of funding for substituted economic activities that permit countries to ease pressure on forest areas, with an emphasis on conditionality for such support.[39] The most important reference to financial assistance, however, is found in Principle 10, which calls for the provision of "[n]ew and additional financial resources" to developing countries to enable them to "sustainably manage, conserve and develop their forest resources." The key element here is the specific endorsement of the need for "new and additional" funds,[40] but no target levels are mandated or suggested.

Despite the apparent progress on these questions at Rio and elsewhere, however, substantial problems remain. It is clear that there is little or nothing by way of definite commitments on this issue in the Forest Principles, especially when we consider that states were not going to be bound by the document in any event. Similar problems exist with the other instruments referred to above. The issues of technology transfer and access to benefits caused controversy both at Rio and afterwards, centred on the question of intellectual property rights.[41] The underlying lack of agreement

38 Forest Principles, Principle 8.

39 Forest Principles, Principle 7(b). The conditionality is reflected in the reference to recipient countries that set aside conservation areas, including "natural forest areas."

40 Similar wording was used in various contexts at Rio, with the phrase "new and additional" inserted "to distinguish the financial resources contained in the conventions [and the Principles] from other bilateral or multilateral aid going to the developing countries." Mensah, *supra* note 19 at 51.

41 On the earlier debate, see generally the following: Chandler, *supra* note 35; D. E. Bell, "The 1992 Convention on Biological Diversity: The Continuing Significance of U.S. Objections at the Earth Summit" (1993) 26 Geo. Wash. J. Int'l L. & Econ. 479; and N. Ashford and C. Ayers, "Policy Issues for Consideration in Transferring Technology to Developing Countries" (1985) 12 Ecol. L. Q. 871, *passim.* At the Feb. 1994 meeting of the Working Group on Technology Transfer and Cooperation (convened to prepare recommendations for the Commission on Sustainable Development), this issue continued to cause divisions: see (1994) 5 Earth Neg. Bull. (No. 14) at 4.

between the North and the South is reflected in the cautious wording of both the Biodiversity Convention and the Climate Change Convention,[42] which resulted in provisions that are at best vague and unenforceable. The scientific research and development measures are largely declaratory in nature, with little by way of defined programs of action. With respect to financial commitments and mechanisms, it is important to note the remaining gaps (particularly with respect to the Climate Change and Biodiversity conventions). The two most critical are first, the absence of actual commitments to certain levels of funding and, second, the failure to address the question of compensation for foregone development opportunities, in that these instruments focus exclusively on financial support for the costs of implementing specific obligations under the treaties, and in some cases only on the "agreed incremental costs" of implementation.[43]

A further problem concerns the careful wording of the financial provisions in the two conventions and in Agenda 21, which leaves an impression that the parties were never truly *ad idem*, but nonetheless wished to reach formal agreement[44] and were prepared to put off settling the thorny details until a later date. This is confirmed by accounts of the final stages of the negotiations on the two conventions, in which the one common element of the opposing positions on financial provisions was that both sides were dissatisfied with the results. It appears that the pressure of time and desire to reach a conclusion may have caused remaining substantive differences to be papered over in the hope that they could be resolved later. It can therefore be said that the final products of the conventions represent diplomatic successes in that agreements were

---

[42] The generally restricted tone is illustrated by the wording of Art. 16(2), which provides that "fair and most favourable" transfer terms include "concessional and preferential terms *where mutually agreed*" [emphasis added]. Specific protection of the contrary interest is also included in Art. 16(2), which provides that "access and transfer shall be provided on terms which recognize and are consistent with the adequate and effective protection of intellectual property rights."

[43] See e.g., Art. 10(1) of the Montreal Protocol and Principle 1(b) of the Forest Principles.

[44] The United States was unprepared to sign the Biodiversity Convention at Rio in any event, although it has since done so. The key United States objections were centred on financing arrangements, technology transfer, and intellectual property issues. For general reviews of these issues see Bell, *supra* note 41, and Chandler, *supra* note 35.

achieved at all, but substantive failures in that no real consensus was reached on key issues, including commitment levels and institutional structures.[45] It has become apparent in the post-UNCED period that negotiators "finessed" underlying disagreements that have since resurfaced, including issues such as control of operations of the financial mechanisms, determination of policies and criteria, and funding levels. Within months of Rio, it had become apparent that "ominous signs [abounded] that even before the ink was allowed to dry on the final Conference documents, governments were proving unable to 'put their money where their mouth was.'"[46] Despite progress on some issues,[47] it is difficult to escape the overall sense of a failure to fulfil the bargain made at Rio.[48]

---

[45] See e.g., E. P. Barratt-Brown, S. A. Hajost and J. H. Sterne, Jr., "A Forum for Action on Global Warming: The UN Framework Convention on Climate Change" (1992) 4 Col. J. Int'l Env. L. & Pol'y 103 at 114. See also J.-F. Pulvenis, "The Framework Convention on Climate Change," in Campiglio et al., *supra* note 4, 71 at 89, on the "closed door" meetings that produced the final draft. Chandler, *supra* note 35 at 169-74, considers that the time-pressured approach to negotiations on the Biodiversity Convention contributed to a vague and ambiguous text. This impression is supported by the illuminating account of the Agenda 21 (Chapter 33) negotiations provided by Ambassador Ricupero of Brazil, co-ordinator of the Contact Group on Finances at UNCED, in R. Ricupero, "Chronicle of a Negotiation: The Financial Chapter of Agenda 21 at the Earth Summit" (1992) 4 Col. J. Int'l Env. L. & Pol'y 82 at 86, which details how "agreement" was reached by half-starved negotiators at two o'clock in the morning, "approving entire pages in a matter of minutes."

[46] See Ricupero, *ibid.* at 100-101, referring to developments such as the following: the attempts to transfer the Montreal Protocol funding functions transferred to the GEF; the omission of any mention of UNCED from the communiqué of the subsequent meeting of the G-7; the failure to establish an "earth increment" as part of the International Development Association replenishment in Dec. 1992.

[47] E.g., agreement was reached in March 1994 on a restructuring of the GEF. This issue had caused substantial controversy, given the general dissatisfaction of developing countries with the role of this UNDP/UNEP/World Bank facility as the interim financial mechanism for the Biodiversity Convention: see, e.g., the summary of discussions at the First Conference of Parties in (1994) 4 Earth Neg. Bull. (No. 55). The agreement on governance, decision-making, and operations cleared the way for the first replenishment of the GEF, in the amount of US$ 2.02 billion. See also the Instrument for the Establishment of the Restructured Global Environment Facility (Report of the GEF Participants Meeting, Geneva, Mar. 14-16 1994) (hereinafter "GEF Restructuring"). Nonetheless, the amount of funding is still not of the scale anticipated in Agenda 21.

[48] Johnson, *supra* note 2 at 7, argues that the contending parties were so far apart on key issues at Rio that in fact the "'global bargain' was never on the table."

THE RELEVANCE OF A LEGAL INSTRUMENT

The post-Rio experience indicates that, while formal agreement may be possible on the development assistance elements of environmental conventions, states are still some distance from a real consensus on what such provisions will mean when they are implemented in concrete terms, especially with respect to financial measures. Any international legal instrument dealing with forests must involve substantive agreement on such issues as funding targets, the institutional home of the funding mechanism, and the nature (voluntary or mandatory) of contributions. These are not merely problems of drafting;[49] they require a degree of political agreement that does not seem likely in the post-UNCED era. If we assume for the sake of argument, however, that these difficulties could be overcome, and that co-operation provisions similar to previous instruments could be agreed upon, what would this accomplishment contribute to the promotion of sustainable forest management and development?

The most striking gap in the existing documents, including Agenda 21, is the absence of any hard financial commitments[50] to particular levels of development assistance in support of agreed obligations. The indefinite commitments that were made at Rio, whether in relation to Agenda 21[51] or to the Biodiversity and Climate Change conventions,[52] do not appear to have been fully

[49] Useful versions of the necessary provisions can be found, e.g., in the *Model for A Convention For the Conservation and Wise Use of Forests,* prepared by the Global Legislators' Organization for a Balanced Environment (GLOBE)(Brussels: GLOBE International, Apr. 1992).

[50] Some have referred to UNCED as creating funding "obligations," but, while this may be so in a moral sense, it is difficult to discern a legal obligation, and assessments such as the following are at best optimistic, even with reference to the finalized conventions: "There is obligation on the part of the North to provide financial resources to the South so that the South can meet its own obligation of implementing the mandate of the Earth Summit." Mensah, *supra* note 19 at 51.

[51] The euphoria, such as it was, surrounding Agenda 21 was remarkably short-lived. Within a few months of UNCED, close observers feared that the necessary money would not be forthcoming. See Ricupero, *supra* note 45 at 100-101; see also M. Strong, "Beyond Rio: Prospects and Portents" (1992) 4 Col. J. Int'l Env. L. & Pol'y 21 at 25.

[52] See e.g., the difficulties experienced at the Intergovernmental Committee on the Convention on Biological Diversity over such issues as the nature of contributions (mandatory or obligatory) and the scale of contributions: (1994) 9 Earth Neg. Bull. (No. 17) at 6-7.

implemented in the post-UNCED period.[53] In general, the flow of development assistance is unlikely to increase significantly in the near future.[54] This fact may by itself create an insurmountable obstacle to the conclusion of a binding forest convention or, if one is concluded, to its effective implementation.

Nevertheless, lack of funds has clearly not been the only problem with the development assistance effort related to forests throughout the past decades.[55] Environmental disasters in the forest sector provided a good part of the impetus for the emergence of "eco-development" concerns.[56] Given the difficulties experienced in this sector, would a binding legal instrument on forests contribute meaningfully to the non-financial issues, and correct the perceived distortions of earlier development efforts, as was the hope of some in the pre-UNCED period?[57] Were these ambitions for a forest

53 The experience of the intervening period has not been any more encouraging; see, e.g., the continuing debate over the need for adequate financial resources at the First Meeting of the Conference of the Parties (COP) to the Convention on Biological Diversity (Nassau, 28/11/94-9/12/94), where even the limited issue of the Secretariat budget caused significant difficulty; for a summary of these discussions see (1994) 4 Earth Neg. Bull. (No. 55). Concern about the failure to deliver on the financial aspects of Agenda 21 has also been clearly stated in discussions related to the UNCSD. In the 1994 session (New York, 16/5/94-27/5/94), members "determined that, although some progress has been made, until there is an increase in official development assistance and an improvement in the international economic climate, it will continue to be difficult to translate the Rio commitments into action": (1994) 5 Earth Neg. Bull. (No. 26).

54 Overall assistance flows have, if anything, fallen in real terms in recent years: UNCSD: Financial Resources, *supra* note 16 at para. 17; see also Ricupero, *supra* note 45 at 101.

55 It was, however, clearly seen as one of the reasons for seeking a binding convention. See, e.g., *Tropical Forestry Action Plan: Report of the Independent Review* 47 (Kuala Lumpur, 1990) (hereinafter, "TFAP Independent Review"). See also The World Bank, *The Forest Sector: A World Bank Policy Paper* (Washington: World Bank, 1991) (hereinafter "The Forest Sector") at 54.

56 See P. R. Muldoon, "The International Law of Ecodevelopment: Emerging Norms for Development Assistance Agencies" (1986) 22 Texas Intl. L. J. 1, *passim.* See also, H. McGee Jr. and K. Zimmerman, "The Deforestation of the Brazilian Amazon: Law, Politics, and International Cooperation" (1990) 21 Inter-Amer. L. Rev. 513, *passim.*

57 See e.g., R. Winterbottom, *Taking Stock: The Tropical Forestry Action Plan After Five Years* 30-31 (Washington: World Resources Institute, 1990): "An international convention and protocols should be negotiated on a range of TFAP-related and parallel actions that are needed to address global deforestation issues, in order to achieve net afforestation within a decade."

convention ever realistic, or did they demonstrate nothing more than a misplaced faith in the normative power of law? In answering this question, it is useful to note some of the major issues identified in pre-UNCED analyses of the sector, and to consider the extent to which a legal instrument would have been able to address those issues, using the existing models discussed above as a basis for what might realistically have been achieved in a forests convention.

Reviews of past experience in the forest sector, particularly with the Tropical Forestry Action Plan (TFAP)[58] and the World Bank's forest-related programs[59] identify a number of common technical requirements, including, *inter alia*, an improved research and information base, better quality control in planning and project activities, enhanced co-ordination of development assistance efforts, improved co-ordination with complementary sectors such as agriculture, restructuring of zoning, and regulation of commercial logging.[60]

These and other measures, many of which are reflected in Agenda 21,[61] might necessitate substantial funding and represent significant challenges, but their implementation would not require the conclusion of a binding legal instrument; real progress towards these goals would depend more upon the re-orientation of develop-

[58] *Ibid.* at 9. The critical importance of the TFAP is in its influence on the national planning of the countries that become part of the TFAP process. By 1990, 70 countries "that together possess roughly 60 per cent of the world's remaining tropical forests have completed or started to prepare national action plans for the forest sector," although not all of these followed FAO guidelines.

[59] The Bank has been a powerful influence in the sector, and as of 1992 had "financed nearly 100 projects in the forest sector, with total commitments of $2500 million." M. Muthoo, *Response to Rio: International Development Agencies, Agenda 21 and Forests* 12 (Rome: FAO, 1993). This does not, of course, include the massive impacts of Bank-funded projects in other sectors upon forests; on this issue, see McGee and Zimmerman, *supra* note 56, *passim.*

[60] See Winterbottom, *supra* note 57 at 27-30. See also The Forest Sector, *supra* note 55 at 12-17; R. Roberts, S. Pringle and G. Nagle, *CIDA Discussion Paper: World Forestry Leadership — An Update* (Ottawa: CIDA, May 1993); TFAP Independent Review, *supra* note 55.

[61] Agenda 21 (UNCED, 1992), reprinted in Johnson, *supra* note 2 at 125-508. Chapter 11, "Combating Deforestation," incorporates programmes or specific actions relevant to many of these concerns, including the following: improvement of scientific knowledge; creation of National Forestry Action Programmes consistent with the Forest Principles; expansion of protected areas; improved management of areas adjacent to forests; obtaining and applying local and indigenous knowledge; promotion of non-wood forest products; use of regulation and economic incentives; increased afforestation efforts.

ment assistance activities that occur outside any legal document. There were and are, however, underlying problems arising from past performance in this sector that might be remedied by a binding global agreement. The first of these problems is lack of integration — that is, the failure to connect effects in the forest sector with their causes in the broader development context.[62] Other outstanding issues would be the terms of trade and the structure of the agricultural sector,[63] but perhaps the most critical is the impact of chronic poverty and inequality.[64]

It is clear that progress on these issues requires action across the spectrum of development activities (as is implicit in the entire approach of Agenda 21), and would involve fundamental changes in the current patterns of indebtedness and reverse capital flows. Experience to date does not, however, indicate a willingness to come to grips with this aspect of the challenge of sustainable development. Certainly the two conventions signed at Rio, in sectors that are characterized by similar degrees of integration, did not fully confront the interrelated nature of the environment and the structural issues; the relationships are recognized but not addressed with funding or programs.[65] If this past experience is a guide, it is likely that a forest convention's main contribution to the problem of integration would be hortatory in nature, a function that can be served by binding or non-binding documents. The lack of real action on this issue in previous agreements was perhaps inevitable, in that specific conventions cannot be everything to all sectors, and such concerns are often better left to a more general agreement. However, given that the UNCED document with the highest degree of integration, Agenda 21, did not incorporate binding commitments to funding levels, developing countries may be left with a difficult Catch-22 situation — that is, while multisectoral integra-

---

62 Thus the following comment on a contradiction that "undermines the TFAP framework" in general: "The plan acknowledges that deforestation is largely driven by forces outside of the forestry sector and by policy decisions, development planning priorities, and programs beyond foresters' control": Winterbottom, *supra* note 57 at 24.

63 *Ibid.* see also The Forest Sector, *supra* note 55 at 17-18.

64 *The Forest Sector, supra* note 55 at 13: "General economic development, including increased diversification of the national economy, reductions in inequality and poverty, and slower population growth, are necessary for a long-term solution to the forestry problem."

65 See, e.g., the non-binding nature of the various references to integration in the Climate Change Convention, including the Preamble, Arts. 3(4) and 4(1)(f).

tion cannot be achieved via a sectoral convention, enforceable agreements are only possible at the sectoral level.

Another category in which previous development efforts have failed incorporates equity concerns in a broad sense. This category includes (1) the rights of indigenous peoples and forest-dwelling communities to participate effectively in decision-making related to forest development,[66] (2) equitable distribution of the benefits of forest resources, and (3) the effective involvement of NGOs in the development planning process.[67] Rooted in social justice concerns and recognizing that effective development depends upon full involvement of the people most directly affected, criticism of this failure focuses on the need for expanded participation in the development process as it applies to forests.[68] Accepting that progress on these problems is a precondition to sustainable forest development, however, what is the role of an international legal instrument in achieving that goal? It is at the very least unlikely that many states will be willing voluntarily to restrict their own internal control over decision-making and other aspects of political participation in the absence of attractive incentives to do so, and if the post-UNCED experience with the Biodiversity and Climate Change Conventions is an accurate guide, those incentives will not be forthcoming in the near future. If at least some states are unlikely to permit the inclusion of effective, binding provisions that they regard as restrictions on their sovereignty, what contribution can be made on this issue by such a convention?

The main usefulness of conventional provisions relating to broader participation in the decision-making process, whether of indigenous peoples, forest dwellers, or NGOs, is in their influence over the policies and programs of development assistance agencies, and that is certainly the primary context in which this idea has been

[66] See Winterbottom, *supra* note 57 at 24, 28; see also TFAP Independent Review, *supra* note 55 at 45-46 on the need to broaden decision making and consultation in the TFAP process.

[67] Winterbottom, *supra* note 57 at 28.

[68] *Ibid.* A distinct issue that has not been dealt with in this paper but forms part of the same milieu is that of participation by women in the forest sector: see The Forest Sector, *supra* note 55 at 53: "Because of the traditional gender division of labour, women have specific needs and interests in forestry that have often been ignored in planning forestry projects. . . . If forestry projects are to successfully involve and benefit women, there is a need for more refined gender-based planning during the preparation phase.

advanced.[69] In this sense, the proposed contribution of a convention, insofar as it relates to the reform of development assistance, consists of a treaty-based expression of environmental conditionality similar to that identified by the proponents of a law of "ecodevelopment" in the practice of development assistance agencies.[70]

POST-RIO DEVELOPMENTS

As is noted above, the failure to conclude a forests convention at Rio did not forestall efforts to discuss the issues surrounding the sustainable development of forests. Apart from the IWGF, at least five initiatives that relate in varying degrees to the work of the UNCSD have continued to deal with the many substantive policy and technical issues that require resolution, regardless of whether a convention is in place:

(1) The Food and Agricultural Organization (FAO), lead agency in preparatory work on forests for the UNCSD, has engaged in a number of consultative and planning activities. These include deliberations at the Committee on Forestry (COFO) and convening a Panel of External Experts in Forestry to advise on the role of FAO in forests.

(2) In Europe, the Helsinki Process has resulted in the development of criteria and indicators for sustainable development of the region's forests.

(3) A workshop hosted by India and the United Kingdom in New Delhi in July, 1994, with thirty-nine countries and numerous agencies and NGOs in attendance, "agree on a standard framework for countries to use in reporting to the [UN]CSD."

(4) The Montreal Process (or the Working Group on Criteria and Indicators for the Conservation and Sustainable Management and Development of Boreal and Temperate Forests) agreed in November 1994 on "a first draft of seven criteria for the

[69] See e.g., Winterbottom, *supra* note 57 at 28; see also TFAP Independent Review, *supra* note 55 at 47.

[70] The Forest Sector, *supra* note 55 at 66. This approach to conditionality is explicit in the Bank's policy paper of 1991: "Other lending operations [other than for conservation and for small-scale farmers] will be conditional on government commitment to sustainable and conservation-oriented forestry.... If these conditions are present, projects will be judged on their individual merits. If they are not present, Bank support will be restricted to operations that directly help countries to achieve them."

sustainable development and management of boreal and temperate forests," with final agreement targeted for February 1995.

(5) The Centre for International Forestry Research (CIFOR) and the Government of Indonesia jointly hosted a "Policy Dialogue on Science, Forests and Sustainability" in December 1994, to "review the results of the various forest initiatives, determine if they adequately incorporate the latest scientific information and determine their implications for future research and information needs."[71]

The IWGF process overlaps to some extent with these other activities, but is distinct in that it is perhaps the broadest in its coverage of issues, coming closest to replicating the range of sectoral concerns reflected in the Forest Principles and in Chapter 11 of Agenda 21. The first meeting decided on a list of five key issue areas, with two more added subsequently, resulting in the following, quite comprehensive list:

(1) forest conservation, enhancing forest cover and the role of forests in meeting basic human needs

(2) criteria and indicators for sustainable forest management;

(3) trade and environment

(4) approaches to mobilizing financial resources and technology transfer

(5) institutional linkages

---

[71] This summary has been drawn from the review of activities related to the UNCSD in (1994) 5 Earth Neg. Bull. (No. 26). In addition, countries of the Amazon basin have engaged in a less formal process of consultation and cooperation dealing with the problems of criteria and indicators. At the time of going to press, two additional initiatives have progressed. First, the UNCSD Third Session in 1995 decided to establish "an open-ended *ad hoc* Intergovernmental Panel on Forests" to pursue implementation matters arising out of the Forest Principles. See United Nations, *Commission On Sustainable Development — Report On The Third Session, New York, April* 11-28, 1995, Economic and Social Council Official Records, 1995 Supplement No. 12 (United Nations: New York, 1995), Doc. E/CN.17/1995/36 at para. 204 and Annex I, Part II. para. 1. Second, the independent World Commission on Forests and Sustainable Development (WCFSD), referred to above, began its operations with a first meeting in June 1995, with a mandate to report before the Fifth Session of the UNCSD. See personal communication, David Drake (Director, International Affairs, Canadian Forest Service, Natural Resources Canada).

(6) participation and transparency in forest management

(7) comprehensive cross-sectoral integration including land use planning and management and the influence of policies external to the traditional forest sector.[72]

If the issues under consideration in the IWGF mirror to a large degree the discussions at UNCED, the process does not. As noted earlier, the working group is intended not as a negotiation but as a forum to "facilitate dialogue and consolidation of approaches to the management, conservation and sustainable development of all types of forests. . . ."[73] In line with this approach, the objective is not a formal legal document but rather a submission of views to UNCSD in the form of "synthesis papers," each of which "crystallizes the key points raised during the Meeting and includes a set of suggested options, approaches and opportunities specific to each topic."[74] It is of course possible that the IWGF, through the creation of common understandings and a higher level of trust, might eventually assist in laying the groundwork for more formal negotiations. It seems clear, however, that only by excluding that possibility from the explicit objectives of the group could some of the more contentious issues have been included for discussion, given the history of the forest negotiations at UNCED.

In assessing the contribution of a process like the IWGF, it is useful to recall that some of the issues under consideration there are also central to the negotiations that have continued since the Biodiversity and Climate Change conventions and at UNCSD in general. Questions of the transfer of financial resources, reporting and criteria, institutional structures, and other practical problems continue to hamper implementation of the "agreements" reached at UNCED, to say nothing of the further steps required to move from the implementation of the conventions to real progress on the ground. It is possible, then, that the non-formal process of the IWGF and other initiatives might serve functions similar to the negotiations undertaken as a follow-up to binding conventions, while ameliorating the concerns of parties that are simply not ready to undertake permanent commitments. The IWGF process has a significant disadvantage in that parties to it do not have access to

---

[72] IWGF Second Meeting Report, *supra* note 8 at 2.

[73] *Ibid.*, 1.

[74] *Ibid.*, 2.

the funding resources of the GEF,[75] but this problem reflects the particular structure of that fund rather than any inherent inadequacy in the non-conventional approach. If, in fact, participants in the IWGF are sufficiently encouraged by the results of the process, there is nothing to prevent the allocation or reallocation of funds to support new programs.

CONCLUSION

It is too early[76] to say whether the IWGF and the other processes noted above will succeed in contributing to the creation of sustainable approaches to the development and management of the world's forests. Negotiations subsequent to the Biodiversity and Climate Change conventions have in some respects been similar to those following the forests dialogue, raising the possibility that the legal and extra-legal options may be equally capable of a normative contribution to the issues surrounding the key causative elements of deforestation. In any event, it seems clear that the situation post-UNCED precluded any attempt to initiate negotiations on a binding convention, given the residue of the debates at Rio and the suspicion generated by lack of progress on other UNCED commitments. The more flexible approaches that have been pursued represented the only way in which constructive discussions could continue. Any attempt to push too soon for formal negotiations could have stifled these contacts and impaired the prospects for change. This experience would argue for caution in assessing any proposals to elevate the current discussions to the formal level; there may be an appropriate time to make such a shift, but the benefits of the present process should not be sacrificed by moving too soon in this direction.

75 The GEF is available for programmes in the "focal areas" of climate change, biological diversity, international waters, and ozone layer depletion. See GEF Restructuring, *supra* note 47 at 2. While forest-related programmes might be funded insofar as they affect climate change or biological diversity, integrated forest activities would presumably not be supported.

76 At the time of writing (Dec. 1994), an imposing calendar of events related to UNCED follow-up awaited for 1995, including the first meeting of the Conference of Parties to the Climate Change Convention (Mar.-Apr.),the Sixth Intergovernmental Negotiating Committee on Desertification, the Third Session of the UNCSD (Apr. 1995) and a host of UNCED-related formal and informal sessions on issues such as financial resources (Kuala Lumpur, Jan. 1995).

Although this comment has concentrated on the issue of forests, some further conclusions might be suggested with respect to the future of all international law-making in the environmental context. First, from a practical perspective, the post-UNCED world presents a very different set of challenges for the negotiation of comprehensive global treaties. Although it is still possible to conclude these agreements,[77] any negotiations must carry some substantial baggage from Rio. Global bargains predicated on action by the South in exchange for future assistance from the North will be viewed with a somewhat jaundiced eye by developing countries, in light of the poor record in delivering on promises made at UNCED.

A second point that emerges from this discussion is the extent to which the significance of binding conventions such as the Biodiversity and Climate Change conventions lies less in the specific obligations that they set out and more in their role as programs of action and blueprints for change. Success or failure should be judged not on whether an agreement is concluded, but on how fully its program is implemented[78] and, further, how that implementation contributes to a solution of the actual problem.[79] It is important that we not focus exclusively on the presence or absence of a convention, even though its negotiation may signify a hard-won legal or diplomatic achievement. In reality, the nature of the instrument or process is less important than the change that it is able to effect. If UNCED is considered part of a process of change rather than a discrete legal event or set of events,[80] then we must be open to many different modes of participation in that process.

[77] See e.g., the *United Nations Convention to Combat Desertification in Those Countries Experiencing Serious Drought and Desertification, Particularly in Africa*, adopted June 17, 1994; opened for signature, Paris Oct. 14, 1994, (1994) 33 I.L.M. 1328 (hereinafter "Desertification Convention").

[78] See e.g., F. Burhenne-Guilman and S. Casey-Lefkowitz, "The Convention on Biological Diversity: A Hard Won Global Achievement" (1993) 3 *Y.B. Int'l Env. L.* 43 at 57: "[T]he Convention, even more than is usual with international legal instruments, is the beginning of a process rather than the end. Implementation action is needed at both international and national levels and it is this process of implementation which will determine the success or failure of the Convention."

[79] Full implementation of a convention and actual progress in the real world are distinct phenomena, and it is possible to have a fully implemented but misconceived convention that would not bring about desired change.

[80] D. Freestone, "The Road From Rio: International Environmental Law After the Earth Summit" (1994) 6 J. Env. L. 193 at 218.

Finally, it is important to remember that an agreement that is not really an agreement at all is not an unmixed blessing. Under pressure of time,[81] and with the world watching, UNCED managed to produce the two binding agreements on biological diversity and climate change, despite important differences among the parties on fundamental issues. The reality of implementation has not, however, matched the promise of Rio, since these differences inevitably re-emerge in the debates on the next steps to be taken. On the positive side, conclusion of the agreements did at least guarantee that further discussions must take place, some funding has been generated through the GEF, and important symbolic advantages are inherent in the commitment represented by such conventions. On the negative side, it is possible that a formal agreement can remove the political pressure to act, in that the document itself may be presented as evidence of progress, regardless of the lack of any practical steps towards its implementation. In addition, when parties crystallize an agreement that papers over underlying differences on key terms, they may in fact hinder their search for a true consensus. Parties with an obstructionist bent will be able to hide behind a formalist approach and insist on adherence to the existing agreement, no matter how flawed it may be.[82]

This paper should not be taken to mean that the negotiation of a forest convention should be permanently discarded as an option, nor that problems experienced in implementing the Biodiversity and Climate Change conventions demonstrate that they should never have been concluded. At some point further formal negotiations on forests will be productive and necessary, and on balance the contributions of the two UNCED-related conventions have been positive. The *caveat* suggested here is simply that we should not

[81] This "pressure-cooker" approach to negotiating complex and difficult documents did not end with Rio. The last session of the Desertification Convention reflected a similar last minute rush to conclude, if not truly agree upon, a final text. As reported in (1994) 4 Earth Neg. Bull. (No. 55): "After three all-night sessions capped by a closing Plenary that did not even begin until 4:00 AM, the Convention was finally adopted. Few delegates were totally pleased with the outcome, yet most were hopeful that this Convention could have some impact on the 900 million people around the world affected by desertification."

[82] In general, the process associated with formal negotiations, particularly in the UN system, lends itself to excessive delay and formalism, as exemplified by the following complaint about the second session of the UNCSD in 1994: "Delegates spent more time negotiating the procedural text on matters relating to intersessional arrangements than they did on any of the substantive issues": (1994) 5 Earth Neg. Bull. (No. 25).

allow concern with form to distract us from the objectives that an agreement is intended to serve, in this case progress towards sustainable forest management and development. Varying processes and forms of agreement will be appropriate to different settings, and the suitability of a given option at a given time should be assessed primarily with reference to how well it serves the ultimate objective.

A binding convention could potentially serve a number of purposes related to the reform and renewal of forest-related development assistance, but under present conditions the probability of a convention making such a contribution must be questioned. Although a convention might be used to stimulate the flow of new and additional financial resources for the sector, the experience to date with other conventions indicates that a legal instrument is no "magic bullet" that can reverse the trend of declining real assistance levels, particularly in the face of structural adjustment programs. As noted above, a convention could make a symbolic statement as to the goal of enhanced integration, but that function could be served as well by a non-binding document. It is true that a convention may have more legal force, but the practical effect of a consensus document to which parties freely agree may be just as significant. Finally, it could be suggested that over-concentration on a forest agreement would divert attention from more important causes of unsustainable forest use that originate outside the forest sector itself.[83]

A key motivation in the drive for a forest convention was the promotion of the equitable development of forests. The latter may be broadly defined to include the distribution of benefits to, and the enhanced participation of those most directly affected by development activities. Use of a convention to achieve these goals was predicated partly on the notion of a "bargain" that included increased and more effective development assistance. Given that developing countries perceive a breakdown of that bargain in the post-UNCED period, it will be difficult under present conditions to make a credible offer of this kind on forests. What is left, then, is the use of a convention to impose more stringent environmental

---

[83] Some observers have questioned whether the very idea of a "forestry" chapter of Agenda 21 is to some degree antithetical to a fully integrated approach. See Roberts *et al.*, *supra* note 60 at 9: "In fact the strong focus of Chapter 11 as the 'forestry chapter' of *Agenda 21* may not have been in the long run interest of the proposed expansion of sector horizons to include a broad sustainable development outlook."

conditions on development assistance that is provided. Without entering into the debate on the merits of conditions of this type, it is worth noting that, while conventional provisions may have more influence on development agencies than internal policies and procedures, a binding treaty is not needed to implement conditions. Furthermore, the lack of a prospective financial incentive gives developing states little reason to formalize environmental restrictions in a convention, even if, in any event, restrictions will eventually be imposed by agency policy.

The discussion to this point suggests that the primary causes of the "forests problem" are more broadly based than a lack of binding legal instruments, and that solutions must be found in measures that address those causes, whether within a formal legal structure or by other means. It is true that the effectiveness of some of the necessary measures might be enhanced by their affirmation in a binding legal instrument,[84] but it should not be assumed that the legal instrument is a necessary condition for implementing the required programs and policies. Furthermore, the incremental gains provided by a convention must be weighed against the potential cost. The possibly divisive effects of a lengthy north-south wrangle on the terms of a forest convention, especially given the difficulties being experienced in bringing other UNCED obligations to fruition, may be more damaging than the potential gains would justify at this time.[85] This assumes, of course, that there are other approaches available that could deliver benefits similar to those of a convention, but without the attendant disadvantages. It is in this light that we should consider the forest initiatives that have developed since Rio.

PHILLIP M. SAUNDERS
Faculty of Law, Dalhousie University

[84] A convention might have more than an incremental effect on the institutional issue; any move to some form of global forest agency would probably necessitate a convention.

[85] See *supra* notes 51-53, and accompanying text.

Sommaire

Les progrès depuis Rio: initiatives récentes touchant les forêts du monde entier

Comme la Conférence des Nations Unies sur l'environnement et le développement (CNUED) faisait face à une scission Nord-Sud sur la question des forêts au Sommet de Rio, elle n'a pas réussi à conclure un accord obligatoire dans ce domaine et s'est contentée à la place d'une "Déclaration de principes non juridiquement contraignante mais faisant autorité, pour un consensus mondial sur la gestion, la conservation et l'exploitation écologiquement viable de tous les types de forêts." Les Principes directeurs sur les forêts ont été vivement critiqués parce qu'ils étaient mal orientés et inefficaces. De plus, le fait qu'aucune convention n'a été conclue a été considéré comme un échec important du Sommet de Rio.

Ce commentaire examine les initiatives touchant les forêts qui ont été prises après la Conférence des Nations Unies, ainsi que le rôle joué par le Canada dans la poursuite d'un dialogue informel ne débouchant pas sur une convention. On soutient que les défis importants auxquels fait face le secteur des forêts concernent le développement et non le droit et que la négociation d'un instrument juridique obligatoire ne devrait pas être considérée comme une condition indispensable à l'accomplissement de progrès en matière de développement durable des forêts. On devrait plutôt juger toutes les formes de négociation et d'entente en fonction de l'importance de leurs contributions à l'utilisation durable des forêts du monde entier. De ce point de vue, les efforts déployés après la conférence sont utiles et pertinents, car il est nécessaire de prendre des mesures pour régler ce grave problème.

Summary

Moving on from Rio: Recent Initiatives on Global Forest Issues

Confronted with a north-south split at Rio on the question of forests, the United Nations Conference on Environment and Development (UNCED) failed to conclude a binding agreement in this sector, settling instead for the "Non-legally binding authoritative statement of principles for a global consensus on the management, conservation and sustainable development of all types of forests." The Forest Principles have been attacked as both toothless and misdirected, and the failure to achive a convention has been identified as a major failing of the Rio process.

This comment examines post-UNCED initiatives on forests, including Canada's role in pursuing a non-formal dialogue with no conventional outcome. It is argued that the major challenges facing the forest sector are developmental rather than legal, and that negotiation of a binding legal instrument should not be viewed as a sine qua non *of progress on sustainable forest development. Rather, all forms of negotiation and agreement should be judged on the substantive contributions they make to ensuring sustainable use of global forests. Viewed in this light, the post-UNCED efforts constitute an appropriate and useful response to the need for further action on this critical problem.*

La procédure des rapports périodiques en application des traités relatifs aux droits de la personne: L'aprés-conférence de Vienne*

INTRODUCTION

L'OBLIGATION DES ÉTATS DE présenter des rapports périodiques apparaît comme un élément essentiel du système de protection des droits de la personne des Nations Unies. Seul mécanisme prévu par tous les principaux instruments internationaux de protection des droits fondamentaux, le système des rapports est aussi l'unique mécanisme qui s'impose automatiquement aux États dès le moment de leur adhésion à l'un de ces traités.

La présentation de rapports par les États comme moyen de contrôle de la mise en oeuvre de leurs obligations internationales trouve son origine dans la pratique de l'Organisation Internationale du Travail. Précédemment, des conventions relatives au travail avaient déjà été établies par la Conférence de Berne en 1906 qui prévoyaient que les États parties se communiqueraient certaines de leurs lois internes et établiraient à l'usage de leurs co-contractants des rapports sur la façon dont ces lois étaient appliquées. En 1919, la Constitution de l'OIT prévoit en son article 22 un système de rapports périodiques sur les mesures prises pour mettre en oeuvre les conventions ratifiées. Dès 1929, le Conseil d'administration de l'organisation approuvait des questionnaires-types servant à l'établissement des rapports. Au niveau international, de nombreux autres systèmes de rapport ont existé ou existent. Ainsi, l'article 22 du Pacte de la Société des Nations prévoyait un mécanisme de rapports annuels, en ce qui concerne les mandats. La Charte des

---

* Remerciements sincères à Jacqueline Loignon pour son assistance à la recherche lors de la préparation de ce texte ainsi qu' Hélène Laporte pour en avoir assumé la révision.

Nations Unies prévoit un système de rapports en ses articles 73 pour les territoires non-autonomes et 88 en ce qui concernait le régime de tutelle. L'article 7 de la Convention contre la discrimination dans l'éducation prévoit la soumission de rapports périodiques à la Conférence générale de l'UNESCO.[1] Au plan régional, ce mécanisme est aussi utilisé au sein du Conseil de l'Europe et prévu notamment par l'article 57 de la Convention européenne des Droits de l'Homme (1950), par les articles 21 et 22 de la Charte sociale européenne (1961) ou encore par l'article 15 de la Charte européenne des langues régionales ou minoritaires (1992). De même, les articles 42 de la Convention américaine des Droits de l'Homme et 62 de la Charte africaine des Droits de l'Homme et des Peuples prévoient la présentation de rapports par les États parties.

Dans le cadre de l'ONU, l'établissement d'un système de rapports pour contrôler le respect par les États des dispositions de la Déclaration universelle des Droits de l'Homme, adoptée le 10 novembre 1948, a été proposé dès 1951. Puis, dans le domaine de la protection des droits de la personne, un premier système de rapports fut mis en place en 1956 par la Commission des Droits de l'Homme par sa résolution 1 (XII). Ensuite, en 1965, la résolution ECOSOC 1074 C (XXXIX) demandait à la Commission des Droits de l'Homme d'établir un comité ad hoc pour étudier et évaluer les rapports périodiques. Enfin, ce système général fut définitivement abandonné en 1977, car il fut progressivement remplacé, à partir de l'adoption en 1965 de la Convention internationale sur l'élimination de toutes les formes de discrimination raciale, par un mécanisme d'établissement et de présentation de rapports reposant sur des obligations spécifiques découlant d'un traité international.[2]

[1] Sur l'historique des systèmes de rapports, voir P. Alston, "Rapport intérimaire sur l'étude des moyens d'améliorer l'efficacité à long terme du régime conventionnel mis en place par les Nations Unies dans le domaine des droits de l'homme," Doc. NU A/CONF.157/PC/62/Add.11/Rev.1, 22 avril 1993, para. 91 et 92 et "Finalité de la présentation des rapports" dans *Manuel relatif à l'établissement des rapports sur les droits de l'homme*, HR/PUB/91/1, Nations Unies (New York, 1992), à la p. 13 [ci-après *Manuel*]. A. Dormenval, *Procédures onusiennes de mise en oeuvre des droits de l'homme: limites ou défauts?* (Paris: Presses Universitaires de France, 1991), aux pp. 13 à 15, K. T. Samson, "Reporting Systems," Recueil des cours de l'Institut des Droits de l'Homme (Strasbourg, 1988), aux pp. 1 à 3.

[2] On peut noter que l'obligation pour les États de présenter des rapports peut être aussi d'origine non-conventionnelle. Ainsi, sur recommandation du Comité pour la prévention du crime et la lutte contre la délinquance, le Conseil

Aujourd'hui, au sein des Nations Unies, neuf conventions de protection des droits de la personne prévoient un système de rapport: la Convention internationale sur l'élimination de toutes les formes de discrimination raciale (article 9), le Pacte international relatif aux droits civils et politiques (article 40), le Pacte international relatif aux droits économiques, sociaux et culturels (article 16), la Convention sur l'élimination de toutes les formes de discrimination à l'égard des femmes (article 18), la Convention contre la torture et les peines ou traitements cruels, inhumains ou dégradants (article 19), la Convention relative aux droits de l'enfant (article 44), la Convention internationale sur l'élimination et la répression du crime d'apartheid (article 7), la Convention contre l'apartheid dans les sports (article 12), ainsi que la Convention internationale sur la protection des droits de tous les travailleurs migrants et des membres de leur famille (article 73).[3]

économique et social des Nations Unies a approuvé, le 25 mai 1984, les "dispositions visant à assurer l'application effective de l'ensemble des règles minima pour le traitement des détenus" qui prévoit notamment pour les États l'obligation d'adresser tous les cinq ans au Secrétaire général un rapport sur la manière dont l'ensemble de ces règles minima est appliqué (Doc. NU ECOSOC, Rés. 1984/47 (25 mai 1984), Disposition 5). De même, des rapports étatiques sont demandés par les rapporteurs spéciaux ou les groupes de travail mis en place dans le cadre de la Commission des Droits de l'Homme des Nations Unies. Cette profusion de rapports tend à augmenter encore la charge de travail des États et à créer certains risques de duplication. Par exemple, les informations demandées par le Rapporteur spécial sur les questions se rapportant à la torture peuvent être essentiellement les mêmes que celles que contient un rapport étatique destiné au Comité contre la torture ou la partie d'un tel rapport concernant l'article 7 du Pacte international relatif aux droits civils et politiques et soumis au Comité des Droits de l'Homme.

3 *Convention internationale sur l'élimination de toutes les formes de discrimination raciale* [ci-après CERD] (660 RTNU 195), adoptée le 21 décembre 1965, entrée en vigueur le 4 janvier 1969, signée par le Canada le 24 août 1966 et ratifiée le 14 octobre 1970; *Pacte international relatif aux droits civils et politiques* [ci-après PDCP] (999 RTNU 171), adopté le 16 décembre 1966, entré en vigueur le 23 mars 1976, adhésion du Canada le 19 mai 1976; *Pacte international relatif aux droits économiques, sociaux et culturels* [ci-après PDESC] (999 RTNU 171), adopté le 16 décembre 1966, entré en vigueur le 23 mars 1976, adhésion du Canada le 19 mai 1976; *Convention sur l'élimination de toutes les formes de discrimination à l'égard des femmes* [ci-après CEDAW] (1249 RTNU 13), adoptée le 18 décembre 1979, entrée en vigueur le 3 septembre 1981, signée par le Canada le 17 juillet 1980, ratifiée le 10 décembre 1982; *Convention contre la torture et les peines ou traitements cruels, inhumains ou dégradants* [ci-après CAT] (AG NU, Rés. 39/46, Doc.A/39/51), adoptée le 10 décembre 1984, entrée en vigueur le 26 juin 1987, signée par le Canada le 23 août 1985 et ratifiée le 24 juin 1987; *Conven-*

Contrairement à l'Organisation Internationale du Travail, qui dispose d'un seul type de procédure pour examiner les rapports et qui charge un seul organe, la Commission d'experts pour l'application des recommandations et conventions de l'OIT, du suivi de quelques 150 conventions, il n'existe, au sein de l'ONU, ni procédure unique, ni organe commun d'examen des rapports étatiques. Ainsi, pour examiner les rapports étatiques dans le cadre des neuf traités des Nations Unies, il est prévu de mettre en place neuf organes distincts dont le statut et la composition sont d'ailleurs différents.[4] Composés de trois, dix, quatorze, dix-huit ou vingt-trois membres, ces organes sont pour la plupart d'origine conventionnelle, sauf pour le Comité des droits économiques, sociaux et culturels, qui a été créé par le Conseil économique et social.[5] Les membres des comités sont des experts dont l'indépendance est garantie par leur convention respective, sauf pour le "Groupe des trois" chargés d'examiner les rapports présentés en application de

---

tion relative aux droits de l'enfant [ci-après CRC] (AG NU, Rés. 44/25), adoptée le 20 novembre 1989, entrée en vigueur le 2 septembre 1990, signée par le Canada le 28 mai 1990 et ratifiée le 12 décembre 1991; *Convention internationale sur l'élimination et la répression du crime d'apartheid* (1015 RTNU 243), adoptée le 30 novembre 1973, entrée en vigueur le 18 juillet 1976, non signée par le Canada; *Convention internationale contre l'apartheid dans les sports* (Assemblée Générale, Résolution 40/64, Document A/40/53) adoptée le 10 décembre 1985, entrée en vigueur le 3 avril 1988, non signée par le Canada; *Convention internationale sur la protection des droits de tous les travailleurs migrants et des membres de leur famille* (Assemblée Générale, Résolution 45/158) adoptée le 18 décembre 1990, non entrée en vigueur, non signée par le Canada.

[4] Il s'agit du Comité des Droits de l'Homme [ci-après Cdh], du Comité des droits économiques, sociaux et culturels [ci-après Cdesc], du Comité pour l'élimination de la discrimination raciale [ci-après Cerd], du Comité pour l'élimination de la discrimination à l'égard des femmes [ci-après Cedaw], du Comité contre la torture [ci-après Cat], du Comité des droits de l'enfant [ci-après Crc], du Groupe des Trois de la Convention internationale sur l'élimination et la répression du crime d'apartheid, de la Commission contre l'apartheid dans les sports et du Comité pour la protection des droits de tous les travailleurs migrants et de leurs familles.

[5] Le Pacte international relatif aux droits, économiques, sociaux et culturels ne contient aucune disposition relative à l'examen des rapports par un organe d'experts indépendants et confie au Conseil Économique et Social [ci-après ECOSOC] le rôle de superviseur (art. 16(2) et 17(1) du PDESC). En 1978, l'ECOSOC a créé en son sein un "groupe de travail de session" chargé d'examiner les rapports (déc. 1978/10 du 3 mai 1978), puis a décidé, en 1985, la mise en place du Comité des droits, économiques sociaux et culturels, composé de 18 experts (Rés. ECOSOC 1985/17 du 28 mai 1985).

la Convention internationale sur l'élimination et la répression du crime d'apartheid, qui est composé de trois représentants d'États, membres de la Commission des Droits de l'Homme désignés par leur président. Cette multiplicité d'organes et de procédures a donc engendré des pratiques différenciées selon chaque traité en fonction de son histoire, du nombre d'États parties, de l'étendue de son contenu normatif, du nombre de membres et de ressources dont dispose chaque organe de supervision.[6] Toutefois, les comités s'influencent réciproquement, les plus récents profitant de l'expérience des anciens, et notamment du Comité des Droits de l'Homme et du Comité pour l'élimination de la discrimination raciale, qui eux-mêmes s'appuient sur la volonté réformatrice des nouveaux organes, comme le Comité des droits économiques, sociaux et culturels ou le Comité des droits de l'enfant.

Les effets peu contraignants qui découlent de l'obligation de produire des rapports expliquent sans doute en grande partie pourquoi cette procédure a été privilégiée par les États. Toutefois, malgré ses insuffisances inhérentes à sa nature même, l'obligation de présenter un rapport remplit plusieurs fonctions importantes. Dans un premier temps, cette obligation signifie nécessairement qu'un État devra passer en revue l'ensemble de ses lois, règlements, procédures et pratiques en vue de s'assurer qu'ils soient conformes au traité.[7] De cet examen, c'est non seulement l'organe conventionnel, mais d'abord et avant tout l'État qui doit tirer un certain

---

6 D'une façon générale, le financement des travaux des organes de contrôle est assuré par le budget ordinaire de l'ONU, sauf pour le Cerd et le Cat dont le financement est assuré partiellement ou totalement par les seuls États parties en application de leur convention respective. Des amendements aux deux Conventions ont été proposés pour que les organes soient financés sur le budget de l'Organisation et ne soient plus subordonnés financièrement aux États parties (voir notamment, Cinquième réunion des présidents des organes créés en vertu de traités relatifs aux droits de l'homme du 19 au 23 septembre 1994, Doc. A/49/537, para. 47 et 48). Cette précarité du statut financier de certains comités, mais aussi la crise financière traversée par les Nations Unies, ont des répercussions sur les travaux des organes de contrôle dont certains ont dû annuler ou écourter plusieurs de leurs sessions (voir Dormenval, *supra* note 1, aux pp. 158 à 167).

7 B. Simma, ''The Implementation of the CESCR'' dans F. Matscher, éd., *La mise en oeuvre des droits économiques et sociaux: aspects nationaux, internationaux et droit comparé* (Kehl am Rhein: N. P. Engel Verlag, 1991), à la p. 88. Voir aussi l'observation générale 1 du Cdesc sur la présentation des rapports des États parties, adoptée à sa troisième session (1989), Doc. NU HRI/GEN/1/Rev.1 à la p. 48.

constat sur les modifications qui s'avéreraient souhaitables.[8] De plus, l'obligation de produire des rapports sur une base périodique devrait être une opportunité pour l'État de mesurer le chemin parcouru.[9] Par ailleurs, un organe de supervision, en constatant par l'examen d'un rapport la non-conformité au traité, peut également motiver un État à modifier ses lois ou pratiques existantes.[10] Le système des rapports permet donc de mettre en place un processus de dialogue entre l'organe de supervision et les États parties. De plus, la pratique des Nations Unies est de publier *in extenso* rapports des États, rapports et observations de l'organe de contrôle et comptes rendus des séances d'examen des rapports. Ces documents sont donc à la disposition de toute personne souhaitant les obtenir.

Dans la Déclaration de la Conférence Mondiale sur les Droits de l'Homme, les États ont fait des recommandations précises en ce qui concerne la procédure de rapports. En particulier, il a été recommandé de "continuer à prendre des mesures pour coordonner les multiples obligations imposées aux États en matière de rapports et harmoniser les directives pour l'établissement des rapports qu'ils doivent soumettre en vertu de chaque instrument et voir si en leur donnant, comme on l'a suggéré, la possibilité de faire rapport en un seul document sur la manière dont ils respectent les obligations auxquelles ils ont souscrit, on n'accroîtrait pas l'efficacité et l'utilité de cette procédure."[11]

Ainsi, autant est-il clair que les États réunis à cette Conférence ne remettent pas en question l'utilité du mécanisme de rapports autant ils semblent préoccupés par la survie du système dans sa forme actuelle. Puisque toute réforme majeure du système nécessitera l'assentiment des États parties et se fera sûrement avec la collaboration étroite des organes conventionnelles, la Conférence mondiale a prudemment et probablement sagement encouragé les efforts pour remédier aux lacunes actuelles. Néanmoins, confronté aux difficultés qui menacent l'existence même du mécanisme des

[8] A. F. Bayefsky, "Making the Human Rights Treaties Work" dans L. Henkin et J. H. Hargrove, éd., *Human Rights: An Agenda for the Next Century* (Washington: Studies in Transnational Legal Policy, n° 26, American Society of International Law, 1994), à la p. 232.

[9] Simma, *supra* note 7, à la p. 89.

[10] Bayefsky, *supra* note 8, à la p. 232.

[11] Rapport de la Conférence mondiale sur les droits de l'homme, Doc. NU A/CONF.157/24, para. 87.

rapports, elle a aussi cru bon d'indiquer qu'il était peut-être temps d'envisager des transformations plus radicales du système.

Dans ce cadre, l'objet de notre étude est, après avoir présenté les traits principaux de la procédure de rapports (A), d'en noter les déficiences les plus marquantes (B), pour analyser enfin les réformes qui peuvent être envisagées pour assurer un meilleur contrôle de la mise en oeuvre des traités internationaux en matière de droits de la personne (C).

I ASPECTS ESSENTIELS DE LA PROCÉDURE DES RAPPORTS

L'existence d'une obligation pour les États de présenter des rapports entraîne logiquement la mise en place d'une procédure minimale pour la préparation et la présentation de ces rapports aux organes concernés. Ainsi, dans les traités relatifs aux droits de la personne qui nous concernent on retrouve quelques dispositions pertinentes à la procédure des rapports, dispositions qui par ailleurs varient de traités à traités.[12] Toutefois, l'essentiel de la procédure de rapports se trouve soit dans le règlement intérieur de chaque organe ou découle de la pratique de ces organes. Que la procédure de rapports soit principalement non conventionnelle signifie que les divers organes peuvent, s'ils le désirent, harmoniser relativement facilement plusieurs aspects de cette procédure.[13] Des initiatives en ce sens ont d'ailleurs déjà été prises, encouragées par des réunions maintenant régulières des "Présidents des organes des Nations Unies créés en vertu d'instruments internationaux relatifs aux droits de l'homme."[14] Par conséquent, même s'il existe

[12] Pour les dispositions pertinentes dans chaque traité, voir le texte *supra*, à la p. 2.

[13] L'art. 39.2 du PDCP prévoit que le Cdh adopte lui-même son propre règlement intérieur; il en est de même pour le Cerd à l'art. 10.1 du CERD; pour le Cedaw à l'art. 19.1 du CEDAW; pour le Cat à l'art. 18.2 du CAT; pour le Crc à l'art. 43.8 du CRC; l'art. 71 du règlement intérieur du Cdesc prévoit que son règlement peut être modifié par le Comité avec l'approbation du Conseil économique et social.

[14] Dès 1984, des réunions des présidents des organes créés en vertu de traités relatifs aux droits de la personne ont été organisées pour assurer un rapprochement entre les organes et une meilleure coordination de leurs travaux (première réunion du 16 au 17 août 1984 (A/39/484), deuxième réunion du 10 au 14 octobre 1988 (A/44/98), troisième réunion du 1er au 5 octobre 1990 (A/45/636), quatrième réunion du 12 au 16 octobre 1992 (A/47/628), cinquième réunion du 19 au 23 septembre 1994 (A/49/537)). À ces réunions participent les présidents ou vice-présidents des six organes de supervision des principaux traités des Nations Unies de protection des droits de la personne

toujours des différences sensibles entre la procédure de chaque organe relativement aux rapports, chacune présente cependant suffisamment d'éléments communs pour qu'on puisse aujourd'hui parler des "aspects essentiels de la procédure des rapports." Nous avons regroupé ces aspects comme suit: (1) la périodicité des rapports, (2) les directives pour la préparation du rapport, (3) les groupes de travail de pré-session, (4) la procédure d'examen par les organes, (5) la participation des agences spécialisés et des ONG à l'examen, (6) les observations finales des organes et (7) la procédure de suivi.

A LA PÉRIODICITÉ DES RAPPORTS

Puisqu'un des rôles des organes est de vérifier si les États ont pris et continuent de prendre des mesures pour assurer le respect des droits garantis par les traités pertinents, il en découle nécessairement que l'obligation de présenter des rapports doit être périodique. Il faut donc déterminer quand sera dû le rapport initial d'un État partie ainsi que ses rapports subséquents. En ce qui concerne le délai pour présenter un rapport initial, il est d'un an ou deux. Sauf pour le Cdesc, ce délai est fixé par le traité.[15] Quant à la périodicité des rapports subséquents, elle est généralement de quatre ou cinq ans; cette périodicité est fixée par le règlement intérieur pour les Pactes et par le traité pour les quatre autres conventions.[16] Bien qu'en vertu de l'article 9(1)(b) de la Convention sur l'élimination de toutes les formes de discrimination raciale les États

ainsi que des représentants des institutions spécialisées des Nations Unies et des ONG. Les présidents ont souhaité que ces rencontres soient institutionnalisées et qu'elles aient lieu tous les ans. La prochaine réunion devrait donc avoir lieu en 1995. Une conférence des organes créés en vertu de traités relatifs aux droits de l'homme est également envisagée (voir cinquième réunion, para. 58 et 59).

15 Délai pour la présentation du rapport initial d'un État: PDCP, 1 an (art. 40(1)(a) du Pacte); PDESC, 2 ans (ECOSOC, Rés. 1988/4 et art. 58.2 du règlement intérieur); CERD, 1 an (art. 9(1)(a) de la Convention); CEDAW, 1 an (art. 18(1)(a) de la Convention); CAT, 1 an (art.19(1) de la Convention); CRC, 2 ans (art. 44.1 (a) de la Convention).

16 Périodicité pour la présentation des rapports subséquents au rapport initial: PDCP, 5 ans (décision du Comité à cet effet dans CCPR/C/19/Rev.1); PDESC, 5 ans (ECOSOC, Rés. 1988-4 et art. 58.2 du règlement intérieur); CERD, 2 ans (art. 9(1)(b) de la Convention); CEDAW, 4 ans (art.18(1)(b) de la Convention); CAT, 4 ans (art. 19(1) de la Convention); CRC, 5 ans (art. 44.1 (b) de la Convention).

s'engagent à présenter un rapport tous les deux ans, le Cerd a décidé, en 1988, que les États parties doivent dorénavant présenter un rapport détaillé tous les quatre ans et de brefs rapports de mise à jour tous les deux ans.[17]

Les dispositions des traités permettent également aux organes de demander des rapports supplémentaires en tout temps.[18] Par exemple, un organe peut demander à un État de compléter certains aspects d'un rapport en lui fournissant de l'information additionnelle dans un délai approprié. Plus important encore, ces dispositions justifient une demande par un organe qu'un État produise un rapport urgent lorsque la protection des droits de la personne s'est rapidement dégradée dans l'État en question. Ainsi, depuis le mois d'avril 1991, lorsque la situation des droits de la personne est gravement compromise dans certains États parties, le Cdh peut demander aux États de présenter d'urgence des rapports sur la situation. Lorsqu'une telle situation survient entre deux sessions, le Président, agissant en consultation avec les membres du Comité, peut demander à l'État concerné de soumettre un rapport. Cette procédure a été officialisée le 8 avril 1993 par l'adjonction d'un nouveau paragraphe 2 à l'article 66 de son règlement intérieur.[19] D'autres organes ont en fait de même. Par exemple, à sa 12e session, le Comité pour l'élimination de la discrimination à l'égard des femmes a demandé des rapports exceptionnels aux États situés sur le territoire de l'ancienne Yougoslavie.[20] De même, à sa 42e et sa 43e session, le Comité pour l'élimination de la discrimination raciale a demandé et examiné des rapports spéciaux de ces mêmes États.[21] Durant ces mêmes sessions, ce comité a adopté le rapport d'un Groupe de travail qu'il avait mis sur pied pour discuter, entre autres, des mécanismes possibles pour prévenir une discrimination raciale sérieuse, persistante ou massive. Ce comité suggère qu'une

---

[17] Rapport annuel du Cerd, Doc. off. AG NU. 43e sess., supp. n° 18, Doc. A/43/18, para. 24c.

[18] PDCP, art. 40(1)(b) du Pacte; PDESC, art. 17 (1) du Pacte; CERD, art. 9(1)(b) de la Convention; CEDAW, art.18(1)(b) de la Convention; CAT, art. 19(1) de la Convention; CRC, art. 44.4 de la Convention.

[19] Rapport annuel du Cdh, Doc. off. AG NU, 49e sess., supp. n° 40, Doc. A/49/40, para. 46.

[20] CEDAW/C/1995/7, para 248.

[21] Rapport du CEDR, Doc. off. AG NU, 48e sess., supp. n° 18, Doc. A/48/18, para. 453 à 516; voir aussi p. 112.

procédure soit clairement établie pour demander des rapports dans une telle situation.[22]

B   LES DIRECTIVES POUR LA PRÉPARATION DU RAPPORT

La forme et le contenu des rapports périodiques sont à déterminer par chaque organe. Chacun d'entre eux a adopté des directives générales exposant aux États le type d'information recherchée. Un tel système facilite la tâche des États et des organes en précisant la nature de l'information exigée et en assurant l'uniformité dans la présentation des rapports. En vertu de ces directives, chaque rapport comprend deux parties: une de nature générale et l'autre spécifique aux droits protégés par le traité pertinent. Afin d'alléger le fardeau des États parties à plusieurs traités relatifs aux droits de la personne exigeant la présentation de rapports périodiques, les organes ont décidé d'harmoniser dans la mesure du possible la présentation des rapports, en recourant à des directives unifiées pour la préparation de la première partie. Il s'agit en fait pour chaque État de préparer et de mettre à jour, périodiquement, un document séparé qui expose certains attributs essentiels.[23]

Évidemment une telle solution n'est pas envisageable pour la deuxième partie du rapport, puisque celle-ci est consacrée aux dispositions de fond propres à chaque traité.[24] Par contre, les États

[22] *Ibid.*, para. 18 et annexe III.

[23] Les directives unifiées divisent la première partie du rapport en quatre composantes: (a) renseignements détaillés sur le territoire et la population, (b) présentation de l'évolution historique de l'État et de sa structure exécutive, législative et administrative, (c) explication du cadre juridique général de la protection des droits de la personne au sein de l'État, (d) précisions sur la diffusion d'information au public et aux autorités compétentes sur les droits protégés et sur les efforts pour encourager le débat public sur la protection de ces droits. Ces directives unifiées sont explicitées dans le *Manuel, supra* note 1. Préparé par le Centre des Nations Unies pour les Droits de l'Homme et l'Institut des Nations Unies pour la Formation et la Recherche (UNITAR), ce manuel contient également des explications détaillées sur la préparation de la deuxième partie des rapports pour chacun des principaux organes créés en vertu de traités des Nations Unis relatifs aux droits de la personne.

[24] "The Assembly, through the item on reporting obligations under human rights activities, has begun to engage in efforts to enhance co-ordination of these reporting procedures. A wide variety of delegations have complained about the onerous burden of reporting which falls upon conscientious States parties to the human rights treaties, and have drawn attention to the need for reform of both reporting guidelines and procedures, as well as for practical assistance,

peuvent avoir recours à la pratique des "renvois" pour éviter les dédoublements inutiles dans la préparation des rapports. Par conséquent, si des informations ont déjà été fournies dans un rapport à un autre organe, un simple renvoi, sous forme d'annexe ou de citation, à ce rapport pourra souvent suffire.[25] Cette méthode est susceptible d'être utilisée lorsqu'un État est partie à deux ou plusieurs traités protégeant des droits identiques ou similaires.[26]

Si la forme et le contenu des directives pour la préparation de la deuxième partie d'un rapport varient d'organe en organe, plus ces directives seront précises plus un organe sera susceptible d'obtenir un constat authentique sur le respect des droits dans un État.[27] En effet, la nature et le détail de l'information exigée par les directives pourront limiter la capacité d'un État de présenter des rapports formalistes, sans relation avec la protection réelle accordée par

especially for developing countries, struggling to meet reporting obligations. Because individual treaties contain specific provisions on reporting requirements, there are, however, limits to the amount of harmonization possible." Dans J. Quinn "The General Assembly into the 90s," dans P. Alston (ed.), *The United Nations and Human Rights: A Critical Appraisal* (Oxford: Clarendon Press, 1992), à la p. 68.

25 Voir la deuxième réunion des présidents A/44/98, annexe, para. 89. Toutefois, une telle pratique ne devrait pas être systématique, chaque organe déterminant dans un cas précis si cette méthode est acceptable. Il a été suggéré que des recommandations précises concernant la méthode des renvois soient incorporées dans les principes directeurs concernant la présentation des rapports par les États parties (voir troisième réunion des présidents A/45/636 para. 22 à 26). Notons que le recours aux renvois est par ailleurs expressément prévu au para. 17.3 du PDESC: "Dans le cas où des renseignements à ce sujet ont déjà été adressés à l'Organisation des Nations Unis ou à une institution spécialisée par un État partie au Pacte, il ne sera pas nécessaire de reproduire lesdits renseignements et une référence précise à ces renseignements suffira."

26 Le droit à l'autodétermination, par exemple, est formulé dans des termes identiques à l'article 1 du PDCP et du PDESC. D'autres droits, bien que formulés différemment, font l'objet de protection dans divers traités. À titre d'exemple, on peut penser au droit à la vie, à la non-discrimination ou encore à celui d'association.

27 Parmi les divers organes créés par des traités relatifs aux droits de la personne c'est actuellement le Cdesc qui a adopté les directives les plus élaborées. Ainsi dans l'introduction à son deuxième rapport sur la mise en oeuvre des articles 10 à 15 du PDESC, le Canada écrit: "les directives élaborées pour la rédaction de ces rapports sont extrêmement détaillées, contrairement aux directives élaborées pour les rapports soumis en vertu des autres instruments." Pacte international relatif aux droits économiques, sociaux et culturels: deuxième rapport du Canada sur les articles 10 à 15, Direction des droits de la personne, Multiculturalisme et Citoyenneté Canada, Ottawa, 1992, à la p. 1.

184   *Annuaire canadien de Droit international 1994*

l'État aux droits pertinents.[28] Par conséquent, même si ces directives n'ont pas de caractère obligatoire, les organes insistent fortement sur les États pour qu'ils s'y conforment.[29]

Le Centre des Nations Unies pour les Droits de l'Homme offre des services consultatifs visant à la formation au niveau national des personnels administratifs chargés de la rédaction des rapports. Le Service des services consultatifs, de l'assistance technique et de la

28 À plusieurs reprises dans le passé les divers organes des droits de l'homme ont critiqué maints États pour la qualité de leur rapports. Si, en général, les rapports canadiens ont fait l'objet d'éloges par ces organes, ils ont aussi été à l'occasion sévèrement critiqués comme l'illustre les commentaires suivants des membres du Cdesc lors de l'examen du 2ᵉ rapport du Canada sur les articles 6 à 9 du PDESC: "Le rapport dont est saisi le Comité est en quelque sorte une anomalie. Tout en étant très sérieux et très détaillé, il est également superficiel et n'apprend rien." (Commentaire de P. Alston, E/C.12/1989/SR.8, para. 30); "M. Simma, comme M. Alston et M. Mrachkov, estime que le rapport du Canada est par trop formaliste et manque d'informations concrètes. Un rapport qui s'attache trop aux aspects juridiques est tout naturellement suspect dans la mesure où l'on soupçonne qu'il pourrait y avoir un écart entre la Loi et la pratique. Le rapport du Canada est cependant moins sujet à caution que les rapports de nombreux autres pays" (commentaire de B. Simma, E/C.12/1989/SR.8, para. 42).

29 Dans ses rapports le Canada indique fréquemment son intention de suivre les directives. Ainsi dans l'introduction à son deuxième rapport sur la mise en oeuvre des articles 10 à 15 du PDESC, *supra* note à la p. 1, le Canada précise qu'il: "s'efforce donc de présenter ses rapports de façon concise tout en tenant compte des directives et des demandes des comités." Dans son troisième rapport préparé en vertu de la Convention sur l'élimination de toutes les formes de discrimination à l'égard des femmes, le Canada souligne: "Les lignes directrices émises par le Comité pour l'élimination de la discrimination à l'égard des femmes ont été suivies dans la mesure du possible." Troisième rapport du Canada sur la Convention sur l'élimination de toutes les formes de discrimination à l'égard des femmes, Direction des droits de la personne, Multiculturalisme et Citoyenneté, août 1992, à la p. 1. Également dans son premier rapport sur la Convention relative aux droits de l'enfant, Direction des droits de la personne, Patrimoine canadien, mai 1994, à la p. 1 le Canada écrit: "Il [le rapport] établit par ailleurs les priorités et les objectifs en ce qui concerne l'application éventuelle de ces droits, conformément aux Directives générales concernant la forme et le contenu des rapports initiaux formulées par le Comité des droits de l'enfant." Par ailleurs, les organes ont, à l'occasion, souligné si le Canada respectait ou non les directives. Ainsi le président du Cdh a indiqué que les rapports étaient présentés par le Canada dans le respect des directives. Voir CCPR/C/SR.1013 (séance du 24 octobre 1990, para. 40). Par contre, un membre du Cerd note que le Canada n'a pas suivi les directives pour la préparation du 11ᵉ rapport. Voir CERD/C/SR.1043, para. 17 (séance du 8 août 1994). Sur les directives, voir aussi l'examen par le Cat du 2ᵉ rapport du Canada CAT/C/139/SR (le 28 avril 1993), para. 17.

formation du Centre pour les droits de l'homme des Nations Unies, a organisé un séminaire sur la présentation des rapports à Abidjan en juin 1994 auxquels ont été conviés 16 pays africains, un stage de 40 personnes en novembre 1994 à Genève et à Turin axé sur la préparation technique des rapports. Il importe en effet que cette assistance ne se limite pas à la formation d'un ou deux fonction-naires qui rédigent le rapport de l'État, mais concerne une audience beaucoup plus large de fonctionnaires, de membres d'ins-titutions spécialisées, d'organisations sociales et d'ONG.[30] Dans un cas, un membre du Comité des Droits de l'Homme s'est rendu dans un État partie pour l'aider, par ses services consultatifs, à établir son rapport.[31]

C LES GROUPES DE TRAVAIL DE PRÉ-SESSION

À l'exception du Cerd et du Cat, tous les autres organes ont mis sur pied des groupes de travail de pré-session, normalement com-posés de cinq personnes, dont le mandat consiste essentiellement à déterminer, lors de séances non publiques, les questions les plus importantes à soulever avec l'État dont on examinera le rapport à la prochaine session. Puisque le temps de rencontre de ces groupes est limité, plusieurs organes ont trouvé plus efficace de confier à chaque membre du groupe la tâche de préparer une liste prélimi-naire de questions pour un certain nombre de rapports plutôt que d'élaborer ces questions à cinq. Lors de ses rencontres, le groupe révise ces listes préliminaires en y ajoutant des questions au besoin.

Les questions ultimement proposées par le groupe de travail sont d'une grande importance, car elles donnent véritablement le ton de l'examen avec un État. Dans ces conditions, la pratique de certains groupes de travail d'accepter une assistance extérieure pour la formulation des questions apparaît souhaitable. Ainsi le groupe de travail pour le Cdesc accepte de l'information d'ONG, par écrit ou en personne.[32] En ce qui concerne le Cdh, les institu-tions spécialisées et les autres organismes des Nations Unies partici-pent au groupe de travail depuis la session de mars 1995.[33] Dans son "Projet d'observation générale sur la procédure de rapport,"

---

[30] Quatrième réunion des présidents, A/47/628 du 10 novembre 1992, para. 75.

[31] Cdh, Rapport annuel, Doc. Off. 49ᵉ sess., Doc. A/49/41, vol. 1, para. 52

[32] Rapport du Cdesc sur les huitième et neuvième sessions, E/C.12/1993/19, para. 30.

[33] CCPR/C/SR. 1374 du 2 novembre 1994 para. 73.

débattu le 11 octobre 1994, le Comité des droits de l'enfant a souhaité la participation des organismes spécialisés et des autres organes au groupe de travail.[34] Quant aux ONG elles peuvent être invitées à fournir des informations par écrit ou oralement.[35]

Ayant dressé une liste de ces questions le groupe de travail en transmettra une copie à l'avance à l'État en lui demandant d'y répondre. Certains organes, comme le Cdesc par exemple, demanderont aux États de répondre par écrit avant la rencontre avec le Comité.[36] D'autres, comme le Cdh, adopteront les listes de questions pour chaque rapport au début de leur session et attendront à l'examen pour recevoir la réponse des États concernés.[37]

Ces groupes se réunissent normalement 5 jours, soit, pour certains, tout juste avant la session ou, pour d'autres, quelques mois auparavant.[38] Il semble que cette dernière pratique soit nettement préférable puisque l'État qui reçoit les questions a alors amplement le temps d'y répondre.

Le but des groupes de travail de pré-session est d'améliorer la qualité du dialogue entre un État et un organe au moment de l'examen et non de se substituer de quelque manière que ce soit à cet organe. Par conséquent, lors de l'examen le Comité n'est d'aucune façon limité à soulever les questions identifiées par un groupe de pré-session.

Comme nous le verrons dans la section consacrée aux réformes, le rôle des groupes de pré-session est susceptible d'élargissement. Notons que déjà le Crc a suggéré dans son "Projet d'observation générale sur les rapports" que si, lors de l'examen d'un rapport par ce groupe, il en conclut qu'il est souhaitable que l'État présente un

---

[34] CRC/C/SR.169 para. 37; notons que le groupe de travail du Cdesc a tenu une rencontre conjointe avec le groupe de travail de pré-session du Crc pour une première fois en 1993 (E/C.12/1993/19 para. 11).

[35] HRI/MC/1994/2, para. 19.

[36] Voir *Manuel*, *supra* note 1 à la p. 58; de même le projet d'observations générales sur les rapports du Crc précise que les réponses écrites de l'État devraient être reçues en avance (CRC/C/SR.169, para. 12).

[37] Voir *Manuel*, *ibid.* à la p. 91.

[38] Par exemple, le Cdesc se réunit un mois et de préférence deux mois avant la session du Comité (p. 58); le Crc a convenu que les rapports des États parties serait initialement examinés deux mois, ou au moins six semaines, avant chaque session par un groupe de travail de pré-session (CRC, A/49/41, para. 11 à 14); le Cdh se réunit une semaine avant les sessions (voir *Manuel*, *ibid.*, à la p. 89).

nouveau rapport, il peut en informer le Comité qui pourra prendre une telle décision.[39]

D   LA PROCÉDURE D'EXAMEN PAR LES ORGANES

Ayant reçu le rapport d'un État, chaque organe procédera à son examen lors d'une séance publique à laquelle les représentants et représentantes de l'État ont le droit de participer activement. En pratique, les organes insistent sur cette participation et ce ne sera qu'exceptionnellement qu'ils procéderont en l'absence de représentation d'un État.

Typiquement, les représentants et représentantes étatiques prendront la parole au début de la séance pour exposer les aspects principaux de leurs rapports, l'information connue postérieurement à la publication du rapport et, si le groupe de pré-session à fait parvenir une liste de questions à l'État, pour répondre à celles-ci. Nous verrons que pour certains organes, des agences spécialisées sont par la suite invitées à commenter ledit rapport. Cela sera suivi d'une période de questions et d'observations par les membres d'un organe.

La pratique de plusieurs organes a été de désigner un de leurs membres pour initier les questions dirigées à l'État lors de l'examen. Il agit en quelque sorte comme un rapporteur désigné pour ce pays. Par la suite tout autre membre peut à son tour poser les questions qu'ils ou elles désirent. Dans le cas du Cerd et du Cat, le rôle de ces "rapporteurs par pays" est particulièrement important, car en l'absence de groupe de travail de pré-session pour ces organes c'est à ces rapporteurs que revient la tâche de préparer une liste de questions qu'il ou elle posera à l'État à la suite de l'exposé introductif de l'État.[40]

L'État aura ensuite l'opportunité de répondre à ces questions, normalement lors de la séance suivante qui se tiendra souvent le jour suivant ou l'après-midi, si un examen est survenu le matin. Si cela s'avère impossible pour l'État de répondre à certaines questions dans l'immédiat, les représentants et représentantes de l'État s'engageront à fournir cette information par écrit aussitôt que possible. Le Comité fera part de ses observations en fin d'examen, désignant pour ce faire un membre spécifique, sans que cela empêche tout autre membre d'ajouter à ces commentaires. Les membres de l'État peuvent alors être autorisés à faire des commentaires finaux.

[39] CRC/C/SR.169, para. 41.

[40] Sur le Cerd, voir *Manuel, supra* note 1 à la p. 104. Pour ce qui est du Cat, voir CAT A/45/44, para. 15.

Pour le meilleur ou pour le pire, il apparaît que la technologie moderne a déjà commencé à modifier quelque peu la procédure d'examen. Le 20 juillet 1992, lors de l'examen du deuxième rapport périodique du Pérou par le Cdh, la délégation gouvernementale a proposé la projection d'une vidéocassette destinée à illustrer, selon elle, "le niveau de violence que l'on a atteint dans le pays." Cette proposition de projection a provoqué un long débat entre les membres du Cdh. Certains membres étaient d'avis que la projection d'une telle cassette n'était pas de nature à fournir d'éléments nouveaux au Comité, qu'elle était contraire au règlement intérieur et qu'elle risquait "de créer un dangereux précédent ouvrant la voie à des pratiques regrettables, alors que le temps du Comité est précieux et que le nombre de séances consacrées à l'examen des rapports de chaque État partie est limité." Toutefois la majorité des membres du Comité étaient favorables à l'idée d'autoriser l'État à projeter une vidéocassette de courte durée dans le cadre de sa présentation orale, soulignant que le Comité ne doit pas s'opposer à l'emploi de moyens nouveaux qui pourront l'aider à avancer dans ses travaux. Il a été souligné, sur le fond, que "l'article 40 du Pacte prévoit que les États parties s'engagent à présenter des rapports, mais il n'est pas dit que le recours aux moyens modernes de communication soit exclu. Il s'agit essentiellement d'assurer le respect de la liberté d'expression des États parties." "Par ailleurs, l'État partie est pleinement en droit de présenter au Comité toutes les informations qui lui paraissent utiles et le Comité n'a aucune raison de vouloir se renseigner à l'avance sur la nature des informations qui lui seront communiquées." Il a toutefois été rappelé que, selon l'article 38 du règlement intérieur du Comité, "le Président peut rappeler à l'ordre un orateur dont les remarques n'ont pas trait au sujet en discussion." Le Comité pourrait en conséquence prendre connaissance du contenu de la cassette, étant entendu que le Président pourra interrompre la projection s'il le juge nécessaire."[41] Notons aussi que, lors de l'examen du second rapport périodique du Canada sur les articles 10 à 15 en mai 1993, le Comité a permis à des ONG canadiennes d'exposer le visage de la pauvreté au Canada par le biais de diapositives.[42]

---

[41] CCPR/C/SR.1158, Séance du 20 juillet 1992, para. 1 à 25.

[42] Voir J. Walsh, "La question de la pauvreté au Canada devant l'ONU" (1993) n° 40 L'Écho de l'ONAP aux pp. 2, 15.

On ne peut par ailleurs exclure que dans un avenir rapproché les examens de rapport se fassent par télé-conférence si un organe juge cette méthode appropriée.

E   LA PARTICIPATION DES AGENCES SPÉCIALISÉES ET DES
    ONG À L'EXAMEN

L'apport des ONG est essentiel pour assurer l'efficacité du système d'examen des rapports étatiques par les organes. Dans bien des cas les membres des organes pourront seulement formuler des questions précises parce que des ONG leur auront officieusement fourni de l'information.[43] Par contre celles-ci ne peuvent officiellement déposer des rapports au Comité et ni davantage y prendre la parole. La situation est différente pour ce qui est du Cdesc. Ainsi, puisque certaines ONG ont un statut consultatif avec le Conseil Économique et Social, Conseil d'où le Comité tire son autorité, les ONG peuvent jouer un rôle actif vis-à-vis le Comité.[44] Par exemple, les ONG qui ont un statut consultatif peuvent présenter au Comité des déclarations écrites.[45] De plus, le Comité réserve une partie du premier avant-midi d'une session publique à des présentations orales par des ONG. Il est aussi possible pour une ONG nationale, sans statut consultatif, de s'exprimer oralement devant le Cdesc en relation avec l'examen du rapport de son État si ce dernier y consent.[46] L'article 45 de la Convention sur le droit des enfants a

---

[43] K. T. Samson, *supra* note 1 à la p. 14; un État peut également fournir lui-même à un organe l'information provenant d'ONG. Par exemple, dans le passé le Cdesc a remercié le Canada d'avoir bien voulu transmettre au Comité des documents émanant de sources non gouvernementales (Commentaire du Comité E/C.12/1989/SR.11 examen du 2e rapport du Canada sur les articles 6 à 9, para. 72.

[44] Voir S. Colliver, "International Reporting Procedures" dans *Guide to International Human Rights Practice*, 2e éd. (Philadelphia: UPP, 1992), à la p. 191; sur le statut des ONG, voir aussi M. N. Posner et C. Whittome, "The Status of Human Rights NGOS" (1994) 25 Col. Hum R. L.R. 269.

[45] Voir ECOSOC Résolution 1987/5 du 26 mai 1987, para. 6); art. 69.1 du règlement intérieur du Cdesc.

[46] Tel que mentionné ci-dessus, des ONG canadiennes ont présenté un rapport oralement au Cdesc lors de l'examen du deuxième rapport du Canada sur les articles 10 à 15 du PDESC. Cet exposé des ONG le matin, en présence de la délégation canadienne, a été suivi dans l'après-midi de l'examen du rapport canadien: *supra* note 42, à la p. 2.

aussi été interprété comme permettant au Comité de consulter officiellement les ONG.[47]

Certaines organisations non gouvernementales se sont regroupées pour former des groupes de coordination auprès de certains organes de supervision. D'une part, a été formé le Groupe des ONG pour la Convention relative aux droits de l'enfant qui a nommé un coordonnateur. Un guide a été élaboré sur la façon dont les ONG peuvent fournir des informations complémentaires au Crc. D'autre part, afin d'améliorer la coordination d'informations de sources non gouvernementales et autres, présentées au Cerd, la communauté des ONG a créé une organisation appelée Service d'information sur la lutte contre le racisme.[48]

Quant aux agences spécialisées, le rôle qu'elles peuvent jouer dans la procédure de rapports varie d'un traité à l'autre. D'une part, les agences spécialisées peuvent consulter des rapports et elles-mêmes en préparer. Ainsi, les organes peuvent communiquer à une agence spécialisée les portions de rapports ayant trait à leur domaine de compétence et provenant d'un État membre de cette agence.[49] De plus, le Cdh peut inviter ces agences spécialisées à présenter par écrits des observations sur les portions du rapport qui leur ont été transmises.[50] Quant au PDESC, il prévoit spécifiquement que les agences spécialisées peuvent présenter des rapports sur les progrès accomplis quant à l'observation des obligations du Pacte sans toutefois prévoir que ces rapports soient préparés en réaction à chaque rapport étatique.[51] Pour ce qui est de la CEDAW, elle peut et d'ailleurs les a invité "à soumettre des rapports sur l'application de la Convention dans les domaines qui entrent dans le cadre de leurs activités."[52]

La participation officielle des agences spécialisées lors de l'examen des rapports est en règle générale très limitée ou prohibée. Encore récemment, le Cdh a réitéré qu'il n'y aurait pas de réunion

---

[47] "Moreover, the drafters agreed that the reference to 'competent' in article 45, which authorizes the Committee to invite the 'specialized agencies, UNICEF and other competent bodies to provide expert advice on the Convention's implementation' — includes NGOs." Voir Colliver, *supra* note 45, à la p. 185.

[48] Doc. HRI/MC/1994/2, para. 19.

[49] Voir, par exemple, l'art. 40.3 du PDCP et l'art. 67.1 de son règlement intérieur; voir aussi l'art. 16(2)(b) de PDESC.

[50] Art. 67.2 du règlement intérieur du PDCP.

[51] Art. 18 du PDESC et art. 66 de son règlement intérieur.

[52] Art. 22 du CEDAW.

comme tel avec des agences spécialisées.[53] De même, si de par la CEDAW, les agences spécialisées "ont le droit d'être représentées lors de l'examen de la mise en oeuvre de toute disposition de la présente Convention qui entre dans le cadre de leurs activités,"[54] elles n'y ont pas droit de parole. Par contre, la pratique du Cdesc est toute autre puisque l'article 68 de son règlement intérieur prévoit que les agences spécialisées peuvent désigner des représentants ou représentantes pour participer aux séances du Comité et précise que ceux-ci "peuvent faire des déclarations générales sur des questions liées au domaine de compétence de leur organisation respective à la fin de l'examen par le Comité du rapport de chaque État partie au Pacte."[55] Ainsi, des agences spécialisées, telle l'OIT, sont invitées à commenter oralement le rapport des États devant le Cdesc au moment de l'examen.

F   LES OBSERVATIONS FINALES DES ORGANES

Les observations finales des organes à la suite de l'examen d'un rapport sont reproduites dans leurs rapports annuels.[56] À l'origine la pratique des organes était de rédiger un compte rendu par ailleurs assez détaillé de leur dialogue avec l'État lors de l'examen d'un rapport.[57] Cette formule a été progressivement remplacée ces dernières années par un format plus structuré. Ainsi, les organes ont généralisé la pratique consistant à adopter des observations reflétant les vues de l'ensemble de ses membres sur chacun des rapports des États parties examinés au cours d'une session donnée. En règle générale, ces observations sont présentées de manière uniforme, comportant une introduction d'ordre général suivie de trois chapitres portant respectivement sur les progrès accomplis, sur les facteurs et difficultés faisant obstacle à l'application de la

---

53 CCPR/C/SR.1374 (2 novembre 1994), para. 73.

54 Art. 22 du CEDAW.

55 Art 68 du règlement intérieur du CDESC.

56 La capacité des organes de faire des observations est prévue aux dispositions suivantes des traités: PDCP, art. 40.4; PDESC, art. 21; CERD, art. 9.2; CEDAW, art. 19.4; CAT, art. 19.4; CRC. art. 45 (d).

57 Par exemple, le *Manuel*, *supra* note 1, à la p. 59 décrit ainsi le résumé du rapport d'un État au Cdesc: "Il contient notamment un résumé de l'examen de chaque rapport avec indication des questions soulevées par les membres du Comité, les renseignements fournis par des institutions spécialisées, les réponses données par les représentants des États parties, ainsi que les observations finales faites par les membres du Comité."

convention et sur les principaux sujets de préoccupation et un chapitre final contenant les suggestions et les recommandations à l'intention de l'État partie concerné.[58]

Cette nouvelle approche pour la formulation des observations finales, intimement liée à l'existence de directives de plus en plus précises, signifie des changements non seulement de forme mais surtout de fond, comme l'a constaté le Canada lorsqu'il a été examiné par le Cdesc en 1993. Dans ses observations, sous la rubrique "principaux sujets de préoccupation," le Comité dénonce la pauvreté persistante au Canada en dépit des richesses de ce pays.[59] Expliquant le nouveau système d'observations au média, le rapporteur du Cdesc pour le Canada, Bruce Simma, offrait les commentaires suivants: "Our monitoring system used to be so weak the committee was unable to give any view at all. . .Now, Canada and other countries will have to get used to hearing opinions, some of them not so nice. It just happened to be Canada's turn when we began using the new system."[60]

Cette pratique a maintenant aussi été officialisée par le Cdh qui, lors de sa quarante-neuvième session, le 21 octobre 1994, a modifié le paragraphe 3 de l'article 70 de son règlement intérieur qui se lit maintenant comme suit: "À la suite de l'examen des rapports et des renseignements soumis par un État partie, le Comité peut faire toutes observations qu'il juge appropriées, conformément au paragraphe 4 de l'article 40 du Pacte."[61]

La pratique du Crc se distingue en ce qu'elle peut établir deux types de recommandations aux États parties. D'une part, le Comité peut formuler des suggestions préliminaires et des demandes complémentaires lorsque l'ensemble des questions ayant trait au rap-

[58] Voir, par exemple, E/C.12/1993/19.

[59] Voir Doc. UN E/C.12/1993/19, para. 101 à 113.

[60] Propos rapportés par D. Fischer, "UN Officials Defend Poverty Report but Tories Claim It Is Flawed," *The Gazette* [Montréal] (3 juin 1993), B8. Après la publication des observations finales du Cdesc, le ministre d'État aux Finances et à la Privatisation, à l'époque, John McDermid, a accusé une fin de non-recevoir aux conclusions du comité, déclarant à la Chambre des communes: "Madam Speaker, I have looked at the report of the United Nations committee which is about six pages long. It is seriously flawed. It did not do a great deal of work or investigation and did not understand the situation in Canada at all." Il s'agit là d'une rare occasion où le gouvernement canadien a remis en question la qualité de son dialogue avec un organe responsable d'un traité relatif aux droits de la personne.

[61] CDH, A/49/40, vol. 1, para. 43.

port n'ont pu être examinées ou lorsqu'un rapport plus complet apparaît nécessaire ou encore si le Comité n'a pas reçu de réponses suffisantes à ses questions. D'autre part, lorsque l'examen du rapport est achevé, le Comité formule des conclusions ou des observations finales dans lesquelles il fait des suggestions et des recommandations. Ces conclusions peuvent être assorties de procédures de suivi dont nous discuterons ci-dessous.[62]

G LA PROCÉDURE DE SUIVI

À la suite d'un examen de rapport, les États parties sont invités à indiquer systématiquement dans le rapport suivant les mesures qu'ils ont adoptées pour donner suite aux observations d'un organe.

Au fil des ans, les organes ont développé diverses méthodes pour assurer le suivi d'un examen: demande lors de l'examen d'information supplémentaire de l'État à être fourni à une date ultérieure; participation de l'État à une séance additionnelle; demande d'un nouveau rapport ou d'un rapport intérimaire; demande qu'une question soit adressée dans le prochain rapport périodique de l'État.[63] En outre, un organe peut identifier dans ses observations les secteurs pour lesquels une assistance technique et des services consultatifs sont nécessaires.

Puisque le Comité des droits de l'homme est, des trois organes habilités à considérer des communications individuelles, celui qui reçoit le plus de ces communications et rend le plus de constatations à cet égard, il a aussi instauré depuis 1990, par le biais des rapports périodiques, une procédure pour s'assurer qu'un État donne un suivi à ses constatations. Ainsi, l'État doit, dans son rapport périodique, préciser les mesures qu'il a pris pour réparer les droits d'un individu dont le Comité aurait constaté que les droits auraient été violés.[64]

II PRINCIPALES DÉFICIENCES DE LA PROCÉDURE DES RAPPORTS

A LES RETARDS

Tout retard heurte le dialogue permanent qui doit s'engager entre l'organe de supervision et l'État concerné. Pourtant, en date

---

[62] A/49/41, para. 359 à 361.

[63] Pour une énumération d'options possibles de suivi voir E/C.12/1993/19.

[64] *Manuel, supra* note 1, à la p. 65.

du 30 juin 1994 on constate que, quelque soit le traité, un nombre important de rapports sont en retard.[65] Pour chacun de ceux-ci, à l'exception de la CRC dont l'entrée en vigueur est récente, la majorité des États parties accusent un retard plus ou moins grand.[66] À cet égard le Canada[67] se distingue: des États parties aux six traités

[65] Nombre de rapports reçus et en retard au 30 juin 1994: PDESC: reçus: 231 — en retard: 105; PDCP: reçus: 316 — en retard: 98; CERD: reçus: 739 — en retard: 381; CEDAW: reçus: 169 — en retard: 117; CAT: reçus: 67 — en retard: 47; CRC: reçus 41 — en retard: 79. Voir HRI/MC/1994/3.

[66] Nombre d'États parties en retard au 30 juin 1994: PDESC: 93 États sur 129 accusaient un retard — 10 de ces États devaient 2 rapports et un en devait 3; PDCP: 77 États sur 127 accusaient un retard — 16 États devaient 2 rapports et 2 en devaient 3; CERD: 124 États sur 139 accusaient un retard — 84 États devaient plus de 2 rapports et 30 d'entre eux 5 rapports et plus; CEDAW: 80 États sur 133 accusaient un retard — 14 États devaient 2 rapports et 12 en devaient 3; CAT: 45 États sur 82 accusaient un retard — 3 États devaient 2 rapports; CRC: 79 États sur 160 accusait un retard — 10 États devaient 2 rapports — 1 en devait 3. Voir HRI/MC/1994/3.

[67] Référence des rapports présentés par le Canada et des séances d'examen par les différents organes de supervision: *Comité des Droits de l'Homme: Rapport initial* CCPR/C/1/Add. 43, volumes 1 et 2; Examen par le Comité CCPR/C/SR. 205, 206, 207, 208 et 211. *Rapport supplémentaire* CCPR/C/1/Add. 64 (présenté après l'adoption de la Charte canadienne des droits et libertés en avril 1982); Examen par le Comité CCPR/C/SR. 558 à 560 et 562. *Deuxième rapport périodique* CCPR/C/51/Add. 1 et *Troisième rapport périodique* CCPR/C/64/Add. 1; Examen conjoint par le Comité CCPR/C/SR. 1010 à 1013. *Comité des droits économiques, sociaux et culturels: Rapport initial sur les articles 6 à 9* E/1978/8/Add.32; Examen par le Groupe de travail E/1982/W.G.1/SR. 1 et 2. *Rapport initial sur les articles 10 à 12* E/1980/6/Add.32; Examen par le Groupe de travail E/1984/W.G.1/SR. 4 et 6. *Rapport initial sur les articles 13 à 15* E/1982/3/Add.34; Examen par le Groupe de travail E/1986/W.G.1/SR. 13, 15 et 16. *Deuxième rapport périodique sur les articles 6 à 9* E/1984/7/Add. 28; Examen par le Comité E/C.12/1984/S.R. 8 et 11. *Deuxième rapport périodique sur les articles 10 à 15* E/1990/6/Add. 3; Examen par le Comité E/C.12/1993/S.R. 5, 6 et 18. *Comité pour l'élimination de la discrimination raciale: Rapport initial* CERD/C/R.25/Add.5 et Coor.1; Examen par le Comité CERD/C/SR. 97 et 98. *Deuxième rapport périodique* CERD/C/R.53/Add.6; Examen par le Comité CERD/C/SR. 188. *Troisième rapport périodique* CERD/C/ R.78/Add.6; Examen par le Comité CERD/C/SR. 297 et 298. *Quatrième rapport périodique* CERD/C/52; Examen par le Comité CERD/C/SR. 425 et 426. *Cinquième rapport périodique* CERD/C/50/Add.6 et Add.7; Examen par le Comité CERD/C/SR. 522. *Sixième rapport périodique* CERD/C/76/Add.6 et Add.7; Examen par le Comité CERD/C/SR. 633 et 634. *Septième rapport périodique* CERD/C/107/Add.8; *Huitième rapport périodique* CERD/C/132/Add.3; Examen conjoint par le Comité CERD/C/SR. 778 et 781. *Neuvième rapport périodique* CERD/C/159/Add.3; *Dixième rapport périodique* CERD/C/185/Add.3; Examen conjoint par le Comité CERD/C/SR. 905 et 906. *Onzième rapport périodique* CERD/C/210/Add.2; *Douzième rapport périodique* CERD/C/240/Add.1; Examen

étudiés, il était parmi les trois à ne pas avoir accumulé de retard en date du 30 juin 1994.[68]

Diverses raisons ont été suggérées pour expliquer l'énormité des retards: (a) le fait qu'un État partie à plusieurs traités ait une multiplicité d'obligations de préparer des rapports,[69] (b) la méconnaissance du devoir qu'ont les États parties de présenter de tels rapports,[70] (c) le manque de personnel compétent au sein de l'État pour la préparation de ces rapports,[71] (d) l'absence de structure administrative efficace et de coordination entre les divers organismes administratifs chargés des mêmes questions,[72] (e) le manque de volonté politique pour remplir ses obligations à cet égard.[73]

---

conjoint par le Comité CERD/C/SR. 1043 et 1044. *Comité pour l'élimination des discriminations à l'égard des femmes: Rapport initial* CEDAW/C/5/Add.16; Examen par le Comité CEDAW/C/SR. 48, 61 et 62. *Deuxième rapport périodique* CEDAW/C/13/Add. 11, volumes 1 et 2; Examen par le Comité CEDAW/C/SR. 167. *Troisième rapport périodique* CEDAW/C/CAN/3. *Comité contre la torture: Rapport initial* CAT/C/5/Add. 15; Examen par le Comité CAT/C/SR. 32 et 33. *Deuxième rapport périodique* CAT/C/17/Add. 5; Examen par le Comité CAT/C/SR. 139 et 140. *Comité des droits de l'enfant: Rapport initial* CRC/C/11/Add.3. Voir HRI/MC/1994/3. Sur les rapports canadiens voir D. Turp, "La préparation et la présentation des rapports du Canada en application des traités relatifs aux droits et libertés," (1986) 24 A.C.D.I. 161; D. Turp, "L'Examen des rapports périodiques du Canada en application du Pacte international relatif aux droits économiques, sociaux et culturels," (1991) 29 A.C.D.I. 330.

68 L'Arménie et la Suède sont les deux autres États. Si l'on considère les États parties à au moins trois des six traités, seul la Géorgie vient s'ajouter à la liste d'États non retardataires. Voir HRI/MC/1994/3.

69 Rapport annuel du Cdh, AGNU Doc. off., 49ᵉ sess., Doc. A/49/40, para. 51. Voir aussi F. Pocar, *Comment favoriser l'application universelle des normes et instruments concernant les droits de l'homme*, Doc. NU A/CONF.157/PC/60/ Add.60/Add.4, para. 19. Une auteure, A. Manin, "De quelques autorités internationales indépendantes" (1989) 35 Ann. fran. dr. int. 229 à la p. 248 souligne, à juste titre, que ce motif est peu convaincant: "Plusieurs raisons ont été avancées pour expliquer les défaillances des États. L'une d'entre elles ne vaut pas pour rendre compte d'une situation constatée dès la mise en place du Comité pour l'élimination de la discrimination raciale et alors qu'il était le seul organe de supervision de ce type à fonctionner."

70 Rapport annuel du Cdh, *ibid.*

71 *Ibid.*

72 *Ibid.*

73 *Ibid.* "Le Président du Comité pour l'élimination de la discrimination raciale, en précisant que certains États n'avaient même pas soumis un seul rapport depuis leur adhésion n'a sûrement pas tort d'en déduire une absence de volonté politique." A. Manin, *supra* note 69, à la p. 248.

Les règlements intérieurs des divers organes prévoient un nombre limité de mesures que peuvent prendre les organes en cas de retards. Dans un premier temps, un organe peut rappeler à un État son obligation de produire un rapport.[74] En pratique, les organes font des appels répétés aux États retardataires. Si un appel reste sans réponse, un organe peut en faire mention dans son rapport annuel.[75] Ces mesures se sont toutefois avérées nettement insuffisantes, puisque le nombre de rapports en retard a continué de s'accroître. Confronté à cet état de choses, les organes ont dû réagir pour éviter que ne soit irrémédiablement minée toute la procédure d'examen des rapports. Des mesures additionnelles ont été prises, telles des recommandations aux réunions des États parties, des contacts avec les représentants permanents des États,[76] la possibilité de combiner tous les rapports dus dans un seul document.[77] D'autres actions beaucoup plus radicales ont été envisagées dont celle de suspendre le droit de vote des retardataires lors des réunions des États parties.[78]

Certains organes, comme le Cerd et le Cdesc, ont adopté une procédure permettant l'examen de la situation d'un État, même en l'absence de présentation d'un rapport. Il s'agit pour chaque comité de sélectionner les États parties qui ont accumulé le plus de retard dans la présentation de leurs rapports, puis de notifier à ces États que le comité va examiner leur situation à l'une de ses futures sessions, et enfin examiner, en l'absence de rapport, la situation des États concernés à la lumière de toute information dont il dispose. Le comité autorise son Président, si un État s'engage à présenter un rapport, à attendre ce rapport et à remettre, dans un délai rappro

---

[74] Art. 69.1 du règlement intérieur du PDCP; art. 59.1 du règlement intérieur du PDESC, où le Comité peut recommander au Conseil économique et social d'adresser un rappel à l'État; art 66.1 du règlement intérieur du CERD; art.47.2 du règlement intérieur du CEDAW; art 64.1 du règlement intérieur du CAT; art. 67.1 du règlement intérieur du CRC.

[75] Art. 69.2 du règlement intérieur du PDCP; art. 59.2 du règlement intérieur du PDESC; art 66.2 du règlement intérieur du CERD; art. 47.3 du règlement intérieur du CEDAW; art. 64.2 du règlement intérieur du CAT; art. 67.2 du règlement intérieur du CRC.

[76] E. Tistounet, ''Amélioration des procédures conventionnelles des Nation-Unies en matière de droits de l'homme'' (1993) 5:5-6 Revue Universelle des Droits de l'Homme, à la p. 149.

[77] Voir, par exemple, le Rapport du Cerd, Doc. off. AG NU, 48ᵉ sess., supp. n° 18, Doc. A/48/18, para. 30.

[78] Tistounet, *supra* note 76, à la p. 149.

ché, l'examen de la situation du pays.[79] Ainsi, à ses quarantième et quarante-deuxième sessions, le Cerd a inscrit à l'ordre du jour la situation de vingt-six États qui n'avaient pas présenté leur rapport depuis longtemps. La situation de dix-neuf de ces États a été examinée en l'absence de délégation, cinq États se sont engagés à soumettre un rapport prochainement, et un seul État a envoyé un représentant lors de l'examen de sa situation.[80]

B LA PÉRIODICITÉ

Pour que l'obligation de produire des rapports ne constitue pas une simple exigence de forme, mais permette réellement à un Comité de constater l'évolution de la situation des droits de la personne dans un État donné, il est impératif que les États soient appelés à présenter de tels rapports sur une base suffisamment régulière.[81] Par contre, il apparaît improductif de demander aux États, en particulier ceux parties à plusieurs traités imposant une obligation de rapporter, de produire de nouveaux rapports dans des délais relativement rapprochés. Non seulement cela risquerait-il de trop taxer les ressources des États plus démunis mais également les États en général pourraient ne pas y investir à tout coup le temps, les montants et l'énergie que requière un bon rapport. Il pourrait aussi s'avérer difficile pour des organes aux ressources limitées d'adéquatement examiner ces rapports.[82]

C LES RESSOURCES LIMITÉES DES ORGANES

Les retards ne sont pas qu'imputables aux États. Les comités ont accumulé des délais souvent importants dans l'examen des rapports. Ce décalage n'encourage certes pas les États à présenter leurs rapports à la date fixée. De plus, ces retards ont entraîné "divers effets préjudiciables, en particulier les rapports perdaient de leur actualité et obligeaient l'État partie à fournir des renseignements complémentaires substantiels."[83]

79 Pour le Cdesc, voir E/C.12/1993/19, para. 44; pour le Cerd, voir Rapport du CERD, Doc. off. AG NU, 48ᵉ sess., supp. n° 18, Doc. A/48/18, para. 28.

80 Voir Tistounet, *supra* note 76 à la p. 149; sur cette pratique du Cerd, Colliver rapporte: "The effort was modestly successful in encouraging delinquent governments to submit information" (Colliver, *supra* note 45, à la p. 179).

81 Samson, *supra* note 1, à la p. 4.

82 *Ibid.*

83 Quatrième réunion des présidents, A/47/628, para. 16.

Ces délais s'expliquent en grande partie par le peu de ressources consacrées aux organes.[84] Ainsi, la durée de leur rencontres annuelles est limitée, variant entre deux et neuf semaines[85] durant laquelle ils doivent se décharger de toutes leurs fonctions dont l'examen de rapports, la formulation d'observations générales et, pour trois d'entre eux, l'examen de plaintes individuelles et inter-étatiques. Le montant d'heures consacrées à l'examen de rapports varie selon les organes de trois à neuf heures.[86]

Devant l'incapacité des organes de s'acquitter de leurs fonctions dans les délais impartis, l'ONU a dû à l'occasion permettre la tenue de sessions additionnelles.[87] Ces solutions ad hoc ne remplacent pas le besoin d'accorder aux organes des moyens suffisants pour

---

84 Il faut aussi reconnaître que le mandat de certains organes est tellement ambitieux qu'il sera difficile à remplir quelles que soient les ressources. "Certains comités se sont vus attribuer des tâches incommensurables. On pense tout particulièrement au Comité des droits économiques, sociaux et culturels. Étant donné l'ambition démesurée de l'instrument dont il est chargé de superviser l'application, il nous paraît qu'il sera forcément pris en défaut, sinon dans son sérieux, du moins dans l'obligation pratique de se choisir des priorités" (Dormenval, *supra* note 1, à la p. 123).

85 Art. 1 du règlement intérieur du Cdesc: "Le Comité des droits économiques, sociaux et culturels se réunit chaque année pendant une période ne dépassant pas trois semaines ou pour une durée fixée par le Conseil économique et social compte tenu du nombre de rapports que le Comité aura à examiner." Bien que l'art. 2.1 du règlement intérieur du Cdh prévoit que le Comité "tient normalement deux sessions ordinaires par an," l'article 1 prévoit que le Comité tiendra le nombre de sessions nécessaires à l'accomplissement de ses fonctions. En pratique le Comité tient trois sessions par an, d'une durée de trois semaines chacune. Voir *Manuel, supra* note 1, à la p. 89; le Cerd tient normalement deux séances par année (art. 1 du règlement intérieur) de trois semaines chacune, bien que des difficultés financières ont souvent bouleversé l'horaire de cet organe: voir *Manuel, supra* note 1, à la p. 102. Exceptionnellement, la CEDAW prévoit, à l'art. 20.1 de la Convention même, que la CEDAW "se réunit normalement pendant une période de deux semaines au plus chaque année"; l'art. 2 du règlement intérieur du Cat prévoit 2 sessions qui normalement durent 2 semaine chacune; l'art. 2 du règlement intérieur du CRC prévoit qu'il tient deux sessions par année, normalement de trois semaines chacune.

86 Par exemple, pour le Cdesc, 3 séances de 3 heures chacune: voir *Manuel, supra* note 1 à la p. 59; pour Cdcp, 2 à 3 séances de 3 heures chacune: voir *Manuel, supra* note 1 à la p. 90.

87 Par exemple le Conseil Économique et Social a autorisé, à titre exceptionnel, une séance supplémentaire de 3 semaines du Cdesc au premier semestre de 1994 ainsi qu'une réunion de 3 jours du groupe de travail de pré-session du Comité: voir E/C.12/1993/19.

accomplir leur tâche ou de risquer que le système perde toute créd-
ibilité.[88]

D LA COMPOSITION DE LA DÉLÉGATION DE L'ÉTAT LORS DE L'EXAMEN DU RAPPORT

L'importance qu'un État attache à son obligation de présenter
des rapports sera reflétée par le calibre de la délégation qui le
représentera à l'examen. Bien que plusieurs auteurs du *Manuel
relatif à l'établissement des rapports sur les droits de l'homme* insistent sur
l'importance de la qualité de la délégation étatique,[89] en pratique
les organes ont formulé peu de remarques officielles à propos de la
composition de la délégation de l'État qu'ils invitent à participer à
l'examen du rapport. Le Comité des droits de l'enfant a toutefois
donné certaines indications en ce domaine en souhaitant que l'État
soit représenté par une délégation impliquée concrètement dans
les décisions stratégiques dans le domaine de la Convention.[90]

Un incident important a eu lieu, lors de la treizième session du
Comité contre la torture, au sujet de la délégation marocaine venue
présenter en novembre 1994 le rapport initial du Maroc. En effet,
réuni à huis clos, le Comité a fait part de sa préoccupation après la
participation en qualité de membre de la délégation marocaine de
Yousfi Kaddouri, directeur de l'administration centrale à la Direction Générale de la Sûreté nationale marocaine. Selon l'Organisation Marocaine des Droits de l'Homme, il est un "ancien responsable du centre de détention et de torture situé au Derb Moulay à
Casablanca" et a été formellement reconnu par trois de ses victimes.[91] Devant la gravité de telles allégations émanant d'organisa-

---

88 Les remarques suivantes sont à cet effet éloquentes: "Le succès de la Convention dépend aussi de l'action du Comité pour l'élimination de la discrimination
à l'égard des femmes, qui est principalement chargé d'examiner les rapports
périodiques des États parties et de formuler des recommandations générales
sur cette base. . . . [B]eaucoup d'États sont actuellement en retard dans la
présentation de leurs rapports."

89 Sur la désirabilité d'un délégation compétente voir le *Manuel, supra* note 1 aux
pp. 57-58, 89 et 139.

90 Projet d'observation générale débattu le 11 octobre 1994 sur la procédure de
rapport (CRC/C/SR.169, para. 15).

91 Voir "Un tortionnaire, délégué au Comité de l'ONU contre la torture" *Le
Monde* (26 novembre 1994) 4. Au cours de la séance d'examen du rapport du
Maroc, Y. Kaddouri avait notamment déclaré "que les responsables de la police
marocaine sont fermement décidés à consolider, au Maroc, l'État de droit et à

tions non gouvernementales, le Comité, choqué par cette situation, a saisi le gouvernement marocain pour lui faire part de sa préoccupation à ce propos. À la suite de cette intervention, les autorités marocaines ont fourni au Comité une réponse dont la teneur n'a pas été rendue publique par le gouvernement.[92]

Il se peut qu'un État, ayant préparé un rapport et ayant été convoqué pour examen par un organe, omette volontairement ou par indifférence d'envoyer une délégation. Dans ces conditions, des organes ont décidé qu'elles pouvaient quand même décider de procéder à l'examen du rapport.[93]

E   LA PARTIALITÉ DES RAPPORTS

Puisqu'il s'agit ici de rapports étatiques préparés presque toujours sans collaboration d'organismes indépendants, il n'est guère surprenant que l'information y est souvent présentée de manière à ce que l'État fasse bonne figure. À la limite l'État peut détourner ce mécanisme en le limitant à l'auto-justification.[94] Il aurait été naïf de s'attendre à autre chose, car peu d'États sont enclins à laisser passer une occasion d'avancer leurs propres intérêts, quelle que soit la tribune. Par conséquent, les membres des organes ont souvent la tâche d'exposer, dans des termes diplomatiques, des réalités

---

assurer le respect des droits de l'homme. On signale parfois des écarts de conduites ou 'bavures,' mais ils ne sont pas le fait de l'institution et toutes garanties sont données aux victimes pour qu'elles puissent poursuivre les coupables. Lorsque les faits sont établis, les coupables sont sanctionnés par l'administration avant d'être présentés à la justice" (Séance du mercredi 16 novembre 1994, CAT/C/SR.204, para. 15).

92 Dans ses conclusions rendues publiques après l'examen du rapport marocain, le Cat indique qu'il est "préoccupé par des allégations de torture et mauvais traitements reçues de diverses organisations non gouvernementales, pratiques qui seraient constatées dans divers lieux de détention et, en particulier, dans les locaux de la police. Le Comité est aussi préoccupé par certaines insuffisances dans l'adoption de mesures préventives adéquates pour combattre efficacement la torture, notamment une certaine timidité constatée pour la diligence des enquêtes et la traduction des auteurs desdits actes devant les tribunaux dont l'indépendance doit être préservée. Cette situation crée une impression de relative impunité des auteurs de ces infractions, impunité préjudiciable à la bonne application des dispositions de la Convention contre la torture" (séance du mercredi 16 novembre 1994, Cat/C/SR.204/Add.2, para. 15).

93 Voir *supra* note 32, para 347.

94 Voir H. Haug, "Instruments de droit international pour lutter contre la torture" (1989) n° 775 Revue Internationale de la Croix-Rouge 18.

cachées. Il ne leur est pas toujours facile de s'acquitter de cette fonction, en particulier lorsque des délégations gouvernementales tentent, pour éviter un examen trop critique de la situation de leur État, de noyer les membres du Comité dans un flot d'informations nouvelles extrêmement spécifiques et détaillées ou au contraire trop générales. Elles espèrent ainsi focaliser l'attention des experts sur des questions peu essentielles tout en sachant que le temps d'examen de chaque rapport est limité.

Enfin, un réel handicap de ces procédures est l'absence de capacité indépendante d'enquête des organes. Dans ces circonstances, les observations formulées par l'organe sont limitées par le caractère partiel de l'échange de vue avec les États et par l'écart inévitable avec la réalité.

III LES RÉFORMES ENVISAGÉES ET DE NOUVELLES PROPOSITIONS
POUR AMÉLIORER LE SYSTÈME DE PRÉSENTATION ET D'EXAMEN
DES RAPPORTS

Dès 1982, les problèmes relatifs à l'application effective des instruments internationaux relatifs aux droits de la personne ont fait l'objet de nombreux examens à travers les multiples instances des Nations Unies, et notamment de l'Assemblée générale.[95] Puis, cet effort de réflexion a été systématisé lors des réunions des présidents des organes créés en vertu de traités relatifs aux droits de la personne. De plus, en 1988, la Commission des Droits de l'Homme a nommé un expert chargé d'étudier "les méthodes envisageables à long terme pour améliorer le fonctionnement des organes qui ont été créés en vertu d'instruments des Nations Unies relatifs aux droits de l'homme."[96]

Dans l'ensemble de cette démarche, la Conférence de Vienne a constitué une étape importante, notamment en demandant "instamment aux organismes et programmes des Nations Unies de coopérer pour renforcer, rationaliser et simplifier les activités qu'ils

[95] Doc. AG NU, Rés. 37/44, adoptée le 3 décembre 1982. Voir aussi Rés. 47/111 et 48/120.

[96] Commission des Droits de l'Homme, Rés. 1989/47 du 6 mars 1989. C'est Philip Alston qui a été nommé expert indépendant. Sa première étude est parue en novembre 1989 (A/44/668) et a été actualisée en 1993, à l'occasion de la Conférence de Vienne (A/CONF.157/PC/62/Add.11/Rev.1, 22 avril 1993).

exécutaient dans le domaines des droits de l'homme.''[97] La Conférence de Vienne avait aussi recommandé à l'Assemblée générale de créer le poste de Haut commissaire des Nations Unies aux Droits de l'Homme qui doit jouer un rôle actif pour impulser et veiller à l'application des réformes dont le but est d'''améliorer la coordination des activités, de renforcer l'efficacité des mécanismes dans le domaine des droits de l'homme et élaborer des directives visant à adapter les dits mécanismes aux besoins actuels et futurs.''[98] À cet égard, le Haut Commissaire ''va entreprendre avec les divers organes concernés, une analyse approfondie des mécanismes de mise en oeuvre, en vue d'en améliorer l'efficacité et la productivité'' et ''considère que le suivi des décisions et recommandations adoptées par ces organes et organismes constitue l'une de ses principales obligations.''[99] Dans cette optique, il s'est adressé en septembre 1994 à la cinquième réunion des présidents des organes de supervision avec lesquels il a eu une discussion.

Il est important de souligner les efforts déjà entrepris par les organes de supervision pour améliorer les procédures de présentation et d'examen des rapports. Par leurs pratiques, comme par l'élaboration de leur règlement intérieur, la rédaction de directives ou d'observations destinées aux États et la mise en place de procédures ad hoc ou de méthodes de suivi, les comités ont constamment et considérablement enrichi le système des rapports. Ainsi, sans que soit remis en cause le cadre conventionnel, les comités peuvent disposer de capacités d'initiatives non négligeables pour améliorer et adapter les procédures.

Dans cette optique, les réunions des présidents des comités ont été des moments importants de confrontation des pratiques et des règles suivies par chaque organe. Elles ont permis d'amorcer une coordination active des différents comités qui peut notamment déboucher sur une coopération thématique. Ainsi, en 1995, au

97 *Questions relatives aux Droits de l'Homme: Application et suivi méthodiques de la Déclaration et du Programme d'action de Vienne,* Suivi de la Conférence mondiale sur les Droits de l'Homme, Rapport du Secrétaire général, Doc. A/49/668 du 15 novembre 1994, para. 7.

98 Doc. A/49/668 du 15 novembre 1994, para. 15. L'Assemblée générale a approuvé la nomination de M. José Ayala-Lasso, qui est devenu le premier Haut Commissaire aux Droits de l'Homme le 14 février 1994 et a pris ses fonctions le 5 avril 1994. Sur le Haut Commissaire, voir A. Clapham, ''Creating the High Commissioner for Human Rights: The Outside Story'' (1994) 5:4 European Journal of International Law 556.

99 Doc. A/49/668 du 15 novembre 1994, para. 15 et 163.

cours de la sixième réunion des présidents, devraient être débattus les "moyens de contrôler plus efficacement l'application des droits fondamentaux de la femme."[100]

De l'ensemble de ces travaux, se dégagent plusieurs propositions de réformes et d'amélioration des mécanismes de supervision. Ces propositions doivent, nous semble-t-il, être classées à deux niveaux.[101] D'une part, les propositions d'amélioration des procédures qui sont engagées ou peuvent être envisagées sans remise en cause du cadre conventionnel. Dans ce cadre, à côté des réformes engagées sur recommandation des présidents des comités (1), nous avons souhaité formuler certaines suggestions qui seraient réalisables pour améliorer le système des rapports (2). D'autre part, certaines réformes proposées imposent par leur caractère global l'accord de l'ensemble des États parties, et des modifications substantielles et coordonnées des traités (3).

A DES AMÉLIORATIONS EN COURS DE RÉALISATION

Plusieurs des propositions formulées par les présidents des comités restent encore à réaliser, et notamment l'examen de la situation des États malgré la non-présentation des rapports, la préparation d'un dossier unique par État et la révision du manuel relatif à l'établissement des rapports.

Ainsi, lors de leur cinquième rencontre, les présidents des organes de supervision ont proposé que la procédure d'examen de la situation des États malgré la non-présentation des rapports, déjà adoptée par le Cerd et le Cdesc, soit étendue à l'ensemble des comités.[102] En effet, à leur avis, même en l'absence de rapport, il est possible d'obtenir à partir d'autres sources appropriées des informations suffisantes pour entreprendre un examen, si possible sous forme de dialogue.[103] Toutefois, la généralisation de cette pratique est loin de faire l'unanimité notamment au sein du Comité des Droits de l'Homme et du Comité contre la torture. Par exemple, sachant qu'il est très peu probable qu'un État accepte d'être représenté lors de l'examen de sa situation alors qu'il n'a pas présenté de rapport,

---

100 Cinquième réunion des présidents, Doc. A/49/537, para. 58. Sur la coopération entre comités, voir aussi quatrième réunion, Doc. A/47/628, para. 26 et 27.22

101 Les réformes étudiées dans ce document ne prétendent pas être exhaustives.

102 Cinquième réunion des présidents du 19 au 23 septembre 1994, Doc. A/49/537 du 19 octobre 1994, para. 18.

103 Quatrième réunion des présidents, Doc. A/47/628 du 10 novembre 1992, para. 71.

Madame Higgins, membre du Comité des Droits de l'Homme, s'est opposée à cette proposition dans les termes suivants:

En l'absence d'une délégation [de l'État], l'examen se réduirait à un échange de vues entre les membres du Comité, et ne permettrait pas de confronter les informations dont dispose le Comité avec celles de l'État partie. En outre, certains États parties pourraient prendre prétexte de cette disposition pour critiquer le Comité, au motif que ses informations ne seraient pas exactes, qu'il n'aurait pas jugé utile d'entendre leur point de vue, etc. Les autorités de l'État partie intéressé pourraient ainsi traiter le Comité comme une ONG, voire lui accorder moins de considération, puisque le Comité, contrairement aux ONG, ne prend pas ses informations directement à la source.[104]

Cette question touchant à la compétence des organes de supervision a fait récemment l'objet d'un très intéressant débat au sein du Comité contre la torture. Pour le Président et d'autres experts, l'obstacle à l'introduction de cette pratique est essentiellement juridique, car, "la Convention ne prévoit rien que le Comité puisse faire si l'État partie n'a pas présenté son rapport dans le délai prévu" et "le fait que d'autres comités chargés d'examiner la situation des droits de l'homme procèdent ainsi ne suffit pas à justifier que le Comité contre la torture fasse de même, en l'absence des bases juridiques nécessaires." Pour un autre membre du Comité, M. Lorenzo, au contraire,

la Convention n'énonce pas non plus de disposition qui limite expressément les compétences du Comité. Le raisonnement par induction autorise à conclure à une compétence générale du Comité l'habilitant à contrôler l'application de la Convention, compétence générale qui n'est pas explicitement définie comme telle, mais qui découle de l'ensemble des dispositions de la Convention. Et cette compétence générale est susceptible d'extension précisément en vertu des dispositions générales de l'acte constitutif du Comité: s'il manque de moyens pour entreprendre diverses actions (faire connaître l'existence de la Convention, se réunir dans d'autres pays, se rendre dans les pays qui l'invitent à le faire), il doit en demander à l'ONU, mais il n'a pas à restreindre de lui-même sa propre compétence. M. Lorenzo pense donc que le Comité a compétence pour examiner la situation régnant dans un État partie en matière de torture sans avoir à s'appuyer sur l'article 19 ni sur l'article 24 (de la Convention),[105] parce qu'il a par principe compétence pour contrôler l'application de la Convention. Il peut par conséquent inventer des procédures non

---

[104] CCPR/C/SR.1384/Add.1 du 18 novembre 1994.

[105] L'article 19 de la Convention contre la torture a trait à l'obligation des États de présenter leur rapport au Comité. L'article 24 concerne la présentation du rapport annuel du Comité aux États parties et à l'Assemblée générale des Nations Unies.

expressément prévues dans la Convention . . . Quand un État partie est en
retard dans la présentation de son rapport, le Comité peut certes signaler le
fait à l'Assemblée générale et aux autres États dans le rapport annuel prévu
à l'article 24 de la Convention, mais il peut certainement aussi, sans
invoquer l'article 19, consacrer une séance à l'examen d'informations
fournies par des organisations non gouvernementales qui seraient invitées à
participer à ces travaux, ainsi que les informations éventuellement envoyées
par l'État partie qui serait également invité à participer à ces travaux.

Alors que traditionnellement on attribue la compétence d'examen
de la situation d'un État sans présentation de rapport sur le fondement du non-respect des obligations conventionnelles par les États
et qu'on la rattache donc expressément aux dispositions du traité
relatives aux rapports,[106] l'expert du Comité contre la torture va
plus loin, car selon lui cette pratique ne découle pas de dispositions
précises du traité, mais d'une interprétation téléologique de la
Convention en vertu de laquelle le comité dispose d'une compétence implicite et générale pour contrôler l'application du traité.
Toutefois, ces compétences ne sauraient être illimitées. En effet,
comme le faisait remarquer un autre membre du Comité: "Mais
quelles seraient les limites de cette compétence? Comment le Comité peut-il 'contrôler' l'application de la Convention? Le terme
'contrôler' a une acception très large et dès que l'on sort du cadre
strict de la Convention, il faut user de prudence."[107]

Quant à la réalisation d'un dossier unique par État, le secrétariat
général a commencé à préparer des dossiers par pays pour différents
comités. Pour mieux assumer l'examen de la situation d'un pays et

106 De même, c'est sur le fondement du manquement des États à leurs obligations
conventionnelles que les comités ont fondé leur compétence à porter à la
connaissance de l'Assemblée générale les retards des États, compétence par
ailleurs affirmée dans leur règlement intérieur (voir *supra* notes 74 et 75).
Certains experts soutenaient au contraire qu'il appartenait à la seule réunion des
États parties de se prononcer et de prendre les mesures appropriées (Comité des
Droits de l'Homme, 201e séance, 21 mars 1980, Annuaire 1979-80, p. 307 et s.).
"La première solution a prévalu à juste titre, en raison des compétences inhérentes des organes de supervision. En effet, l'obligation prise par les États de
présenter des rapports s'appuie sur une des clauses dont les comités surveillent
l'application et, indiscutablement la plus importante d'entre elles puisqu'elle
conditionne l'ensemble de l'activité de supervision. En outre, la présentation des
rapports par les États étant essentielle pour que les comités s'acquittant
eux-mêmes de leur mandat, la pratique suivie est irréprochable" (Manin, *supra*
note 69 aux pp. 247-48).
107 Document Cat/C/SR/206 Add. 1 du 17 novembre 1994, para. 6 à 18. Sur le
débat au sein du Comité contre la torture, voir aussi Cat/C/SR.176 du 22 avril
1994, para. 31-39.

faciliter le travail du secrétariat, les présidents des organes de supervision souhaitent que chaque comité dispose, lorsqu'il examine le rapport d'un État, d'un dossier unique par pays qui comprend la totalité des documents ONU présentant un intérêt direct, sources non gouvernementales et articles de presse pertinents.[108]

Enfin, les présidents des organes de comités souhaitent que le manuel relatif à l'établissement des rapports sur les Droits de l'Homme soit révisé notamment pour y intégrer un nouveau chapitre relatif à la Convention relative aux droits de l'enfant, ainsi que pour tenir compte des pratiques nouvelles adoptées par les différents organes.[109] Les présidents ont souhaité que ce manuel soit présenté sous forme de feuillets volants avec mise à jour régulière et soit assorti d'un index.[110]

B   DES SUGGESTIONS NOUVELLES

Pour alléger le travail des comités, il nous paraît souhaitable de généraliser les *groupes de travail* de pré-session auxquels pourraient participer les institutions spécialisées et les autres organes des Nations Unies concernées. Avant l'examen du rapport en séance publique, le groupe de travail pourrait adresser à l'État des *demandes d'explication*, notamment si certaines insuffisances étaient constatées dans le rapport envoyé par l'État ou si certains compléments d'informations apparaissaient nécessaires au vu des remarques reçues de toutes sources extérieures. Le groupe de travail pourrait, si nécessaire, demander à l'État de répondre *à l'avance et par écrit* à ces demandes d'explication. Il est en effet souhaitable d'introduire une certaine dose de procédure écrite préalable dans le processus d'examen des rapports, pour que, lors de la séance publique, un dialogue véritable puisse avoir lieu entre le comité et la délégation.[111] Dans cette optique, le groupe de travail pourrait

---

[108] Quatrième réunion des présidents, A/47/628 du 10 novembre 1992, para. 54. Voir aussi HRI/MC/1994/2, Rapport du Secrétaire Général, 12 août 1994, para. 17.

[109] Cinquième réunion des présidents du 19 au 23 septembre 1994, Document A/49/537 du 19 octobre 1994, para. 57.

[110] *Ibid.*

[111] Ainsi E. Tistounet note qu'il faut veiller à ce que la majeure partie de la séance d'examen du rapport ne soit pas consacrée uniquement à la présentation de son rapport par l'État partie et à la réponse à la liste de questions transmises par le groupe de travail (*supra* note 76 à la p. 152).

saisir l'organe conventionnel ou son président qui pourrait adresser des *observations préliminaires* à l'État concerné.

Il nous semble aussi possible que *l'examen des rapports étatiques soit assuré en groupe de travail.* De la même façon que le Conseil économique et social chargé conventionnellement de l'examen des rapporteurs a créé en son sein d'abord un groupe de travail, puis le Comité des droits économiques, sociaux et culturels, les organes créés par les autres traités des Nations Unies pourraient confier l'examen des rapports à des groupes de travail désignés en leur sein et qui devraient leur en rendre compte. De même, des comités prévoient dans leurs règlements intérieurs la possibilité de créer des organes subsidiaires pour l'accomplissement de leurs fonctions.[112] Ainsi, lors d'une session, un comité pourrait désigner en son sein plusieurs groupes de travail pour examiner simultanément la situation de plusieurs États, augmentant ainsi considérablement ses capacités de travail. Toutefois, à tout moment de la procédure, l'organe conventionnel ou, en cas d'urgence, son président pourrait décider, au vu de l'importance d'une question ou de difficultés particulières, de confier l'examen du rapport en séance publique à l'ensemble du Comité.

Dans le cas de l'examen du rapport étatique par un groupe de travail, ce groupe serait habilité, au nom de l'organe de supervision, à formuler publiquement des *observations immédiates* à la délégation de l'État concerné. Le groupe de travail ferait rapport à la prochaine réunion plénière de l'organe de supervision qui adopterait une *évaluation générale* qui serait transmise à l'État et rendue publique. Dans le cadre de la procédure, les décisions majeures, telles que le rapport de l'examen de la situation d'un État, la demande d'un rapport supplémentaire, la nomination d'un rapporteur spécial, les propositions de services consultatifs ou d'assistance technique, les propositions de visites sur place devraient être prises par le Comité réuni en plénière.

Dans un autre ordre d'idées, plusieurs organes des Nations Unies ont souhaité que les populations soient associées le plus largement possible à la procédure des rapports. En effet, la préparation d'un rapport périodique devrait être en soi un outil pour informer la population et l'inviter à évaluer le respect par l'État de ses obligations internationales.[113]

---

112 Art. 62 du règlement intérieur du Cdh; art. 56 du règlement intérieur du Cdesc; art. 61 du règlement intérieur du Cerd.

113 Voir Simma, *supra* note 7, à la p. 89.

Selon la Commission des Droits de l'Homme, il s'agit même d'assurer la "participation" des populations et des institutions nationales de défense des droits de la personne à l'élaboration des rapports.[114] Toutefois, cette participation du public à la préparation des rapports est discutée, car la tâche de rédaction des rapports apparaît essentiellement devoir être une responsabilité gouvernementale.[115] En effet, il est souhaitable que le gouvernement soit le seul responsable de la rédaction de ses rapports, ne serait-ce que pour apprécier sa sensibilité envers les droits protégés par les conventions.

Il est par contre tout à fait nécessaire que le public soit vivement encouragé à réagir au contenu du rapport présenté par l'État. Si diverses mesures ont été prises pour élargir la participation des organisations non gouvernementales, il nous semble qu'il reste encore beaucoup à faire. De nouvelles pistes nous paraissent devoir être explorées pour assurer une visibilité plus grande de ces procédures à l'égard du grand public, des institutions nationales de protection des droits fondamentaux, des parlementaires. Dans cette optique, deux propositions nous paraissent réalisables: assurer la diffusion du rapport de l'État auprès du public avant son examen et développer l'expertise *in loco* des comités en mettant en place une procédure d'examen sur place des rapports étatiques.

D'abord, pour assurer *la publicité du rapport de l'État avant son examen par le comité*, l'intervalle entre la présentation du rapport par l'État et la session du comité devrait être utilisé pour assurer une véritable procédure de diffusion et de consultations sur le rapport de l'État avant son examen. Ainsi, le rapport étatique serait rendu public par le gouvernement concerné et par les Nations Unies dès sa réception par l'organe de supervision. Cette publication donnerait le temps au public, aux parlementaires, aux organismes

114 Voir notamment la Rés. 1993/14 de la Commission des Droits de l'Homme. De même, il est noté que les organes de supervision "ne peuvent pas s'acquitter efficacement de leurs mandats si les renseignements concernant leurs activités ne sont communiqués qu'aux gouvernements et que des efforts devraient être donc déployés pour que ces informations soient présentées par des moyens accessibles à la collectivité dans son ensemble. Il est suggéré entre autres que, pour en débattre, les collectivités en soient informées par les institutions nationales, les ONG, les établissements scolaires, la presse et d'autres organes d'information." (Doc. HRI/MC/1994/2, Rapport du Secrétaire général, para. 21).

115 "Their preparation is a governmental task, and involvement of nongovernmental organizations or members of the public is an unreasonable expectation"(Bayefsky, *supra* note 8, à la p. 232).

nationaux chargés de la protection des droits fondamentaux, aux organisations non gouvernementales d'analyser le rapport de l'État et de faire part de leurs remarques non seulement au comité, mais publiquement. Ainsi, la présentation du rapport serait envisagé comme un processus dynamique et de débat "en encourageant et en facilitant la participation du public à l'élaboration et à l'examen de la politique gouvernementale."[116]

Cette discussion pourrait se faire sous l'auspice d'une institution nationale concernée par les droits de la personne ou encore devant un comité parlementaire.[117] L'État pourrait faire parvenir le rapport de cette institution au comité ou aux organes concernés. Enfin, il nous apparaît important que les organes clarifient le rôle pour l'instant quelque peu ambigu des ONG au moment de l'examen d'un rapport d'État. À cet égard, nous faisons nôtre la suggestion de P. Alston que chaque organe confirme officiellement, combien il est vital pour l'efficacité de la procédure d'obtenir des informations continues d'ONG.[118]

Il nous paraît aussi possible et souhaitable de développer, dans le cadre de la procédure de rapport, une véritable procédure d'examen sur place de la situation du pays. De prime abord, il n'apparaît pas que la procédure d'examen des rapports étatiques implique de la part de l'organe de supervision de réaliser une visite sur place dans l'État concerné. De plus, aucun des traités concernés ne prévoit dans le cadre de l'examen des rapports un tel type de contrôle. Toutefois l'expertise *in loco* s'affirme de plus en plus comme un outil essentiel de protection des droits fondamentaux, car elle est un moyen privilégié pour établir les faits et mieux appréhender la réalité, mais aussi pour ajuster au mieux les recommandations des organes de protection des droits de la personne à la situation réelle des États.[119]

---

116 CRC, Rapport annuel à l'Assemblée Générale, 49ᵉ sess., Doc. off. A/49/41, para. 36.

117 Pour d'autres suggestions sur des forums appropriés de discussion, voir Alston, *supra* note 1 à la p. 43. Sur ce sujet, voir aussi Colliver, *supra* note 45, à la p. 188: "Norway, for example, has established an Advisory Committee on Human Rights, which includes NGOs representatives and human rights researchers, one whose main function is to comment on draft human rights reports to international bodies."

118 Alston, *supra* note 1, à la p. 81.

119 Certains traités ont prévu de tels mécanismes d'enquêtes sur place, notamment pour le Comité contre la torture, la Commission américaine des Droits

Dans le cadre de son mandat, le Comité des droits de l'enfant a développé la pratique des réunions informelles en dehors de Genève, notamment au plan régional. Une première réunion a eu lieu pour la région de l'Amérique latine et des Caraïbes à Quito, en juin 1992. Elle a permis à la fois de mieux faire connaître aux États les dispositions de la Convention et la fonction de surveillance du Comité, mais aussi aux membres du Comité d'évaluer sur place la situation des enfants dans la région, grâce à des visites et à des contacts, et, ainsi, d'en mieux appréhender les réalités. Le Comité a donc décidé de faire de ce type de visites et de rencontres une de ses activités régulières. Une deuxième réunion a eu lieu en Asie du 23 au 29 mai 1993, qui a mieux fait comprendre le système de rapports aux pays devant soumettre sous peu leur rapport sur la Convention (Thaïlande et Philippines). Pour le Vietnam, la visite a complété l'examen du rapport initial de ce pays et assuré le suivi des recommandations du Comité. Les autorités ont pu adresser des demandes précises de services consultatifs, notamment dans le domaine de l'administration de la justice pour mineurs.[120] Enfin, une troisième mission a été réalisée en Afrique en juillet 1994.[121] Lors de leur quatrième réunion, les présidents des organes de contrôle ont souhaité insister sur l'importance qu'il y a à organiser des réunions des organes ailleurs qu'à Genève, Vienne ou New York, tout en observant que des obstacles financiers rendent le coût de ces réunions prohibitifs.[122]

Ces expériences positives nous paraissent devoir être développées et intégrées à la procédure de rapport. Il est en effet possible d'organiser, avec l'accord de l'État concerné, des visites sur place d'une délégation de l'organe de supervision qui seraient très utiles pour assurer le suivi des recommandations du comité, vérifier les informations données par les États et mieux adapter les recommandations du comité à la réalité du pays. Telle est la voie sur laquelle s'est déjà engagé le Comité des droits économiques, sociaux et

---

de l'Homme ou le Comité européen pour la prévention de la torture et des peines ou traitements inhumains ou dégradants. Au sein des Nations Unies, dans un cadre non-conventionnel, plusieurs organes d'enquêtes par pays ou à caractère thématique, ainsi que des rapporteurs spéciaux peuvent effectuer de telles visites avec l'accord de l'État concerné.

[120] CRC, Rapport annuel à l'Assemblée Générale, 49ᵉ sess., Doc. off. A/49/41, para. 337 à 354.

[121] CRC/C/S.R.166 10 octobre 1994.

[122] Doc. A/47/628 du 10 novembre 1992, para. 86.

culturels. En effet, les visites *in loco* peuvent être utilisées pour établir des faits ou pour recueillir des renseignements. Ainsi, si le Comité des droits économiques, sociaux et culturels ne reçoit pas de réponse à des renseignements qu'il a sollicités, il peut demander à l'État d'accepter la visite de membres du Comité afin que ceux-ci puissent recueillir l'information nécessaire. Cette proposition a déjà été faite dans le cas du Panama et de la République dominicaine qui n'ont pas répondu à cette demande.[123]

Il nous paraît qu'il est concevable d'aller encore plus loin. Il serait en effet envisageable d'inviter les États à accepter la tenue d'une véritable *session nationale d'examen du rapport étatique*. Ce rapport ayant été diffusé suffisamment longtemps à l'avance, le comité ou une délégation composée de plusieurs de ses membres pourrait tenir dans le pays concerné une session publique d'examen du rapport qui pourrait se dérouler en deux parties. Une première partie serait consacrée à l'audition par le comité d'experts nationaux, de parlementaires ou membres de commissions parlementaires, de représentants d'institutions spécialisées dans le domaine des droits de la personne, d'ONG, le groupe de travail ou le secrétariat du comité ayant la charge de sélectionner les intervenants. La deuxième partie serait consacrée à l'examen du rapport étatique avec les représentants du gouvernement. Certaines visites sur place peuvent s'avérer nécessaires dans des lieux ou des institutions intéressant particulièrement les domaines d'activité du comité. À la fin de la session, la délégation pourrait formuler des observations immédiates ou des suggestions préliminaires, le comité émettant en réunion plénière ses propres conclusions générales sur la base du rapport de visite établi par sa délégation. La tenue d'une session publique d'un organe des Nations Unies aurait un impact important dans les médias et parmi le public. Cette proposition aurait l'immense avantage d'accroître la visibilité de la procédure aux yeux de la population. Même si une telle procédure n'est acceptée que par quelques États qui apparaîtraient novateurs en la matière, une dynamique nouvelle serait créée valorisant l'ensemble du système des rapports. La réunion d'une telle session sur place se faisant sur la base du volontariat des États, les frais d'organisation seraient à la charge de l'État invitant. En effet, il ne paraît pas plus coûteux pour un État d'organiser une telle session sur place que d'envoyer une délégation parfois nombreuse à Genève.

[123] Doc. E/C.12/1993/19, para. 40.

Dans tous les cas, que la session d'examen du rapport ait lieu à Genève ou dans l'État concerné, il nous paraît envisageable que les séances publiques puissent être retransmises à la télévision nationale. En outre, l'organe de supervision pourrait recommander à l'État que certaines de ses conclusions soient à titre particulier adressées et diffusées le plus largement possible auprès de certains publics-cibles désignés dans ses observations finales (responsables de l'application des lois, fonctionnaires, institutions ou secteurs de la population). Les comptes rendus des séances d'examen du rapport ainsi que les recommandations du comité pourraient notamment faire l'objet d'une publication spéciale destinée à l'ensemble des parlementaires de l'État concerné.[124] On pourrait également envisager qu'un comité parlementaire ou une institution nationale se charge d'assurer un suivi des recommandations des organes, car, sans un suivi sérieux, l'exercice perd une grande partie de sa raison d'être.

C   DES SOLUTIONS GLOBALES DIFFICILEMENT RÉALISABLES

La création d'un organe unique de supervision des traités et la présentation d'un rapport unique global sont deux réformes de caractère général qui ont été mentionnées.[125] Mais, pour certains, l'unification des organes ou des rapports dissoudrait les spécificités de chaque convention et remettrait en cause l'évolution bénéfique et nécessaire qu'a représentée l'adoption d'instruments spécifiques ou thématiques s'attachant à protéger une catégorie particulière de droits ou de personnes particulièrement vulnérables.[126] En outre, toute réforme qui nécessite la révision simultanée des différents traités et la réunion de l'accord préalable de tous les États parties à ces amendements, a peu de chance de voir le jour. De plus, il est à craindre qu'un réexamen des traités ne soit l'occasion pour certains États d'obtenir des contreparties substantielles à leur acceptation d'un aménagement procédural, en tentant de négocier la suppres-

---

[124] "Déjà, certains comités suggèrent dans leurs observations finales aux États parties d'établir un document unique comprenant le rapport de l'État partie, les comptes rendus analytiques et observations finales sur l'examen du rapport, et de le diffuser aussi largement que possible" (Doc. HRI/MC/1994/2, para. 20).

[125] Voir entre autres, Pocar, *supra* note 69, para. 25.

[126] Pour A. Dormenval, une telle unification "risquerait aussi d'amoindrir la qualité de la supervision effective des différentes obligations contractées jusqu'ici assurée" (*supra* note 1, à la p. 220).

sion de certaines clauses qui leur paraissent trop contraignantes. Au lieu de renforcer le système de protection des droits fondamentaux, une telle initiative aurait paradoxalement pour conséquence de l'amoindrir. Malgré ces objections majeures, il nous apparaît important d'étudier ces projets en ce qu'ils permettraient d'améliorer le mécanisme des rapports.

La plus radicale de ces mesures est la création d'un organe unique, ce qui réduirait subséquemment le nombre des rapports exigés. Pour E. Tistounet, par exemple, "le but ultime de toutes les adaptations des mécanismes de supervision des traités relatifs aux droits de l'homme est. . . de rationaliser la procédure de telle sorte que ne demeure qu'un Comité unique semi-permanent se réunissant en chambres particulières pour examiner les rapports au titre des divers traités ou des rapports globaux sur l'ensemble des dits textes. Le système de protection conventionnelle des droits de l'homme se trouverait ainsi unifié face au contrôle politique représenté par la Commission des droits de l'homme et permettrait un traitement uniforme et cohérent de l'ensemble des traités en vigueur ou à venir. Il permettrait aussi d'intégrer successivement tous les développements envisagés des normes internationales."[127] Dans le même sens, P. Alston étudie une unification plus limitée à deux ou trois comités au lieu de six.[128]

Telle n'est pas la voie qui semble prévaloir au sein des Nations Unies. Ainsi, les différents traités ont confié les tâches de supervision à chaque fois à des organes différents. Cette différenciation est apparue nécessaire pour tenir compte des spécificités de chaque convention. Lors de la présentation en 1978 du projet de convention contre la torture et autres peines ou traitements cruels, inhumains et dégradants, la Suède avait proposé que le Comité des Droits de l'Homme soit désigné comme l'instance d'examen des rapports étatiques.[129] Cette option fut abandonnée pour des raisons pratiques et juridiques, "tenant notamment au fait que les États parties au Pacte (international relatif aux droits civils et politiques) ne seraient pas nécessairement ceux qui adhéreraient à la future

---

[127] Tistounet, *supra* note 76, à la p. 150, para. 32.

[128] Alston, Doc. A/CONF.157/PC/62/Add.11/Rev.1, para. 166.

[129] Au cours des négociations qui ont précédé l'adoption de la Convention contre la torture, l'URSS a combattu la création d'un organe spécifique, soulignant que les États étaient déjà liés par les dispositions du PDCP et notamment son article 7 qui prohibe la torture. À cet égard, elle observait que la création d'un Comité spécifique contre la torture ne s'imposait pas, car il "n'aurait guère à faire" (Doc. E/CN.4/1983/63, para. 30).

convention.''[130] C'est pourquoi il fut envisagé de créer un comité spécifique.

De plus, on peut ajouter que loin de démultiplier les ressources des organes de contrôle, l'unification aurait l'effet fâcheux de diminuer le nombre des experts, sauf à créer un organe unique pléthorique.

La deuxième option à long terme, à savoir l'établissement d'un rapport unique "global" par l'État partie, semble plus facilement réalisable. Pour P. Alston en effet, "il semblerait possible aujourd'hui tout au moins dans le principe, qu'un État donné adopte unilatéralement une telle approche en n'établissant qu'un seul rapport global qu'il présenterait à peu près en même temps."[131] Selon cet expert, cette approche éviterait un amendement des traités qui "ne semble ni urgent, ni même essentiel."[132] La proposition du rapport "global" a reçu un accueil favorable. Ainsi, pour les présidents des organes de supervision, "il faudrait envisager, au moins à plus long terme, la possibilité de permettre aux États parties à plus d'un instrument international de préparer un rapport unique, 'global,' pour répondre à ses obligations en la matière découlant des divers instruments concernés."[133] De même, dans sa résolution 1994/19 relative au "bon fonctionnement des organes créés en application des instruments des Nations Unies relatifs aux droits de l'homme," adoptée le 25 février 1994, la Commission des Droits de l'Homme demande qu'il soit envisagé la possibilité de "présenter des rapports globaux uniques et de remplacer les rapports périodiques par des rapports spécifiques et des rapports thématiques."[134]

Il apparaît donc essentiel d'évaluer si une telle solution est susceptible d'améliorer de façon significative le système des rapports tant dans ses aspects substantifs que procéduraux. Quant à l'aspect substantif, un seul rapport aurait nécessairement pour conséquence d'élargir considérablement la dimension des droits par le biais d'un seul rapport et, en adoptant une approche unifiée, permettrait aux Comités et aux États de mettre en lumière l'universalité, l'indivisibilité et l'interdépendance des droits de la personne.

[130] Manin, *supra* note 69, à la p. 237.

[131] A/CONF.157/PC/62/Add.11/Rev.1, para. 168.

[132] *Ibid.*

[133] Quatrième réunion, A/47/628, para. 73.

[134] E/CN.4/1994/132, para. 6.d). Voir aussi HRI/MC/1994/2, rapport du Secrétaire général, para. 32 et 37.

Cette approche aurait aussi l'avantage de remplir l'un des objectifs majeurs de la Conférence mondiale, soit l'intégration des droits des femmes et des enfants dans l'ensemble du système des droits de la personne. Au surplus, les États ne pourraient ou n'auraient plus à choisir à quel rapport il leur faudrait donner priorité au détriment des autres en termes de préparation. Par conséquent, dans le cadre du processus d'élaboration des rapports, les droits se verraient accorder la même importance.

Sur le plan procédural, il est évident qu'un rapport unique faciliterait la rédaction pour les droits qu'on retrouve dans plusieurs conventions. Il va toutefois de soi que chaque comité resterait totalement libre d'examiner un État sur le respect de ces droits concordants. Un autre avantage serait la plus grande visibilité du rapport global et, par voie de conséquence, la plus grande importance qu'y attacheraient l'État et le public. On peut aussi penser que des économies d'échelle et d'efforts seront réalisés par la rédaction d'un seul rapport.

Il serait toutefois illusoire de croire qu'un rapport global apporterait une solution à tous les problèmes et n'en créerait pas de nouveaux. Ainsi, s'il est vrai qu'après un arrangement initial entre les comités serait éliminé le besoin de coordonner les directives existantes, il serait tout de même nécessaire d'ajuster périodiquement les directives de rédaction du rapport et de coordonner les procédures d'examen par les différents comités. Davantage préoccupant serait le délai qui s'écoulerait pour un État entre la présentation de chaque rapport global dont la périodicité pourrait être de cinq ans. Ce délai paraît en effet déraisonnable pour contrôler la situation des droits de la personne dans un État. À cet égard, P. Alston suggère que les comités pourraient, au besoin, demander des rapports supplémentaires aux États.[135] Une autre alternative serait de combiner deux des suggestions de cet expert, à savoir la remise d'un rapport global alors qu'un Comité pourrait solliciter un rapport thématique sur une question ou une situation particulière.[136] Cela devrait s'avérer moins exigeant que la préparation d'un nouveau rapport exhaustif sur tous les droits couverts par un traité.

135 A/CONF.157/PC/62/Add.11/Rev.1, para. 171.
136 Sur la proposition de remplacement des rapports périodiques détaillés par des rapports thématiques, voir A/CONF.157/PC/62/Add.11/Rev.1, para. 174 à 182.

CONCLUSION

La mécanique de mise en oeuvre du système des rapports semble se gripper inexorablement, condamnée à l'inefficacité, confrontée au mal chronique de rapports toujours en retard ou simplement non présentés. D'un autre côté, toute amélioration de cette situation créera un fardeau disproportionné pour des comités manquant de temps et de ressources. Face à ce dilemme, les Nations Unies n'ont pas d'autres choix que d'augmenter de façon substantielle les ressources des organes de supervision et procéder à des améliorations du système existant, tout en envisageant et en préparant des réformes plus radicales.

Les multiples réunions et les textes préparatoires à la Conférence de Vienne, la Conférence elle-même, ainsi que la réflexion qui l'a suivie permettent d'espérer que des solutions innovatrices viendront combler des lacunes héritées d'une époque où la souveraineté étatique s'imposait par-dessus tout.

Depuis quelques années nous avons assisté à l'affirmation d'une opinion publique qui exerce une pression non négligeable sur les gouvernements et les organisations internationales pour que les droits fondamentaux soient respectés. Toutefois, il reste toujours vrai qu'au-delà de tous les projets de réformes, si ingénieux soient-ils, et malgré les pressions des ONG, la volonté politique des États demeure encore un facteur important d'une mise en oeuvre efficace des instruments de protection des droits de la personne. À cet égard, plusieurs réformes souhaitables en la matière pourraient être soutenues ou, encore mieux, initiées par des États tels que le Canada.

YVES LE BOUTHILLIER ET DIDIER ROUGET
Université d'Ottawa and Université de Lille

Summary

The Proceedings of Periodic Reports in the Application of Human Rights Treaties: The Preconference of Vienna

Member states to a human rights treaty have an obligation to provide periodic reports. These reports allow the United Nations to verify that states are complying with the treaty. After discussing the essential procedural aspects of these reports, the authors disclose the problems of this system and conclude with some potential reforms designed to enhance the protection of human rights in the implementation of these international treaties.

Sommaire

La procédure des rapports périodiques en application des traités relatifs aux droits de la personne: L'après-conférence de Vienne

Lors de la ratification d'un traité international en matière de droits de la personne, les États adhérants ont une obligation de présenter aux Nations Unies des rapports périodiques. Ce système permet de savoir si les États se conforment effectivement aux obligations de la convention. Les auteurs exposent les aspects essentiels de la procédure des rapports et dévoitent les principales déficiences de ce système. Ils concluent par une étude des différentes réformes envisagées pour améliorer la protection des droits de la personne dans la mise en oeuvre de ces traités.

International Efforts to Secure the Return
of Stolen or Illegally Exported Cultural Objects:
Has Unidroit Found a Global Solution?*

INTRODUCTION

THIS NOTE REVIEWS RECENT international efforts to combat the rapidly expanding problem of illicit trade in cultural objects, and focuses on the latest international instrument developed with a view to curtailing this activity — namely, the draft Convention on the International Return of Stolen or Illegally Exported Cultural Objects.[1]

The draft Convention was prepared under the auspices of the Rome-based International Institute for the Unification of Private Law (Unidroit). A diplomatic conference has been convened for June 1995, at which time governments will have an opportunity to consider, and perhaps adopt, Unidroit's draft. The impact of this latest multilateral effort will depend upon whether the diplomatic conference successfully adopts a convention, and if it does, what the final version of that instrument provides.

MULTILATERAL EFFORTS TO PROTECT CULTURAL OBJECTS

Throughout history, art, antiquities, and cultural objects have been taken from their countries of origin as trophies of war. They have also been "borrowed" from colonized territories, and removed "for preservation purposes" so as not to risk deterioration if left

---

* The views expressed are those of the authors and do not necessarily represent the views of the Department of Justice.

---

[1] Unidroit, CONF. 8/3, Dec. 20, 1994.

in situ.[2] Today, "the international market in works of art, which has developed in a remarkable manner since the Second World War . . . has become . . . the main cause of the impoverishment of the cultural heritage of some nations to the advantage of others."[3]

PROTECTION OF CULTURAL PROPERTY IN TIME OF WAR

International law has long sought to protect cultural property in time of war. Vattel and Wheaton admonished warring armies to spare monuments and works of art unless their destruction was necessary to advance the cause of war.[4] The Hague Peace Conventions of 1899 and 1907 called for the protection of artistic property.[5] These instruments, however, proved to be of little value during the First and Second World Wars, which saw the systematic plunder, confiscation, and destruction of art and cultural objects. Fortunately, some of the cultural booty was returned to the countries of origin as required under peace treaties and other agreements.

The Hague Convention for the Protection of Cultural Property in the Event of Armed Conflict,[6] adopted in 1954, and its Protocol[7] and Regulations[8] were intended to enhance the protection afforded under the Hague Conventions to cultural property during wartime, taking into account the inadequacies of the earlier instruments and the realities of modern warfare.[9] The Convention, which also applies during armed conflicts of a non-international character

2 Napoleon Bonaparte, Lord Elgin, and Hermann Goering are some of the more famous figures in this history.

3 International Institute for the Unification of Private Law (Unidroit), *Uniform Law Review, Biannual,* vol. II, 33 (Rome: Unidroit, 1990).

4 E. de Vattel, *The Law of Nations* and H. Wheaton, *Elements of International Law,* cited in S. Williams, *The International and National Protection of Movable Cultural Property: A Comparative Study* 5-6, 15 (New York: Oceana Publications, 1978).

5 *Ibid.,* 17-18.

6 (1956) 249 U.N.T.S. 240. The Convention came into force on Aug. 7, 1956.

7 (1956) 249 U.N.T.S. 358. The Protocol deals with the obligations of occupying States. It was adopted at the same time as the Convention, and also came into force on Aug. 7, 1956.

8 Regulations for the Execution of the Convention for the Protection of Cultural Property in the Event of an Armed Conflict (1956) 249 U.N.T.S. 270.

9 The Convention also contains provisions that apply during peacetime. E.g., Art. 3 calls on parties to take appropriate measures during peacetime for the safeguarding of cultural property situated within their own territory against foreseeable effects of an armed conflict. Parties are also, in time of peace, to introduce into their military regulations provisions that may ensure observance of the Convention.

and during occupation, was developed under the auspices of the United Nations Educational, Scientific and Cultural Organization (UNESCO).

Under the Convention, parties undertake to respect cultural property situated within their own territory as well as within the territory of other parties by refraining from any use of that property that is likely to expose it to destruction or damage in the event of armed conflict, and by refraining from any act of hostility directed against such property (Article 4(1)). As in the days of Vattel, imperative military necessity permits a waiver of these obligations (Article 4(2)). Parties must also prohibit theft, pillage,or misappropriation of, and acts of vandalism directed against, cultural property, and shall refrain from any act directed by way of reprisals against cultural property (Article 4(4)).

The Convention specifies the obligations of occupying powers with respect to the preservation of cultural property (Article 5), provides for the designation in an international register of refuges having "special protection" (Article 8), and prescribes rules for transporting cultural property under special protection (Articles 12 and 13). The Convention also calls for the use of a distinctive emblem as a means of identifying certain cultural property (Articles 16 and 17). And the parties are obliged "to take, within the framework of the ordinary criminal jurisdiction, all necessary steps to prosecute and impose penal or disciplinary sanctions upon those persons, of whatever nationality, who commit or order to be committed a breach of the present Convention" (Article 28).

Although the Convention has numerous parties (eighty-five as of October 31, 1994), major art market countries like the United Kingdom and the United States are missing from the list, as is Canada. Moreover, it suffers from vague provisions that have been interpreted differently by different parties,[10] and the breaches that it sanctions are not specifically described. UNESCO is now working towards improving and reinforcing the application of the Convention, probably by embodying new provisions in a protocol, to bring it into line with current international requirements and to improve and modernize its terms. UNESCO has also resolved to harmonize its activities in the field of protection of cultural heritage with United Nations peacekeeping activities.[11]

---

10 E.g., there are differing approaches to Art. 28. Some parties interpret it to operate extraterritorially, while other parties do not.

11 UNESCO, Information Note, 1954/1, June 1994 at 4.

Despite its drawbacks, the 1954 Hague Convention must nevertheless be regarded as an important achievement. In particular, it represents international recognition of the importance of having respect for and preserving cultural property, regardless of where it is located, for the benefit of all humanity.[12] Moreover, it underlines that "such protection cannot be effective unless both national and international measures have been taken to organize it in time of peace" (Preamble).

CURBING ILLICIT TRAFFIC IN CULTURAL OBJECTS

Recent years have seen a proliferation in instruments seeking to combat illicit trade in art and cultural objects. The illegal trade, a crime that is increasingly international in character, has nonetheless continued to expand at an alarming rate. Efforts to curb it have been thwarted by various factors, including the extraordinary increase since the Second World War in the value of works of art and the consequent expansion in the number of rich and eager clients and markets, the increasingly sophisticated methods of international communication and electronic transfer of information, and the ease in crossing international borders. Another concern is that the trade in works of art is often linked to the international traffic in drugs and international money laundering activities.[13] An observation by the Unidroit Secretariat is particularly apt:

While it is evident that the greater the difficulties put in the way of legal traffic the more illegal traffic will prosper, on the other hand, for as long as illegal traffic has not been stopped, it is politically difficult to encourage legal commerce. The two measures go hand in hand.[14]

The lack of success in dealing with the illegal traffic in cultural objects is also due to the inability of the international community to achieve a workable compromise between the two diametrically

12 The Preamble states that "damage to cultural property belonging to any people whatsoever means damage to the cultural heritage of all mankind," and notes that "the preservation of the cultural heritage is of great importance to the peoples of the world and it is important that this heritage should receive international protection."

13 Unidroit Secretariat, Diplomatic Conference for the Adoption of the Draft Unidroit Convention on the International Return of Stolen or Illegally Exported Cultural Objects, *Text of the Draft Convention and Explanatory Report*, Unidroit, CONF. 8/3, *supra* note 1 at 8.

14 *Ibid.*

opposed approaches to solving the problem. On the one hand, in countries where the art trade is prospering and where investment capital is abundant while cultural treasures are not, strong arguments are made for a generally unfettered market with sanctions for only very serious abuses. The advantages are said to be both economic and cultural:

> Apart from the economic advantages which it offers, a free trade market in art — it is said — is likewise beneficial and desirable from the cultural point of view as the circulation of works of art across frontiers will indisputably contribute to that dialogue between national cultures which many see as the principal element directed towards concord among the peoples of the world and ultimately peace.[15]

On the other hand, countries rich in cultural property but poor in terms of economic wealth promote a solution calling for the return of stolen or illegally exported cultural property to its country of origin, and believe that international instruments governing such return should operate retroactively.

The practical problems are as follows. In the case of a theft of cultural property, the conflict between the dispossessed owner and the *bona fide* purchaser for value is resolved differently by different jurisdictions in accordance with their own legal systems. Some states would resolve the matter in favour of the dispossessed owner, citing the principle of *nemo dat qui non habet*, to the effect that the thief could not pass good title to the purchaser. Other jurisdictions would protect the good faith purchaser and the dispossessed owner would be out of luck.[16]

The other problem concerns illegally exported items. Many states refuse to order the return to the state of origin of an item exported contrary to that state's export laws. States are reluctant to give effect to the export laws of other states because, they argue, international law does not recognize the extraterritorial effect of these measures.[17]

Although attempts have been made to achieve a compromise between the above two schools of thought, some of the major art importing states have been reluctant to sign international instruments drawn up to deal with the problem of illegal traffic in cultural property.

15 *Supra* note 3 at 33.

16 See e.g., the oft-cited case of *Winkworth v. Christie, Manson & Woods Ltd. and another*, [1980] 1 All. E. R. 1121.

17 See *Attorney-General of New Zealand v. Ortiz and Others*, [1984] A.C. 1.

UNESCO's Activities to Protect Cultural Property

The first multilateral attempt to create international rules for dealing with stolen or illegally exported cultural property is found in the Convention on the Means of Prohibiting and Preventing the Illicit Import, Export and Transfer of Ownership of Cultural Property,[18] adopted in 1970 by UNESCO. The Convention establishes in its declarative section the duty of every state to "protect the cultural property existing within its territory against the dangers of robbery, clandestine excavation and illicit export" and notes that "the protection of cultural heritage can be effective only if organized both nationally and internationally among States working in close cooperation."

The Convention defines cultural property as that specifically designated by a state as being of importance for archaeology, prehistory, history, literature, art, or science and that falls within a prescribed list of categories, including rare collections of fauna and flora, property relating to military and social history, archaeological discoveries, elements of dismembered monuments, antiquities more than 100 years old such as coins, objects of ethnological interest, rare manuscripts, archives, and furniture or musical instruments more than 100 years old (Article 1). Parties are required to:

(1) establish national services within their territories to, e.g., draft laws designed to secure the protection of the cultural heritage and to prevent illicit import, export, and transfer of ownership

(2) develop and maintain a list of important public and private cultural property whose export would constitute an appreciable impoverishment of the national cultural heritage

(3) take educational measures to foster respect for the cultural heritage of all states, and give appropriate publicity to the disappearance of any item of cultural property (Article 5)

(4) require exported cultural property to be accompanied by a certificate authorizing the export (Article 6).

[18] (1971) 10 I.L.M. 289. Although other conventions dealing with the protection and preservation of cultural heritage preceded the 1970 Convention — see, e.g., the European Cultural Convention (1954) 218 U.N.T.S. 139 and the European Convention on the Protection of the Archaeological Heritage (1969) 8 I.L.M. 739 — the 1970 Convention was the first to seek to deal specifically with the return of property illegally removed from the country of origin.

Article 7 of the Convention also obliges importing parties to do, *inter alia*, the following:

(1) take the necessary measures to prevent museums within their territories from acquiring illegally exported cultural property

(2) prohibit the import of cultural property stolen from a museum or public monument, provided that such property is listed in the museum's inventory

(3) at the request of the state of origin, take steps to recover and return such stolen cultural property, provided that the requesting state pays just compensation to an innocent purchaser.

Parties are to require antique dealers to maintain registers recording the origin of each item of cultural property, as well as information about the supplier and the price paid (Article 10). Parties are to facilitate restitution of illegally exported cultural property to its rightful owner (Article 13).

Canada became a party to the 1970 UNESCO Convention in 1978 and adopted very progressive legislation to implement it.[19] Australia and the United States are also parties, as are more than sixty other states. However, most countries with large art markets (in western Europe) have not become party to the Convention, so that its utility has been marginal.

One major obstacle to becoming a party to the Convention is the requirement that states take steps to recover and return stolen cultural property, regardless of when the property was stolen, and that states of origin pay just compensation to an innocent purchaser, a term that is not defined. As noted above, states have approached these matters in varied ways in their national laws, some providing protection to the original owner, others giving priority to the *bona fide* purchaser.

Criticism of the UNESCO Convention has come from both sides of this argument: it is regarded as having severely eroded the principle of protection of the *bona fide* purchaser, as prejudicing original owners who may have to pay inflated prices as compensation for recovering their cultural objects, and as favouring international protection of cultural property at the expense of ensuring freedom and security in international commerce. The UNESCO

19 Cultural Property Export and Import Act, R.S.C. 1985, c. C-51. This legislation, which came into effect in 1977, makes it an offence to import into Canada foreign cultural property that has been illegally exported from a country with which Canada has concluded a cultural property agreement.

Convention has also been criticized as putting the entire burden of protection of cultural property on states with large art markets.

Activities of the Economic and Social Council

The Economic and Social Council adopted a resolution in 1989,[20] deciding that the topic of transnational crime against the cultural patrimony of countries should be included on the agenda of the Eighth United Nations Congress on the Prevention of Crime and the Treatment of Offenders. The objective was to have participants explore possibilities for formulating policies of international co-operation for the prevention of these offences. The Congress, which took place in Cuba in 1990, considered a draft Model Treaty for the Prevention of Crimes that Infringe Upon the Cultural Heritage of Peoples in the Form of Movable Property.[21]

The model treaty defines movable cultural property as that which has been designated by a state as being subject to export control by reason of its importance for archaeology, prehistory, history, literature, art, or science. The property must also belong to one or more categories, such as products of archaeological excavations, antiquities, materials of anthropological or ethnological interest, paintings, archives, etc. Under the treaty, states must take measures to prohibit the import and export of movable cultural property that has been stolen or illegally exported. They must also introduce a system whereby the export of movable cultural property is authorized by export certificate. States must impose sanctions upon persons or institutions responsible for the illicit import or export of movable cultural property, or that knowingly acquire or deal in stolen or illicitly imported movable cultural property. The draft also establishes a procedure for recovery and return of such property.

The Eighth Congress adopted a resolution recommending to states that they consider the model treaty "as a framework that may be of assistance to interested States in negotiating and drawing up bilateral agreements designed to improve co-operation in the area. . . ."[22] The Congress also adopted a resolution, proposed by Canada and co-sponsored by twenty-three other states, calling for the creation of an automated information exchange service access-

20 Resolution 1989/62 of May 24, 1989.

21 *Report of the Eighth United Nations Congress on the Prevention of Crime and the Treatment of Offenders*, Havana, Cuba, Aug. 27 - Sept. 7, 1990. A/CONF.144/28, Oct. 5, 1990 at 112-16.

22 *Ibid.*, 111.

ible to states for the purpose of ensuring international dissemination of information on stolen or illegally exported cultural property. The resolution noted that "the swift international exchange of computerized data concerning stolen or illegally exported movable cultural property is a valuable tool in the prevention of crimes against cultural heritage and the apprehension of offenders."[23] The resolution accordingly requested that the Secretary-General of the United Nations "make arrangements . . . for the establishment of national and international computer data bases that would be used by competent authorities for the purposes of preventing and combating crime against cultural heritage. . . ."[24] The data bases would contain information on stolen and illegally exported movable cultural property around the world, and also include national legislation and international instruments related to the protection of cultural heritage.

Canada has a computerized data base, the "Register for Stolen Art and Artefacts" (ROSA), developed by the Canadian Heritage Information Network of Heritage Canada and the Interpol Section of the RCMP. It contains information in English and French on national and international thefts, seizures, and forgeries of works of art and artefacts, and includes an optical disc for storing images of art works. Currently there are some 19,000 records on the data base, 15,000 of which are supported by images. Each year, an average of 2,000 entries are added to the system by Canadian police agencies and Interpol bureaus around the world.[25]

The Ninth Congress on the Prevention of Crime and Treatment of Offenders will take place in Cairo in April and May 1995. Participants can expect to learn whether the model treaty considered at the Eighth Congress has proved useful, and whether the resolution on the establishment of national and international computer data bases has led to concrete results.

The Efforts of the Commonwealth

At their 1993 meeting, held in Mauritius, the Commonwealth Law Ministers adopted a "Scheme for the Protection of Cultural

---

23 *Ibid.*, 142.

24 *Ibid.*

25 Interpol Ottawa, *Theft of Cultural Property in Canada, 1994* 4 (Ottawa: Royal Canadian Mounted Police Public Affairs Directorate, 1994). Another example of a computerized data base is the "Art Loss Register," which was created in 1990 and has offices in New York and London.

Heritage within the Commonwealth.''[26] The Scheme was developed by a working group (on which Canada was represented) acting on a proposal of the New Zealand Minister of Justice and Attorney General made at the 1983 Meeting of Commonwealth Law Ministers.[27] The Scheme governs the return by one Commonwealth country to another of illegally exported cultural property. To that end, it:

(1) sets out a definition of items covered

(2) requires states to prohibit the export of these items without an export permit

(3) calls for the designation of central authorities for the making and receiving of requests for return of items

(4) stipulates that an innocent purchaser be paid fair and reasonable compensation as a condition of returning the item

(5) establishes a limitation period for claiming return of an item of five years from the time the whereabouts of the item was known.

Law Ministers agreed that Commonwealth jurisdictions should take early steps to give effect to the new Scheme in their domestic legislation.[28] Implementation in Canada will require minor changes to the *Cultural Property Export and Import Act.*[29]

The Work of the European Union

The Council of the European Communities issued a directive on the return of cultural objects unlawfully removed from the territory of a member state in March 1993.[30] This action was necessary in the light of the establishment on January 1, 1993 of an internal market within the Union in which the free movement of goods, persons, services, and capital was assured.

[26] *Communiqué,* Nov. 19, 1993, LMM(93)70, points 18-22 and attachment.

[27] 1983 Meeting of Commonwealth Law Ministers, Colombo, Sri Lanka, Feb. 1983, *Minutes of Meeting* 71-73 (London: Commonwealth Secretariat). Of interest in this regard is the fact that the *Ortiz* case (*supra* note 17) concerned the illegal export from New Zealand of a Maori carving.

[28] The Attorney General of the United Kingdom expressed his support for action in this area and encouraged those in a position to do so to implement the Scheme. He noted, however, that the United Kingdom was not in a position to implement the Scheme at that time.

[29] *Supra* note 19.

[30] Council Directive 93/7 of Mar. 15, 1993, J.O., Mar. 27, 1993, No. L74/74.

Under Article 36 of the Treaty Establishing the European Economic Community, member states are entitled to maintain regulations on the import and export of "national treasures possessing artistic, historic or archaeological value." With the disappearance of customs controls, there was concern that existing regulations would be evaded. It was necessary, therefore, to introduce arrangements enabling member states to secure the return of cultural objects, classified as national treasures within the meaning of Article 36, that had been unlawfully removed from their territory.

The directive defines cultural objects as objects that have been classified under national legislation as national treasures possessing artistic, historic, or archaeologic value and that belong to one of the listed categories, including archaeological objects, paintings, mosaics, and sculptures. Some objects must meet specified age and value thresholds. Cultural objects that have been unlawfully removed from the territory of a member state are to be returned in accordance with the procedure provided for in the directive. The return procedure permits states to bring actions before foreign courts, provided stipulated limitation periods have not expired. Where the return of an object is ordered, the possessor may be awarded compensation, provided that due care was exercised in acquiring the object.

The Council of the European Communities also promulgated a regulation on the export of cultural objects in December 1992.[31] The regulation noted the need to establish uniform rules for exporting cultural objects (using the same definition as in the directive) to states outside the European Community, and stipulated that an export permit was required to export such objects beyond Community territory. Permits can be refused for objects protected under national legislation or for the protection of national treasures possessing artistic, historic, or archaeological value. The return procedure set out in the directive would apply to objects exported contrary to this regulation.

THE UNIDROIT DRAFT CONVENTION ON THE INTERNATIONAL RETURN OF STOLEN OR ILLEGALLY EXPORTED CULTURAL OBJECTS

Originally established in Rome in 1926 as an auxiliary organ of the League of Nations, Unidroit was re-established in 1940 as an independent governmental organization. Membership is now close

---

[31] Council Regulation (EEC) No. 3911/92 of Dec. 9, 1992, J.O., Dec. 31, 1992, No. L395/1.

to sixty states drawn from all regions of the world and representing various legal systems. Canada has been a member of Unidroit since 1968 and a Canadian has served on its Governing Council[32] since 1984.[33]

The purpose of Unidroit as set out in Article 1 of its statute, "is to examine ways of harmonising and co-ordinating the private law of States and of groups of States, and to prepare gradually for the adoption by the various States of uniform rules of private law." Unidroit does this by preparing drafts of laws, conventions, and agreements on private law matters that may be adopted by states, thus fostering the development of uniform internal law. Unidroit also undertakes studies in comparative private law, organizes international conferences and publishes works on private international law and unification of law.

GENESIS OF THE DRAFT UNIDROIT CONVENTION

In 1974 Unidroit completed a draft Uniform Law on the Acquisition in Good Faith of Corporeal Movables. UNESCO thought that the 1974 draft could serve as a useful starting point for drawing up rules applicable to the illegal traffic in cultural property, and it requested Unidroit to study the issue in the light of the 1974 draft Uniform Law and the 1970 UNESCO Convention on the Means of Prohibiting and Preventing the Illicit Import, Export and Transfer of Ownership of Cultural Property.[34] Unidroit appointed Gerte Reichelt of the Vienna Institute of Comparative Law to undertake this work. She produced two studies.[35] In addition, the then President of Unidroit, Riccardo Monaco, prepared a document propo-

---

[32] Every five years the member states of Unidroit elect the 25 members of the Governing Council. The Council is responsible for drawing up the work program of the Institute and determining the methods for carrying out the Institute's mandate. E.g., the Council establishes study groups and committees to develop international instruments or to carry out studies.

[33] T. Bradbrooke Smith of Stikeman, Elliott in Ottawa and former Assistant Deputy Attorney General of the Department of Justice served on the Governing Council from 1984 through 1988. Madam Justice Anne-Marie Trahan of the Quebec Superior Court and former Associate Deputy Minister for Civil Law and Legislative Services of the Department of Justice has served on the Council since 1989.

[34] *Supra* note 18.

[35] G. Reichelt, "The Protection of Cultural Property," Study 70 -Doc. 1 (Unidroit, 1986); G. Reichelt, "International Protection of Cultural Property," C.D. - Doc. 8 (Unidroit 1988).

sing an outline for a private law convention on the international protection of cultural property. The paper "stressed the need for striking a balance between the interests of the countries of origin of cultural property and those referred to as importing countries."[36]

In 1986, the Governing Council of Unidroit decided to include the subject of the international protection of cultural property on the Institute's work program, and in 1988 it set up a study group to consider the feasibility and desirability of drawing up uniform rules on the international protection of cultural property. Over the next four years the study group prepared a preliminary draft convention on stolen or illegally exported cultural objects, including the concept of the right to payment and restitution. The Governing Council submitted the draft for consideration to a Committee of Governmental Experts.

The Committee, composed of representatives of some sixty states, including Canada, as well as a number of international organizations such as UNESCO, Interpol, and the Hague Conference on Private International Law, met on four occasions during the period 1991 to 1993. At its fourth session it adopted the draft Convention on the International Return of Stolen or Illegally Exported Cultural Objects.

THE DRAFT UNIDROIT CONVENTION

The Convention sets out rules for the return of stolen or illegally exported cultural property, as defined in the Convention, provided that certain conditions are met. The questions of compensation for *bona fide* purchasers and limitation periods for bringing actions are addressed, as is the issue of the proper jurisdiction in which to bring a claim. The draft Convention is divided into five chapters, each of which will be dealt with separately.

Chapter 1: Scope of Application and Definition

Article 1 provides that the Convention applies to claims of an international character for the restitution of stolen cultural objects or for the return of illegally exported cultural objects. In other words, the Convention does not apply to domestic claims. Where illegally exported cultural objects are concerned, the Article specifies that the objects must have been exported contrary to a law that

36 *Supra* note 3 at 31.

prohibited their export because of their cultural significance. Thus, they must have been exported contrary to a law that places conditions on or prohibits the export of objects because they are culturally significant.

Article 2 defines cultural objects for the purposes of the Convention. The definition is very broad and includes objects that, on religious or secular grounds, are of importance for archaeology, prehistory, history, literature, art, or science. The definition refers by way of example to the list of classes of objects found in the definition of cultural property in the 1970 UNESCO Convention. The definition does not refer to specific qualities of the object such as age, nor to the degree of importance of the object.

The definition Article was vigorously debated during the sessions of the Committee of Governmental Experts. Some participants pressed for a detailed definition listing categories of objects, a formulation said to facilitate matters before the courts, while others suggested that it would be sufficient to refer to objects that have been designated in national legislation as being of importance because of their cultural significance.[37] Proponents of the latter approach argued that such a definition recognizes the right of each state to decide for itself what is culturally significant for that state.

Chapter 2: Restitution of Stolen Cultural Objects

Article 3 of the Convention places an obligation on the possessor of a stolen cultural object to return it. In addition, the Article specifies that objects that have been unlawfully excavated, or lawfully excavated but unlawfully retained, are deemed to have been stolen. It also contains provisions for limitation periods for actions for restitution of stolen cultural objects.

The length of the limitation periods appears in square brackets in the draft Convention because the Committee of Governmental Experts could not reach a consensus on the appropriate period. The two options for the principal limitation period are one and three years from the time when the claimant knew or ought reasonably to have known the object's location and the identity of its possessor. This means that a person wanting to make a claim to get property back would have to do so within one or three years from the time of becoming aware of the object's location and its possessor's name, depending on the period that is eventually stipulated

[37] The Canadian Cultural Property Export and Import Act, *supra* note 19 follows this approach.

in the final version of Article 3. The options for the absolute limitation period are thirty and fifty years from the time of the theft.

Shorter limitation periods favour possessors, and would therefore tend to bring greater certainty to the trade in cultural objects. A buyer of a cultural object would face less risk of being sued and hence be less concerned about eventual restitution. By contrast, longer limitation periods are to the advantage of claimants who have been unlawfully deprived of their property. Some states do not want to include any limitation periods, arguing that the passage of time should not operate to legalize theft. This issue will likely give rise to considerable debate at the diplomatic conference.[38]

Paragraph 4 of Article 3, which currently appears in square brackets because the Committee of Experts did not reach consensus as to whether it should be included, provides that claims for restitution of a stolen cultural object belonging to a public collection are subject to two possible options, both appearing in square brackets: either to no limitation period or to a limitation period of seventy-five years.

A proposed definition of "public collection" for purposes of the longer limitation period appears in square brackets in the Convention, as follows:

For the purposes of this paragraph, a "public collection" consists of a collection of inventoried cultural objects, which is accessible to the public on a [substantial and] regular basis, and is the property of (i) a Contracting State [or local or regional authority], (ii) an institution substantially financed by a Contracting State [or local or regional authority], (iii) a non profit institution which is recognized by a Contracting State [or local or regional authority] (for example by way of tax exemption) as being of [national] [public] [particular] importance, or (iv) a religious institution.

Article 4 of the Convention provides that a possessor of a stolen cultural object who is required to return it is entitled to fair and reasonable compensation to be paid by the claimant. There are two conditions that a possessor must meet in order to be eligible for compensation. First, the possessor must show that he or she neither knew nor ought reasonably to have known that the object was

---

38 The Canadian Cultural Property Export and Import Act, *ibid.*, provides that no limitation period applies to actions for recovery of illegally *exported* cultural property brought in the Federal Court of Canada. However, under existing federal legislation, an action brought in one of the superior courts of the provinces would be subject to provincial limitation periods.

stolen. Second, the possessor must show that he or she exercised due diligence when acquiring the object.

Paragraph 4(2) states that, in determining whether the possessor exercised due diligence, consideration should be given to the circumstances in which the object was acquired. Those circumstances are described as including the character of the parties, the price paid, and whether the possessor consulted any reasonably available register of stolen cultural objects.

Paragraph 4(3) states that a possessor who acquired an object by inheritance or by gift shall not be in a more favourable position than the person from whom he or she acquired the object. In other words, a possessor is not excused from returning a stolen cultural object by the fact that he or she inherited it or received such an object as a gift.

Chapter 3: Return of Illegally Exported Cultural Objects

Article 5 sets out the conditions for the return of an illegally exported cultural object. It is the contracting state (as opposed to the individual or institution that has been deprived of its cultural object) that makes the request for the return of the object. Paragraph 5(1) provides that the object must have been exported in violation of that state's law regulating the export of cultural objects because of their cultural significance. In other words, that state must have enacted legislation that places conditions on or prohibits the export of cultural objects because those objects are culturally significant, and the export must have been contrary to that legislation.

A contracting state may also request the return of an object that was temporarily exported under a permit and has not been returned in accordance with that permit. This might occur when a cultural object was exported for purposes of an exhibition, and the object was not returned when the exhibition was over.

The request for return must be made to a court or other competent authority of another contracting state, such as a government minister or a designated official. There was some debate during the meetings of the Committee of Governmental Experts as to whether it should be possible to make such a request to a body other than a court of law. One delegation expressed the view that the courts provide a better guarantee of impartiality, and the fact that they are bound by precedent would add certainty to the process.

Under paragraph 5(2), to have the object returned after illegal export the requesting state must establish that the removal of the object from its territory significantly impairs one or more of the following four interests:

(1) the physical preservation of the object or its context

(2) the integrity of a complex object

(3) the preservation of information of, for example, a scientific or historical character

(4) the use of the object by a living culture.

In the alternative, the requesting state must establish that the object is of "outstanding cultural importance" for the requesting state. The above provisions gave rise to vigorous debate during the meetings of governmental experts. A number of participants have argued that the burden of proof placed on the requesting state is too rigorous and that it should be sufficient for a requesting state to prove that the object has been exported contrary to its laws protecting cultural objects.[39] Many of the art importing countries, however, have made it clear that this provision is a *sine qua non* for their adoption of the Convention.

Paragraph 5(3) places an obligation on the requesting state to provide any information of a factual or legal nature to assist the court or other competent authority in determining whether the requirements of paragraphs 5(1) and (2) are met. Claimants are required to file information with the court or competent authority, or possibly to provide expert witnesses about export laws, on such matters as whether the object forms part of a larger cultural object, and the use of the object.

The last paragraph of Article 5 contains the limitation periods for requests for return of illegally exported cultural objects. As with the provisions relating to stolen objects, options for limitation periods appear in square brackets. The principal limitation period is either one or three years from the time when the requesting state knew or ought reasonably to have known the location of the object and the identity of its possessor. The absolute limitation period is either thirty or fifty years from the date of the illegal export.

Article 6 states the circumstances in which a court or other competent authority of the state may refuse to order the return of

[39] Under Canada's Cultural Property Export and Import Act, *ibid.*, the foreign State need show only that the cultural property was illegally exported from that State, and therefore illegally imported into Canada.

illegally exported cultural objects, even where all of the requirements of Article 5 have been satisfied. The principal ground for such refusal is that the object has a "closer connection" with the culture of the state to which the request for return has been made.[40]

This provision was also the subject of lengthy debates during the meetings of governmental experts. Some delegations considered that the inclusion of Article 6 would render it more difficult for courts or other competent authorities to decline to return an object, while other delegations believed that the provision would have the opposite effect. The debate will no doubt be resurrected during the diplomatic conference.

Article 6 also contains a provision in square brackets that would allow the court or other competent authority to refuse to order the return where the object was unlawfully removed from the state addressed before it was unlawfully removed from the territory of the requesting state.

Article 7 states that a contracting state may not make a request for the return of an illegally exported cultural object where the export is no longer illegal at the time of the request. Paragraph 2 also provides that no request for return may be made for two types of objects: those that were exported during the lifetime of the person who created them (a provision in square brackets states "or within a period of [five] years following the death of that person"); and, where the creator is not known, those that were less than twenty years old at the time of the export. The period of five years following the death of a known creator is intended to permit the timely winding up of the creator's estate. Some delegations thought that the provision would not prove useful because the time of death of the artist would often be difficult to determine or to prove.

In addition, Article 7 contains a provision in square brackets that would allow a contracting state to request the return of an object made by a member of an indigenous community for use by that community, even though the creator is still alive or, where the creator is not known, the object is less than twenty years old at the time of the export. There was reluctance to adding this provision on the part of several delegations, because the term "indigenous" was not defined and was subject, in their view, to very broad interpretations. The provision was added late in the day, and there was

---

40 The Article would not apply, however, in the case of objects that were exported under a temporary export permit and have not been returned according to the terms of the permit.

insufficient time for discussion; it may be deleted from the final version. In any event, the Convention is intended to deal with cultural objects in general and is not designed to cover all aspects of aboriginal cultural objects. These are being dealt with in conventions or in fora that deal specifically with aboriginal concerns — for example, the United Nations Working Group on Indigenous Peoples, which is currently studying cultural and intellectual property rights.

As with stolen cultural property, there is a provision providing for fair and reasonable compensation to a possessor who is required to return an illegally exported cultural object. Article 8 requires the possessor to show that he or she neither knew nor ought reasonably to have known at the time of acquisition that the object had been unlawfully removed from the requesting state. However, unlike the possessor of stolen cultural property, the possessor of illegally exported cultural property does not need to offer proof of due diligence in acquiring the object to get compensation. The Committee of Governmental Experts resolved that purchasers of stolen objects should be subject to a greater burden, because theft is universally recognized as a criminal act whereas export rules differ from country to country.

Article 8 includes a square-bracketed paragraph on the subject of export certificates. Under this paragraph, where a contracting state has instituted a system of export certificates, the purchaser of an object is put on notice that an object has been illegally exported if the object is not accompanied by an export certificate. The Convention does not, however, require contracting states to institute a system of export certificates for cultural objects.

Export certificates are referred to in several of the international instruments that deal with the protection of cultural property.[41] Such a system, it is argued, provides for control over the legal export of cultural objects, and the absence of an export certificate can signal that the object came into the hands of the possessor illegally. The presence or absence of an export certificate can be important when determining the *bona fides* of an acquirer of an object. However, opponents of export certificates argue that such systems can be administratively burdensome and enormously costly, particularly for countries with large art markets. Thus, there is

41 Canada has set up a system of export permits for cultural property in the Cultural Property Export and Import Act, *supra* note 19, to meet the requirements of the 1970 UNESCO Convention.

considerable reluctance to including such a provision in the Unidroit Convention.

Paragraph 3 of Article 8 provides that, as an alternative to compensation, a possessor who is required to return an illegally exported cultural object may nevertheless retain title of the object, or may transfer title to a person residing in the requesting state "who provides the necessary guarantees." "Necessary guarantees" are not defined. This provision demonstrates the paramount importance of having cultural objects, rather than legal titles thereto, returned to their countries of origin.

Article 8 places the cost of returning the object on the requesting state. The article concludes by stating that a possessor shall not be in a more favourable position than the person from whom the object was acquired by way of gift or inheritance.

Chapter 4: Claims and Actions

Article 9 provides that a claim may be brought in the place where the cultural object is located. This is a special ground of jurisdiction, since there is currently no general rule providing for jurisdiction based solely on the location of a movable object. Normally, jurisdiction would be based on the residence of the possessor or, in the case of stolen cultural objects, where the theft had occurred. This special ground of jurisdiction is important because it may often be easier to locate a stolen or illegally exported cultural object than to find the person who has or purports to have title to it.

This special ground of jurisdiction does not prevent claimants from relying on other, more traditional, grounds of jurisdiction, since the article states that the special ground exists without prejudice to the jurisdictional rules either in the ordinary law of states parties to the Convention or in international conventions. Therefore, claims could still be brought where the possessor resides.[42]

Paragraph 2 of Article 9 states that the parties may agree upon the jurisdiction to which to submit their dispute, or they may agree to go to arbitration rather than to court. Finally, paragraph 3 permits parties to have resort to interim measures for the protection of the object that are available under the law of the contracting state where the object is located, even if the request for return of the object is brought in a different contracting state.

---

[42] Under the Cultural Property Export and Import Act, *ibid.*, claims may be brought in Canada when the object in question is in Canada.

Chapter 5: Final Provisions

Article 10 allows parties to apply rules that are more favourable to the international return of stolen or illegally exported cultural objects than those found in the Convention. For example, a state can enact legislation stipulating less stringent limitation periods. In its final version, this chapter will also set out the procedures for states to become parties and the numbers required to bring the Convention into force. There will also be a federal state clause to enable federal states to become party to the Convention, extending its application to those of their territorial units that have adopted implementing legislation.

Other Issues

Debates on matters not reflected in the draft Convention also occurred during the meetings of the Committee of Governmental Experts. One such issue was the question whether states should have the option of implementing only that part of the Convention dealing with illegally exported cultural objects. In other words, some states have proposed that the Convention permit opting out of the part dealing with stolen cultural property, because the Convention's provisions are vastly different from their national laws dealing with stolen property.

Another issue is whether the Convention should operate retroactively. States that have lost art treasures and items of cultural heritage have vigorously promoted retroactivity, while art market states have refused to consider any such proposal. This issue is likely to be debated at length during the diplomatic conference. It is doubtful, however, in the light of the considerable opposition that has been expressed against it, that retroactivity will find its way into the final version of the Convention.

CONCLUSION

The illicit trade in cultural property has continued to flourish in the face of increasing numbers of international instruments designed to control it. These instruments have not succeeded because they have not reconciled the opposing views of the proponents of an unfettered art market and the advocates of countries that continue to suffer from the impoverishment of their cultural heritage through theft and illegal export. As the Unidroit Secretariat has explained, "States naturally tend to adopt a position more favourable to the defence of their own particular interests. If a satisfactory solution is to be reached, however, it will be necessary to look beyond these purely egoistic considerations. Regard will have to be had to all the competing interests and an attempt made somewhere to strike a fair balance."[43] Although Unidroit's draft on cultural property is of considerable interest to a number of countries, participants have thus far demonstrated limited willingness to compromise on key issues. Thus, there is a risk that the diplomatic conference will fail to adopt a final convention along the lines of Unidroit's draft.

Nevertheless, recent regional instruments such as the European Community Directive and the Commonwealth Scheme for the Protection of Cultural Heritage Within the Commonwealth provide some basis for believing that progress can be made. True success, however, lies in a multilateral approach such as the draft prepared by Unidroit. Only universal or near universal action will result in curbing an illegal trade that has become internationalised. The means to struggle against this must also be international.

If a convention is adopted on the basis of the Unidroit draft that has the support of art importing and art exporting countries, Unidroit's effort will represent the most significant achievement to date in the international effort to protect cultural property.

VALERIE HUGHES AND LAURIE WRIGHT
Department of Justice, Ottawa

Sommaire

La collaboration internationale visant à assurer la restitution de biens culturels volés ou illicitement exportés: Est-ce qu'Unidroit a trouvé une solution globale?

La protection internationale des biens culturels a commencé par des efforts visant à limiter l'appropriation illicite des biens culturels et les dommages qui leur étaient causés en temps de guerre. Le principal exemple de ces efforts est la Convention de La Haye de 1954 pour la protection des biens culturels en cas de conflit armé. Par la suite, on s'est préoccupé de mettre en place des mesures de répression du trafic illicite et international des biens culturels, telles que celles prévues dans la Convention de l'UNESCO de 1970 concernant les mesures à prendre pour interdire et empêcher l'importation, l'expor-

---

[43] *Supra* note 3 at 36-37.

tation et le transfert de propriété illicites des biens culturels. Le Canada est partie à cette convention qu'il a intégrée à son droit interne en adoptant la Loi sur l'exportation et l'importation de biens culturels. Mais comme la plupart des pays dotés d'un important marché de l'art (en particulier ceux de l'Europe de l'Ouest) ne sont pas parties à la convention de l'UNESCO, son utilité est marginale. Unidroit a présenté un projet de convention pour une collaboration internationale visant à assurer la restitution des biens culturels volés ou illicitement exportés. Le projet de convention, qui sera examiné à l'occasion d'une conférence diplomatique en juin 1995, s'efforce de trouver un équilibre entre les intérêts des pays d'origine des biens culturels et ceux des pays importateurs, ce qui constituerait le succès le plus important obtenu jusqu'à maintenant par la communauté internationale dans le domaine de la protection des biens culturels. Mais cette convention risque de ne pas être adoptée, car les participants ne se sont pas montrés très disposés à faire des compromis sur des questions fondamentales.

Summary

International Efforts to Secure the Return of Stolen or Illegally Exported Cultural Objects: Has Unidroit Found a Global Solution?

The international protection of cultural objects began with efforts to reduce damage to and unlawful appropriation of cultural objects in time of war. The primary example of such efforts is the 1954 Hague Convention for the Protection of Cultural Property in the Event of Armed Conflict. Subsequently, attention was turned to curbing the international illicit traffic in cultural objects, as in the 1970 UNESCO Convention on the Means of Prohibiting and Preventing the Illicit Import, Export and Transfer of Ownership of Cultural Property. Canada is a party to this Convention, which is implemented domestically through the Cultural Property Export and Import Act. However, since most countries with large art markets (particularly in Western Europe) are not parties to the UNESCO Convention, its utility is marginal. Unidroit has produced a draft Convention on the International Return of Stolen or Illegally Exported Cultural Objects, which will be considered at a diplomatic conference in June 1995. The draft Convention, which strives to strike a balance between the interests of countries of origin of cultural property and those of importing countries, would represent the most significant achievement to date in the international effort to protect cultural property. However, there is a risk that this convention will not be adopted, since participants have demonstrated a limited willingness to compromise on key issues.

The Status of Indigenous Peoples under International Law: Greenland and the Right to Self-Determination

INTRODUCTION

THE TOPICS ADDRESSED IN contemporary social science and in the media normally reflect actual or emerging political, economic, social, or cultural problems in society. When basic national characteristics are under pressure to yield to new paradigms, we tend to reflect on our history, and the national characteristics of others are compared, appraised, and criticized in order to assess our perception of who we are. For most Europeans, the process of putting together a European Union with enough vision and viability to meet the demands of the next century certainly includes a tremendous challenge to our truly "national" qualities. Are Danes (to take my own nationality), first of all a Nordic people, or are the Nordic countries really (finally, some would argue) becoming an integrated part of Europe? Can we preserve and develop our cultural identity if we merge deeply and decisively with larger social creations? Canadians, I take it, are equally beset by these issues in the ongoing cacophony on constitutional unity.

This line of thinking applies as well to indigenous peoples and to the current debate on their status under international law and their right to self-determination, both of which have now become regular issues on the international agenda. Reflection over cultural heritage and national identity is surely as important to the Inuit, or to the Dene Nation of the Northwest Territories, as "Danishness" is for Danes in a rapidly changing Europe. The issue of self-determination has become one legal tool that indigenous peoples can use to bring their political and cultural distress in their home countries to the attention of the international community.

Two Aspects of Self-Determination

After the decolonization of most overseas possessions throughout the 1960s, indigenous peoples within the old metropolitan states were largely left to the national policies of those states. The decolonization process and the Cold War gave impetus to the idea of sovereignty, and states largely subjected their indigenous peoples to policies of national assimilation. The problem is that, as long as indigenous peoples are subjected to national assimilation (or even repression), or have insufficient autonomy programs, many indigenous cultures are likely to vanish.

The international legal response to this problem proposed by indigenous peoples has been to explore the possibility of finding a basis for the extension of the concept of self-determination to indigenous peoples and perhaps even to minorities. However, the identification of the subjects and the content of this concept have so far remained elusive.

Two main challenges to states, seemingly pointing in different directions and offering different conclusions, are implied by indigenous peoples' pursuit of self-determination. First, self-determination for indigenous peoples raises the issue of how states can accommodate the preservation and development of cultural diversity without sacrificing general principles of nondiscrimination and the protection of the environment. Providing self-determination for indigenous peoples implies a degree of difference in treatment between the indigenous and the non-indigenous. The task for states, therefore, lies in finding a justification for differential treatment in their policies. This would suggest solutions that give preference to the constitutional entrenchment of political autonomy for indigenous peoples within states (the cultural approach). This approach is based partly on the premise that full respect must be given to the lives and cultures of the indigenous people concerned, and partly on the assumption that cultural diversity is a life value in itself, just as we assert that biological diversity is important to the survival of humanity.

Second, indigenous self-determination defies constitutional unity and challenges the internal sovereignty of states whose territories were originally occupied by indigenous peoples. Most states, and in particular multicultural societies like Canada, the United States, Russia, or India, are sensitive to claims for self-government made by indigenous peoples, because such claims may potentially entail a risk of segmentation into ethnically based subdivisions of society, loss of political control, and ultimately national dissolution. On the basis of these considerations, solutions favourable to the preservation of constitutional coherence and state control should be given maximum priority in any final self-government arrangements to be established for indigenous peoples (the static approach).

Contemporary legal discourse on self-determination has swung between these two approaches and has mainly, but inconclusively, focused on attempts to identify the beneficiaries and ingredients of this concept. The relative fruitlessness of these ventures would seem to call for a novel approach.

This note first summarizes an alternative view of the concept of self-determination in order to find new ways to overcome the present deadlock in this endeavour, and then outlines the status of Greenland's "Home Rule" provisions. Since Greenland's model of autonomy partly embodies the law on self-determination, it may have a particular interest for Canada's indigenous peoples.

SELF-DETERMINATION AS A PROCEDURAL NORM

Many scholars, while searching for substantive rights pertaining to self-determination, have furnished the concept with certain basic elements of autonomy — notably, secession and the transfer of legislative, executive, and judicial powers over local issues, land rights, ownership of natural resources, participation in public decision-making, financial support, etc.

In my view, however, although such rights may accommodate the needs of some indigenous peoples, they may be either insufficient or too comprehensive for others. It is questionable, in other words, whether we can identify universal rights that are fit to meet the concerns of all indigenous peoples, and whether, indeed, we should. The risk, of course, is that globally applicable standards might end up being so diluted that they really provide very little of substance. The present situations of indigenous peoples are far too dissimilar to build a case for one unique concept of self-determination. In fact, the degree and possibilities of autonomy depend in each case on very different political, economic, demographic, cultural, and climatic conditions. By contrast, too many variations in the content of self-determination might further complicate attempts to give content to the idea of autonomy.

A closely related consideration is that of defining the possible subjects of these rights. States will inevitably, for fear of national disruption, seek to limit the beneficiaries of self-determination to the smallest possible number of groups in society, especially as long as the right of secession remains a part of the concept of self-determination. This concern of states is the basic reason for the distinction between indigenous peoples (who may enjoy the right of self-determination) and minorities (who may not). Both indigenous peoples and minorities, not surprisingly, have rejected this distinction and suggested that "self-identification" and "historical relationship with the territory" be established instead as the fundamental criteria for entitlement to self-determination. This view now seems to be acquiring more general acceptance.[1]

If a viable interpretation of self-determination for indigenous peoples is to be found, I believe that it would be worthwhile considering an exclusion of the immediate right of secession from that concept. This particular element cannot, of course, be denied to indigenous peoples, but it should not remain an integral component of the right of self-determination because it tends to petrify further progress on the issue. Secession is an option only for peoples with a right to national independence who are in a position to maintain full-scale statehood and a reasonable level of territorial integrity. If an indigenous people has sufficient resources and can develop an economy that will support it as an independent state, it is no doubt entitled to do so. This might be the situation for indigenous peoples that are geographically separated from a later-established nation state.

Nevertheless, this is not the usual situation. In my view, it would generally be helpful to exclude secession as an *inherent* element of self-determination for domestic indigenous peoples. Self-determination for indigenous peoples, in other words, would be taken to include a variety of substantial political autonomy arrangements other than secession, which would then remain an option only for former colonies and overseas territories. The United Nations Declaration on International Legal Principles for Friendly Relations and Co-operation between States does provide, however, that secession is one among several options for exercising self-determination. In order to surmount the firm resistance by many states to recognizing the right of self-determination for indigenous peoples, however, I suggest that this provision should be interpreted to imply that secession is not necessarily available to any indigenous people at any time, but rather to indigenous peoples for whom

[1] See e.g., International Labour Organization, Convention 169 on Indigenous Peoples, Art. 1, para. 2.

national independence is not only economically feasible but also politically and legally indispensable for the defence and development of their culture. I believe that accepting this limitation would be a fair exchange for obtaining the commitment of states to actively promote self-determination for their indigenous peoples.

States, furthermore, are themselves increasingly engaged in international integration of their domestic affairs. International supervision of indigenous self-determination would therefore not fall out of line with the trend towards the increased internationalization of internal matters. Sovereignty, in many other ways, is being rearranged in the process of adjusting national economies to changing world market conditions, and it is no longer given that issues like self-determination for indigenous peoples can and should exclusively fall within the province of individual states. Cross-border co-operation and common self-determination arrangements between indigenous peoples in neighbouring states, for instance, could perhaps turn out to be far more constructive and cost-effective solutions for all parties involved.

Furthermore, rather than trying to substantiate the content of self-determination, I suggest that this concept be understood as a procedural norm that includes two elements:

(1) States have a duty to promote autonomy for indigenous peoples in good faith. This statement may seem void of any content, but in fact the world community can, by establishing a simple international legal principle, exert pressure on states that, in words or in practice, refuse to establish any form of self-determination for their indigenous peoples. States will be obliged to prove that they are doing whatever is possible to accommodate the needs of their indigenous peoples and to convince the international community that self-determination is provided for to the fullest possible extent. The burden of proof should lie with the states themselves, and not with the indigenous peoples.

(2) Once established, self-determination arrangements for indigenous peoples can never be unilaterally withdrawn, reduced, or amended by states. This provision would offset the threats that many indigenous peoples have experienced when they have exercised their autonomy in a contentious manner. Indigenous peoples will therefore always be able to increase their autonomy, but can never be forced to surrender it.

These two procedural elements, in my view, offer a more workable response to the issue of self-determination than the cultural or static approaches outlined above. Applying self-determination as a procedural norm rather than one of substance with a fixed or identifiable content has two advantages: it blurs the adversarial relationship between the two interpretations of self-determination, which otherwise tend to neutralize each other; and it allows for a flexible solution in each case by excluding the terror of the secessionist argument and leaving the burden of proof on the shoulders of the state.

GREENLAND'S HOME RULE

In the following sections I will outline the features of the Greenland Home Rule model in order to assess the usefulness of my approach to self-determination.

BACKGROUND

Greenland has approximately 55,000 inhabitants, 45,000 of which are Greenlandic Inuit, while the rest are Danish or foreigners. The climate is arctic and subarctic and most of the population lives along the southwestern coast of Greenland, where an offshoot of the Gulf Stream makes human life sustainable. Nuuk, the capital of Greenland, has a population of 12,000.

Greenland was colonized in 1721 by Denmark through a joint operation by the Danish King, the Church, and Danish-Norwegian trading companies. Until then, Greenland's waters had been sailed by whale hunters from Spain, Portugal, and England. Dutch and German missionaries had been in regular contact with the Greenland Inuit, who were living in small settlements scattered along the coast. The Danish King's move to establish a permanent Lutheran Mission and a small Danish colony in 1721 was thus designed to exclude foreigners from Greenland and its surrounding waters, and from the profits gained by trade with oil and blubber from sea mammals. This policy was successful, and Greenland remained isolated from the outside world and inaccessible to foreigners until 1953, when its colonial status was finally rescinded.

THE ESTABLISHMENT OF HOME RULE

After Greenland was brought into the European Community with Denmark's admission in 1973, despite an overwhelming majority in Greenland against membership, and after Denmark began granting concessions for oil exploration off western Greenland, a movement to establish local autonomy emerged in Greenland. In 1975 a Greenland committee recommended Home Rule along the same lines as that established for the Faroe Islands in 1948. In 1978, a joint Danish-Greenlandic "Home Rule Commission" finally submitted a comprehensive report that included a bill for a Greenland Home Rule Act. The Danish legislature adopted the Home Rule Act for Greenland in 1978, after approval by a referendum in Greenland, and Home Rule was subsequently introduced in Greenland on May 1, 1979.

The Home Rule Act establishes a Greenlandic government (the "Landsstyre") and an elected Greenlandic Parliament (the "Landsting"), and transfers full administrative and legislative powers within certain areas to these institutions. These areas (17 in all) are specified in an annex to the Home Rule Act and the powers have all by now been assumed by the Greenland government. One of the powers transferred under Home Rule is that of taxation. The Home Rule government collects all taxes and duties in Greenland; these are an important source of revenue to cover the expenditures of Home Rule. Since the underlying principle in the transfer of areas from Denmark to Greenland was that Denmark should neither lose nor gain financially from handing over jurisdiction, Denmark provides for annual block grants to the Greenland government to help pay for public services that were previously administered and controlled by Denmark.

The Greenlandic Home Rule government consists of a premier and six ministers, each in charge of a department of administration. The government must enjoy the support of the parliament at all times. The premier and the majority of the ministers must be members of parliament. The parliament numbers twenty-seven members who are elected for four years, although irregular elections may be held if the government loses the parliament's confidence. The parliament adopts the legislation prepared and tabled by the administration and each bill is debated three times before final adoption. The Greenland parliament's laws are binding on everyone with permanent residence in Greenland and cannot, presumably, be unilaterally withdrawn or amended by Danish authorities.

Political parties have surfaced and are now represented in parliament. The biggest party is the social democratic Siumut Party that, in coalition with the left-wing party Inuit Ataqatigiit, has held power since the inauguration of Home Rule. The liberal Atassut Party is the second largest party and forms the opposition in parliament together with a small right-wing party.

THE EXTENT OF HOME RULE POWERS

The Constitutional Issue

Home Rule is a system of political autonomy or self-determination that allows Greenland to set out its own policies and adopt its own laws within a number of specified areas, yet remain with Denmark and the Faroe Islands in the community of the Danish realm. Home Rule is not mentioned in the Danish Constitution Act. However, Faroese Home Rule, which preceded the current constitution of 1953, was believed to be in conformity with the old constitution of 1915, and this view was also taken when Greenland achieved Home Rule in 1978. Thus, the Home Rule Act serves partly as a constitution for Greenland, although some parts of the Danish constitution, notably those relevant to the Danish currency, the Monarch, and rights and freedoms, are still common to the entire Danish realm and are therefore in force in Greenland.

The lack of any reference in the 1953 constitution to Home Rule has led to much debate about the constitutional character of Home Rule powers. The Danish constitution establishes a monostructural model with all powers vested in the Danish executive, the Danish legislature, and the Danish judiciary. Thus, according to the traditional view, administrative and law-making powers are only delegated under Home Rule, which implies that they can be withdrawn or amended unilaterally by Denmark at any time. According to this approach, since judicial powers cannot be delegated, the judiciary cannot be transferred to the Greenland Home Rule government, and thus the last word in legal conflicts will remain with the Danish Supreme Court in Copenhagen. This, in fact, was the view of the Home Rule Commission in 1978, and the courts in Greenland are thus established by Danish law and fall under the authority of the Danish Ministry of Justice.

The Greenland interpretation is, however, somewhat different. According to the Greenlandic view, the powers transferred under Home Rule are exclusive and have been irrevocably assumed by the Home Rule authorities, with the consequence that Denmark is no longer entitled to interfere with Home Rule legislation. Danish invalidation of any piece of Greenland's internal legislation would be seen as a violation of contemporary international law regarding self-determination for indigenous peoples.

Also, according to the Greenland view, the judiciary cannot be excluded from the areas assumed under Home Rule; any autonomous legal system has the right to establish a judicial structure for the solution of legal conflicts within the system itself. The Greenland authorities therefore believe that they are entitled to establish a separate Greenlandic judiciary with independent courts. So far, however, the existing Danish courts have proved to be loyal to the Home Rule legislation and there has been no incentive to institute a parallel and costly separate system of courts. If, however, a Danish court in Greenland disregarded Home Rule legislation and gave supremacy to Danish law in an area within Home Rule jurisdiction, this peaceful state of affairs would break down immediately and Greenland would establish its own courts. This would not be a transfer of authority from Danish to Greenland courts, since a few Danish courts would probably still remain in Greenland to solve legal conflicts that are under Danish jurisdiction. It would rather be the exercise of the right of the Greenland authorities to establish their own judicial system under Home Rule.[2]

If Greenland's understanding of its powers is correct, the Danish constitution would have undergone a significant change by customary practice, in that the Danish realm would no longer consist of one, coherent area of regulation, but rather of three separate parts — Denmark, Greenland, and the Faroe Islands — each with its own autonomous legislative and administrative authority.

A more appropriate view is that, constitutionally, the 1978 Home Rule Act for Greenland and the 1948 Home Rule Act for the Faroe Islands rank above the level of ordinary Acts of the Danish Parliament to the extent that Home Rule legislation cannot be directly and unilaterally repealed or amended by Danish legislation. The implication of this assumption is that the Home Rule Act has the status of a constitutional appendix that is superior to ordinary Danish legislation but remains under the Danish constitution.

External Relations

In principle, the Home Rule government has no power to conclude treaties or otherwise to maintain links with foreign govern-

---

[2] The same issue arises in repect of the police in Greenland, who are also Danish and governed by the Danish Ministry of Justice. A Greenlandic police force, too, may be established under Home Rule if there is ever a conflict of loyalty for the existing Danish police in Greenland.

ments.[3] In practice, however, the Home Rule government has concluded agreements with neighbouring countries on matters that fall exclusively within Home Rule powers. The bilateral Greenland-Norway fisheries agreement of September 24, 1991 and the trilateral fisheries agreement between Greenland/Denmark, Norway, and Iceland of June 12, 1989, are examples of such agreements. In both cases the Home Rule government concluded international agreements in its own right on matters in which it had the exclusive jurisdiction to implement the provisions of an international agreement. The Danish government has tacitly accepted these treaties as true international agreements, indicating that only the Home Rule government could be held responsible in case of breaches. It is understood, however, that this limited international treaty-making power applies only to local Greenlandic matters under Home Rule jurisdiction that have no general implications for Danish foreign policy and external security. The alternative practice is exemplified by Denmark's ratification of International Labour Organization Convention 169, which was done by the Danish government after it had secured the consent of the Home Rule authorities.

When Greenland decided to withdraw from the European Community in 1985 (after a referendum held in Greenland in 1982), the Home Rule government formed part of the delegation that negotiated the terms of withdrawal in Brussels, and the final agreement was signed by representatives of the European Community, Denmark, and Greenland. Greenland then acquired the status of an associated Overseas Country and Territory within the European Community under Part 4 of the Treaty of Rome.

Exploitation of Mineral Resources

One of the most serious problems facing the Home Rule Commission was that of ownership of mineral resources, including oil and gas, in Greenland. In contrast to most other places in the world, private ownership of land and subsurface resources does not exist in Greenland. Land and non-living resources are publicly owned — meaning, in effect, ownership by the state. This system has prevailed since time immemorial.

The Danish government officially took the position that jurisdiction over mineral resources could not be transferred to any particular part of the country, since these resources were common assets of the

[3] Section 19 of the Danish Constitution and section 10 of the Home Rule Act.

entire Danish realm. Greenland, on the other hand, has maintained that all resources in Greenland's territory are the property of Greenland's population. A compromise between these positions was found in Section 8 of the Home Rule Act, which provides that the permanent population of Greenland has "fundamental rights" over natural resources in Greenland. Rather than providing for the interpretation of this term, agreement was reached on equal sharing between Denmark and Greenland of all revenues from the exploitation of mineral resources in Greenland. Apart from deposits of cryolite, lead, and zinc, the mining of which have now been exhausted, no exploitation of mineral resources is currently taking place in Greenland.

Concessions to explore and exploit mineral resources in Greenland are formally issued by the Danish Minister of Energy, but only after approval by a joint Danish-Greenland Mineral Resources Board, which consists of a chair appointed by the Queen, five persons appointed by the Danish parliament, and another five persons appointed by the Greenlandic parliament. In effect, the Home Rule authorities have a veto in all matters pertaining to the mining of natural resources in Greenland.

The administration of mineral concessions and control of the mining companies, however, is vested with the Mineral Resources Department for Greenland, which is an administrative body in the Danish Ministry of Energy. Since the minister holds the power to issue mineral concessions, this department falls under his responsibility. The Mineral Resources Department negotiates the terms of exploration and exploitation, maintains links directly with the mining companies, and also advises both the minister and the joint board in their decisions.

Because the Home Rule government has no direct influence over the powerful Mineral Resources Department, recent claims have been voiced to transfer the power of granting concessions from the minister to the joint board, and thereby remove the Department from the minister's authority to an intermediate position under the joint board. This issue is currently under negotiation.

While the Danish Government had always maintained that jurisdiction over mineral resources could never be handed over to any part of the country, in December 1992 it suddenly changed its position by allowing for the Faroese Home Rule authorities to assume all responsibilities over natural resources. The reasons for this new position have remained obscure, but it now seems that Greenland, too, could if it wished take full jurisdiction over natural resources. Whether the

Greenland Home Rule authorities will eventually decide to do so depends, among other things, on their capacity and willingness to assume the financial costs of running the Department.

CONCLUSION

Greenland's Home Rule model seems to comply well with the self-determination theory discussed above. A substantial transfer of legislative and administrative powers from Danish to Greenlandic authorities has taken place, and it is assumed that judicial powers could be transferred to the Home Rule authorities as well.

Since Greenland is an overseas territory with an indigenous people, the Greenlanders would no doubt be entitled to national independence and full statehood if they so preferred. Greenland's insufficient economic foundation, however, makes the Home Rule model a more appropriate form of indigenous self-determination.

One crucial issue still remains to be settled: namely, the constitutional status of Home Rule within the Danish realm. The prevailing interpretation of the Danish constitution is that the two Home Rule Acts for Greenland and the Faroe Islands respectively, both pieces of Danish legislation, are included by constitutional custom in the Danish constitution at a level above the authority granted to the Danish legislature. This implies that Greenlandic (and Faroese) law constitute separate and distinct legal systems within the Danish realm, and that the Danish parliament accordingly has no power to interfere with the laws established by them. In constitutional and international legal terms, therefore, Denmark is a somewhat peculiar creature: it is neither a federation (since it lacks a treaty to this effect), nor is it a confederation. Nor can Denmark be classified as a "suzerain state," since Greenland and the Faroe Islands enjoy a higher status than mere vassals. A proper union or commonwealth would, however, require a more independent status for the two overseas territories.

The existing relationship between the three parts of the Danish realm therefore seems to be unique. It is a community of three culturally and ethnically different parts, tied together by history and a common constitution that establishes separate and autonomous legal systems for each of the three parts, but leaves Denmark with certain hegemonial and common powers.

FREDERIK HARHOFF
Faculty of Law, University of Copenhagen

Sommaire

Le statut des peuples autochtones

L'autodétermination des peuples autochtones suscite la controverse en droit international contemporain depuis que le processus de décolonisation s'est achevé, à la fin des années 1960. Parce qu'ils craignaient avant tout des désordres nationaux, de nombreux pays ont refusé de reconnaître que les peuples autochtones ont le droit de se séparer du territoire national et d'obtenir leur indépendance. Cependant, même la reconnaissance d'un droit moins vaste, soit un droit de recevoir un statut spécial et d'obtenir l'autonomie politique dans le cadre des frontières étatiques existantes, demeure une question litigieuse, car aucune définition claire des bénéficiaires et de la substance de ces droits ne peut être établie. De toute façon, la disparité des conditions politiques, économiques, sociales et climatiques dans lesquelles vivent les peuples autochtones du monde entier rend futile la création d'un seul et unique concept d'autodétermination qui s'appliquerait au monde entier. Pour sortir de cette impasse, on propose d'adopter une approche procédurale, au lieu d'essayer de fixer ces questions dans des termes juridiques stricts.

Le fait de qualifier le concept d'autodétermination de processus, au lieu de le décrire comme étant une série de règles exactes et préétablies, a pour avantage d'apporter un élément de flexibilité, car il permet aux deux parties, c'est-à-dire les États et les peuples autochtones, de trouver des appuis pour défendre leurs intérêts et d'imaginer une solution viable qui tienne compte des circonstances particulières de chaque cas. Mais toutes les parties concernées devraient tout d'abord accepter trois conditions préalables:

(1) Le droit de sécession immédiate et d'indépendance complète, en tant qu'aspect du droit à l'autodétermination, devrait être réservé aux peuples autochtones des territoires d'outre-mer.

(2) Les États ont le devoir de favoriser l'autonomie de leurs peuples autochtones et le fardeau de prouver qu'ils offrent la plus grande autonomie possible aux peuples autochtones vivant sur leurs territoires.

(3) Une fois que des ententes relatives à l'autonomie ont été conclues, les États ne peuvent pas les révoquer, les abréger ou les modifier unilatéralement.

L'auteur de cette note examine ensuite le régime d'autonomie du Groenland et conclut que ce régime semble satisfaire aux critères énoncés, bien que la question du statut actuel du Groenland (et des îles Faroe) au sein du royaume danois demeure incertaine sur le plan constitutionnel. Le régime d'autonomie implique un transfert irrévocable des pouvoirs législatifs et administratifs des autorités danoises aux autorités du Groenland, ce qui a pour effet de créer un régime juridique indépendant au Groenland. Par ailleurs, il est entendu que le régime d'autonomie du Groenland permet d'établir un système judiciaire indépendant, si les tribunaux danois du Groenland ne reconnaissent pas la validité de la Loi d'autonomie du Groenland.

Summary

The Status of Indigenous Peoples under International Law: Greenland and the Right to Self-Determination

Political self-determination for indigenous peoples has been a controversial issue in contemporary international law ever since the completion of the decolonization process by the end of the 1960s. For fear of national disruption, first of all, many states have denied that indigenous peoples have a right to secede from national territory and gain independence. But even the less dramatic right of being granted a special status and achieving political autonomy within the existing state-boundaries has remained a contentious issue, since no clear definition of the beneficiaries and the substance of such rights can be identified. In any case, the disparity in political, economical, social, and climatic conditions among the world's indigenous peoples would render futile the possibility of establishing one single and globally applicable concept of self-determination. In order to circumvent this deadlock, it is suggested that a procedural *approach be adopted rather than trying to fix these issues in hard law terms.*

Characterizing the concept of self-determination as a process *instead of a predetermined set of exact rules carries the advantage of flexibility by allowing for both parties — states as well as indigenous peoples — to find support of their interests and to establish a viable solution that takes into account the particular circumstances of every single case. Three preconditions, however, would need the prior acceptance of all parties involved. First, the right of immediate secession and full national independence — as part of the right of self-determination — should be reserved for indigenous peoples in* overseas *territories. Second, states have a duty to promote autonomy for their indigenous peoples and have the burden of proof that a maximum level of autonomy is being provided for indigenous peoples living within their territories. Third, self-determination arrangements once established cannot be withdrawn, reduced, or amended unilaterally by states.*

The article then reviews the Greenland Home Rule system and concludes that this system seems to meet these criteria, although some constitutional

legal uncertainty still remains about the current status of Greenland (and the Faroe Islands) within the Danish Realm. The Home Rule implies an irrevocable transfer of legislative and administrative powers from Danish to Greenlandic authorities, thereby creating an independent legal system in Greenland. It is understood, moreover, that an independent Greenlandic judiciary may be established by the Greenland Home Rule if the Danish courts (in Greenland) fail to recognize the validity of the Home Rule's legislation.

The Principle of Non-Encroachment: Implications for the Beaufort Sea*

INTRODUCTION

CANADA AND THE UNITED STATES have four maritime boundaries yet to be determined: the landward and seaward extensions of the Gulf of Maine, seaward of the Strait of Juan de Fuca, seaward of Dixon Entrance, and the Beaufort Sea.[1] Because of the huge potential for oil and gas exploration in the Beaufort Sea,[2] this last delimitation is the most important. Exploration in the Beaufort has revealed potentially vast reserves, and it seems only a matter of time before a major discovery or an increase in oil prices will make immediate delimitation necessary.[3] Rather than waiting for this eventuality, as many fear the two governments will do,[4] it would seem preferable to resolve the issue during a period when it is less politically charged. While a negotiated solution is always preferable, political realities between the two nations[5] make arbitration likely.

---

* The author would like to thank Professor Judith Swan for her helpful advice and Professor Ian Brownlie and Dr. Christine Gray whose seminars and materials inspired an interest in this subject.

---

1 Kindred, Hugh, M. et al., *International Law, Chiefly as Interpreted and Applied in Canada* 716 (5th ed., Toronto: Emond Montgomery, 1993).

2 Rothwell, D., *Maritime Boundaries and Resource Development: Options for the Beaufort Sea* 25-30 (Calgary: The Canadian Institute of Resource Law, 1988).

3 *Ibid.* Fisheries in the Beaufort Sea area are relatively unimportant due to a lack of commercial exploitation. See Lawson, Karin L., "Delimiting Continental Shelf Boundaries in the Artic: The U.S.-Canada Beaufort Sea Boundary," (1981) 22 Va. J. Int'l L. 221 at 227.

4 Bergman, Brian et al., "Parting the Waters," *Maclean's* (Aug. 12, 1991) 14.

5 As demonstrated by the negotiations regarding the Gulf of Maine dispute: Kindred, *supra* note 1 at 719.

Canada argues that the maritime boundary in the Beaufort Sea should be the 141st meridian of longitude, which would extend the existing land boundary out into the sea (see Map 1). The United States position is that the equidistance line should be the boundary. Because of the concave nature of the coastline in the vicinity of the

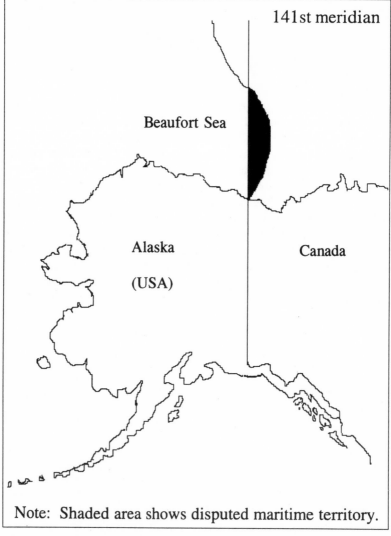

Note: Shaded area shows disputed maritime territory.

Map 1   Beaufort Sea dispute

land boundary, use of the equidistance line would cause the maritime boundary to swing out towards Canada, restricting the area of its maritime projection. The shaded area on Map 1 shows the resulting disputed maritime territory.

The parties have each made a number of arguments supporting their respective positions, which have been discussed elsewhere.[6] What has not been considered, however, is the importance of the equitable principle of non-encroachment for the Beaufort Sea delimitation. In the light of its gradual development into one of the few consistently-applied principles in maritime boundary delimitation and the manner in which it has been applied in similar geographical situations, non-encroachment seems likely to have a great effect on the outcome. This comment traces the development of the related principles of natural prolongation and non-encroachment. It then examines the crucial interaction between non-encroachment and the direction of coastal projection. Finally, it explores the specific implications of the principle for a future delimitation in the Beaufort Sea.

THE PRINCIPLES OF NATURAL PROLONGATION AND NON-ENCROACHMENT

The idea that maritime areas off the shores of coastal states "appertain" to them was stated in the *Grisbadarna* arbitration to have originated in the seventeenth century.[7] The method of expressing such appertenance through the related ideas of natural prolongation and non-encroachment, however, is of more recent origin. The first formal statement of the two principles was in the *North Sea Continental Shelf Cases*,[8] in which the International Court of Justice defined the "fundamental norm" of customary international law applicable to maritime boundary delimitation as follows:

---

[6] On the issues of the treaties of 1825 and 1867, the sector theory, equidistance, and claims of U.S. acquiescence, see Lawson, *supra* note 3; Pharand, D., *Canada's Arctic Waters in International Law* 17, 18 (Cambridge: Cambridge University Press, 1988); Prescott, J. R. V., *The Maritime Political Boundaries of the World* 268 (New York: Methuen, 1985); and Rothwell, *supra* note 2. On historic Inuit usage of the area, see VanderZwaag, D. and Pharand, D., "Inuit and the Ice: Implications for Canadian Arctic Waters" (1983) 21 *Canadian Yearbook of International Law* 53. On the possibilities for commercial and environmental joint development zones, see Lamson, C. and VanderZwaag, D., "Arctic Waters: Needs and Options for Canadian — American Cooperation" (1987) Ocean Dev. & Int'l L. 49.

[7] (1910) 4 Am. J. Int'l L. 226 at 231.

[8] [1969] ICJ Rep. 4.

. . . delimitation is to be effected by agreement in accordance with
equitable principles, and taking account of all relevant circumstances, in
such a way as to leave as much as possible to each party all those parts of
the continental shelf that constitute a natural prolongation of its land
territory into and under the sea, without encroachment on the natural
prolongation of the land territory of the other.[9]

The concave coastline of Northern Europe at the point in question meant that application of the equidistance principle would
have enclaved the Federal Republic of Germany, greatly limiting its
maritime territory and cutting off its seaward extension. The court
held that the equidistance principle was not a compulsory norm of
customary international law,[10] and that its application in this case
would be inequitable. It further held that Article 6 of the 1958
Continental Shelf Convention, which enshrines the "equidistance/
special circumstances" rule, was not applicable because Germany
had not ratified the Convention, and Article 6 did not represent
customary international law. The ultimate lines negotiated by the
parties extended Germany's maritime territory well beyond the
enclave that would have resulted from a delimitation based on
equidistance.

The *North Sea Cases* took two fundamental steps in defining the
related concepts of natural prolongation and non-encroachment.
The first was to emphasize the geological and geomorphological
aspect of natural prolongation. The court stated that the rights of
coastal states over adjacent areas of the continental shelf proceed
from the recognition of a physical fact: that the land territory of the
state extends beneath the surface of the sea.[11] This emphasis on the
geological basis for such rights was to have an impact on delimitation jurisprudence for decades, and continues to be cited in argument today. Even though it emphasized the geological basis of
continental shelf rights, the court did not endorse the mechanistic
application of geological arguments. It noted that Norway was
accepted by the parties as enjoying continental shelf rights over
areas of the North Sea separated from its coast by 80-100 kilometres
of the Norwegian Trough.[12] Such areas, the court held, could not be
viewed in any physical sense as representing the natural prolonga-

9 *Ibid.*, para. 101.

10 *Ibid.*, para. 8.

11 *Ibid.*, paras 95-96.

12 *Ibid.*, para. 45.

tion of the Norwegian land mass. Lack of geological continuity was therefore not necessarily fatal to claims to areas of the continental shelf.

The second fundamental step taken by the court in the *North Sea Cases* was its refusal to endorse a concept of natural prolongation according to which all areas of the continental shelf closest to a state inevitably appertained to that state.[13] Adoption of this concept would have amounted to the paramountcy of the equidistance principle. In rejecting this approach, the court noted that, in certain geographical configurations,[14] the strict application of equidistance would result in one state "cutting off" or encroaching on the coastal front of another state. Such a result was seen as inequitable. The International Court thus endorsed the view that a coastal area had a right to a reasonable projection into the maritime areas onto which it fronted, even if those areas were technically closer to another state. Although it would not become clear until after its consistent application in later cases, this caused the principle of non-encroachment to trump equidistance in the definition of an equitable result for a given geographical situation.

North Sea also made it clear that the application of the principle of non-encroachment is intimately linked to the concept of natural prolongation: if two states are adjacent, at which point does one state's natural prolongation begin to encroach on the natural prolongation of the other? The court's answer to this question has evolved since 1969, and has reflected the changes in view that emerged at the Third United Nations Conference on the Law of the Sea (UNCLOS III) and in state practice about the package of rights enjoyed by coastal states over adjacent maritime areas. As coastal state rights have moved from the exploration and exploitation of the continental shelf to exclusive rights over an economic zone (the "EEZ"), natural prolongation has changed from a concept based upon geological unity to one based upon distance and spatial coastal projection.

In the *Anglo/French Continental Shelf Case*,[15] the Court of Arbitration continued to develop the concept of natural prolongation and implicitly supported the principle of non-encroachment. The court

[13] *Ibid.*, paras. 8, 42-45.
[14] Such as concave coastlines or where small islands are located close to mainland shores.
[15] (1977) 54 I.L.R. 6.

was called upon to delimit the continental shelf between France and the United Kingdom, including the area around the Channel Islands. Both parties presented geologically-based natural prolongation arguments. The strongest of these was the English contention that the boundary in one sector should follow the Hurd Deep Fault Zone, which ran roughly parallel to the median line. The court rejected the geological arguments of both parties, and stressed the fundamental unity of the shelf.[16] It went on to discuss the nature of the continental shelf as the natural prolongation of the land territory of coastal states. The court noted that geologically the continental shelf of the English Channel/La Manche could be said to be the natural prolongation of either of the parties. The question for the court to decide was the extent of each state's natural prolongation in a legal sense. The court held that natural prolongation was a juridical concept that could not be evaluated exclusively on the basis of physical facts, but for which legal rules also were required.[17] It thus moved away from *North Sea*'s emphasis on geology and geomorphology towards a more complex view of natural prolongation.

The boundary resulting from the *Anglo/French* arbitration also reflects the principle of non-encroachment in the enclave drawn around the Channel Islands. A particular concern of France was the security, defence, and navigational problems presented by having foreign maritime territory so close to its shores.[18] The result of limiting the Channel Islands to an enclave implicitly reflects the reluctance of the court to award anything but the minimum amount of maritime territory that will encroach on the coastline of another state.

In the *Tunisia/Libya Continental Shelf Case*, the International Court took significant steps towards a more modern view of natural prolongation and non-encroachment.[19] By the time the case was heard, discussions at UNCLOS III were well advanced and the concept of the EEZ was emerging. The EEZ, which would encompass most continental shelf rights, was to be based exclusively on distance; as a result, the geological basis of claims to continental shelf rights was to become of much less significance.

---

[16] *Ibid.*, paras. 104-109.

[17] *Ibid.*, paras. 191-92.

[18] *Ibid.*, paras. 175-88.

[19] (1982) ICJ Rep. 3; see Map 2.

The court, which was asked to delimit the continental shelf between Tunisia and Libya in the Mediterranean Sea,[20] rejected both the geological plate tectonics argument of Libya and the bathymetry/geomorphology argument of Tunisia. It held, as the court of arbitration had done in the *Anglo/French Case*, that the shelf was one continuous unit in which boundaries could not be defined by geological features.[21] In addition, and more significantly, the court rejected the Libyan contention that a delimitation that accorded with the physical facts of geology must inevitably be equitable.[22] The court instead emphasized geographical features such as coastal formation and islands, as well as the need to prevent the maritime boundary from encroaching on maritime areas. It did, however, maintain that under certain circumstances geology could still be an important factor in defining an equitable solution.[23]

Judge *ad hoc* Jiménez de Arechaga traced the development of the concept of natural prolongation, and noted the incompatibility of a geological definition with claims to continental shelves by states such as Norway and Chile.[24] He noted that the principles of natural prolongation and non-encroachment are complementary, and that their definitions are inextricably intertwined.[25] While the basis of title to continental shelf areas rests on the view that the shelf is the natural appurtenance of the state in front of whose coast it lies, this title is limited by the converse "principle of non-encroachment, a fundamental principle of equity."[26] Judge de Aréchaga's recognition of the importance of the principle of non-encroachment is reflected in the result of *Tunisia/Libya*, and also in the case law following it.

The relevance of the principle of non-encroachment can be seen in both sectors of the maritime boundary in *Tunisia/Libya*. The inner segment of the line is drawn outwards from the land boundary between the two states. At this point, the relationship between them is one of adjacency, and in fact the shape of the coast closely

[20] Technically speaking, the court was asked to define the applicable principles and rules, but in fact a line did result from its conclusions.

[21] *Supra* note 19, paras. 61-68.

[22] *Ibid.*, para. 44.

[23] *Ibid.*

[24] Separate Opinion of Judge *ad hoc* Jiménez de Arechaga; *ibid.*, 102-105.

[25] *Ibid.*, 111-12.

[26] *Ibid.*, 109-10.

resembles that of Canada and Alaska in the Beaufort Sea area. In this inner sector, the court adopted a line that approximated to a perpendicular to the coast.[27] If this perpendicular had been continued in a straight line, it would have encroached on Tunisia's Sahel Promontory. The court therefore deflected the outer sector of the line eastwards, following a line parallel to the change in coastal direction.[28] The court thus applied the principle of non-encroachment emphasized by Judge de Arechaga.

By the time of the *Gulf of Maine Case,*[29] UNCLOS III had been concluded and the 1982 Law of the Sea Convention had been signed. The idea of a 200-mile EEZ based solely on distance was becoming accepted as a norm of customary international law, and had been included in Part 5 of the new Convention.[30] The idea of natural prolongation with respect to the continental shelf had also been included, in Article 76(1). Against the background of these developments, a Chamber of the International Court was asked to delimit a single maritime boundary in the Gulf of Maine between the coasts of Maine (United States) and Nova Scotia (Canada) on the eastern seaboard of North America.[31] The Chamber noted that the development of EEZ rights following UNCLOS III would make single maritime boundaries for the shelf and water column more common. As a result, neutral factors such as distance and geography would predominate over those pertaining to strictly one aspect of the delimitation, such as the geomorphology of the shelf.[32] In the same vein, the Chamber held that the notion of adjacency, or distance, now better expressed the basis of a state's title to areas of adjacent submerged land than the concept of natural prolongation.[33]

The principle of non-encroachment played a substantial role in *Gulf of Maine,* effectively trumping American arguments relating to both geomorphology and primary/secondary coasts. The United

[27] *Supra* note 19, paras. 118-19.

[28] Half-effect was also given to the Kerkennah Islands.

[29] (1984) 71 I.L.R. 58.

[30] United Nations Convention on the Law of the Sea (New York: UN Documents, 1982); Churchill R. R. and Lowe, A. V. *The Law of the Sea* 133-38 (2nd ed., Manchester: Manchester University Press, 1988).

[31] See Map 2.

[32] *Supra* note 29, paras. 194-96.

[33] *Ibid.,* paras. 102-103.

States had argued that the maritime boundary should take account of a geological depression known as the Northeast Channel, which lies just off the coast of Nova Scotia. It supported this position by contending that the coast of Nova Scotia represented a "secondary" coast, deviating from the general direction of the "primary" coast of North America, which followed the direction of the coast of Maine. Adoption of the line advocated by the American arguments would have resulted in a maritime boundary encroaching on the south-western seaward projection of Nova Scotia. The Chamber accordingly rejected both of the United States arguments, the former as relating only to the shelf aspect of the delimitation, and the latter as putting a dubious human construction on the facts of geography.[34]

The Chamber held that the relevant circumstances in the area were, first, proportionality between maritime areas and relevant coastal length, second, islands, and, third, the need to avoid encroachment on any coastal area.[35] The line adopted by the Chamber — the bisector of the angle made by the two coastlines in the inner sector and a line perpendicular to the general direction of the coast in the outer sector — shows the Chamber's emphasis on avoiding any form of encroachment in either sector. The Chamber was careful to note, however, that it was not elevating the principle of non-encroachment to the status of a "rule" of boundary delimitation.[36] Delimitation was still to be achieved in accordance with the fundamental norm, which required in the absence of agreement an equitable result based upon the relevant circumstances.[37] While the need for flexibility in responding to each separate delimitation prevents the adoption of rigid and mechanistic rules, the decision confirmed that the principle of non-encroachment is of fundamental importance.

In the year following *Gulf of Maine*, the International Court delimited the maritime boundary between Libya and the island-state of Malta in the *Libya/Malta Continental Shelf Case*.[38] It took this opportunity to dispel finally any lingering influence that the geological view of natural prolongation could have had. After referring to statements in *North Sea* and *Tunisia/Libya* that accorded a

---

[34] *Ibid.*, paras. 108-109.

[35] *Ibid.* paras 194-96.

[36] *Ibid.* para. 110.

[37] *Ibid.* paras 110-12.

[38] (1985) I.C.J. Rep. 13.

continuing role to geology, the court stated that natural prolongation, "in spite of its physical origins has throughout its history
become more and more a complex and juridical concept."[39] It went
on to state that, for delimitations within 200 miles of each of the
two coastal states, geological factors were to play no role.[40] Features
common to the EEZ and the shelf (such as proximity or distance)
were to be emphasized over those (such as the geomorphology of
the shelf) that related to only one of them. The court also under-
lined the intimate relationship between the principles of natural
prolongation and non-encroachment, which had been noted by
Judge Jiménez de Aréchaga in *Tunisia/Libya*.[41]

In the same year that the court decided *Libya/Malta*, an arbitral
tribunal, whose three members were also judges of the International Court, was called upon to delimit a single maritime boundary
between Guinea and Guinea-Bissau.[42] The concave shape of the
West African coast in this area, combined with the large number of
small coastal states, meant that application of the equidistance
principle would have resulted in Guinea-Bissau being enclaved. As
the International Court had done in the *North Sea Cases*, the arbitral
tribunal rejected equidistance as a method that was capable of
producing an equitable result in these circumstances. It noted that
an enclave would have produced an undesirable "cut-off effect" for
Guinea-Bissau, and would have prevented it from extending its
maritime territory as far seaward as international law permitted.[43]
The tribunal therefore found that each state's coastal front projected out into the sea at an angle perpendicular to the general
direction of the coast. In this way, the maritime boundaries would
all run parallel and would not encroach on any one state.

By recognizing Guinea-Bissau's right to a maritime projection,
the tribunal was not only repeating the *North Sea* finding that being
reduced to an enclave is inequitable, but also extending the definition of natural prolongation and non-encroachment to include the
notion of a "coastal opening." This concept, which had first been
introduced in *Libya/Malta*,[44] essentially states that an equitable

[39] *Ibid.* para. 34.
[40] *Ibid.* para. 77.
[41] *Ibid.* para. 46.
[42] (1985) 77 I.L.R. 636.
[43] *Ibid.* at 679-81.
[44] *Supra* note 38, para. 49.

delimitation is one that allows where possible each state to "extend" its maritime rights to the fullest extent permitted by international law, in at least one direction. This "opening" may be narrow, due to the presence of nearby states, but encroachment onto a state's seaward projection in its designated direction will almost always be viewed seriously and as potentially inequitable by a court. In *Guinea/Guinea-Bissau*, the court also emphasized its rejection of the geological view of natural prolongation by summarily rejecting geological arguments from both parties.[45]

The principles of natural prolongation and non-encroachment assumed perhaps their greatest importance in the 1992 *Canada/France Maritime Boundary Arbitration* that concerned delimitation between Canada and the French islands of Saint-Pierre and Miquelon[46] (hereafter "*Saint-Pierre and Miquelon*"). The islands lie off the east coast of Canada, in an area characterized by the intermingled projections of several coastlines. The five-member court of arbitration, of which Mr. Jiménez de Aréchaga was President, held that all coasts in the area projected in a southerly direction perpendicular to the general direction of the south coast of Newfoundland. In this manner, it could be ensured that each coastal area had an opening in at least one direction, and no projection encroached on that of another area. The islands of Saint-Pierre and Miquelon were accordingly given a full 200-mile EEZ in a corridor lying directly to their south. To the west, however, the islands were limited to a 24-mile EEZ, since westward extension would encroach on Newfoundland's southerly projection. The court even expressed concern about this 12-mile extension beyond the territorial sea, but noted that some encroachment is inevitable in all delimitations.[47] The seriousness with which even this minor encroachment was treated indicates that a tribunal is likely to accord similar gravity to any United States claim to an equidistance line that would encroach on Canada's frontal projection in the Beaufort Sea.

The court of arbitration in *Saint-Pierre and Miquelon* applied a view of natural prolongation that was entirely divorced from geological facts, and was based upon distance, proximity, and the idea of "coastal projection."[48] In defining the southern corridor of

[45] *Ibid.* at 685-87.
[46] (1992) I.L.M. 1149.
[47] *Ibid.* paras 66-74.
[48] *Ibid.* paras 46-47.

the EEZ around the islands of Saint-Pierre and Miquelon, the court also endorsed the concept of a "coastal opening" employed in *Libya/ Malta* and in *Guinea/Guinea Bissau.*[49] The designated direction of projection in this case was held to be southwards. In this direction, coastal areas enjoy — without encroachment — the full seaward extension of their maritime rights. The southerly corridor for the islands illustrates this principle in action. The concept of a "coastal opening" is a natural result of the court's jurisprudence relating to concave coastlines, natural prolongation, and non-encroachment.

This review of the development and application of the related principles of natural prolongation and non-encroachment in the jurisprudence of the International Court and of international tribunals leads to the following conclusions:

(1) Non-encroachment is now a fundamental equitable principle that is applied consistently, and almost without exception trumps other competing equitable principles.

(2) Natural prolongation and non-encroachment together contribute greatly to our conception of what constitutes an equitable solution in each case.

(3) Natural prolongation and non-encroachment are now essentially based upon the related ideas of adjacency, proximity, distance, and coastal projection; the former geological/geomorphological basis is now obsolete.

(4) Each coastal area is entitled to a "coastal opening," or a full extension seaward of its maritime rights in at least one direction. This principle is particularly important where delimitations involve adjacent states.

(5) The direction in which a coastline is seen to project is now of crucial importance.

COASTAL PROJECTION AND THE BEAUFORT SEA

What are the implications of these principles for the Beaufort Sea? If a court or tribunal wishes to protect the seaward extension of a land mass from encroachment, it is necessary to determine the direction in which the coast projects. When this projection was based on geological prolongation, the task was (in theory) scientific. With the modern view of projection being complex, and primarily based on distance, the direction must be determined by

[49] *Ibid.* paras 60 and 80, and citing *Libya/Malta supra* note 38, para. 49.

other means. A coastline could be seen to project radially (the same amount in each direction),[50] or along some predetermined set of parallel lines, such as those perpendicular to the general direction of the coast, or in some other direction. In cases involving a number of intermingled projections (such as *Gulf of Maine* or *Libya/Tunisia*), the direction in which each coast is seen to project becomes important. If the shape of the coastline is concave (as in *North Sea*, *Guinea/ Guinea Bissau*, and to a certain extent in the Beaufort Sea area), it can determine a state's claims (see Map 2 for an example of court and arbitral tribunal findings on coastal projection).

The Committee of Experts of the International Law Commission in 1953 noted three possible directions for the projection of a maritime frontier: lines perpendicular to the direction of the coast at the point of intersection between it and the land frontier, lines perpendicular to the general direction of the coast, and equidistance.[51] The difference between the first two perpendiculars should be noted: one refers to the general direction of the coast, the other to its direction at the point of the land frontier. The length of the coastal strip that is examined in determining the direction of the projection can thus vary widely. In the Beaufort Sea area, given the concave nature of the Alaska/Yukon coast at the point of the land frontier but the relatively straight (west-east) nature of the overall coastline, this issue will be crucial. If a narrow strip were to be selected, the resulting line would be even more skewed towards Canada than would an equidistance line (see Map 1). If a wider strip is used, the line will approximate the 141st parallel (the boundary claimed by Canada). Therefore, the length of coast considered by the court in defining the projection will determine the extent to which the delimitation line "encroaches" on the "natural prolongation" of the Canadian land mass.

How is Coastal Direction Determined?
State Practice and Judicial Decisions

The discussion of the Beaufort Sea demonstrates the importance of the direction in which coastlines are seen to project. It is therefore useful to look at state practice and at the views of past tribunals on the projection of land masses. Allan Willis has examined state

[50] See the dissenting opinion of Prosper Weil in the *Saint-Pierre and Miquelon* case *supra* note 46.

[51] See *Libya/Tunisia, supra* note 19, para. 119.

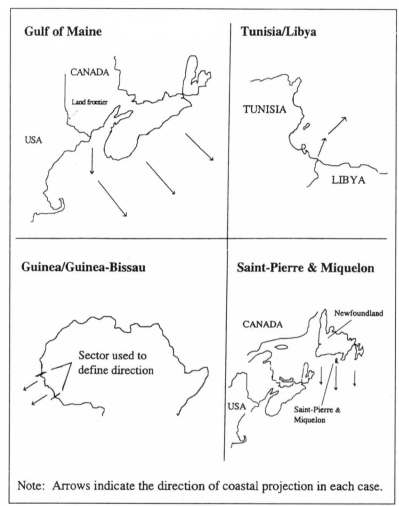

Note: Arrows indicate the direction of coastal projection in each case.

Map 2 Direction of coastal projection

practice on the issue of coastal projection, and found a number of delimitations that employ the perpendicular to the general direction of the coast.[52] He has also noted that several have used parallels

---

[52] These are, Uruguay-Brazil, Brazil-France, Senegal/Guinea-Bissau, Umm al Quaiwan-Sharjah, and Dubai-Abu Dhabi: Willis, L. Allan "Delimitation in State Practice Generally;" in D. Pharand and U. Leanza (eds), *The Continental Shelf and The Exclusive Economic Zone: Delimitation and Legal Regime,* 65-79 (The Netherlands: Kluwer, 1993).

of latitude or meridians.[53] Willis further observes that such lines are most common where adjacent states share a coastline. Ample practice therefore exists to support the adoption of a perpendicular by a tribunal for the Beaufort Sea.

Past decisions discussing coastal projection are also informative of the likely approach to be taken. In the *Grisbadarna* arbitration of 1910, an international tribunal was called upon to delimit a maritime boundary that extended outwards from the land frontier between Norway and Sweden.[54] The tribunal rejected the contention that the land boundary should follow the median line. Rather, citing international legal opinion dating back to the seventeenth century, the court held that the boundary should follow a line perpendicular to the general direction of the coast.[55] The tribunal noted the necessity of examining the direction of the coast on both sides of the land boundary to demarcate the perpendicular.

This early acceptance of the perpendicular to the coastline as defining the maritime boundaries of adjacent states continued in the jurisprudence. In *Gulf of Maine*,[56] the Chamber made an interesting finding with respect to direction of coastal projection (see Map 2). For the inner sector of the line, it adopted the bisector of the angle formed by the closing line of the Bay of Fundy and the direction of the American coastline.[57] For the outer sector, the Chamber adopted a line perpendicular to the closing line of the Gulf, which approximates the general direction of the coast.[58] The *Gulf of Maine* result demonstrates the court's affinity for projection at a perpendicular to the general direction of the coast, but also makes it clear that such a direction will not be adopted if it would result in an encroachment on another coastal area.

The inner sector of the *Gulf of Maine* line displays a slight variation on the perpendicular: the use of the bisector of the angle between two adjacent coasts. This method has also been approximated in the *Dubai/Sharjah* arbitration.[59] In the Beaufort Sea

---

53 *Ibid.* Columbia-Panama, Columbia-Honduras, Kenya-Tanzania, and Chile-Argentina. See also the U.S./Russia maritime boundary in the Bering Sea.

54 *Supra* note 7.

55 *Ibid.* at 232.

56 *Supra* note 29.

57 *Ibid.* paras 207-14.

58 *Ibid.* paras 224-28.

59 (1981) 91 I.L.R. 543.

context, if the angle of the concave "V" shape was to be transposed to the land boundary, and its bisector taken as the direction of projection, the result would be a line bending towards the western side of the 141st meridian — that is, towards the United States side. For the reasons relating to the principle of non-encroachment discussed above, this seems as unlikely a result as an equidistance line.

In *Guinea/Guinea Bissau*,[60] the tribunal also considered the issue of the direction of coastal projection (see Map 2). In that case, because of the concave nature of the coastline and the intermingled projection of several states, the tribunal held that the projection should be perpendicular to the general direction of the West African coastline. The section of coastline considered in establishing the direction encompassed the coastal areas of five states — Senegal, Gambia, Guinea-Bissau, Guinea, and Sierra Leone — and the tribunal stated that it was appropriate to consider both the general direction of the coastline and further delimitations in the area.[61] In such delimitations between adjacent states, each coastal state will clearly desire a "coastal opening," and to facilitate these claims a line approximating the perpendicular is appropriate.[62]

The decision in the Saint-Pierre and Miquelon[63] delimitation has special relevance because of the consideration given to the issue of coastal projection by the court (see Map 2). It will be recalled that the court of arbitration considered the coastlines to project in a southerly direction perpendicular to the south coast of Newfoundland, resulting in a narrow "corridor" EEZ for the islands. The court could have viewed all coastal projections as parallel to the general direction of the North American continent, as in the outer segment of the *Gulf of Maine* or in *Guinea/Guinea-Bissau* with respect to the West African coastline. Instead, however, it selected a smaller strip of coastline to define the direction of the coastal projection. This implies that the potential projections for the Beaufort area, which were discussed earlier, are possible.

---

[60] *Supra* note 42.

[61] *Ibid.*

[62] In the similar enclave situations of the *North Sea Continental Shelf Cases* and the *Nicaragua-Honduras* (Gulf of Fonseca) case ((1992) I.C.J. Reports 351), while it was not practical for the court to adopt perpendiculars, the "enclaved" state was granted an enhanced form of coastal projection to ensure some seaward reach.

[63] *Supra* note 46.

It is interesting to note that both the Canadian judge, Allan Gotlieb, and the French judge, Prosper Weil (who both dissented although on different grounds) criticized the projection aspect of the court's decision in *Saint-Pierre and Miquelon*.[64] Gotlieb argued that the southerly projection of Newfoundland was encroached upon by the 24-mile EEZ that Saint-Pierre and Miquelon were granted to the west by the decision of the court. Weil criticized the direction as arbitrary, and favoured radial projection. If one considers the directions of coastal projection in the *Gulf of Maine* and the *Saint-Pierre and Miquelon* decisions together, it is evident that the southerly EEZ corridor of the French islands overlaps the coastal projection of the Canadian province of Nova Scotia, as defined in *Gulf of Maine* (see Map 2). Given the concern of the court voiced in *Guinea/Guinea-Bissau* regarding potential future delimitations with third states in the region, it would seem desirable for courts to be more attentive to such potential conflicts in the future. Presumably, the court of arbitration in *Saint-Pierre and Miquelon* felt that the overlap was small enough and at a sufficient distance from the coast that it would not result in any significant encroachment on Nova Scotia's seaward projection.

The court's finding in *Saint-Pierre and Miquelon* is also significant for the Beaufort Sea for a more technical reason. It will be noted from the geodetic report of the case that, while the 200-mile corridor proceeds in a southerly direction, it does not precisely follow the meridian.[65] This result has particular significance in the arctic context, because it demonstrates the possibility that a court can draw a line very close to the 141st meridian without precisely following it. In this manner, the court can avoid being seen to endorse the "sector theory." This theory has been intermittently advanced by Canada as a basis for asserting sovereignty over the entire "sector" of the arctic encompassing its islands, and bordered on the west by the 141st meridian. Pharand has analyzed the various arguments in favour of sector theory and, while he concludes that it cannot serve as a valid basis for sovereignty, he points to enough state practice in the arctic and antarctic to make any tribunal wary in dealing with the principle.[66] An implied adoption of the sector theory would be beyond the purview of a delimitation

---

[64] *Ibid.*

[65] *Ibid.*, appendix following the report.

[66] Pharand, *supra* note 6 at 1-79.

tribunal, and would also contradict the only statement of the International Court of Justice on the issue — a strong rejection of it by Judge Ammoun in the *North Sea Continental Shelf Cases.*[67] Thus, *Saint-Pierre and Miquelon's* use of a north/south corridor coming close to, but not precisely following, the meridian will facilitate a future tribunal's delimiting the Beaufort Sea boundary somewhere close to the meridian.

The delimitations examined indicate that both judicial and arbitral decisions and state practice in situations of adjacency display an affinity for coastal projection in a direction perpendicular to the general direction of the coast (whether attained through a calculation or by use of a meridian or parallel of latitude). This is particularly true where the equidistance or other proposed line would encroach upon or enclave one of the states, as in *Gulf of Maine* and *Guinea/Guinea Bissau.* For the Beaufort Sea, the cases suggest that the direction of projection will approximate the perpendicular or 141st meridian, and that the potential encroachment over this line by an equidistance line will be an important consideration.

CONCLUSION

The rich resource potential of the Beaufort Sea indicates that a delimitation of the maritime boundary in the area will be necessary in the near future. While many legal arguments and other factors will play a part, the related principles of natural prolongation and non-encroachment are likely to have a substantial impact on the outcome. Natural prolongation has developed from a geologically-based principle to one based on proximity, distance, and coastal projection. When combined with a defined direction of coastal projection and the principle of non-encroachment, the result demonstrates a powerful principle of maritime boundary delimitation. While mechanistic rules of delimitation are undesirable, the principle of non-encroachment has become an equitable principle, consistently applied, that conditions our view of what an equitable result is in a given situation, and is rarely if ever superseded. For the Beaufort Sea, the principle suggests that an equidistance line will be rejected because of its encroachment on the coastal projection of the Canadian land mass. The exact line selected will depend on the sector of coastline considered by the court in defining the

[67] *Ibid.* at 39.

direction of the coastal projection. While sectors exist to justify projections ranging eastward and westward of the 141st meridian, the emphasis of courts and tribunals on the principle of non-encroachment, combined with frequent projections perpendicular to the general direction of the coast, militate in favour of a line approximating the meridian.

ROGER GILLOTT
Student-at-Law
Tory, Tory, DesLauriers and Binnington, Toronto

Sommaire

Le principe du non-empiètement: les conséquences sur la délimitation de la Mer de Beaufort

Ce commentaire traite des principes connexes de prolongement naturel et de non-empiètement et de leurs conséquences sur une future délimitation de la frontière maritime entre le Canada et les États-Unis dans la Mer de Beaufort. L'auteur décrit l'évolution du principe du prolongement naturel, qui reposait d'abord sur la géologie et la morphologie du plateau continental pour se définir maintenant en grande partie par les concepts de distance et de proximité. L'auteur constate aussi que, même si le non-empiètement n'est pas une règle de délimitation mécanique et contraignante, il est devenu un principe équitable qui est rarement ou pour ainsi dire jamais supplanté par des principes équitables concurrents. Par conséquent, la direction de la projection côtière est devenue un aspect capital de toute délimitation. L'auteur discute ensuite de l'impact de ces conclusions sur la délimitation de la Mer de Beaufort.

Summary

The Principle of Non-Encroachment: Implications for the Beaufort
Sea

*This comment deals with the related principles of natural prolongation and
non-encroachment and their implications for any future delimitation of the
maritime boundary between Canada and the United States in the Beaufort
Sea. The evolution of the principle of natural prolongation is traced from one
based in the geology and geomorphology of the continental shelf to one based
primarily on concepts of distance and proximity. The conclusion is reached
that, while not a binding or mechanistic rule of delimitation, non-encroachment is an equitable principle that is rarely if ever superseded by competing
equitable principles. For this reason, the direction of the coastal projection
has become a key aspect of any delimitation, including the Canada/United
States negotiations on the Beaufort Sea.*

Chronique de Droit international économique en 1993 / Digest of International Economic Law in 1993

I Commerce

préparé par

MARTIN ST-AMANT*

L'ANNÉE 1993 AURA ÉTÉ une année relativement importante en ce qui concerne l'action juridique du Canada en matière de commerce international. Un événement a d'abord et avant tout retenu notre attention au cours de l'année; l'approbation et la promulgation par le Canada de la loi de mise en oeuvre de l'Accord de libre-échange nord-américain (ALÉNA).[1] Cette loi donne effet

---

* Avocat, Joli-Coeur, Lacasse, Lemieux, Simard, St-Pierre (Québec); Doctorat en Droit commercial international, Université de Paris I (Panthéon-Sorbonne).

---

[1] Loi portant mise en oeuvre de l'Accord de libre-échange nord-américain, L.C. 1993, c. 44. Cette loi fut adoptée par la Chambre des communes, le 27 mai et par le Sénat le 23 juin. Elle comprend trois parties et couvre tous les amendements législatifs nécessaires à la mise en oeuvre de l'Accord. La première partie prévoit notamment que les lois fédérales mettant l'Accord en oeuvre doivent être interprétées d'une manière conforme à l'Accord et établit le droit du parlement du Canada de légiférer de nouveau pour satisfaire à une quelconque obligation du Canada aux termes de celui-ci. La seconde partie suspend les dispositions pertinentes de la Loi de mise en oeuvre de l'Accord de libre-échange tant et aussi longtemps que l'ALÉNA sera en vigueur entre le Canada et les États-Unis. Des amendements sont, en outre, apportés à 29 lois et ce, afin de les rendre conformes à l'Accord. La troisième partie prévoit les modalités d'entrée en vigueur. La loi de mise en oeuvre de l'ALÉNA est entrée en vigueur le 1er janvier 1994. Voir Décret fixant au 1er janvier 1994 la date d'entrée en vigueur de la Loi à l'exception de l'article 177, TR/94-1, Gaz. C. 1994.II.604.

en droit interne à cet accord, lequel est entré en vigueur le 1er janvier 1994.[2] Soulignons par ailleurs que suite aux pressions de l'administration américaine, des accords parallèles à l'ALÉNA sur la protection environnementale, le travail et les mesures d'urgence contre la hausse subite des importations furent signés le 14 septembre par les trois chefs de gouvernement.[3] Ces accords sont également entrés en vigueur le 1er janvier 1994.[4]

Mis à part ces événements, cette chronique fera état des conflits et des activités survenus dans le cadre du GATT au cours de l'année 1993 qui ont impliqué le Canada, ainsi que du déroulement de la cinquième année de mise en oeuvre de l'Accord de libre-échange Canada-États-Unis.

I Conflits et activités dans le cadre du GATT

Dans le cadre du GATT, les contentieux impliquant le Canada ont nettement diminué par rapport à l'année dernière. Un seul dossier a connu un dénouement positif par l'adoption d'un rapport d'un Groupe spécial. C'est ainsi qu'en ce qui concerne les mesures compensatoires appliquées par les États-Unis aux importations de bois de construction résineux en provenance du Canada, le Comité de subventions et des droits compensateurs a adopté, le 27 octobre, le rapport du Groupe spécial chargé d'examiner ce différend.[5]

Le Groupe spécial a formulé deux conclusions. Il fut premièrement d'avis que les mesures compensatoires provisoires prises en 1991 par les États-Unis en vertu de la section 301 de la législation américaine, ne pouvaient se justifier au regard de l'article 4:6 du

---

[2] Notre prochaine chronique sera d'ailleurs consacrée à l'Accord de libre-échange nord-américain.

[3] Accord nord-américain de coopération dans le domaine de l'environnement entre le gouvernement du Canada, le gouvernement des États-Unis d'Amérique et le gouvernement des États-Unis du Mexique, 13 septembre 1993, Ottawa, Approvisionnements et Services Canada; Accord nord-américain de coopération dans le domaine du travail entre le gouvernement du Canada, le gouvernement des États-Unis d'Amérique et le gouvernement des États-Unis du Mexique, 13 septembre 1993, Ottawa, Approvisionnements et Services Canada; Entente entre les parties à l'Accord de libre-échange nord-américain en ce qui concerne le chapitre Huit: Mesures d'urgence, 13 septembre 1993, Ottawa, Approvisionnements et Services Canada.

[4] Sur ces accords, voir notre prochaine chronique.

[5] Voir le texte du rapport du Groupe spécial dans le document du GATT: SCM/150 (1993).

Code sur les subventions et les droits compensateurs. Selon le Groupe spécial, le mémorandum d'entente sur le bois d'oeuvre entre les gouvernements canadien et américain ne constitue pas un "engagement" au sens de cette disposition et, par conséquent, la décision du Canada de mettre fin à ce dernier n'équivaut pas à une violation d'un engagement pouvant justifier l'application immédiate de mesures provisoires.[6] Le Groupe recommande donc le remboursement des sommes perçues de la sorte. Par ailleurs, concernant la décision des États-Unis d'amorcer une enquête sans que l'industrie en ait préalablement fait la demande, le Groupe spécial conclut que cette ouverture d'enquête n'est pas incompatible avec les prescriptions du Code sur les subventions et les droits compensateurs et plus précisément avec l'article 2:1. Dans l'esprit du Groupe, le Département du commerce américain possédait suffisamment de preuves de l'existence d'une subvention quant aux politiques d'établissement du prix de vente des droits de coupe et suffisamment de preuves de l'existence d'une menace de préjudice suite à la décision canadienne de mettre fin au mémorandum.

D'autre part, le Canada et les États-Unis ont informé le Conseil qu'ils avaient conclu, le 5 août, un mémorandum d'entente assurant la mise en oeuvre du rapport du Groupe spécial du GATT sur les pratiques canadiennes de commercialisation de la bière.[7] Ce mémorandum prévoit notamment la levée des mesures de représailles réciproques imposées en juillet 1992, l'élimination immédiate de droits de douane canadiens sur la bière originaire des États-Unis, l'accès de la bière américaine aux points de vente ontariens, la diminution du prix minimum de l'Ontario ainsi que la possibilité de dénoncer l'Accord, en tout ou en partie, à l'égard de l'ensemble du Canada ou uniquement de certaines provinces, si

6 On se rappellera à cet égard que le 4 octobre 1991, le Canada décidait de mettre fin au mémorandum d'entente sur le bois d'oeuvre résineux puisqu'il avait selon lui donné les résultats escomptés. Conformément au mémorandum et pour éviter la menace imminente de l'imposition par les États-Unis d'un droit compensateur sur le bois d'oeuvre résineux canadien, le Canada avait, en 1986, provisoirement assujetti certains produits du bois d'oeuvre destinés aux États-Unis à une taxe à l'exportation de 15p.100. Le mémorandum faisait en sorte que les recettes découlant de ces droits restent au Canada au lieu d'être expédiées aux États-Unis. Voir Mémorandum of Understanding of Dec. 1986, for the Secretary of Commerce and the United States Trade Representative, 52 Fed. Reg. 231 (1987).

7 Au sujet de ce rapport, voir M. St-Amant, "Chronique du Droit international économique," (1993) 31 Ann. can. dr. int. 313-315.

une nouvelle mesure ou la modification d'une mesure existante compromettait les avantages accordés aux États-Unis.[8]

Par ailleurs, peu de progrès significatifs ont été accomplis par les États-Unis pour donner effet aux recommandations du Groupe spécial chargé d'examiner certaines pratiques américaines de commercialisation de la bière, du vin et du cidre.[9] Quelques états ont manifesté un certain intérêt pour une éventuelle mise en oeuvre de ces recommandations mais, dans les faits, seulement le Nouveau-Mexique a adopté en 1993 une législation pour se conformer au rapport du Groupe spécial.[10]

Mentionnons finalement que le Canada a notifié aux États-Unis qu'il retirait sa plainte à l'égard de la décision américaine d'ouvrir une enquête sur le magnésium en provenance du Canada en raison de la décision finale du Département du commerce américain concluant à l'absence de subvention dans le cadre d'une procédure de révision pour changement de circonstances.[11]

II Mise en oeuvre de l'Accord de libre-échange
    Canada-États-Unis

Cinq années après l'entrée en vigueur de l'Accord de libre-échange Canada-États-Unis,[12] on peut constater que la mise en oeuvre de l'Accord a été menée à bien et s'est faite de façon harmonieuse pour l'essentiel; les calendriers prévus, notamment les calendriers de réductions tarifaires, ont normalement été respectés.

8 Voir Ministre du Commerce extérieur, Communiqué de presse, no 152, 5 août 1993; *Int'l Trade Rep.* (BNA) 1319 (1993); *Inside U.S. Trade,* vol. II, no 31, p. 1 (1993). Dès la conclusion de l'entente, certains brasseurs américains ont cependant réagi négativement en faisant valoir que l'entente ne prévoyait pas l'élimination de la taxe environnementale sur les bières vendues par l'Ontario ainsi que les prix minimums établis pour l'ensemble des bières canadiennes. *Ibid.* La mise en oeuvre de cette entente s'est en outre avérée des plus difficiles eu égard, entre autres, à la complexité du système de distribution et de fixation des prix de la bière au Canada. Voir *Inside U.S. Trade,* Vol. II, no 32, p. 1 (1993). Pour la mise en oeuvre de cette entente en droit canadien, voir Décret de remise des droits de douane sur la bière originaire des États-Unis de 1993, DORS/93-418, Gaz. C. 1993.II.3511.

9 Sur les conclusions de ce Groupe spécial, voir M. St-Amant, *supra* note 7, à la p. 315.

10 Voir *Focus, Bulletin d'information du GATT,* no 99, 1993, p. 5.

11 Voir *GATT — Activités,* 1993, p. 49.

12 Accord de libre-échange entre le gouvernement du Canada et le gouvernement des États-Unis d'Amérique, 2 janvier 1988, R.T. Can. 1989 no 3, 27 I.L.M. 281 [ci-après Accord de libre-échange] (en vigueur le 1er janvier 1989).

Ce sont certes les différends commerciaux et leur règlement dans le cadre de l'Accord qui ont par ailleurs suscité le plus d'intérêt et requis le plus d'attention de la part des deux gouvernements. Soulignons comme décevant, toutefois, le fait que certains travaux techniques complémentaires à l'Accord de libre-échange, tels que les huit groupes de travail sur les règlements techniques et les normes touchant les produits agricoles, n'ont fait que peu de progrès[13] et que les échanges de statistiques prévus sur les marchés publics n'ont pas eu lieu.[14] Quoi qu'il en soit, de 1988 au premier semestre de 1993, la valeur des exportations canadiennes à destination des États-Unis a augmenté de 35p.100 tandis que les exportations à destination du reste du monde sont demeurées inchangées.[15] La part des États-Unis dans l'ensemble des échanges commerciaux canadiens atteignait quant à elle un sommet de 76,4p.100 au premier semestre de 1993.[16]

Il reste que les analyses sont très partagées quant aux effets économiques de l'Accord. La difficulté d'isoler l'effet de l'Accord de l'effet d'autres variables explique assurément cet état de fait. Il apparaît cependant raisonnable de conclure à l'efficacité de l'Accord en tant qu'instrument juridique visant à faciliter le commerce entre les deux pays.

A   MISE EN OEUVRE LÉGISLATIVE

L'Accord prévoit qu'en 1988, les droits de douane seront éliminés entre les deux pays.[17] Au 1er janvier 1993, tous les droits ont été éliminés pour les produits appartenant à la catégorie B[18] et une cinquième réduction tarifaire de 10p.100 s'est opérée à la même

---

13 Sur la création de ces groupes de travail, voir *Accord de libre-échange, ibid.*, art. 708.4.

14 Tel que le prévoit pourtant l'Accord de libre-échange. *ibid.*, art. 1306.2. Notons également que l'entente expérimentale sur l'inspection de la viande découlant de l'article 708 de l'Accord n'a jamais été mise en oeuvre par les États-Unis.

15 Voir A. Côté, ''L'évolution récente du compte courant: une comparaison avec le cycle précédent,'' (1993-94) Revue de la Banque du Canada 21.

16 *Ibid.*

17 Accord de libre-échange, *supra* note 12, art. 401 (2). La tarification des obstacles non tarifaires dans le domaine agricole à la suite de l'Uruguay Round constitue une exception.

18 *Ibid.*, art. 401 (2)(b). Les voitures de métro, les pièces de rechange pour automobiles, les meubles, le papier et les produits de papier entrent donc par exemple maintenant en franchise de droits de part et d'autre de la frontière.

date sur la catégorie d'échelonnement C.[19] La troisième série sur
l'élimination accélérée des droits de douane est d'autre part entrée
en vigueur le 1er juillet et couvre plus de 600 produits représentant
environ 1 milliard de dollars d'échanges commerciaux bilatéraux.[20]
Dans le secteur de l'agriculture, les deux gouvernements se sont
entendus pour modifier l'Appendice 2 de l'annexe 705.4 de
l'Accord de libre-échange pour y inclure de nouveaux programmes
canadiens et une méthodologie afférente pour le calcul des niveaux
de soutien gouvernemental.[21]

B   MISE EN OEUVRE JURISPRUDENTIELLE

Les deux principaux mécanismes de règlement des différends
prévus par l'Accord de libre-échange ont de nouveau démontré
leur utilité pour les exportateurs canadiens. Dans le cadre du

[19] *Ibid.*, art. 401 (2)(C). Soulignons en outre la réduction de l'écart de majoration des prix du vin supérieur qui, le 1er janvier 1993, ne devait plus dépasser
20p.100 de l'écart de base entre l'écart de majoration appliqué par les autorités
en 1987 et l'écart des frais de service réels. *Ibid.*, art. 803 (2)(e). Par ailleurs,
l'élimination complète des restrictions à l'importation des automobiles d'occasion dès le 1er janvier 1993, autorise maintenant l'admission en franchise de
ces dernières. *Ibid.*, art. 1003 (e). Finalement, les redevances pour opérations
douanières ont été comme prévu réduites et elles ne représentent plus que
20p.100 des redevances par ailleurs applicables. *Ibid.*, art. 403 (3)(d).

[20] Gouvernement du Canada, Communiqué de presse, n° 141, 5 juillet 1993. La
mise en vigueur formelle de cette entente fut finalisée par un échange de
lettres entre les deux gouvernements. Échange de Lettres entre le gouvernement du Canada et le gouvernement des États-Unis d'Amérique concernant
l'accélération de l'élimination des droits applicables à certains produits aux
termes de l'article 401.5 et la modification des sections XV et XVI de l'annexe
301.1 du chapitre 3 de l'Accord de libre-échange entre le Canada et les États-
Unis (avec appendices), Washington, 30 juin 1993. Parmi ces produits on
retrouve par exemple les pièces de moteur, certaines boissons alcoolisées, les
tissus en denim et les fibres discontinues. Rappelons par ailleurs que cette
élimination accélérée ne portait que sur les produits pour lesquels l'élimination de droits se devait d'être effectuée après une période de 10 ans.

[21] Échange de lettres entre le gouvernement du Canada et le gouvernement des
États-Unis d'Amérique constituant un Accord modifiant l'appendice 2 de
l'annexe 705.4 (tel que modifié; *RTC 1999/50, 1991/13 et 1992/25) de l'Accord
de libre-échange*, Washington, 30 avril 1993. Soulignons, en outre, que des
modifications mineures ont été apportées aux règles d'origine et ce en vertu de
l'article 303 de l'Accord de libre-échange. Voir Échange de lettres entre le
gouvernement du Canada et le gouvernement des États-Unis d'Amérique,
supra note 20. Pour la mise en oeuvre de ces modifications en droit canadien,
voir par ailleurs le Règlement sur les règles d'origine des marchandises bénéfi-
ciant du tarif des États-Unis: Modification, DORS/93-378, Gaz C. 1993.II.3180.

chapitre 18, outre la demande par le Canada de la création d'un groupe spécial d'experts en ce qui concerne la vente de blé américain au Mexique,[22] deux groupes spéciaux d'experts auront rendu leur décision en 1993. Le premier groupe, institué à la demande des États-Unis pour interpréter l'article 701.3 de l'Accord de libre-échange en ce qui concerne son application aux ventes de blé dur de la Commission canadienne de blé, a déposé son rapport le 9 février.[23] Le Groupe a statué notamment que le prix d'achat des produits mentionnés à cet article englobe uniquement l'acompte à la livraison payé par la Commission canadienne du blé, que seuls les frais d'entreposage et de manutention assumés par ladite Commission devraient être inclus dans l'établissement des coûts visés par cette disposition et que l'expression "ou autre [frais] qu'elle aura dû assumer" ne visait pas les coûts d'administration.[24] Le second groupe institué à la demande du Canada pour statuer sur l'importation, la distribution et la vente de lait UHT du Québec à Porto Rico, a, quant à lui, déposé son rapport le 4 juin.[25] Bien que ce dernier concluait que les États-Unis n'avaient violé aucune des dispositions de l'Accord de libre-échange, il déterminait toutefois, en vertu de l'article 2011 de l'Accord, qu'en fermant le marché portoricain pendant que des négociations bilatérales étaient en cours, la partie américaine avait annulé ou compromis des avantages auxquels le Canada était en droit de s'attendre aux termes de l'Accord.[26]

[22] Voir Gouvernement du Canada, Communiqué de presse, n° 208, 22 octobre 1993. Cette demande du Canada faisait suite à l'annonce par l'administration américaine des projets au titre du programme d'encouragement des exportations (EEP). Les États-Unis comptaient ainsi subventionner l'exportation de 1.4 millions de tonnes de blé vers le Mexique, client traditionnel du Canada.

[23] *Dans l'affaire de l'interprétation et de l'application par le Canada de l'article 701.3 relativement au blé dur* (9 février 1993), CDA-92-1807-01 (Ch. 18 Groupe spéc.).

[24] *Ibid.* Le Groupe spécial a aussi recommandé qu'un groupe de travail soit établi pour superviser les vérifications périodiques des ventes de blé dur aux États-Unis effectuées par la Commission canadienne du blé.

[25] *Dans l'affaire de la réglementation de Porto Rico sur l'importation, la distribution et la vente de lait UHT du Québec* (4 juin 1993), USA-93-1807-01 (Ch. 18 Groupe spéc.).

[26] *Ibid.* Les dispositions de l'Accord de libre-échange, *supra* note 12, invoquées au soutien des prétentions du Canada sont les suivantes: articles 407, 501, 703, 708, 710 et l'appendice 11 du chapitre 7. Les parties ont par ailleurs convenu de mettre en oeuvre les conclusions du rapport en trois étapes. D'abord, une étude d'équivalence accélérée sera réalisée relativement aux normes de production de lait UHT dans les deux pays. Une étude de plus long terme sera par

Relativement au mécanisme particulier de règlement des différends en matière de droit antidumping et compensateur, on doit en premier lieu souligner qu'un Comité de contestation extraordinaire a rejeté, le 8 avril, les allégations américaines selon lesquelles le Groupe spécial aurait manifestement outrepassé ses pouvoirs en rendant sa décision dans le quatrième examen administratif de l'ordonnance d'imposition des droits compensateurs à l'égard des porcs vivants du Canada.[27] Selon le Comité, le Groupe spécial n'aurait pas omis d'appliquer le critère prévu par le droit américain pour un examen judiciaire et de ce fait il conclut que les États-Unis n'ont pas apporté la preuve requise pour donner ouverture à une procédure de contestation extraordinaire.[28] Fondamentale est toutefois la conclusion du Comité sur le rôle octroyé par l'Accord de libre-échange aux groupes spéciaux binationaux. Ces groupes doivent, selon le Comité, appliquer le droit en vigueur et non pas le créer ou le faire évoluer; ils se doivent de comprendre les limites assignées à leur rôle. Ils ne sont pas des tribunaux d'appel et ils doivent déférence aux décisions des organismes d'enquête. Quant au rôle de ces derniers, les conclusions du Comité sont claires: ils doivent reconnaître que les décisions des groupes spéciaux sont obligatoires tout en prenant soin de répondre à chacune de leurs directives.[29]

Par ailleurs, la grande majorité des groupes spéciaux binationaux ayant rendu leurs décisions en 1993 avait pour but d'examiner les décisions administratives du Département du commerce des États-Unis (DOC) ou les décisions judiciaires de la Commission américaine du commerce international (ITC). À cet égard, les ordon-

---

la suite entreprise sur l'équivalence des systèmes réglementaires et d'inspection des produits laitiers au Québec et aux États-Unis. Finalement, une troisième étude de long terme portera sur l'équivalence de ces systèmes mais province par province. Ces deux dernières études seront menées sous l'égide des groupes de travail prévus à l'article 708 de l'Accord de libre-échange, *supra* note 12.

27 *Dans l'affaire des porcs vivants du Canada* (8 avril 1993), ECC-93-1904-01 USA (Comité con. extr.). Concernant le rapport du Groupe spécial, voir M. St-Amant, *supra* note 7, à la p. 322.

28 L'Accord de libre-échange, *supra* note 12, prévoit implicitement à son article 1904 (13) que si un Groupe spécial omet d'appliquer le critère propre à un examen judiciaire, il outrepasse ses compétences. Dans le cas en l'espèce, le Comité est d'opinion que le Groupe spécial a non seulement exprimé adéquatement ce critère mais l'a discuté et mentionné plusieurs fois.

29 *Dans l'affaire des porc vivants du Canada*, *supra* note 27, aux pp. 15-16.

nances des Groupes spéciaux sur le bois d'oeuvre résineux furent assurément les plus importantes; ce produit faisant l'objet depuis plus d'une décennie d'un différend commercial entre les deux pays. Le premier Groupe spécial, formé pour examiner la décision sur le "subventionnement" dans ce dossier, a ainsi demandé au DOC le 6 mai, de refaire ses devoirs, notamment quant à savoir si les droits de coupe conféraient un avantage déloyal ou non aux producteurs de bois d'oeuvre canadien et quant à leur effet de distorsion sur les marchés américains.[30] Suite à cette ordonnance, le DOC rendait une nouvelle décision, le 17 septembre réitérant le caractère spécifique et préférentiel des droits de coupe provinciaux.[31] Toutefois, le Groupe spécial appelé à se prononcer de nouveau donnait, dans une seconde ordonnance, des instructions précises au DOC se résumant à déclarer la non-compensabilité des droits de coupe provinciaux ainsi que des restrictions aux exportations imposées par la Colombie-Britannique.[32] Le second Groupe spécial, chargé lui d'étudier la décision de préjudice de l'ITC, a rendu son ordonnance le 26 juillet. Sa principale conclusion est à l'effet que l'ITC n'a pas démontré, de façon satisfaisante, que les importations de bois d'oeuvre canadien sont à l'origine d'un préjudice pour l'industrie américaine.[33]

[30] Certains produits de bois d'oeuvre en provenance du Canada (6 mai 1993), USA-92-1904-01 (Ch. 19 Groupe spéc.).

[31] Softwood Lumber from Canada, 59 Fed. Reg. 30,774 (Dep't Comm. 1993). Les restrictions aux exportations de billes de bois, en vigueur en Colombie-Britannique, constituaient également une subvention selon le DOC. Le taux de subvention augmentait d'autre part de 6,5 p.100 à 11,54 p.100 par rapport à l'enquête originelle.

[32] Certains produits du bois d'oeuvre en provenance du Canada (17 décembre 1993), USA-92-1904-01 (Ch. 19 Groupe spéc.). L'absence de preuve quant à la spécificité des programmes provinciaux de droit de coupe et des distorsions des marchés occasionnées par ces programmes est à la base de l'ordonnance du Groupe spécial.

[33] Certains produits de bois d'oeuvre du Canada (26 juillet 1993), USA-92-1904-02 (Ch. 19 Groupe spéc.). Le Groupe spécial fut dans ce dossier exceptionnellement critique quant à l'analyse par l'ITC du lien de causalité. En l'absence d'une augmentation des parts de marchés ou d'autres indices, le volume des importations ne constitue pas à lui seul, selon le Groupe spécial, une preuve substantielle d'un préjudice en raison des importations. Soulignons que l'ITC, dans sa décision sur renvoi, confirmait le 25 octobre que les importations de bois d'oeuvre du Canada causaient un préjudice à l'industrie américaine. Voir Softwood Lumber from Canada, Inv. No 701-TA-312 (Remand) USITC Pub.2689 (oct. 1993).

Trois autres groupes spéciaux binationaux ont d'autre part été créés pour reconsidérer les décisions du DOC et de l'ITC dans l'affaire du magnésium. Le premier groupe, dont le mandat consistait à réviser la décision du DOC sur le "subventionnement," rendit son ordonnance le 16 août.[34] À cette occasion, le Groupe spécial a renvoyé le dossier au DOC pour une nouvelle décision, lequel pour sa part confirmait par la suite ses précédentes déterminations.[35] Le 14 décembre, dans sa seconde ordonnance, le Groupe spécial maintenait intégralement cette décision du DOC et se dissolvait par le fait même.[36] Le deuxième Groupe, formé pour examiner la décision de dumping du DOC, s'est quant à lui rapidement dissout en entérinant la proposition unilatérale du DOC de réduire, suite à son enquête, les droits antidumping de 31,33 p. 100 à 21 p. 100.[37] Finalement, le troisième Groupe qui a rendu son ordonnance le 27 août sur le préjudice a renvoyé le dossier à l'ITC pour nouvelle décision.[38] Selon les instructions du Groupe, l'ITC devait examiner chaque industrie américaine séparément dans le but de déterminer si les importations de magnésium pur causent préjudice à l'industrie américaine produisant ce produit et si les importations d'alliages de magnésium causent préjudice à l'industrie américaine produisant ces derniers produits.

Notons en terminant, sur les décisions américaines contestées, la seconde ordonnance du Groupe spécial dans le cinquième examen

---

[34] *Magnésium pur et alliage de magnésium en provenance du Canada (droits compensateurs)* (16 août 1993), USA-92-1904-03 (Ch. 19 Groupe spéc.).

[35] Le DOC était d'avis qu'une analyse de la spécificité entreprise par entreprise s'avérait justifiée en l'espèce et que la période d'amortissement choisie pour répartir les bénéfices était conforme avec la politique administrative américaine car elle reflétait la réalité commerciale.

[36] Magnésium pur et alliage de magnésium en provenance du Canada (droits compensateurs) (14 décembre 1993), USA-92-1904-03 (Ch. 19 Groupe spéc.).

[37] Magnésium pur et alliage de magnésium en provenance du Canada (dumping) 6 octobre 1993), USA-92-1904-04 (Ch. 19 Groupe spéc.). Cette ordonnance du Groupe spécial fait suite à une "redétermination" par le DOC des coûts de production et des frais généraux de vente et d'administration de l'entreprise en cause, Norsk Hydro.

[38] Magnésium en provenance du Canada (préjudice), (27 août 1993), USA-92-1904-05 (Ch 19 Groupe spéc.). Soulignons que le 26 octobre, l'ITC maintenait sa décision de préjudice. Voir Magnesium from Canada, Inv. Nos 701-TA-309 et 731-TA-528 (Remand), USITC Pub. 2696 (nov. 1993).

administratif des droits compensateurs à l'égard des porcs vivants du Canada.[39]

Trois décisions canadiennes seulement auront par ailleurs été portées devant un Groupe spécial: la décision du Tribunal canadien du commerce extérieur après le renvoi dans l'affaire de la bière,[40] la décision finale du même tribunal dans l'affaire des tapis[41] et la décision de Revenu Canada, Douanes et Accises concernant ce dernier produit.[42]

[39] *Dans l'affaire des porcs vivants* (26 août 1992), USA-91-1904-04 (Ch. 19 Groupe spéc.). Le Groupe spécial confirmait ici la majeure partie de la décision du DOC quant à la compensabilité des programmes en cause.

[40] *Dans l'affaire de la bière originaire des États-Unis d'Amérique* (26 août 1992), CDA-91-1904-02 (Ch. 19 Groupe spéc.). La question portée à l'étude du Groupe spécial concernait le lien de causalité entre le dumping et le préjudice. Le Groupe spécial confirma intégralement la décision du Tribunal canadien du commerce extérieur.

[41] *Dans l'affaire des tapis produits sur machines à touffeter originaires ou exportés des États-Unis* (7 avril 1993), CDA-92-1904-02 (Ch. 19 Groupe spéc.). Eu égard aux critères d'examen figurant au paragraphe 28 (1) de la Loi sur la Cour fédérale, les questions examinées portaient sur le lien de causalité entre le dumping et le préjudice et plus précisément sur l'analyse macro et micro économique du Tribunal démontrant le lien causal, sur la menace de préjudice, sur l'exclusion de certains producteurs de la branche de production nationale et sur la notion de marchandises similaires. Le Groupe confirmait en partie et renvoyait en partie la décision du Tribunal.

[42] *Dans l'affaire des tapis produits sur machines à touffeter originaires ou exportés des États-Unis* (19 mai 1993), CDA-92-1904-01 (Ch. 19 Groupe spéc.). Parmi les questions portées à l'étude du Groupe figurait l'exception de la chose jugée, le prix prédominant et l'exclusion de certaines ventes dans le calcul de la valeur normale, la période visée par l'enquête, la notion de marchandises similaires, le calcul du montant des bénéfices et les rectifications selon le niveau du circuit de distribution.

II Le Canada et le système monétaire international en 1993

préparé par

BERNARD COLAS*

L'ANNÉE 1993 A ÉTÉ MARQUÉE par l'aggravation de la crise économique dans les pays de l'ex-URSS et par l'évolution impré-
visible des marchés de capitaux et obligataires. Pour éviter les
tensions internationales qui pourraient découler de ces situations,
le Canada a continué de soutenir les efforts des pays engagés dans
la transition vers l'économie de marché (I) et a pris part aux
discussions destinées à modifier l'Accord de Bâle de 1988 sur les
fonds propres (II).

I SOUTIEN AUX RÉPUBLIQUES DE L'EX-UNION SOVIÉTIQUE

Pour une quatrième année consécutive, les pays de l'ex-URSS ont
vu leur production baisser et le déséquilibre de leur balance des
paiements se creuser.[1] Face à la gravité de cette situation, le Canada
a encouragé la communauté internationale à mettre à leur disposition des ressources supplémentaires. En 1993, dans le cadre du
Fonds monétaire international (FMI), il a approuvé la création de
la Facilité de transformation systémique (FTS). Ce nouveau guichet
financier est conçu de façon à aider les pays qui ont des problèmes
de balance de paiements en raison d'une forte baisse de leurs

---

* Avocat au Barreau du Québec, Consultant auprès de l'Organisation de coopération et de développement économiques (OCDE), Vice-président de la Société
de droit international économique (SDIE). Les opinions exprimées n'engagent
que leur auteur.

---

[1] *Rapport annuel de la Banque des règlements internationaux* (1994), aux pp. 62-75.

exportations ou d'une forte augmentation des coûts de l'énergie importée.[2] Cette même année, huit pays issus de l'ex-URSS, notamment la Russie qui a effectué le plus gros achat (2,2 milliards de DTS), trois pays d'Europe centrale et orientale ainsi que deux pays asiatiques (Cambodge et Viet-Nam) ont pu en bénéficier.

Par ailleurs, le Canada a favorisé le renouvellement de la Facilité d'ajustement structurel renforcée (FASR), qui arrivait à terme en novembre 1993. Initialement créée en 1988 pour une période de cinq ans, la FASR accordait des prêts à des conditions concessionnelles aux pays à faible revenu qui acceptaient d'entreprendre des programmes de réforme économique destinés à renforcer leur balance des paiements et améliorer leurs perspectives de croissance. Satisfaits de l'expérience des pays qui avaient conclu des arrangements dans le cadre de cette facilité, les pays du Groupe des Sept[3] ont proposé, lors de leur sommet économique de Tokyo en juillet 1993, sa prorogation et son élargissement. La décision à cet effet fut prise en décembre 1993 par le Conseil d'administration du FMI.[4] Les modalités de la FASR sont les mêmes que celles de la facilité qui l'a précédée. Elle doit être financée par un compte de capital de cinq millions et un compte de subventions de deux millions de DTS. Le Canada a accepté d'y contribuer[5] en insistant sur le fait que les programmes prévus dans le cadre de la FASR accordent une plus grande attention aux filets de sécurité sociale et mettent davantage l'accent sur la qualité des dépenses publiques.

Malgré les initiatives prises dans le cadre du FMI et d'autres organisations internationales auxquelles le Canada participe,[6] les problèmes économiques des pays d'Europe orientale sont demeurés

[2] Ministère des Finances du Canada, *Rapport sur les opérations effectuées en vertu de la Loi sur les accords de Bretton Woods et des accords connexes 1993* (1993), aux pp. 16-17.

[3] Le Groupe des Sept réunit les Chefs d'États ou de gouvernements de l'Allemagne, du Canada, des États-unis, de l'Italie, du Japon, de la France et du Royaume-Uni. Le Président de la Commission et le Président du Conseil des ministres de la Communauté européenne sont en général associés à ces réunions.

[4] *Rapport annuel du FMI* (1994), aux pp. 143-44.

[5] *Ibid.*, aux pp. 181-82.

[6] Parmi les principales mentionnons la Banque mondiale (BIRD), la Banque européenne pour la reconstruction et le développement (BERD), et l'Organisation de coopération et de développement économique (OCDE). Elles n'ont adopté en 1993 aucun mécanisme particulier qui ait pu retenir l'attention de cette chronique annuelle.

préoccupants. En effet, certains d'entre eux se sont trouvés dans l'impossibilité d'honorer les engagements contractés auprès de banques commerciales. Pour éviter que leur défaillance n'affecte la solvabilité des banques canadiennes, le Bureau du surintendant des institutions financières a exigé, en 1993, qu'elles conservent des provisions sur les titres de créance à l'égard de certains pays de l'ex-URSS et de la Yougoslavie.[7] Le Chili s'est vu cette même année retirer de la liste des pays à l'égard desquels l'établissement de provisions sur les prêts et d'autres engagements est exigé.

II Normes prudentielles relatives aux risques de marché

La stabilité du système bancaire et financier international a continué de faire l'objet des discussions des autorités de contrôle et des banques centrales du Groupe des Dix auquel le Canada fait partie. Réunies au sein du Comité de Bâle sur le contrôle bancaire,[8] ces autorités ont diffusé le 30 avril 1993 auprès des banques soumises à leur juridiction un ensemble de propositions pour fins de discussions.[9] Subdivisées en trois documents, ces propositions ont porté sur le traitement prudentiel de la compensation, des risques de marché et du risque de taux d'intérêt. Les deux premières visaient à modifier l'Accord de Bâle de 1988 sur les fonds propres;[10] la troisième proposait une méthode commune d'évaluation du risque de taux d'intérêt.[11]

---

[7] Canada, *Rapport annuel du Bureau du Surintendant des institutions financières* (1993), à la p. 14 [ci-après *Surintendant des institutions*].

[8] Ce Comité regroupe les hauts représentants des autorités de contrôle et des banques centrales du Groupe des Dix (Allemagne, Belgique, Canada, États-Unis, France, Italie, Japon, Luxembourg, Pays-Bas, Royaume-Uni, Suède et Suisse). Il se réunit habituellement au siège de la Banque des règlements internationaux à Bâle.

[9] Ces propositions ont été transmises aux chefs de la direction des banques canadiennes par le Bureau du surintendant des institutions financières le 29 avril 1993 [P2825-1]. Ils avaient jusqu'à la fin de l'année 1993 pour faire part de leurs observations.

[10] Cet accord est également connu sous le titre "Convergence internationale de la mesure et des normes de fonds propres" du 11 juillet 1988. Il a été amendé le 6 novembre 1991.

[11] Cette méthode d'évaluation permettra de déterminer, de façon approximative, la mesure dans laquelle la valeur de la banque serait défavorablement affectée par les fluctuations de taux d'intérêt.

Rappelons que l'Accord de Bâle de 1988, commenté dans des chroniques antérieures, est entré en vigueur le 31 décembre 1992. Il a pour principal objectif d'établir des normes minimales de fonds propres destinées à fournir une protection à l'égard du risque de crédit (risque de défaillance de la contrepartie)[12] aux banques opérant à l'échelle internationale. À la suite de son adoption, des études ont notamment été menées sur l'évaluation des risques de crédit des systèmes de compensation interbancaire ainsi que sur les exigences de fonds propres destinées à pallier aux risques de marché.[13]

En ce qui concerne les mécanismes de compensation des ordres de paiement interbancaires et des engagements contractuels à terme, le Rapport Lamfalussy[14] a démontré qu'ils permettaient d'améliorer l'efficacité et la stabilité des règlements interbancaires. En effet, ce Rapport a précisé que ces mécanismes de compensation réduisaient non seulement les coûts mais également les risques de crédit et de liquidité, sous réserve de l'observation de certaines conditions. S'appuyant sur ce Rapport, le Comité a proposé en 1993 d'amender l'Accord de 1988 en vue de reconnaître, outre la compensation par novation,[15] d'autres formes de compensation bilatérale des risques de crédit, dans la mesure où de tels mécanismes sont efficaces selon la loi en vigueur et sont conformes aux normes minimales décrites dans le Rapport.[16] Cette proposition a pour objet de permettre aux banques de pondérer en termes nets plutôt que bruts les créances nées de swaps et de contrats similaires avec les mêmes contreparties. Elle a reçu l'appui des autorités canadiennes, d'autant plus que sa mise en oeuvre se traduira pour les banques par une réduction de l'obligation globale de fonds propres. La compensation multilatérale n'a donné lieu qu'à des réflexions préliminaires.

[12] Risque qu'une contrepartie à un contrat financier n'exécute pas ses obligations contractuelles.

[13] Les risques de marché sont les risques de pertes sur position de bilan et hors-bilan découlant des variations des prix du marché, liées notamment à des mouvements de taux d'intérêt, des cours de change et de la valeur des actions.

[14] *Rapport Lamfalussy sur les systèmes de compensation interbancaire,* 1990.

[15] La compensation par novation pour la même monnaie et la même date de valeur était déjà couverte par l'Accord de Bâle de 1988.

[16] Pour la version définitive de l'amendement à l'Accord de Bâle de 1988 issue de cette proposition, lire l'Accord de Bâle sur les fonds propres: Traitement du risque de crédit lié à certains instruments de hors-bilan, juillet 1994.

Par ailleurs, la seconde proposition tente d'élargir la portée de l'Accord de 1988 afin d'intégrer les risques de marché encourus par les banques au ratio de solvabilité. Cette proposition est justifiée par les nouveaux risques auxquels les banques sont exposées compte tenu de l'accroissement de leurs activités sur les marchés financiers. Elle établit une méthode d'évaluation explicite des exigences de fonds propres pour les risques liés aux fluctuations des prix (risques de marché) dans les cas des positions ouvertes sur titres de créance et titres de propriété (et sur les produits dérivés qui y sont liés) des portefeuilles de négociation, ainsi que sur devises. La méthodologie et l'essentiel de ses particularités sont identiques à celles de la Directive européenne sur l'adéquation de fonds propres de 1993 qui, pour sa part, s'applique à la fois aux établissements de crédit et aux opérateurs sur titres.[17]

Cette proposition ne semble pas aboutir puisque les banques internationales, y compris les banques canadiennes, ont émis un jugement négatif sur l'approche proposée par le Comité. Celle-ci leur semble trop complexe et ne permet pas de mesurer les risques assumés par les grandes institutions financières diversifiées.[18] Elles reconnaissent l'utilité de constituer des provisions au titre des risques de marché mais préfèrent, à la méthode proposée, utiliser leurs propres "modèles" pour évaluer ces risques; position en faveur de laquelle le Canada semble se ranger.[19]

D'autre part, il aurait été préférable, pour des raisons d'égalité de concurrence, que cette proposition soit élargie aux autres intermédiaires financiers et notamment aux opérateurs sur valeurs mobilières. En effet, ceux-ci traitent des produits identiques à ceux de certaines banques sur des marchés internationaux décloisonnés et supportent des risques de marché équivalents. Malgré ce fait, les discussions engagées depuis 1989 entre le Comité de Bâle et l'Organisation internationale des commissions de valeurs (OICV) ne sont pas parvenues à dégager un accord qui aurait permis d'instituer des exigences minimales de fonds propres communes.

---

17 Christian Gavalda, dir., *Les défaillances bancaires* (Paris Association d'économie financière, à paraître).

18 *Surintendant des institutions, supra* note 7, à la p. 6.

19 Dans sa lettre du 29 avril 1993, le Bureau du Surintendant des institutions financières considère comme insuffisante la seconde méthode proposée par le Comité de Bâle pour calculer les exigences des fonds propres dans le cas du risque de change.

Cet accord ne saurait toutefois tarder. La pression exercée par la réalité du marché devrait permettre d'atténuer les différences d'approches[20] et d'instituer un régime juridique plus homogène.[21]

[20] L'approche prudentielle spécifique des autorités de marché, à laquelle la Securities and Exchange Commission semble particulièrement attachée, s'inscrit dans une perspective de très court terme justifiée par une extrême volatilité des marchés. Quant à l'approche prudentielle bancaire, elle tend à s'inscrire davantage dans une optique de moyen terme et de continuité de l'exploitation.

[21] A noter la publication en 1993 par le groupe de la Politique de surveillance du Bureau du surintendant des banques des "Lignes directrices sur les limites régissant les engagements importants et les exigences en matière de fonds propres, à l'intention des sociétés de fiducie et de prêt à charte fédérale." Celles-ci fixent des normes semblables à celles applicables aux banques; *Surintendant des institutions, supra* note 7, à la p. 14.

III Investissement

préparé par

PIERRE RATELLE*

I Mise en oeuvre de l'Accord de libre-échange Canada-États-Unis

L E 1ᵉʳ janvier 1993 marquait le quatrième anniversaire de l'Accord de libre-échange entre le Canada et les États-Unis (ALÉ), mais aussi le début de sa cinquième période de transition devant conduire à sa pleine réalisation en matière d'investissement.[1] À cet égard, il convient de noter que, dans le cadre de la Loi sur Investissement Canada (LIC),[2] le seuil donnant ouverture à l'examen de l'acquisition directe du contrôle d'une entreprise canadienne par une entreprise américaine a été établi à 150 millions de dollars canadiens, en dollars constants de 1992.[3] Rappelons que, depuis le 1ᵉʳ janvier 1992, l'acquisition indirecte du

---

* Avocat au Barreau de Montréal; Chargé de cours aux départements des Sciences juridiques, des Sciences administratives et de Science politique de l'Université du Québec à Montréal; Docteur en droit international économique de l'Université Panthéon-Sorbonne (Paris 1); DEA de droit international économique de l'Université Panthéon-Sorbonne (Paris 1); DEA de droit international public et européen de l'Université Panthéon-Assas (Paris 2); LL.B. de l'Université Laval.

---

[1] ALÉ, 22 décembre 1987, R.T. Can. 1989 n° 3 (Partie A, Annexe à la Loi de mise en oeuvre de l'Accord de libre-échange entre le Canada et les États-Unis d'Amérique, S.C. 1988, c. 65).

[2] *L.I.C.*, S.C. 1985, c. 20.

[3] ALÉ, *supra* note 1, Annexe 1607.3, art. 2 § (a) (i) (E).

contrôle d'une entreprise canadienne par une entreprise américaine n'est plus assujettie à un examen de l'agence Investissement
Canada.[4]

Les investissements étrangers autres qu'américains ne bénéfi-
cient pas de ces mesures et restent assujettis aux seuls actuels de la
LIC, lesquels sont fixés à cinq millions de dollars canadiens pour les
acquisitions directes et à 25 millions de dollars canadiens pour les
acquisitions indirectes.[5]

II ADOPTION DE LA LOI DE MISE EN OEUVRE DE L'ACCORD DE
LIBRE-ÉCHANGE CANADA-ÉTATS-UNIS-MEXIQUE

Le 23 juin 1993, la Chambre des communes du Canada a adopté
la loi de mise en oeuvre de l'Accord de libre-échange nord-américain avec les États-Unis et le Mexique (ALÉNA).[6] Cet accord, qui
doit entrer en vigueur le 1er janvier 1997, est la plus importante
convention multilatérale jamais conclue par le Canada en matière
d'investissement.

La loi de mise en oeuvre de l'ALÉNA inclut les dispositions de cet
accord concernant les investissements effectués entre les trois pays,
notamment celles que l'on retrouve au chapitre sur l'investissement, soit le chapitre 11. Dans ce chapitre, l'on retrouve l'ensemble
des droits et obligations qui s'appliqueront aux investisseurs d'un
pays de l'ALÉNA et à leurs investissements et, dans le cas des
prescriptions de résultats et des mesures environnementales, à tous
les investissements étrangers effectués sur le territoire d'un pays de
l'ALÉNA, quelle que soit leur origine.[7]

III CONVENTIONS SUR LA PROMOTION ET LA PROTECTION DES
INVESTISSEMENTS

Au cours de 1993, deux conventions sur la promotion et la
protection des investissements (CPPI) sont entrées en vigueur au

---

[4] *Ibid.*, art. 2 § (a) (ii) (D).

[5] *L.I.C.*, *supra* note 2, art. 14 et 15.

[6] Voir Loi portant mise en oeuvre de l'Accord de libre-échange nord-américain,
S.C. 1993, c. 44.

[7] Pour un résumé des dispositions du chapitre 11 de l'ALÉNA, voir P. Ratelle,
"Investissement" (1993) 31 Ann. can. dr. int. 339-42.

Canada.[8] Le réseau canadien de CPPI compte maintenant six conventions en vigueur.[9]

Le corpus des CPPI conclues avec l'Argentine et la Hongrie ressemble *mutatis mutandis* à celui des autres CPPI. Les termes "investissement,"[10] "investisseur,"[11] "revenus"[12] et "territoire"[13] sont tout d'abord définis. Suivent ensuite les règles concernant l'admission,[14] le traitement,[15] la protection[16] et la compensation pour pertes[17] des investissements. Des dispositions concernant le transfert des fonds,[18] la subrogation[19] et le règlement des différends[20] sont également prévues par ces CPPI.

IV CONCLUSION DE L'URUGUAY ROUND DU GATT

Le 15 décembre 1993, sept ans après le début des négociations commerciales multilatérales de l'Uruguay Round à Punta del Este, en Uruguay, le Canada et les autres parties contractantes du GATT

---

[8] Voir Accord entre le Gouvernement du Canada et le Gouvernement de la République d'Argentine sur l'encouragement et la protection des investissements, 5 novembre 1991, R.T. Can. 1993 n° 11 [ci-après CPPI-Argentine] (en vigueur le 29 avril 1993); Accord entre le Gouvernement du Canada et le Gouvernement de la République de Hongrie sur l'encouragement et la protection des investissements, 3 octobre 1991, R.T. Can. 1993 n° 14 [ci-après CPPI-Hongrie] (en vigueur le 21 novembre 1993).

[9] Les autres CPPI ont été conclues avec l'ex-URSS, l'Uruguay, la Pologne et la Tchécoslovaquie. Au sujet de ces CPPI, voir P. Ratelle, "Investissement," (1993) 31 Ann. can. dr. int. 337-38; (1992) 30 Ann. can. dr. int. 337; (1991) 29 Ann. can. dr. int. 446-47; (1990) 28 Ann. can. dr. int. 453-54.

[10] Voir CPPI-Argentine, *supra* note 8, art. 1 (a); CPPI-Hongrie, *supra* note 8, art. 1 (b).

[11] Voir CPPI-Argentine, *ibid.*, art. 1 (b); CPPI-Hongrie, *ibid.*, art. 1 (b).

[12] Voir CPPI-Argentine, *ibid.*, art. 1 (c); CPPI-Hongrie, *ibid.*, art. 1 (d).

[13] Voir CPPI-Argentine, *ibid.*, art. 1 (d); CPPI-Hongrie, *ibid.*, art. 1 (c).

[14] Voir CPPI-Argentine, *ibid.*, art. 2 (2) et 3; CPPI-Hongrie, *ibid.*, art. 1 (d).

[15] Voir CPPI-Argentine, *ibid.*, art. 3-4; CPPI-Hongrie, *ibid.*, art. 2.

[16] Voir CPPI-Argentine, *ibid.*, art. 5; CPPI-Hongrie, *ibid.*, art. 3.

[17] Voir CPPI-Argentine, *ibid.*, art. 6; CPPI-Hongrie, *ibid.*, art. 5.

[18] Voir CPPI-Argentine, *ibid.*, art. 8; CPPI-Hongrie, *ibid.*, art. 7.

[19] Voir CPPI-Argentine, *ibid.*, art. 9; CPPI-Hongrie, *ibid.*, art. 8.

[20] Voir CPPI-Argentine, *ibid.*, art. 10 et 22; CPPI-Hongrie, *ibid.*, art. 9 et 11.

sont parvenus à conclure ce cycle.[21] Ils sont tombés d'accord sur un texte d'Acte final reprenant les résultats de ces négociations.[22]

Dans l'Acte final, on retrouve un accord, portant sur un des domaines de négociation cités dans la Déclaration de Punta del Este, qui aura un impact tant sur la réglementation des pays d'accueil des investissements canadiens situés hors de la zone de libre-échange nord-américaine, que sur la réglementation canadienne à l'égard des investissements étrangers originant hors de cette zone.

L'Accord relatif aux mesures concernant les investissements et liées au commerce, plus communément appelé dans le jargon du GATT "l'Accord sur les TRIMS," reconnait que certaines mesures concernant les investissements peuvent avoir des effets de restriction et de distorsion des échanges.[23] Il dispose qu'aucune partie contractante n'appliquera de mesures concernant les investissements liées au commerce qui soient incompatibles avec les dispositions de l'article 3 (traitement national) et de l'article 11 (élimination générale des restrictions quantitatives) de l'Accord général.[24] À cette fin, une liste indicative de TRIMS, dont il a été convenu qu'elles étaient incompatibles avec ces articles, est annexée à l'Accord.[25] Cette liste comprend des mesures qui exigent qu'une entreprise étrangère achète un certain volume ou une certaine valeur de produits d'origine locale (prescriptions relatives à la teneur en éléments d'origine locale) ou qui limitent le volume ou la valeur des importations que cette entreprise peut acheter ou utiliser à un montant lié au volume ou à la valeur des produits locaux qu'elle exporte (prescriptions relatives à l'équilibrage des échanges).[26]

Cet Accord prévoit ensuite la notification obligatoire de toutes les mesures concernant les investissements et liées au commerce qui ne sont pas conformes.[27] Il prévoit également leur élimination dans un

21 Voir "Le succès; les négociations les plus ambitieuses qui aient jamais été engagées s'achèvent," dans *Focus: Bulletin d'information du GATT,* n° 104, décembre 1993 à la p. 1.

22 Voir "L'Acte final de l'Uruguay Round; résumé pour la presse," dans *Nouvelles de l'Uruguay Round,* NUR 080, 14 décembre 1993 [ci-après "Acte final"].

23 "Acte final," *ibid.,* à la p. 15.

24 *Ibid.*

25 *Ibid.*

26 *Ibid.*

27 *Ibid.*

délai de deux ans pour les pays développés, de cinq ans pour les pays en développement et de sept ans pour les pays moins avancés.[28]

De plus, l'Accord crée un comité des TRIMS qui sera chargé, entre autres choses, de surveiller la mise en oeuvre des engagements.[29] Enfin, l'Accord prévoit que l'on examinera, à une date ultérieure, s'il devrait être complété par des dispositions relatives à la politique en matière d'investissement et de concurrence de manière plus large.[30]

[28] *Ibid.*

[29] *Ibid.*

[30] *Ibid.*

Canadian Practice in International Law / La pratique canadienne en matière de droit international public

At the Department of Foreign Affairs in 1993-94 / Au ministère des Affaires étrangères en 1993-94

compiled by / préparé par
PHILIPPE KIRSCH*

INTERNATIONAL ECONOMIC LAW

NAFTA Cultural Exemption — Application of Right of Retaliation

In a memorandum dated August 12, 1993, the Legal Bureau wrote:

Annex 2106 of the NAFTA provides that "any measure adopted or maintained with respect to cultural industries . . . and *any measure of equivalent commercial effect taken in response*, shall be governed *exclusively* in accordance with the provisions of the Canada - United States Free Trade Agreement" [emphasis added]. Article 2005 of the FTA provides that "[c]ultural industries are exempt from the provisions of this Agreement. . . ." This means that measures relating to cultural industries under the NAFTA, including those relating to copyright, are exempt from the

* Philippe Kirsch, Legal Adviser, Department of Foreign Affairs, Ottawa. The extracts from official correspondence contained in this survey have been made available by courtesy of the Department of Foreign Affairs. Material appearing in the House of Commons debates is not included. Some of the correspondence from which extracts are given was provided for the general guidance of the inquirer in relation to specific facts that are often not described in full in the extracts within this compilation. The statements of law and practice should not necessarily be regarded as a definitive statement by the Department of Foreign Affairs of that law or practice.

disciplines of the NAFTA. Article 2005 of the FTA also provides that "a Party may take measures of equivalent commercial effect in response to actions that would have been inconsistent with this Agreement but for [the exemption]." This allows for retaliatory action by the U.S. when the cultural exemption is invoked under the FTA. But since Annex 2106 of the NAFTA effectively incorporates those same words from Article 2005 of the FTA, and since copyright is not covered under the FTA (except insofar as relates to cable retransmission), there can be no "inconsistency" with the FTA. As a result, there can be no right of retaliation by the U.S. (or Mexico, for that matter). . . .

NAFTA Procurement Chapter — Modification of Coverage

In a memorandum dated February 16, 1994, the Legal Bureau wrote:

The word "coverage" in Article 1022 must be construed broadly. Article 1022 is not intended to be limited just to a change in the list of covered entities or exclusions in the Annexes, but extends also to the monetary thresholds set out in Article 1001. Article 1022 is worded more broadly than Article XXVIII of the GATT. The drafters of NAFTA could have worded Article 1022 to state that a Party may not modify "its list of covered entities" or "the Annexes to Article 1001." Instead, they chose broader language, prohibiting a Party from modifying "its coverage under this Chapter," except in exceptional circumstances.

The setting of monetary thresholds, as well as the establishment of the lists of covered entities and exceptions, was a result of an assessment made by each Party of the share of the market, calculated in dollar terms, that the Chapter would open up for its suppliers. Canada agreed to the liberalization of its own procurement practices at a certain level, in part as a result of an evaluation of the quantum of procurement contracts that Canadian suppliers would secure in the U.S. market. The use of set-asides cannot substantially undermine the bargain agreed to by the Parties in setting the thresholds in Article 1001.

NAFTA — Telecommunications

In a memorandum dated February 24, 1994, the Legal Bureau wrote:

Article 1301 makes it clear that Chapter 13 applies only to (a) access to and use of the public telecommunications network; (b) provision of enhanced services; and (c) telecommunications standards-related measures. It has been suggested that access to and use of the public network means access for the purpose of providing any service, including a basic service. This cannot be. Chapter 13 does not guarantee the provision of services; it only disciplines Parties' ability to restrict the matters mentioned above. Only services covered by Chapter 12 requiring access to the public network are services permitted for the purposes of ensuring such access under Chapter 13.

NAFTA — Obligations Arising from Liberalization of Provincial Measures

In a memorandum dated February 14, 1994, the Legal Bureau wrote:

. . . [C]oncerning the national treatment obligation in the areas of investment and cross-border trade in services (Articles 1102 and 1202), for a province this obligation means treatment accorded to Americans or Mexicans that is no less favourable than the most favourable treatment that that province accords, in like circumstances, to any Canadians (Articles 1102(3) and 1202(2)). Annex I reservations taken under Articles 1206 or 1108 with respect to a particular measure removes that measure, as it existed on January 1, 1994, from the application of the national treatment obligation. But a new measure or an amendment to the existing measure that is more discriminatory may not be made. Moreover, if the measure is now liberalized, a "ratchet" requirement prevents a Party from restoring the measure to its previous level of discrimination (Articles 1108(1)(c) and 1206(1)(c)).

If a province reduces the level of discrimination for *all* out-of-province investors or service-providers, then of course there is no problem. If instead it reduces the level of discrimination only for other *Canadian* out-of-province investors or service-providers, then there is also no problem in that it need not extend the same treatment to Americans or Mexicans. This is because the obligation for a province in Articles 1102(2) and 1202(2) is to accord national treatment to Americans or Mexicans, not to Canadians in other provinces. Consistent with this, a province is bound in its reservations to its existing level of discrimination vis-a-vis Americans or Mexicans only, and not other Canadians. Articles 1108(c) and 1206(c) allow a reservation to continue in respect of an amendment to a measure so long as the measure does not "decrease the conformity" of the measure, i.e., make it more discriminatory for Americans or Mexicans. But liberalizing (or "increasing the conformity") of the measure for other Canadians does not mean that there is less conformity for Americans or Mexicans. Nothing would have changed under the reservation vis-a-vis Americans or Mexicans. Previously, they were precluded from national treatment because the reservation protected the better treatment of in-province residents. Under amendments that liberalized the measure for other Canadians, they would still be precluded from national treatment, the difference merely being that the reservation would now be protecting the better treatment of all Canadians.

*GATT, GATT Agreement on Technical Barriers to Trade — Treaty
Interpretation and Priority of Agreements*

In a memorandum dated May 1, 1994, the Legal Bureau wrote:

... [I]t may be useful to outline the principles of treaty interpretation as
laid down in the *Vienna Convention on the Law of Treaties.* This Convention
is widely accepted as codifying the previously existing customary rules of
treaty interpretation. . . . The US government has recognized that the
Vienna Convention is generally recognized as the authoritative guide to
current treaty law and practice (*Restatement of the Law - The Foreign Relations Law of the United States* (1987), Vol. 1, at pp. 144-145). In the FTA
Panel report, *In the Matter of the Interpretation of and Canada's Compliance
with Article 701.3 with Respect to Durum Wheat Sales* (February 8, 1993), it is
recorded, at p. 7, that, in that case, the USA agreed, in answer to a
specific question by the Panel concerning the law applicable to the
dispute, that the Panel should refer to "the principles memorialized in
the Vienna Convention on the Law of Treaties". . . .

According to Article 31, paragraph 3(b) of the same Convention, one
should take into account "any relevant rules of international law applicable in the relations between the parties." This clearly includes the GATT
1947 text. This raises the question of what the structural relationship is
between Article IX of the GATT 1947 and the 1979 TBT Code.

In respect of the relationship between the GATT 1947 and the 1979
TBT Code it can be argued that the TBT Code is a further articulation of
GATT norms contained in Articles III, XI and XX, and that thus Article
IX operates as a carve-out from the TBT Code. Professor John H. Jackson,
in *World Trade and the Law of GATT* (1969), at p. 461, supports the
interpretation that Article IX operates as an exception to the national
treatment obligation of Article III. . . .

The new *Agreement Establishing the World Trade Organization,* in a general
interpretative note relating to the Agreements listed in Annex IA,
provides that in case of inconsistency between the GATT 1994 and any of
the Agreements of Annex IA, the specialized agreements (in this case the
new TBT Agreement) will prevail over the GATT 1994 to the extent of
such inconsistency. This provision would not have been included if the
Agreements of Annex IA were not considered as elaborations of certain
provisions of the GATT 1994. The question under consideration here is
an example of a situation in which an interpretation of a specialized
Agreement of Annex IA [if it were not for the elimination of the definition of "marking" in the 1990 ISO/ECE Guide] might result, in effect,
in an override of a provision of the GATT 1994. . . .

LAW OF THE SEA

*Internal Waters — Access to Ports in International Law —
Fishing Vessels*

In a memorandum dated July 22, 1994, the Legal Bureau wrote:

There is a presumption that all ports used for international trade are open to all merchant vessels, but this is a practice only, based upon convenience and commercial interest; it is *not* a legal obligation. Ports are situated in a State's internal waters, which form part of its territory, and which consequently are subject to the State's territorial sovereignty. Limitations to sovereignty cannot be presumed and there is no evidence of any limitations in state practice in relation to sovereignty over ports. Pursuant to this sovereignty, States have absolute control over access to their ports. The only exception is for vessels in distress, which have a right to take refuge in the nearest port. The right to designate only certain ports as being open is not questioned, nor is the right to impose conditions upon entry.

Moreover, fishing vessels are not included in the presumption that ports are open to trade and they are specifically exempted from the freedom of access to ports stipulated in certain bilateral and multilateral conventions. Indeed, the existence of these conventions in themselves is an indication that there is no general right of free access in customary international law. In state practice, there are numerous instances of ports being closed without protest. Conversely, there is no evidence in state practice of a customary right of access. Several decades ago, a few authors claimed the existence of such a right, but this claim has been decisively shown to be based upon faulty or no authority. In any event, not even these authors believed that the right extended to fishing vessels.

There is a possibility that a prohibition on entry into ports for the purposes of transshipment might be contrary to Article V of the GATT, but the closure of ports even to transshipment could fall under the general exception in Article XX(g), if the purpose of the closure was to promote the conservation of exhaustible natural resources. This would include the closure of ports to vessels that are undermining the effectiveness of measures for fisheries conservation.

Internal Waters — Control of Access

In a memorandum dated June 2, 1994, the Legal Bureau wrote:

Essentially, foreign vessels have a right of "innocent passage" in the territorial sea, meaning that they can pass through the territorial sea unhindered provided that they do not disturb the peace, good order or security of the coastal state. Hence, the ability of coastal states to control normal passage is extremely limited. In the instant case, we could not bar or impose a licensing requirement upon foreign fishing vessels that were merely transiting through our territorial sea.

On the other hand, states have complete sovereignty over their internal waters, including their ports. Under the Law of the Sea Conventions of 1958 and 1982, internal waters include the waters landward of the baselines by which the territorial sea is measured, ports and historic bays. Under customary law, waters historically considered as internal might also be included.

Consequently, we could bar foreign ships from these waters or impose conditions or restrictions upon entry. Therefore, a licensing requirement for entry into the internal waters and ports of Canada would be fully consistent with international law. There is a possible exception for transhipment rights in ports, which may be protected under Article V of the GATT. However, the boats concerned are unlikely to wish to tranship in Canadian ports and access to all other port facilities may be denied or controlled.

L'origine de la Convention sur le plateau continental de 1958

Dans le cadre d'une opinion rendue le 12 octobre 1994, le Bureau des affaires juridiques expliquait:

... Or si l'expression "plateau continental" fut utilisée pour la première fois par un géographe en 1898, il s'agissait alors d'un terme géographique et non d'un concept légal. Sa consécration juridique dans la sphère internationale remonte en fait à la proclamation que le Président Truman fit le 28 septembre 1945. Il s'agissait d'une déclaration unilatérale américaine créant un précédent en matière de revendication étatique puisqu'elle établissait la juridiction des États-Unis sur le plateau continental entourant leurs côtes de même que sur les richesses naturelles, biologiques et minérales, de ce dernier. C'est cette déclaration qui inspira par la suite les travaux de la Commission du droit international et ceux de la Conférence de Genève sur le droit de la mer qui se sont soldés par l'élaboration de la Convention sur le plateau continental de 1958.

Définition juridique du terme sédentaire: Art. 2(4) de la Convention sur le Plateau continental de 1958

Le 31 octobre 1994, le Bureau des affaires juridiques écrivait:

S'il est clair et non contesté que le Canada a effectivement juridiction exclusive sur les espèces sédentaires qui peuplent son plateau continental, la définition du terme sédentaire que l'on retrouve à l'article 2(4) de la Convention sur le Plateau continental de 1958 (la Convention de 1958) de même que l'absence de liste d'espèces visées ouvrent la porte à de nombreuses interprétations. En effet, l'un des principaux problèmes que pose cette définition est: "whether by immobility is meant incrustation in the soil or attachment to it, or whether it includes presence on the sea-bed with minimal powers of locomotion."

Définition juridique du terme sédentaire

De nombreux auteurs se sont penchés sur la question et ont scruté les commentaires des rédacteurs de l'article suscité. S'il est une chose à retenir des délibérations de ces derniers, c'est bien leur refus de trancher la question et leur volonté de céder la place aux experts scientifiques dans ce domaine.

Parmi les travaux préparatoires figure une étude préparée à la demande des Nations Unies par la FAO (Organisation des Nations Unies pour l'alimentation et l'agriculture) sur les rapports qui existent entre les ressources biologiques aquatiques et le lit de la mer du plateau continental, tel qu'il est défini à l'article 67 du projet relatif au droit de la mer adopté par la Commission de droit international (CDI) en 1956 et qui est devenu par la suite l'article 1 de la Convention de 1958. Sans prétendre avoir effectué une étude exhaustive de la question, les auteurs de cette étude ont toutefois mis en lumière sa complexité et proposent une classification des organismes qui font normalement partie de la population du plateau continental.

Afin de faciliter la compréhension du lecteur, les auteurs ont annexé un glossaire à leur étude et c'est au sein de cette liste de termes spéciaux que l'on peut lire "Sédentaire (adj.): Se dit des organismes vivants au fond et qui sans y être fixés *se déplacent à peine* [en anglais: . . . *move little if at all*].

Cette définition tendrait donc à appuyer la thèse qui veut que le terme *immobile* que l'on retrouve à l'article 2 suscité n'impliquerait pas nécessairement l'incrustation ou l'attachement au sol. On pourrait ainsi dire d'un organisme qui vit sur le fond qu'il est sédentaire et immobile bien qu'il possède des pouvoirs de locomotion minimaux. De plus, en discutant de l'intention des rédacteurs de l'article 68 du projet de la CDI mentionné au paragraphe 9 ci-dessus, qui devint par la suite l'article 2 de la Convention de 1958 cité au paragraphe 6, le professeur Bailey, membre de la délégation australienne à la Conférence qui adopta cette Convention, s'exprimait en ces termes: "It would be senseless to give coastal States exclusive rights over mineral resources such as the sands of the seabed but not over the coral, sponges and the living organisms which never move more than *a few inches or a few feet* on the floor of the sea."

Le professeur O'Connell est d'avis que le cheminement des rédacteurs démontre bien que la définition doit recevoir une interprétation plus large et qu'*immobilité* ne veut pas dire *immobilité totale* et *emplacement permanent*. Il rappelle de plus l'existence d'une théorie comparant les espèces sédentaires aux *fruits* du fond marin devant être récoltés et non chassés comme les poissons. Il explique:

> The pearl oyster, for example, affixes itself early in life to the sea bed by means of a byssus and does not thereafter move. Although it derives its life from the sea and not from the subsoil, it bears a close analogy to a tree or plant in that it depends upon its intimate association with the sea bed for continued existence. If removed and exposed it will suffocate; if detached, it will immediately affix itself again.

Overfishing on the High Seas

On April 25, 1994, the Legal Bureau wrote:

> The United Nations Convention on the Law of the Sea recognizes a coastal State's sovereign rights concerning, *inter alia*, the conservation and management of living marine resources within the 200-mile exclusive economic zone (EEZ). Beyond the EEZ of the coastal State, however, the nationals of all States have the right to engage in fishing on the high seas, subject to the relatively ineffective obligations of concerned States to "seek. . . to agree upon," or to "co-operate" with regard to, conservation measures for straddling fish stocks and highly migratory fish stocks.

Conservation and management effort within a State's EEZ are undermined in the case of straddling fish stocks and highly migratory fish stocks where fisheries for these stocks on the high seas just beyond the EEZ are unregulated. Overfishing on the high seas has contributed to sharply declining stocks around the world. In addition, highly migratory fish stocks (such as tunas) have become increasingly vulnerable throughout their ranges. Such ranges may cover entire oceans, both on the high seas and within the EEZ of many States.

The international community has begun to respond to this problem. At the United Nations Conference on Environment and Development, held in Rio in 1992, States decided to convene a UN Conference on Straddling Fish Stocks and Highly Migratory Fish Stocks to deal with the overfishing issue. While the UN Conference has not yet decided on the legal form of its outcome, the vast majority of participants seek a convention. Canada and most coastal States believe a convention is indispensable in order to ensure an effective regime of conservation and management of straddling fish stocks and highly migratory fish stocks on the high seas, supported by an effective system of surveillance and control and compulsory recourse to binding dispute settlement.

Some coastal-State governments have come under pressure from domestic fisheries interests to unilaterally extend their jurisdiction beyond the EEZ to ensure effective conservation and management on the high seas. A non-binding outcome would do little to ease such pressure. However, a convention containing legally binding obligations would go a long way towards removing the need for unilateral action. It would also provide general rules for regional fisheries conservation organizations and arrangements, thereby facilitating the establishment and operation of such organizations and arrangements for all States.

Article 92(1) of UNCLOS and Stateless Vessels

In November 1993, the Legal Bureau wrote:

Article 92 of UNCLOS is entitled "Status of ships." Its first paragraph reads as follows:

1. Ships shall sail under the flag of State only and, save in exceptional cases expressly provided for in international treaties or in this Convention, shall be subject to its exclusive jurisdiction on the high seas. A ship may not change its flag during a voyage or while in a port of call, save in the case of a real transfer of ownership or change of registry.

It has been suggested that this provision and in particular the first few words, requires all vessels to fly the flag of a State: i.e. that it is illegal for any vessel to be stateless. The question is whether this is a correct interpretation, or whether Article 92(1) simply requires that vessels which choose to fly a flag must not fly more than one.

A brief review of the legislative history of Article 92(1) leaves no indication that the drafters of that provision and its precursors considered statelessness in and of itself to be contrary to international law. On the contrary, the evolution of the wording indicates that the statelessness was discussed, at least briefly, and in terms that suggested it was a legal condition. If the numerous experts who conceived and refined UNCLOS over a period of some thirty years had considered the failure to sail under a flag to be repugnant to the history, goals or purposes of international law, they had every opportunity to say so in the clearest of terms. As it was, one delegate to the Geneva Conference suggested that the assembly require every vessel to have a nationality, but no formal proposal was ever made to this effect.

PEACE AND SECURITY

Nuclear Non-Proliferation — Safeguards in the Model Canadian Nuclear Co-operation Agreement

In a memorandum of February 23, 1994, the Legal Bureau wrote:

Article I(a) of the model Canadian NCA [Nuclear Co-operation Agreement] provides as follows:

The "Agency's Safeguards System" means the safeguards system set out in the International Atomic Energy document INFCIRC/66 Rev 2 as well as any subsequent amendments thereto that are accepted by the Parties.

The expression "The Agency's Safeguards System" is used once in the model Nuclear Co-operation Agreement in Article VII (2), which provides as follows: "With respect to nuclear material, the commitment contained in paragraph (1) of the Article shall be verified pursuant to the *safeguards agreement between each Party and the International Atomic Energy Agency, in connection with the [Nuclear Non-Proliferation] Treaty.* However, if for any reason or at any time the International Atomic Energy Agency is not administering such safeguards within the territory of a Party, that Party shall forthwith enter into an agreement with the other Party for the establishment of *IAEA safeguards* or *of a safeguards system that conforms to the principles and procedures of the Agency's Safeguards System and provides for the application of safeguards to all items subject to this Agreement"* (our emphasis.)

Article VII(2) of the model NCA provides for three alternative types of safeguards. In the first instance, safeguards must be applied by each party pursuant to the safeguards agreement between the party and the International Atomic Energy Agency in connection with the *Treaty on Non-Proliferation of Nuclear Weapons* (NPT). Those are the safeguards agreements required by Article III of the NPT and modelled on IAEA INFCIRC/153. In the event that the NPT safeguards are not applied, the parties are obliged to conclude an agreement for the application of fallback safeguards. Two types of fallback safeguards are envisaged. The first type mentioned in Article VII(2) is "IAEA safeguards." These IAEA fallback safeguards could involve parties additional to the Parties to the NCA and the IAEA, if all concerned parties agree. The provision for fallback IAEA safeguards neither requires nor precludes the adoption of safeguards on the INFCIRC/153 model. The alternative type of fallback safeguards mentioned is a "safeguards system that conforms to the principles and procedures of the Agency's Safeguards System and provides for the application of safeguards to all items subject to this Agreement." This safeguards system could involve just the two parties to the NCA, or it could involve additional parties. The model NCA envisages that this fallback safeguards [system] would conform to the system described in INFCIRC/66 Rev 2.

STATE RESPONSIBILITY

Defences — The Doctrine of Necessity

In a memorandum dated April 19, 1994, the Legal Bureau wrote:

An act that would otherwise constitute a breach of an obligation is not wrongful if taken in a state of necessity, where an essential interest of the state is threatened by a grave and imminent peril and there is no other means of averting it. The severe depletion of the fish stocks in the Northwest Atlantic is a grave and imminent peril threatening the livelihood of scores of thousands of Canadians and the economy of the Atlantic provinces. If the flag of convenience vessels are allowed to continue fishing, the fish stocks may be permanently wiped out. In the short term enforcement action on the high seas is the only way to stop the fishing and save the stocks.

General Principles

Vital Interests

Unlike self-defence and counter-measures, which also preclude wrongdoing, the operation of the doctrine of necessity does not presuppose the existence of a wrongful act committed by another State whose right is infringed by the State acting out of necessity. In circumstances of necessity, the other State may be innocent or guilty. What is required is that the State relying on the plea is acting in a situation of urgency, of "abnormal conditions of peril," of grave and imminent danger that threatens an essential or "vital" interest of the State.

This vital interest need not be such that it threatens the very existence of the State, but it must be at the level of an economic calamity, something endangering the survival of at least a portion of the population, an ecological disaster, and so forth, that creates an imperative necessity to act. This act is a conscious deliberated choice. For the action adopted to avoid the taint of wrongfulness, it must be the only effective means of averting the imminent peril. If some other means is available that does not constitutes the breach of an international obligation, that means must be chosen.

The "Torrey Canyon" Disaster

Also apposite to our own case is the Torrey Canyon oil pollution disaster. On March 18, 1967 a Liberian tanker carrying 117,000 tons of crude oil went aground off the Cornish coast, outside British territorial waters. Soon, 30,000 tons of oil had leaked into the sea from a hole in the hull. The British Government tried in vain to disperse the oil using detergents on the surface of the sea. Then, it tried to assist a salvor engaged by the owner, but salvage proved to be impossible when the hull broke and more oil was released into the sea. Finally, the UK decided to bomb the wreck to ignite the oil and burn it off before it could spread and pollute the nearby coast. This strategy was successful and almost all the oil was burned.

Although the British authorities did not claim any legal justification for bombing the ship, in public statements it emphasized the danger was extreme and that it had decided to bomb the ship only after all other methods of preventing pollution had proved impossible. That it was generally accepted that a state of necessity existed was evidenced by the fact that no one protested the action, not the shipowner, the flag State, nor any other State. Alerted to the possible consequences of a major oil tanker accident, within a couple of years Member States of the IMO had adopted conventions on liability for oil pollution damage and intervention on the high seas in cases of oil pollution casualties. Eventually the right of a coastal State to intervene on the high seas in accidents threatening pollution by oil and other substances was incorporated into the Law of the Sea Convention in Article 221. Intervention in such a situation may now be considered as a right under customary international law.

In its comments on the case, the ILC draws a general principle from this particular incident, holding that:

> . . . a state of necessity can still be invoked, in areas not covered by these rules, as a ground for state conduct not in conformity with international obligations in cases where such conduct proves necessary, by way of exception, in order to avert a serious and imminent danger which, even if not inevitable, is nevertheless a threat to a vital ecological interest, whether such conduct is adopted on the high seas, in outer space or—even this is not ruled out—in an area subject to the sovereignty of another state.

Other Instances of Necessity

Since the beginning of the nineteenth century, the validity of the plea of necessity has been recognized in a number of judicial decisions and arbitral awards, even where it has not formed the basis of the decision. In 1902, the doctrine was applied in the *Orinoco* arbitration, to absolve Venezuela from a charge of breach of contract in relation to the grant of mineral concessions to a French company. Much earlier, in 1832, on the advice of its law officers, the British Government had declined to press a claim against Portugal regarding the seizure of property of British subjects on account of a state of pressing necessity. In this century, the validity of the plea was admitted but not applied in the *Oscar Chinn* case, the *Wimbledon* case, the *Properties of Bulgarian Minorities in Greece* case, and the case concerning the *Rights of Nationals of the United States in Morocco*. It has also been referred to in a number of cases concerning the non-payment of State debts, such as the *Russian Indemnity* case and the *Société Commerciale de Belgique* case.

These examples reveal a number of common elements or conditions precedent before a plea of necessity can be accepted as a circumstance precluding the wrongfulness in international law of an act or omission by a putative wrongdoing State. These are:

(1) an "essential" interest of the State must be involved (what is essential will depend upon the circumstances);

(2) the peril must be extremely grave and must have been a threat to the interest at the actual time, and the action complained of must definitively have been the only means of warding off the extremely grave and imminent peril;

(3) the State claiming the benefit of the state of necessity must not itself have provoked, either deliberately or by negligence, the occurrence of the state of necessity, and

(4) the interest of the State towards which the obligation existed must itself be a less essential interest of the State in question.

TREATIES

Initialling of Texts of Treaties

On August 18, 1993, the Legal Bureau wrote:

Initialling of the text of a treaty by negotiators usually serves to record their agreement on the substance of the treaty and to authenticate the negotiated text. Non-substantive changes can still be made to the text at any time prior to signature. Initialling by negotiators "*ad referendum* to Governments" means that it is still possible for either Government to re-open the text by proposing changes of a substantive character, but that would mean that the negotiating process would recommence. When the text of an agreement is initialled by a minister in the sense described in this paragraph, the legal effect is no different than when it is initialled by an official. However, ministerial initialling, even when clearly stated to be *ad referendum*, is bound to create a presumption in the mind of the other party that the minister's government is politically committed to signing the initialled text.

. . . .

In Canadian practice, there are two alternative approaches to initialling a negotiated text for a bilateral agreement. They are as follows:

(1) Each page of the text is initialled by both negotiators. The representative of one country would initial each page in the bottom right corner, and the representative of the other country would do the same in the bottom left-hand corner.

(2) The negotiated text can be attached to an "agreed minute," prepared in two original copies. The agreed minute is signed by both negotiators. One copy would be retained by each country. The copy of the agreed minute for one country would mention it first and have its representative's signature on the left-hand side. The copy for the other country would mention it first and have its representative's signature on the left-hand side. Occasionally, the attached negotiated text is also initialled by the negotiators. Although this is perhaps good practice, it is not necessary.

The text initialled or attached to the agreed minute would be only in the language in which it has been negotiated.

Incompatibility of Treaty Provisions — Proposed Rule for European
Energy Charter Basic Agreement

In a memorandum of March 15, 1993, the Legal Bureau wrote:

Article 18 of the negotiating text for the European Energy Charter Basic
Agreement provides:

Where two or more Contracting Parties have entered into a prior international agreement, or enter into a subsequent international agreement,
whose terms in either case concern the subject matter of Part V [invest-
ment liberalization and protection] or V [dispute settlement] of this
Agreement, nothing in Part IV or V of this Agreement shall be construed
to supersede any incompatible provision of such terms of the other
agreement, and nothing in such terms of the other agreement shall be
construed to supersede any incompatible provision of Part IV or V of this
Agreement, where any such incompatible provision is more favourable to
the Investor or Investment.

Article 18 has been presented as a rule to address incompatibility
between the investment provisions of the BA and the investment provisions of other agreements between states party to the BA. In the event
that provisions in two treaties deal with the same subject-matter and yield
contradictory or incompatible results, the provisions of one treaty will be
inapplicable. International law allows the parties to a treaty to specify
explicitly which provisions will prevail in instances of incompatibility
between that treaty and other agreements to which they are party.

In our view, Article 18 does not establish a workable rule of priority. . . .
The intent of the "most favourable" rule is unclear. It could be intended
to mean:

(1) that a tribunal would resolve instances of incompatibility between
    the BA and another treaty by referring to a notional ideal standard;
    or
(2) that an investor may choose to invoke either the terms of the BA or
    the terms of the other agreement, according to the investor's deter-
    mination of which terms are "more favourable to the Investor or the
    Investment."

. . . interpretation A would be difficult to apply and would lead to uncertainty about prevailing rights and obligations and. . . interpretation B is
unworkable in the face of incompatible treaty provisions and unnecessary
in the absence of incompatibility.

. . . It is difficult to understand how reference to a notional ideal standard
of "more favourable to the investor or investment" would assist in the
determination of whether the BA or another agreement would prevail in
the event of incompatibility. The determination of which provisions will
be more favourable to the investor or the investment would be subjective
and dependent upon particular circumstances. For example . . . procedural and substantive treaty provisions cannot be easily divorced, and
provisions that would be more favourable to an investor in one situation
might be less favourable in another. . . . It seems unlikely that there can

be a universally valid abstract conception of what is more favourable to investors or investments. Consequently, were the "most favourable" rule intended to establish a national standard, it would provide little guidance to Contracting Parties or to investors about which treaty provisions prevail where the provisions of the BA and another treaty are incompatible. In our view, one of the principal objectives of a rule to address the relationship between two treaties is to remove uncertainty about which treaty provisions are applicable. The "more favourable" rule would defeat the objective of certainty, and it would be an open invitation to use dispute settlement to resolve incompatibility between the BA and other agreements.

. . . [Article 18] is unworkable if the rule is aimed at resolving situations where the provisions of the BA are incompatible with the provisions of another agreement. The "more favourable" rule suggests that more than one rule on the same particular subject-matter can apply at the same time between the same states; otherwise there would be no choice to be made. However, only one treaty rule on the same subject-matter can apply between states that are party to both the BA and another agreement. International law will not admit that in any given situation the applicable rule will be at once "do X" and "do not do X." Where two rules are incompatible, in the absence of a prior express choice by the states concerned, the applicable rule will be determined by the rules of the *Vienna Agreement* and customary international law. . . . As only one rule would apply in a given situation, the investor would have no choice to make. On the other hand, if there is no incompatibility between the provisions of the BA and the provisions of another agreement, then there is no need for a rule of priority. The provisions of both agreements would apply, and the investor would not be required to choose between them. . . .

Parliamentary Declarations in 1993-94 / Déclarations parlementaires en 1993-94

compiled by / préparé par
LAURIE WRIGHT*

I Les droits de la personne / Human Rights

(a)   Le Mexique / Mexico

L'hon. André Ouellet (ministre des Affaires étrangères): Monsieur le Président, il est important de rappeler à tous les députés qu'en 1990, le président Salinas a créé la Commission nationale des droits de la personne, qui fait maintenant l'objet d'une loi. Je crois que les autorités mexicaines elles-mêmes veulent prendre des mesures afin de veiller au respect des droits de la personne dans leur pays.

Deuxièmement, je tiens à assurer aux députés que, dans le cadre de l'ALÉNA, le Canada s'occupera maintenant d'un certain nombre de questions en relations plus étroites avec nos amis mexicains. Nous espérons que les Mexicains respecteront les critères établis ici au Canada et aux États-Uni touchant les droits de la personne.

Il est clair que, grâce à l'ALÉNA, nous serons peut-être en mesure de contribuer à remédier à la situation là-bas. Il est à espérer que les Mexicains fassent participer leurs citoyens à ce processus et que l'ALÉNA se révélera avantageux pour les plus pauvres au Mexique.

(House of Commons Debates, January 19, 1994, p. 27)
(Débats de la Chambre des communes, le 19 janvier 1994, p. 27)

Mr. Bill Blaikie (Winnipeg Transcona): . . . What is the government prepared to do if the human rights situation does not improve in Mexico?

---

* Counsel, Constitutional and International Law Section, Department of Justice / Section de droit constitutionnel et international, ministère de la Justice.

Are we going to continue in this agreement regardless of what the Mexican army and government do to people who feel these agreements are destroying their lives?

Right Hon. Jean Chrétien (Prime Minister): . . . we are following very closely what is happening at this moment in Mexico. We are putting pressure on its government to respect human rights. We will keep pressuring. . . .

We have to see how the situation develops there. We have confidence that the grievances that exist in that society have no relation to the signing of NAFTA.

(House of Commons Debates, January 19, 1994, p. 28)

(Débats de la Chambre des communes, le 19 janvier 1994, p. 28)

(b)   Haïti / Haiti

Mme Maud Debien (Laval-Est): . . . Ma question est la suivante: Pour s'assurer du respect de l'embargo par la communauté internationale, incluant les pays voisins d'Haïti, quels moyens concrets le gouvernement entend-il développer en collaboration avec les pays amis d'Haïti pour renforcer le blocus commercial et favoriser ainsi le retour du président élu, M. Aristide?

L'hon. André Ouellet (ministre des Affaires étrangères): . . . Il est évident que dans le contexte actuel où Haïti a principalement quatre amis qui essaient, à l'intérieur des Nations Unies, de faire avancer le cause de la démocratie dans ce pays, nous manquons d'appui et de soutien.

L'un des objectifs que nous poursuivons est d'élargir le cercle des amis d'Haïti et d'y inclure un certain nombre de pays des Caraïbes en particulier, voisins d'Haïti qui pourraient, en collaboration avec les quatre amis traditionnels d'Haïti, aider à s'assurer qu'un blocus total et complet soit vraiment efficace.

Mme Maud Debien (Laval-Est): . . . [L]e gouvernement canadien entend-il contribuer à la formation et à l'entraînement des forces policières haïtiennes qui auraient pour mandat d'assurer le restauration des institutions démocratiques? Et y a-t-il eu des engagements fermes qui ont été pris par le ministre avec M. Aristide à ce sujet lors de leurs entretiens?

L'hon. André Ouellet (ministre des Affaires étrangères): Cette question, M. le Président, a été discutée par le premier ministre lors de sa rencontre à Paris avec le secrétaire général des Nations Unies. Nous pensons qu'il serait opportun d'avoir, sous l'égide des Nations Unies, un tel programme d'entraînement pour des corps policiers dans des pays qui subissent la dictature militaire.

Cette proposition, mise de l'avant par le Canada, est une qui pourrait bien sûr s'appliquer d'abord à Haïti mais qui pourrait s'appliquer aussi dans plusieurs autres pays où il y a des dictatures militaires et où un contrepoids, telle une force policière, peut être utile à l'instauration et au respect de la démocratie. Par conséquent, dans nos discussions hier avec le président Aristide, nous avons obtenu son aval pour une telle initiative.

Il est évident que nous ne pouvons faire ceci sans l'approbation du gouvernement haïtien. Nous l'avons obtenue. Nous allons nommer un représentant qui, avec le représentant du président Aristide, étudiera les modalités d'application d'un tel programme de formation de policiers.

(House of Commons Debates, January 25, 1994, pp. 302-303)

(Débats de la Chambre des communes, le 25 janvier 1994, pp. 302-303)

Mr. Bob Mills (Red Deer): . . . Can the Minister of Foreign Affairs explain the specific criteria that he will now utilize to determine whether Canada should provide peacekeepers, especially to a place like Haiti? How does the safety of our peacekeepers factor into this decision?

Hon. André Ouellet (Minister of Foreign Affairs): Mr. Speaker, I want to remind the hon. member that according to the Governors Island agreement, under the United Nations a mission of police officers was supposed to be sent to Haiti to assist the Haitian authorities in forming a police corps that could complement the work of the government in ensuring a stable democratic government in counterbalance to the influence of the military forces.

It is in this spirit of the Governors Island agreement that Canada has agreed to send RCMP officers to take part in this operation. Indeed, we will honour our commitment in this regard whenever the forces return.

We have not talked about sending military forces and this is not an option that we are considering at the moment.

(House of Commons Debates, May 10, 1994, p. 4134)

(Débats de la Chambre des communes, le 10 mai 1994, p. 4134)

(c) Iraq / l'Iraq

Mrs. Carolyn Parrish (Mississauga West): . . . Will our government consider requesting United Nations peace observers to visit the southern Iraq marshes to report on the following: Measures being taken to stop the free flow of water to the marshes and effectively destroying their ecostructure; a blockade around the marshes which restricts the movement of food, people and medical care; the systematic torture and murder of women, children and the elderly.

Hon. André Ouellet (Minister of Foreign Affairs): Mr. Speaker, I certainly share the view expressed by the hon. member about the terrible situation imposed on the people living in Iraq and the persistent violation of human rights by the authorities there.

The representative of Canada at the United Nations, particularly at the Human Rights Commission, has proposed resolutions to send monitors, particularly to that region of Iraq, to assist these people who are abused by the authorities. Unfortunately, in order to achieve a remedy we need the co-operation of the authorities who have systematically refused United Nations missions or United Nations observers being sent there.

We will pursue this matter and hope that through perseverance the Iraqi authorities will accept the United Nations monitors.

(House of Commons Debates, April 21, 1994, p. 3334)
(Débats de la Chambre des communes, le 21 avril 1994, p. 3334)

(d)   La Birmanie / Burma

M. Réal Ménard (Hochelaga-Maisonneuve): . . . On nous apprend au ministère du Commerce international qu'en raison des violations des droits de la personne en Birmanie, aucune compagnie canadienne n'est encouragée à y faire affaires. Cependant, la Chine, pays voisin, qui approvisionne la junte militaire en armes, ne fait l'objet d'aucune restriction commerciale. Comment la vice-première ministre justifie-t-elle le double langage de son gouvernement? . . .

Hon. Sheila Copps (Deputy Prime Minister and Minister of the Environment): Mr. Speaker, I had an opportunity to personally meet with the leaders of the democracy movement yesterday.

They congratulated the Canadian government and in particular the Department of Foreign Affairs for the work we were doing in assisting them in getting their case brought to the United Nations through the auspices of the human rights commission headed by Mr. Ed Broadbent in Montreal; for the strong stand we have taken in ensuring that no direct government assistance goes to the Government of Burma; and for promoting at the ASEAN meeting that is going to be coming up very shortly a renewed call for the return of democratic government in Burma.

(House of Commons Debates, June 10, 1994, pp. 5158-59)
(Débats de la Chambre des communes, le 10 juin 1994, pp. 5158-59)

(e)   Les lesbiennes et homosexuels / Lesbians and Gays

Mr. David Chatters (Athabasca): . . . in July of last year Canada's representative on the United Nations' Economic and Social Council voted in favour of granting roster status to the non-governmental organization called the International Lesbian and Gay Association, which is an umbrella group representing a number of organizations, including the North American Man-Boy Love Association. This organization promotes sexual freedom between men and boys and opposes age of consent laws and other restrictions which deny men from having sex with boys.

I would like to ask the minister if his government endorses the decision of Canada's representative on the United Nations committee that voted in favour of granting status to this umbrella group.

Hon. André Ouellet (Minister of Foreign Affairs): . . . when Canada, the United States and western European countries voted in favour of giving consultative status to the ILGA, they were not aware the North American Man-Boy Love Association was affiliated with the International Lesbian and Gay Association.

I am now informed that corrective action has been taken.

Mr. David Chatters (Athabasca): . . . I would like to ask the minister if he would instruct Canada's representative on the United Nations committee to rescind our endorsement of this umbrella organization.

Hon. André Ouellet (Minister of Foreign Affairs): . . . the goal of the ILGA in seeking consultative status at the United Nations was to raise the issue of human rights abuses against lesbians and gay men.

Irrespective of the affiliations of which we were not aware, we believed it was important that corrective measures be taken and this was done to our satisfaction. I also understand it is to the satisfaction of other countries who supported the same resolution.

(House of Commons Debates, February 9, 1994, p. 1106)

(Débats de la Chambre des communes, le 9 février 1994, p. 1106)

(f) Les femmes / Women

L'hon. Sheila Finestone (secrétaire d'État (Multiculturalisme) (Situation de la femme)): . . . Le Canada est certes reconnu comme un des chefs de file mondiaux de la promotion de l'égalité des femmes. Le Canada a aidé à faire reconnaître les droits des femmes comme un "élément inaliénable, intégral et indivisible des droits universels de la personne" à la Conférence mondiale sur les droits de la personne, qui a eu lieu à Vienne l'année dernière. . . .

Le Canada est aussi à l'origine d'une déclaration des Nations Unies sur l'élimination de la violence faite aux femmes, adoptée en décembre 1993. La semaine dernière, la Commission des Nations Unies des droits de l'homme a annoncé son intention de nommer un rapporteur spécial sur la violence faite aux femmes. . . .

Next year the world will be looking at our progress and at that of other nations at the fourth United Nations conference on women in Beijing, China. We should think of the consequences if we do not work to improve the situation for women in Canada. What will we say to our daughters and granddaughters who look to their elected representatives to help lead the way in this process for change? We cannot ask our daughters to hold back their aspirations until we are ready for them. . . .

(House of Commons Debates, March 8, 1994, pp. 1957-58)

(Débats de la Chambre des communes, le 8 mars 1994, pp. 1957-58)

(g) Les enfants / Children

Mr. Paul E. Forseth (New Westminster-Burnaby): . . . Last week the minister confirmed that section 43 of the Criminal Code, which allows parents to use reasonable physical discipline, was being reviewed. The former Minister of Justice stated in May 1993 that the general direction of the departmental review was to investigate the possibility of children receiving the same protection against assault as adults have under the Criminal Code.

Would the minister tell us if the department is still following this direction? . . .

Hon. Allan Rock (Minister of Justice and Attorney General of Canada): Mr. Speaker, the review that is now under way in the Department of Justice was undertaken following this country's signing of the United Nations accord with respect to the rights of children. This international convention committed Canada along with other civilized countries of the world to prohibitions against the use of excessive force toward children in any context.

As a signatory to that United Nations convention, Canada became obligated to review its own domestic laws to ensure they reflect that international principle of basic decency. That is the reason for the review. That is its purpose and that is its scope.

Mr. Paul E. Forseth (New Westminster-Burnaby): . . . What are the reasons for the government to interfere with the freedom of parents to effectively raise their children by spending significant amounts of taxpayers' money on reviewing legislation which a majority of parents feel should remain the same?

Hon. Allan Rock (Minister of Justice and Attorney General of Canada): . . . As I have said, it is linked directly to our international obligations to ensure that our domestic laws reflect the accord among all civilized nations of the world that we prohibit the use of excessive force against children. That is exactly what we are looking at in this study.

(House of Commons Debates, June 14, 1994, pp. 5306-07)

(Débats de la Chambre des communes, le 14 juin 1994, pp. 5306-07)

2   *Les différends internationaux et le maintien de la paix / International Disputes and Peacekeeping*

(a)   La Bosnie / Bosnia

L'hon. Lucien Bouchard (chef de l'opposition): . . . Cinq jours après le massacre du marché central de Sarajevo, les 16 membres du Conseil de l'OTAN se réunissent aujourd'hui à Bruxelles, pour étudier une proposition américaine visant à forcer, d'ici 10 jours, la levée du siège de Sarajevo. Et une dépêche tombe à l'instant sur le fil pour annoncer, et je cite: "Les pays de l'OTAN ont aujourd'hui convenu d'adresser un ultimatum aux Serbes de Bosnie en les menaçant de raids aériens s'ils ne retirent pas leurs armements lourds de la région de Sarajevo dans les 10 jours qui viennent."

Je demanderais au premier ministre si cette information est exacte, et si, par le fait que ces décisions doivent se prendre d'une façon unanime, le Canada a appuyé l'expédition d'un ultimatum aux Serbes.

Le très hon. Jean Chrétien (premier ministre): Monsieur le Président, nous avons souscrit à la proposition de faire une zone de 20 kilomètres à partir du centre de Sarajevo pour que les armes qui sont là, contrôlées par les Serbes bosniaques et par les Musulmans bosniaques, tombent sous le contrôle des Nations Unies. Nous avons souscrit à cet ultimatum.

Je vois dans les dépêches de dernière minute que le militaire en charge des Forces à Sarajevo, M. Rose, a dit qu'il avait eu une entente il y a quelques minutes avec les Serbes, qui ont accepté de mettre leurs armes dans la région de Sarajevo sous le contrôle des Nations Unies. Je crois comprendre que la même chose sera faite par les Musulmans, ce qui veut dire que si on accepte cet ultimatum, les raids aériens dans cette région ne seront pas nécessaires.

L'hon. Lucien Bouchard (chef de l'opposition): . . . Est-ce qu'on peut demander au premier ministre, tout de même, quels sont les termes de l'ultimatum? De quoi menace-t-on précisément les Serbes au cas où il serait rejeté?

Le très hon. Jean Chrétien (premier ministre): Monsieur le Président, lors de résolutions au mois d'août, et renouvelées le 11 janvier, nous avons dit — et nous avons souscrit à cet élément — que si on allait continuer l'étranglement de Sarajevo, l'on pourrait avoir recours aux forces aériennes pour libérer d'une certaine façon cette ville.

À la suite des massacres inacceptables de la fin de semaine, les seize pays de l'OTAN ont décidé de donner un ultimatum et de créer une zone démilitarisée de 20 kilomètres à partir du centre de Sarajevo. Les Musulmans, apparemment, seraient prêts à l'accepter, de même que les Serbes de la région, ce qui veut dire que la menace d'attaques aériennes n'aurait pas à être exécutée, si ce que j'ai vu dans la dépêche est vrai.

L'hon. Lucien Bouchard (chef de l'opposition): Monsieur le Président, cela signifie que le Canada vient de franchir un pas important dans sa démarche vis-à-vis de la question des frappes aériennes puisque, jusqu'à maintenant, si j'ai bien compris, le Canada n'avait accepté que le principe de raids aériens rapprochés, pour des fins défensives concernant la sécurité des Casques bleus. Je comprends que dans ce cas-ci, le gouvernement a décidé d'appuyer le principe d'une frappe aérienne contre une force belligérante pour dégager la ville de Sarajevo.

Je voudrais demander au premier ministre, dans ce cas-là, quelles sont les conditions de sécurité qu'il a obtenus pour s'assurer que les Casques bleus canadiens ne seraient pas l'objet d'effets négatifs à la suite de l'ultimatum?

Right Hon. Jean Chrétien (Prime Minister): Mr. Speaker, when we were in Brussels a month ago we were very concerned about the Canadian troops that were on the other side of the line in Srebrenica. The situation has evolved naturally there. The Bosnian Serbs have accepted the Canadians being replaced by the Dutch before the end of this month.

The situation there is progressing normally. According to the news I heard a few minutes ago, the Serbs have agreed to accept the ultimatum in relation to Sarajevo so there will be no need for a strike. We have accepted to protect the civilians in Sarajevo and, in order to avoid a repetition of the massacre of last weekend, we gave that ultimatum to the military forces in the area.

(House of Commons Debates, February 9, 1994, pp. 1100-1101)
(Débats de la Chambre des communes, le 9 février 1994, pp. 1100-1101)

Mr. Ted McWhinney (Vancouver Quadra): . . . Given the sustained failure of United Nations and western European diplomatic efforts to end the armed conflict in Bosnia-Hercegovina, will the minister consider utilizing the provisions of the Treaty of St. Germain-en-Laye, which created Yugoslavia in 1919 and of which Canada is a full legal party, to ensure a peaceful solution to state succession problems in Yugoslavia, including, in addition to Bosnia-Hercegovina, the Skopje region?

    Hon. André Ouellet (Minister of Foreign Affairs): Mr. Speaker, I thank the hon. member for his suggestion. I think he based his question on the premise that the efforts of the United Nations and NATO will not be successful.

    Obviously we are hoping the decision taken yesterday will lead to a peaceful solution, but if it fails I certainly will consider very carefully the element of le traité de Saint-Germain-en-Laye.

(House of Commons Debates, February 10, 1994, p. 1188)

(Débats de la Chambre des communes, le 10 février 1994, p. 1188)

L'hon. Lucien Bouchard (chef de l'opposition): . . . Le ministre peut-il nous confirmer si le Canada a donné son appui à la résolution de l'OTAN de procéder à de nouvelles frappes aériennes et, en plus, nous indiquer s'il est vrai que le Canada a émis des doutes quant à leur efficacité?

    L'hon. André Ouellet (ministre des Affaires étrangères): Monsieur le Président, nous sommes énormément préoccupés par la détérioration de la situation en Bosnie. Il est évident que la demande formulée par le secrétaire général des Nations Unies de demander à l'OTAN de passer à des frappes aériennes de caractère offensif, plutôt que des frappes aériennes de caractère exclusivement défensif, est une décision lourde de conséquence.

    En effet, en fonction du changement de cette démarche, les troupes qui servent au nom des Nations Unies ne seront plus là exclusivement pour assurer le maintien de la paix et pour aider à l'acheminement de convois humanitaires. Nous prendrons à ce moment-là une position afin d'imposer la paix. C'est une question qui fait présentement l'objet de discussions entre les différents représentants membres de l'OTAN et quand une décision finale aura été prise, il me fera plaisir de la communiquer en cette Chambre.

(House of Commons Debates, April 20, 1994, pp. 3272-73)

(Débats de la Chambre des communes, le 20 avril 1994, pp. 3272-73)

L'hon. André Ouellet (ministre des Affaires étrangères) propose: . . . en février dernier, le Canada avait émis des réserves quant à l'utilisation des frappes aériennes pour protéger Sarajevo. Mais en fin de compte, nous étions arrivés à la conclusion que c'était le seul moyen de réagir à une situation qui devenait de plus en plus grave. Les préoccupations canadiennes avaient été prises en considération dans la décision de l'OTAN en février. Nous avions, par ailleurs, indiquée de façon très claire qu'advenant un changement important dans la nature des opérations des

Nations Unies en Bosnie, où nos troupes ne seraient plus là en tant que troupes de maintien de la paix, nous pourrions reconsidérer la présence de nos troupes en Bosnie.

J'aimerais souligner que le représentant canadien au Conseil de l'OTAN a réitéré hier les réserves du Canada quant à l'utilisation des frappes aériennes. La puissance aérienne ne peut, à elle seule, résoudre le problème en Bosnie. Nous devons situer nos décision dans le cadre de nos objectifs stratégiques qui demeurent avant tout la paix et les négociations. . . .

(House of Commons Debates, April 21, 1994, pp. 3348-50)

(Débats de la Chambre des communes, le 21 avril 1994, pp. 3348-50)

(b)   Le Rwanda / Rwanda

M. Bill Graham (Rosedale): . . . Pourquoi ne pas utilise nos bons offices auprès des institutions internationales, surtout l'Organisation de l'unité africaine, pour établir un corridor humanitaire aux 20 000 âmes présentement retenues à Kigali de sortir et de chercher refuge en Tanzanie, jusqu'à ce que la situation se stabilise et que le boucherie cesse?

L'hon. André Ouellet (ministre des Affaires étrangères): . . . Je voudrais en effet confirmer à l'honorable député que notre représentant, notre mission à Addis-Abeba a fait des représentations auprès de l'Organisation de l'union africaine, afin qu'elle s'implique davantage et qu'elle essaie de trouver des moyens pour venir en aide à une population tout à fait ravagée par cette guerre civile absolument inacceptable.

Je peux assurer l'honorable député que le Canada est disposé à intervenir pour participer avec d'autres à une mission humanitaire dans ce coin du monde qui en a besoin.

(House of Commons Debates, April 28, 1994, p. 3652)

(Débats de la Chambre des communes, le 28 avril 1994, p. 3652)

M. Philippe Paré (Louis-Hébert): . . . Vendredi, le Secrétaire général des Nations Unies a exhorté le Conseil de sécurité à envisager un recours à la force pour mettre un terme au massacre de milliers d'innocents, même si cela nécessite des renforts de Casques bleus.

Alors qu'un dépêche de ce matin rapporte que le ministre de la Défense nationale hésite à appuyer cette démarche du Secrétaire général de l'ONU, le ministre des Affaires étrangères peut-il indiquer si le Canada entend appuyer ou non cette démarche?

L'hon. André Ouellet (ministre des Affaires étrangères): Monsieur le Président, il est évident que le massacre qui continue au Rwanda ne peut être ni toléré ni même accepté par les pays qui ont eu par le passé des programmes de coopération avec cette population.

Le Canada est donc parmi les pays qui essaient, au sein des Nations Unies, ou au sein de l'Organisation de l'unité africaine, de trouver des moyens pour ramener à la raison ces factions qui s'entre-tuent actuellement.

Je voudrais dire à l'honorable député que les discussions préliminaires qui ont eu lieu aux Nations Unies n'ont pas apporté les résultats escomptés. C'est pourquoi nous pensons que peut-être un autre forum, l'OUA en particulier, pourrait être mieux placé pour jouer un rôle de conciliation afin d'amener les parties à la raison pour cesser de s'entre-tuer. Toute démarche à cet effet sera certainement supportée par le Canada. . . .

(House of Commons Debates, May 2, 1994, p. 3765)

(Débats de la Chambre des communes, le 2 mai 1994, p. 3765)

Mr. Ted McWhinney (Vancouver Quadra): . . . With the tragic communal strife in Rwanda now transcending national boundaries, will the minister ask the United Nations Secretary-General Boutros-Ghali to request the Security Council for emergency action under chapter six of the United Nations charter?

L'hon. André Ouellet (ministre des Affaires étrangères): Monsieur le Président, j'ai eu l'occasion de discuter de cette question aujourd'hui avec l'ambassadeur américain à l'ONU, Madeleine Albright, qui était de passage à Ottawa. Je lui ai rappelé que le Canada trouve regrettable que le Conseil de sécurité des Nations Unies n'ait pas décidé d'envoyer un contingent plus important que celui qui est présentement au Rwanda pour assister le général Dallaire qui tente d'intervenir entre les parties pour les amener à un cessez-feu.

Je rappellerai à l'honorable député que, vendredi, le Canada a demandé à la Commission des droits de l'homme des Nations Unies de se pencher de toute urgence sur la question rwandaise et de faire une série de recommandations à cet effet. Finalement, je rappellerai que le Canada a mis à la disposition des Nations Unies et des organismes qui oeuvrent pour des fins humanitaires deux avions militaires qui sont à Nairobi et qui peuvent en tout temps acheminer des médicaments ou de la nourriture pour soulager la population affligée de Kigali et de la région.

(House of Commons Debates, May 9, 1994, p. 4058)

(Débats de la Chambre des communes, le 9 mai 1994, p. 4058)

Mr. Jesse Flis (Parliamentary Secretary to Minister of Foreign Affairs): . . . CIDA is . . . examining what further response may be made to the requests of the Canadian NGOs and the United Nations High Commissioner for Refugees. In addition, Canada took the initiative in arranging an intervention in Rwanda by the United Nations High Commissioner for Human Rights and for a special session of the human rights commission.

Canada has also provided the force commander for UNAMIR, General Romeo Dallaire, and six other officers. General Dallaire's actions in particular have commanded uniform attention and approval.

As noted by the Minister of Foreign Affairs in an earlier intervention, Canada has interceded with members of the Security Council to encourage the dispatch of a strengthened UNAMIR contingency to Rwanda. The council will consider a draft resolution envisaging an enlarged

UNAMIR force of 5,500 to support groups affected by the fighting and to assist with the provision of assistance by humanitarian agencies.

(House of Commons Debates, May 12, 1994, pp. 4303-4304)
(Débats de la Chambre des communes, le 12 mai 1994, pp. 4303-4304)

Mme Maud Debien (Laval Est): . . . Avant que l'aide humanitaire ne se rende au Rwanda que le contingent de la force canadienne, est-ce que le ministre peut nous dire si le Canada souscrit à la proposition de la France, présentement débattue au Conseil de sécurité de l'ONU, et qui préconise, elle, l'envoi d'une force d'intervention militaire au Rwanda?

L'hon. André Ouellet (ministre des Affaires étrangères): Monsieur le Président, la position du Canada à cet égard est bien connue. Nous pensons que notre participation doit être au sein de forces de paix des Nations Unies. Par conséquent, nous sommes mieux disposés à répondre positivement à la demande des Nations Unies que de participer à une opération militaire.

(House of Commons Debates, June 21, 1994, pp. 5659-60)
(Débats de la Chambre des communes, le 21 juin 1994, pp. 5659-60)

(c)   Haïti / Haiti

L'hon. André Ouellet (ministre des Affaires étrangères): . . . Je suis encouragé par l'action énergique de l'Organisation des États américains qui, unanimement, a pris la position mise de l'avant par le représentant personnel du Secrétaire général des Nations Unies, M. Caputo. Deuxièmement, je suis encouragé aussi par la décision des autorités de la République dominicaine de permettre la mise en place d'un système plus sûr, plus efficace pour contrôler la frontière entre Haïti et la République dominicaine.

Voilà des éléments qui me permettent de croire qu'enfin, l'embargo total pourra être efficace et amener les militaires à céder le pouvoir.

(House of Commons Debates, June 14, 1994, p. 5303)
(Débats de la Chambre des communes, le 14 juin 1994, p. 5303)

(d)   Les Nations Unies / United Nations

M. Jean-Marc Jacob (Charlesbourg): . . . Dans le contexte de la révision de la politique étrangère canadienne et de la politique de défense, le ministre accueille-t-il favorablement cette recommandation visant à créer une unité canadienne de rétablissement de la paix?

L'hon. André Ouellet (ministre des Affaires étrangères): Monsieur le Président, il s'agit d'une proposition très intéressante qui sera certainement étudiée à son mérite par le comité parlementaire mandaté justement pour une révision de notre politique étrangère et de notre politique de défense.

M. Jean-Marc Jacob (Charlesbourg): . . . Le ministre peut-il également nous dire s'il est d'accord avec une autre proposition de ce comité visant à augmenter le nombre de membres au Conseil de sécurité de l'ONU afin d'y faire une plus grande place aux pays en développement?

L'hon. André Ouellet (ministre des Affaires étrangères): Monsieur le Président, le député doit savoir que justement des études se font actuellement au Conseil de sécurité des Nations Unies. Au fait, à l'occasion de la dernière réunion des Nations Unies, un comité spécial a été mandaté pour revoir la composition du Conseil de sécurité. Actuellement, plusieurs propositions sont à l'étude.

Le Canada s'intéresse grandement à un Conseil de sécurité qui refléterait davantage la réalité présente des Nations Unies, compte tenu du fait qu'un nombre important de pays se sont ajoutés depuis le moment où le premier Conseil de sécurité a été créé. Le Canada n'a pas présenté de proposition particulière, mais nous étudions très activement diverses propositions qui sont présentement à l'étude. Lorsque ce comité spécial fera rapport, il est certain que le Canada sera à l'avant-garde d'une réforme importante du Conseil de sécurité.

(House of Commons Debates, June 16, 1994, p. 5431)
(Débats de la Chambre des communes, le 16 juin 1994, p. 5431)

(e)   La politique du maintien de la paix / Peacekeeping Policy

L'hon. André Ouellet (ministre des Affaires étrangères) propose:

. . . Au fil des années, le Canada a développé des lignes directrices guidant sa participation aux opérations du maintien de la paix. J'en résume les grandes lignes.

Il faut d'abord un mandat clair et réalisable provenant d'une autorité politique compétente, comme le Conseil de sécurité.

Il faut ensuite que les parties au conflit s'engagent à respecter un cessez-le-feu et évidemment acceptent la présence de troupes canadiennes.

Également, l'opération de paix doit soutenir un processus de règlement politique du conflit.

Enfin, le nombre de troupes et la composition internationale de l'opération doivent être appropriés au mandat. L'opération doit être adéquatement financée et son organisation logistique doit être satisfaite. . . .

Il nous apparaît que, dans le passé, le niveau du risque encouru par nos soldats était rarement un problème. Malheureusement, ce n'est plus le cas aujourd'hui et le facteur risque est devenu un élément essentiel dans nos prises de décisions. . . .

Si ces lignes directrices que je mentionnais plus tôt demeurent valables, il faut reconnaître que le contexte international dans lequel les opérations de maintien de la paix se déroulent à changé radicalement depuis 1989 et, je le pense, continuera à évoluer. . . .

Traditionnellement . . . les opérations de maintien de la paix ont été lancées lorsque les parties à un conflit ont conclu que la réalisation de leurs objectifs ne serait pas servie par la continuation d'un conflit armé mais plutôt par un règlement négocié avec l'aide d'une tierce partie. Ces opérations étaient par conséquent déployées pour vérifier un cessez-le-jeu ou pour vérifier le retrait de troupes hors de zones disputes.

Mais en 1989-90, des opérations beaucoup plus considérables ont vu le jour, visant à aider les parties à un conflit à mettre en vigueur un règlement négocié de ce conflit. Au Cambodge, par exemple, les Nations Unies ont eu pour mandat de désarmer des factions, d'assurer la sécurité à travers le pays, de rapatrier des réfugiés, de faire respecter les droits de la personne, de superviser les ministères clés d'une administration nationale et, finalement, d'organiser des élections provisoires. On se rend donc compte qu'une composante civile très importante s'est alors ajoutée au traditionnel volet militaire.

En Bosnie et en Somalie, un nouveau concept a vu le jour: celui de l'intervention humanitaire. Nos soldats n'ont pas été envoyés là pour maintenir un cessez-le-feu ou une paix qui de toute évidence n'existait pas et n'existe pas encore. Leur mandat est de faciliter l'acheminement de convois humanitaires. L'exemple de la Somalie, en particulier, montre que ce type d'intervention peut avoir des résultats très positifs, car malgré les problèmes que l'on sait et qui affectent essentiellement Mogadiscio, la cris humanitaire en Somalie a largement été surmontée dans le reste du pays.

Le Secrétaire général des Nations Unies a reconnu cette évolution dans son agenda pour la paix, en cette déclaration qu'il a faite intitulée "Agenda pour la paix," qui part du principe que la gestion des conflits exige toute une gamme d'outils dont le maintien de la paix en est un parmi d'autres. Les objectifs de la communauté internationale sont donc devenus beaucoup plus ambitieux: prévenir les conflits, consolider ou rétablir la paix par des moyens diplomatiques comme par la médiation ou les bons offices, mais aussi maintenir la paix ou encore assumer la reconstruction politique et sociale de sociétés effondrées.

Certaines opérations reflètent un mélange de ces divers éléments. Le terme "maintient de la paix" a pris un caractère que je qualifierais de quelque peu élastique; on s'éloigne bien souvent du concept des forces d'interposition que l'on a connu à Chypre, par exemple.

Il est important de noter le contexte international qui a permis cette évolution. La fin de la confrontation entre les deux superpuissances a permis — au moins jusqu'ici — un degré de consensus sans précédent au sein du Conseil de sécurité. Traditionnellement, dans le passé, les membres du Conseil de sécurité utilisaient leur droit de veto pour empêcher plusieurs interventions.

Donc, plus récemment, grâce à ce nouveau consensus, le Conseil de sécurité a donc pu, ces dernières années, exercer une autorité qui lui est bien sûr reconnue par la Charte des Nations Unies, mais qui était restée sans effet jusqu'à là.

Il faut reconnaître que cette évolution chamboule nos idées préconçues sur la nature du maintien de la paix et sur la façon dont la communauté internationale doit répondre. Je dirais, sans vouloir faire la sèche terminologie, que je pense qu'il est important de souligner que les nouveaux concepts utilisés par le Secrétaire général dans "Agenda pour la paix" ne sont pas interchangeables. Le terme "rétablissement de la paix," "peacemaking," comme on le dit en anglais, se réfère à des activités essentiellement diplomatiques employées pour résoudre un conflit, alors que celui "d'imposition de la paix" caractérise les situations où la communauté internationale utilise résolument la force contre un état membre comme ce fut le cas lors de la guerre du Golfe.

Monsieur le Président, vous constaterez que ce qui complique singulièrement les choses, c'est qu'un élément de force est de plus en plus souvent introduit dans les résolutions du Conseil de sécurité mandatant des opérations de maintien de la paix en quelque sorte à des opérations d'imposition de la paix. C'est évidemment le cas de la Somalie et celui aussi de la Bosnie. . . .

Essentially there are two distinct scenarios for air strikes. The first envisages the case where United Nations troops are directly under attack. In this specific case NATO agreed in June that the commander of the UNPROFOR could call on the United Nations Secretary General to authorize an air strike to assist United Nations troops where they are under attack.

The fact that the United Nations Secretary General would be the ultimate authority for an air strike under these conditions was insisted upon by Canada in view of the highly charged political considerations which would surround such decisions. There would be no debate within NATO before the strike was carried out as time would be of the essence.

We agree with this procedure. We think it is appropriate that if our troops are under attack we should be able to respond. An air strike under these circumstances might be necessary and we are fully in agreement with this.

The second type of air strike would be intended to remove an obstacle to UNPROFOR's performance of its duties in circumstances where there was no direct threat to UNPROFOR troops. The proposed air strike would thus be less time urgent. Under these circumstances the commander of UNPROFOR would submit a request for such an air strike to the Secretary General of the United Nations who must give his authorization as in the first case. The request would also be discussed in the North Atlantic Council of NATO. The North Atlantic Council must agree to support the request.

The North Atlantic Council operates by means of consensus. Therefore no decision to launch an air strike under these circumstances could be made unless all allies agreed to it. Canada's position on this question is well known and would guide our representative to the North Atlantic Council in such debate.

We have said and we repeat that in the second case we do not believe that an air strike would be conducive to solving current situations. In fact we have said on numerous occasions that air strikes should be the last resort. We believe the use of an air strike could jeopardize the humanitarian aid process and put our soldiers in great danger.

We want it abundantly clear that obviously this is a decision that would have to be discussed and agreed to within NATO by unanimous consent, including obviously the acceptance by Canada. . . .

(House of Commons Debates, January 25, 1994, pp. 263-66)

(Débats de la Chambre des communes, le 25 janvier 1994, pp. 263-66)

3   *Les relations diplomatiques* / *Diplomatic Relations*

(a)   Les missiles de croisière et le désarmement nucléaire /
Cruise Missiles and Nuclear Disarmament

M. Gilles Duceppe (Laurier-Sainte-Marie): . . . est-ce que le ministre peut nous dire si le gouvernement a pris une décision et qu'attend-il pour nous faire connaître sa position?

Hon. David Michael Collenette (Minister of National Defence and Minister of Veterans Affairs): . . . Members will know that in August 1993 the previous government authorized the 1994 test and the planning was well under way when we took office. Given this and given the fact that we will be having foreign policy and defence reviews in the next year where all matters including testing of weapons systems can be debated, the government has decided to proceed with the two tests in 1994, beginning this month.

I should also tell members that we have communicated this in the last hour to the United States government. We have stressed the fact that it should make no presumption about the outcome of the defence and policy reviews Parliament will be seized of later this year, given the very strong feelings on the matter of cruise testing both within the country and certainly within our party.

M. Gilles Duceppe (Laurier-Sainte-Marie): . . . Est-ce que le ministre des Affaires étrangères pourrait nous donner les détails de cette entente et la déposer à la Chambre?

Hon. David Michael Collenette (Minister of National Defence and Minister of Veterans Affairs): . . . It was renewed in 1993 and it does provide for individual tests to be conducted bilaterally. The actual tests can be agreed on or cancelled at any time within the framework of that agreement.

All we are doing today is verbally acceding to the request of the United States to have two more tests in 1994 in the same way as we have had tests in the past nine years.

(House of Commons Debates, February 3, 1994, pp. 888-89)
(Débats de la Chambre des communes, le 3 février 1994, pp. 888-89)

Mr. Ted McWhinney (Vancouver Quadra): . . . will the Minister of Foreign Affairs consider intervening in the World Health Organization process now pending before the World Court in The Hague on the illegality of nuclear weapons?

Hon. Michel Dupuy (Minister of Canadian Heritage): . . . I am informed that it is up for consideration by the foreign minister who will make a decision in due course. However, there is no evidence in sight that Canada is going to change its traditional support for non-proliferation and to stop its fight against nuclear weapons.

(House of Commons Debates, April 29, 1994, p. 3709)
(Débats de la Chambre des communes, le 29 avril 1994, p. 3709)

M. Stéphane Bergeron (Verchères): . . . Le ministre des Affaires étrangères peut-il nous indiquer si le Canada souscrit sans réserve à la position américaine quant à l'embargo sur l'importation et l'exportation d'armes en provenance de la Corée du Nord, ainsi qu'à la panoplie de sanctions commerciales envisagées contre ce pays?
L'hon. André Ouellet (ministre des Affaires étrangères): . . . le Canada soutient la position américaine; que si besoin est, nous ferons campagne auprès des autres membres du Conseil de sécurité pour que cette résolution soit passée par le Conseil de sécurité et, certainement, que si les Nations Unies appliquent des sanctions contre la Corée du Nord, nous les respecterons intégralement.
M. Stéphane Bergeron (Verchères): Monsieur le Président, le ministre peut-il nous indiquer quelles interventions ont été faites, jusqu'à présent, par le gouvernement canadien pour amener la Corée du Nord à réintégrer les rangs de l'Agence internationale de l'énergie atomique et s'assurer que le programme nucléaire de ce pays respecte les dispositions du traité de non-prolifération?
L'hon. André Ouellet (ministre des Affaires étrangères): Monsieur le Président, nous n'avons pas de relations diplomatiques avec ce pays. Nous n'avons donc pas la possibilité d'exprimer directement notre point de vue. Nous l'avons fait, évidemment, par des déclarations publiques. Nous l'avons fait, également, indirectement en soutenant ce point de vue auprès des personnes qui parlent régulièrement avec les autorités nord-coréennes.
En particulier, lors de la récente visite du ministre des Affaires étrangères de la Corée du Sud, tant le premier ministre que moi-même avons expliqué à notre visiteur l'importance que nous voyons dans le respect intégral de ce traité de non-prolifération, de l'importance de le voir reconfirmé, reconduit, par toutes les nations du monde et l'importance de faire comprendre aux autorités de la Corée du Nord qu'elles ne peuvent pas s'isoler ainsi et qu'elles devraient s'intégrer avec l'ensemble des pays de la Terre, qui veulent non plus que nous utilisions des armes nucléaires, mais que nous respections ce traité de non-prolifération des armes nucléaires.

(House of Commons Debates, June 16, 1994, p. 5428)
(Débats de la Chambre des communes, le 16 juin 1994, p. 5428)

(b)   La politique des affaires étrangères / Foreign Affairs Policy

L'hon. André Ouellet (ministre des Affaires étrangères): . . . Premièrement, le gouvernement ratifiera bientôt la Convention sur le droit de la mer. Nous reconnaissons le désir des Canadiens et des Canadiennes, en particulier ceux des régions atlantiques, de voir un mécanisme international de contrôle des pêcheries en haute mer plus efficace. . . . Par ailleurs, j'ai demandé aux fonctionnaires de mon ministère de produire un document de travail sur les grandes questions touchant la réforme de l'Organisation des Nations Unies.

(House of Commons Debates, March 15, 1994, p. 2254)
(Débats de la Chambre des communes, le 15 mars 1994, p. 2254)

4   Le droit de la mer / Law of the Sea

(a)   Les pêcheries / Fisheries

Mr. Harbance Singh Dhaliwal (Parliamentary Secretary to Minister of Fisheries and Oceans): . . . The amendments to the Coastal Fisheries Protection Act [in Bill C-8] provide authority to use disabling force against a foreign fishing vessel that is fleeing so as to arrest the person commanding the vessel. This legislation relates to foreign fishing vessels, it does not relate to Canadian vessels. . . . Let me outline when disabling force could be used. The legislation sets out three conditions: First, a duly authorized Canadian official referred to as a protection officer is proceeding lawfully to arrest the person in command of a foreign fishing vessel. The vessel takes flight to avoid the arrest and the protection officer believes on reasonable grounds that force is necessary to make the arrest. Thus, Parliament would define in the legislation when disabling force could be used. . . . This would be done in regulations. . . . In general terms the regulations would provide for the use of disabling force at sea in compliance with international practice. This is what would happen: A foreign vessel has fished contrary to Canadian laws. Various methods of warning the vessel are used. Internationally accepted flags are hoisted to request communication with the vessels and to order the vessel to heave to. Flashing lights and whistles are used to order the master to stop his vessel. Internationally accepted codes are used to signal the vessel to heave to. Repeated orders to stop are also made via radio communication. Only if these are unsuccessful — and I repeat that — only if these are unsuccessful are warning shots fired.

If all of those attempts to get the vessel to stop are failed, those aboard the vessels are told that disabling force will be used. . . . Canada has never used disabling force against a foreign fishing vessel. We hope we will never have to, but we must be prepared to do so where circumstances warrant.

M. Yvan Bernier (Gaspé): . . . J'ai cru comprendre que le renforcement proposé dans la loi serait pour lui une façon d'arrêter ce qu'il appelle la surpêche à l'extérieur de la zone des 200 milles, sur le nez et la queue du Grand Banc à l'est de Terre-Neuve. Je dois lui rappeler cependant, que le nez et la queue du Grand Banc de Terre-Neuve est à l'extérieur de la zone des 200 milles. Donc, ce n'est pas de juridiction canadienne. Ce n'est pas le renforcement ou l'encadrement de la loi proposée ici présentement qui va régler ce problème. . . .

Mr. Harbance Singh Dhaliwal (Parliamentary Secretary to Minister of Fisheries and Oceans): . . . This law does not deal with beyond the 200-mile limit.

(House of Commons Debates, February 14, 1994, pp. 1316-17) (Débats de la Chambre des communes, le 14 février 1994, pp. 1316-17)

Mr. Fred Mifflin (Parliamentary Secretary to Minister of National Defence and Minister of Veterans Affairs): . . . [Bill C-8] applies in the case of a foreign fishing vessel that is to be arrested. . . . Certainly there are precedents for arresting foreign vessels on the high seas. . . . the country that has the coastline adjacent to the high seas . . . has a right, a duty and a responsibility on the high seas with respect to a straddling stock. . . . If we have to stand on guard quietly and watch our fish disappear under some rubric that we are not really allowed to go outside the 200-mile limit, this government is not going to stand for it. . . . I do not expect to live the rest of my life with a 200-mile limit. I have gone from 3 miles to 200 miles so I can assume, in the interest of avant-garde international law, we may well go beyond the 200-mile limit. . . .

(House of Commons Debates, February 14, 1994, pp. 1333-35, 1337)

(Débats de la Chambres de communes, le 14 février 1994, pp. 1333-35, 1337)

M. Stéphane Bergeron (Verchères): . . . Comment le gouvernement explique-t-il que les membres de l'OPANO ne se soient entendus que pour un moratoire d'un an alors que le Canada, de son côté, faisait valoir la nécessité d'un moratoire de trois ans pour reconstituer les stocks de morue?

Hon. David Anderson (Minister of National Revenue): . . . we had a vote. It was not a unanimous vote. . . . We now have the beginning of an agreement.

It would be unfortunate if we attempted at this point to ask for too much.

M. Stéphane Bergeron (Verchères): . . . le moratoire aura une portée limitée en raison de l'abstention de la Norvège et de l'Union européenne, qui ont refusé de participer au moratoire décidé par les autres pays membres de l'OPANO?

Hon. David Anderson (Minister of National Revenue): . . . it is true there were three abstentions, but we believe even when nations abstained in the past they did not necessarily go against the majority decision of NAFO.

(House of Commons Debates, February 18, 1994, pp. 1554-55)
(Débats de la Chambre des communes, le 18 février 1994, pp. 1554-55)

Hon. Brian Tobin (Minister of Fisheries and Oceans): . . . we have received assurances from the European Union, Denmark and Norway, even though they abstained on the vote which put in place a moratorium on 3NO cod stocks, it is their intention to abide by the decision of NAFO not to use the objection procedure.

(House of Commons Debates, February 21, 1994, p. 1617)
(Débats de la Chambre des communes, le 21 février 1994, p. 1617)

Mr. Ted McWhinney (Vancouver Quadra): . . . Pending conclusion of his proposed new high seas fisheries convention prohibiting overfishing by foreign vessels operating just outside Canada's 200-mile fishing zone, will the minister of fisheries remind states that Canada has the legal right under already existing international law to apply stringent fisheries conservation measures and penal sanctions where necessary against delinquent foreign vessels and their crews?

Hon. Brian Tobin (Minister of Fisheries and Oceans): . . . We are taking every measure to try to ensure that international law is binding, that we can develop binding dispute settlement mechanisms, and that Canada can through agreement put an end to the problem of foreign overfishing. . . . if we cannot resolve this problem by agreement we will resolve it by unilateral action by Canada.

(House of Commons Debates, March 21, 1994, p. 2545)

(Débats de la Chambre des communes, le 21 mars 1994, p. 2545)

Mr. Derek Wells (South Shore): Mr. Speaker, my question is for the Minister of Fisheries and Oceans. There continue to be reports of Spanish and Portuguese vessels taking undersized cod outside the 200-mile limit on the nose and tail of the Grand Banks.

Will the minister tell the House what the government is doing to stop this activity?

Hon. Brian Tobin (Minister of Fisheries and Oceans): . . . these catches of undersized fish are in violation of the conservation rules that we would apply to ourselves and in violation as well of NAFO conservation rules.

This morning I spoke to the European Fisheries Commissioner. I brought this matter to his attention and sought and received his assurance that member states of the European Union will prosecute and penalize those who engage in this kind of improper and illegal fishing activity.

(House of Commons Debates, April 11, 1994, p. 2858)

(Débats de la Chambre des communes, le 11 avril 1994, p. 2858)

Hon. Brian Tobin (Minister of Fisheries and Oceans): . . . We propose a measure today to give us the ability to enforce the conservation measures necessary to protect endangered species not just for ourselves but for the world. . . . Our legislation says: "The bill will enable Canada to take the urgent action necessary to prevent further destruction of straddling stocks and to permit their rebuilding while continuing to seek effective international solutions."

Lest anyone be in doubt, let me affirm once again three fundamental commitments by the Government of Canada. First, Canada is committed to the rule of international law. Second, Canada's goal remains effective international controls over high seas fishing. Third, the Government of Canada will use the powers under this legislation only where other means to protect threatened straddling stocks have failed.

Our commitment to the third principle is no less strong than our commitment to the first two; that is, the rule of law and our desire to seek effective international controls to deal with the problems of high seas fishing.

That is why, even as we propose a measure that allows us to go beyond 200 miles and to use the force required to ensure that NAFO conservation rules and other conservation measures are respected, we continue to work at the United Nations Conference on High Seas Fishing which will undertake its third session in August in New York to seek a permanent solution to the problem of overfishing.

The measures we take today under Bill C-29 are an interim measure, a temporary measure. They are necessary now because if we do not act those fish stocks will disappear, perhaps forever.

The world needs, and Canada needs, not a temporary solution taken by one nation but a permanent solution taken by all nations under the auspices of the United Nations. That is why Canada has worked hard at the United Nations both last summer and again this spring and we will do so again in August to get a new convention on high seas fishing. . . .

(House of Commons Debates, May 11, 1994, pp. 4212-14, 4221, 4222)

(Débats de la Chambre des communes, le 11 mai 1994, pp. 4212-14, 4221, 4222)

Mr. Joe McGuire (Egmont): . . . I see by the map that the legislation covers the nose and tail of the Grand Bank. Adjacent to it is the Flemish Cap, a very important breeding ground for cod and other groundfish.

Could the minister explain why the legislation stops short of the Flemish Cap and whether he has confidence that NAFO with the agreements he secured a month and a half ago is in a position to police that area?

Hon. Brian Tobin (Minister of Fisheries and Oceans): . . . The legislation gives the Parliament of Canada the authority to designate any class of vessel for enforcement of conservation measures. The legislation does not categorize whom we would enforce against. The legislation makes clear that any vessel fishing in a manner inconsistent with good, widely acknowledged conservation rules could be subject to action by Canada. We cite as an example the NAFO conservation rules. Any vessel from any nation fishing at variance with good conservation rules could under the authority granted in the legislation be subject to action by Canada. There are no exceptions. . . . the areas outlined on the map are NAFO regulatory areas. They cover straddling stocks and stocks regulated by NAFO. The area that is not outlined on the map, including the Flemish Cap, is not part of the straddling stocks that affect Canada. That is why we have not claimed any territory beyond those affected or covered by our own straddling stocks.

As I said, this is not an extension of jurisdiction; this is a conservation regime that we are introducing today.

(House of Commons Debates, May 11, 1994, p. 4216)

(Débats de la Chambre des communes, le 11 mai 1994, p. 4216)

Mrs. Jean Payne (St. John's West): . . . On May 12, amendments to the Coastal Fisheries Protection Act received royal assent. This legislation will allow Canada to take action against foreign fishing vessels fishing contrary to conservation measures on the Grand Banks outside Canada's 200-mile limit.

Can the minister advise this House when and how we can expect to see this measure enforced?

Hon. Brian Tobin (Minister of Fisheries and Oceans): Mr. Speaker, the regulations to bring the new Act into force were approved by cabinet this week and will come into effect the week of May 30.

All stateless and all flag of convenience vessels are being notified of the new legislation. We are already receiving indications as a result of boardings that have taken place over the last few days that many of these vessels will leave voluntarily. We hope that all vessels will leave voluntarily because those that do not will be seized and charged under a new Canadian law.

(House of Commons Debates, May 25, 1994, p. 4394)
(Débats de la Chambre des communes, le 25 mai 1994, p. 4394)

Mr. John Cummins (Delta): Mr. Speaker, my question is for the Minister of Fisheries and Oceans. Last week six American fishing vessels accompanied by a 150-foot American coast guard cutter conducted a black cod fishery while 15 miles south of the Canada-United States border between Alaska and British Columbia.

Was the minister aware of this incursion into Canadian territory? If so, why did he do nothing?

Hon. Brian Tobin (Minister of Fisheries and Oceans): . . . Indeed we are aware of the American vessels in the area of AB line and the Dixon Entrance.

The member knows it is not unusual over the years that both Canadian and American vessels are in this disputed zone and that each nation conducts its fishery and enforces its own fishery in this disputed zone.

(House of Commons Debates, June 21, 1994, p. 5663)
(Débats de la Chambre des communes, le 21 juin 1994, p. 5663)

(b) Law of the Sea Convention / la Convention sur le droit de la mer

Hon. Charles Caccia (Davenport): . . . Will the minister inform the House when Canada, after nine years of inaction, will ratify the law of the sea?

Hon. André Ouellet (Minister of Foreign Affairs): . . . there are a few difficulties in regard to the convention. We are diligently working to improve it and will hopefully be able to ratify it in the near future.

(House of Commons Debates, February 2, 1994, pp. 792-93)
(Débats de la Chambre des communes, le 2 février 1994, pp. 792-93)

(c)   Security of Marine Transportation / la Sûreté du transport maritime

Mr. Joe Fontana (Parliamentary Secretary to Minister of Transport): . . . The Marine Transportation Security Act is intended to address a long standing omission in federal regulatory powers and in so doing better equip the government and the marine transportation industry to respond to any threat to the security of people, goods, vessels, ports and facilities in the Canadian maritime marine environment. . . .

. . . [T]he International Maritime Organization, or IMO, the United Nations agency that deals with maritime matters, passed a recommendation that cruise ships on international voyages carry out security screening of passengers, analogous to that at airports, together with a variety of other complementary measures.

Canada was a strong supporter of that recommendation but has lacked the legislative authority to require the considerable cruise ship trade in Canada to comply. Attempts to achieve broad compliance with these measures on a voluntary basis have also been unsuccessful. These same IMO recommendations called on governments to review their national legislation to determine its adequacy. . . .

The international standards are intended to be the basis for the major element of a Canadian regulatory regime. . . . The bill is designed to apply to vessels, ports and marine facilities in Canada and to Canadian registered vessels anywhere, as well as to marine installations and structures, primarily drilling rigs and platforms on the continental shelf. . . .

(House of Commons Debates, June 14, 1994, pp. 5292-93, 5296)
(Débats de la Chambre des communes, le 14 juin 1994, pp. 5292-93, 5296)

5   *Environmental Law / Le droit de l'environnement*

(a)   Great Lakes / les Grands Lacs

Mrs. Karen Kraft Sloan (York-Simcoe): Mr. Speaker, the IJC today released a report that claims governments have not done enough to clean up pollution in the Great Lakes. . . . Does the government have any specific plans to resolve this serious problem?

Hon. Sheila Copps (Deputy Prime Minister and Minister of the Environment): . . . We expect to have a timetable and a framework in place within the next six months. We are very concerned that we sign the second phase of the Canada-United States water quality agreement to ensure that the decrease in sperm levels and the increase in breast cancer are dealt with very directly by elimination of toxins.

(House of Commons Debates, February 17, 1994, pp. 1503-1504)
(Débats de la Chambre des communes, le 17 février 1994, pp. 1503-1504)

(b) Migratory Birds / Les oiseaux migrateurs

Mr. Clifford Lincoln (Parliamentary Secretary to Deputy Prime Minister and Minister of the Environment): . . . Bill C-23 . . . will replace and repeal the current Migratory Birds Convention Act which was enacted 77 years ago in 1917. . . . The amendments proposed in Bill C-23 are designed to ensure the sustainable life of migratory birds and their enjoyment by Canadians. They also address our international commitments to the wise management of an internationally shared resource, and are consistent with the objectives of the Convention on Biological Diversity.

The Convention on Biological Diversity is one of the most tangible and important results of the earth summit in Rio two years ago. It was ratified by Canada in December 1992 and requires that countries regulate or manage biological resources to ensure their conservation and sustainable use and that countries establish a system of protected areas to conserve biodiversity. . . .

En modifiant la Loi sur la convention concernant les oiseaux migrateurs, on nous a donné l'occasion de nous tourner vers une possibilité d'avenir pour réagir contre les menaces aux oiseaux migrateurs. En accord avec la Convention sur la diversité biologique, le sperme, les embryons et les cultures de tissus d'oiseaux migrateurs sont maintenant assujettis à la loi. Les oeufs sont déjà protégés en vertu de la Loi. Même si dans ce domaine, il n'y a pas de menace immédiate pour les oiseaux migrateurs, les nouvelles utilisations de matériels biologiques continuent de se développer. . . .

From a point of view of both practicality and effectiveness the issue of enforcement is one in which a co-ordinated federal-provincial approach makes the most sense. There are many other areas for which this approach generates benefits, where the objectives and concerns are shared and where building on each other's strengths through co-operative action improves environmental results.

An excellent example of such a partnership is the international North American Waterfowl Management Plan. The plan, originally signed in 1986, is an initiative to protect and enhance wetland and upland habitat on a continental basis so as to stem the decline of waterfowl. The NAWMP has evolved from a plan focused on waterfowl conservation to one that incorporates benefits toward biodiversity conservation.

The plan exemplifies sustainable development in action by involving private land owners and resource sectors to integrate wildlife conservation practices with sustainable economic development, particularly through soil and water conservation initiatives.

Partners include the United States federal and state governments, NGOs and certainly all Canadian provinces. As well, Mexico is now a full partner, making the North American Waterfowl Management Plan a truly continental conservation plan.

On June 9 of this year the Deputy Prime Minister and Minister of the Environment signed the update to the plan extending Canada's commitment for another five years. . . . Le projet de loi C-23, celui-ci, qui modifie la Loi sur la convention concernant les oiseaux migrateurs, représente un pas en avant considérable envers la protection et la conservation des oiseaux migrateurs et envers le respect de nos engagements dans le cadre de la Convention sur la diversité biologique. . . .

(House of Commons Debates, June 13, 1994, pp. 5227-30, 5240) (Débats de la Chambre des communes, le 13 juin 1994, pp. 5227-30, 5240)

(c) La faune / Wildlife

M. Clifford Lincoln (secrétaire parlementaire à la vice-première ministre et à la ministre de l'Environnement): . . . C'est donc avec plaisir que je présente la troisième lecture du projet de loi visant à modifier la Loi sur la faune du Canada. . . . The marine ecosystem and its biodiversity remain largely unprotected from the habitat perspective. Presently application of the act is limited to the territorial 12-mile limit.

Critical wildlife habitat, including areas with significant concentration of seabirds and breeding and feeding grounds for whales exist or extend beyond the territorial sea. Such areas include polynyas, openings in the ice cover, and sea mounts, upwellings of nutrients in the ocean and other areas associated with Canada's continental shelf.

We therefore have a provision to allow for the establishment of protected areas within the area bounded by the territorial sea and the 200-nautical mile limit so that this would contribute to sustaining the biodiversity and associated benefits of the marine ecosystems. . . .

Le projet de loi C-24 remplacera la définition de faune. . . .

La nouvelle définition rend aussi la loi conforme à la politique fédérale-provinciale pour les espèces sauvages au Canada, adoptée en 1990, et la Convention sur la diversité biologique, que le Canada a signé en 1992 au Sommet de la terre à Rio de Janeiro. . . .

Bill C-24 will enable Canada to meet its commitments and international agreements. One such key agreement is the 1975 Ramsar Convention on Wetlands of International Importance which Canada signed in 1981. This is one of the most widely adopted conservation treaties in the world and over 80 nations have agreed to promote the conservation and wise use of wetland habitat, particularly for waterfowl. . . . Canada's Ramsar wetlands cover 13 million hectares, which is over 30 per cent of all the wetland areas designated under the convention. . . .

(House of Commons Debates, June 13, 1994, pp. 5240-42, 5249) (Débats de la Chambre des communes, le 13 juin 1994, pp. 5240-42, 5249)

6 *Trade / Le commerce*

(a) Free Trade Agreement / l'Accord de libre-échange

Mrs. Diane Ablonczy (Calgary North): Mr. Speaker, could the minister state conclusively that the text of the [Canada-United States Free Trade] agreement which has been made public is in fact the true and complete text? . . .

Hon. Roy MacLaren (Minister for International Trade): Mr. Speaker, the text made available by the previous government is, in my understanding, the actual text.

(House of Commons Debates, January 20, 1994, p. 103)
(Débats de la Chambre des communes, le 20 janvier 1994, p. 103

(b) NAFTA / L'ALENA

Mr. Peter Milliken (Parliamentary Secretary to Leader of the Government in the House of Commons): . . . Last summer, Canada, the United States and Mexico concluded two agreements which were additional and complementary to the North American Free Trade Agreement. One of these agreements is the North American agreement on environmental co-operation. This agreement commits the three countries to environmentally sustainable economic growth, to effective enforcement by each country of its environmental laws and regulations and to increased co-operation in the development of such laws and regulations.

The other is the North American agreement on labour co-operation, which promotes improvement of working conditions in the North American work place for all workers.

En vertu de ces ententes accessoires, les trois pays sont tenus non seulement d'appliquer réellement leurs lois en matière de main-d'oeuvre et de l'environnement, mais également de rectifier toute tendance à ne pas appliquer effectivement ces lois existantes. Ces ententes accessoires ont créé des obligations internationales pour le Canada.

In order to enforce these obligations, each agreement provides for the establishment of panels to make findings of fact and determinations. In carrying out these functions a panel may in its determination require a country to adopt an action plan to correct any failures to enforce its own laws or standards. In certain cases the panel determination may require the offending party to pay a fine.

The proposed amendments to the Crown Liability and Proceedings Act, for which the Minister of Justice is responsible, are before us today to permit domestic enforcement by the Federal Court of Canada of determinations relating to Canada's international obligations which may be made by these trinational panels. Without these amendments, no mechanism exists in Canadian law whereby our domestic courts can be employed to require the government to live up to its international obligations.

Le Canada estime et respecte la primauté du droit. Il n'a pas de difficulté à mettre son cadre juridique national au service de l'application des droits internationaux et des obligations internationales. . . . Because this is a strictly international determination which calls for particular expertise and complex international issues, Canadian courts would not be allowed to override the panel's determination.

The bill also contains a privative clause to exclude domestic judicial review of the panel proceedings, panel determinations, enforcement proceedings taken in the Federal Court, and orders and decisions made by the Federal Court in any enforcement proceedings.

This provision is similar in some respects to one already in place concerning the North American Free Trade Agreement.

(House of Commons Debates, February 4, 1994, pp. 949-50)
(Débats de la Chambre des communes, le 4 février 1994, pp. 949-50)

Hon. Audrey McLaughlin (Yukon): . . . since April 21 we have seen a deterioration in our trade relations with the United States. . . . Canadians on a wide variety of fronts know what they have lost from Liberal trade policy. Can the representative explain what exactly Canadians have gained?

Mr. Lyle Vanclief (Parliamentary Secretary to Minister of Agriculture and Agri-food): . . . With respect to grains, the United States has chosen to pursue the matter of Canadian exports to the United States under the GATT and not NAFTA.

On May 3 the United States officially notified the GATT of its intentions to renegotiate tariffs on wheat and barley under the GATT Article XXVIII. This notification triggers a 90-day period in which Canada and the United States will continue to attempt to reach a mutually satisfactory settlement of several agriculture trade issues.

If no agreement is reached following the 90-day period and the United States does proceed with restrictions on Canadian wheat and barley, Canada has the right under GATT to retaliate. If necessary we will exercise our GATT rights in response to the United States trade action. . . .

(House of Commons Debates, May 26, 1994, pp. 4502-4504)
(Débats de la Chambre des communes, le 26 mai 1994, pp. 4502-4504)

Mr. Bill Blaikie (Winnipeg Transcona): . . . a question that I asked of the government a couple of weeks ago. . . . had to do with the testimony in committee of someone representing the tobacco industry who threatened to use the North American free trade agreement and the protection of trademark and the property rights entrenched therein to get in the way of the government's apparent intention to bring in plain packaging of cigarettes. . . .

Mr. Mac Harb (Parliamentary Secretary to Minister for International Trade): . . . NAFTA contains provisions allowing exceptions to trademark rights. NAFTA also includes provisions that recognize Canada's right to adopt or maintain sanitary measures and standard related measures for the protection of human health. As well, the government will ensure that any measure it chooses to adopt will not only achieve our goal of protecting the health of Canadians but will also be consistent with our international obligations.

(House of Commons Debates, June 6, 1994, pp. 4903-4904)
(Débats de la Chambre des communes, le 6 juin 1994, pp. 4903-4904)

(c) GATT / le GATT

Hon. Douglas Peters (for the Minister of Finance): . . . The legislation I am introducing today seeks to extend the general preferential tariff, commonly referred to as the GPT, for another 10 years. The GPT is a tariff preference granted to developing countries for goods originating in those countries. . . . The GPT provides for a reduction in tariffs of up to one-third of the most favoured nation rates on certain types of goods from developing countries.

In the case of the least developed developing countries, that is the poorest countries known as the LDDCs, the tariff reduction is even larger. These countries are entitled to duty free treatment on all of their GPT eligible exports to Canada.

In all, more than 180 countries and territories are entitled to zero or low tariffs on a wide range of products, primarily manufactured and semi-manufactured goods.

In order for particular items to qualify for GPT they must comply with the rules of origin and other regulations. More particularly goods would only qualify for the GPT if at least 60 per cent of the factory price of the goods exported to Canada originated from one or more GPT countries. In the case of the LDDCs, the poorest countries, the content requirement is 40 per cent.

In order to ensure that GPT products do not have an adverse impact on Canadian producers, a safeguard system is authorized by the Minister of Finance to withdraw GPT treatment for particular goods. . . .

(House of Commons Debates, February 18, 1994, pp. 1539-40, 1547)
(Débats de la Chambre des communes, le 18 février 1994, pp. 1539-40, 1547)

M. Stéphane Bergeron (Verchères): Monsieur le Président, le ministre peut-il éclairer cette Chambre quant aux dispositions qui prévaudront en matière de litiges commerciaux entre le Canada et les États-Unis, à savoir si le GATT aura oui ou non préséance sur l'ALENA et pourrait-il déposer en cette Chambre les avis juridiques sur lesquels il appuie sa réponse?

Hon. Roy MacLaren (Minister for International Trade): Mr. Speaker, I can assure the hon. member that Canada's position has been clearly conveyed to the United States on numerous occasions. That is that our belief, our conviction and our best legal advice without question is that the GATT rules take precedence over the NAFTA.

(House of Commons Debates, May 5, 1994, pp. 3956-57)
(Débats de la Chambre des communes, le 5 mai 1994, pp. 3956-57)

Treaty Action Taken by Canada in 1993 / Mesures prises par le Canada en matière de traités en 1993

compiled by / préparé par
CÉLINE BLAIS*

* Treaty Registrar, Legal Advisory Division, Department of Foreign Affairs/ Greffier des Traités, Directions des consultations juridiques, Ministère des Affaires étrangères.

I: BILATERAL

Argentina
Convention between the Government of Canada and the Government of the Argentine Republic for the Avoidance of Double Taxation and the Prevention of Fiscal Evasion with Respect to Taxes on Income and on Capital (with Protocol). Buenos Aires, April 29, 1993.

Agreement between the Government of Canada and the Government of the Republic of Argentina for the Promotion and Protection of Investments. Toronto, November 5, 1991. *Entered into force* April 29, 1993. CTS 1993/11.

ASEAN
Agreement between the Governments of the Member Countries of the Association of Southeast Asian Nations and the Government of Canada on Economic Co-operation. Singapore, July 28, 1993.

Austria
Agreement between the Government of Canada and the Austrian Federal Republic on Air Transport (with Annex). Vienna, June 22, 1993. *Entered into force* September 1, 1993. CTS 1993/19.

Hong Kong
Agreement between the Government of Canada and the Government of Hong Kong for the Surrender of Fugitive Offenders. Hong Kong, September 7, 1993.

Exchange of Notes between the Government of Canada and the Government of Hong Kong constituting an Agreement to Extend the Canada/ Hong Kong Agreement concerning the Investigation of Drug Trafficking and Confiscation of the Proceeds of Drug Trafficking. Done, August 1993.

Hungary
Agreement between the Government of Canada and the Government of the Republic of Hungary for the Promotion and Reciprocal Protection of Investments. Ottawa, October 3, 1991. *Entered into force* November 21, 1993. CTS 1993/14.

Indonesia
General Agreement on Development Co-operation between the Government of Canada and the Government of the Republic of Indonesia (with Annexes). Ottawa, May 21, 1991. *Entered into force* June 28, 1993. CTS 1993/21.

Jordan
Exchange of Notes between the Government of Canada and the Government of the Hashemite Kingdom of Jordan constituting an Agreement amending the Annex to their Agreement on Air Transport signed May 10, 1990 (with Annex). Amman, April 14, 1993. *Entered into force* April 24, 1993. CTS 1993/22.

Mexico
Exchange of Letters between the Government of Canada and the Government of the United Mexican States constituting a bilateral Agreement pertaining to the 1992 North American Free Trade Agreement. Mexico, October 19, 1993.

Netherlands
Protocol Amending the Convention between Canada and the Kingdom of the Netherlands for the Avoidance of Double Taxation and the Prevention of Fiscal Evasion with Respect to Taxes on Income, with Protocol. The Hague, March 4, 1993.

New Zealand
Exchange of Notes constituting an Agreement between the Government of Canada and the Government of New Zealand amending their Agreement on Film and Video Relations signed at Vancouver, October 16, 1987. Wellington, June 17, 1993. *Entered into force* June 17, 1993. CTS 1993/12.

North Pacific Anadromous Fish Commission
Headquarters Agreement between the Government of Canada and the North Pacific Anadromous Fish Commission. Ottawa and Vancouver, October 29, 1993. *Signed* at Ottawa October 29, 1993 and at Vancouver on November 3, 1993. *Entered into force* November 3, 1993. CTS 1993/16.

North Pacific Science Organization (PISCES)
Headquarters Agreement between the Government of Canada and the North Pacific Science Organization (PISCES).

Victoria, January 8, 1993. *Entered into force* January 8, 1993. CTS 1993/3.

Portugal
Agreement between the Government of Canada and the Government of Portugal on their Mutual Fishery Relations. Ottawa, July 29, 1976. *Entered into force* July 18, 1977. CTS 1977/21. *Terminated* July 18, 1993.

Romania
Agreement between the Government of Canada and the Government of Romania concerning Military Relations. Ottawa, June 7, 1993.

Agreement between the Government of Canada and the Government of Romania concerning the Guarantee of a Loan. Bucharest, March 11, 1993.

Russia
Treaty on Concord and Co-operation between Canada and the Russian Federation. Ottawa, June 19, 1992. *Entered into force* April 4, 1993. CTS 1993/23.

Agreement between Canada and the Russian Federation on Economic Co-operation. Moscow, May 8, 1993.

Agreement between the Government of Canada and the Government of the Russian Federation concerning Environmental Co-operation. Moscow, May 8, 1993. *Entered into force* May 8, 1993. CTS 1993/7.

Agreement between the Government of Canada and the Government of the Russian Federation on the Establishment of a Direct Protected Telephone Line between Ottawa and Moscow. Moscow, May 8, 1993. *Entered into force* May 8, 1993. CTS 1993/6.

Switzerland
Treaty between Canada and the Swiss Confederation on Extradition. Berne, October 7, 1993.

Treaty between Canada and the Swiss Confederation on Mutual Assistance in Criminal Matters. Berne, October 7, 1993.

Ukraine

Exchange of Notes between the Government of Canada and the Government of Ukraine constituting an Agreement to extend for two years, as between Canada and Ukraine, the 1956 Trade Agreement between Canada and the Union of Soviet Socialist Republics. Kiev, April 18, 1993. *Entered into force* April 18, 1993. CTS 1993/26.

United Kingdom

Exchange of Notes between the Government of Canada and the Government of the United Kingdom of Great Britain and Northern Ireland constituting an Agreement to amend their Treaty on Mutual Legal Assistance in Criminal Matters (Drug Trafficking) done at Ottawa on June 22, 1988. London, March 26, 1992. *Entered into force* September 17, 1993. CTS 1993/15.

Exchange of Letters between the Government of Canada and the Government of the United Kingdom of Great Britain and Northern Ireland constituting an Agreement Establishing the Terms and Conditions of Reciprocity in Social Security between Canada, Jersey and Guernsey (with Schedule). Ottawa, February 12, 1993. *Letters signed* February 5 and February 12, 1993.

United States of America

Exchange of Notes between the Government of Canada and the Government of the United States of America constituting an Agreement further amending their 1959 Agreement concerning the Application of Tolls on the St. Lawrence Seaway (with Memorandum of Agreement). Washington, December 13, 1993. *Notes signed* November 8, 1993 and December 13, 1993. *Entered into force* December 13, 1993. CTS 1993/25.

Exchange of Letters between the Government of Canada and the Government of the United States of America constituting an Agreement amending Schedule 2 of Annex 705.4 as amended, of the Free Trade Agreement. Washington, April 30, 1993. *Entered into force* April 30, 1993. CTS 1993/4.

Exchange of Letters between the Government of Canada and the Government of the United States of America regarding the acceleration of the elimination of tariffs on goods under Article 401.5 and the amendment of Sections XV and XVI, Annex 302.1 of Chapter 3 of the Free Trade Agreement (with Annexes). Washington, June 30, 1993. *Entered into force* June 30, 1993. CTS 1993/18.

Exchanges of Letters between the Government of Canada and the Government of the United States of America constituting bilateral Agreements pertaining to the 1992 North American Free Trade Agreement. Washington and Ottawa, December 30, 1993.

Exchange of Notes between the Government of Canada and the Government of the United States of America constituting an Agreement concerning the Reciprocal Testing and Evaluation of Weapons Systems. Washington, February 10, 1993. *Entered into force* February 10, 1993. CTS 1993/17.

Exchange of Notes between the Government of Canada and the Government of the United States of America constituting an Agreement to Amend their Memorandum of Arrangement concerning the Operation of Pilotage Services on the Great Lakes. Washington, June 17, 1993. *Notes signed* October 24, 1992 and June 17, 1993. *Entered into force* June 17, 1993. CTS 1993/29.

Exchange of Letters between the Government of Canada and the Government of the United States of America constituting an Agreement concerning Co-operation on the Non-Proliferation Assurances to Canadian Uranium Retransferred from the United States of America to Taiwan (with Annex). Washington, March 5, 1993. *Letters signed* February 24 and March 5, 1993. *Entered into force* March 5, 1993. CTS 1993/5.

Exchange of Notes between the Government of Canada and the Government of the United States of America providing Privileges and Immunities to the Administrative and Technical Staffs of the Embassy of the United States in Ottawa and the Embassy of Canada in Washington. Washington, September 2, 1993. *Signed* at Ottawa August 26, 1993 and at Washington September 2, 1993.

USSR

Trade Agreement between the Government of Canada and the Government of the Union of Soviet Socialist Republics and Protocols of Extension. Ottawa, February 29, 1956. *Entered into force* May 26, 1956. CTS 1956/1. *Terminated* April 17, 1993. *Still in force* for Ukraine.

Venezuela

Agreement between the Government of Canada and the Government of the Republic of Venezuela for the Avoidance of Double Taxation Regarding Shipping and Air Transport. Caracas, June 26, 1990. *Entered into force* July 13, 1993.

ADDENDUM

Chile

Exchange of Notes between the Government of Canada and the Government of Chile constituting an Agreement concerning the Employment of Dependents of Employees of each Government Assigned to Official Missions in the Other Country. Santiago, January 21, 1991. *Entered into force* February 28, 1992. CTS 1992/38.

II: MULTILATERAL

Aviation

Protocol for the Suppression of Unlawful Acts of Violence at Airports Serving International Civil Aviation. Montreal, February 24, 1988. *Signed* by Canada February 24, 1988. *Ratified* by Canada

August 2, 1993. *Entered into force* for Canada September 1, 1993. CTS 1993/8. Note: Supplements the Convention for the Suppression of Unlawful Acts against the Safety of Civilian Aviation concluded at Montreal September 23, 1971.

Conservation

Convention for the Conservation of Anadromous Stocks in the North Pacific (with Annex). Ottawa, September 20, 1991. *Signed* by Canada February 11, 1992. *Ratified* by Canada November 6, 1992. *Entered into force* for Canada February 16, 1993. CTS 1993/13.

Defence

Document of the States Parties to the Treaty on Conventional Armed Forces in Europe (with Annexes). Vienna, February 5, 1993. *Signed* by Canada February 5, 1993. *Entered into force* for Canada July 6, 1993.

Administrative Agreement to implement Article 60 of the Agreement dated August 3, 1959 to Supplement the Agreement between the Parties to the North Atlantic Treaty regarding the Status of their Forces with respect to Foreign Forces stationed in the Federal Republic of Germany, as amended by the Agreements of October 21, 1971 and May 18, 1981 as well as by the Revised Supplementary Agreement. Bonn, March 18, 1993. *Signed* by Canada March 18, 1993.

Agreement between the Federal Republic of Germany, Canada and the United Kingdom of Great Britain and Northern Ireland on the Termination of the Agreement of 3 August 1959 concerning the Conduct of Manoeuvres and Other Training Exercises in the Soltau-Lünenburg Area as amended by the Agreement of 12 May 1970. Bonn, March 18, 1993. *Signed* by Canada March 18, 1993.

Agreement to amend the Agreement to Supplement the Agreement of June 19, 1951 between the Parties to the North Atlantic Treaty regarding the

Status of their Forces with respect to Foreign Forces stationed in the Federal Republic of Germany of August 3, 1959 as amended by the Agreements of October 21, 1971 and May 18, 1981. Bonn, March 18, 1993. *Signed* by Canada March 18, 1993.

Agreement to implement Paragraph 1 of Article 45 of the Agreement dated August 3, 1959 to Supplement the Agreement between the Parties to the North Atlantic Treaty regarding the Status of their Forces with respect to Foreign Forces stationed in the Federal Republic of Germany, as amended by the Revised Supplementary Agreement signed March 18, 1993. Bonn, March 18, 1993. *Signed* by Canada March 18, 1993.

Disarmament
Convention on the Prohibition of the Development, Production, Stockpiling and Use of Chemical Weapons and on their Destruction (with Annexes). Paris, January 13, 1993. *Signed* by Canada January 13, 1993.

Environment
Agreement Establishing the Inter-American Institute for Global Change Research. Montevideo, May 13, 1992. *Signed* by Canada March 25, 1993.

Convention on Biological Diversity (with Annexes). Rio de Janeiro, June 5, 1992. *Signed* by Canada June 11, 1992. *Ratified* by Canada December 4, 1992. *Entered into force* for Canada December 29, 1993. CTS 1993/24.

North American Agreement on Environmental Co-operation (with Annexes). Ottawa, September 14, 1993. *Signed* by Canada September 14, 1993. Note: *Signed* at Ottawa September 12 and 14, 1993, at Mexico September 8 and 14, 1993, and at Washington, D.C. September 9 and 14, 1993.

Fisheries
Protocol to amend Paragraph 2 of the International Convention for the Conservation of Atlantic Tunas (ICCAT). Madrid, June 5, 1992. *Signed* by Can-

ada September 22, 1993. *Ratified* by Canada September 22, 1993.

International Convention for the High Seas Fisheries of the North Pacific Ocean (with Annex) as amended April 25, 1978. Tokyo, May 9, 1952. *Signed* by Canada May 9, 1952. *Ratified* by Canada June 12, 1953. *Entered into force* for Canada June 12, 1953. CTS 1953/3. *Terminated* February 21, 1993.

Industrial Development
Constitution of the United Nations Industrial Development Organization. Vienna, April 8, 1979. *Signed* by Canada August 31, 1982. *Ratified* by Canada September 20, 1983. *Entered into force* for Canada June 21, 1985. *Denunciation* by Canada December 3, 1992, *with effect* December 31, 1993.

International Maritime Organization
Amendments to the Convention on the International Maritime Organization (Institutionalization of the Facilitation Committee). London, November 7, 1991. *Acceded to* by Canada June 24, 1993.

Labour
Convention concerning Minimum Standards in Merchant Ships (ILO Convention 147). Geneva, October 29, 1976. *Ratified* by Canada May 25, 1993.

North American Agreement on Labour Co-operation (with Annexes). Ottawa, September 14, 1993. *Signed* by Canada September 14, 1993. Note: *Signed* at Ottawa September 12 and 14, 1993, at Mexico September 8 and 14, 1993, and at Washington, D.C. September 9 and 14, 1993.

Law (Trusts)
Convention on the Law Applicable to Trusts and on their Recognition. The Hague, July 1, 1985. *Signed* by Canada October 11, 1988. *Ratified* by Canada October 20, 1992 with Declarations and Reservation. *Entered into force* for Canada January 1, 1993. CTS 1993/2.

Marine Pollution
Protocol, as amended, relating to the 1973 International Convention for the

Prevention of Pollution from Ships (MARPOL 73/78). London, February 17, 1978. *Acceded to* by Canada November 16, 1992 with Declarations. *Entered into force* for Canada February 16, 1993. CTS 1993/14.

Maritime Safety
Protocol for the Suppression of Unlawful Acts against the Safety of Fixed Platforms Located on the Continental Shelf. Rome, March 10, 1988. *Signed* by Canada March 10, 1988. *Ratified* by Canada June 18, 1993. *Entered into force* for Canada September 16, 1993. CTS 1993/9.

Convention for the Suppression of Unlawful Acts against the Safety of Maritime Navigation. Rome, March 10, 1988. *Signed* by Canada March 10, 1988. *Ratified* by Canada June 18, 1993. *Entered into force* for Canada September 16, 1993. CTS 1993/10.

Organization of American States
Protocol of Amendments to the Charter of the Organization of American States "Protocol of Washington." Washington, December 14, 1992. *Signed* by Canada December 14, 1992. *Ratified* by Canada October 4, 1993.

Protocol of Amendment to the Charter of the Organization of American States "Protocol of Managua." Managua, June 10, 1993. *Signed* by Canada June 10, 1993. *Ratified* by Canada October 4, 1993.

Pacific Settlement of International Disputes
Convention on Conciliation and Arbitration within the CSCE (Conference on Security and Co-operation in Europe). Stockholm, December 15, 1992. *Signed* by Canada March 31, 1993.

Postal Matters
Fifth Additional Protocol to the Constitution of the Postal Union of the Americas, Spain and Portugal. Montevideo, June 23, 1993. *Signed* by Canada June 23, 1993.

Science
Agreement to Establish a Science and Technology Center in Ukraine. Kiev, October 25, 1993. *Signed* by Canada October 25, 1993.

Telecommunications
Partial Revisions of the Radio Regulations and the Appendices thereto. Malaga-Torremolinos, March 3, 1992. *Signed* by Canada March 3, 1992 with Declaration. *Approved* by Canada June 21, 1993. *Entered into force* for Canada October 12, 1993. CTS 1993/27.

Optional Protocol on the Compulsory Settlement of Disputes Relating to the Constitution of the ITU, to the Convention of the ITU and to the Administrative Regulations, Nice, 1992. Geneva, December 22, 1992. *Signed* by Canada December 22, 1992 with Declaration. *Ratified* by Canada June 21, 1993.

Constitution and Convention of the International Telecommunication Union (ITU). Geneva, December 22, 1992. *Signed* by Canada December 22, 1992 with Declaration. *Ratified* by Canada June 21, 1993.

Textiles
Protocol Maintaining in Force the Arrangement Regarding International Trade in Textiles (GATT). Geneva, December 9, 1992. *Signed* by Canada December 21, 1992. *Ratified* by Canada March 31, 1993. *Applied provisionally* by Canada January 1, 1993. *Entered into force* for Canada March 31, 1993. CTS 1993/20.

Protocol Maintaining in Force the Arrangement Regarding International Trade in Textiles (GATT). Geneva, December 9, 1993. *Signed* by Canada December 21, 1993.

United Nations
Resolutions adopted by the United Nations Security Council acting under Chapter VII of the Charter of the United Nations on the situation in Angola, Haiti, Iraq/Kuwait, Libya, Somalia and the former Yugoslavia and the mandate of United Nations Forces in Angola (UNAVEM II), Somalia (UNOSOMII) and the former Yugoslavia (UNPROFOR). New York,

beginning February 5, 1993. *Effective and binding* on Canada from the dates passed.

ADDENDUM

Environment
Amendment to the Montreal Protocol on Substances that Deplete the Ozone Layer (with Annexes). London, June 29, 1990. *Acceded to* by Canada July 5, 1990. *Entered into force* for Canada August 10, 1992. CTS 1992/39.

I: BILATÉRAUX

Argentine
Convention entre le gouvernement du Canada et le gouvernement de la République d'Argentine en vue d'éviter les doubles impositions et de prévenir l'évasion fiscale en matière d'impôts sur le revenu et sur la fortune (avec Protocole). Buenos Aires, le 29 avril 1993.

Accord entre le gouvernement du Canada et le gouvernement de la République d'Argentine sur l'encouragement et la protection des investissements. Toronto, le 5 novembre 1991. *En vigueur* le 29 avril 1993. RTC 1993/11.

ASEAN
Accord de coopération économique entre le gouvernement du Canada et les gouvernements des États Membres de l'Association des Nations de l'Asie du Sud-Est. Singapour, le 28 juillet 1993.

Autriche
Accord sur le transport aérien entre le gouvernement du Canada et le gouvernement fédéral d'Autriche (avec Annexe). Vienne, le 22 juin 1993. *En vigueur* le 1er septembre 1993. RTC 1993/19.

Commission des poissons anadromes du Pacifique Nord
Accord de Siège entre le gouvernement du Canada et la Commission des poissons anadromes du Pacifique Nord. Ottawa, le 29 octobre 1993. *Signé* à Ottawa le 29 octobre 1993 et à

Vancouver le 3 novembre 1993. *En vigueur* le 3 novembre 1993. RTC 1993/16.

États-Unis d'Amerique
Échange de Lettres entre le gouvernement du Canada et le gouvernement des États-Unis d'Amérique concernant l'accélération de l'élimination des droits applicables à certains produits aux termes de l'article 401.5 et la modification des sections XV et XVI de l'annexe 302.1 du chapitre 3 de l'Accord de libre échange entre le Canada et les États-Unis (avec appendices). Washington, le 30 juin 1993. *En vigueur* le 30 juin 1993. RTC 1993/18.

Échange de Notes entre le gouvernement du Canada et le gouvernement des États-Unis d'Amérique constituant un Accord modifiant l'appendice 2 de l'Annexe 705.4 tel que modifié, de l'Accord de libre-échange. Washington, le 30 avril 1993. *En vigueur* le 30 avril 1993. RTC 1993/4.

Échanges de Lettres entre le gouvernement du Canada et le gouvernement des États-Unis d'Amérique constituant des Accords relatifs à l'Accord de libre-échange nord-américain *(ALÉNA)* de 1992. Washington, le 30 décembre 1993.

Échange de Notes entre le gouvernement du Canada et le gouvernement des États-Unis d'Amérique constituant un accord relatif à l'essai et à l'évaluation reciproques de systèmes d'armes. Washington, le 10 février 1993. *En vigueur* le 10 février 1993. RTC 1993/17.

Échange de Notes entre le gouvernement du Canada et le gouvernement des États-Unis d'Amérique constituant un Accord modifiant leur Accord de 1959 concernant l'application des taux de péage sur la voie maritime du Saint-Laurent (avec Mémorandum d'accord). Washington, le 13 décembre 1993. *Notes signées* les 8 novembre 1993 et 13 décembre 1993. *En vigueur* le 13 décembre 1993. RTC 1993/25.

Échange de Notes entre le gouvernement du Canada et le gouvernement des États-Unis d'Amérique constituant un Accord modifiant leur Accord concernant le pilotage dans les Grands Lacs (avec Mémoire d'accord) constitué par l'échange de Notes des 23 août 1978 et 29 mars 1979, tel que modifié. Washington, le 17 juin 1993. *Notes signées* les 24 octobre 1992 et 17 juin 1993. *En vigueur* le 17 juin 1993. RTC 1993/29.

Échange de Lettres entre le gouvernement du Canada et le gouvernement des États-Unis d'Amérique constituant un Accord concernant la coopération à l'égard des garanties de non-prolifération applicables à l'uranium canadien retransféré des États-Unis d'Amérique au Taiwan (avec Annexe). Washington, le 5 mars 1993. *En vigueur* le 5 mars 1993. RTC 1993/5.

Échange de Notes entre le gouvernement du Canada et le gouvernement des États-Unis d'Amérique accordant des privilèges et immunités au personnel administratif et technique de l'ambassade des États-Unis à Ottawa et à celui de l'ambassade du Canada à Washington. Washington, le 2 septembre 1993. *Notes signées* à Ottawa le 26 août 1993 et à Washington le 2 septembre 1993.

Hong Kong
Accord entre le gouvernement du Canada et le gouvernement de Hong Kong sur la remise des délinquants. Hong Kong, le 7 septembre 1993.

Échange de Notes entre le gouvernement du Canada et le gouvernement de Hong Kong constituant un Accord prorogeant l'Accord Canada-Hong Kong concernant les enquêtes sur le trafic des drogues. Fait en août 1993.

Hongrie
Accord entre le gouvernement du Canada et le gouvernement de la République de Hongrie sur l'encouragement et la protection réciproque des investissements. Ottawa, le 3 octo-bre 1991. *En vigueur* le 21 novembre 1993. RTC 1993/14.

Indonésie
Accord général de coopération au développement entre le gouvernement du Canada et le gouvernement de la République d'Indonésie (avec Annexes). Ottawa, le 21 mai 1991. *En vigueur* le 28 juin 1993. RTC 1993/21.

Jordanie
Échange de Notes entre le gouvernement du Canada et le gouvernement du Royaume hachémite de la Jordanie constituant un Accord modifiant l'Annexe de l'Accord sur le transport aérien signé le 10 mai 1990 (avec Annexe). Amman, le 14 avril 1993. *En vigueur* le 14 avril 1993. RTC 1993/22.

Mexique
Échange de Lettres entre le gouvernement du Canada et le gouvernement des États-Unis Mexicains constituant un Accord bilatéral relatif à l'Accord de libre-échange nord-américain (ALÉNA) de 1992. Mexique, le 19 octobre 1993.

Nouvelle Zélande
Échange de Notes constituant un Accord entre le gouvernement du Canada et le gouvernement de la Nouvelle-Zélande modifiant leur Accord sur les relations cinématographiques et audio-visuelles signé à Vancouver le 16 octobre 1987. Wellington, le 17 juin 1993. *En vigueur* le 17 juin 1993. RTC 1993/12.

Organisation pour les sciences marines dans le Pacifique Nord (PICES)
Accord de Siège entre le gouvernement du Canada et l'Organisation pour les sciences marines dans le Pacifique Nord (PICES). Victoria, le 8 janvier 1993. *En vigueur* le 8 janvier 1993. RTC 1993/3.

Pays-Bas
Protocole modifiant la Convention, y compris son Protocole, entre le Canada et le Royaume des Pays-Bas en vue d'éviter les doubles impositions et de prévenir l'évasion fiscale en

matière d'impôts sur le revenu. La Haye, le 4 mars 1993.

Portugal
Accord entre le gouvernement du Canada et le gouvernement du Portugal sur leurs relations mutuelles en matière de pêche. Ottawa, le 29 juillet 1976. *En vigueur* le 18 juillet 1977. RTC 1977/21. *Terminé* le 18 juillet 1993.

Roumanie
Accord entre le gouvernement du Canada et le gouvernement de la Roumanie au sujet des relations militaires. Ottawa, le 7 juin 1993.

Accord entre le gouvernement du Canada et le gouvernement de la Roumanie concernant une garantie d'emprunt. Bucarest, le 11 mars 1993.

Royaume-Uni
Échange de Notes constituant un Accord modifiant le Traité d'entraide en matière pénale (Trafic de drogue) entre le gouvernement du Canada et le gouvernement du Royaume-Uni de Grande Bretagne et d'Irlande du Nord, fait à Ottawa le 22 juin 1988. Londres, le 26 mars 1992. *En vigueur* le 17 septembre 1993. RTC 1993/15.

Échange de Lettres constituant un Accord entre le gouvernement du Canada et le gouvernement du Royaume-Uni de Grande Bretagne et d'Irlande du Nord établissant les termes et conditions de réciprocité en matière de sécurité sociale entre le Canada, Jersey et Guernesey (avec Annexe). Ottawa, le 12 février 1993. *Lettres signées* les 5 et 12 février 1993.

Russie
Traité d'entente et de coopération entre le Canada et la Fédération de Russie. Ottawa, le 19 juin 1992. *En vigueur* le 4 avril 1993. RTC 1993/23.

Accord de coopération économique entre le Canada et la Fédération de Russie. Moscou, le 8 mai 1993.

Accord de coopération dans le domaine de l'environnement entre le gouvernement du Canada et le gouvernement de la Fédération de Russie. Moscou, le 8 mai 1993. *En vigueur* le 8 mai 1993. RTC 1993/7.

Accord entre le gouvernement du Canada et le gouvernement de la Fédération de Russie sur l'installation d'une ligne téléphonique directe pour communications protégées entre Ottawa et Moscou. Moscou, le 8 mai 1993. *En vigueur* le 8 mai 1993. RTC 1993/6.

Suisse
Traité d'entraide judiciaire en matière pénale entre le Canada et la Suisse. Berne, le 7 octobre 1993.

Traité d'extradition entre le Canada et la Confédération Suisse. Berne, le 7 octobre 1993.

Ukraine
Échange de Notes entre le gouvernement du Canada et le gouvernement de l'Ukraine, prorogeant de deux ans, entre le Canada et l'Ukraine, l'Accord commercial de 1956 entre le Canada et l'Union des Républiques socialistes soviétiques. Kiev, le 18 avril 1993. *En vigueur* le 18 avril 1993. RTC 1993/26.

URSS
Accord commercial entre le gouvernement du Canada et le gouvernement de l'Union des Républiques socialistes soviétiques et Protocoles de prorogation. Ottawa, le 29 février 1956. *En vigueur* le 26 mai 1956. RTC 1956/1. *Terminé* le 17 avril 1993. *Demeure en vigueur* pour l'Ukraine.

Venezuela
Accord entre le gouvernement du Canada et le gouvernement de la République de Venezuela tendant à éviter la double imposition dans le domaine du transport maritime et aérien. Caracas, le 26 juin 1990. *En vigueur* le 13 juillet 1993.

ADDENDUM
Chili
Échange de Notes entre le gouvernement du Canada et le gouvernement du Chili constituant un accord relatif

à l'emploi de personnes à la charge des employés de chaque gouvernement en poste dans des missions officielles dans l'autre pays. Santiago, le 21 janvier 1991. *En vigueur* le 28 février 1992. RTC 1992/38.

II: MULTILATÉRAUX

Aviation
Protocole pour la suppression des actes illicites de violence dans les aéroports servant à l'aviation civile internationale. Montréal, le 28 février 1988. *Signé* par le Canada le 24 février 1988. *Ratifié* par le Canada le 2 août 1993. *En vigueur* pour le Canada le 1ᵉʳ septembre 1993. RTC 1993/8. Note: Complète la Convention pour la répression d'actes illicites dirigés contre la sécurité de l'aviation civile, faite à Montréal le 23 septembre 1971.

Conservation
Convention concernant la conservation des espèces anadromes dans l'océan Pacifique Nord (avec Annexe). Ottawa, le 20 septembre 1991. *Signée* par le Canada le 11 février 1992. *Ratifiée* par le Canada le 6 novembre 1992. *En vigueur* pour le Canada le 16 février 1993. RTC 1993/13.

Défense
Document des États parties au Traité sur les forces armées conventionnelles en Europe (avec annexes). Vienne, le 5 février 1993. *Signé* par le Canada le 5 février 1993. *En vigueur* pour le Canada le 6 juillet 1993.

Accord administratif portant application de l'Article 60 de l'Accord du 3 août 1959 modifié le 21 octobre 1971 et le 18 mai 1981 complétant la Convention entre les États parties au Traité de l'Atlantique Nord sur le statut de leurs forces, en ce qui concerne les forces étrangères stationnées en République d'Allemagne, dans sa version modifiée par l'Accord complémentaire revisé. Bonn, le 18 mars 1993. *Signé* par le Canada le 18 mars 1993.

Convention portant application du paragraphe 1 de l'article 45 de l'Accord du 3 août 1959 complétant la Convention entre les États parties au Traité de l'Atlantique Nord sur le statut de leurs forces, en ce qui concerne les forces étrangères stationnées en la République fédérale d'Allemagne, dans sa version modifiée par l'Accord complémentaire revisé. Bonn, le 18 mars 1993. *Signée* par le Canada le 18 mars 1993.

Accord modifiant l'Accord complétant la Convention du 19 juin 1951 entre les États parties au Traité de l'Atlantique Nord sur le statut de leurs forces en ce qui concerne les forces étrangères stationnées en la République fédérale d'Allemagne, signé le 3 août 1959 et modifié le 21 octobre 1971 et le 18 mai 1981. Bonn, le 18 mars 1993. *Signé* par le Canada le 18 mars 1993.

Convention entre la République fédérale d'Allemagne, le Canada et le Royaume-Uni de Grande-Bretagne et d'Irlande du Nord portant abrogation de la Convention du 3 août 1959 relative à l'exécution de manoeuvres et autres exercices militaires dans la région de Soltau-Lüneburg, modifiée par l'Accord du 12 mai 1970. Bonn, le 18 mars 1993. *Signée* par le Canada le 18 mars 1993.

Désarmement
Convention sur l'interdiction de la mise au point, de la fabrication, du stockage et de l'emploi des armes chimiques et sur leur destruction (avec Annexes). Paris, le 13 janvier 1993. *Signée* par le Canada le 13 janvier 1993.

Développement industriel
Acte constitutif de l'Organisation des Nations Unies pour le développement industriel. Vienne, le 8 avril 1979. *Signé* par le Canada le 31 août 1982. *Ratifié* par le Canada le 20 septembre 1983. *En vigueur* pour le Canada le 21 juin 1985. *Dénonciation* par le Canada le 3 décembre *avec effet* à compter du 31 décembre 1993.

Droit (Trust)
Convention relative à la loi applicable au trust et à sa reconnaissance. La Haye, le 1er juillet 1985. *Signée* par le Canada le 11 octobre 1988. *Ratifiée* par le Canada le 20 octobre 1992 avec Déclarations et Réserve. *En vigueur* pour le Canada le 1er janvier 1993. RTC 1993/2.

Environnement
Accord relatif à la création d'un institut interaméricain de recherches sur les changements à l'échelle du globe. Montevideo, le 13 mai 1992. *Signé* par le Canada le 25 mars 1993.

Convention sur la diversité biologique (avec Annexes). Rio de Janeiro, le 5 juin 1992. *Signée* par le Canada le 11 juin 1992. *Ratifiée* par le Canada le 4 décembre 1992. *En vigueur* pour le Canada le 29 décembre 1993. RTC 1993/24.

Accord nord-américain de coopération dans le domaine de l'environnement (avec Annexes). Ottawa, le 14 septembre 1993. *Signé* par le Canada le 14 septembre 1993. Note: *Signé* à Ottawa, les 12 et 14 septembre 1993, à Mexico, DF, les 8 et 14 septembre 1993 et à Washington, DC, les 9 et 14 septembre 1993.

Nations Unies
Résolutions adoptées par le Conseil de sécurité des Nations Unies, agissant en vertu du Chapitre VII de la Charte des Nations Unies concernant la situation en Angola, Haïti, Iraq/Koweït, Libye, Somalie et ancienne Yougoslavie, et le mandat des forces des Nations Unies en Angola (UNAVEM II), Somalie (UNOSOM II) et l'ancienne Yougoslavie (UNPROFOR). New York, à compter du 5 février 1993. *En vigueur* pour le Canada à la date d'adoption.

Navigation (Sécurité)
Convention pour la répression d'actes illicites contre la sécurité de la navigation maritime. Rome, le 10 mars 1988. *Signée* par le Canada le 10 mars 1988. *Ratifiée* par le Canada le 18 juin 1993. *En vigueur* pour le Canada le 16 septembre 1993. RTC 1993/10.

Navigation (Pollution)
Protocole de 1978, tel que modifié, relatif à la Convention internationale de 1973 pour la prévention de la pollution sur les navires (MARPOL 73/78). Londres, le 17 février 1978. *Adhésion* par le Canada le 16 novembre 1992 avec Déclarations. *En vigueur* pour le Canada le 16 février 1993. RTC 1993/14.

Organisation des États Américains (OÉA)
Protocole d'amendements à la Charte de l'Organisation des États Américains "Protocole de Washington." Washington, le 14 décembre 1992. *Signé* par le Canada le 14 décembre 1992. *Ratifié* par le Canada le 4 octobre 1993.

Protocole d'amendements à la Charte de l'Organisation des États Américains "Protocole de Managua." Managua, le 10 juin 1993. *Signé* par le Canada le 10 juin 1993. *Ratifié* par le Canada le 4 octobre 1993.

Organisation maritime internationale (OMI)
Amendements à la Convention portant création de l'Organisation maritime internationale (institutionnalisation du comité de la simplification des formalités). Londres, le 7 novembre 1991. *Adhésion* par le Canada le 24 juin 1993.

Pêche
Convention internationale concernant les pêcheries hauturières de l'Océan Pacifique Nord (avec Annexe) tel que modifiée le 25 avril 1978. Tokyo, le 9 mai 1952. *Signée* par le Canada le 9 mai 1952. *Ratifiée* par le Canada le 12 juin 1953. *En vigueur* pour le Canada le 12 juin 1953. RTC 1953/3. *Terminée* par le Canada le 21 février 1993.

Protocole visant à amender le paragraphe 2 de l'article X de la Convention internationale pour la conservation des thonidés de l'Atlantique. Madrid, le 5 juin 1992. *Signé* par le Canada le 22 septembre 1993. *Ratifié* par le Canada le 22 septembre 1993.

Postes

Cinquième protocole additionel à la Constitution de l'Union postale des Amériques, de l'Espagne et du Portugal. Montevideo, le 23 juin 1993. *Signé* par le Canada le 23 juin 1993.

Questions maritimes

Protocole pour la répression d'actes illicites contre la sécurité des plates-formes fixes situées sur le plateau continental. Rome, le 10 mars 1988. *Signé* par le Canada le 10 mars 1988. *Ratifié* par le Canada le 18 juin 1993. *En vigueur* pour le Canada le 16 septembre 1993. RTC 1993/9.

Règlement pacifique des différends internationaux

Convention relative à la conciliation et l'arbitrage au sein de la SCE (Conférence sur la sécurité et la coopération en Europe). Stockholm, le 15 décembre 1992. *Signée* par le Canada le 31 mars 1993.

Science

Accord instituant un centre pour la science et la technologie en Ukraine. Kiev, le 25 octobre 1993. *Signé* par le Canada le 25 octobre 1993.

Télécommunications

Revision partielle du Règlement des radiocommunications et des appendices audit Règlement. Malaga-Torremolinos, le 3 mars 1992. *Signée* par le Canada le 3 mars 1992 avec Déclaration. *Ratifiée* par le Canada le 21 juin 1993. *En vigueur* pour le Canada le 12 octobre 1993. RTC 1993/27.

Protocole facultatif concernant le règlement obligatoire des différends relatifs à la Constitution de l'Union internationale des télécommunications, à la Convention de l'Union internationale des télécommunications et aux Règlements administratifs, Nice 1992. Genève, le 22 décembre 1992. *Signé* par le Canada le 22 décembre 1992 avec Déclaration. *Ratifié* par le Canada le 21 juin 1993.

Constitution et Convention de l'Union internationale des télécommunications (UIT). Genève, le 22 décembre 1992. *Signées* par le Canada le 22 décembre 1992 avec Déclaration. *Ratifiées* par le Canada le 21 juin 1993.

Textiles

Protocole portant maintien en vigueur l'arrangement concernant le commerce international des textiles. Genève, le 9 décembre 1992. *Signé* par le Canada le 21 décembre 1992. *Ratifié* par le Canada le 31 mars 1993. *Appliqué* à titre provisoire à compter du 1er janvier 1993. *En vigueur* pour le Canada le 31 mars 1993. RTC 1993/20.

Protocole portant maintien en vigueur de l'arrangement concernant le commerce international des textiles. Genève, le 9 décembre 1993. *Signé* par le Canada le 21 décembre 1993.

Travail

Convention concernant les normes minima à observer sur les navires marchands (Convention de l'OIT 147). Genève, le 29 octobre 1976. *Ratifiée* par le Canada le 25 mai 1993.

Accord nord-américain de coopération dans le domaine du travail (avec Annexes). Ottawa, le 14 septembre 1993. *Signé* par le Canada le 14 septembre 1993. Note: *Signé* à Ottawa, les 12 et 14 septembre 1993, à Mexico, DF, les 8 et 14 septembre 1993 et à Washington, DC les 9 et 14 septembre 1993.

ADDENDUM

Environnement

Amendement au Protocole de Montréal relatif à des substances qui appauvrissent la couche d'ozone (avec Annexes). Londres, le 29 juin 1990. *Adhésion* du Canada le 5 juillet 1990. *En vigueur* pour le Canada le 10 août 1992. RTC 1992/39.

Canadian Cases in Public International Law in 1993-94 / La jurisprudence canadienne en matière de droit international public en 1993-94

compiled by / préparé par
KARIN MICKELSON*

Criminal law — extradition — jurisdiction of requesting state

United States of America v. *Lépine*, [1994] 1 S.C.R. 286, 111 D.L.R. (4th) 31. Supreme Court of Canada.

The respondent was allegedly involved in the planning of a scheme to procure cocaine in Colombia for distribution in Canada. No acts associated with the scheme had been carried out in the United States except for an unsuccessful attempt to finance the larger deal through the purchase of a small amount of cocaine in New York, also to be sold in Canada. The plane that was to carry the drugs from Colombia to Canada was stopped in Pennsylvania. The respondent was not on the plane, having remained in Canada throughout the time frame of these events. The United States requested extradition of the respondent on a charge of conspiracy to distribute cocaine; the extradition judge dismissed the application on the grounds that the United States did not have jurisdiction to prosecute the offence charged.

La Forest, J., writing for the majority, held that a judge at an extradition hearing does not have the authority to consider whether the state requesting extradition has jurisdiction to prosecute the offence charged. The judge's role is limited to the "modest" one of determining whether the evidence would have warranted the accused's committal for trial under Canadian law. In other words, the question to be asked is whether the acts alleged

* Faculty of Law, University of British Columbia.

would constitute a crime in Canada had they been committed here (the "double criminality" rule), not whether they would constitute a crime if some of the conduct had been committed here and some abroad (the "mirror image" approach). The "double criminality" rule is intended for the protection of the individual, a duty assigned to the courts. While there is a role for Canada in monitoring whether a state requesting extradition has gone beyond the terms of a treaty in exercising jurisdiction, that role is one for the executive rather than the courts. In any event, if the "mirror image" approach were the correct one to apply, it is clear that even if only the specific acts committed in the United States had taken place in Canada, jurisdiction could have been exercised under Canadian law under the "real and substantial link" test articulated in *R. v. Libman*, [1985] 2 S.C.R. 178.

In a minority opinion, Sopinka, J. (with Iacobucci, J. concurring) held that the question of whether the requesting state has jurisdiction over the offence is a proper inquiry for the extradition judge, being a question of mixed fact and law that is appropriately resolved in a judicial proceeding. That this is the proper approach is supported by the importance accorded to safeguarding individual liberty within the scheme in the Extradition Act, R.S.C. 1985, c. E-23. Sopinka, J. agreed with La Forest, J. that the application of the "mirror image approach" to the present case would justify the United States' exercise of jurisdiction over the offence charged.

Human rights — refugees — interpretation of Convention refugee

Zolfagharkhani v. Canada (Minister of Employment and Immigration), [1993] 3 F.C. 540. Federal Court of Appeal.

In this appeal from a decision of the Immigration and Refugee Board, the Court of Appeal held that the Board's refusal to grant the appellant's claim for refugee status was invalid. The appellant, who had served in the Iranian military for over two years, was being trained to act as a paramedic in an offensive against the Kurdish movement when he learned that chemical weapons might be used in the course of combat. For reasons of conscience, he deserted the army and fled the country, claiming refugee status on the basis of persecution for political opinion.

In an attempt to provide guidance as to the question of when the enforcement of an ordinary law of general application can amount to persecution (fear of persecution being an essential element in the definition of a Convention refugee), the Court of Appeal articulated four general propositions. First, it is the intent or principal effect of an ordinary law of general application, rather than the claimant's motivation in disobeying such a law, that is relevant to the determination of persecution. Second, the neutrality of an ordinary law of general application vis-a-vis the five grounds for refugee status must be judged objectively by Canadian courts and tribunals. Third, there should be a presumption that an ordinary law of general application, even in a non-democratic society, is valid and neutral; the claimant will have to show that such a law is either inherently or for some other reason persecutory. Finally, the claimant must show not only that a particular regime is generally oppressive but that the law in question is persecutory in relation to a Convention ground.

Applying these propositions to the present case, the Court of Appeal noted that the use of chemical weapons is contrary to customary international law, and that the possibility of punishment for refusal to participate in a military action that is contrary to the basic rules of human conduct could be regarded as persecution. The Court held that the appellant's refusal to participate in the military action against the Kurds would be treated by the Iranian government as the expression of an unacceptable political opinion. In these circumstances, the potential consequences associated with defying the ordinary Iranian conscription law would amount to persecution under the Convention definition.

Human rights — war crimes and crimes against humanity

R. v. Finta, [1994] 1 S.C.R. 701, 112 D.L.R. (4th) 513. Supreme Court of Canada.

The respondent, a captain in the Royal Hungarian Gendarmerie while Hungary was under German occupation, was alleged to have been involved in the implementation of the infamous "Baky Order," a plan for the purging of all Jews from Hungary, while acting as commander of an investigative unit in the city of Szeged. Pursuant to this order, 8,617 Jewish people in Szeged were confined, had their possessions confiscated, and were later sent to concentration camps. The respondent was charged with having committed the offences of unlawful confinement, robbery, kidnapping, and manslaughter in relation to these events, under the Criminal Code existing at the time the offences were committed.

The indictment added that the offences constituted crimes against humanity and war crimes under what is now section 7(3.71) of the Criminal Code, R.S.C. 1985, c. 30 (3rd Supp.). The respondent was acquitted on all counts. One of the main issues on appeal was whether section 7(3.71) created new offences of war crimes and crimes against humanity or merely removed barriers to the exercise of jurisdiction of Canadian courts over the underlying offences.

Writing for the majority, Cory J. held that a distinction must be drawn between the jurisdictional issue of situs, a determination for the judge, and the jurisdictional issue of whether the essential elements of an offence have been proven, a determination that must be left to the jury. Given that an accused convicted under section 7(3.71) will suffer the opprobrium and stigma associated with war crimes or crimes against humanity, the question cannot be merely whether the accused is morally innocent, but must be whether his or her conduct is sufficiently blameworthy to justify conviction for a crime of this nature. Thus, these must be treated as new offences, and the question of whether the acts constituted war crimes or crimes against humanity goes to proof of essential elements of the offences. The jury was required to determine not only whether the accused committed the acts alleged, but also whether the accused knew or ought to have known that the surrounding circumstances would bring those acts within the definition of a crime against humanity or war crime.

In dissent, La Forest, J. (with L'Heureux-Dube and McLachlin, JJ.) held that the fact that the act constituted a war crime or crime against humanity is not an essential element of the offence, but is merely the jurisdictional link grounding prosecution for the underlying offence by a Canadian court. That determination is a question of law to be decided by the judge. While there is a mental element required, the definition of the underlying domestic offence will include the requisite mental element for the war crime or crime against humanity in almost all cases; in other words, all that is required is that the accused intended the factual element of the offence.

Both Cory, J. and La Forest, J., in rejecting the respondent's argument in cross-appeal that the charges of crimes against humanity or war crimes violated the rights of an accused by reason of vagueness, indicated that the fact that the body of international law is not codified and that reference must be made to the opinions of experts does not make the offences themselves vague or uncertain.

Cory, J. noted that the abhorrent nature of crimes against humanity and war crimes is such that there cannot be said to be any significant uncertainty as to their definition and scope.

Immunité du souverain

Note. Veuillez voir *R. c. Cobb*, [1993] A.J.Q. 580, N° 1845 (C.Q.) (arrestation de marins sur un navire de guerre américain amarré au Québec, relativement à une accusation d'agression sexuelle; renonciation des autorités américaines à l'immunité).

Sovereign immunity — State Immunity Act — "agency of a foreign state"

Walker v. *Bank of New York Inc.* (1994), 111 D.L.R. (4th) 186, 16 O.R. (3d) 504. Ontario Court of Appeal.

The plaintiff had been the target of a "sting" operation set up by United States government officials who contacted him to find suppliers of arms for destinations prohibited by the United States Arms Export Control Act, 22 U.S.C.S. §§ 2751 *et seq.* (1993). Employees of the Bank of New York co-operated in the operation by representing the Bank as banker for *bona fide* potential corporate purchasers, and the United States government agent involved as an authorized representative of those corporations. The plaintiff was lured onto a plane to the Bahamas, arrested during a stopover in New York, and charged with violations of the Arms Export Control Act. The plaintiff pleaded guilty and was permitted to return to Canada on an assurance that he would return for sentencing. He did not do so, and later commenced an action in Ontario claiming damages from the United States government, the Bank of New York, and several employees of each of these entities; causes of action including conspiracy, unlawful imprisonment, fraud, and misrepresentation. While all of the appellants claimed immunity under the provisions of the State Immunity Act, R.S.C. 1985, c. S-18, their motions to stay the respondent's action against them were dismissed.

The first issue on appeal concerned whether the immunity provided in the Act extended to the bank and its employees. The Act confers immunity on an "agency of a foreign state," defined as "any legal entity that is an organ of the foreign state but that is separate from the foreign state." The Court of Appeal held that the term "organ of the foreign state" was wide enough to cover the bank and its employees in this situation. The employees involved had not acted on their own initiative, but had acted at the request of and under instructions from United States law enforcement officials. The use of the broad term "organ" in the Act is an indication of the intention of Parliament to protect individuals and institutions who act at the request of a foreign state in situations where that state itself would enjoy immunity from the jurisdiction of Canadian courts.

The second issue concerned the applicability of the exception to immunity set out in section 6 of the Act, which provides that a foreign state is not immune from the jurisdiction of a court in proceedings relating to, *inter alia,* personal injury that occurs in Canada. While noting that the scope of the personal injury exception could extend to cover mental distress, emotional upset, and loss of liberty, the Court held that the injury here had occurred in the United States and not in Canada. Given this view of the facts, the Court did not have to reach a decision on the appellants' argument that the Act was not intended to alter the common law, and that the section 6 exceptions to immunity ought therefore to be read as applying only to situations where the injury results from private acts of the foreign state. However, the Court expressed clear misgivings about this interpretation of the Act as representing a mere codification of the common law.

Sovereign immunity — State Immunity Act — employees of foreign state

Jaffe v. *Miller* (1993), 103 D.L.R. (4th) 315. Ontario Court of Appeal.

The appellant alleged that the respondents, all of whom were functionaries of the State of Florida, were responsible for laying false criminal charges against him for the purpose of coercing him into settling a civil suit that had been brought against a company controlled by him. At trial, the judge had granted a motion to dismiss the action on the ground of sovereign immunity. The Court of Appeal held that the fact that the State Immunity Act, R.S.C. 1985, c. S-18 does not explicitly confer immunity on employees of the foreign state does not exclude immunity being granted to them, but is an indication that Parliament wished to determine which employees are entitled to immunity determined at common law. Here, the officials being sued by Jaffe were state functionaries exercising powers created by the Florida state constitution, and were entitled to claim sovereign immunity when acting within the scope of their duties and in furtherance of a public act. The Court rejected the appellant's argument that the respondents had lost immunity because the alleged acts involved some illegality; the illegal and malicious nature of the acts does not move them outside the scope of the official duties of the respondents. When immunity exists, either at common law or under the Act, it is absolute.

Note. One issue on appeal related to the holding that section 6 of the State Immunity Act did not apply because the personal injuries complained of predated the coming into force of the Act. While it was alleged that some of the tortious acts had in fact occurred after that date, this was not clearly established in the pleadings, and the Court declined to exercise jurisdiction in those circumstances.

In light of the argument raised in *Walker,* discussed above, it is worth noting that the Court of Appeal here clearly indicates that section 6 is a statutory innovation, introducing statutory exceptions to immunity not recognized at common law.

Treaties — interpretation of implementing statute

Minister of National Revenue v. Seaboard Lumber Sales Co. (1994), 74 F.T.R. 231. Federal Court, Trial Division.

The main issue concerned the interpretation of the term "United States" in the Softwood Lumber Products Export Charge Act, R.S.C. 1985, c. 12 (3rd Supp.), which was passed in implementation of a 1986 Memorandum of Understanding between Canada and the United States regarding the export of certain softwood lumber products to the United States. Seaboard had sought a refund of export charges paid on the sale of softwood to Puerto Rico, on the grounds that "United States" as used in the Act did not include Puerto Rico. The Minister had disallowed the application; the Canadian International Trade Tribunal allowed Seaboard's appeal from that decision.

In allowing the appeal from the Tribunal's decision, Dubé, J. referred to the decision of the Supreme Court of Canada in *National Corn Growers' Association v. Canadian Import Tribunal,* [1990] 2 S.C.R. 1324 (noted in (1991), 29 *Canadian Yearbook of International Law* 540), in holding that it is reasonable to make reference to an underlying international agreement not only to clarify any uncertainty in the domestic implementing statute but also to determine at the outset whether there is in fact any ambiguity in the domestic legislation. Here, the Act contained a latent ambiguity as to the scope of the term "United States," arising from the fact that different statutes and conventions have defined that term differently. There is a presumption of compatibility between international agreements and their implementing statutes, such that it is clear that the term "United States" in the Act was intended to have the same scope as the term's definition in the Memorandum of Understanding.

In reaching his decision, Dubé, J. did not address the Minister's submission that the inclusion of Puerto Rico in the United States for the purposes of the Act arises from the application of fundamental principles of international law, which dictate that statutes are to be interpreted so as not to be inconsistent with the comity of nations or the established rules of international law.

Canadian Cases in Private International Law in 1993-94 / La jurisprudence canadienne en matière de droit international privé en 1993-94

compiled by / préparé par
JOOST BLOM*

A. *Jurisdiction / compétence des tribunaux*

1. Common Law and Federal

(a) Jurisdiction *in personam*

Attornment to the jurisdiction of the local forum

Note. See *Nathanson, Schachter & Thompson* v. *Sarcee Band of Indians*, [1994] 6 W.W.R. 213, 90 B.C.L.R. (2d) 1 (C.A.). In addition to finding that the Alberta-resident client had attorned to the jurisdiction of the British Columbia court, the court held that the British Columbia solicitor's action for fees was within the jurisdiction of the British Columbia court because of the special status of such actions under the Legal Profession Act, S.B.C. 1987, c. 25, ss. 70-76, which gives the court power to review the fees.

Service ex juris — *claims for which service is authorized* — *general*

Note. The rules of court of most provinces allow service *ex juris* without leave in certain listed cases, and with leave in any other case. In *Upper Lakes Shipping Ltd.* v. *Foster Yeoman Ltd.* (1993), 14 O.R. (3d) 548, 17 C.P.C. (3d) 150 (Gen. Div.), claims for breach of fiduciary duty (for which the rules did not authorize service *ex juris* without leave, unless breach of fiduciary duty was a "tort" under the rules) were so closely linked to the claims for breach of contract

---

* Faculty of Law, University of British Columbia.

(for which the rules did authorize service without leave) that they were allowed to stand. It would have been senseless to deny the plaintiff leave to include them.

Service ex juris — *claims for which service is authorized* — *defendant carrying on business in the province*

Note. A foreign corporation that carries on business in the province through a more or less fixed place of business is present in the province according to the common law, and so can be served there. In addition, Rule 17.02(p) of the Ontario Civil Procedure Rules provides that a defendant who carries on business in the province may be served *ex juris* without leave. This was applied in *Applied Processes Inc.* v. *Crane Co.* (1993), 15 O.R. (3d) 166 (Gen. Div.), to a foreign corporation that sold its products in Ontario but had no presence there beyond regular visits by a travelling representative. Its regular marketing efforts in the province were held to amount to carrying on business for the purposes of the rule.

Service ex juris — *claims for which service is authorized* — *necessary or proper party*

Note. See *Hanson* v. *E & D Aircraft Services Ltd.* (1993), 148 A.R. 120 (Q.B. (Master)).

Declining jurisdiction — *agreed choice of another forum*

Note. A defendant by counterclaim was held to have waived its right to invoke an exclusive choice of forum clause by itself, bringing an action in Canada in breach of that clause: *Maersk Inc.* v. *Coldmatic Refrigeration of Canada Ltd.* (1994), 74 F.T.R. 70 (F.C.T.D.).

Declining jurisdiction — *forum non conveniens* — *defendant served in the jurisdiction* — lis alibi pendens

Guarantee Co. of N. America v. *Gordon Capital Corp.* (1994), 18 O.R. (3d) 9. Ontario Court, General Division.

Gordon took out a fidelity bond in February 1991 for $25 million from Guarantee Co., and excess insurance for $10 million each from Laurentian and Chubb. Gordon's business was in Ontario and the bonds were issued in that province. In June 1991 Gordon gave written notice to Guarantee that it had suffered a loss that might be covered by the bond, and in March 1992 it delivered a formal proof of loss in an amount over $39 million. Guarantee took the position that the bond was avoided on the ground of misrepresentations made when it was applied for. When Gordon had not brought an action by June 1993, Guarantee also relied on the expiry of a two-year limitation period in the bond. In July 1993 Gordon commenced an action against Guarantee in Quebec, where Guarantee and Laurentian had their head offices. The Quebec Civil Code provided for a three-year limitation period, although the parties took contrary positions as to whether it would override the contractual limitation. Two weeks after Gordon brought the action in Quebec, Guarantee brought an action in Ontario for declarations that it was not liable on the bond on various grounds, including the expiry of the contractual limitation period. Guarantee subsequently sought a stay in Quebec of the proceedings there. This was refused. The Quebec Court of Appeal gave leave to appeal. The appeal was still pending at the time of the present decision in Ontario.

This decision was on Gordon's application for dismissal or a stay of Guarantee's action in the Ontario Court for declaratory relief. Gordon argued, *inter alia*, that the continuation of Guarantee's action was an abuse of the process of the court because it duplicated issues that would be tried in the Quebec action. Guarantee, having challenged the jurisdiction of the Quebec court on grounds akin to *forum non conveniens* and failed, should not now be able to maintain an action in Ontario designed to counter an action properly before the Quebec court. In support of this argument, Gordon invoked the principle of comity, as expounded in *Morguard Investments Ltd.* v. *De Savoye*, [1990] 3 S.C.R. 1077 (noted in (1991), 29 *Canadian Yearbook of International Law* 556), and *Amchem Products Inc.* v. *British Columbia*, [1993] 1 S.C.R. 897 (noted in (1993), 31 *Canadian Yearbook of International Law* 405).

Ground, J. held that Guarantee's action should continue. Ontario was clearly the *forum conveniens*, given all the connections between the facts of the case and Ontario. Gordon's juridical advantage in suing in Quebec, in the form of the (according to Gordon) longer limitation period, was offset by Guarantee's corresponding advantage in suing in Ontario. The Supreme Court had said that comity should be a guide to deciding whether a foreign court had properly or appropriately exercised jurisdiction. But even where the foreign court's taking of jurisdiction met that test, it did not mean that a parallel local action should necessarily be stayed. The Quebec court had not been shown to be a more appropriate forum for the litigation. If only one of the actions should proceed, it was not for this court to decide which one.

Note. Despite the fact that all or most of the subject matter of the litigation had taken place elsewhere, arguments of *forum non conveniens* were rejected in *Tomlinson* v. *Turner* (1993), 108 Nfld. & P.E.I. R. 346 (P.E.I. C.A.) (local resident sued for out-of-province automobile accident); *Pietzsch* v. *R-Tek Corp.* (1993), 87 Man. R. (2d) 298 (Q.B.) (German resident sued on counterclaim relating to a contract governed by German law and to be performed in Germany); and *Abus KG* v. *Secord Inc.* (1992), 8 C.P.C. (3d) 343 (Ont. Gen. Div.) (two local firms and one German firm sued by German shipper for failure to pay for, or obtain payment for, goods). Stays were also refused, primarily on the basis that the plaintiff had a legitimate juridical advantage in the local forum, in *Marchand (Guardian* ad litem *of)* v. *Alberta Motor Assn. Ins. Co.,* [1994] 5 W.W.R. 764, 89 B.C.L.R. (2d) 293 (C.A.) (higher no-fault insurance benefits available in the local forum), and *Byers* v. *Higgin,* [1993] 6 W.W.R. 511, 80 B.C.L.R. (2d) 386 (S.C.) (claim barred in the alternative forum by workers' compensation statute).

In *Bank van Parijs en de Nederlanden België N.V.* v. *Cabri* (1993), 19 C.P.C. (3d) 362 (Ont. Gen. Div.), a stay was granted, although the defendant was a local resident, because all the other elements of the action were connected to Belgium.

Declining jurisdiction — forum non conveniens — *defendant served* ex juris

Note. Two actions against American defendants were stayed on the ground of *forum non conveniens* because the claims, in contract and in tort respectively, had much more to do with the foreign jurisdiction than with Ontario: *Bailey & Co.* v. *Laser Medical Technology Inc.* (1993), 15 O.R. (3d) 212 (Gen. Div.); *Bluewater Agromart Ltd.* v. *Paul's Machine & Welding Corp.* (1993), 16 O.R. (3d) 404 (Gen. Div.). A Nova Scotia action against a former local resident, who now lived in Ontario, for negligence in a motor vehicle accident in Maine, was allowed to continue in *Donovan* v. *Boucher* (1993), 123 N.S.R. (2d) 359 (C.A.), because the plaintiff's claim was barred in Ontario under the no-fault insurance legislation there.

(b)   Actions relating to property

Bankruptcy and insolvency — effect of foreign bankruptcy proceedings

Best Electric & Heating Ltd. v. *MacKillop* (1993), 17 C.P.C. (3d) 55.
British Columbia Supreme Court.

Lundy's Sports Catering Inc. provided catering services at the
1992 Vancouver Indy Race for Canadian Indy Motor Sports. A
creditor of Lundy's Sports Catering obtained an order garnishing
the Canadian firm's debt to Lundy's. Two months earlier, Lundy's,
along with its parent corporation and associated corporations, had
filed in Connecticut for Chapter 11 protection under the United
States Bankruptcy Code. Lundy's contended that the action should
be stayed on the basis of comity vis-à-vis the United States bankruptcy proceedings, and the garnishing order set aside. Evidence of
United States law was to the effect that the commencement of
Chapter 11 proceedings created an estate comprised of all legal
and equitable interests of the debtor, wherever located and by
whomsoever held. If no trustee in bankruptcy was appointed, and
none had been here, a debtor could act as a debtor-in-possession
over its own estate.

Saunders, J. held that the present situation was distinguishable
from those where a trustee or receiver was appointed in a foreign
jurisdiction. Lundy's was a debtor-in-possession, able to continue
using its funds without court adjudication or appointment of an
outsider to oversee the business. There was as yet no court order in
the Chapter 11 proceedings, nor any appointment that the court
was obliged to recognize or in respect of which it should give
comity. There was simply the commencement of proceedings by a
defendant in the present action without any formal external
adjudication on which the court could base a declension of jurisdiction. Moreover, the materials filed by Lundy's in Connecticut did
not disclose the asset in question in the present case, nor the debt
on which the plaintiff was suing. It was unclear whether it was
intended that the Chapter 11 proceedings would apply in British
Columbia, or whether a United States bankruptcy court could
intend to encompass these assets within any order it made. At this
stage of the American judicial proceedings it would be unjust to set
aside the garnishing order.

(c)   Matrimonial actions

Divorce — jurisdiction to vary corollary order

Note. The provisions of the Divorce Act, R.S.C. 1985, c. 3 (2nd Supp.), relating to jurisdiction to vary corollary orders, were applied in *Gartner* v. *Gartner* (1993), 146 A.R. 84 (Q.B.) (court took jurisdiction because the respondent wife had long been resident in the province and had limited means for litigation elsewhere), and *Snider* v. *Kennedy* (1994), 118 Sask. R. 178 (Q.B.) (jurisdiction taken on basis of respondent's attornment).

Support obligations

Note. Because neither party resided in the forum any more, there was no jurisdiction to vary a support order although it was originally made in the forum: *Miller* v. *Miller* (1994), 119 Sask. R. 158 (Q.B.).

(d)   Infants and children

Custody and access — jurisdiction

Jurisdiction to decide custody was declined in *Sturkenboom* v. *Davies* (1993), 142 A.R. 144 (Q.B.), because the mother and children were now living in the United Kingdom. Their move out of the province, albeit surreptitious, had not been in breach of any court order. Jurisdiction was also declined in *Martini* v. *Martini* (1993), 142 A.R. 321 (Q.B.), mainly because the respondent father could not be heard in Canada owing to his having been barred from entering the country.

Custody and access — enforcement of extraprovincial custody order

Note. A New Brunswick court held it had jurisdiction to confirm the terms of an Ontario custody order, in *A.(C.)* v. *L.(J.W.)* (1993), 131 N.B.R. (2d) 337 (Q.B.). The child could not be considered habitually resident in New Brunswick because it had lived there only a month, but the mother intended the stay to be permanent and so the child did have a real and substantial connection with the province.

Child abduction — Hague Convention

S. (J.W.) v. *M. (N.C.)* (1993), 12 Alta. L.R. (3d) 379, 145 A.R. 200 (*sub nom. D.(H.A.)* v. *M.(N.C.)*). Alberta Court of Appeal.

The child in question in this case was born in the State of Georgia, U.S.A. When he was eight days old his mother delivered him in California to a husband and wife resident in Alberta. They immediately took him to Alberta. Two months later, with the mother's consent, the Alberta couple obtained a court order in Alberta appointing them sole guardians of the baby and giving them sole custody of him. Five months after that, the baby's biological father began an action in Alberta claiming guardianship and custody of his son, and an order under Article 3 of the Hague Convention on the Civil Aspects of Child Abduction (implemented by the International Child Abduction Act, S.A. 1986, c. I-6.5), declaring that the baby had been wrongfully removed from the United States and directing that the Central Authority for Alberta return him to the United States. This action was tried together with an application by the Alberta couple to adopt the baby. At the trial the biological father did not pursue his request under the Hague Convention and sought only an order for guardianship and custody. This was denied by the judge, who made the adoption order in favour of the Alberta couple. The appeal was dismissed.

One point that the biological father argued on the appeal was that, although he himself had not claimed it at the trial, the judge should have considered on his own motion whether the Hague Convention required that the Central Authority be ordered to return the child on the ground that the child had been wrongfully removed from the United States. The Court of Appeal rejected this on two grounds. First, Article 16 of the Convention said that the judicial or administrative authorities of the state where the child was present could proceed to decide as to the child's custody, even after notice of a wrongful removal was communicated to them, if "an application under this Convention is not lodged within a reasonable time following receipt of the notice." There was no Convention application before the judge, and the biological father's application for guardianship and custody was inconsistent with such an application.

Secondly, the removal of the child was not wrongful under the Convention. Article 3 defined wrongful as meaning that the removal was in breach of rights of custody attributed to a person under the law of the state in which the child was habitually resident immediately before the removal. The baby in this case, the court held, was never habitually resident in the United States because he was only eight days old when he was taken to Alberta. Moreover, the biological father did not have rights of custody under the relevant American laws, but only the right to apply for rights of custody.

Adoption

Re Birth Registration No. 1480 (1994), 112 D.L.R. (4th) 53, [1994] 5 W.W.R. 323. British Columbia Supreme Court.

The father and mother were married in British Columbia in 1980. They moved to the State of New York, U.S.A., where the child was born in 1982. The family moved to Ontario in 1983. Two years later the parents separated and in 1986 the mother moved with the child to British Columbia. She and the father agreed that the mother would have sole custody, with the father to have reasonable access. They were divorced in 1987. Soon afterwards the mother married a man from Victoria, B.C. who was then employed in Chile. She moved to Chile with him. From 1989 to 1990 they lived in Kuwait, while the husband worked in Saudi Arabia. In 1991 the mother and her husband jointly filed the adoption petition. At that time the mother and the child had been living in Victoria for nearly a year. The husband had come to Victoria with them but meanwhile had returned to live and work in Saudi Arabia. The mother declared that it was likely that the family would continue to live abroad for the foreseeable future. Later that year she and the child returned to Kuwait, but continued to spend holidays at least once a year in Victoria. In a 1993 affidavit the mother deposed that she and her husband intended to live abroad for the time being, but to settle down eventually in British Columbia. The child's natural father opposed the adoption and argued that the British Columbia court had no jurisdiction to grant it because the parties were domiciled in Kuwait.

Drost, J. noted that the Adoption Act, R.S.B.C. 1979, c. 4, said nothing about the jurisdiction of the court. The laws of most Canadian provinces, by contrast with English law, did not rely on the domicile of the parents or the child as jurisdictional tests. That being so, the right approach to the issue of jurisdiction was to ask whether there was a sufficient connection between the child and his adoptive parents and the province to allow the purposes of the statute to be served. As a rule the presence of the parties for a reasonable period before the order was made should be sufficient. In the conflict of laws, however, the law of the adoptive parents' domicile, or the child's, or both, were referred to in determining whether an adoption should be recognized. This meant that it was relevant to consider whether the law of the domicile would recognize the adoption, as a factor in determining the best interests of the child.

Here, the parties had sufficient connection with British Columbia to give the court jurisdiction. The mother and the child had been in Victoria for nearly a year when the petition was filed, and both petitioners as well as the child had roots in British Columbia. The parents of both petitioners lived there. The petitioners had also adduced expert evidence as to the law of Kuwait. It showed that the adoption would be regarded as valid in Kuwait on the basis that the parties were domiciled, according to Kuwaiti law, in British Columbia. It also showed that the parties could not obtain permanent residence in Kuwait and could not apply to the courts of that country for an adoption. The British Columbia court should accept jurisdiction for these reasons, and because it was able, on the evidence before it, to ascertain the adoptive parents' ability to bring up, maintain, and educate the child properly, and to determine the propriety of the adoption having regard to the welfare of the child and the interest of the child's parents. On the merits, Drost, J. decided the adoption should be granted.

2.   Québec

(a)   Lieu de l'introduction de l'action

Défendeur étranger — application de la loi ancienne en l'art. 68 C.P.

Morissette c. *Entreprises de systèmes Fujitsu du Canada Inc.*, [1994] R.J.Q. 976. Cour supérieure du Québec.

En 1992 le demandeur était l'employé de Philips à Halifax, Nouvelle-Écosse. Le défenderesse, qui avait son siège social à North York, Ontario, a acheté une partie des actifs de Philips. Elle a soumise au demandeur une offre d'emploi par un écrit sur papetrie portant son adresse à North York. Le poste qu'elle lui a offert était de "branch support" à Halifax. Le demandeur a apposé sa signature à l'acceptation et confié l'offre acceptée à un courrier pour remise au bureau d'affaires de la défenderesse à Montréal, Québec, d'où l'offre lui a été envoyé. L'année suivante, le demandeur a reçu un avis de terminaison par un écrit sur papetrie du bureau de la défenderesse á Montréal. Le demandeur a intenté la présente action devant la Cour supérieure du Québec. L'action est signifiée à la défenderesse le 16 novembre 1993 à son établissement à Montréal. Après l'entrée en vigueur du nouveau Code civile au 1 janvier 1994, la défenderesse a présenté une exception déclinatoire de la compétence de la Cour, se basant sur l'article 1348 du nouveau Code civil, L.Q. 1991, c. 64, qui se lit comme suit:

Dans les actions personnelles à caractère patrimonial, les autorités québécoises sont compétentes dans les cas suivants:

(1) Le défendeur a son domicile ou sa résidence au Québec;

(2) Le défendeur est une personne morale qui n'est pas domiciliée au Québec mais y a un établissement et la contestation est relative à son activité au Québec;

(3) Une faute a été commise au Québec, un préjudice y a été subi, un fait dommageable s'y est produit ou l'une des obligations découlant d'un contrat devait y être exécutée;

(4) Les parties, par convention, leur ont soumis les litiges nés ou à naître entre elles à l'occasion d'un rapport de droit déterminé;

(5) Le défendeur a reconnu leur compétence.

Cependant, les autorités québécoises ne sont pas compétentes lorsque les parties ont choisi, par convention, de soumettre les litiges nés ou à naître entre elles, à propos d'un rapport juridique déterminé, à une autorité étrangère ou à un arbitre, à moins que le défendeur n'ait reconnu la compétence des autorités québécoises.

La Cour a rejeté l'exception déclinatoire. Certes, l'action du demandeur ne pouvait être portée devant les tribunaux du Québec selon l'article 3148. L'exigence que la contestation soit relative à l'activité au Québec de la corporation y ayant un établissement, est substituée à celle de la possession de biens au Québec tel que prévu à l'article 68 C.P. Des exigences de l'article 3148 C.C.Q. — qu'une faute ait été commise au Québec, un préjudice y ait été subi, un fait dommageable s'y soit produit ou l'une des obligations découlant du contrat dût y être exécutée — sont substituées à celle de la naissance au Québec de toute la cause d'action tel que prévu à l'ancien article 68 C.P. La preuve n'avait pas démontré qu'une faute avait été commise au Québec, qu'un préjudice y avait été subi, qu'un fait dommageable s'y était produit ou que l'une des obligations du contrat d'emploi devait y être exécutée.

Mais c'était l'ancien article 68 C.P. qui s'appliquait ici. Les faits allégués par le demandeur, ayant été accomplis avant le 1er janvier 1994, donnaient ouverture aux droits que conférait la loi en vigueur au moment de leur survenance. Selon l'article 2 de la Loi sur l'application de la réforme du Code civil, L.Q. 1992, c. 57, la loi nouvelle n'a pas d'effet rétroactif. L'article 3 édicte que la loi nouvelle est applicable aux situations juridiques en cours lors de son entrée en vigueur. Les lois déterminant les attributions des tribunaux sont des lois de procédure, et selon l'article 9 les lois de procédure s'appliquent même aux instances en cours. Mais de donner dans les circonstances à l'article 3148 C.C.Q. un effet immédiat dans les instances en cours aurait comme conséquence de le rendre rétroactif. Le principe de la non-rétroactivité de la loi nouvelle devait avoir priorité sur celui de l'effet immédiat. Le maintien de la validité de l'assignation de la défenderesse par le demandeur répondait à une interprétation de l'article 9 telle que tempérée par la règle de non-rétroactivité de l'article 2 et par la règle de l'effect immédiat de l'article 3. L'action était conforme à l'article 68 C.P. tel qu'il se lisait avant le 1ᵉʳ janvier 1994 puisque la défenderesse avait des biens au Québec, ce qui était alors suffisant pour intenter une action contre elle au Québec.

Note. Voir *Masson* c. *Thompson*, [1994] R.J.Q. 1033 (C.S.), dans lequel l'ancien article 68 C.P. est aussi appliqué pour attribuer compétence au Tribunal. Un groupe d'ex-employés d'une compagnie en faillite a poursuivi en recours collectif certains anciens administrateurs de la compagnie. Les employés ont toujours travaillé au bureau de la compagnie au Québec. Leur recours était fondé sur la responsabilité statutaire imposée aux administrateurs en vertu de l'article 119 de la Loi sur les sociétés par actions, L.R.C. 1985, c. C-44. Les défendeurs ne résidaient pas au Québec et n'y avaient pas de biens, mais toute la cause d'action est née au Québec parce que les faits qui étaient générateurs du droit d'action se sont produits dans la province.

(b) Demande en matière familiale

Enfants — garde — Convention de La Haye

W.(V.) c. *S.(D.)* (1993), 58 Q.A.C. 168. Cour d'appel du Québec.

Pendant leur mariage, le père et la mère habitaient au Maryland, É.-U. Le mariage éclata. Le père alla vivre au Michigan avec l'enfant, dont il avait le droit de garde. La mère requérit au Maryland la modification de ses droits de visite. Le père consentit à amener l'enfant au Maryland pour une évaluation psychiatrique et des visites avec la mère, mais il déménagea au Québec avec l'enfant. La mère demanda au Maryland un changement de garde et demanda à la Cour supérieure du Québec que l'enfant fût retourné au Maryland. Elle invoqua la Loi sur les aspects civils de l'enlèvement international et interprovincial d'enfants, L.R.Q. 1977, c. A-23.01, qui incorpore la Convention de La Haye sur les aspects civils de l'enlèvement international d'enfants (1980).

La Cour supérieure a accueilli la requête de la mère, et la Cour d'appel a rejeté l'appel du père. Le sens donné aux mots "droit de garde" dans la Loi et dans la Convention n'était pas nécessairement le même que celui qui pouvait être prêté aux mêmes mots dans d'autres lois québécoises. Ce que importe surtout, aux termes de la Loi, c'est le droit, exclusif ou non, de déterminer la résidence de l'enfant. Ces deux parents revendiquaient farouchement leur droit de visiter l'enfant en recouraient aux tribunaux dès que l'autre parent eût entravé son droit. Si le père s'était engagé à amener l'enfant à la mère à des dates fixes et à la conduire chez un psychiatre pour une évaluation, cette entente comportait une clause nécessairement implicite interdisant le déménagement dans un lieu où les termes explicites de l'entente ne pouvaient être réalisés. De plus, tant en vertu du droit du Maryland que du droit québécois, le père n'avait plus, en déménageant au Québec, qu'un droit de garde précaire. Un tel déménagement sans entente préalable entre les parties est une circonstance justifiant une révision de l'ordonnance de garde pour vérifier si l'intérêt de l'enfant est protégé. Les principes généraux d'application de la Loi, et principalement ceux visant à une application au plus grand nombre de cas possible pour favoriser le retour à la juridiction d'origine, couplés avec le contexte factuel particulier du présent dossier permettaient de conclure que la mère était investie d'un droit de garde, au sens de la Loi, lui donnant qualité pour demander le retour de l'enfant au Maryland.

Le père a invoqué l'article 20 de la Loi, qui dicte que, si la demande est introduite après l'expiration d'un an à partir du déplacement ou du non-retour, le retour de l'enfant doit être ordonné à moins qu'il ne soit établi que l'enfant s'est intégré dans son nouveau milieu. Le juge de première instance avait fait appel à un critère psychologique pour l'application de l'article 20, et avait conclu que l'enfant ne s'était pas intégré dans son milieu au Québec. Il n'y avait aucune erreur de droit à cet égard.

(c)   Forum non conveniens — art. 3135 C.C.Q.

Note. L'article 3135 du nouveau Code civil du Québec a introduit, pour la première fois, la doctrine du *forum non conveniens* dans le droit international privé québécois. Cet article se lit comme suit:

> Bien qu'elle soit compétente pour connaître d'un litige, une autorité du Québec peut, exceptionnellement et à la demande d'une partie, décliner cette compétence si elle estime que les autorités d'un autre État sont mieux à même de trancher le litige.

Dans l'affaire *Banque Toronto-Dominion c. Cloutier*, [1994] R.J.Q. 386 (C.S.), la Cour a estimé que puisque la question de compétence relève davantage du droit judiciaire que du droit substantif, on peut conclure que la doctrine du *forum non conveniens* serait assimilable à de la procédure et est conséquemment applicable aux instances en cours le 1er janvier 1994, selon l'article 9 de la loi d'application. Pourtant, le Tribunal était d'avis qu'il n'y avait pas lieu de l'appliquer aux circonstances de l'affaire.

B. Procedure / Procédure

1. Common Law and Federal

(a) Pre-trial procedure

Interlocutory orders — international arbitration

Trade Fortune Inc. v. *Amalgamated Mill Supplies Ltd.* (1994), 113 D.L.R. (4th) 116, 24 C.P.C. (3d) 362. British Columbia Supreme Court.

The plaintiff Greek shipowners claimed demurrage from the defendant charterer, a British Columbia firm, in connection with a shipment of logs from Venezuela to Korea. Arbitration proceedings were begun in London, England, pursuant to an arbitration clause in the charterparty. Subsequently, the plaintiffs began an action in British Columbia on the same claim, and caused a garnishing order to be issued in respect of the defendant's bank account in Williams Lake, British Columbia. The bank paid the amount claimed into court. The defendant applied to set aside the garnishing order and to stay the British Columbia action, on the ground that the court was obliged to take both steps under the International Commercial Arbitration Act, S.B.C. 1986, c. 14, which enacts the UNCITRAL Model Arbitration Law in British Columbia.

Bouck, J. held that the garnishing order could stand because section 9 of the Act (article 9 of the Model Law) provides that it "is not incompatible with an arbitration agreement for a party to request from a court, before or during arbitral proceedings, an interim measure of protection and for a court to grant that measure." Interpreting the statute in the light of the documents of UNCITRAL and its working group on the Model Law, it was clear that interim measures of protection were meant to include pre-award attachments to secure an eventual award.

The plaintiffs insisted that the stay of the British Columbia action, which they conceded had to be ordered, should be without prejudice to their rights to pursue the interim measures of protection referred to in section 9. The defendant argued that, according to the relevant statute, money subject to a garnishing order could only be paid out to a "judgment creditor," and that the plaintiff could never be a judgment creditor because the eventual arbitration award was not the same thing as a judgment. Bouck, J. rejected this argument, pointing out that a cause of action is not merged in an arbitration award or foreign judgment, so there was no substantive law that prevented the plaintiffs from pursuing their lawful demands until they were paid in full. The stay was therefore ordered on the terms proposed by the plaintiffs.

(b)   Proof of foreign law

*Foreign judicial decisions subsequent to trial in the forum —
admissibility*

MacDonald v. *Travelers Indemnity Co. of Canada* (1993), 63 O.A.C.
167. Ontario Court of Appeal.

Travelers issued an Ontario insurance policy to an Ontario resident whose daughter was at university in Michigan. She travelled back to university as a passenger in a van that had been rented in Ontario. She was gravely injured when the van ran out of control on a Michigan highway. She claimed no-fault benefits under her father's policy, since she was named in it as an occasional driver. In other proceedings the Ontario Court held liability for the no-fault claims was governed by the law of Michigan, under which no-fault benefits were unlimited, rather than by the law of Ontario, under which they were limited to $25,000. The victim was awarded benefits far exceeding $250,000. In third party proceedings, Travelers claimed the excess from MCCA, a Michigan statutory body that was obliged to indemnify member insurers for no-fault payments in excess of $250,000. The judge from whose decision the present appeal was taken interpreted the Michigan statute and held that Travelers qualified as a member of MCCA by virtue of its having filed a certificate that out-of-state insurers were entitled to file, accepting the personal and property protection insurance system created by the Act. The judge therefore held MCCA liable. On appeal MCCA sought to adduce, as new evidence that was not discoverable before the end of trial, decisions of Michigan courts, rendered subsequent to the judge's decision, that showed that

Travelers did not meet the statutory conditions for membership in MCCA. The Ontario Court of Appeal held that this new evidence was admissible on the appeal and was conclusive on the issue of Michigan law, so that the trial judgment had to be reversed.

(c)   Remedies

Claims for losses in foreign currency — conversion date

Note. Canadian courts still apply differing conversion dates when they determine the Canadian dollar equivalent of a claim denominated in foreign currency. In *American Savings & Loan Assn.* v. *Stechishin* (1993), 14 Alta. L.R. (3d) 255 (Q.B. (Master)), the relevant date was the date of initiation of the local proceeding. In *Promech Sorting Systems BV* v. *Bronco Rentals & Leasing Ltd.*, [1994] 4 W.W.R. 374 (Man. Q.B.), it was the date of filing of the defence because, the court reasoned, that was when the plaintiff knew that its claim would be contested, and that it should accordingly secure protection against the possible fall of the Canadian dollar.

(d)   Evidence obtained locally for foreign proceeding

Letters rogatory

Note. Letters rogatory from United States courts for the taking of evidence in Canada were enforced in *Somerset Pharmaceuticals Inc.* v. *Interpharm Inc.* (1994), 109 D.L.R. (4th) 493 (Ont. Gen. Div.), and *Gourmet Resources Int'l Inc. Estate* v. *Paramount Capital Corp.* (1993), 14 O.R. (3d) 139*n* (C.A.).

2.   Québec

(a)   Poursuite dans un pays étranger — effect au Québec

Action en garantie — non-recevabilité

North Country Union High School c. *Stanstead College*, [1993] A.J.Q. 798, N° 2353. Cour supérieure du Québec.

Par un contrat verbal, l'intimée, une école située au Vermont, É.-U., a emprunté son aréna à la requérante, une école située au Québec près de la frontière américaine, pour une partie de hockey qui a eu lieu en février 1989. Lors de cette partie, une spectatrice a été blessée au visage par une rondelle. La victime a poursuivi l'intimée en dommages dans l'État du Vermont. L'action en garantie de l'intimée contre la requérante avait pour but d'engager cette dernière dans l'action intentée par la victime au Vermont, d'où la requête en irrecevabilité de la requérante pour absence d'intérêt. La requête est accueillie.

La simple existence de procédures judiciaires à l'étranger ne peut entraîner des conséquences juridiques immédiates au Québec. Le droit international privé québécois n'autorise pas la reconnaissance des actes juridiques étrangers, sauf exception. De plus, la règle générale veut qu'un jugement étranger ne produise aucun effet au Québec, à moins qu'il ne soit judiciairement reconnu à la suite d'une action en exemplification, qui ne peut être accordée qu'à certaines conditions. Il faut notamment que la partie québécoise ait été partie à l'action à l'étranger, ce qui n'était pas le cas en l'espèce. De plus, la compétence d'un tribunal du Vermont ne peut être étendue par l'ordonnance d'un tribunal québécois. La compétence d'un tribunal est régie par la loi de sa juridiction. Or, le tribunal du Vermont n'avait pas compétence pour entendre une action en responsabilité opposant la victime à la requérante. Une ordonnance de la Cour supérieure ne pourrait rien y changer. L'action de l'intimée était prématurée: ses obligations à l'égard de la victime étaient pour l'instant conditionnelles à ce qu'un jugement favorable à cette dernière intervienne. Advenant la réalisation de cette condition, elle pourra poursuivre la requérante au Québec.

(b) Saisie-arrêt — biens situés au Québec

Biens reçus à titre d'aliments — accident du travail survenu dans un autre pays

Note. Voir *Centre d'Aide aux entreprises du Témiscouata Inc.* c. *Thériault,* [1994] R.J.Q. 1640 (C.S.), dans laquelle une saisie-arrêt de quelques sommes d'argent déposées dans des comptes d'épargne est annulée au motif que les sommes avaient été reçues par le débiteur soit à titre d'aliments, soit à titre de prestations d'invalidité à la suite d'un accident du travail survenu aux États-Unis. La Cour a appliqué la loi de l'État de Maine pour déterminer que le caractère alimentaire des sommes reçues ou à recevoir par le requérant existait et continuait à exister, qu'il soit dans le Maine ou au Québec. L'insaisissabilité de ces indemnités décrétée par les lois d'un autre pays devait être respectée en vertu des principes généraux des lois québécoises, plus particulièrement de l'article 553, paragraphe 12 C.P.

C. Foreign Judgments / Jugements Étrangers

1. Common Law and Federal

(a) Conditions for enforcement by action or registration

Finality

> *Note.* See *Arrowmaster Inc.* v. *Unique Forming Ltd.* (1993), 17 O.R. (3d) 407, 29 C.P.C. (3d) 65 (Gen. Div.) (stay of enforcement action pending appeal of the Illinois judgment).

Jurisdiction of original court — submission during the proceedings

> *Note.* Where the defendant's sole action in the foreign jurisdiction was to attempt an appeal of the judgment, only to have it dismissed on procedural grounds, there was no submission during the proceedings: *Lafarge Canada Inc.* v. *Clearwater Concrete Products (2000) Ltd.* (1993), 114 Sask. R. 314 (Q.B.).

Jurisdiction of original court — submission by agreement

> *Note. Re Foder* (1993), 15 Alta. L.R. (3d) 263 (C.A.) suggests that becoming a director of a British Columbia company carries with it an implied agreement to submit to the jurisdiction of the provincial Director of Employment Standards to make orders, with the force of judicial judgments, against directors for unpaid wages. Earlier cases, however, are virtually unanimous that an agreement to submit to a foreign court's jurisdiction must be express in order to make the foreign judgment binding. The Director's order was enforceable in any event on the basis of the real and substantial connection that the "action" had with British Columbia.
>
> In *Tramp's Music & Books Inc.* v. *Diamond Comic Distributors Inc.* (1993), 111 Sask. R. 232 (Q.B.), a party was held precluded from bringing an action for breach of contract in Saskatchewan by a prior default judgment against it, on the same issues, from a Maryland court. The party was bound by that judgment on the basis of an agreement that the Maryland courts should have jurisdiction over disputes arising out of the contract.

Jurisdiction of original court — sufficient connection with the foreign jurisdiction

Moses v. *Shore Boat Builders Ltd.* (1993), 106 D.L.R. (4th) 654, [1994] 1 W.W.R. 112. British Columbia Court of Appeal. (Leave to appeal refused, 3 March 1994 (S.C.C.).)

The plaintiff, a fisherman resident in Alaska, ordered a fishing boat from the defendant, a British Columbia company that had no physical presence in Alaska and did not carry on business there. The contract was approved and the purchase financed by the State Department of Commerce of Alaska. The boat was built in British Columbia and delivered to a common carrier in Seattle. The Department of Commerce paid the plaintiff the purchase price of US$105,000. During the first season the starboard engine was damaged by sea water entering through a defective exhaust port. The defendant replaced the engine under warranty. The next year, a similar problem occurred with the port engine. The defendant denied liability because the damage was outside the warranty period. The plaintiff repaired the defect and brought action in Alaska state court against the defendant for his loss, plus costs and attorneys' fees. The defendant received notice of the proceeding but did not appear. In December 1987 judgment was given against it in default, for US$58,627.23. The plaintiff brought an action in British Columbia on the judgment.

The plaintiff relied on *Morguard Investments Ltd.* v. *De Savoye,* [1990] 3 S.C.R. 1077, 76 D.L.R. (4th) 256 (noted in (1991), 29 *Canadian Yearbook of International Law* 556), which departed from long-standing authority and held that a default judgment from another Canadian province was enforceable, although the defendant neither had been served in the original province nor submitted to the jurisdiction of its court, if a real and substantial connection existed between the litigation and the original forum. In the present case the Court of Appeal held: (1) that the *Morguard* doctrine applied to judgments from outside Canada; (2) that the required real and substantial connection existed on the facts; and (3) that two alleged errors by the court in Alaska were irrelevant.

(1) It was true that the Supreme Court in the *Morguard* case had justified its new rule in part by Canadian constitutional considerations. These included the intent to create a common market within Canada, the right of citizens to move between parts of Canada, the fact that all superior court judges in Canada were federally

appointed, and the Supreme Court of Canada's power to review decisions of the courts from all the courts of the provinces. At the same time, however, the Supreme Court had emphasized the importance of comity among judicial systems, a notion that was not limited to Canada, although it was especially strong among Canadian courts because of the considerations just mentioned. The court had pointed out in *Morguard* that modern means of international travel and communications made the old rules on the enforcement of foreign judgments appear parochial and too restrictive. The present case arose out of international commerce, and comity supported the extension of the real and substantial connection test to the circumstances here. This was also in accord with the Supreme Court's view, expressed in *Moran* v. *Pyle National (Canada) Ltd.*, [1975] 1 S.C.R. 393, 43 D.L.R. (3d) 239, that it was fair that a manufacturer should assume the burden of defending its products wherever they caused harm, as long as the forum was one that it reasonably ought to have had in contemplation when it put its goods on the market. Finally, the case was one in which a British Columbia court could have assumed jurisdiction in parallel circumstances.

(2) The trial judge had summarized the situation by saying that the courts of either British Columbia or Alaska would have been a reasonable forum for the purchaser's action. In relation to the connections with Alaska, she had referred to the facts that the purchaser, to the seller's knowledge, was resident in Alaska, had obtained financing there, would use the boat there, and might wish to sue there for an eventual breach of contract. She also noted that if the seller had wanted to restrict the forum for such an action it could have done so by agreement. It was not necessary, she said, that Alaska should be the territory with which the action had the most significant contacts, only that there be such contacts as constitute a real and substantial connection to make reasonable Alaska's taking and exercise of jurisdiction in the absence of any objection by the defendant. The Court of Appeal said that the judge had had ample evidence for her conclusion.

(3) The defendant said that a notice from the Alaska Department of Commerce, which was filed with the original court, was defective, and that service of process had been improper under Alaska law. The Court of Appeal held that these did not constitute a "manifest error" on the face of the judgment, which, according to a line of British Columbia cases, might prevent enforcement of a default judgment. It also observed that the "manifest error" doctrine was of dubious legitimacy and its reach was not to be extended. In any event, it was clear law that an error by the foreign court as to its own procedure was no ground for treating its judgment as invalid.

Note 1. This was one of several reported cases this year that were spawned by the *Morguard* decision. It was the first in which an appellate court addressed the question whether default judgments from outside Canada could now be enforced pursuant to the new rule. First instance judgments that decided this issue the same way were: *Stoddard* v. *Accurpress Mfg. Ltd.* (1993), [1994] 1 W.W.R. 677, 84 B.C.L.R. (2d) 194 (S.C.) (a Connecticut judgment on a tort claim by an employee against the British Columbia manufacturer of the machine that had injured him); *Allen* v. *Lynch* (1993), 111 Nfld. & P.E.I. R. 43, 21 C.P.C. (3d) 99 (P.E.I. T.D.) (a Massachusetts judgment in an action on a loan where the debtor, at the time the debt was incurred, resided in that state); and *American Savings & Loan Assn.* v. *Stechishin* (1993), 14 Alta. L.R. (3d) 255 (Q.B. (Master)) (a Hawaiian judgment for deficiency in action for foreclosure of a mortgage on property in Hawaii). A case that disagreed, and refused to extend *Morguard* to an English default judgment, was *Evans Dodd* v. *Gambin Associates* (1994), 17 O.R. (3d) 803, 26 C.P.C. (3d) 189 (Gen. Div.). It was an action by English solicitors against a firm of Ontario solicitors to recover fees for work that one of the Ontario solicitors' partners, since departed from the firm, had instructed the plaintiffs to do. In refusing to follow the other first instance cases that had applied *Morguard* to non-Canadian judgments, the judge was influenced by the fact that the defendants had not defended the English action, believing (correctly on the law as it then stood) that the judgment would not be enforceable in Ontario. In addition, the defendants said they had a good defence on the merits and, alternatively, a claim over against a third party that could only be made in an Ontario court.

A rare case in which the "real and substantial connection" criterion was held not to have been met was *First City Trust Co.* v. *Inuvik Automotive Wholesale Ltd.*, [1993] N.W.T.R. 273 (S.C.). A Northwest Territories firm had leased equipment from an Alberta lessor by an agreement that was negotiated over the telephone but signed in the Northwest Territories. The equipment was delivered to the lessee in the Northwest Territories. The lessor obtained a default judgment in Alberta for breach of the lease agreement, but the Northwest

Territories court refused to enforce it, on the ground that the only real connection with Alberta was the plaintiff's own office. The plaintiff should not be able to conduct business in the Territories, but then claim the benefit of going to court in its own province.

Note 2. The Supreme Court of Canada made important comments on the *Morguard* rule in *Hunt* v. *T & N plc.*, [1993] 4 S.C.R. 289, 109 D.L.R. (4th) 16. The actual decision concerned the constitutional validity of a Quebec statute barring the removal of business records from Quebec at the behest of courts outside the province. The court held that the statute was constitutionally inapplicable to orders of other Canadian courts for the production of evidence. To apply it would violate the obligation of comity that was owed by courts in one province towards the courts elsewhere in Canada. This requirement of comity had been invoked in *Morguard* as a reason for expanding the common law rules for the enforcement of judgments, and it was based in part on what the court saw as the implication of Canada's federal structure. What *Hunt* makes clear is that the "full faith and credit" rule (so named by analogy with Art. IV, § 1 of the United States Constitution) laid down in *Morguard* was not just a matter of common law, but a constitutional imperative. In other words, where a Canadian court takes jurisdiction on the basis of a sufficient connection with its province or territory (which, according to *Hunt*, itself reflects the constitutional limits on provincial judicial authority), the recognition and enforcement of its judgment elsewhere in Canada is beyond the power of any provincial legislature to override. Only the "modalities" for recognition (at 324 S.C.R., 41 D.L.R.) might be regulated by statute.

La Forest, J., who gave the judgments in both *Morguard* and *Hunt,* also rejected the criticism that the "real and substantial connection" test adopted in the earlier case was unduly vague. He said it was "not meant to be a rigid test, but was simply intended to capture the idea that there must be some limits on the claims to jurisdiction" (at 325 S.C.R., 41 D.L.R). He added that "no test can perhaps ever be rigidly applied" and that, "though some of these may well require reconsideration in light of *Morguard,* the connections relied on under the traditional rules [by which courts take jurisdiction] are a good place to start." Beyond this, there would be "the gradual accumulation of connections defined in accordance with the broad principles of order and fairness" (at 325 S.C.R., 42 D.L.R.).

In the *Stoddard* case, referred to in Note 1, the judgment debtor sought an extension of the time to file an appeal, arguing that the Supreme Court's affirmation that the *Morguard* principle was rooted in the constitution was reason for a re-examination of the assumption in *Moses* v. *Shore Boat Ltd.* that the principle should extend to non-Canadian judgments. A further ground for the debtor's application was that the Connecticut court had awarded non-pecuniary damages on a far higher scale than a Canadian court could do, and that personal injury judgments, unlike contract judgments (which made up all the judgments enforced under *Morguard* until then), might call for some review of the merits. A panel of three judges of the Court of Appeal granted the extension (Dec. 3 1993, Vanc. Reg. No. CA017775), but the action is understood to have been settled.

(b)   Enforcement by registration under uniform reciprocal enforcement of judgments legislation

Conditions for registration — jurisdiction of original court

Note. The uniform reciprocal enforcement of judgments statute, which is in force in all provinces and territories except Quebec, provides in effect that a defendant who did not submit to the court's jurisdiction has a defence to registration so long as he or she was neither carrying on business nor ordinarily resident in the original state. In *Wilson* v. *Hull* (1993), [1994] 3 W.W.R. 648, 15 Alta. L.R. (3d) 286 (Q.B.), it was held that the carrying on business test is to be applied as of the time the cause of action arose, not the commencement of the original proceeding. This seems anomalous, since at common law the presence or absence of the original court's jurisdiction over a non-consenting defendant is always determined as of the time proceedings were commenced.

Conditions for registration — effect of judgment's enforceability by action at common law

Note. The effect of *Morguard Investments Ltd.* v. *De Savoye*, [1990] 3 S.C.R. 1077, 76 D.L.R. (4th) 256 on the application of the uniform reciprocal enforcement of judgments statutes is very limited. The expansion of the common law recognition rules by *Morguard* cannot be applied in the face of the listed defences in the statute, which more or less replicate the pre-*Morguard* rules about when the original court has jurisdiction. See *Sims* v. *Bower* (1993), 108 D.L.R.

(4th) 677 (N.B.C.A.). In *Land Management Corp. of N. America Inc.* v. *Wilson* (1993), 135 N.B.R. (2d) 129 (Q.B.), the court seems to have thought that *Morguard* somehow does expand the range of judgments that can be registered under the statute, but the reasoning is unclear.

Effect of registration — execution of judgment registered ex parte

Note. The restrictions on executing a judgment registered *ex parte* under the uniform reciprocal enforcement of judgments statute were discussed in *Cominco American Inc.* v. *Duval* (1993), 89 B.C.L.R. (2d) 83 (S.C.).

Effect of registration — judgment against uninsured non-resident defendant — claim arising out of accident in the province

Note. In *Holm* v. *Christensen*, [1994] 5 W.W.R. 298, 119 Sask. R. 45 (Q.B.), an Ontario-resident victim of a Saskatchewan motor vehicle accident obtained a judgment in Alberta against an Alberta-resident defendant. He registered the judgment in Saskatchewan. It remained unsatisfied. His claim against the uninsured motorist fund under the Saskatchewan automobile accident insurance legislation was upheld, because he was a judgment creditor in Saskatchewan and the legislation was intended to compensate victims of accidents that took place in Saskatchewan.

(c)   Enforcement by registration under reciprocal enforcement of maintenance orders legislation

Confirmation proceeding — foreign order varying local order

Cain v. *Cain* (1993), 109 D.L.R. (4th) 251, [1994] 2 W.W.R. 559. Saskatchewan Queen's Bench.

This case concerned the interrelationship between the maintenance provisions of federal divorce legislation, the uniform provincial reciprocal enforcement of maintenance orders statutes, and the powers of courts outside Canada to vary maintenance orders made in Canada against persons resident abroad. In 1984 a judge of the Saskatchewan Queen's Bench made an order corollary to divorce proceedings that the husband should pay the wife $450 a month for the maintenance of the parties' son. By this time the husband had been deported to England. He made no payments to the wife. In 1991 the Saskatchewan order was registered in England under the Maintenance Orders (Reciprocal Enforcement) Act 1972 (U.K.). Subsequently, the husband obtained three successive orders from the Magistrates' Court in England, provisionally varying the order to reduce his obligations. The last of these reduced the child maintenance to a token amount and remitted part of the arrears, on the ground that the husband had lost his job and could not pay. Each of these provisional orders in turn was submitted for confirmation by the Saskatchewan court under the Reciprocal Enforcement of Maintenance Orders Act, 1983, S.S. 1983, c. R-4.1 (the REMO Act), s. 6(2). Confirmation of the first two was refused. In the present case, Klebuc, J. held that he had no power to confirm the third, and that even if he had the power he would have refused to do so.

The reason Klebuc, J. found that the court lacked jurisdiction was that maintenance orders made pursuant to the Divorce Act, R.S.C. 1985, c. 3 (2nd Supp.), could be varied only by the procedure given in the Act, not under provincial reciprocal enforcement legislation. Orders made under federal legislation were expressly excluded from the provisional order and confirmation procedure of the REMO Act by its section 8(2). Sections 18 and 19 of the federal Act provided that courts in Canada could provisionally vary or confirm orders made under the Act, but made no provision for recognition of provisional orders made by a foreign court. Klebuc, J. examined the relevant English statutes and concluded that the Magistrates' Court had jurisdiction by English law to vary foreign maintenance orders. It therefore appeared that a legal hiatus existed between the laws of Canada and Saskatchewan and between the laws of Canada and the United Kingdom. The judge suggested that the Divorce Act should be amended to recognize provisional orders and confirmation orders made in a country that was a reciprocating state under the provincial REMO Act, and that the REMO Act be amended to include support orders made under the Divorce Act. Alternatively, the Divorce Act could be amended to recognize provisional orders and confirmation orders made by a superior court of a foreign state.

The judge went on to consider the merits of the provisional order. The English Magistrates' Court had been right to apply English law to decide whether the Canadian order should be varied but, Klebuc, J. thought, the English court had incorrectly applied its own law to the facts as they appeared. It had failed to take into account the husband's flagrant disregard of his obligations to his son under the Canadian order, and his having accumulated additional real and personal property for his use and benefit while he ignored his primary obligation to support the son. Thus, had the REMO Act applied, the judge would have ordered that the provisional order be referred back to the English court in order that further evidence could be taken by it regarding the husband's assets and financial transactions. Alternatively, if the English court could be shown to have applied its own law correctly, the Saskatchewan court should still refuse confirmation of the order because, according to Saskatchewan law, the husband would have been required to dispose of several major assets and apply the proceeds to his maintenance obligations before there could be any remission of arrears or reduction of future payments.

Confirmation proceeding — effect of local limitation law

Note. An Ontario court made a provisional child maintenance order against a putative father resident in Alberta. The Alberta court refused to confirm it, because, *inter alia*, the Alberta limitation period for affiliation proceedings had expired. Even if the law of Ontario was applicable to the claim, which was unclear, the Alberta limitation rule applied because it was procedural: *E.(N.)* v. *D.(D.R.)* (1993), 109 D.L.R. (4th) 747 (Alta. Q.B.).

(d)   Enforcement of arbitral awards

Enforcement under UNCITRAL Model Law or New York Convention

Note. See *Dunhill Personnel Systems Inc.* v. *Dunhill Temps Edmonton Ltd.* (1993), 13 Alta. L.R. (3d) 241 (Q.B.) (award in international commercial arbitration enforced under UNCITRAL Model Law).

2.   Québec

Exemplification de jugement — conditions

Finalité

Canetti-Calvi c. *Assicurazioni Generali S.P.A.*, [1994] R.J.Q. 1269. Cour d'appel du Québec.

La compagnie d'assurances intimée a émis une police d'assurance-accident au nom du mari de l'appelante par laquelle elle s'engageait à indemniser l'assuré pour des accidents, y compris la mort résultant d'actes agressifs ou violents. L'assuré a été assassiné et sa veuve, l'appelante, a intenté, en Italie, une action en réclamation d'indemnités d'assurance. Un jugement a été rendu condamnant la compagnie d'assurances. Ce jugement a été porté en appel et la compagnie d'assurances a procédé à l'enregistrement du jugement et en a payé le coût d'enregistrement. Elle a alors intenté un recours contre l'appelante, lui réclamant la moitié de la taxe ainsi payée. En défense, l'appelante a soutenu qu'elle ne devait pas la somme réclamée; par demande reconventionelle, elle a demandé l'exemplification du jugement italien et réclamé les bénéfices de la police d'assurance. Le premier juge a rejeté cette demande reconventionelle aux motifs, d'une part, que la demande d'exemplification était prématurée puisque le jugement italien n'était pas final ni exécutoire et, d'autre part, qu'il n'y avait pas de lien de connexité entre l'action et la demande reconventionelle.

La Cour a rejeté l'appel. Le jugement italien n'avait plus d'effet au Québec qu'il n'en avait dans son pays d'origine. Ce jugement n'était pas sujet à l'exécution suivant le droit qui le gouvernait, pas plus qu'il ne l'était suivant le droit du Québec. La demande était prématurée.

En ce qui concernait le lien de connexité, il y avait absence totale de connexité entre la source de la réclamation de la compagnie d'assurances — un impôt d'enregistrement dû au ministère des Finances en vertu d'une loi fiscale italienne — et celle de l'appelante — une prestation résultant d'une police d'assurance. On ne pouvait réunir un litige fondé sur l'interprétation d'une loi fiscale concernant des débiteurs solitaires et un autre litige reposant sur l'application d'une police d'assurance. On ne retrouvait aucun rapport de dépendance ou de similitude entre la demande principale et la demande reconventionelle. Les considérations fondant une interprétation large et généreuse de l'article 172 C.P. au regard du maintien d'une demande reconventionelle, telles la commodité, la réduction des coûts, l'efficacité judiciaire, la suppression des jugements contradictoires, la simplification des recours, étaient sans objet en l'espèce, la source de la demande principale étant très éloignée de la demande reconventionelle.

Note. Dans l'affaire *Bond Architects & Engineers Ltd.* c. *Compagnie de Cautionnement Alberta*, [1994] R.J.Q. 1603 (C.S.), la Cour a refusé d'exemplifier un jugement de Terre-Neuve pour des dépens au montant de $244 000. Le jugement avait été porté en appel. La Cour a précisé qu'un jugement étranger ne peut être considéré comme définitif puisqu'un appel est pendant, parce qu'il n'a jamais acquis l'autorité de la chose jugée. La Cour s'est ainsi exprimée contre la position prise par la common law, dans l'affaire *Nouvion* c. *Freeman* (1890), 15 App. Cas. 1 (H.L.). La Cour supérieure a appliqué l'ancienne loi dans les articles 178-81 C.P. parce que le jugement de Terre-Neuve était déjà rendu lors de l'entrée en vigueur du nouveau Code civil au 1er janvier 1994. Veuillez comparer l'article 3155 paragraphe 2 du nouveau Code civil, L.Q. 1991, c. 64, qui se lise:

Toute décision rendue hors du Québec est reconnue et, le cas échéant, déclarée exécutoire par l'autorité du Québec, sauf dans les cas suivants.
2. La décision, au lieu où elle a été rendue, est susceptible d'un recours ordinaire, ou n'est pas définitive ou exécutoire.

Compétence du tribunal étranger — révision — ordre public

Pier Augé Produits de beauté c. *Importations Cimel ltée* (1992), [1993] A.J.Q. 453, N° 1499. Cour supérieure du Québec.

La demanderesse, une société française spécialisée dans la fabrication de produits de beauté, voulait que soit déclaré exécutoire au Québec un jugement rendu en France qui résilia un contrat de distribution exclusive de ses produits. Le contrat a été conclu en France, en 1982, avec la défenderesse, une compagnie ayant son siège social à Montréal. Outre la résiliation du contrat, ce jugement ordonna à la défenderesse d'interrompre la distribution au Canada des produits de la demanderesse à compter de la signification du jugement, laquelle a eu lieu le 20 octobre 1986. Par la suite, la demanderesse intenta contre la défenderesse une action en injonction permanente et une action sur compte, visant à percevoir les sommes d'argent qui lui étaient dues pour les marchandises déjà vendues et livrées. Pour sa part, la défenderesse contesta la demande en exemplification du jugement de France, soutenant que les faits exposés devant le tribunal de France ne donnaient nullement ouverture à la conclusion retenue, soit la résiliation du contrat. Elle demanda, au plus, la délivrance d'une injonction permanente ordonnant à la demanderesse de respecter les termes de leur contrat.

La Cour a accueilli les actions en exemplification et sur compte de la demanderesse. Il était évident que, aux termes du contrat, seuls les tribunaux de France étaient compétents pour l'exécution du contrat. Deuxièmement, l'ordre public était respecté et le tribunal français a rendu un jugement réputé contradictoire compte

rendu jugement, toutes les conditions sauvegardant les droits d'un défendeur de comparaître et de se défendre avaient été respectées.

D.   Choice of Law (Including Status of Persons)/Conflits de lois (y compris statut personnel)

1.   Common Law and Federal

(a)   Characterization

Procedural and substantive rules — legal personality

Note. In *Hal Commodities Cycles Mgmt.* v. *Kirsh* (1993), 17 C.P.C. (3d) 320 (Ont. Gen. Div.), the issue whether a dissolved corporation has the status to bring an action was held procedural in nature. The court therefore refused to apply a rule in the state of original incorporation, Arizona, that would have allowed the plaintiff to commence and continue lawsuits although its charter had been revoked.

(b)   Exclusion of foreign law

Revenue law

Stringam v. *Dubois* (1992), 135 A.R. 64, 48 E.T.R. 248. Alberta Court of Appeal.

In 1983 the testatrix died domiciled and resident in Arizona, leaving a total estate of US$1.9 million, of which US$430,000 represented a wheat farm in Alberta. The wheat farm was left to her niece, Dubois, who brought this action against the administrator with will annexed of the estate in Alberta, for an order that he convey the farm to her. The administrator acted under power of attorney from the executor of the estate in the United States, an Arizona bank. The bank had obtained an order from an Arizona court in 1987, apportioning the total estate taxes. The order was that 36.85 per cent of the taxes be paid out of the probate assets, as distinct from non-probate assets, which were in joint tenancies and trusts and made up US$1.3 million of the estate. The probate assets included the wheat farm. The taxes payable on the probate assets exceeded the value of the assets in the United States, leaving US$143,000 to be paid out of the wheat farm. The administrator claimed that he was entitled to withhold this amount out of the bequest to Dubois.

The Court of Appeal held that Dubois was entitled to a conveyance of the wheat farm without deduction by the administrator of any amount in respect of United States estate taxes. The general principle that the beneficiary should bear the burden of the costs incidental to ownership incurred by the trustee was subject in this case to the rule that a Canadian court would not enforce, directly or indirectly, a foreign tax claim. The court disagreed with *Re Reid* (1970), 17 D.L.R. (3d) 199 (B.C.C.A.), which held that the foreign taxes in that case could be deducted by the trustee on the basis that they had already been paid, so the time of enforcement was past. The timing of the payment of the taxes could not be relevant to the result. Also, a situation like the present one illustrated exactly one of the traditional justifications for the rule against enforcement of foreign tax claims — namely, that it avoided the local forum having to pronounce on whether the foreign claim was consistent with its own public policy. Various issues, including the reason for taxes to remain outstanding despite a substantial United States estate, and the apportionment of the taxes between probate and non-probate assets, left questions as to whether the tax claimed would be in accord with the policy of this country. Nevertheless, the court noted that the rule about tax claims had been subject to considerable criticism, and that the Supreme Court of Canada might wish to re-examine the problem in the light of more modern international notions of comity.

(c)   Tort

Tort outside the province

Note. In *Bowes* v. *Chalifour* (1992), 18 C.P.C. (3d) 391 (Ont. Gen. Div.), adoptive parents and grandparents, resident in Ontario, of a child who had been injured in an accident in British Columbia before he came to live with them, invoked the statutory cause of action that exists in Ontario for the loss suffered by a family member through the injury of the primary victim. The court held that the Ontario statute was inapplicable. These statutory claims were derivative from the claim and circumstances of the primary victim and so did not apply to this accident, the rights arising out of which were governed by British Columbia law.

(d)   Property

Movables — intangible — beneficial interest in trust

Note. Interesting issues as to which of several provinces' laws governed beneficiaries' rights in respect of a pension fund surplus

of women; and (iv) to make international human rights law more effective for women (Rebecca Cook, p. 4).

The Consultation discussions took place within the framework of the legal obligation to eliminate all forms of discrimination against women as a fundamental tenet of international human rights law. Generally, sex is a prohibited ground of discrimination in various United Nations and regional human rights instruments. More specifically, the 1979 *Convention on the Elimination of All Forms of Discrimination Against Women* ("Women's Convention") moved beyond earlier conventions to address the pervasive and systematic discrimination against women. Hence, the development, interpretation, and implementation of the Women's Convention serves as the background or focus for many of the papers in this book.

Overall, the scope of the volume is wide. This is made clear in the first paper, which is a concentrated report of the views and consensus of the participants to the Consultation. In this paper, entitled "Women's International Human Rights Law: The Way Forward," Professor Rebecca Cook explores what legal rights have the potential to offer women, whether women's rights can be truly universal, how rights can be legitimized or "indigenized" in various cultures, and how international human rights law can be recharacterized to be gender-conscious. She also suggests approaches to how the specific rights of women can be guaranteed. In particular, she refers to rights concerning nationality, rights to ownership of real and personal property (with special reference to how structural adjustment problems burden women), health and reproductive care rights, and rights to liberty and security (including protection from gender-based violence). Furthermore, Professor Cook addresses the issues of state responsibility and accountability for violations of women's rights and discusses the development of legal methods for the protection of women's human rights through United Nations bodies, regional mechanisms, and domestic remedies.

Examples of the themes to which certain papers are devoted follow, but are necessarily inadequate in a review of this length. The examples are intended to demonstrate the tremendous range of subjects, disciplines, and perspectives represented in the book.

A survey of challenges to implementing the human rights of women is provided in the second paper by Radhika Coomaraswamy, United Nations Special Rapporteur on Violence Against Women and Director of the International Centre for Ethnic Studies, Colombo, Sri Lanka. Initially, she warns against falling into the "orientalist trap," according to which the world is divided into two categories, one of which is superior, by virtue of its being either more progressive on human rights, or more communal and less self-centered (at 40). According to her, an ideological resistance to human rights for women has been a barrier in some countries. For human rights to be effective, they must go beyond the normative and textual and become part of the legal culture of a given society, as well as part of the popular consciousness (pp. 39, 55).

Abdullahi Ahmed An-Na'im, Executive Director, Human Rights Watch - Africa, endorses the need for internationally recognized standards of human rights to be validated in terms of the values and institutions of each culture as well as through a "cross-cultural dialogue" among the various cultural traditions of the world (p. 174).

In an excellent essay on "What are Women's Human Rights?" Hilary Charlesworth, Professor of Law, University of Adelaide, asserts that, despite critiques by feminists and proponents of critical legal studies, the language of rights has an important and recognized vocabulary with which to frame injustices against women (p. 61). While listing the doctrinal hurdles, she also details the practical obstacles that exist for women, from the lack of effective channels that would carry women's concerns into the mainstream human rights law-making arena to the public/private distinction that entrenches women's subordination (pp. 63, 69). Celia Romany, Professor of Law, City University of New York Law School, in the fourth paper, also concentrates on the public/private distinction in international human rights law, asserting that it "cripples women's citizenship" (p. 94). Of course, Charlesworth notes, differences of class, race, and nationality result in differing power relationships among women, and no monolithic "women's point of view" can be assumed (p. 63). Nevertheless, she maintains that the essential challenge is "to ensure that women's voices find a public audience, to reorient the boundaries of mainstream human rights law so that it incorporates an understanding of the world from the perspective of the socially subjugated. . .[and] to challenge the gendered dichotomy of the public and private worlds" (p. 76).

The parallels between torture, which is prohibited by international instruments and condemned universally, and domestic violence are drawn by Rhonda Copelon, Professor of Law, City University of New York Law School.

Kenneth Roth, Executive Director, Human Rights Watch, New

Cook and the Consultation participants/contributors for having provided such a rich and impressive source of material.

MARCIA V. J. KRAN
*International Centre for Criminal Law Reform
and Criminal Justice Policy at the
University of British Columbia*

Reconceiving Reality: Women and International Law. Edited by Dorinda G. Dallmeyer. Washington, D.C.: American Society of International Law, 1993. (Studies in Transnational Legal Policy No. 25.) Pp. 294. (U.S.$18 plus 10 per cent postage and handling) ISSN 1057-0551.

The scope of the work under review is captured by its ambitious title. Indeed, feminism can be said to involve a fundamental challenge to traditional international legal scholarship, demanding a profound rethinking of the international legal system, its actors and participants, and their respective roles, rights, and responsibilities. The papers in this collection were presented at a day-long session sponsored by the Women in International Law Interest Group of the American Society of International Law, and held in conjunction with the Society's 87th Annual Meeting in 1993. As stated in the preface to this volume, the papers presented were intended to answer the challenge posed by the ground-breaking article by Hilary Charlesworth, Christine Chinkin, and Shelley Wright, "Feminist Approaches to International Law," that was published in the American Journal of International Law in 1991. All three of those authors contributed papers to the present volume, and many of the other authors represented are engaged in an extension or critique of that earlier work.

This book also includes a foreword, which comprises a brief but useful discussion of some of the difficulties involved in setting up a course in women's international human rights law, and highlights the importance of curricular development in this area.

The volume is divided into three parts. The papers in the first part, which provide an overview of the current state of feminist analysis of international law, reveal a number of differences of opinion among the scholars working in the area. In the opening chapter, Hilary Charlesworth tackles the basic issue of what a "feminist" analysis of international law actually involves. Charlesworth notes that developing such a theoretical perspective requires that feminists be willing to take risks, to challenge the mainstream. In her contribution, on the other hand, Moira McConnell takes issue with the very labelling of certain approaches as "theoretical," arguing that accepting such a label inevitably involves an acceptance of marginalization as against a mainstream that is characterized not as the product of theory but as embodying reality.

The second part of the book consists of a number of papers that examine the implications of the public/private distinction in the international legal sphere and its impact upon women. Rebecca Cook, for example, looks at the issue of how international law might be made to respond to the reality of women's oppression within the private sphere, through a recognition of state accountability for violations of women's rights by non-state actors. The chapter by Karen Engle is particularly interesting, in that it "problematizes" the feminist critique of the public/private distinction. While acknowledging the usefulness of the critique, and identifying its many positive effects, Engle cautions against an application of the critique that does not guard against a number of potential pitfalls. Among these, she identifies the tendencies to reify both the public and private spheres, to assume that women are still relegated to the private sphere, and to assume that the unregulated private realm is necessarily bad for women. Engle emphasizes that, beyond theorizing, the primary focus must be on "strategizing women's rights."

In the third and last section, a number of authors outline feminist approaches to war and peace. It is here that some of the most topical issues are addressed, including the treatment of rape in warfare. In focussing on the impact of various forms of armed conflict upon the lives of women, the authors in this section raise fundamental questions regarding the extent to which international law in this area does anything more than skim the surface of existing problems. One of the writers, Christine Chinkin, raises the even more troubling question of how we can neatly draw a line between violence against women in wartime and violence that occurs daily around the globe. This section includes chapters by two political scientists; Robin Teske, an international relations scholar, offers an examination of power from an interdisciplinary perspective.

Gender inequality and related issues have long occupied a marginal position within the mainstream literature of international law.

international du Liban est précisé dans un premier temps, du Protocole d'Alexandrie qui, en 1944, consacre son existence en tant qu'Etat indépendant à la participation à la Ligue arabe qui confirme cet état de fait. K. Boustany analyse également les accords du Caire (1969) et de Melkart (1973), qui constituaient le cadre juridique de la présence palestinienne en territoire libanais. Elle expose sous ce titre les diverses violations du droit international — universel autant que régional — qu'ont représentées les différentes interventions étrangères au Liban et les réactions extrêmement discrètes que celles-ci ont entraîné au sein de la communauté internationale. Il est vrai que, comme l'auteur le souligne, le conflit apparaissait aux yeux de cette dernière comme essentiellement interne — à l'exception notable des interventions israéliennes qui faisaient l'objet de condamnations régulières — et que les divisions persistantes qui affectaient le gouvernement libanais rendaient la planification d'une action internationale concrète (le modèle de l'ONUC est évoqué à cet égard) des plus difficiles. Le coeur même du problème est ensuite atteint avec la discussion des liens entre la structure de l'État et le concept de maintien de la paix. Cette question apparaît en effet fondamentale dans la réflexion sur l'adéquation des opérations de maintien de la paix — dont il ne faut pas oublier qu'elles ont initialement été conçues à une toute autre fin — à l'objectif de pacification d'un conflit intraétatique. L'auteur aborde successivement pour ce faire les rapports entre la déstructuration de l'État et le maintien de la paix, d'une part, ainsi qu'entre l'ordre public interne et la paix internationale, de l'autre, en appuyant également son analyse sur les deux précédents où l'ONU était intervenue dans des conflits similaires: l'ONUC au Congo et l'UNFICYP à Chypre. Paradoxalement, ce rapport entre rétablissement de l'ordre public interne et maintien de la paix internationale n'est pas établi dans le cas du Liban et la force des Nations Unies mise sur pied dans ce pays en 1978 le sera en fin de compte essentiellement pour tempérer le conflit avec Israël.

Les tentatives mêmes de pacification du conflit sont abordées dans la deuxième partie de l'ouvrage. Les opérations régionale (Force arabe de dissuasion — FAD), d'une part, multinationale (Forces multinationales I et II — FM) et universelle (Force intérimaire des Nations Unies au Liban — FINUL), de l'autre, sont traitées à tour de rôle. L'étude des bases juridiques de création de la FAD, ainsi que de la définition et du déroulement de son mandat fournit un exemple très évocateur des potentialités, et plus encore des limites — si ce n'est des dangers — des initiatives régionales de maintien de la paix. Comme le montre K. Boustany de façon très convaincante, l'absence de cadre juridique précis dans lequel ce type d'opération pourrait être menée, de même que la nette prédominance dans les circonstances des considérations politiques sur les principes juridiques au sein de l'organisation concernée ont fait que l'opération régionale a véritablement été détournée de ses objectifs et confisquée à son profit par la puissance la plus intéressée de la région: la Syrie. Jusqu'à sa dissolution en 1982, la FAD a coexisté pendant plusieurs années avec la FINUL dont le but premier était de s'interposer entre Palestiniens et Israéliens dans le sud du Liban et, brièvement, avec la FM qui avait plutôt pour mission d'apaiser le conflit libano-palestinien, essentiellement dans et autour de Beyrouth. Le mandat de l'une ou l'autre de ces opérations comprenait toutefois également l'assistance au gouvernement libanais pour lui permettre de restaurer son autorité sur l'ensemble du territoire, se rapprochant par là de celui des deux opérations de l'ONU évoquées plus haut.

Les deux opérations sont détaillées de manière parallèle en ce qui concerne leur établissement, leur fonctionnement, leur composition, leur mandat et leurs moyens d'action. La Force multinationale constitue un cas intéressant à cet égard, puisqu'elle revêt un caractère atypique par rapport aux opérations de maintien de la paix de l'ONU, dont elle ne possède pas le caractère institutionnalisé, en même temps que certains de ses traits l'en rapprochent. Il est ainsi plus particulièrement du consentement de l'État territorialement concerné et de ses moyens d'action, limités à la légitime défense, comme dans le cas des forces des Nations Unies. Mais au-delà de cette approche théorique, K. Boustany se livre à une excellente analyse des raisons de l'échec de ces opérations, en montrant entre autres comment elles ont elles-mêmes été affectées par le conflit intraétatique. L'influence des conditions géopolitiques d'ensemble (évolution du conflit moyen-oriental, bien sûr, mais plus généralement aussi rapports est-ouest), l'état extrême de désagrégation des structures étatiques libanaises, ainsi que la perte progressive de neutralité de la FM constituent autant d'éléments qui expliquent la disparition de cette dernière. Le constat final de l'auteur à propos de ces différentes initiatives est donc cruel, puisqu'elle observe que les trois opérations de maintien de la paix étudiées sont en fin de compte elles-mêmes devenues des facteurs conflictuels supplémentaires au Liban.

On le comprend, l'ouvrage de K. Boustany offre donc une matière abondante pour nourrir la réflexion sur les opérations de maintien de la paix et, plus précisément, sur le bien-fondé de leur création dans le cadre de conflits intraétatiques, voire strictement internes. Il serait ainsi très intéressant de voir dans quelle mesure les conclusions atteintes par l'auteur trouveraient un écho dans l'analyse des opérations de maintien de la paix mises sur pied par l'ONU en ex-Yougoslavie, au Cambodge, en Amérique centrale ou en Somalie, pour ne prendre que ces exemples. De la même manière, il faudrait tenter de déterminer dans quelle mesure les très nettes réserves qu'elle exprime sur les opérations régionales de maintien de la paix ont été rencontrées par la pratique récente du Conseil de securité particulièrement en ce qui concerne le mandat que cet organe a confié à la CEDEAO au Libéria en vertu du Chapitre VIII de la Charte. Mais tout cela est assurément, comme l'on dit, une autre histoire. Il faut, à ce stade, être reconnaissant à K. Boustany de nous avoir fourni, au fil de son étude minutieuse et exhaustive du conflit intraétatique libanais, une grille de lecture des conflagrations de ce type, de même que d'avoir mis en évidence les nombreux aléas susceptibles d'affecter le fonctionnement et l'efficacité des opérations de maintien de la paix instituées pour y mettre fin.

PIERRE KLEIN
Boulton Fellow, Faculté de droit, Université McGill

North American Free Trade Agreements. Compiled and edited by James R. Holbein and Donald J. Musch. Dobbs Ferry, New York: Oceana Publications, Inc. 1993. (U.S.$450) ISBN 0-379-01038-0.

When the North American Free Trade Agreement[1] ("NAFTA") came into force on January 1, 1994 it was the most comprehensive trade treaty in the world, covering issues not previously addressed in the context of trade (for example, intellectual property), as well as traditional trade law matters, like tariffs. The implementation of NAFTA required sweeping changes to the domestic laws of Canada, the United States, and Mexico. The scope of NAFTA both reflects and facilitates the increasing integration of the economies

[1] (1993) 32 I.L.M. 670.

of the party states and the corresponding trend toward the internationalization of formerly national economic issues. Because of its wide ranging implications, understanding how the treaty operates is both challenging and critical, not just for academic and practising trade lawyers, trade policy officials, importers, and exporters, but also for business people and lawyers in a variety of practice areas.

North American Free Trade Agreements is an important contribution to understanding NAFTA. Published in five regularly updated volumes, it is a comprehensive collection of the basic documents relating to NAFTA, including the decisions made under the dispute settlement provisions of the Free Trade Agreement[2] ("FTA"), complemented by one complete volume devoted to commentary. There are certain ways in which the extensive material presented could have been made more accessible, and there are some gaps in the Canadian material included, but there is no question that *North American Free Trade Agreements* is a very useful resource.

The two *Treaties* volumes contain the official texts of NAFTA, including the voluminous chapter annexes, and the FTA, as well as the agreements on environmental and labour co-operation. The Canadian and American legislation implementing NAFTA is also included. No comprehensive implementing legislation was passed in Mexico,[3] but *North American Free Trade Agreements* does provide a translation of the complete text of Mexico's Foreign Trade Law, which gives effect to some of Mexico's commitments under NAFTA.[4] The United States Statement of Administrative Action, which sets out the American government's view of its obligations under NAFTA, is an extremely useful inclusion. The omission of the comparable Canadian document, the Canadian Implementation Statement,[5] is unfortunate, but the authors will remedy this omission in their first release in 1995.

The materials relating to dispute settlement are particularly comprehensive. The second *Treaties* volume contains a complete set of

[2] (1988) 27 I.L.M. 281. The dispute settlement provisions of the FTA were continued and expanded under NAFTA.

[3] No such legislation was necessary, since treaties are the supreme law of the land under the Mexican Constitution (Art. 133).

[4] E.g., those regarding tariffs, unfair trade practices, safeguards, and certain non-tariff barriers, including import and export licences, quotas, and country of origin.

[5] Canada Gazette, Part I, Jan. 1, 1994.

the relevant materials on dispute settlement: that is, the rules adopted by the NAFTA parties, and Codes of Conduct for both the general dispute settlement procedure under Chapter 20 and the dumping and countervailing duty review procedure under Chapter 19.[6] In addition, the Special Committee Rules under Article 1905[7] of the NAFTA have been included. In the two *Dispute Settlement* volumes, the complete text of all decisions rendered by dispute settlement panels under the general dispute settlement procedure and the subsidies and dumping review procedure of the FTA are provided. These basic materials are complemented by three extremely useful articles in the *Commentary* binder: of these, two address the implications of Chapter 19 dispute settlement for United States business and the United States legal system, and the third is a summary of the panel decisions rendered under the FTA.

In addition to dispute settlement the *Commentary* binder contains a diverse collection of general informational material as well as an exhaustive guide to customs, tariffs, and rules of origin under NAFTA by Harry Endsley and Steven Baker, and a very thorough piece on the antidumping and countervailing duty regime in Mexico by Craig Giesze. The general material consists of a brief but effectively written summary of NAFTA, a summary of the United States legislative history, a substantial bibliography of the burgeoning literature on NAFTA, the "NAFTA Implementation Resource Guide" and "Official Contacts and Inquiry Points." The last two items list contact people and their addresses in the three NAFTA party states and a wealth of other practical information. Together, these general materials provide invaluable keys to finding further information and analysis regarding discrete questions related to NAFTA.

While the commentary provided to date is of high quality, the overall subject area coverage is limited. This is not surprising, given the relatively recent implementation of the agreement. The authors intend to remedy this situation over time with releases that address issues arising under all the major headings of NAFTA. They have advised the writer that they plan releases on at least agriculture and

---

[6] The equivalent FTA documents have also been included. These are relevant not just for historical purposes but also for the purposes of the various subsidies and dumping panel reviews that commenced before the coming into force of NAFTA and are still continuing.

[7] Art. 1905 deals with dispute settlement in situations where it is alleged that the domestic law of one party state interferes with the operation of the Chapter 19 dispute settlement process.

energy in 1995. From a Canadian point of view it would be desirable if more material focussing on Canada were included.[8]

North American Free Trade Agreements could be made more accessible in a variety of ways. A topical index or at least a more detailed table of contents would help the reader find his or her way through this massive work. Similarly, it would be helpful to add some commentary that would briefly describe each included document and, perhaps, link it to other included materials. The bibliography would be more useful if it were organized by subject categories, by author, or by date of publication. In its present form, there is no discernible order and finding references can be difficult and time consuming.

It would, however, be unfair to focus on these criticisms. *North American Free Trade Agreements* is a very useful resource. It fills a gap in the literature on trade that is becoming wider in Canada with the recent discontinuation of some of the loose leaf services covering the FTA.[9] It is a comprehensive collection of basic documents that is helpful both as a starting point for research and as a guide to the resolution of practical problems.

J. ANTHONY VANDUZER
Faculty of Law, University of Ottawa

Third Parties in International Law. By Christine Chinkin. Oxford: Clarendon Press, 1993. Pp. xxvii, 385. ($121.50).

In the editor's short preface, Ian Brownlie informs the reader that the author will focus in considerable depth on three areas in international law that concern third parties: namely, treaties, the work of international tribunals, and armed conflict coupled with acts of aggression.

This book originated in the author's research towards a Ph.D degree, and represents a final revision of her successful thesis. The

[8] Even in the bibliography, there are some surprising gaps in the Canadian materials referred to. While there is a fairly complete listing of Canadian periodicals, there is no reference to Canadian government materials like Finance Canada's *Economic Assessment of the NAFTA* (Supply and Services: Ottawa, 1992), and the *Canadian Government Backgrounder* (Supply and Services: Ottawa, 1992). There may be similar gaps in relation to Mexican government documents.

[9] E.g., the *Free Trade Law Reporter* (CCH Canadian: Don Mills, 1991) and the *Canadian Trade Law Reporter* (CCH Canadian: Don Mills, 1989), both discontinued in 1994.

research in this book is current, involving the political and legal events up to March 1992. Hence, discussion of the International Court of Justice judgment in the *Land, Island and Maritime Frontier Dispute* (El Salvador/Honduras; Nicaragua Intervening), the first case before the World Court in which a third state was permitted to intervene, is not incorporated in the appropriate body of the text, but is briefly noted by the author in the acknowledgments. Professor Chinkin's publishing deadline also prevented her from including the multi-state humanitarian intervention in Somalia and the collective sanctions imposed against Libya, Liberia, and Serbia that are of current continuing interest to the international community.

Essentially the book is divided into three parts. Part One examines the modern application of the *pacta tertiis* rule, which was designed to protect non-parties to a treaty from having the treaty imposed upon them. Nevertheless, if a third party finds that it has been adversely affected by the traditional bilateral model of international legal relations, it has usually found itself without any available forum to lodge substantive claims. Discussion of this issue leads into Part Two, which considers third party claims before international adjudicative and arbitration tribunals. In this Part, Profess Chinkin categorizes the third party claims with respect to international procedures according to the third party's right to participate in the proceedings, to submit information to the tribunal, and to affect the disposition of the case when it is not afforded a presence.

In Part One, Professor Chinkin demonstrates that the limitations traditionally placed on third parties with regard to treaties have been circumvented by characterizing the problem as involving other areas within international law — for example, the law of state responsibility. Also, she provides many examples of exceptions to the *pacta tertiis* rule, and explains how the rule has been manipulated by more powerful states (albeit with sensitivity to avoid offending weaker states and to marshal their support). The new flexibility in practice that permits third parties to participate in proceedings before international tribunals is discussed further in Part Two. However, Professor Chinkin does show that, in the main, courts have been extremely conservative and do not massage procedures in typical interstate cases. In 1966, the International Court of Justice rejected the existence of an *actio popularis* in the South West Africa cases. Almost thirty years later, Professor Chinkin hints that, in the East Timor case, with Portugal as the colonial power, the International Court of Justice might be willing to stand in the public interest, resting upon the obligations of the international community as a whole to respect the rights of East Timorese. In this situation, other states could participate in the proceedings.

In his preface, Ian Brownlie points out that "the conceptual umbrella of 'third parties' may shelter too many items for some tastes." It is in Part Three, which concerns armed conflicts and the concept of criminality of the state in the use of force, that I think Professor Chinkin makes her greatest contribution. Acts of aggression, she suggests, are contrary to the *jus cogens,* and impinge upon all international actors, not just on those directly involved.

When not initially a direct participant in an armed conflict, the third party has a range of options: it can (1) remain neutral and act in the collective self-defence of a state that it perceives to be the victim; (2) ignore the situation on the basis that the conflict has minimal impact on itself; (3) express its displeasure and attempt to punish the perceived wrongdoer or use coercive measures that will bring the offensive conduct to an end; (4) mobilize a collective response through regional or global institutions; or, (5) make use of institutional resolutions. Professor Chinkin evaluates each of the above third party unilateral or collective responses in relation to conflicts that took place in the 1980s and early 1990s — particularly, the "contra" struggle in Nicaragua, the invasion of Grenada, the Iraq-Iran war and the Gulf War following Iraq's invasion of Kuwait, as well as the developing conflict in East Timor.

Each Part of the book ends with Professor Chinkin's evaluation of the legal developments on the particular subject. Then, in a general conclusion, she tries to convince the reader of a unifying thread that has linked the three areas considered. Although I struggled to find this link, I was unsuccessful. Nonetheless, its absence does not discount the great worth of this book. Professor Chinkin has given us prodigious research, careful in-depth thought and analysis, and skilled writing. She has provided a beacon and guidance for continued developments in this branch of international law.

Other attributes of the book include useful tables of cases, United Nations resolutions, treaties and other documents. The bibliography on this subject appears to be exhaustive, and the index quite workable. It is a book that anyone associated with international law will want to consult on a regular basis.

DANIEL C. TURACK
Law and Graduate Center, Capital University

Principes de droit des conflits armés. Par Éric David. Bruxelles: Établissements Émile Bruylant, S.A., 1994. Pp. 792. (FB 4.670) ISBN 2-8027-0897-X.

Éric David est un homme prudent. Non content de modestement intituler son livre *Principes de droit des conflits armés*, et non "Traité" ou "Manuel," il préface encore l'oeuvre avec un avertissement sévère au lecteur pour souligner le caractère nécessairement incomplet de cet ouvrage de presque huit cents pages, vu la vastitude du sujet abordé. Le calibre et la profondeur de l'analyse qui suit cette entrée en la matière viennent admirablement réfuter la vision pessimiste de l'auteur quant à la portée de son oeuvre monumentale.

Le livre consiste en une analyse systématique du droit des conflits armés, ou *jus in bello*. L'ampleur même du sujet force l'auteur à écarter de son étude certains aspects plus spécialisés de ce droit, par exemple le droit de la guerre sur mer ou dans les airs, de même que certaines règles connexes parfois incluses dans ce genre d'ouvrage, tel que le droit de la neutralité ou le problème réfugiés. Se limitant aux éléments essentiels du droit international humanitaire, l'ouvrage aborde successivement le champ d'application du droit des conflits armés, ses principales règles de substance, les instruments de mise en oeuvre et de contrôle, la réparation des violations et finalement les raisons qui expliquent pourquoi le droit des conflits armés est si souvent violé.

Il n'y que peu à dire sur la longue introduction dans laquelle l'auteur effectue un survol des principes généraux et de l'évolution historique du droit des conflits armés, pour conclure à l'importance toujours très actuelle de ce droit dans les relations internationales contemporaines. Suivent deux sections forts brèves sur les sources conventionnelles et coutumières du droit humanitaire. On peut déplorer quelque peu le traitement superficiel — à peine trois pages — de la formation et du rôle de la coutume, qui demeure un élément-clef de l'application du droit humanitaire malgré le fait que pratiquement tous les États soient aujourd'hui parties aux Conventions de Genève de 1949. Non seulement n'en est-il pas de même pour les Protocoles additionnels de 1977, que plusieurs grandes puissances militaires refusent toujours de ratifier, mais encore le statut coutumier de ces règles a-t-il une importance critique pour leur application interne dans les pays à tradition dualiste, pour l'effet des réserves, nombreuses, aux instruments conventionnels, et pour la possibilité de dénoncer ces traités. De plus, l'évolution coutumière du droit humanitaire soulève des problèmes particuliers à ce système, découlant entr'autres de la fréquence des violations des normes par rapport à la rareté apparente de leur application conforme. On s'étonne à cet égard de ne voir mentionné ni dans cette section, ni même dans la bibliographie générale en fin de volume, le livre de Theodor Meron, *Human Rights and Humanitarian Norms as Customary Law* (Oxford: Clarendon, 1989), devenu une référence pratiquement incontournable dans ce domaine.

Le premier chapitre situe le droit des conflits armés par rapport à d'autres règles du droit international, y compris le droit de la paix et, surtout, le droit international de la personne.[1] L'auteur consacre de nombreuses pages à une étude soulignant les rapports souvent difficiles à cerner entre droit humanitaire et droits de la personne, insistant à juste titre sur la nature cumulative et supplétive de ces deux systèmes malgré le "no man's land humanitaire" qui séparent les notions de conflit armé et de danger public menaçant la vie de la nation (pp. 73-84, 171).

À cette discussion succède une analyse de l'application de la notion de *jus cogens*. Plutôt hardiment, l'auteur conclut que l'ensemble du droit des conflits armés appartient au *jus cogens* (p. 92)! Cette affirmation, qui en surprendra plus d'un, repose en large partie sur l'obligation des Hautes Parties Contractantes de "faire respecter" le droit humanitaire "en toutes circonstances," sur l'impossibilité de suspendre les normes conventionnelles humanitaires en vertu de l'Article 60(5) de la Convention de Vienne sur le droit des traités, et sur la formulation de diverses dispositions des Conventions de Genève et Protocoles additionnels. On ne saurait sans difficultés se rallier à cette position qui semble relever plus du prosélytisme humanitaire que d'une stricte application du concept de *jus cogens* tel qu'accepté en droit international. La validité incontestée des réserves, la possibilité de dénoncer la plupart des conventions pertinentes et la légalité de suspension par représailles de la plupart des normes (seuls certains groupes de victimes éventuelles étant protégés de leurs effets) s'allient pour

---

[1] On se doit ici de saluer l'utilisation de l'expression "droits de la personne" pour désigner ce que beaucoup en Europe appelle toujours "droits de l'homme." La Belgique constituerait-elle la tête de pont québécoise dans notre croisade pour moderniser cette expression que beaucoup considère comme vieux jeu, sinon comme exclusive?

soulever un doute certain quant à la validité de cette conclusion de l'auteur.

L'analyse des règles substantielles du droit des conflits armés dans le chapitre II suit une division entre, d'une part, le droit "de La Haye" relatif à la conduite des hostilités et, d'autre part, le droit "de Genève" relatif au traitement des personnes au pouvoir de l'ennemi. Il s'agit là d'une division géographique sinon obsolète, du moins traditionnelle, du droit des conflits armés, que l'auteur adopte à titre de "raccourcis terminologiques commodes pour désigner des réalités distinctes" (p. 65). On peut s'interroger sur la nécessité d'une telle distinction qui déjà au début du siècle ne reflétait pas adéquatement le contenu respectif des conventions de Genève et de La Haye, et qui se justifie maintenant d'autant moins avec l'adoption des Protocoles de 1977, dans laquelle se mélangent indistinctement des éléments "de Genève" et "de La Haye."

Dans le cadre de cette structure quelque peu artificielle, l'auteur procède à une analyse méthodique des règles particulières du droit des conflits armés. L'exposé s'avère à la fois clair et instructif, illustré de nombreux exemples tirés de la pratique ancienne et récente. Par exemple, la règle exigeant la proportionnalité entre, d'une part, l'avantage militaire concret et direct attendu et, d'autre part, les pertes et dommages aux civils résultant d'un bombardement (Art. 51(5), Protocole I) est illustrée par des références aux bombardements d'Hiroshima, de Nagasaki et de Dresde durant la seconde guerre mondiale, et de l'Iraq en 1991. L'utilisation abondante de la pratique s'avère essentielle pour ancrer dans la réalité ces règles qui souvent paraissent d'une simplicité s'accordant mal avec l'horreur du contexte dans lequel elles doivent trouver application.

Dans le même esprit, l'auteur utilise à intervalles réguliers dans l'ensemble de l'ouvrage des extraits littéraires afin de donner vie aux principes étudiés. On peut ainsi lire des passages des mémoires d'un grognard de l'armée napoléonienne (*Le conscrit* de 1813), d'*À l'ouest rien de nouveau* d'Erich Maria Remarque à propos de la guerre 1914-18, et des diverses expériences du Dr Junod, délégué du Comité international de la Croix-Rouge pendant la guerre d'Espagne et la seconde guerre mondiale (*Le troisième combattant*). Ces témoignages souvent poignants soulignent à la fois les limites et les succès de l'entreprise humanitaire que représente le droit des conflits armés.

L'auteur enseigne à l'Université Libre de Bruxelles, et l'on retrouve tout au long de l'exposé des règles de droit international de nombreuses références à la pratique et législation belge pertinente. Il s'agit d'un aspect qui, loin de réduire l'attrait de l'oeuvre, lui ajoute une dimension supplémentaire tout-à-fait enrichissante, même pour un lecteur étranger. Un bon exemple de l'intérêt de ces annotations à couleur plutôt locale est fourni par la loi belge de 1993 sur la répression des infractions graves aux Conventions de Genève et Protocoles additionnels. L'auteur, qui a agi à titre de consultant pour la rédaction du projet de loi, souligne l'aspect novateur de cette loi qui criminalise non seulement les infractions graves aux Conventions de 1949 et au Protocole I, mais aussi au Protocole II applicable lors des conflits armés non-internationaux (pp. 553-56, 646-49). Or, le Protocole II ne prévoit pas de responsabilité pénale individuelle pour violation de ses dispositions! C'est donc dire que la loi belge ajoute au droit international en dotant ce pays d'une compétence universelle pour un "crime" qui n'existe qu'en droit belge. La pratique belge en ce domaine se trouve par ailleurs confirmée depuis la publication du livre par l'attribution au Tribunal pénal international pour le Rwanda d'une compétence pour punir les violations graves du Protocole II et de l'Article 3 commun des Conventions de 1949.[2]

Le dernier chapitre du livre constitue sans doute la partie la plus inhabituelle pour un ouvrage consacré au droit des conflits armés. Sans prétendre apporter toutes les réponses à un problème largement extra-juridique, l'auteur y souligne néanmoins de manière succincte mais convaincante certains éléments sociologiques, psychologiques, anthropologiques et économiques qui peuvent expliquer la violation du droit des conflits armés à grande et petite échelles. On y lit entr'autres de nombreux témoignages de criminels de guerre, soldat américain à Mylai, tortionnaire français en Algérie, ou milicien libanais psychopathe, qui illustrent bien les limites inévitables d'un droit qui cherche à réglementer l'activité humaine à son plus inhumain.

Ce livre d'Éric David représente un effort de systématisation remarquable du droit des conflits armés. Le texte est clair, bien

[2] Article 4, Statut du Tribunal pénal international pour le Rwanda, Doc. ONU S/RES/955, 8 novembre 1994, Annexe. Ce faisant, le Conseil de sécurité de l'ONU passait outre aux commentaires de sa propre Commission d'experts chargée d'enquêter sur les violations du droit humanitaire en Yougoslavie, qui avait conclu à peine six mois plus tôt qu'il n'existait pas en droit international de responsabilité pénale individuelle pour violation du droit humanitaire dans le cadre d'un conflit armé non-international: Doc. ONU S/1994/674, 27 mai 1994, paras. 52-54.

écrit, décrivant de manière simple et éminemment compréhensible les concepts d'un droit dont la logique interne n'apparaît pas toujours évidente. De nombreux tableaux en fin de chapitre viennent récapituler les éléments-clefs de la discussion et permettent de saisir d'un seul coup d'oeil les implications d'une situation. Malgré les quelques critiques formulées ci-dessus, il s'agit d'un excellent traité sans doute appelé à devenir un ouvrage de référence standard en droit des conflits armés.

RENÉ PROVOST
Faculté de droit, Université McGill

Choice-of-Law Problems in International Commercial Arbitration. By Horacio A. Grigera Naón. Tübingen: J. C. B. Mohr (Paul Siebeck), 1992. (Max-Planck-Institut für ausländischen und internationalen Privatrecht: Studien zum ausländischen und internationalen Privatrecht, 29.) Pp. xii, 337 including tables. (DM 129.00) ISBN 3-16-145636-X.

Dr. Grigera Naón is an Argentinian scholar who did most of his work on this study in Hamburg, at the research institute under whose imprint it appears, and at Harvard, where the core of it formed his S.J.D. thesis. He has tackled one of the most elusive areas of private international law — namely, the choice of law methods that should be used by arbitrators in international commercial disputes. Problems of choice of law are complicated enough for national judges, but at least they know for certain that the system of conflicts rules they are supposed to apply is that of their own jurisdiction. For arbitrators in an international commercial dispute, there is the added problem of deciding which country's system of conflicts rules, if any, they should use in the first place.

There is no consensus on this issue. Three basic approaches are possible. The first avoids the choice of law issue altogether, by maintaining that an international arbitrator's function is not to choose among national legal rules, but to give effect to the rules of *lex mercatoria* or, more broadly, a body of private legal rules that has its source in the international legal order rather than in any national system of law. The second, at the other end of the spectrum, envisages that arbitrators select a national conflict of laws system from among the countries involved in the dispute, and then follow that system's rules in order to choose the domestic legal rules to apply to the case before them. This is the solution adopted in Article 28(2) of the UNCITRAL Model Law on International Commercial Arbitration for cases in which the parties have not chosen the rules of law to apply to the substance of the dispute. The article states that, in these cases, the tribunal "shall apply the law determined by the conflict of laws rules which it considers applicable." (By contrast, if the parties have agreed on which rules of law shall be applied, their choice governs.) The third, intermediate, approach acknowledges that arbitrators, in deciding their case, apply rules drawn from national legal orders, but allows them to choose those rules free from the restraint of any particular choice of law system. That is, broadly speaking, the line taken in the provincial and federal statutes that implement the UNCITRAL Model Law throughout Canada. They have modified Article 28(2) to read (in the case of British Columbia's International Commercial Arbitration Act, S.B.C. 1986, c. 14, s. 28(3), which is typical of the rest), that the "tribunal shall apply the rules of law it considers to be appropriate given all the circumstances surrounding the dispute." This formula is wide enough to embrace the first approach as well as the third, because a tribunal might decide that the appropriate "rules of law" for a particular dispute are to be found in *lex mercatorie* or the international legal order.

Dr. Grigera Naón surveys the arbitral laws and practices of many countries, as well as many arbitral awards. He does so, not as a neutral reporter, but as a firm opponent of the first of these approaches and an enthusiastic advocate of the third. His denial that the rules applied in international commercial arbitration are to be found in the international legal order rests on two premises, both of which are convincing. One is that international arbitrators have to strike a bargain, as it were, with national legal orders. The arbitrators' awards are toothless unless they are given effect by national courts, and those courts are entitled to insist, as a condition of their assistance, that at least some account be taken of national legal rules — other countries' as well as their own — that embody important state policies. The other premise is that the international legal order simply cannot supply appropriate solutions to private legal disputes. Those disputes concern activities that take place within the boundaries of national states. No supranational *lex mercatoria*, or collection of general principles common to the legal systems of the international community, is suited to providing a just solution because it cannot reflect the legal responses to the economic and social, as well as private, issues at stake. These responses can be provided only by national laws.

One especially useful context in which the author pursues this argument is that of state contracts. In an extensive analysis (pp. 113-51), he contends that even these cannot be regarded as being governed by rules drawn from public international law. Referring to, among other sources, United Nations resolutions that show a stronger sovereign consciousness on the part of developing states, he concludes that no choice of law method can legitimately allow the contract to be placed wholly outside the reach of the public and constitutional law of the state party.

The major theme of the work is that the third approach referred to above, in which arbitrators choose national legal rules without being bound by any one nation's choice of law system, is the only one that meets the needs both of the parties to the disputes and of the community of states. But, beyond that, Dr. Grigera Naón is concerned to show that there is a right way in which arbitrators should address questions of choice of law. It is the "functional" approach, meaning that the rules used to resolve a dispute should be "functionally compatible — in the light of the issue in dispute — with legal rules and principles of countries connected with the dispute which are normally applied by the courts of such country to the substance of the dispute or to the results of the arbitration or to determine the jurisdiction or competence of arbitral tribunals in order to conclude whether the resulting awards should be recognized and enforced in such country" (p. 100). Therefore, functional compatibility is most likely to be attained if the tribunal incorporates in its analysis not only the substantive legal rules of the states concerned, but also their conflict of laws rules and their rules for the recognition and enforcement of arbitral awards. All of these may shed light on the degree to which a state's legal system sees it as important that its substantive rule be applied to the issue in question in the dispute. Only by analyzing the full range of these indicators and giving them such weight as seems appropriate can an arbitral tribunal make a decision that strikes the right balance between the different private and public interests that may be at stake.

In developing this thesis, the author argues both from principle and (pp. 154-219) from the observed fact that the functional approach is to be found, albeit to widely varying degrees, in every major choice of law system. French private international law has the powerful (but still ill-defined) concepts of *lois de police* and *lois d'application nécessaire*, two categories of legal rules of the forum, and possibly of foreign states, that demand to be applied even at the sacrifice of the general choice of law principles. The "proper law of the contract" idea in English law arguably reflects, and certainly can accommodate, functional concerns. The much-discussed Article 7 of the Rome Convention (1980), the European Union's attempt at a uniform solution to the choice of law problem in relation to contractual obligations, also gives a court the power to apply, where it finds it justified, a mandatory domestic or foreign legal rule at the expense of the rule that would ordinarily govern the issue. (But, as the author notes (p. 215), individual states may make a reservation to the convention that excludes Article 7. Germany and the United Kingdom have done so.) The choice of law rules of the socialist jurisdictions and of Argentina are also canvassed. Most notably, in the United States the functional approach has to a large extent been elevated from the exception to the rule. It lies at the heart of the *Second Restatement on the Conflict of Laws* (1971), and of much of the case law of the past twenty-five years.

In making his case for a functional approach to choice of law in international commercial arbitration, the author has the same problem that confronts anyone who deals with the functional approach — namely, that the arguments *why* it should be used are so much clearer than exactly *how* it should be used. It is singularly difficult to describe just how, logically, each of the many factors that one is supposed to embrace in one's decision should be related to all of the others. The author does not advance this discussion very much, but he did not set out to do so. What he has done is to provide both a comprehensive analytical framework and a comparative legal context for the choice of law problem in international commercial arbitration. The framework is clear, and the comparative material, drawn from arbitral as well as court jurisprudence, is extensive. This book will be an essential source for anyone who wishes to understand this tantalizing subject.

JOOST BLOM
Faculty of Law, University of British Columbia

International Law: A South African Perspective. By John Dugard. Ken-
wyn: Juta & Co., 1994. Pp. xxxviii, 372. (R135,00 or R99,00
paper) ISBN 0-7021-3164-4; ISBN 0-7021-3071-0 (paper).

In a certain sense this book signals the end of an era. As the
author notes, South Africa's contribution to international law has
been "enormous, although unintended" (p. 18). Much of this
contribution, as this book confirms, has been through violations of
international law (for example, see Chapter 19, "The Use of Force
by States"). But the coming of a new constitution, a multiracial
government, and the end of apartheid provide the opportunity for
a new beginning, a new South Africa in the international legal
arena. It is, therefore, possible to look back on South Africa and
international law with some perspective.

Professor Dugard, who over the years has chronicled South
Africa's progress (or lack thereof) in relation to international law,
clearly has these thoughts in mind, and there is an optimistic tone
running throughout the work. It is therefore quite understandable
to find in a discussion of the international protection of human
rights the statement, "Human rights and international law will play
a substantial role in the new South African legal order" (p. 230).
Some of the reasons for this optimism are set out in a postscript on
the new South African constitution (pp. 339-54).

The book is essentially an introductory work for students, but its
interest goes beyond this audience because of the substantial references to South African material — in particular, to decisions of
courts that have been confronted with international legal arguments. As a student text, the book presents a fairly orthodox view of
international law. A graduate of Cambridge, Professor Dugard has
been strongly influenced by the intellectual legacy of Sir Hersch
Lauterpacht, in terms both of idealism and of pragmatism. Professor Dugard is clear, as he has been in the past, on where the
South African government has been wrong, and in the spirit of a
new beginning in South Africa he is gentle with South African
colleagues who have sought to provide an international legal
rationale for the indefensible.

This, then, is a book that South African students will read with
profit in their introductory courses on international law. They will
gain some insight into this field, and find food for reflection about
South Africa's past place in international law (for example, in the
long-running issue over Namibia), and about its potential place.
However, those who stumble over the issue of enforceability in

international law are not likely to be convinced by the suggestion that the punishment of individuals for international crimes provides evidence for the existence of sanctions in international law (p. 7). Moreover, subsequent editions will no doubt have to take into account other areas, such as economic and trade law, as South Africa re-establishes its position in the international community.

For those outside South Africa, this book provides an interesting insight into the intersection between international law and domestic courts. This has been a fertile area in South African jurisprudence since evolving international norms continued to provide ammunition for attacking the policies of the South African government. However, it is not surprising that judges appointed by the South African government would not entertain arguments about the international illegitimacy of what the regime was doing either in the light of general human rights standards or of specific rulings, decisions, or resolutions of international organizations. But they were able to apply international law, and did so when they deemed it appropriate. In fact, Professor Dugard concludes that overall there is "support for the harmonization theory with a monist bias" (p. 57).

Although the South African government provided numerous opportunities for them to do so, it does not appear that South African courts made any important intellectual contribution to international law. This does not mean that judges did exactly what the government said. At times they showed independence in rather odd ways. For example, one court was able to conclude that the illegal regime in Southern Rhodesia was a state, even though the South African government had not recognised it (p. 88)! Indeed, the South African experience seems to indicate that domestic judges simply pick and choose in their use of international law.

This raises some interesting issues for further research both within and beyond South Africa about the role of the judiciary in controlling regimes that move so far from generally accepted international standards. It also reinforces the importance of devoting attention to the use of international law at the domestic level at a time when so many hitherto domestic issues have implications beyond the nation state. In this regard, the attention given in the new South African constitution to the reception of customary international law and of treaties is of particular interest (pp. 339-46).

In the end, while this is an optimistic book, it contains so much of the past that it is also a disturbing book for anyone concerned about the meaning of the rule of law both within states and among members of the international community. In this respect, the book provides an interesting contrast between the value-free way in which the parameters of international law are often described, and the value-loaded content of what goes under the name of international law.

Professor Dugard has built a career as an international lawyer and as a human rights lawyer under particularly adverse conditions. His courage, as well as his intellectual contribution to the field of international law, make him a product of which the "Cambridge school" (p. ix) can be rightly proud.

D. M. McRae
Faculty of Law, University of Ottawa

Manual of European Environmental Law. By Alexandre Kiss and Dinah Shelton. Cambridge: Grotius Publications, 1993. Pp. xxxvi, 5,250. U.S.$49. ISBN 1-85701-019-1; ISBN 1-85701-018-3 (paper).

Authors Kiss and Shelton set out "to provide teaching materials and a reference work for university and professional courses in environmental law." To this end, they have assembled a comprehensive text that consists of a series of sectoral chapters supported by an extensive introductory survey of institutions, concepts, and techniques of environmental law and concludes with a survey of such sectoral issues as integrated environmental protection and public participation in environmental decision-making.

The first part of the volume provides an overview of the legal framework of European environmental law with reference to national laws, international law, and the basic environmental provisions of the European Union. A related chapter briefly describes national, international, and European institutions insofar as these participate in environmental management and decision-making. Two other introductory chapters deal with concepts such as the "polluter pays" principle and the principle of "precaution," and techniques of environmental law, respectively.

The second and major part of the volume consists of five sectoral chapters. These deal with biodiversity and the protection of nature, protection of the soil, fresh waters, the marine environment, and atmospheric pollution. Each chapter consists of a brief overview followed by a discussion of particular legal issues. In relation to atmospheric pollution, for example, the *Manual* surveys general legislation with applicability to air pollution as well as special measures directed at air pollutants. Regulations associated with particular activities or facilities are addressed alongside provisions focused on specific pollutants. The role of air quality standards and zoning provisions is also considered.

In the third section of the book, Kiss and Shelton consider some miscellaneous issues in environmental regulation, including the control of hazardous substances and facilities, waste management, noise, and nuclear radiation. There is a short chapter on planning and integrated environmental protection, and a further short chapter on the role of the public and of non-governmental organizations.

An important feature of each chapter in the *Manual* is the inclusion of detailed case studies by independent contributors. For example, the atmospheric pollution chapter includes short descriptions by Jose Just on the protection of the atmospheric environment by international law, by Ludwig Kramer on the European Community and atmospheric pollution, and by Owen Lomas on air pollution control in the United Kingdom.

Each chapter is also supported by documentary material and a short but useful bibliography. Those interested in using the *Manual* for teaching purposes may find the questions and problems section associated with each chapter of considerable assistance. However, despite the high quality of the discussion and analysis, some readers may be frustrated by the lack of detailed references to sources for further information and authority.

The indexing is in general quite satisfactory. Used in combination with the detailed table of contents, the table of national laws and cases, and a chronological table of international and European Union documents accompanied by page references, the overall finding system is generally workable. There are, however, some limitations and possible sources of frustration for the less-than-patient reader. Anyone looking for discussion of CFCs would be disappointed by the absence of reference to CFCs or chlorofluorocarbons in the index, although one might, by accident, come upon a reference to "CFC ban" under the general subject of Sweden. "Integrated pollution control" and "integrated protection" appear as index entries but "integrated planning," a subject heading found within page references for "integrated protection," does not appear on its own in the index. Also, there is no reference in the index to planning, urban planning, or rural planning, although cross-references to "land use" will eventually lead the reader to appropriate sections of the text.

Non-European readers may be struck by the lack of discussion of such issues as corporate liability and directors' and officers' responsibilities, which have become central issues in the environmental law regimes of Canada and the United States.

JAMIE BENIDICKSON
Faculty of Law, University of Ottawa

Droit international privé: Travaux du Comité français de droit international privé, années 1991-1992, 1992-93. Paris: Éditions A. Pédone, 1994. Pp. 282. ISBN 2-233002-57-1.

The Comité français de droit international privé is a unique institution, and the envy of conflicts scholars in other countries. It consists of some 200 judges, scholars, and advocates who are, in the words of its constitution (reprinted in this volume), "les jurisconsultes spécialisés en France dans l'étude du droit international privé." As the list of members (also included) shows, every notable scholar in the field belongs to it, as do judges of the highest courts. It is rigorously French in its membership, but far from parochial in its concerns. The papers that are delivered at its meetings, which are held four times a year, include some given by foreign legal scholars concerning developments in their legal system, and others in which French scholars view private international law from a comparative perspective. The papers are generally of the highest quality and make the *travaux* of the Comité a pre-eminent source of scholarly literature on French and European private international law.

The present volume is graced by two outstanding tributes to the late Henri Batiffol, who for some decades was the undisputed *doyen* of private international law in France. Professor Pierre Gothot, of the Faculté de droit de Liège (and, as a Belgian, a non-member of the Comité), assesses "La place d'Henri Batiffol dans la doctrine" and Professor Yves Lequette, of the University of Paris II, analyzes "L'influence de l'oeuvre d'Henri Batiffol sur la jurisprudence française." These are moving pieces, because of the way in which each author is able to give a sense of Batiffol's personal qualities almost entirely through an analysis of Batiffol's thought. Batiffol was above all a great synthesizer, able to bridge disparate theories as well as theory and practice. Professor Gothot observes (p. 30) that Batiffol was so successful in integrating the best aspects of various schools of thought that it is difficult to say precisely where his originality, which he undoubtedly had in full measure, lay. The two essays are valuable for more than their immediate subject. They will interest any comparative lawyer for the insight they give into how the scholarly tradition in French law views itself and its role today.

Professor Hervé Synvet, of the University of Paris II, contributes a discussion of letters of credit and guarantees in private international law, focusing on the choice of law issues as well as on the determination of the place of payment. He draws on common law sources as well as French ones. Three other papers also deal with commercial subjects. "L'actualité de l'autonomie de la clause compromissoire" by Mr. Jean-Pierre Ancel, a judge of the Cour de cassation, discusses the severability of arbitration clauses from the contracts in which they are found. The French courts have probably taken this principle further than anyone else. The original impulse for this came from the fact that agreements to arbitrate future disputes were until 1981 generally invalid under French domestic law. The courts seized on the autonomy principle as a ground for treating arbitration clauses as valid, irrespective of the national law that might otherwise govern the surrounding contract, provided that the contract could be considered an international one. Their decisions go so far as to suggest that the clause functions independently, not only of its contract, but also of any system of domestic law.

Mr. Cyrille David provides a wide-ranging analysis of the current state of international taxation of financial instruments, testimony to the breadth of interest of French private international lawyers. And Mr. Jean-Pierre Remery, referendary judge of the Cour de cassation, surveys the *jurisprudence* on international bankruptcy. This intricate subject evidently exercises the courts of France as much as those of other jurisdictions, and clear guidance from the cases tends to be the exception rather than the rule.

Two essays deal with the law of the European Union (then still the European Communities). Professor Laurence Idot, of the University of Paris I, discusses "Le domaine spatial du droit communautaire des affaires." The rubric *droit des affaires* embraces the European rules relating to a business's freedom of access to all parts of the common market, and the rules relating to competition. The territorial reach of the Union's law on these subjects is defined by various connecting factors, including the place where goods and services are marketed, the effect on the market (especially in the case of restrictions on conduct), and, to some extent, the domicile or place of incorporation of those who claim the benefit of rights. Professor Konstantinos Kerameus, of the University of Athens, deals with international judicial jurisdiction under the Brussels Convention in matters of delict, examining the decisions both of the Court of Justice of the European Communities and of national courts.

The collection is rounded out by a paper devoted to a foreign system of private international law. Professor Juan Antonio Carrillo Salcedo, of the University of Seville, examines the evolution of Spanish private international law since the legislative reform of 1974. He traces, among other things, how the new Spanish constitution of 1978 has had profound effects in the area of family law, not only because it mandates the replacement of the religious foundations of the law with secular ones, but also because it enacts a principle of non-discrimination between persons.

As always in these volumes, each paper is followed by a verbatim report of the discussion that followed among the participants in the session. These discussions often provide interesting sidelights on the paper, or a valuable elaboration by the author of some of its themes.

JOOST BLOM
Faculty of Law, University of British Columbia

ANALYTICAL INDEX /
INDEX ANALYTIQUE

THE CANADIAN YEARBOOK OF
INTERNATIONAL LAW

1994

ANNUAIRE CANADIEN
DE DROIT INTERNATIONAL

(A) Article; (NC) Notes and Comments;
(C) Chronique; (PR) Practice; (R) Review
(A) Article; (NC) Notes et commentaires;
(C) Chronique; (PR) Pratique; (R) Recension de livre

INDEX OF CASES /
INDEX DES AFFAIRES

435